MW00808527

JOHN LENTHALL

The Life of a Naval Constructor

Stephen Chapin Kinnaman

Series in American History

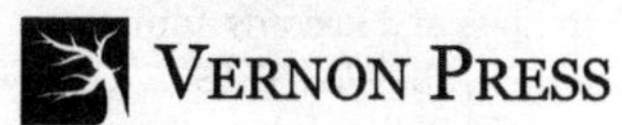

www.vernonpress.com

In the Americas:
Vernon Press
1000 N West Street,
Suite 1200, Wilmington,
Delaware 19801
United States

In the rest of the world:
Vernon Press
C/Sancti Espiritu 17,
Malaga, 29006
Spain

Series in American History

Library of Congress Control Number: 2021950204
ISBN: 978-1-64889-348-3

Also available:
978-1-64889-418-3 [Hardback, Premium Color]

Cover design by Vernon Press.

Images on the front cover: (Above) *Constructor John Lenthall.* Image 527130, courtesy of the National Archives and Records Administration. (Below) *Dale, Bow Profile.* John Lenthall Collection, Ship Plan FI L90.43.107, courtesy of the Independence Seaport Museum, Philadelphia, PA for the Franklin Institute.

Image on the back cover: *Scene on the Delaware at Philadelphia.* Lithograph by James Queen, Digital ID ppmsca19644, courtesy of the Library of Congress.

To Thomas Hornsby of Cheltenham, Pennsylvania
You showed the way.

TABLE OF CONTENTS

LIST OF ILLUSTRATIONS

MAPS

IMAGES

PLANS

ACKNOWLEDGEMENTS

Many people helped me to tell the story of John Lenthall and it is my great pleasure to be able to acknowledge their assistance. Taking them in the order I met them, I must start with Craig Bruns, the chief curator of Philadelphia's Independence Seaport Museum. During my several trips to his museum, I was graciously looked after by his two archives and library assistants, Sarah Stopper and Debbie Lovell, who by Craig's direction, accorded me full access to the wonders of the John Lenthall Collection. He encouraged my efforts to research the life of John Lenthall and to write this book. For that I am very grateful.

Although I did not meet him, I must acknowledge the debt this book owes to the prior work of Thomas Hornsby. A Philadelphia-area builder of ship models and author of numerous articles published in the *Nautical Research Journal*, Hornsby's decades-long effort to research the professional achievements of John Lenthall culminated in a manuscript titled *The Career of John Lenthall, Naval Constructor*. This manuscript circa 1958 and Hornsby's prolific research notes are housed in the Independence Seaport Museum's archives. I can state without hesitation that if he had published his manuscript, this book would have been simply an update of a good biography. It is for this reason that I dedicate my book to Thomas Hornsby.

The City of Brotherly Love was also the site of additional help from Susannah Carroll, the assistant director of collections at The Franklin Institute. The Institute's deepest archives were opened to my enquiries, and during a late spring day, Susannah helped me navigate their musty ledgers and other conserved records.

In the nation's capital, the staff at the National Archives and Records Administration (NARA) were unfailingly productive, directing my general enquiries toward the correct call number and the right reel of microfilm. In particular, I well remember Kim McKeithan, Adebo Adetona and Chris, archives specialists, for their repeated assistance. I also wish to acknowledge the patient staff of NARA's Room 203, the location of many hours of investigation into thousands of documents related to John Lenthall and much else.

At the Smithsonian Institute's National Museum of American History, Dr. Paul F. Johnston, curator of maritime history, assisted me obtaining copies of Howard I. Chapelle's iconic ship plans of *Relief, Raritan* and *Germantown.*

Across town toward the Anacostia River lies the Washington Navy Yard where I was greeted by the cheerful Sandra Fox, reference librarian at the Navy Department's library. Sandi and her assistant, Dennis Wilson, ably opened the library's archives to my research and rendered assistance with copying documents and accessing their microfilm collections.

It was also in Washington, D.C., that I met Dr. Larrie D. Ferreiro, author, naval architect and historian, who shares my enthusiasm for the work of naval constructors. Fluent in French, Larrie has been very helpful to my efforts tracing Lenthall's footprints in Paris and many other places. His landmark book, *Ships and Science,* was an inspiration to my treatment of Lenthall's education and how it was influenced by the French pioneers of naval architecture.

I can't leave the Washington area without a nod to the former archivist of the Church of the Epiphany, Tripp Jones, although I suspect he no longer lives in the capital city. Thank you for your very helpful insights into the Lenthall family's footprint as parishioners of your church.

Moving to the United States Naval Academy Museum at Annapolis, I cannot thank enough Tracie Logan, senior curator, and the irrepressible Baltimore photographer, Roger Miller, who, at my request, organized the photographing of each and every item in the Ives Collection. I couldn't have written this book without their efforts. My hat is off to Tracie and Roger.

Further afield, Lucas R. Clawson, reference archivist/Hagley historian, rendered great service obtaining copies of Samuel Francis Du Pont's private letters to John Lenthall in the collection of the Hagley Museum and Library, Wilmington, Delaware. Also, to Erin Weinman, manuscript librarian and Charina Castello, assistant, at the New-York Historical Society, for arranging for drawing copies of the Navy Department's never-built iron-plated steam batteries.

Closer to home in Texas, I must acknowledge the constant encouragement given by Ira Gruber, professor emeritus of history at Rice University. Our Holly Street walks discussing naval history and much else will always be cherished.

Across the pond, Robert Thorp has helped with his 'Photoshopping' of plans, maps and images, and proof reading, always giving his fullest encouragement to my writing efforts.

And I can never give enough praise to my dear wife, Maureen Carroll, who suffered through my many hours of inattention while focused on pounding out my Lenthall manuscript … and then took the time to read it and offer comments.

Many thanks to all of you and to those I have unwittingly left out. Your assistance made this book possible. Any errors of concept, fact or interpretation, however, are mine alone for which I accept full responsibility.

Stephen Chapin Kinnaman
Chappell Hill, Texas
November 2021

INTRODUCTION

Naval constructors are rarely accorded biographies, but John Lenthall merits the happy exception. His life story delivers the human elements of triumph and tragedy. Even better, a study of his career reveals how his arcane craft—naval architecture—was practiced in his time. His biography combines both elements into a compelling tale of American naval history.

Constructor John Lenthall was active in the mid-nineteenth century and rose to become the chief of the U.S. Navy's Bureau of Construction and Repair, a post he held before, during and after the Civil War. Most students of American maritime and naval history familiar with famous naval architects of that period such as William Webb, George Steers and Donald McKay, pause when they hear the names of the Navy's skilled constructors—not only John Lenthall but also Samuel Humphreys and Francis Grice to cite but a few. For various reasons, the nation's illustrious corps of naval constructors, laboring within the walled confines of government navy yards, became only partially illuminated by the limelight cast on their better-known commercial contemporaries. The vessels they created were, after all, called warships for a good reason, and the nation was largely at peace during the period of John Lenthall's story. The careers of the frigates and sloops they built had little of the publicity of ships like Webb's legendary *Challenge* or McKay's record-breaking *Flying Cloud,* or of Steers' racing yacht *America.* But they were the primary instruments of America's projection of power and, in that role, competed just as fiercely with their foreign peers as did clippers striving to make record passages around Cape Horn. The constructors who created them were talented men whose stories deserve to be told. And of all of them, none has a more compelling life story than John Lenthall. In human terms, he endured more than his share of a family tragedy. As an accomplished constructor, Lenthall's considerable body of extant drawings and calculations allow an unfiltered appreciation of his consistently successful warships.

Born in Washington, D.C. during Thomas Jefferson's second term as president, Lenthall was the son of an English emigrant of considerable ability who was killed in a freak accident when young John was but one year old. Raised by his mother and her King family uncles, John Lenthall aspired to become a naval constructor. It was his good fortune to come under the guidance of Samuel Humphreys, the Philadelphia naval architect whose genius became indelibly imprinted on the "Gradual Increase" warships of the U.S. Navy—and on his willing pupil. An apprenticeship was soon followed by a tour of Europe's dockyards, which initiated Lenthall's life-long affinity with France, the most scientific of maritime powers. On his return to America, John Lenthall was hired in 1835 by the Navy's prickly Commodore John Rodgers and began a stellar career as a naval constructor.

From the beginning, John Lenthall demonstrated a commitment to his chosen profession, whether it was the severe labor of a ship carpenter or the endless hours of Navy board meetings. An insatiable bibliophile, Lenthall took advantage of opportunities for self-education wherever and whenever he could, tapping the skills of his surveyor uncles, shipbuilder mentors such as Captain William Easby and the resources of Philadelphia's Franklin Institute. As his career developed, he displayed an unmatched numerical proficiency, capable of performing prodigious volumes of repetitive calculations, and honed the instincts necessary to succeed within of the Navy's bureau system of administration.

John Lenthall's accomplishments in the primary business of a constructor, designing and building ships, ranged far and wide. The first ship he built was the humble storeship *Relief,* and he designed the last sailing warship launched by the U.S. Navy, the 22-gun sloop *Constellation.* She is afloat today in Baltimore's inner harbor, the only example of Lenthall's art still in existence. John Lenthall's masterpiece, the 60-gun *Merrimack* class steam frigates, created excitement in Europe and provoked a British counter in the form of Walker's Big Frigates. And after being derided for doubting the efficiency of Ericsson's *Monitor,* Lenthall produced the finest example of that class fielded by the Navy during the Civil War, the double turreted *Monadnocks*. His sheer volume of activity made him the best documented of the early naval constructors, much to the modern historian's advantage and delight.

John Lenthall's administrative achievements were equally impressive. He served as chief of the Bureau of Construction and Repair and its predecessor for over seventeen years, a record that has never been equaled. Lenthall's longevity is even more remarkable when it is remembered that in his first year as a bureau chief, 1853, the Navy was composed largely of wooden-hulled sailing vessels mounting smoothbore guns firing round shot. By the time he was forcibly retired in 1871, the Navy had progressed to powerful ironclad war steamers armed with huge shell-firing and rifled guns. Lenthall's ability to deliver at a time of crisis was without peer. At the end of the Civil War's first year, 1861, under his guidance the Navy Department had begun construction of forty-nine warships of six widely different classes. These vessels, including the famous 'ninety-day gun boats' and the 'double-enders', formed the backbone of a victorious navy. Often overlooked was Lenthall's ability to survive no fewer than five presidential administrations and as many secretaries of the navy. From the exemplary James C. Dobbin to the shady George M. Robeson, John Lenthall dealt with them all. Most eventful were his years serving under President Lincoln's navy secretary, Gideon Welles, which required Lenthall and his fellow bureau chiefs to adjust to the insertion into the Navy Department of the new and very energetic assistant secretary, Gustavus Vasa Fox.

This brings us to the most controversial period of John Lenthall's career, his handling of the Navy's introduction of ironclads. He was severely criticized by his contemporaries and by later historians for his tepid embrace of ironclads and his vocal criticism of Ericsson's monitors. Close examination of the record tells a different story. Lenthall, as a conservative engineer, well understood the pitfalls of a hasty rush into a new, transformational technology and was keenly aware of the ironclad developments made at great cost in both France and England. He also had prior experience working with John Ericsson during the construction of the steam sloop *Princeton* at the Philadelphia Navy Yard. The world's first warship to be *designed* with a screw-propeller, *Princeton* has been usually credited to John Ericsson, but the plans of her hull were drawn up by and her construction was supervised by Constructor John Lenthall. He well knew the Swedish inventor and when, eighteen years later, Ericsson submitted a proposal to the Navy for his unorthodox ironclad steam battery—later known as *Monitor*—Lenthall's bureau checked his calculations and found them wanting. After the Battle of Hampton Roads and the onset of Monitor fever, Lenthall together with his brilliant engineer-in-chief, Benjamin Isherwood, saw only too clearly that the Navy's rush to build *only* monitors would cripple its ability to perform its core strategic mission, defending America. They believed that mission was best accomplished at the enemy's doorstep rather than from within harbors guarded by unseaworthy monitors and coastal fortifications. But their Mahanian advice went unheeded and so the U.S. Navy passed through its decades of decline—its Dark Ages—before fielding the armored ocean-going war vessels that allowed it to emerge as a world power.

Briefly returning to John Lenthall's personal life, it has also been largely overlooked that he was a rare native of the District of Columbia—he was born and grew up there, worked in Washington most of his life and is buried in Rock Creek Cemetery. His father was a federal employee, his King uncles were public servants of the District and many early role models—the architect Benjamin Latrobe and Captain Easby of the Washington Navy Yard—were also federal employees during much of their careers. Lenthall had, from his earliest years a familiarity with the responsibilities, duties and burdens of government employees, and the benefit of hearing everyday conversations from those in public service. His exposure to such informative sources allowed him to prosper and succeed in the distinctly unique environment of the U.S. Navy's bureaucracy, and to navigate its clashes between line and staff officers.

John Lenthall was late to marry. An Episcopalian, his choice of a Roman Catholic wife had its invisible social tensions. And his first child, a son, died in infancy. The Lenthalls rebounded and took pride in raising their daughter Jenny. But soon after his retirement his wife passed away and then, little over two years later, his daughter died at age twenty-eight. Lenthall's close-knit family, especially his two sisters, allowed him to recover from his losses and take pleasure in raising his three grandchildren. The eldest of them, Anny, was his particular favorite. Many decades after Lenthall's passing, it was she who donated the invaluable Ives Collection to the U.S. Naval Academy.

The career of John Lenthall spanned so many years, events and subjects that in writing his biography an author is forced to make choices about what to cover and what to leave out. Of the latter category, with a few brief exceptions, mention of the ironclads and other vessels built by the U.S. Navy on the western waters has been largely ignored. Lenthall figured only marginally in their story. Further, it was never the intention for this treatment of John Lenthall's life to be a design history of the U.S. Navy's warships of his era. For that purpose, the interested reader is referred to the many fine works by naval historian Donald L. Canney which were extensively consulted during the preparation of this book.

A few final remarks about sources. Any scholar embarking on a study of John Lenthall will soon find themselves overwhelmed by the vast volume and scope of available sources, the opposite problem that many researchers encounter. First and foremost is the John Lenthall Collection housed in Philadelphia's Independence Seaport Museum, which consists of over 500 drawings, some eighty folders of technical documents and Lenthall's fabulous 360 volume book collection. A largely untapped but hugely rich source of Lenthall's personal correspondence is the U.S. Naval Academy Museum's Ives Collection. On the order of 1,000 letters, documents, calculations and miscellanea populate this priceless trove. Think of the Independence Seaport Museum's John Lenthall Collection as the contents of his Navy Department office while the Ives Collection is what Lenthall saved in his home's desk drawers. Then there are the endless numbers of official government documents held in the National Archives and Records Administration, mainly in Record Groups 19 and 45, and the Navy Department's library at the Washington Navy Yard. And there were many others, all as listed in the bibliography.

A recent catalogue of John Lenthall Collection drawings opens with the statement that "John Lenthall was not the sort of individual who inspires biographies." I heartily disagree! Let the story of Lenthall, his times and his achievements speak to you. Allow yourself to slip back into his nineteenth-century world and experience the remarkable life of Constructor John Lenthall. It is a journey you will not regret.

* * *

FAMILY TREE

The Lenthall family tree traces three main families that merged through John Lenthall and his wife Mary Dugan Eck: the Lenthalls shown in the center, the Kings to the left and the Ecks on the right. Note the three different religious affiliations of each branch. The generation of John Lenthall Sr. was paralleled by the growth of the family of Nicholas King, his wife's brother. Of John Lenthall's generation, the families of his sister Elizabeth Lenthall Stone as well as his brother-in-law Joseph Eck are also plotted. Thereafter, the Waggaman family becomes the central focus. Names of this period were subject to varying spellings and in several cases, reliable sources indicate two possibilities. Decisions for making choices between options were guided by the inscription on that person's headstone.

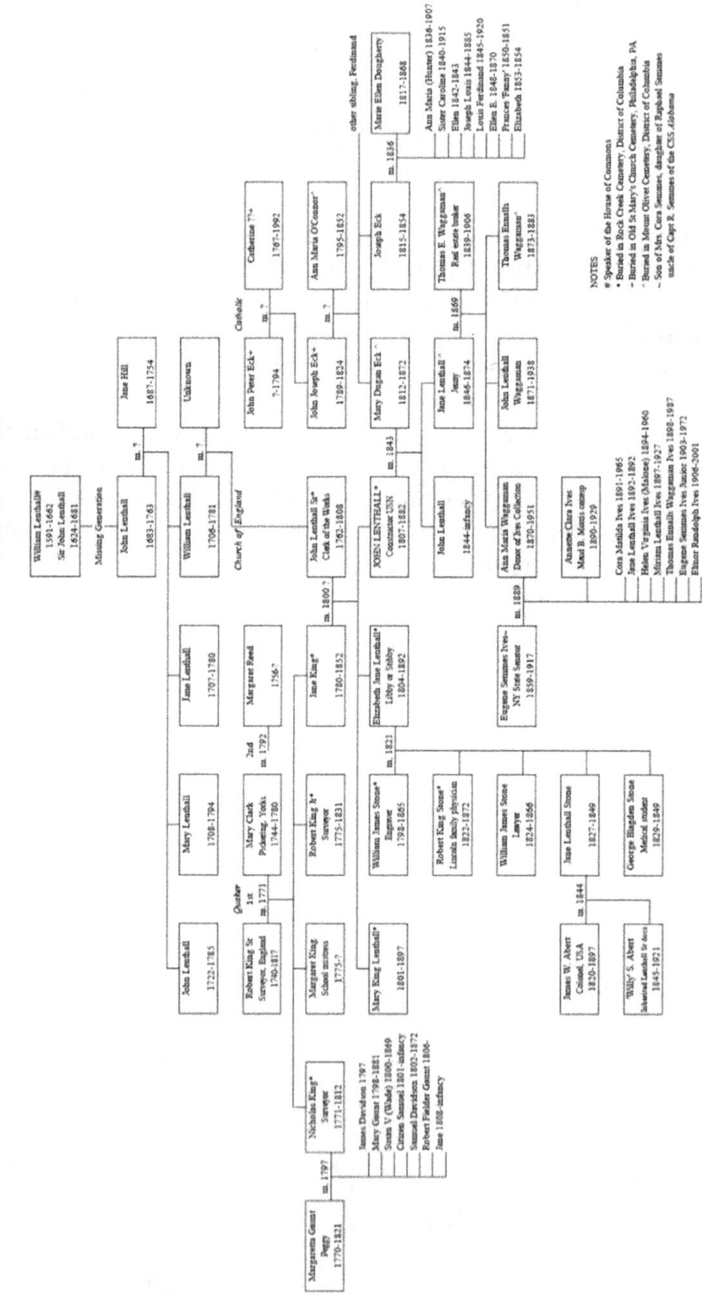

John Lenthall Family Tree

MAPS

No. 1 *Washington D.C., 1818*

Lenthall's Uncle Robert King was the creator of this engraved map of Washington. Its quality set the standard until the eve of the Civil War. Land fill gradually removed Tiber Creek and its canal system from the Mall. The Lenthall family's F Street home of many years was located below the F marking the street's name. (Robert King's *Map of the City of Washington*, 1818. Digital ID ct006189r, courtesy of the Library of Congress).

No. 2 *Philadelphia, 1836*

The city of Philadelphia was the scene of young John Lenthall's apprenticeship and earliest experiences as a constructor. Southwark and its navy yard are on the Delaware at the bottom right, downtown Philadelphia is at the center and to the upper right is Kensington, site of many private shipyards (from H. S. Tanner's *A New Universal Atlas*, 1844. Digital ID gcws0193, courtesy of the Library of Congress).

No. 3 *Philadelphia Navy Yard*

The compact grounds of the Philadelphia Navy Yard, hemmed into the Southwark district and bounded by the Delaware river are clearly shown in this map inset. Smallest of the navy yards, it was finally closed in 1876 and its facilities moved to League Island (from Samuel Smedley's *Atlas of the City of Philadelphia*, 1862, Section 3. Image ID MSMDAA00008, courtesy of the Free Library of Philadelphia, Map Collection).

No. 4 *The United Kingdom and France*

This map features the two countries that were the prime focus of John Lenthall during his 1831-34 European dockyard tour. After returning from Russia and the Baltic, he toured the north of England, then pivoted through the Isle of Wight to France where he stayed for fifteen months (By the Author, Katherine Bolding and Robert Thorp).

No. 5 *U.S. Eastern Seaboard*

Shown on this map is the eastern seaboard of the United States, the principal area of operations of John Lenthall during his career as a naval constructor and bureau chief. Centered first in Philadelphia then Washington, he frequently travelled to New York and less so to the other navy yards in Portsmouth, Boston and Norfolk (By the Author, Katherine Bolding and Robert Thorp).

No. 6 *Central Washington, 1851*

The focus of this map inset is the President's House, or White House as it is now called. Immediately to the west of it is the old Navy Department building, and across 17th Street, the Winder Building. John Lenthall had offices in both places during his long career with the U.S. Navy. His F Street home was on the north side of block 143. On the south side of block 252, to the east of the President's house, is the G Street location of Church of the Epiphany, the spiritual home of Lenthall and his sisters (from Lloyd Van Derveer's *Map of the City of Washington, D.C.*, 1851. Digital ID ct000754, courtesy of the Library of Congress).

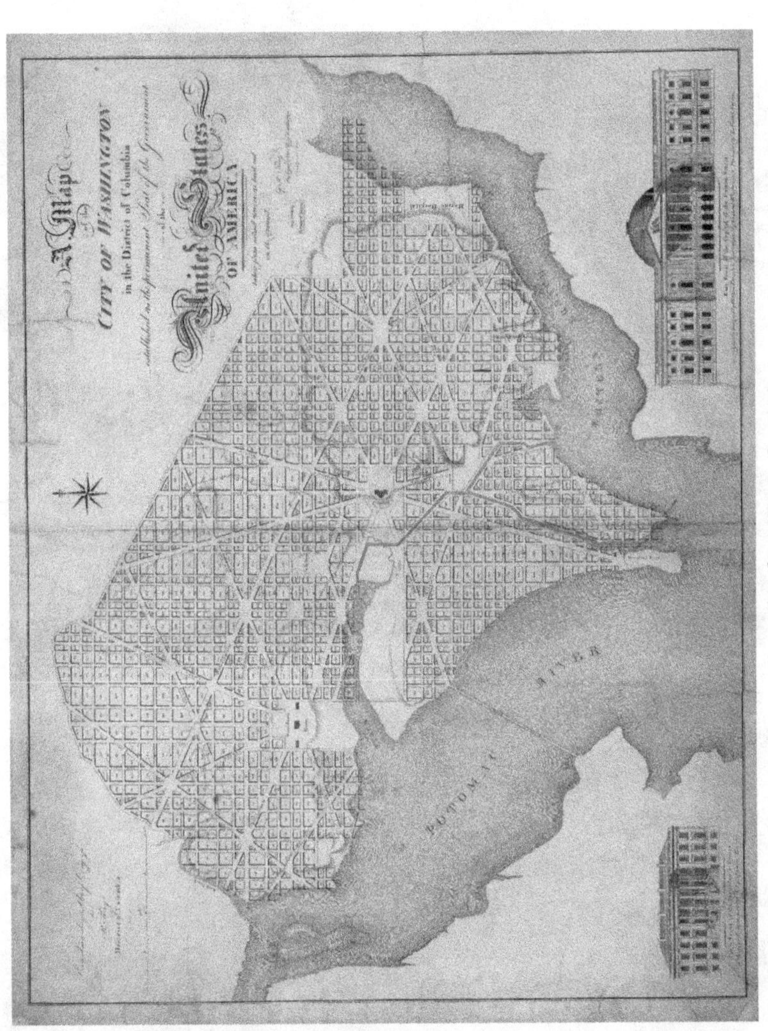

No. 1 *Washington, D.C., 1818*

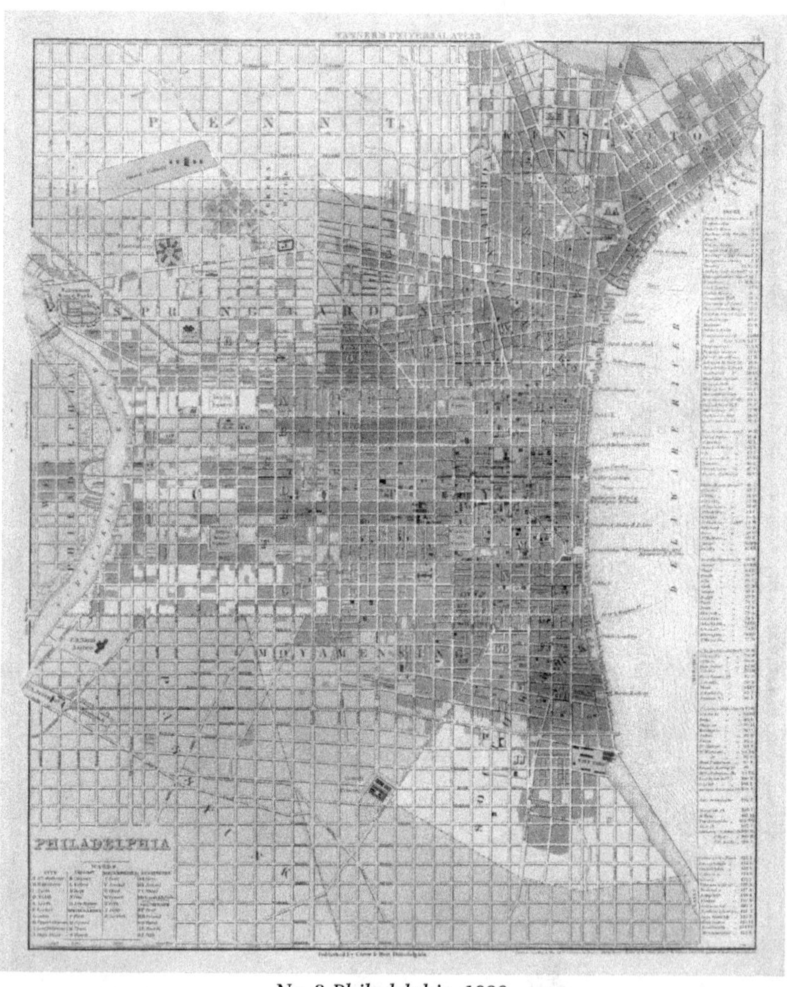

No. 2 *Philadelphia, 1836*

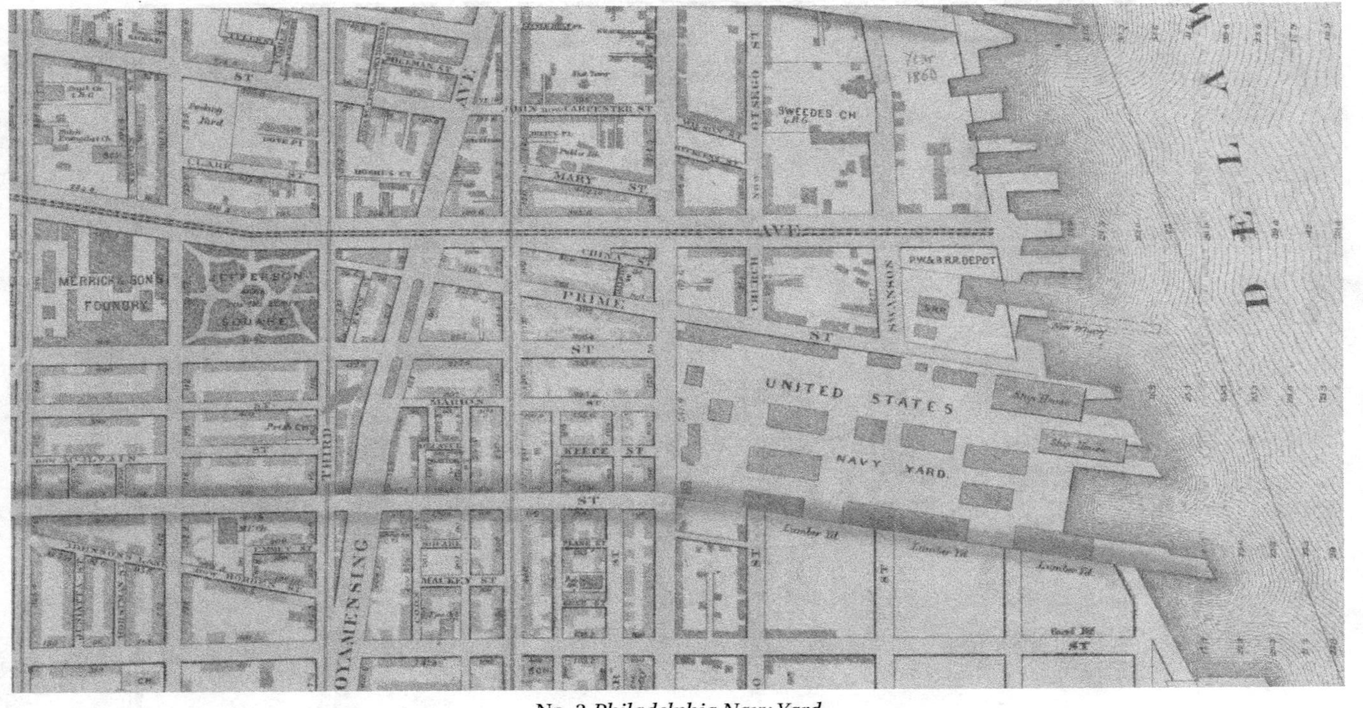

No. 3 *Philadelphia Navy Yard*

No. 4 *The United Kingdom and France*

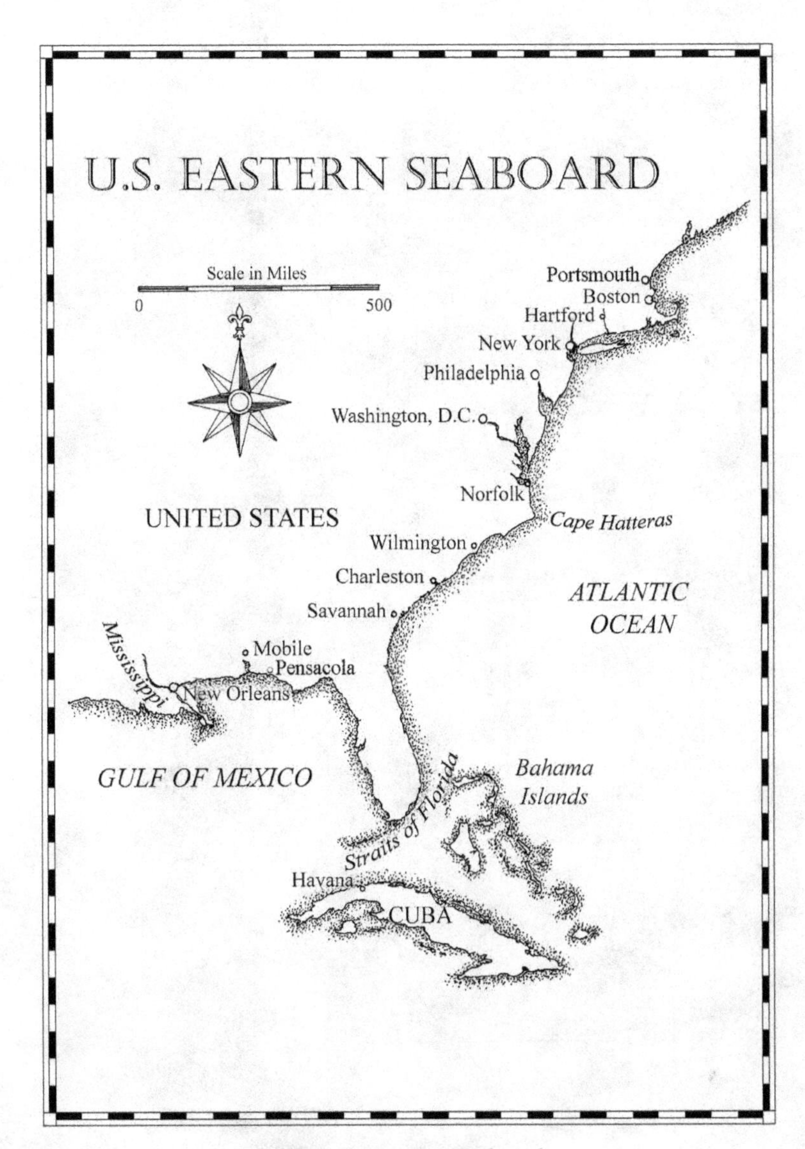

No. 5 *U.S. Eastern Seaboard*

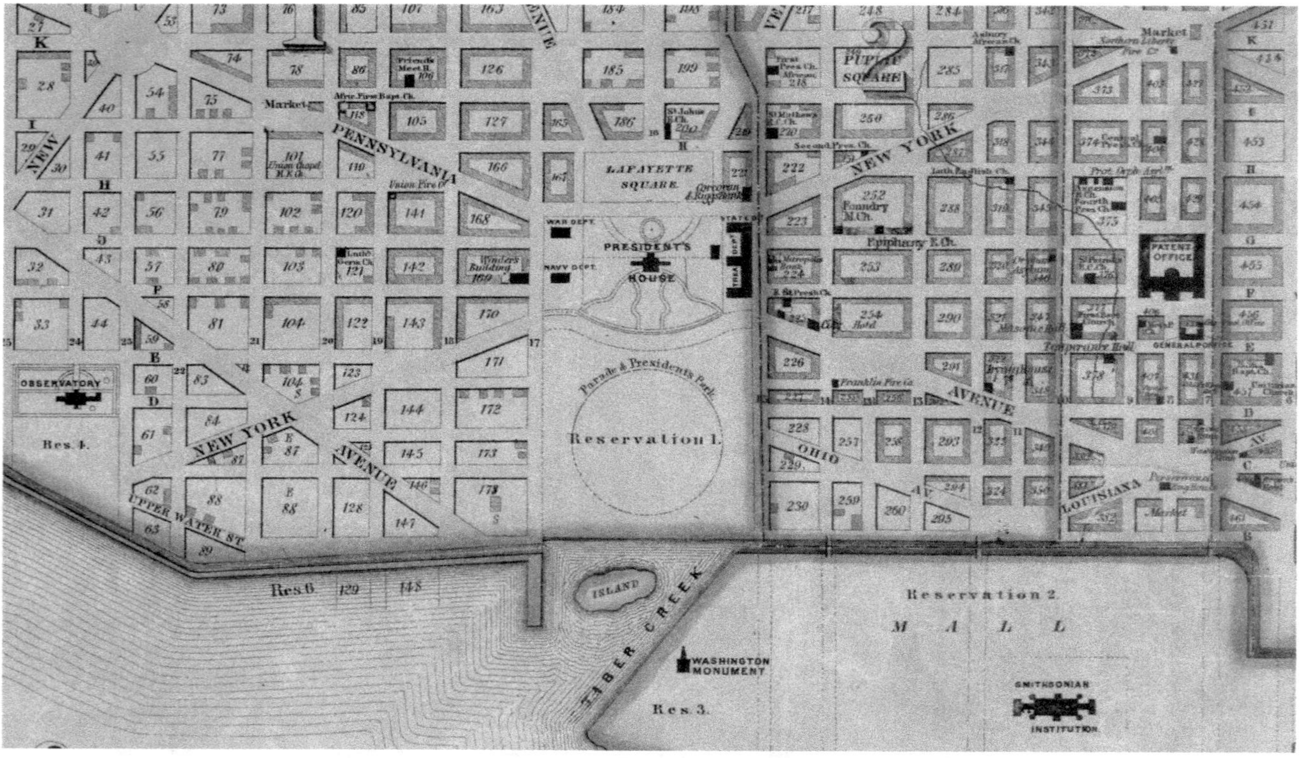

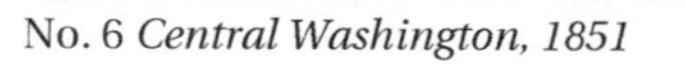

No. 6 *Central Washington, 1851*

BOOK ONE
Apprentice

CHAPTER 1

Washington City

Any biography of Constructor John Lenthall must necessarily begin in Washington, D.C.—he was born there in 1807, his family lived and flourished in the city, he spent the majority of his professional career working within sight of the White House, and after a brief retirement, he died and was buried in the District of Columbia. In those formative years that shaped young John Lenthall's life, the nation's capital grudgingly yielded a precarious existence to its earliest residents. More a village than a city, Washington was sparsely populated, over-promoted and indifferently governed by the whims of an often-absent Congress. The trajectory of Washington's growth was unlike that of any other city. But one feature it did share with other American urban centers of that era was the dominance of foreign-born artisans. While the federally controlled District of Columbia was a unique creation of the United States government, it was largely built by the hands of many skilled immigrants.

French émigré and Revolutionary War veteran Pierre Charles L'Enfant drafted the original plan of the nation's capital.[1] That was in 1791, the year after Congress created the new federal district to replace the existing capital of the United States which was then located in Philadelphia.[2] L'Enfant was followed in 1792 by the Irishman James Hoban, whose design was selected for the President's House (now called the White House). The next year, a gifted amateur architect born in the British West Indies, Dr. William Thornton, won the competition for the U.S. Capitol's design. With the federal district's street plan mapped out and its principal buildings designed, a series of foreign-born architects were hired to supervise the erection of its new structures, the most famous of which was the Briton, Benjamin Henry Latrobe. Appointed in 1803 by President Jefferson as surveyor of the public buildings, his legacy would loom large over both the capital's buildings and the men who assisted him.[3]

Because of the tangible achievements of the capital's first architects and the ever-present promise of a building boom, others were encouraged to follow in their footsteps. Scores of lesser-known artisans populated the first ranks of those whose labor turned Washington into a federal city. Among them were the English-born builder John Lenthall Sr. and his fellow countryman, surveyor Robert King Sr. From these two men sprang the family which brought Constructor John Lenthall into this world.

* * *

One of the earliest of the intrepid artisans, John Lenthall Sr., the future Constructor John Lenthall's father, emigrated to America in either 1792 or 1793, probably through Philadelphia.[4] He was about thirty years old at the time, having been born in Chesterfield, Derbyshire in 1762. His reasons for leaving England are opaque. During the years of his emigration, the tensions arising from the French Revolution caused increasingly hostile relations between Britain and France, war being finally declared in February 1793. The uncertainties of a wartime economy may have been a factor, but there were other motivations. By the end of the eighteen century, the Lenthall family was in decline. Long the proprietors of two country estates, Burford Priory in Oxfordshire and Besselsleigh in Berkshire, the family's proud heritage extended deep into British history. John Lenthall Sr. was the great-great-grandson of Sir John Lenthall (1624-1681), a member of Parliament, who was the son of the best-known of the venerable family, William Lenthall (1591-1662), Speaker of the House of Commons during the Long Parliament of the English civil war period. Speaker Lenthall won fame for his principled defiance of King Charles I in favor of the rights of Parliament. Although endowed with an esteemed lineage, by the early 1790s John Lenthall Sr. saw his future not as an heir to a diminished ancestral heritage but as an entrepreneur in a brash new country across the Atlantic. He would never look back.[5]

John Lenthall Sr. arrived in Washington with ample experience in a wide range of allied professions. Perhaps the best description of his abilities was provided by his future employer, Benjamin Latrobe:

> He was brought up to the business of a carpenter. He was much in his youth employed in mines and knew much of the machinery used in that part of England. He was not less acquainted with the cotton works, and joined an insatiable desire of knowledge to a strong memory and sound judgement. His acquaintance with the arts and sciences not immediately connected with his trade was very extensive. He was also a superior draughtsman and a perfect master of his own business.[6]

Just what John Lenthall Sr. did during his first years in Washington is difficult to discern. As he thought of himself a builder—that defining title would be engraved on his headstone—he was likely hired as a general or sub-contractor in support of public and private construction projects.[7] John Lenthall Sr. was documented in 1798 and 1799 as being associated with the planning and perhaps construction of George Washington's North Capital Street town houses.[8] And then there are his most visible and enduring private creations of this period, the Lenthall houses. Built sometime during the late 1790s—the accounts vary—these paired Federal-style homes were originally erected at (using modern street numbering) 612-614 19th Street NW. The relentless press of urban renewal caused them in 1978 to be moved *in toto* by their current owners, the George Washington University, to a site a few blocks to the west, where they currently stand at 606-610 21st Street.[9] The presumption is that John Lenthall Sr. built them and may have briefly lived in one of them, No. 614. The example was staring him in the face—during this period he assisted the nation's first president to build his own speculative town houses. A charming tale has been handed down by descendants of the Lenthall family:

> There is the usual tradition that George Washington stopped in the 19th St. house when he was studying the plans of Washington. We have a mirror supposed to have hung in his room.[10]

This story has a ring of truth given John Lenthall Sr.'s connection to George Washington and, as will be related, the family of surveyors who created the earliest plans of Washington City.

In the closing months of 1799, a new government facility was founded within the federal district that would cast a long shadow over John Lenthall Sr.'s namesake, the Washington Navy Yard.[11] Situated at the south-eastern side of the District of Columbia, on the north bank of the Potomac's Eastern Branch, the shipyard would in time become Washington's largest employer. Some accounts say John Lenthall Sr. worked there although no record has been found to document these claims. But as he was active in the district, it is entirely plausible that he participated in the construction of the many structures required by a navy yard.

By 1800 John Lenthall Sr. was established as a well-regarded builder in a growing city where "he had invested his earnings of many laborious years."[12] In that year the District of Columbia was a still struggling urban enclave of 14,093 inhabitants of which only 3,210 lived in Washington proper. But optimism burned bright for on the 17th of November, the "Grand Council of the Nation"—Congress—met for the first time in the new federal district.[13]

* * *

The next foreign-born artisan of interest to reach Washington was not an individual but a family, the Kings. They brought to America the maternal wellspring from which issued the future Constructor John Lenthall. Robert King Sr., the family patriarch, was born in 1740 in Old Malton in the Vale of Pickering, Yorkshire. His profession, and indeed of his male heirs, was that of a surveyor. The late 1700s found England in the midst of a land enclosure movement and a surge of canal building. Each of these activities required experienced surveyors: land enclosures demanded knowledge of cadastral or land title surveying and navigational projects required topographical surveying skills. Robert King was proficient in both specialties.[14]

Unlike John Lenthall Sr., on the eve of his emigration to the new world Robert King Sr. was the father of a modestly sized family: his eldest son, Nicholas (b. 1771), had been followed by daughter Margaret (b. 1775), a second son Robert Jr. (b. 1775) and a second daughter, Jane (b. 1780). King's first wife died in 1780, possibly during childbirth; he remarried in 1792 to Margaret Reed. Both sons trained with their father as surveyors and, as will be seen, were attentive pupils and became skilled cartographers in their own right.[15]

The King family arrived in America piecemeal. Their urge to emigrate could well have flowed from the same source as John Lenthall Sr.'s, to avoid fall-out from the growing war between England and France. It seems that the youngest son, Robert Jr., may have been first. One account indicates he was hired by Treasury Secretary Albert Gallatin in 1794 as draftsman of public surveys in the land office.[16]

Next was Nicholas who emigrated in the spring of 1796. His travels brought him to Washington where on 24 September 1796, he was appointed a city surveyor, thus beginning the federal district's King era of mapmaking. Nicholas clearly anticipated his father's coming to Washington the following year, for he made his hiring conditional on his resigning his office upon the arrival of Robert King Sr. so that his more experienced father could take up the office's work.[17] In his short time as the city's principal surveyor, Nicholas King established a reputation as a meticulous draftsman who embellished his plans with artistic watercolor highlights.[18]

As expected, Robert King Sr. emigrated to the United States in 1797, accompanied by his family. Just who travelled with him is somewhat uncertain. Most accounts name his son Robert Jr. as coming to Washington at this time, and his second daughter, Jane, and wife can also be confidently included with those who made the journey.[19] However, it is not clear if his first daughter Margaret also emigrated. She was certainly alive and well, and appears in later accounts of the family.

Robert King Sr. assumed his son Nicholas' duties at Washington City's surveyor's office, his appointment dated 12 September 1797.[20] King Sr. was reckoned to be the most experienced surveyor employed during Washington's earliest years. In the meantime, first son Nicholas began working for private interests to manage their land businesses. In that pivotal year, Nicholas also took a wife, marrying Margaretta Gaunt (or Gantt) and started a family.[21]

The King family that remained under the aegis of father Robert Sr.—his wife, son Robert Jr., daughter Jane and perhaps Margaret—settled into a home a few blocks to the west of the site of the President's House. Just when they built the house and what it looked like is shrouded in the mists of time; it may even have started out as two, separate smaller 'bricks' that were later merged. The present address (using modern street numbering) of 1818 F Street NW has long been completely overrun by newer construction. Today the General Services Administration building covers the entire block on which the King house once stood.[22] The deed for the purchase of this property, in the names of Robert King Sr. and Robert King Jr., was eventually recorded on 23 April 1801, sometime after the Kings originally occupied their home.[23]

At the turn of the century, the King families were comfortably situated within their adopted city, both socially and professionally. Robert Sr., his wife and son Robert Jr. were thriving on F Street, and his eldest son Nicholas and wife were adding children with each passing year. And very soon another family member, the youngest daughter Jane, would succumb to the temptations of marriage.

* * *

A delightful recollection of the Lenthall family descendants relates just how Jane King chose her future mate:

> It seems that Jane King ... did live in the F Street house before she married John Lenthall [Sr.]. In fact there is a legend, that she observed him one day passing by with a friend and decided then and there that she would one day marry him, although they had not as yet met.[24]

The romantic wish of twenty-something Jane King soon became reality. She and John Lenthall Sr. joined in wedlock on or about the year 1800. No fully documented date is available; the same Lenthall descendent, Annette Ives, who related the above legend dated the marriage "about 1796." [25] The one researcher who dug deepest into Washington's archives in search of Lenthall-King documentation, Maud Burr Morris, suggests John Lenthall

Sr.'s connection with the King family did not occur before 1801.[26] Leaving the ambiguity of dates aside, Morris' narrative does usefully speculate on the circumstances that shaped the newly-weds' first year of marriage:

> After Jane King had selected her future husband with such nice perception, she evidently brought him home to this house [King house on F Street], perhaps with the intention of remaining there only until the erection of a home (if it was not already completed) on the Nineteenth Street lot, which Mr. Lenthall had purchased about the time of his marriage.[27]

* * *

CHAPTER 2

Father and Son

The Lenthalls started their new life together on F Street, choosing to remain in the King house rather than move elsewhere. It must have been a magnificent home, finer than the superbly finished Lenthall houses, or perhaps it was simply that the Lenthall houses had been leased out and their hands were tied.[1] However, other circumstances were changing around them, which may have influenced their decision. Jane was soon pregnant with her first child. The birth occurred in the King House on 18 July 1802.[2] It was a girl, and she was named Mary King Lenthall, probably in honor of Jane's late mother.

Just one month later, Jane's father, Robert King Sr., began his return to England. He resigned his position as Washington City surveyor on 13 August 1802, submitted an inventory of all the books, plans and instruments in his care and soon after, together with his wife, left for the old country.[3] Sons Nicholas and Robert Jr. stayed in Washington. Why did he choose to go at this time? King was now sixty-two and may have had thoughts of retiring. The Treaty of Amiens had been recently signed, bringing a pause in the war between England and France, perhaps encouraging hopes for prosperity. Regardless of the cause of his departure, the result was that he, together with his son Robert Jr., conveyed the King house property on F Street to John Lenthall Sr., the deed being dated the day after King's resignation.[4] Reviewing the chronology of events since the Lenthalls' marriage, it may have been that Robert King Sr.'s departure was long anticipated, making their continuity of residence in the King house eminently logical.

* * *

Near the end of the momentous year of 1802, the influence of the brilliant engineer-architect Benjamin Latrobe began to exert itself on the landscape of Washington and, very soon thereafter, upon the life of John Lenthall Sr. Latrobe's first acquaintance with the federal district had come four years before when he travelled through Washington and was introduced to the designer of the Capitol building, Dr. William Thornton. Now he returned at the behest of America's third president, Thomas Jefferson, to design a mammoth-covered drydock capable of housing all of the United States' warships. This was Latrobe's first brush with the Navy and the Washington Navy Yard. It would be the beginning of a long relationship that would gradually reshape the haphazard footprint of the capital city's infant navy yard into an efficiently organized industrial establishment.[5]

On 29 November 1802, while in Washington to develop his plans for the drydock, Latrobe was invited to dinner with the president.[6] But Jefferson had another, more urgent motive for sharing dinner with Latrobe that evening. Work on the Capitol building had been stalled for some time now—none of the appointed architects lasted long on the job—and he was looking for the right man to take charge. And in the thirty-eight-year-old Benjamin Latrobe, Thomas Jefferson found a lot to like. Originally trained for the ministry, Latrobe had spent his formative years studying in Europe. But ultimately, Latrobe's inquisitive mind lost interest in the Divine and instead, he pursued professions that guided him for the rest of his life. He studied under the renowned engineer John Smeaton—builder of the treacherously located Eddystone Lighthouse—and then worked in the offices of London architect S. P. Cockerell. So in addition to his formal education, which had included mathematics, logic, ethics and music, he quickly learned the fundamentals of engineering and architecture. And like so many young Englishmen of this same period, the loss of opportunity and changing political conditions caused by the French wars would, late in 1795, impel Benjamin Latrobe to seek his fortune in the New World.[7]

Little over three months after Latrobe's meeting with the president, Congress voted additional funds to restart construction of the unfinished south wing of the Capitol building. That was on 3 March 1803, and just three days later, Thomas Jefferson offered Benjamin Latrobe the office of surveyor of public buildings. Latrobe quickly accepted. It was a seismic boost for the young architect. Just seven years after his arrival in America, he had now been appointed to his profession's most prestigious position.[8]

Propelled by the same Congressional momentum, on 4 March 1803, Nicholas King was appointed by President Jefferson to his former post as surveyor of the City of Washington, filling the vacancy created by his father's departure.[9] The continuity of the Kings as Washington's leading surveyors was again ensured. Nicholas would remain in office for the next decade.

* * *

Events in the capital moved quickly. As Latrobe did not at that time envisage moving to Washington—he was then living in Philadelphia—it was vital that he select just the right man for the all-important position of "clerk of the works and principal surveyor." This supporting superintendent's duties were substantial. He must represent Latrobe in his absence and during such periods, report construction progress to the president.[10] Further, he had to be the on-site judge of materials and workmanship, manage the hiring and discharge of all employees, and produce detailed drawings under the architect's direction.[11] But who should Latrobe choose to fill such a position?

Less than a month after accepting the president's commission, Benjamin Latrobe asked John Lenthall Sr. to be his clerk of the works. Lenthall's appointment was dated 7 April 1803.[12] His selection in such a short time for the all-important superintendent's role together with their earliest, familiar correspondence suggests a prior acquaintance, or at the very least, a strong personal recommendation. Latrobe's previous business in November at the Washington Navy Yard—the drydock commission never came through—may have brought him in touch with John Lenthall Sr. Or Lenthall could have been introduced by Washington builders or architects familiar to Latrobe. Both Lenthall and Latrobe were English-born and in the business of building, so they must have been well known to many in their expatriate professional community. Or possibly they met through the newly appointed principal surveyor of Washington City, Nicholas King, Lenthall's brother-in-law. Whatever the reason, John Lenthall Sr. was an excellent choice. From long experience, he knew all of the local district builders, tradesmen and artisans and, as Latrobe had observed, was the perfect master of his own business.

Latrobe later recorded his impressions at the time of both Washington and Lenthall. Washington City he described as "an anomalous kind of settlement, neither village, town nor city," adding that "Speculators of all degrees of honesty and of desperation made a game of hazard of the scheme." Of John Lenthall Sr.'s circumstances, he penned a telling image. "I found him here nearly as badly off as any of the rest, who had sunk their prosperity into buildings. I wish I could reward his merit as it deserves."[13] Latrobe's estimation of Lenthall made it clear he held him in the highest regard. "I gave you the office from no motive whatever but a conviction that in skill and integrity I could not find your superior."[14] As for the personality of his new clerk of the works—the future father of Constructor John Lenthall—Latrobe leaves a carefully nuanced portrait:

> Though of very moderate stature, his personal strength and activity were unequalled, and the command he acquired of all those who

> were placed under him was achieved by his own superior ability. The full utility of so many and such extraordinary qualifications of mind and body, so seldom united in the same man, was somewhat abated by a reserved exterior, & a rigid adherence to his own principles and opinions, which nothing could bend; and on a slight acquaintance his character was not conciliatory. In the execution of his public duty he was inflexibly just, so far as to be often thought harsh, but when acting in his individual character, the benevolence of his heart could not be mistaken and he was by all those who had known him long, as much loved as respected.[15]

* * *

Less than a year after John Lenthall Sr. assumed his role as the Capitol building's clerk of the works, he and his wife welcomed a second member to their growing family. On 2 March 1804, "when Washington must have seemed almost a part of the surrounding wilderness, a little girl, Elizabeth Jane Lenthall was born ... at the Lenthall homestead on F Street."[16] The child's second name was clearly meant to honor her mother but the source of Elizabeth is not obvious. Her family affectionately called her Libby, which in her later correspondence she styled to read "Stibby" or "SLibby," possibly a shorthand for Sister Libby.

In this same year, as if he weren't busy enough with the Capitol construction and his other private commissions, Benjamin Latrobe was designated as the "engineer of the Navy Department." He was asked to prepare a comprehensive plan for developing the Washington Navy Yard. Progress with the improvements was gradual and often languished, but its trajectory was firmly guided by Latrobe's vision until the War of 1812's catastrophic intervention. During this period more than double the funds allocated to any other navy yard went to Washington.[17] Between British destruction and subsequent development, little remains of Latrobe's handiwork in the Washington Navy Yard beyond its residual footprint. Benjamin Latrobe's intensive focus on the Washington Navy Yard during these years, involving frequent contacts with its English-born commandant, Captain Thomas Tingey, must have nourished the links connecting the Lenthall family to the United States Navy. In time and after the birth of the family's next child, they would grow stronger.

The press of Latrobe's work and his growing commitments in Washington caused him, during the summer of 1807, to at last move his family to the nation's capital. But instead of smooth sailing he was now forced to deal with problems caused by intemperate outbursts from his moody clerk of the works. Diligent and capable he may have been, but John Lenthall Sr.

was at times excessively thin-skinned and prone to bouts of sulking. The latest target of his anger was, surprisingly, his former partner during his work on George Washington's town houses, master mason George Blagden. Latrobe was finally compelled to write to Lenthall, "reproving him for his uncivil actions and his constant complaints, and asking him if he wished to resign." The date was 5 September 1807. Thinking he had been too harsh. Latrobe quickly sent a second message to his clerk of the works in which he revealed the stunning admission that President Jefferson had been prejudiced against Lenthall's original appointment, but Latrobe had stood by his choice. He further declared his despair at trying to find Lenthall an acceptable assistant. But then Latrobe lightened up. "Whether you remain or not depends not on me. If you remain till I desire you to go, you will go only to sleep with your fathers." [18] They would prove to be prophetic words.

Such turmoil could not have come at a more uncomfortable time for John Lenthall Sr. His wife, then twenty-seven years old, was heavy with their third child. In the midst of the back-and-forth tensions between the clerk of the works and his benevolent boss, she gave birth to the Lenthalls' first son. The baby was delivered at their F Street home on Wednesday, 16 September 1807.[19] Thus began the life of the future naval constructor. The boy was named John Lenthall in honor of his father and many other Lenthall ancestors who had come before.

* * *

In the months that followed, the issues that had estranged relations between John Lenthall Sr. and Benjamin Latrobe gradually eased their grip. The press of work on the Capitol continued apace, exerting its claim on their attention and calming exchanges between the two. As the year of 1808 dawned, their former easy-going, close cooperation resumed. Friendship had prevailed.

During July and most of August, Benjamin Latrobe was away from Washington. It was in this period that his clerk of the works suggested a seemingly minor change to the construction of the Supreme Court chamber's vaults, all in the interests of saving time and labor. Latrobe agreed to Lenthall's proposal although with reservations. As the turn of events later demonstrated, both Lenthall and Latrobe shared varying degrees of responsibility for the tragic accident that followed. The oft-related event resulted in the sudden, violent death of John Lenthall Sr. on 19 September 1808, three days after his son's first birthday. He was forty-six years old. Because of its central place in Lenthall family biographies, it is instructive to view this story through the different lenses of those who were affected. The starting point is the Lenthall descendants' version:

> The first John Lenthall was under-architect at the Capitol, conducting the work in the absence of his chief, when it was ordered that the part under construction should be ready at a given date for the trial of Aaron Burr. John Lenthall remonstrated "the masonry would not have time to set and that the archway leading into the interior of the room would crumble if the wooden supports were removed." His suggestions were not considered, so at the appointed time the framework was taken down, excepting the main support. This was sawed or cut by the young architect himself, and the archway caved in on top of him.[20]

The day after the vault's collapse and now in Washington, a subdued Benjamin Latrobe penned a lengthy account of the accident which was published in the 23 September 1808 edition of the *National Intelligencer*:

> Yesterday (Monday) the vaults of the Court Room in the North wing of the Capitol fell down. Several workmen under the direction of Mr. John Lenthall ... were under the vault, lowering down that part of the center which still stood under it, just before it fell. A loud crack gave notice of the danger and all escaped out of the windows or under the adjoining vault, except Mr. Lenthall, who to judge from the place in which his body was found, wanted only a single step to have secured his retreat, but being under that part of the arch, the center of which had been removed on Friday, he was suddenly buried under many tons of bricks and must have been instantly deprived of all sensation and life. As all the butments of the vault are standing without the smallest failure, it is not easy satisfactorily to account for the sudden falling of the work. ... It was always the opinion of Mr. Lenthall that, to use his own words,–this vault had not fair play. Having been absent in the months of July and August a few weeks, I received a letter from him on the subject, in which he did not explain this hint, but while discharging the work on Friday last he mentioned a number of facts ...

Here Latrobe digresses and mentions suspicions of sabotage or foul deeds contributing to the collapse, but quickly downplayed the possibility of such "thankless villainy:"

> I mention these facts in justice to the opinion of Mr. Lenthall, and as only *one* of the causes of failure, without attaching any suspicion to any individual. ... The real causes of failure, I conceive to have been a too early removal of the centers and perhaps a removal not

> altogether judicious. And in so far as I might have controlled the judgment of any of those who are in trust under me, the error of confiding too much in the experiences of others against my own opinion ought to relieve every other person engaged in the work from blame. But after having safely constructed many infinitely bolder and more dangerous vaults without any accident, Mr. Lenthall's intrepidity occasioned frequent alarms for his safety, and his activity was such that he often had incurred considerable risk alone, before anyone was apprized of his intention. That he at least fell victim to his zeal for the public service, which always outstripped his own interest, convenience and safety, is most sensibly deplored by all who acted with him.[21]

A close analysis of Latrobe's remarks reveals that he accepted overall responsibility for the vault's collapse. He further suggested Lenthall's removal of the centers may well have been an impulsive, last-minute act. No mention is made of just who if anyone ordered the centers' removal that fatal Monday.

Three days later, on 23 September, when the emotions of the disaster had abated, Latrobe penned an explanation of the accident's cause to President Jefferson. Including a sketch to clarify his words, he described the vaults' original design and the alterations that led to their collapse. A summary of Latrobe's account was later written by his biographer, Talbot Hamlin:

> The original conception had contemplated a ribbed semi-dome; the ribs were to have had conical vaults built over and between them to support the Senate chamber floor above. ... Lenthall suggested another scheme that would save a great deal in centering and labor; instead of the conical vaults radiating from the center, annular barrel vaults would be run over the lower semi-dome circumferentially. ... The Lenthall system had brought heavy concentrated loads on the dome at places ill-adjusted to receive them, and when the supports were removed the whole collapsed.[22]

As a postscript, Glenn Brown, the author of *History of the United States Capitol* published in 1900, wrote that "Latrobe had considerable difficulty in keeping the arched ceilings from falling." He cited sharp comments from Dr. William Thornton, the original Capitol architect, on this same subject.[23] In fairness to Latrobe—and Lenthall—the Capitol building is composed of countless arches, vaults, domes and like structures, and it is not surprising that difficulty was experienced with their erection over the many years of its construction. The ultimate tragedy is that despite foreshadowings of disaster, John Lenthall Sr. found himself beneath a weakened vault at just the wrong time.

* * *

It is painful to even try to imagine the scene at the Lenthall's home on that dreadful Monday. Jane Lenthall must have been overwhelmed with grief at her loss, then anxiety for the future of her family. In a blink she was a widow, the mother of three young children: Mary, age six; Elizabeth, age four; and the baby John, just one. But she did have an unwavering source of support that comforted her in those first hours, days and years to come—her brothers Nicholas and Robert.

Once the tons of rubble had been pulled away, John Lenthall Sr.'s crumpled body was removed from the Supreme Court chamber and brought to his home. There it was prepared for interment. His funeral took place from the house on F St. "He was buried with military honors ..." amongst the tall cedars and black headstones of Washington's public burying ground. In time Jane Lenthall, a widow at twenty-eight, was awarded a pension.[24]

John Lenthall, a boy of just one year, had been robbed of his father. Little John never really knew his dad. He was denied the wisdom, encouragement and imparted experience that is a father's greatest gift to a son. But nurtured by his close-knit family, he would thrive and grow into a capable, intelligent youth, always guided by the loving attentions of his mother and his King family uncles.

Jane Lenthall's brothers supported her at every turn, in every way, doing all they could to fill the role of her children's missing father. Nicholas, the eldest, was then active as the City of Washington's surveyor. He also sat on the Washington City council and is said to have been the founder of the city's first public library. By the year of his brother-in-law's death, he had fathered seven children, five of whom survived infancy. A very busy man indeed and a wonderful role model he must have been for the young Lenthall children. But sadly, Nicholas King lived fewer than four years beyond John Lenthall Sr.'s death, dying before reaching forty-one on 21 May 1812.[25]

That left Brother Robert to fill the gaps. Exactly one year after Nicholas died, Robert King Jr. was appointed to his position.[26] A third member of the family now sustained the King era of Washington City surveyors. Robert had been continuously employed since 1797 (if not before) as a draftsman of public surveys at the Treasury Department. He now worked both jobs.[27] Another busy brother.

It also fell to Robert King, Jr. to carry on as the Lenthall family's surrogate father. Aged thirty-seven in the year of Nicholas' passing, Robert had never married. And he was utterly devoted to his sister and her children.[28] At some point in time, Robert moved back into the F Street house, the same property that he and his father had sold to the Lenthalls in 1802. He was documented as living at that address in the 1820 federal census and by that date, he had probably been there for many years.[29] Despite the loss of her husband, Jane Lenthall and her family were able to get on with life in their familiar, comfortable home, supported by the presence of a strong male. The children's Uncle Robert would remain an integral part of the Lenthall-King family for the rest of his life.

* * *

CHAPTER 3

The War of 1812

By the end of the first decade of the 1800s, the District of Columbia and the cities it encompassed had grown considerably. In ten years, the federal district's population increased seventy percent to a total of 24,024 residents, and Washington City by even more, leaping 150 percent to 8,208 persons. But the district was hardly larger than a respectable town and, in the words of one of its historians, was an "outwardly primitive little capital."[1] Benjamin Latrobe's son later recorded his recollections of Washington at that time:

> Pennsylvania avenue was little better than a common country road.... In dry weather the avenue was all dust; in wet weather, all mud ... The Capitol itself stood on a steep declivity, clothed with old oaks and seamed with numerous gullies. Between it and the navy-yard were few buildings, here and there, over an arid common. Following the amphitheater of hills from the south-east around to the heights of Georgetown, houses few and far between indicated the beginning of the present city. The Patent and Post Offices, in one huge, unornamental barn-like edifice, occupied the place of their successors, and at the other end of the avenue the White House had become a conspicuous object, with the adjacent public offices. Still following the amphitheater around, the eye caught a glimpse of Alexandria and rested on the broad expanse of water where the Eastern Branch joined the Potomac.[2]

The Lenthall's home—the King house—standing on the south side of F Street, between 18th and 19th Streets, was one of the "houses few and far between." It was located on the second city block to the west of the large rectangle of land reserved for the President's House and its grounds. Their home was quite close to one of the public offices mentioned by Latrobe, the building that housed the State, War and Navy Departments—the "old

War office"—which sat on the rectangle's western edge. The Treasury Department occupied a building on the opposite side, to the east of the President's House.[3] The proximate locations of these federal departments well served Robert King Jr., and in a later era, would be of inestimable convenience to Constructor John Lenthall.

Despite Benjamin Latrobe's best efforts, the Capitol building was still incomplete. Both of its north and south wings were finished, but the central connecting structure that would, in time, support the distinctive Capitol dome, had yet to be erected. The grounds surrounding the seat of Congress, disfigured by the detritus of on-going construction, were undeveloped and unkempt.[4] Although still a work in progress, perhaps Latrobe was more pleased with his achievements at the Washington Navy Yard. During the first decade of the new century, the steady pressure of construction had resulted in the raising of workshops of all kinds and even a steam engine, which provided power for the foundry and much else.[5]

The navy yard's new facilities had also borne fruit. Standing apart from the Jefferson-era gunboats being built by the yard, the first true sea-going warship to rise from one of its slipways, the sloop of war *Wasp*, was launched on 21 April 1806.[6] That same year, 1807, saw the yard complete its refit of the 36-gun frigate *Chesapeake* for service in the Mediterranean. Under the flag of Commodore James Barron, the hastily commissioned frigate made her way to Norfolk before belatedly taking her departure from the Virginia Capes on 22 June. There she was confronted by H.M.S. *Leopard*, a 50-gun two-decker, and forced to undergo the humiliation of having four of her seamen removed at gun-point. The British claimed they were Royal Navy deserters. When the news reached Washington, the nation was outraged. Demands for revenge stoked the fires that, five years later, would ignite the War of 1812.[7]

* * *

The *Chesapeake-Leopard* affair was just one of many events in a steady drum-beat of tensions between Great Britain and the United States that led to conflict. Constantly at war with Napoleon since 1803, Britain had adopted increasingly oppressive economic measures to strangle its continental rivals, France and its satellites, and they bore most harshly on the vigorous neutral merchant marine of the United States. In the space of four years, hundreds of American ships had been seized by each belligerent. The Royal Navy's dearth of manpower added yet another but very emotional layer to America's pain. Its none-too-scrupulous captains felt entitled to stop U.S. flagged merchantmen and impress any sailors they deemed British subjects. In that era, it was difficult to tell an American from an Englishman, as the Kings or Lenthalls could have attested. The United States' confused response to British Orders in Council and Napoleon's Continental system proved ineffectual and self-defeating. Jeffersonian Republicans' reflexive instinct for economy—laying-up the frigates and building coastal gunboats—resulted in a defense posture that did nothing to protect the nation's far flung merchant marine. The non-importation laws, then the trade embargo and the non-intercourse act that followed did more damage to America's economy than to their targets, Britain and France. And they also served to further polarize America's domestic politics and regional factions, undermining the image of government unity in the face of foreign threats.[8] Broadsheets crying "Free Trade and Sailors' Rights" captured the populist sentiments of the day. They also neatly encapsulated a cornerstone of American foreign policy that would carry into the decades that followed, a preoccupation with neutral rights. But beneath the broadsheets' rousing oratory lurked intractable international differences that, in the minds of an aroused public, could only be resolved by force of arms.[9] And so, on 18 June 1812, the United States declared war on Great Britain. Reflecting the fractured state of American politics, Congress' vote for war passed by the narrowest of margins.[10] It was hardly an auspicious beginning for a conflict with the world's superpower.

* * *

America was woefully unprepared for war, especially one with Britain's tip of the spear, the Royal Navy. In the year 1812, nearly 600 British men-of-war cruised the seas and another 300 were under refit or in harbor service. This was the invincible navy that had clipped Napoleon's maritime wings, defeated the French and Spanish fleets at Trafalgar and whose blockade had, over ten long years, squeezed the lifeblood of commerce from European ports. Facing that colossus, the United States Navy mustered at most fifteen commissioned sea-going warships—frigates, sloops and brigs—and could add only two more before the year was out. No sustained program of new building or dockyard expansion had been promulgated in expectation of hostilities.[11] It was the classic plight faced by warriors since the dawn of time—you fight with the forces you have.

But the United States' situation wasn't as hopeless as the numbers might suggest. The small navy it did possess was a professional service led by ambitious officers of proven ability. In its short life, the U.S. Navy had gained considerable experience on distant seas as a cruising navy, first during the Quasi-War fighting France in the West Indies and then over the many years of Barbary wars in the Mediterranean. Officers such as Isaac Hull, Stephen Decatur and William Bainbridge had gained renown during those campaigns, and they would be heard from again.

Further, the men-of-war fielded by the U.S. Navy were superb ships, well-founded and typically larger and more heavily armed than comparable foreign designs of the same class. These latter qualities—size and force—were a consequence of the Navy's accepting and understanding that as a smaller naval power with few assets, each ship it got to sea had to be superior to its rivals. By comparison, driven by its need to operate enough warships to guard a worldwide trading empire, the Royal Navy consistently chose to build the greatest numbers of ships for the least expense, giving their squadrons the smallest warships of their class.

The core of the U.S. Navy's fighting strength was its original six frigates, authorized by Congress in 1794.[12] Three of these ships, the 44-gun frigates *United States, Constitution* and *President,* were designed specifically to meet the challenges expected to be faced by America's new navy. The remaining three, the 38-gun *Congress* and *Constellation* and 36-gun *Chesapeake,* were big ships but modeled closer to contemporary practice. The concept for the 44-gun frigates grew from the fertile mind of the Navy's first constructor, Joshua Humphreys of Philadelphia, whose family's heritage would soon loom large over the life of young John Lenthall. Humphreys was well-known to the Navy, having designed a number of the Continental Navy's frigates and built the first of its class to get to sea, *Randolph.* He proposed the construction of a type of warship that could overpower any existing frigate yet was weatherly enough to evade an enemy of superior power. The worldly Joshua Humphreys had in his mind's eye just what was wanted, a man-of-war built to a design "similar with those adopted by France ... they having cut down several of their 74s to make heavy frigates." Thus was born the American 'super frigate'.[13]

The new frigates took shape slowly, as deliveries of live oak allowed, the first 44-gun ship launched being the *United States* from the yard of Joshua Humphreys. She was huge, 175 ft long and stoutly constructed of live oak, using scantling sized for a 74-gun ship. Such extreme measures were necessary to ensure her structural integrity and prevent hogging. The big frigate was pierced to carry thirty 24-pdr guns on her main deck, and could mount nearly a full broadside of smaller guns on her spar deck.[14] The contrast between Humphrey's 44-gun frigate and a comparable British frigate, the 38-gun *Lively,* reveals the power of the American creation. A large frigate for the Royal Navy when introduced in 1799, *Lively's* design was influenced by the proportions of captured French frigates—increased length and reduced breadth and depth. On her 150 ft long main deck, she mounted a battery of twenty-eight 18-pdr guns.[15] So by every measure—length of hull, number of cannon and weight of broadside—the American

44-gun frigates were an overmatch for their British opponents. The Royal Navy would soon learn just how lethal they could be.

* * *

A natural complement to a weaker power's motivation to build individually superior fighting ships is the strategy of *guerre de course*, or war of the chase. Rather than seeking battle with its enemy's larger and more numerous squadrons, a smaller navy should instead focus its scarce resources on the destruction of its foe's valuable commerce. This same strategy had been employed by the infant Continental Navy, and with war now declared against Great Britain, it was unhesitatingly adopted by the U.S. Navy.

American frigates, sloops and brigs fanned out over the Atlantic Ocean in search of rich prizes. The British knew what the game was about, and mobilized their war vessels to counter the treat. It was only a matter of time before one sighted the other. The first contact leading to a duel between the two navies' frigates occurred on 19 August 1812, off the coast of Nova Scotia. The U.S.S. *Constitution,* commanded by Isaac Hull, sighted H.M.S. *Guerriere,* known to be one of a British squadron covering the port of New York. Hull immediately gave chase and *Guerriere,* a 38-gun frigate under her experienced captain, James Dacres, chose to wait and give battle. The ensuing contest, during which *Constitution* earned her nickname of "Old Ironsides," saw Dacres's 18-pdr frigate hammered into submission, completely dismasted by *Constitution*'s heavier 24-pdr guns. *Guerriere,* a former French vessel of lighter scantling, was damaged beyond repair and so, once her crew had been transferred, she was burned. Hull's celebrated action was the first major naval victory of the war and a welcome tonic for the American public. The lessons learned were clear. A well-drilled Royal Navy crew, firing three 18-pdr broadsides to two of its American antagonists, were no match for the destructive power of 24-pdr guns. Nor could their cannon easily damage the bigger ship's heavier timbers.[16]

The second frigate duel of the war with significance to a biography of Constructor John Lenthall was fought in October of that year. Cruising in the mid-Atlantic, toward the island of Madeira, the 44-gun frigate *United States* sighted a masthead on the horizon. Captain Stephen Decatur immediately closed on the ship which proved to be a lone British frigate, H.M.S. *Macedonian,* Captain John Carden in command. The recently refitted *Macedonian* was a sister to the *Lively* class of 38-gun, 18-pdr frigates.[17] She had a clean hull and good turn of speed. Her captain could have avoided battle, but instead, he chose to fight. And he lost. During a long-range cannonade, *United States*' 24-pdrs shot away *Macedonian*'s mizzen mast and both her fore and main topmasts, inflicting a frightful butcher's bill. Although his ship was still capable of combat and her hull intact, Carden stuck his colors. Decatur boarded the frigate, raised a jury rig and sent her into New York, giving the U.S. Navy its first 'trophy ship' of the war. The navy's lesson from this contest was a reinforcement of its confidence in the decisive power of the heaviest guns in a fight. Even one of the best English-built 18-pdr frigates was no match for an American super frigate.[18] Now a U.S. Navy prize and soon to be commissioned as one of its warships, *Macedonian*'s hull would give its naval constructors a first-hand look at the arts of the English shipwright.

The third of the frigate encounters of interest was really no contest at all—the engagement of the U.S.S. *Chesapeake,* 36-guns, with H.M.S. *Shannon,* 38-guns. Although *Chesapeake* was of heavier scantling, both ships were nearly the same size and armed with 18 pdrs, but there the similarities end. Captain Philip Broke of the *Shannon,* a gunnery fanatic, had the best-trained crews in the Royal Navy while his foe, Lawrence, putting out from Boston to engage Broke, trusted to brave men who had not yet coalesced into a team. In just eleven minutes, *Shannon*'s murderous broadsides destroyed *Chesapeake*'s fighting cohesion and despite Lawrence's dying words, "Don't give up the ship," her colors were struck. America's winning streak was over. Now the British had a trophy ship of their own. The lesson was that when equal ships engage, rigorous training trumps enthusiasm.[19]

Britain's *Shannon* would have piqued the interest of American naval constructors. One of the *Leda* class frigates—in time they would become numerically the largest in the Royal Navy—her hull was based on the famed French frigate, *Hébé,* captured back in 1782. *Hébé* was one of the first big 40-gun French 18-pdr frigates, designed by their very capable naval constructor, Jacques-Noël Sané.[20] This age of naval warfare must have been stimulating for constructors of all the maritime powers. Warships of their enemies, often the best of their class, were regularly captured and put into service alongside ships of their own design. Sailing together in all conditions and under the watchful eyes of observant officers, features to emulate quickly demonstrated themselves—speed, stiffness, weatherliness, tendency to pitch or roll, wetness, hull strength and ability to stow provisions. Naval architects like nothing better than to have a proven 'go-by' to guide their next project, and in this era, they had ample opportunity to learn much from their rival designers. And as can be seen from this brief analysis of three significant naval actions fought during the War of 1812, the Royal Navy's constructors were enormously influenced by the superior qualities of their captured French frigates.

* * *

To the Lenthall-King family, comfortably distant in Washington City, the war's high seas frigate actions must have seemed remote indeed. But closer to home and filling the columns of their papers, news of the Royal Navy's 1813 campaign of invasion, harassment and burning of American towns throughout the Chesapeake Bay was impossible to ignore. One name never failed to make the headlines, Rear Admiral Sir George Cockburn. Mastermind of the British destruction, Cockburn reserved a particular hatred of irregular American snipers who resisted his attacks. As the new year of 1814 morphed into spring then summer, the capital city's residents must have anxiously wondered if the war would come to Washington.[21]

Such a question was sensible. The biggest target on the bay was Baltimore, a prosperous port and home to scores of despised privateers. But while Washington was strategically insignificant, its navy yard excepted, to the British, the psychological value of capturing the enemy's capital was priceless. Further, the sudden neutralization of Napoleon—now exiled to Elba—meant that thousands of Wellington's "Invincibles" were sailing to join Cockburn and empower his dream of taking Washington. It wasn't until August that the British were ready; then they struck. In a dramatic display of the reach of sea power, a Royal Navy squadron ascended the Patuxent River to the inland port of Benedict, disembarked nearly 4,000 soldiers under Major General Sir Robert Ross and started marching north, supported by Cockburn and his sailors. Their objective was still opaque to the hastily mustering local militia. Would it be Baltimore or Washington? To the Americans' consternation it soon became clear the capital was the target. General Winder supported by the Navy's Joshua Barney attempted to stop them at the bridgehead of Bladensburg, but was roughly shoved aside. That was on the morning of 24 August; by that evening, British forces had overrun Washington. The national nightmare had begun.[22]

Robert King Jr. and Jane Lenthall had no doubts about what must be done. In a past life, the 'redcoats' would have been fellow countrymen, but now they were the enemy. Robert had worked nearly his entire life for the federal government and Jane's husband died building its Capitol. It was simply too risky to allow the Lenthall children to remain in a fallen city. That night Mary, age twelve, Elizabeth, age ten and little John, almost seven, were hastily put in a cart and driven north to safety at the Holmead farm on Mount Pleasant.[23]

The British briskly began their destruction, first touring, then looting and finally smashing and burning the American government's public buildings. The incomplete Capitol, with its magnificent Senate and House of Representatives chambers and the Library of Congress, was their first target, followed quickly by the President's House and Treasury building. All were set afire. At the Washington Navy Yard, Commandant Tingey hastily evacuated what he could, then with a heavy heart, torched his dockyard. The next morning, Ross' and Cockburn's men destroyed even more, burning the old War office, leveling the arsenal at Greenleaf's Point and setting fire to the navy yard buildings that escaped Tingey's arson. And what the British didn't loot, the lawless locals stole with glee, even prying hinges from doors.

Flames lit the skies over Washington, visible afar to its many shocked citizens and the residents of nearby towns. One diarist, transfixed by fireballs billowing from the navy yard's inferno, described their "almost meridian brightness." No one slept that night. All were numbed by the enormity of it all, the awesome disgrace of witnessing their capital's destruction.[24] One wonders just what young John Lenthall made of it. How did he react to the sight of demoralized American troops streaming through his neighborhood? Did he question why soldiers carrying the flag of his parents' homeland were vandalizing the city he had grown up in?

The British began their retreat from Washington the evening of the 25th, retracing their steps back to Benedict and their ships. Only ten days had elapsed from their landing to their disembarkation, ten days of infamy and national humiliation. The Lenthall-King family returned to find their F Street home whole, a huge relief considering its proximity to the still smoking President's House and adjacent federal buildings. And they must have taken heart to learn that, despite fires set by the British in the Supreme Court chamber, the rebuilt vaulting—the same that had collapsed and killed John Lenthall Sr.—withstood the abuse and remained standing. [25]

On 24 December 1814, American commissioners met with their British opposites and signed the Treaty of Ghent, concluding a war that both countries were glad to end. Back in Washington, after some hesitation over whether the nation's capital should be moved, Congress voted to rebuild the damaged Capitol, President's House and other federal buildings. In hindsight, some residents said the British assault was a blessing in disguise. Congress' action had firmly committed the nation to keeping the seat of American government in Washington.[26]

The Washington Navy Yard was a smoldering ruin. Only Latrobe's Gate, the Commandant's House and the Second Officer's Quarters had escaped the fires. What buildings weren't wholly destroyed were, at best, blackened shells. Initial estimates of the cost of the navy yard's destruction were equal to those for all the other public buildings combined.[27] But the war was over and in time, both Washington and the navy yard would rise from their ashes like the phoenix.

* * *

The United States Navy's very visible successes during the War of 1812 convinced the public of the need to maintain a strong navy. The nation was proud of its accomplishments and a groundswell of support ensured the Navy's rebuilding and future growth.[28] And not just as the gunboat-frigate force of pre-war years, but as one that could thwart a European power's attempt to blockade America's ports. Early in the war, Congress had grasped this new reality. In addition to authorizing construction of three new 44-gun frigates, it had approved the building of up to four 74-gun ships of the line; by the end of hostilities, two of them were nearly complete.[29] And in a nod to the future of naval warfare, in March of 1814, Congress further sanctioned a novel blockade-busting craft, Robert Fulton's steam battery, *Demologos.*[30]

The navy that grew in the wake of the War of 1812 would differ from its predecessor in more ways than just its new fighting ships. Little more than a month after the war's end, on 7 February 1815, an act of Congress created a new Board of Navy Commissioners to assist the Secretary of the Navy in his management of the service. Consisting of three senior captains, one of whom was designated as its president, the board's control over the design and construction of new vessels would become nearly absolute. Together with the establishment of the board, the Navy's organization of its naval constructors also evolved. Each of its six navy yards—Portsmouth (Kittery), Boston (Charlestown), New York (Brooklyn), Philadelphia, Washington and Norfolk (Gosport)—was allowed a resident constructor, all of whom reported to the board. The board was initially composed of Isaac Hull and David Porter, with John Rodgers appointed as its president. All were senior captains and had gained fame during the late war, but Rodgers stood out from the very beginning as the Board's most influential member. One senator wrote of him, "His very figure and face were those of the naval hero ... combining in the perfect degree the idea of strength and endurance." Commodore Rodgers would serve for more than nineteen years as the board's president.[31]

Also in February of 1815, the new secretary of the navy, Benjamin Crowninshield, voiced his vision of the future:

> The destinies of the nation appear to be intimately connected with her maritime power and prosperity; and as the creation of a Navy is not a work to be quickly performed, it seems necessary not only to cherish our existing [naval] resources, but to augment them gradually and steadily.[32]

The following year Congress heeded his call. On 29 April 1816, an "Act for the Gradual Increase of the Navy of United States" was passed, which appropriated annual expenditures of one million dollars over the next eight years for the construction of nine new ships of the line and twelve 44-gun frigates, all to be built in navy yards. It was a turning point in the nation's history; its government had committed to an expansion of naval power during a period of peace.[33]

Although a youngster at the time, the War of 1812 loomed large over Constructor John Lenthall. Its outsized legacy shaped the United States Navy for the decades that followed, the same years during which he learned then practiced the arts of a naval constructor. The war created the navy he would soon serve and it long exerted its influence over the navy he would build.

* * *

CHAPTER 4

Apprentice Ship Carpenter

With the excitement of the British assault still fresh in their memories, the Lenthall children pressed their attentions back to what for their young minds must have seemed an unending chore, their education. Few details survive of how or what they were taught, but one memoir tells that Jane Lenthall, a "mother of rare intelligence and refinement," with the aid of her brothers, managed to give them "not only a thorough but finished education." This same source, Elizabeth Lenthall Stone's biographer, gives us the following picture:

> In early childhood the three children used to attend school in a little house which stood on the site of the present National Hotel, tripping gaily along the country paths which led through the huckleberry bushes by the side of the road, which we to-day know as Pennsylvania avenue. Later, the two sisters went for drawing lessons in an unfinished building connected with the White House … Here they were taught by a Mr. André, one of the foreign artists employed by the government.[1]

The influence of expatriate government employees over the lives of the Lenthall children was foreshadowed in their earliest years. Closest to home, their uncle Robert must have given significant guidance to them, especially to young John. It was likely from Robert, the principal draftsman of the General Land Office and surveyor of the City of Washington, that he learned the basics of drafting, geometry and mathematics.[2] But there were others who contributed, as much by role model and inspiration as through the actual teaching of lessons.

Chased away by the war, Benjamin Latrobe returned to Washington in April of 1815 and resumed his duties as architect of the Capitol. In September, he gained the additional role of surveyor of Washington, alongside Robert King Jr. The close presence of his father's former boss, a gifted architect, engineer and as of late, a builder of steamboats for Robert Fulton, must have added an extra dimension to Lenthall's learning experience. And many other men of talent followed on Latrobe's coattails. One example is a French military engineer with the larger-than-life name of Guillaume Tell Lavalloe Poussin. Emigrating to America after the fall of Napoleon, the twenty-year-old Poussin was hired by Latrobe as a draftsman.[3] Within two years, he was commissioned as a U.S. Army officer and then worked as a topographical engineer. [4] Many years later, Poussin would write John Lenthall letters of introduction for his stay in France. But for the present, Poussin was one of many skilled expatriates who likely enlarged Lenthall's knowledge of the world. Maybe it was Poussin or an émigré like him who taught young John the basics of the French language.

* * *

It is at this point that a biographer of Constructor John Lenthall is obliged to pose the question: what drew him to the Navy? Perhaps it was simply the romance of the late war's frigate actions and their rousing tales of brave American sailors. After all, the Washington Navy Yard was just a few miles from Lenthall's F Street home; with but a few steps, the tall masts of famous fighting ships could be glimpsed from afar. And the old War office was only two blocks away, making it commonplace to encounter naval officers in their gold-trimmed blue uniforms. Pausing to consider those who were closest to him—his Uncle Robert, his late father and their immediate associates—logic would suggest that Lenthall should have become a surveyor, or a builder or possibly an architect, a land-based profession that required the disciplines he had probably already mastered—mathematics, geometry, drafting and a smattering of engineering.

But by his early teens, John Lenthall clearly had decided he wanted to be a builder of ships. And not any ordinary craft, say merchant ships, fishing boats or the like, but naval vessels—warships. It was a narrowly focused choice. It could be speculated that a mentor interested in John Lenthall's education or a person he looked up to as a role model, someone involved with the business of building warships, inspired his decision to become a naval constructor. Two names rise as possibilities, men who almost certainly knew Lenthall's father and may have worked with him before his untimely death: the Washington Navy Yard's commandant, Thomas Tingey and its boatbuilder, William Easby, also known as Captain Easby. Both were English-born and both rendered material assistance to Constructor John Lenthall's later career.

Commodore Thomas Tingey, the more speculative candidate, was twelve years older than Lenthall's father. A former Royal Navy officer, he captained merchant ships for a number of years before becoming a U.S.

Navy officer during the Quasi-War with France. Assigned as commandant of the Washington Navy Yard at its founding, Tingey was active in Washington's society and well-known both personally and professionally to that other presence in the Kings' and Lenthalls' lives, Benjamin Latrobe. Tingey would remain the yard's commandant for twenty-nine years.[5] The other possible mentor candidate was William Easby, an energetic and educated Yorkshireman who had worked at the navy yard since 1805 if not before. He was about sixteen years older than young John Lenthall. Easby was the perfect master of his profession, and later in his career as a shipbuilder, took apprentices under his supervision. A demonstrated patriot, Easby served under Joshua Barney at Bladensburg. He was an avid bibliophile, eventually accumulating over 2,500 volumes in his library; Lenthall, in time, also became a collector of books.[6] Easby and Lenthall enjoyed a relation of mutual respect and admiration which was certainly evident in the first year of Lenthall's hiring by the Navy. Whether it was Tingey or Easby or someone else who nudged him along on his chosen vocation will probably never be known, but whatever the source John Lenthall was growing into an inspired and very focused young man.

* * *

Washington recovered briskly from its ordeal of invasion and destruction. In June 1816, just under two years after its burning, the Washington Navy Yard celebrated its resurrection by laying down the keel of *Columbus*, a 74-gun ship of the line, the first to be constructed under the Navy's "Gradual Increase" program.[7] Commodore Tingey must have been proud.

Close to the Lenthall-King home, rebuilding of the burned-out old War office had been completed the year before, allowing the State, War and Navy Departments to reoccupy it. But it was already too cramped—the Board of Navy Commissioners was forced to rent a small house for their own use—so two new buildings were begun to house the War and State Departments. These were complete by 1820, leaving the Navy as the sole inhabitants of their original quarters, now called the "old Navy Department building" or officially the Southwest Executive building.[8]

Benjamin Latrobe had made astonishing progress rebuilding the fire-damaged Capitol. In just two and a half years, he achieved more than he had during the six years before the British assault. Sadly, for both Latrobe and the nation, the architect abruptly resigned his government appointments in November 1817 after a spat with the Capitol's commissioner. It would take eleven more years before the building was finally completed.[9]

Meanwhile Robert King Jr. capped an era by resigning his position as surveyor of Washington in the same year as Latrobe. Then in 1818, he published a map of Washington and the District of Columbia (Map No. 1). It was one of the earliest engraved maps of the city and the most accurate to date, not to be improved upon until the eve of the Civil War. It also got caught up in a famous copyright infringement lawsuit. King sued a local printer who had copied his map, but because King neglected to place the copyright date on the face of his original map, his lawsuit failed. Its precedent has guided publishers ever since.[10]

The capital's burning and the financial panic that followed in 1819 made little difference to the growth of Washington City. Congress' decision to keep the United States' government in the District of Columbia ensured its future. By the year 1820, Washington's population had increased to 13,117, a sixty percent jump over the previous ten years. An upward trajectory, yes, but it was still a small, sparsely populated city that hosted America's capital.[11]

As the new decade of the 1820s dawned, the King-Lenthall family celebrated the first marriage of one of its children. It was their second-born daughter who stole the march. Vows were exchanged on 22 October 1821 between Elizabeth Jane Lenthall, seventeen and a half years old, and William James Stone, twenty-three. William Stone was born in England but emigrated as a boy with his family to America. He learned the art of line engraving in New York City, and came to Washington at the close of the war, establishing in 1820 what would prove to be a very successful business. Stone was also an ardent patron of the arts and an accomplished sculptor in his own right.[12]

* * *

In the year after the Stone-Lenthall wedding, another Lenthall family member embarked on a new path in life. Son John began his apprenticeship as a ship carpenter. From the best reconstruction of imperfect documentation, it appears that John Lenthall started his apprenticeship on or about the date of his fifteenth birthday, 16 September 1822, at the Washington Navy Yard. Shortly thereafter, due to the influence of Samuel Humphreys, the resident naval constructor at Philadelphia's navy yard, he was transferred to that city. As each element of this seemingly straight-forward statement is tainted by varying degrees of uncertainty, some explanations are necessary.

First the start date. From the Philadelphia Navy Yard's payroll of mechanics and laborers, it is documented that John Lenthall worked as a carpenter "on the ship of the line now on the stocks of the yard," earning $0.50 per day, during April 1823 and very likely from 1 January of that year.[13] So he was serving as an apprentice at age fifteen, helping to build the Humphreys designed 120-gun ship of the line *Pennsylvania* which had been laid down the year before, a vessel that will again feature prominently in Lenthall's life.[14] One source suggested he started his apprenticeship at age twelve, but this seems too early.[15] In that era, a common age to begin an apprenticeship was sixteen, so fifteen would be a good fit. And there is compelling physical evidence that ties Lenthall's start date to 1822—two of his books on naval architecture. Lenthall was a life-long collector of books, nearly 400 of which he donated to the Franklin Institute and are now deposited at Philadelphia's Independence Seaport Museum (see Appendix 10).[16] He had the habit of signing his books, usually on the title page, often noting the date and place where he acquired them. Two of his books, *Encyclopedia Methodique, Marine,* 1783 and *Vocabulaire des Termes de Marine, Anglois-François* [sic] *et François-Anglois ...,* by Lescallier, 1799, were 'signed-in' by John Lenthall and dated 1822, the latter of which is also marked "Washington City." That these two books were in Lenthall's hands in 1822—both in French, one an encyclopedia of naval subjects and the other a dictionary to aid in translations—suggests that Lenthall had already mastered the basics of French and that someone familiar with a naval constructor's education had recommended them.

Second the location. From the above discussion, it is clear that Lenthall was, in early 1823, serving his apprenticeship in Philadelphia. Still, some accounts suggest he "learned the trade of ship carpenter at the Washington Navy Yard" without a mention of Philadelphia.[17] A memoir by William Easby's youngest daughter, Wilhelmina, states that "In 1823 John Lenthall was employed in the mould loft at the [Washington] navy yard ...under my father's supervision."[18] Since Lenthall's home was in Washington, it is reasonable to believe that he commenced his apprenticeship in its navy yard. And his supervisor, Samuel Humphreys, was often there dealing with the Navy Board of Commissioners, so it follows that he spent a fraction of his years as an apprentice at the Washington Navy Yard. Fortunately, Humphreys brings closure to this matter, later writing that his apprentice, John Lenthall, worked "the greater part of his time in the Philadelphia Navy Yard, the last year in the navy yard at this place [Washington]." [19]

Third, all sources agree that John Lenthall served his apprenticeship under the aegis of Samuel Humphreys.[20] Given that, the open questions are: how did Lenthall come to Humphreys' notice and why wasn't he assigned to the Navy's resident constructor at the Washington Navy Yard, William Doughty. As will be seen, John Lenthall was something of a math prodigy, with an incredible affinity for the tedious calculations employed by naval constructors of that era. He also had a natural gift for the art of drafting. In the small world of Washington and its close-knit naval community, word that the son of John Lenthall Sr., the late clerk of the works of the Capitol and nephew of Washington surveyor and map maker, Robert King, was so endowed may have reached Humphreys' ears who, after meeting young John and sizing him up, decided he might just make a suitable assistant. As for Doughty, the more senior constructor and already comfortably established, perhaps he simply had no desire to assume the burden of a new apprentice.

The final element of Lenthall's employment that begs further elucidation is the form of his apprenticeship. A common device for specifying the structure of an apprenticeship was an indenture, a legally binding, written contract between a master craftsman and the guardian (usually the father) of the apprentice, under the terms of which the apprentice became all but the property of the master. The apprentice promised to do the master's bidding and never to betray his secrets. In return, the master agreed to teach his apprentice the art and mystery of his trade. When the apprentice reached the age of twenty-one, he was released from the contract. In the meantime, the master was responsible for his room, board and moral education.[21] During the time of Lenthall's apprenticeship to Samuel Humphreys, as many as fifty boys were apprenticed to other masters—blacksmiths, boatbuilders, carpenters—at the Washington Navy Yard.[22]

Such apprentice indentures executed in the District of Columbia were notarized by a court clerk and filed. A search of a compilation of the district's records has not revealed an indenture for John Lenthall, nor has an examination of his private papers in the U.S. Naval Academy Museum's Ives Collection or in the Independence Seaport Museum's John Lenthall Collection.[23] This suggests that the articles of apprenticeship binding John Lenthall were less formal than an indenture, more on the lines of a letter agreement. And in fact, soon after John Lenthall was appointed a naval constructor in 1838, one of his first apprentices, George S. Much, was bound to Lenthall by just such a device.[24] A generic rendering of this document reads:

> [Name of constructor] and [name of apprentice's guardian] of [city of residence], Entered into an Agreement that [name of constructor] take his son [name of apprentice], an Apprentice to teach him the Art, Trade & Mystery of the Shipwright business commencing [date of agreement] until he was of age [apprentice's twenty-first birthdate] and [name of constructor] to pay unto [name of guardian] one half of his wages, and find him [name of apprentice] all tools suitable for that business, and his father [name of guardian] to find him board and clothing and in case he had no work for him to receive no pay; so says I [name of guardian], [date of agreement].

It can be seen that the above agreement specifies all the basic conditions of an apprentice indenture but is absent the more legally binding terms and responsibility for room and board. Such an accord may have governed the relationship between apprentice John Lenthall and Constructor Samuel Humphreys.

What sort of a man was Lenthall's new master? Samuel Humphreys was the son of the Navy's first constructor and progenitor of the American super frigate, Joshua Humphreys. A native of Philadelphia, he was born in November 1778, making him forty-four years old when he entered John Lenthall's life. From an early age, Humphreys worked in his father's Southwark shipyard and helped to build the celebrated frigate *Philadelphia* and the first of the Navy's 44-gun frigates, *United States.* Before the War of 1812, he was a noted designer of merchant and naval vessels. After the outbreak of the war and Congress' authorizing the construction of 74-gun ships of the line, he was appointed a naval constructor at the Philadelphia Navy Yard. There his firm, Humphreys and Penrose, built the liner *Franklin* to his design, the first vessel constructed in that yard. At the war's end, Samuel Humphreys and William Doughty in Washington were the Navy's only constructors. A very competent naval architect, Humphreys drafted the plans for the world's largest ship, the 120-gun *Pennsylvania,* which was laid down at Philadelphia in 1822, the year Lenthall began his apprenticeship.[25]

Historian Howard Chapelle left a brief sketch of Humphreys' personality:

> Samuel Humphreys appears as an executive of much ability, but somewhat vain and pompous. He was quick to resent slights and stood on his dignity. His relations with the constructors seem to have been very friendly and pleasant, however there is little evidence of any close personal relationship, except with those who had been his apprentices.[26]

Samuel Humphreys maintained a home in Philadelphia on "Front Street, a few squares above the navy yard."[27] In the year 1822, he and his wife Letitia's household consisted of three children, sons Andrew, age twelve, and Joshua, nine, and daughter Jane, also nine. A stepson from his wife's previous marriage, Henry Yonge, age seventeen, may also have been a resident.[28] Whether apprentice John Lenthall lived with the Humphreys family or was lodged in separate quarters is not known.

* * *

In the same year that John Lenthall began his apprenticeship, Judah Delano published a *Washington Directory,* "Showing the Name, Occupation, and

Residence of each Head of Family and Person in Business." Its listings for King, Lenthall and Stone were: [29]

> King, Robert, draughtsman general land office, No. 15, 1st floor state dept—dw s side Fn btw 18 and 19w
>
> Lenthall, Mrs. widow, s side Fn btw 18 and 19w
>
> Stone, William J. engraver and copperplate printer, n side Penn av btw 12 and 13w

These addresses confirm the widowed Jane Lenthall and her brother, Robert King Jr., were dwelling at the same F Street address. Additionally, King's office location in the State Department building is also given. And William Stone, husband of the former Elizabeth Lenthall, was now doing business as an engraver on Pennsylvania Avenue.

With the arrival of the new year, a close relative of the King-Lenthall family was married in Washington. On 18 January 1823, Nicholas King's youngest living daughter, Susan, was joined in matrimony with William Wade, an Army ordnance officer.[30] It is not known whether her cousin, John Lenthall, laboring in frosty Philadelphia, was able to attend. He was, by then, a very busy apprentice.

* * *

CHAPTER 5

The Philadelphia Navy Yard

The navy yard that greeted apprentice John Lenthall was very different from that of his hometown. A narrow parallelogram of land of just 546 feet wide and little over twice as long, its cramped footprint lay uneasily between the busy commercial streets of Philadelphia's Southwark district and the waters of the Delaware River. The Philadelphia Navy Yard lacked the measured elegance of Benjamin Latrobe's Washington creation. Of all the navy yards, it was by far the smallest. In the winter of 1822-23 two ship houses—enormous wooden sheds designed to shelter a vessel's hull during its construction—dominated the navy yard and indeed all of Philadelphia: a smaller 'frigate house' at the center of the river bank's run and a larger, still incomplete 'ship house' hugging the yard's boundary just to the north of it. Various buildings, some of brick or stone and others of wood, two or three stories tall, were scattered about the yard's interior. Stacks of timber lay everywhere. And it was noisy. The thumps of mallets, rasps of saws, workmen's shouts and the braying of draft animals filled its damp air.

The Philadelphia Navy Yard was the creation of the two Humphreys, father Joshua who had proposed its Southwark site and expedited its purchase by the government, and son Samuel who had brought order within during the construction of the yard's first warship, *Franklin*. The elder Humphreys' private shipyard had been located just to the north, close by Old Swedes' Church. His long experience gave Humphreys strong reasons for recommending the navy yard's site. It was within practical sailing distance of the Georgia-grown live oak so necessary for a ship's frame and sheltered by the Delaware River from fierce storms and the harmful effects of saltwater on wooden hulls. Southwark was also surrounded by an abundance of skilled workmen and close to Philadelphia "where naval architecture is carried on in an extensive way."[1] This latter point is most germane: the Navy's two most senior constructors, Samuel Humphreys and William Doughty, were both products of Philadelphia's community of shipbuilders, as were their fathers and others of the

Penrose, Hutton and Grice clans. A wealth of men steeped in the traditions of shipwrights and their allied professions were readily available on this long-settled stretch of the Delaware.

However, once the yard's site had been purchased in 1801 by the out-going Adams' administration, its development stalled under Jefferson's Republican economies. Scarce federal dollars flowed instead to the Washington Navy Yard while Philadelphia languished. The exigencies of the War of 1812 brought renewed activity. Revolutionary war veteran Alexander Murray was named as the yard's first commandant, and the firm of Humphreys and Penrose was contracted to build the big liner *Franklin*, but little substantial progress occurred. The threat of a British attack, as actually happened at Washington, stalled the yard's development while local defense needs further deflected attention from long-term planning. It wasn't until the year after the war ended, 1815, that *Franklin*'s keel was finally laid down. And yet the yard lacked many of the most basic facilities.[2]

The boost of the "Gradual Increase" naval build-up revived the Philadelphia yard's fortunes. A new 74-gun ship, *North Carolina*, was begun in June 1816. Designed by William Doughty as an enhanced version of his *Columbus* building in Washington, *North Carolina*'s progress lagged due to delayed deliveries of her live oak frame. By the time she was launched in September 1820, the Navy's priorities had again changed, bringing a virtual halt to the building of big, expensive frigates and ships of the line. Now favored were smaller schooners and brigs to fight the rising tide of piracy in the West Indies. The pause in new construction ironically accelerated development of facilities within the Philadelphia Navy Yard. The keel and frame of the newly laid-down frigate *Raritan* and timbers assembled for the mighty *Pennsylvania* needed to be preserved from the elements, and it was judged to be more economical to erect ship houses to cover their unfinished skeletons than to continue their building.[3] Complimenting these enormous structures, a mast sheers 'A' frame was raised at the water's edge, stone wharfs constructed and within the yard, much-needed sheds, workshops, houses and office buildings were completed, mostly by private contractors. Behind the massive ship sheds that now faced the Delaware's waters, an organized dockyard gradually coalesced. After the death in late 1821 of the yard's first commandant, Alexander Murray, War of 1812 hero William Bainbridge was appointed in his place. Thus, it would have been to Commodore Bainbridge that in the last days of 1822, Constructor Samuel Humphreys introduced his new ship carpenter apprentice, John Lenthall.[4]

* * *

A later official Navy statement summarizing Lenthall's career stated that "the days of his apprenticeship were spent in the severe manual labor of the dockyard."[5] Such a characterization is hardly an exaggeration when the nature of a shipwrights' work of that era is understood. Nearly every task necessary to build a wooden ship was performed manually. With the exception of a steam engine to drive a saw or turn grindstones, and draft animals to haul or lift heavy loads, human muscles powered everything. The splitting or cutting of wood shapes required the use of an ax; for its fine trimming or 'dubbing' another bladed tool, an adz, was deftly wielded. Long holes were drilled through frames with hand-cranked augers; mallets drove home the iron or copper bolts that fastened them together and raps of hammers firmly clenched the bolts' ends. Pairs of sawyers cut logs into planks and beveled frames to fit a hull's curvature; planes and drawknives further shaped their contours. Each piece of the ship's structure was carried to the slipway, lifted up and manually set into its place. This work went on from sunrise to sunset, in fair weather or foul, throughout all the seasons. No doubt blistered hands, aching bones and sore muscles lingered as painful memories of Lenthall's first days at the navy yard.

Each apprentice had different abilities, and it must have been clear to all that in addition to a strong back, John Lenthall possessed an exceptional aptitude for mathematics and geometry. This would have encouraged his master, Samuel Humphreys, to assign him for long spells in the indoor, more cerebral atmosphere of the yard's mould loft. Each shipyard had such a place and as its name implies, it occupied the upper floor or loft of a building large enough to lay out the shape of a ship's hull in full size. The Philadelphia Navy Yard's mould loft was located in its south-west quarter, close by the Federal Street entrance and the yard's administrative offices.[6] Here shipwrights marked out the shapes of a ship's frame in full scale on the loft's floor, and fashioned molds and marked the bevels of each of its components to guide the trimming and erection of the frame's pieces on the ship's hull. Such work required an intuitive grasp of the arcane geometry employed by naval architects to specify a ship's hull form. Commercial shipyards relied on hand-carved representations of a vessel's hull called 'half-models' to capture its signature geometry, but United States naval constructors of this period were more progressive and made extensive use of 'draughts' or specialized ship plans for this purpose. Therefore, an apprentice needed to possess an unshakable understanding of the conventions used by these plans if he were to access the drawings' graphic data. The only way to gain such an understanding was by learning and practicing the art of drafting. Typically, apprentices were trained by tracing or copying existing plans, then graduated to developing new drawings from tables of offsets, the raw three-dimensional measurements that delineated a hull's form. Lenthall no doubt was set to work copying plans handed to him by Samuel Humphreys. Not only would his labors improve his mechanical drafting skills and grasp of naval architecture, but they also provided Constructor Humphreys with much-needed copies of important drawings.

The earliest known drawing by John Lenthall was created during his first year as an apprentice (Plan No. 1). It is a 'lines plan' of a small merchant brig, and it may have been an early effort by Lenthall, then about sixteen years old, to emulate the types of plans he had seen in the mould loft. His drawing adheres to the conventions of the day for drafting ships' lines. Shown are the three traditional views: a half breadth plan, a sheer plan (side elevation), and a body plan (sectional elevations) which was unconventionally rotated by ninety degrees. The drawing is neatly executed in ink, its line control satisfactory but in some places uneven, especially in its use of dashed lines. Lenthall's lettering is crisp and he employs the accepted convention for frame station numbering: a circled X marking the 'dead flat' or midship section, with lettered stations running forward and numbered aft. Most delightful is the scrawled note in Lenthall's hand "No 1, The first draws made by JL in 1823."[7]

During the years John Lenthall spent as an apprentice at the Philadelphia Navy Yard, 1823 through 1827, the yard's new building activity was severely limited. Only two large vessels were on the stocks. Rising slowly under the big ship house was the frame of the massive 120-gun ship of the line *Pennsylvania,* which wouldn't be launched until 1837. Inside the smaller frigate house stood the incomplete hull of the 44-gun frigate *Raritan*; she would wait until 1843 before entering her natural element.[8] During the later phases of his career, as a master builder then a naval constructor, John Lenthall would be involved with both ships' launchings. But for now, he and his fellow apprentices marked their time, slowly adding to each ship's structure as the Navy's economies and priorities dictated. Although such a lethargic pace must have tried the souls of energetic naval constructors, there was a certain logic behind the hulls' halting progress. The country was at peace and the U.S. Navy needed no warships in addition to those already in service. Furthermore, shipwrights knew well that allowing a ship's frame to slowly season on the stocks greatly enhanced a wooden hull's longevity.

* * *

The city that John Lenthall found himself living in must have appeared to possess everything Washington did not. Philadelphia was large, cosmopolitan and a thriving center of commerce. Its densely populated streets confronted the first-time visitor at every turn with arresting manifestations of young America's earliest history—stately brick buildings with their tall white-painted windows. And although the federal government had decamped more than two decades before, the nation's former capital still exuded a lingering imperial charm that could only have stimulated the young apprentice's senses.

As American cities go, Philadelphia was long established by the time Lenthall arrived. Founded in 1682 by William Penn as a Quaker community, its attractions as a place of settlement were initially defined by the rivers that bounded it. The Delaware, flowing down the city's eastern border, gave access to the distant Atlantic while the Schuylkill, wrapping around its western perimeter, offered a route to Pennsylvania's interior lands. Rich soil and plentiful forests surrounded the City of Brotherly Love which prospered in the decades before the American Revolution. That seminal event brought Philadelphia to the fore when the thirteen colonies' representatives gathered there to declare their independence from Great Britain. The years of war that followed all but wiped out the city's commerce, especially its sea-borne trade. But its prestige as a regional center of naval architecture ensured that of the thirteen new frigates ordered for the Continental Navy, four of them were built in Philadelphia. The 32-gun *Randolph* came from the yard of Wharton and Humphreys—the same Joshua Humphreys that was the Navy's first constructor—and the 28-gun *Effingham* was built by Francis Grice, whose namesake grandson will play a prominent role in Lenthall's future career.[9]

During the post-war federal era Philadelphia achieved its greatest prominence among American cities. From 1790 to 1800 it was the capital of the United States. The city's commerce quickly regained its lost vigor. And although New York's growth had edged it out as America's most populous city, Philadelphia's cultural richness and inventive genius ensured its continuing national influence. How could a ship carpenter apprentice not be intrigued by steamboat pioneer John Fitch's ungainly craft configured to "paddle like a crew of Indians." But soon enough, the novelty of steamboats had faded and they became a reality of everyday river transport.[10]

The ugly trade embargoes and non-intercourse acts leading up to the War of 1812, followed by a relentless British blockade, crushed Philadelphia's maritime commerce. Even after the peace that followed, the city never regained its former prominence. Filling the vacuum, New York drew even further ahead—its harbor was ice-free year-round and ships coming and going had no need to chance the Delaware's one hundred miles of shoal-laden navigation. Packet lines offering scheduled liner service increasingly chose New York City as their base.

However, Philadelphia could still flex its muscles in the newly industrializing economy that was reshaping America. Coal mined from Pennsylvania's rich seams began arriving by canal in 1820, and in time would make Philadelphia a major exporter of the fuel. The city's many talented and ambitious citizens propelled Philadelphia's entry into the new age. One entrepreneur who persevered as a shipowner was Thomas P. Cope. In 1821 he founded an eponymously named line of packets offering direct service to Liverpool. John Lenthall undoubtedly caught glimpses of Cope's first ship, the 290 ton *Lancaster,* as she sailed by on the Delaware. His memories must have remained vivid; in the years to come, he would turn his hand to designing vessels for Cope. Another Philadelphian who continued to embrace the sea was renowned ship carver William Rush. By 1824 he was mature in his years but still vigorous enough to fashion the elegant carvings that began to grace the stern of *Pennsylvania.* Again, Lenthall could hardly but fail to notice the handiwork of a true artisan.[11]

* * *

The later years of Lenthall's apprenticeship in Philadelphia coincided with a flourishing of its intellectual and arts communities causing it to be dubbed "the Athens of America." One of its sacred ornaments was the American Philosophical Society. Founded by Benjamin Franklin in 1743, its influence rapidly expanded so that by the eve of the nineteenth century, it was considered to be the nation's leading scientific institution.[12] Looking far into the future, Constructor John Lenthall would be invited to present a paper to its members on the 100-year anniversary of the society's founding.[13] But very much in the present, a brash new organization sprang into existence that would materially shape Lenthall's education and, ultimately, his legacy to the nation. On 5 February 1824, a founding meeting was convened that brought the Franklin Institute into existence "for the purpose of promoting the mechanic arts, and of improving the condition, character and prospects of the industrious class of society by whom they are exercised."[14] Such an organization couldn't have been a better fit for a precocious apprentice like John Lenthall and there is strong evidence that he availed himself of the opportunities offered by the fledgling institute.

Continuing the thread of a previously quoted Navy statement addressing Lenthall's apprenticeship, it says that "his evenings [were spent] in the study of French, mathematics and drawing, in which he became proficient."[15] During the fall of 1824, Lenthall's second year in Philadelphia, the Franklin Institute opened a drawing school, with evening classes offered twice a week. The curriculum focused on architectural drawing, mechanical drafting, lettering and landscape and ornamental drawing. In April of the next year, a school of mathematics was opened and by September 1826, the institute had inaugurated its High School Department which offered full-time classes throughout the week. The Franklin Institute's archives contain no records of its course enrollments, but given Lenthall's later memberships in the institute and his significant gift on his death—the core of his personal library—it is reasonable to assume that the young apprentice's education benefitted from the institute's early course offerings.[16]

It would be remiss to leave the year 1824 without mention of two other events of significance that bear on Lenthall's apprenticeship. Sometime that year while in Philadelphia, Constructor Samuel Humphreys was presented with a wholly unexpected offer from the Russian Ambassador. If he would go to Russia and help organize the emperor's navy, a fabulous salary, town and country residences, carriages, servants and more would all be his. Humphreys listened to the proposal with silence, then offered to give his answer the next morning. He duly returned and after opening pleasantries, firmly declined the offer, concluding that "whether my merit be great or small, I owe it all to the flag of my country, and that is a debt I must pay."[17]

The second event was the navy yard's feting of the Revolutionary War hero, General Lafayette, during his triumphal tour of America. On Saturday morning, 2 October, a goodly part of Philadelphia came to a standstill as its streets filled with joyous marchers celebrating the general's return. Constructor Humphreys led the civic portion of the procession, which slowly snaked its way to the navy yard. There Lafayette received a twenty-one-gun salute after which he and his entourage were led to the festively decorated mould loft for a sumptuous banquet. One wonders whether John Lenthall got to practice his French on an obliging Lafayette.[18]

* * *

As the years slipped by Lenthall's proficiency in the work of the ship carpenter steadily increased. Late in 1826, the Navy Department under whose auspices he labored as an apprentice was confronted with the need to institute some changes to its organization. In the face of an uptick of new ship orders and in an effort to improve its administrative oversight, it decided to formally appoint one of its constructors as the Navy's chief constructor and base him in Washington. The resident constructors assigned to each of the navy yards would then report through him to the board. William Doughty, the Washington Navy Yard's constructor, was most senior and the logical heir to such a position, but he declined the job and the extra work it would entail. So the position was offered to Samuel Humphreys who accepted. On 26 November 1826, he was appointed the Navy's chief constructor.[19] And where Humphreys went, his assistant soon followed, which explains why the last year of Lenthall's apprenticeship was spent in Washington. The disposition of the Navy's other constructors at this time was: John Floyd at Portsmouth, Josiah Barker at Boston, Samuel Hartt at New York, James Keen at Philadelphia, Francis Grice at Norfolk, and Charles Brodie at the newly established navy yard in Pensacola.[20]

In the next year and just days after his twentieth birthday, Lenthall decided to treat himself to a new book. His chosen volume was an English language classic of his profession, Marmaduke Stalkartt's *Naval Architecture, or the Rudiments and Rules of Shipbuilding ...,* published in 1781. Most helpful to curious historians is the sales receipt left inside the book's cover—this tome resides in the Independence Seaport Museum's John Lenthall Collection—which reads "Received of John Lenthall twenty five [dollars] in full for Stalkartt's Naval Architecture, Washington 26th September 1827" /s/ C. Schwarz.[21] But Conrad Schwarz was no ordinary bookseller. He was then employed as a draftsman at the Navy Department and nine years before, had worked with Lenthall's Uncle Robert King Jr. as the engraver of his landmark map of Washington, D.C.[22] A small world indeed!

As the following year progressed, John Lenthall faced the coming of the day when his apprenticeship would end. Anyone who has attended a school can attest that at first, the full-term commitment appears to stretch far into the future, but once graduated, the years feel like they've flown by. So it must have been for John Lenthall on 16 September 1828 when the term of his regular apprenticeship finished.[23] Some weeks later, Samuel Humphreys wrote a letter of recommendation to the Navy board in the hope of obtaining employment for Lenthall. The postscript at the bottom was later added in Lenthall's hand:

Washington Oct 3, 1828

Sir
The bearer Mr John Lenthall has served his apprenticeship with me to the ship building business the greater part of his time in the Philadelphia Navy Yard, the last year in the Navy Yard at this place. He has been employed altogether on ships of war & I am happy to say, he was on all occasions correct in his conduct and anxious to acquire a full knowledge of his profession. His application has been attended with considerable success, particularly in the business of the Mould Loft. A little time devoted to the actual building will enable him at no distant period to undertake the construction of ships of war & I beg leave to recommend him to the notice of your department.

I have the honor to be
Very respectfully Sir
Your humble servant
/s/ S. Humphreys

Commodore John Rodgers
President of the Navy Board

This letter was given a few days after the expiration of my appointment and was handed to Com Rodgers on the 11th inst and was then enquiry by the board. JL[24]

Historian Howard Chapelle suggests that in this same year, Humphreys nominated Lenthall to the post of assistant naval constructor at the Philadelphia Navy Yard.[25] If so, it is not readily obvious in the above letter; perhaps it was through a separate communication. In any event, despite Humphreys' recommendation and the optimism of Lenthall's postscript, no appointment was awarded to the newly matriculated ship carpenter. The Navy board's president, John Rodgers, acknowledged that Lenthall successfully served his apprenticeship and was a man of integrity, but the hard truth was that there were no available permanent navy yard positions to offer the former apprentice. Without a foothold in the Navy's hierarchy, twenty-one-year-old John Lenthall faced an uncertain future, obliged to accept whatever casual work was offered him. It was not the path ahead that the heir to the Lenthall and King family legacies had imagined.

* * *

CHAPTER 6

The Science of Naval Architecture

Lenthall did find work and while it lasted, he earned much more than he had during his early apprentice days. In late February 1829, he received payment of seven dollars for three days of drafting on the 'rebuilt' sloop of war *John Adams.*[1] This work was probably performed in the Washington Navy Yard, which had just been plunged into mourning at the death of its long-standing commandant, Thomas Tingey.[2] Two months later, Lenthall found employment in the yard's mould loft, this time earning $1.76 a day.[3] One of his fellow loftsmen, John Murry, was probably the same John Murray who nine months later wrote Lenthall from Portsmouth, New Hampshire, where he hoped to soon "commence" a new steamboat and canal boat. Could Lenthall draw plans of the steamboat and calculate her displacements, both light and with engines installed? [4] Other independent commercial assignments came his way, but it was not what Lenthall craved most: to design and build men of war.[5]

Sometime in 1830, Lenthall was invited to perform just such work. Although it wasn't a permanent job, it was a step in the right direction. The offer could only have come from Samuel Humphreys, who the year before had drafted plans for a replacement of the aging British trophy frigate, *Macedonian.* Over the past decade, the Navy had developed the sleight-of-hand practice of administratively 'rebuilding' a decrepit ship, but in actual fact it designed and built an entirely new hull in her stead. The new vessel was often of different dimensions than the original and in some cases, of altogether another class. Repair funds for laid up ships were pooled together to fund reconstructing of the most urgent of the basket cases, and with the old frigate *John Adams* dealt with, it was now the turn of *Macedonian.* Humphreys designed a handsome and very sharp modeled, double banked frigate which, although it was pierced for fifty-eight guns, was rated at 36-guns to preserve the fiction of rebuilding the old British warship.[6] Construction of the new frigate would wait until 1832-33, but

Humphreys needed her naval architectural properties calculated. And that is where John Lenthall came in.

* * *

The calculations Lenthall performed for Humphreys in 1830 have been preserved and are available to scholars in the Independence Seaport Museum's John Lenthall Collection. The personal papers folder holding them is titled "Macedonian (USS) Razee 1851-53," but this is misleading.[7] The folder also contains the new frigate's building instructions, calculations and specifications for her later conversion into a spar deck sloop of war, cost data for the frigate, its alteration into a sloop and more, even estimates for recasting *Macedonian* into an auxiliary steamer (which never happened). But with care, a core of calculations labeled "Macedonian 1830" can be identified, many of them initialed JL. They provide the first close look at naval architect John Lenthall's proficiency at numerical analysis and document the form of calculations a U.S. Navy constructor was expected to produce for ships of war.

At the core of Lenthall's calculations are two nearly identical sets of hydrostatic data summaries, covering about one and a half pages each, the longer one with cross-outs, smudged ink and numerous pencil notes. As the principal calculated quantities are identical, it is likely the shorter one is a fair copy. *Macedonian*'s length (163.5 ft), breadth (42.1 ft) and design draft (18.625 ft, floating line to lower edge of rabbet of keel) are documented. Notes also confirm that the ship's appendages—keel, post, rudder, stem and cutwater—are "not taken, calculations to outside of plank," informing the user that the hull properties include the volume of its planking's thickness. Lenthall's list of data encompassed the hull's volume and displacement, in cubic feet and tons using an assumed water density of 34.8 ft^3/ton, its longitudinal and vertical centers of buoyancy (LCB and VCB) and longitudinal center of floatation (LCF). Areas of the ship's design water line (A_{WP}) and of the midship section marked as ¤ (A_M) are provided, as are the principal form coefficients, block (C_B), waterplane (C_{WP}) and midship (C_M). All properties are calculated to at least two decimal places and coefficients to four or more. The data layout is similar to although not identical to that shown for the Store Ship *Relief* in Appendix 2.

Of great interest are Lenthall's calculations of *Macedonian*'s heights of metacenter, a key measure of a ship's initial stability. If a vessel's vertical center of gravity (VCG) exceeded its metacentric height, it would be unstable and capsize. The metacenter also provided an indication of a hull's resistance to roll and pitch and was a determining factor as to whether a warship would exhibit 'easy' motions and therefore be a suitable gun platform. Lenthall provided both transverse and longitudinal (pitching) metacenters (BM_T and BM_L). One of Lenthall's loose calculation sheets contains the notation "Don Juan, Meta Center Pt" likely referring to the Spanish naval constructor, Jorge Juan y Santacilia, who first proposed the calculation of longitudinal metacenters.[8] The recognizable portions of his metacenter calculations use the formula identified by the French scientist Pierre Bouguer in his seminal work, *Traité du Navire* of 1746, and later popularized by Swedish constructor Fredrik af Chapman, $BM = \int \frac{2}{3} y^3 dx/D$ (see Appendix 2 for an explanation of terms).[9] Previous evaluations of U.S constructors' work suggest the earliest calculations of this sort that have been found were performed in about 1842.[10] This is not surprising as the methods used for these calculations, involving cubic functions to determine the waterplane's moments of inertia, were extremely laborious. But now it is clear that John Lenthall, a former ship carpenter apprentice, had by 1830 mastered the mechanics of calculating metacenters. And if he was performing such analyses, it is likely the other constructors were too.

As to Lenthall's methodology of analysis, he makes use of established formulae, namely Atwood's 3rd rule (Simpson's 2nd rule), and to achieve accuracy when dividing large numbers, effortlessly applies base 10 logarithms.[11] His calculations are laid out largely in tabular format, always with copious side additions, multiplications and divisions of the tables' data. And all of his work is in ink with a minimum of cross-outs, demonstrating his self-confidence. It shows him to be a true mathematical virtuoso.

What do Lenthall's calculations tell us about the U.S Navy's design practices of this era? Constructors were certainly capable of accurately calculating the full range of a ship's hydrostatic data. This would allow them to ensure the ship floated at her intended draft—assuming that she wasn't overloaded which happened all too frequently. A key measure of a warship's ability to fight in a seaway, the height of her lowest gunport sills above the design waterline, could also be accurately predicted. And with the tools to calculate metacentric heights, not only could the stability of a vessel be evaluated but it was also possible to estimate its roll and pitch motions. Finally, the fact that hull coefficients of form were routinely calculated strongly suggests that the hull properties of different ships were closely compared.

* * *

With the advantage of perspective in time, the calculations John Lenthall performed in 1830 for Samuel Humphreys can be more fully appreciated. His work documents the application of relatively recent analytical methodologies to the age-old quest of accurately predicting a ship's physical properties. The earliest of the naval architectural treatises cited in the above evaluation, Bouguer's *Traité du Navire*, was first published in

1746, some eighty-five years before Lenthall's application of its postulates. Jorge Juan y Santacilia's *Examen Maritimo* came next in 1771, and Chapman's *Tractat om Skepps-byggeriet* in 1775. And they were written in, respectively, French, Spanish and Swedish, raising the bar for both wide dissemination and popular application of their tenets. In contrast, at the time of writing this book almost two hundred years later, today's naval architects still use the same basic analytical methods and formulae as Lenthall did, which explains why the flow of his cursive calculations' logic can be so readily grasped by modern eyes.[12]

Lenthall came of age in the afterglow of the previous century's Scientific Revolution. He directly benefitted from the fruits of its persevering philosopher scientists who collectively gave birth to the discipline of naval architecture. While the pioneers of naval science were independently creative, they were influenced by each other's work, by their fellow scientists and by the naval policies of the nations in which they lived. During the eighteenth century, certain countries more than others, especially France, Spain and Sweden, fostered the strong institutional development of naval architecture through the support of scientific societies, encouragement of individual talents and the practical application of their work, both within professional schools and for the designs of their warships. A focused example of this phenomenon occurred in France from the 1720s through to mid-century under the guiding hand of the Count of Maurepas, the minister of the navy. An enlightened administrator during a crucial period of French naval resurgence and an active supporter of the Academy of Sciences, Maurepas recognized the benefits to be gained by the application of new scientific developments to France's naval establishment. He laid the groundwork for France's scientific approach to naval architecture which, over time, helped produce those wonderful frigates that were so admired by the British.[13]

And where were the British during the birth of the scientific revolution? The dominant naval power of this period, the Royal Navy was by the first decade of the eighteenth century firmly in the grip of its "establishment of dimensions" rating system, giving rise, for example, to H.M.S. *Victory* being deemed a "first rate." The Royal Navy's successes and the superiority of its seamanship gave little urgency to an introspection of its ships' designs. This together with a government less supportive of its scientific establishment than France's, led to a stagnation in the application of naval science to its men of war.[14] And in turn, the inevitable outcome fed the perception of British naval officers that French ships were better than their own.

A snapshot of the relative influence of the French versus the British on the science of ships during this period is provided by examining the books and pamphlets that once formed Lenthall's library and are now part of the John Lenthall Collection at the Independence Seaport Museum (see Appendix 10). If the books are sorted by their dates of publication and an end point of 1830 is chosen, it will be seen that a majority of his collection were in the French language, sixty-two compared to fifty-seven in English. It's not until twenty years later that English language books dominate. In the matter of the influential books, it is ironic that of the major naval architecture treatises called out in this overview of Lenthall's *Macedonian* calculations—Bouguer's *Traité du Navire,* Santacilia's *Examen Maritimo* and Chapman's *Tractat,* none of them are present today in the John Lenthall Collection.[15] The question of why they and other key books cannot be found there is discussed in Appendix 10.

So there were many reasons why Lenthall would have been attracted to the body of work produced by French scientists and naval constructors. The work of Pierre Bouguer, the "father of naval architecture," frigates built by Constructor Jacques-Noël Sané, the "naval Vauban," and the publications by many other Frenchmen that lined John Lenthall's growing library, were all inspirations to the young ship carpenter who dreamed of becoming a U.S. naval constructor. Naval architects love nothing better than to gossip about why one ship is better than another. There must have been many such conversations in the mould lofts, with Samuel Humphreys, William Doughty, William Easby and others, that delved into the relative performance of the warships that fought during the War of 1812 and those that followed. In their colorful stories, one can imagine a special aura surrounding the French frigates, their technology and superior qualities. Perhaps, Lenthall reasoned, he should travel to Europe, tour the principal naval dockyards and find out the truth of the matter for himself.

* * *

John Lenthall's decision to make just such a trip was well remembered by his descendants:

> At the age of twenty-one, realizing that he could not advance without a knowledge of higher mathematics, engineering and foreign languages, he went to France where he remained several years.[16]

In early 1830 Lenthall was twenty-two years old, but his family's recollection certainly conveys sentiments he must have felt at the time. In its obituary overview of Lenthall's career, the Navy Department added that "Not content with this [his work and studies as an apprentice] he determined to go to Europe for further instructions."[17] Pause to consider these explanations. By now, Lenthall was a prodigy at mathematics, a demonstrably capable engineer and reasonably competent in French. Using these three measures, John Lenthall already compared favorably to his contemporary naval constructors (see Appendix 12). There was something more to Lenthall's decision. Looking ahead to the letters of recommendation he solicited, his appeal to the president of the United States captured his logic:

> Having acquired such practical knowledge of the subject as our navy yards afford means of training, I am now about to depart for Europe, for the purpose of visiting the dock yards and other naval installations, in order to acquire further information and instruction in the science of naval architecture, in the hope of being able to return to my native country better prepared to contribute to public service.[18]

Lenthall's last line gives the clue. After all his arduous labors as an apprentice, the many years of self-study and his unquestionable ability to perform the most complex of naval architectural calculations, he was frustrated at not having received an appointment as an assistant constructor to one of the Navy's dockyards. The son of a family of renowned public servants, John Lenthall sought that same recognition. An element of pride was involved. And if the Navy couldn't yet grant him such a position—the Board of Navy Commissioners only appointed constructors to fill vacancies—what better time to embark on an odyssey of further education.

The other side of motivation is encouragement. Was he encouraged by his fellow constructors to make such a journey? One undocumented source says that advice from Samuel Humphreys helped prompt Lenthall's decision.[19] It probably did, as would the urgings of the other constructors. The draw of a grand tour of Europe was as strong then as now, and as anyone who has undertaken such a journey knows, there is no better time to go than when one's education is largely complete and before a career's commitments have taken hold.

Perhaps as an incentive, that year John Lenthall indulged in the purchase of two books calculated to help him on his journey: Duhamel du Monceau's classic curriculum for French naval constructors, *Élémens de L'Architecture Navale,* and Charles Romme's sumptuously illustrated *L'Art de la Marine.*[20] Someone was giving him excellent advice on what to buy.

* * *

With his decision made, Lenthall's next step was to solicit and gather letters of introduction, without which he could not expect many doors to open to him. This he did with incredible efficiency, demonstrating that he must have been planning his trip for some time. Ranging from the president, secretary of state, navy and army officers on down to merchants, Lenthall tapped them all for their coveted recommendations:

18 April 1830 Letter by John Gardiner (a Philadelphia merchant), To (his cousin), Dr. John Walker, Vaccine House, London.
Introduction of Lenthall who seeks "admission into your dockyards in London, Portsmouth, &c."[21]

19 April 1830 Letter by John Anderson (a Philadelphia merchant), To William P. Preble (U.S. Minister in the Netherlands).
Introduction of Lenthall, "already one of the first Draughtsman in this country and whose family & connections are of the most respectable in this city."[22]

20 April 1830 Letter by John Lenthall,
To the president of the United States (Andrew Jackson)
Introduction and reasons for trip. Requests suitable letters from the departments to the ministers and consuls abroad.[23]

20 April 1830 Letter by John Rodgers, president of the Board of Naval Commissioners,
To all whom it may concern,
Confirmation that Lenthall completed his apprenticeship, referencing Humphreys, vouched for his integrity, connections and that he is worthy of esteem.[24]

21 April 1830 1st Letter by J. J. D'Lagnel (a Frenchman in America),
To his brother Mr. Alf d'Lagnel de St Julien at the Ministére de la Marine, Paris (an under-clerk employed at the ministry).
Introduction for Lenthall who "desires to see arsenals, depots and other places of naval construction."
2nd Letter by M. Van Buren, State Dept. (secretary of state),
To Louis McLane, London (U.S. minister to the United Kingdom).
Introduction of Lenthall, recommendations, give "him your attention."[25]

21 April 1830 1st Letter by M. Van Buren (secretary of state),
To W. C. Rives, Paris (U.S. minster to France).
2nd Letter by Louis Goldsborough (U.S. naval officer),
To Isaac Cox Barnett, U.S. Consul in Paris.
Both are introductions of Lenthall.[26]

24 April 1830 Letter by John H. Hall (a Philadelphia attorney),
To Hon. Wm. Pitt Preble (U.S. Minister in the Netherlands).
Introduction of Lenthall, written at the request of Major Wade of the Ordnance.[27]

29 April 1830 1st Letter by Brig. Gen. Bernard (U.S. Army engineer),
To Colonel Laire, Corps Royal des Constructeurs de Vaisseaux, Paris.
2nd Letter by Brig. Gen. Bernard (U.S. Army engineer),
To Colonel Bagére, Corps Royal des Ingenieurs Militaires.
Both are introductions of Lenthall.[28]

1 May 1830 1st Letter by (Maj. William Tell) Poussin (U.S. Army engineer),
To Mons. F. Debrotournie, Bibliothécaire,
à St. Génevieve à Paris.
2nd Letter by Maj. William Tell Poussin (U.S. Army engineer),
To Mons. Guerard (professor of mathematics),
L'École Polytechnique, Paris.
Both are introductions of Lenthall.[29]

15 July 1830 Letter by G. Bomford (U.S. Army),
To Baron Hyde de Neuville, Paris (French politician, diplomat).
Introduction of Lenthall, his European travels.[30]

23 July 1830 Letter by Chas. W. Varthaus (a Philadelphia merchant),
To Franz Diederich, Hamburg.
Introduction of Lenthall, a stay on return from St. Petersburg.[31]

1 Aug 1830 Letter by C. Gratiot, Br. Gen'l. of (U.S. Army) Engrs., To Adm. Jurien (senior French navy admiral). Introduction of Lenthall, his European travels.[32]

Lenthall's appeal to the president was a necessary first step to unlock responses from officials and officers of the State, War and Navy Departments. Flowing from that request came letters by Secretary of State Martin Van Buren, naval officers Rodgers and Goldsborough, and army officers Bernard, Poussin, Bomford and Gratiot. That Lenthall's F Street home was only a few blocks from all of these department offices simplified the logistics of gathering letters, and Uncle Robert still held an office at the State Department. A few of Lenthall's letter writers bear closer examination. General Bernard was a former French army office and veteran of the Napoleonic Wars. He is best known as the engineer who built Fortress Monroe, the "Gibraltar of the Chesapeake Bay." [33] Major Poussin, also a former French army officer who emigrated to the United States with Bernard, was Latrobe's former draftsman and now an army topographical engineer; he would remain close to Lenthall for many more years[34]. Poussin's recommendations to a librarian at the Bibliothèque à Sainte-Géneviève and the math professor who tutored the French king's third son, a distinguished naval officer in his own right, Prince de Joinville, are truly intriguing. More down to earth, the letter by Jean-Jules D'Lagnel to his brother Alf promised to give Lenthall an entrée to the Depot de la Marine, the French navy's repository of drawings and documents. Lenthall most likely met D'Lagnel in Philadelphia, where he no doubt became acquainted with the merchants of that city who also wrote letters for him.[35]

Most of the extant letters of recommendation are, on close examination, copies of the originals. In some cases, two and three letters are transcribed onto the same sheet, probably by Lenthall himself. The few letters that appear to be originals are directed towards places that it is believed Lenthall did not visit, for example, Hamburg and Amsterdam. In combination, these letters clearly demonstrate the high esteem in which Lenthall was held, his family's social prominence and the far reach of their influential connections.

* * *

By the first of May, in the span of a few short weeks, Lenthall had gathered all the key letters of recommendation needed for his dockyard tour. In the opening of his letter to the president, he confidently claimed he was "now about ready to depart for Europe." Three more letters were picked up in late July, and still he hadn't started his trip. In fact, he wouldn't depart from the United States until after nearly a year had passed, leaving in May 1831. What caused the delay?

The significant event that occurred during this hiatus was the death of Lenthall's Uncle Robert. A surrogate father to the Lenthall family, Robert King Jr. died on 28 January 1831 at the age of fifty-five. It may have been that Uncle Robert was ailing since the year before and his deteriorating condition caused Lenthall to postpone his travel plans. By the terms of Robert King Jr.'s will, his entire estate passed to his sister, Jane Lenthall.[36] Linking these two circumstances together provides a creditable explanation of Lenthall's delay and also yields a clue as to where the funds may have come from to cover his considerable expenses for three years' travelling throughout Europe.

Then in early March 1831, still in Washington, Lenthall received a reply to a letter he had written to former naval constructor Henry Eckford, now a shipbuilder in New York City. Eckford thanked Lenthall for the news about his plans for overseas travel and remarked "I infer the loss of your uncle defeats the objects you had." He then told Lenthall that he cannot "give you any employment at shipbuilding at present. But should you be disposed to going out in my ship ... in May, something might turn up which might enable me to promote your views."[37] This was the big break Lenthall needed. Eckford was planning to deliver a warship he had built, the 30-gun sloop *Kensington,* under the command of his uncle, Captain Ramsey, to the Russian Navy at the Baltic port of Kronstadt. With Eckford's offer in hand, Lenthall now had a cost-free way of expeditiously getting to Europe. And what better way to go than in a ship of war.

* * *

CHAPTER 7

European Dockyard Tour

John Lenthall stood confidently on the deck of the sloop of war *Kensington*, his new-found sea legs continuously adjusting to her sinuous motions, his ears tuned to her hull's every creak and groan, his eyes aloft surveying her taut spread of canvas. It was the first time Lenthall had sailed on the high seas and it must have been exhilarating. Beyond that, it was an education in itself. He had been inside and out of ships of war for nearly nine years, familiar with every stick of their structure. But to experience a vessel at sea, in her own element and handled by professional mariners, added an entirely new and different dimension to his understanding of his chosen profession.

On reporting to Captain Ramsey in New York, Lenthall must have been impressed by his appointment as *Kensington*'s purser, a sinecure that allowed him an official place on the ship's papers and a seat in her wardroom.[1] However, his new ship was no surprise. As an apprentice, he must have seen her following her completion at Philadelphia in 1825. It would be impossible to miss *Kensington*—she was a rakish, flush deck sloop of war and almost as big as the 44-gun frigate *Constitution.* Conceived by Henry Eckford for the Mexican Navy and built under subcontract by Jacob Tees, she had been turned down by the Mexicans and after languishing on the Delaware, was finally sold to Russia.[2] *Kensington*'s destination was Kronstadt, an island fortress guarding the approaches to the imperial capital of St. Petersburg and the base of the Russian Navy's Baltic fleet.

After departing New York sometime in May 1831, *Kensington* headed east then more northerly on the great circle route across the Atlantic. She was dismasted during her passage and a jury rig raised, the whole incident being no doubt fascinating to Purser Lenthall. Even under reduced canvas, the sloop managed speeds of eleven knots, demonstrating her reputation for speed.[3] Once in English waters, she touched at Cowes, Isle of Wight. A small port on the Solent and famous as a yachting center, Cowes must have made an indelible first impression on John Lenthall of his mother and father's homeland. While *Kensington* lay at anchor, Captain Ramsey probably sought new masts and spars to make good his losses. Lenthall enjoyed the company of fellow American Thomas D. Watter, possibly a passenger on *Kensington* or newly introduced in Cowes, who would later write Lenthall with detailed advice for his future trip to France.[4] One of the focal points for contacts ashore was the U.S. consul at Cowes, Col. Robert R. Hunter. Consul Hunter, who is said to have been a relative of Lenthall's, would prove to be invaluable during Lenthall's later visits to Cowes.[5]

* * *

Repairs complete *Kensington* got underway, sailing east past Spithead and up the English Channel. Then her course took her across the North Sea and into the Baltic, finally arriving at her Russian destination, Kronstadt, in the ebb of mid-summer's endless days. Painstakingly constructed on a low, small island at the mouth of the River Neva, by 1831 Kronstadt was one of the world's most strongly defended ports, famous for its surrounding string of 'three decker' island fortresses and an impressive concentration of naval dockyard facilities. Ten miles to the east lay the city of St. Petersburg, the Russian capital founded by Peter the Great at the beginning of the eighteenth century. Here John Lenthall went ashore, the first stop of his dockyard tour.

It is striking that of the many letters of introduction Lenthall obtained, not one is directed to anyone in Russia. However, his cover as the purser of *Kensington* together with Eckford's contract to deliver her to the Russian Navy, gave him an entrée to the U.S. minister, the U.S. consul at St. Petersburg and for his admission to the Russian dockyards. Save for his 'pass ticket' to depart Kronstadt, no extant documentation has been discovered that yields a clear view of just where he lived, what he did and how much he learned. But one clue exists. In a later pitch to the Board of Naval Commissioners, Lenthall offered to "present a paper and plans on … the application of camels to ships of war in Russia."[6] Camels were sets of pontoons which when lashed to each side of a ship and then de-ballasted, allowed a deep draft vessel to pass safely over a bar. He must have observed their use in Kronstadt's shallow inner harbors.

The Baltic's Gulf of Finland begins to ice up in late November. To avoid being trapped through the winter in Russia, Lenthall made arrangements to depart Kronstadt on 10 October as passenger on the English ship *Clisson*. He sailed the next day, headed back toward England.[7] It is likely that Lenthall took advantage of his return voyage's passage through the Oresund, the narrow strait between southern Sweden and the Danish island of Sjælland, to visit the Royal Naval Dockyard at Copenhagen.

Visible to anyone arriving by sea, the distinctive features of the dockyard's facilities would have been a strong temptation for Lenthall. Again, no documentation has been found of such a visit at this period, but given it was one of the naval building centers he was said to have inspected, it fits into the logistics of his European travels.[8]

* * *

From the end of 1831 through to the middle of 1832, Lenthall's travel itinerary can only be speculatively assembled through the paper trail of letters written to him by his new-found English relatives. Often these letters were addressed to a post office of one city or town, then forwarded to another, further confusing the picture. And it should also be remembered that Lenthall's journeys were made before the rapid growth of railways that so revolutionized Victorian-era travel. He was witness to the sunset of England's coaching days.

Lenthall sailed to England at the end of 1831 and headed to Yorkshire and the homes of his King relatives. His first visit was to his Aunt Margaret, a school head mistress living in the seaside town of Scarborough.[9] Just to the east, through the Vale of Pickering, was the village of the same name where so many of the Kings had been born. Writing after his departure, Margaret chided Lenthall for thinking himself a "dull sort of chap" and in passing touched on his plans to travel to York, Sheffield and France. Next, in January, he visited Leon Simpson of York, another distant relative. Then late that month he passed through Leeds on his way to Chesterfield, Derbyshire, the place of his father's birth.[10] It is not known with whom he stayed during his nearly two months in Chesterfield or if he visited the Lenthall family seat in Oxfordshire, further to the south. Lenthall's descendants bring up a related point in their family-directed lament:

> We have always thought it curious that during great-grandfather's residence abroad three years, part of which was spent in England, that there was no mention about his father's people, there is not one citation in reference to them.[11]

By April Lenthall was in Sheffield, enjoying the hospitality of his Wood cousins. But soon he was on his way again, evidently passing through the industrial city of Birmingham, headed to London.[12] Here he paused, certainly long enough to collect forwarded mail and to take in the sights of the British capital. Lenthall may have resided in the home of W. G. Athling, New London Street, to whom some of his mail was addressed. A packet of forwarded letters from the Isle of Wight must have been received at this point for on 25 May, he opened an envelope from Sister Libby and received a rude shock. Dated 11 January 1832, her long letter opened innocuously enough with pleasantries about life in Washington. Soon enough, it segued to an evening tea party meant to honor a visiting sea captain named Morrell and which included Libby's husband (Mr. Stone), Lenthall's mother and likely other family members, and a friend named David Adams and his colleague, U.S. Navy Lieutenant Gedney:[13]

> Accordingly all hands came and while at her table, Mother asked Lt. Gedney if he remembered her son (you) then a little boy. He said yes, he did and asked if you had not been with Mr. H. [Humphreys]), to which Mother answered yes. Lt. G. then said you had done one thing, which he regretted very much, he thought it unfortunate. At which as you may suppose, we were all put in a fluster, and exclaimed, What! There was a dead pause for a moment when Lt. G. replied, that he understood that you had given, while in Cowes, the dimensions of all our ships of war, and that Mr. H. had told him the Commissioners had overhauled him, asking how JL had gotten possession of these documents. The Lt. named several of the vessels Mr. H. stated as having been given. All of us exclaimed, impossible! Mr. S.' eyes were ready to pop out of his head. I felt quite wrathy, and the rest of us had enough. Mr. S. immediately produced the Work, saying the piece therein might have been misunderstood, but Lt. said it was not that, but worse, as the information had been given after your arrival in Cowes, but he would ascertain the facts and let us know next day. Captain Morrell said it must have been exaggerated by some enemy of yours. Mr. S. said you could not have given such information as he had your large stock of drafts, calculations, etc. in his possession. ... Lt. G. said it could not be the work of an enemy as you had none. The Commissioners [were] not your enemies, and Mr. H. spoke in the highest terms of you, saying that he had done as much for you, as a child of his own.
>
> What made us feel worse about it was David had the same story told him by Mr. Sims [?] of his office, who was also informed by Mr. H. The Lt. seemed to feel that what you were said to have done was very imprudent and ill-advised, but on searching into the matter ... the next day, found it originated from the piece in the Naval Work. Mr. H. from the above had made no secret of it. The Commissioners are highly offended about it, and Mr. S. and D. think it would be a fair opportunity for you to write to them and explain matters to

> them ... to let them know of some information you have obtained since away, which will be beneficial to your country.[14]

Further adding to the carnage, a note on the left-hand side of the first page read:

> I entertain for you sentiments of very high respect. /s/ SDK [a King cousin?] Don't trust the old Philadelphia fox. I fear he will not help you forward, so collect what you can to close his mouth if necessary.

This was appalling news! Lenthall must have been aghast. Sitting in England, thousands of miles away, he was unable to determine the truth of the matter or to defend himself. Taken at face value, the Board of Naval Commissioners were highly offended by Lenthall's alleged indiscretion and his mentor, Samuel Humphreys, was not to be trusted. As the letter excerpt's final paragraph indicates, the apparent root of the matter was an article of Lenthall's that had appeared in the "Naval Work," a set of papers on naval architecture published the year before and which presented the offending warship dimensional data. Copies had been delivered to Lenthall's home soon after his departure for Europe.[15] How or to whom Lenthall responded is not known and nothing more about it emerged in later correspondence. It appears the whole incident was overblown and that little if any lasting damage occurred, but still, it must have been a troubling time for a very isolated John Lenthall.

* * *

The dialogue within Lenthall's relatives' letters gives the impression that he intended to cross over to Paris soon after his arrival in London. Since late the year before, his various correspondents had been warning of the outbreak of revolution in the French capital. And now it happened. During the two days of 5 and 6 June 1832, Paris was rocked by a violent anti-monarchist rebellion which gave the inspiration to Victor Hugo's classic, *Les Misérables.* Although quickly crushed, the uprising must have caused John Lenthall to rethink his travel plans. Up till now, although he had resided in England for a good six months, his time had been filled with visits to relatives and seeing cities and sites of interest. That he actually took a pause and refocused his energies on inspections of London area naval dockyards in the months of June and July is speculation based on clues extracted from his correspondence. The evidence is that he finally crossed over to France by September 1832, and it is known that he visited the Portsmouth naval dockyard much later, in January 1834. Generic accounts of his years in Europe claim he visited "all the principal dockyards" of various countries, including Great Britain.

Which of H.M.'s Dockyards did John Lenthall visit? Sorting by geography indicates that he may have directed his attentions to the nearby home dockyards (in order of their proximity to central London) of Deptford, Woolwich, Sheerness and Chatham. The first two were on the Thames and the latter two somewhat more removed on the Medway, all (then) in north Kent. However, by 1832 Deptford was temporarily closed, suggesting Woolwich as Lenthall's first choice. A Royal Navy dockyard since the early sixteenth century, Woolwich was heir to a long and storied history of building warships, earning it the accolade of "the Mother Dock of all England." By 1831 the yard had become specialized as a center for steam engineering, with the subsequent erection of supporting shops, foundries, forges and creation of steam basins.[16]

A link tying Lenthall to Woolwich is the existence of a set of plans in the John Lenthall Collection of the side-wheel steamer *Medea*.[17] Although not identified by the Collection *Guide* as a Royal Navy vessel, the principal dimensions match those of the paddle sloop *Medea* which was built at Woolwich, her keel having been laid down in April 1832.[18] Perhaps Lenthall was allowed to trace her 'draughts' during an extended visit; his initials appear on two of the plans.

* * *

By mid-summer of 1832, John Lenthall was again in Cowes and in the care of Consul Robert Hunter. The news from France must have been encouraging, for Lenthall redirected his energies toward getting to Paris, the principal object of his European tour. Armed with a fresh letter of introduction from Consul Hunter to the U.S. minister in France, W. C. Rives, which declared Lenthall's desire to gain access to the French naval dockyards at Brest, Cherbourg and Toulon, he began his passage across the Channel and up the Seine to Paris, probably in late August or early September.[19] It is likely Lenthall followed the itinerary outlined by his friend of the previous fall, Thomas Watter, transcribed below, which yields a superb overview of his journey and its costs (first in pounds, shillings and pence then in francs and sous):[20]

		£	S	D						
From Cowes to Southampton		"	3	"						
"	Southampton to Havre	2	2	"						
"	Dinner and servants on board	"	6	"		£	S	D		
"	Havre one day & night	"	9	"	=	2	19	"	=	$14.75

		F	S		
"	Havre to Rouen per Steam Boat	13	"		
"	Dinner on board at any price	"	"		
"	Rouen day & night	12	"		
"	Rouen to Paris in Diligence	23	"		
"	Dinner on the road	2	"	F S	
"	Extras say	12	"	= 62 "	= about $12.11

It is a pity John Lenthall did not record his first impressions on entering Paris in 1832. It would be more than two decades before the vision of Louis Napoleon and Baron Haussmann created the open boulevards, sweeping vistas and the harmonious architecture so characteristic of today's central Paris. In the early years of the reign of King Louis Philippe, the heart of the city was clustered tightly around its medieval core, the Île de la Cité. Its surrounding maze of narrow, crowded streets fronted by the time-worn buildings of centuries past exuded a certain picturesque charm but they also harbored dark, unhealthy pockets of squalor and crime. Blemished it may have been, it was still the fabled city of Paris, "the Babylon of modern times," and its imperial splendors—magnificent public buildings, monuments, palaces and gardens—beckoned to its intensely curious American visitor.

Probably on the advice of his contacts in Paris, John Lenthall took lodgings at Madame Potel's *pension* at Rue Monsieur Le Prince No. 49.[21] Her boarding house was well known to travelers from America; the poet Longfellow stayed there in 1826 and again in 1836. Located in the 6th arrondissement on the Seine's left bank, Madame Potel's establishment was close by the Luxembourg Gardens, the Pantheon and the present-day Sorbonne University. Just a handful of boarders, all Americans, were accommodated by Madame Potel, and they were required to speak only French during meals. She charged thirty-six dollars a month for room and board, and to Lenthall's delight, the *pension* was "finely suited for a student—within five minutes of public lectures on all subjects."[22] John Lenthall was now where he had dreamed of being for so long, in the heart of Paris, ready to drink in all that France offered.

* * *

One activity that engaged Lenthall from the start was making friends. The Ives Collection contains a number of letters written to him from other American students, possibly fellow boarders at Madame Potel's. One, by

Charles Stewart, is full of a young man's swagger, teasingly addressing Lenthall as an "artiste mechanique, vulgarly named a mechanic, or ship builder"; another was penned by Thomas Logan, who sent fond remembrances of his Parisian compatriots following his return to Charleston, South Carolina.[23]

Reverting back to an earlier Navy statement regarding Lenthall's post-apprenticeship European travels, it says that "he passed fifteen months in Paris, devoting himself to studying and copying draughts of ships at the Depot de la Marine, attending scientific lectures and perfecting himself in the French language. On his return, he presented himself at the Navy Department with about 300 draughts of all the best English, French, Spanish and Dutch ships-of war…"[24] Given that he arrived in Paris in September 1832 and appears to have left by December 1833, the fifteen months calculus is correct. And due to the location of Madame Potel's *pension*, Lenthall's access to public lectures together with his many letters of introduction to esteemed librarians and academicians, ensured he was in a position to pursue his quest to master both the language and the science of France.

John Lenthall's activities at the Depot de la Marine and his production of so many draughts deserve closer scrutiny. Since the late eighteenth century, the French ministry of the navy occupied a magnificent building on Rue Royale (now facing the Place de la Concorde), originally named the Hôtel du Garde-Meuble and later, after it had been fully occupied by the navy, the Hôtel de la Marine. Although far grander and boasting a façade epitomizing French elegance, this *hôtel* was the functional equivalent of the Navy Department's humble digs in Washington so familiar to Lenthall. However, as a relic of the ministry's former residence at Versailles—the location of the king's chateau—the Depot de la Marine remained housed in the Hôtel des Affaires étrangères et de la Marine, close by the chateau's entrance. This building, an imposing structure that embodied royal authority, was famous in its own right as the place where the Treaty of Paris that ended the wars of the American Revolution was negotiated. By 1832 it was still functioning as the navy's repository for nautical charts, maps, navigational logs and archived drawings, but because of bureaucratic neglect was in deplorable condition: its leaking roof threatened the loss of its many stored documents.[25] In the pre-railway era, the dozen miles between Versailles and central Paris could only have been transited using available coach services. By contrast, Madame Potel's *pension* was within walking distance of the Hôtel de la Marine. The geographic remoteness of the Depot de la Marine places Lenthall's drive to study and copy its archived ship plans in a sobering perspective. He must have been a very determined individual to have regularly endured such a grueling regimen of traveling and tracing.

The other aspect of Lenthall's accomplishments in France and, indeed, at the other dockyards he visited in Europe, was the enormous number of drawings he is said to have returned with—300. If his many months afloat, in transit and visiting relatives are deducted, of his nearly three-year-long tour, he probably had only twenty months free to devote to his studies. Assuming two-thirds of the draughts he returned with were tracings of his own making, this equates to an average of one drawing produced every third day, a prodigious output. The ultimate fate of these hundreds of plans is unknown. Examination of the 518 ship plans and drawings catalogued in today's John Lenthall Collection reveals at best a handful that might have originated from his dockyard tour years.[26]

* * *

Not all of John Lenthall's time during his fifteen months in France was spent in the capital. If he was to visit the nation's dockyards, journeys afar were required. Of the three dockyards that Consul Hunter declared of interest to Lenthall—Brest, Cherbourg and Toulon—there is no reliable evidence that he actually visited them. The oldest naval arsenals, Brest and Toulon, were far from Paris, Brest at the western end of the Breton peninsula and Toulon well to the south, on the Mediterranean coast. The newer dockyard at Cherbourg, laid out within an artificial harbor, faced the English Channel. Although closer it was still a good journey from Paris. Lenthall would have learned much about the art of French naval constructors by inspecting vessels being built in these dockyards.[27]

Lenthall pulled off a coup of sorts by getting invited to attend the steam trials of the paddle aviso (dispatch vessel) *Crocodile.* Conducted on 5 January 1833 from Indret, the French navy's "steam factory" at Paimboeuf on the Loire, *Crocodile*'s day-long trials were minutely observed by Lenthall: he recorded her weights, dimensions, steam pressures, fuel consumption, speeds, and weather and tide conditions, all to his usual two-decimal accuracy. *Crocodile* was a vessel of substance.[28] One of the *Sphinx* class of war steamers, *Crocodile*'s 151.78 ft length, 26.25 ft breadth and 17.72 ft depth compared closely to the dimensions of *Princeton,* the U.S. Navy's first steam screw sloop. She also carried a real bite, mounting "three bomb cannons" or Paixhans shell guns, which were just entering naval service.[29]

John Lenthall moved on from Madame Potel's establishment sometime in mid-1833. An engraved invitation to join his fellow citizens at Lointier's Restaurant, Rue Richelieu, for a 4th of July celebration was addressed to him at 5 Rue du Colisée. This placed him in the 8th arrondissement, on the right bank of the Seine, during his last six months in Paris.[30]

Documentation of Lenthall's other journeys outside Paris suggest that in late July 1833, he considered visiting the small shipyard at St. Servan near St. Malo on the coast of Brittany.[31] And perhaps on the back of that trip, a stamped and signed Marine Royale pass dated 22 July demonstrated that he toured the former Compagnie des Indies shipyard at Lorient, then a major naval dockyard.[32]

* * *

John Lenthall must have concluded his activities in France very late in 1833, for by the new year, he was actively corresponding from Portsmouth, England. In a letter dated 2 January 1834, responding to Lenthall's query from the day before, the U.S. chargé d'affaires to the United Kingdom, Aaron Vail, informed him that "I have made an application for your admission to the Portsmouth Yard."[33] This would prove to be Lenthall's final dockyard inspection and what a splendid way to conclude his European tour. The naval dockyard at Portsmouth long held the reputation of being the world's largest industrial complex. Its system of stone-lined drydocks opening into an enclosed basin set the standard for other navies' yards, and its sprawling grounds boasted every facility demanded by constructors serving the world's largest navy.[34]

Soon enough, Lenthall wrapped up his inspections and set in train arrangements for his return to America. During his years in Europe, he managed to save much of his considerable correspondence, which now resides in the Ives Collection. And he continued to add volumes to his growing library. Some of the more significant books procured in this period are listed below, noting the year and (if known) place of purchase:

1832, … : *Philosophical Transactions*, 'The Construction and Analysis of Geometric Properties …' , George Atwood, 1796.

1832, Paris: *Principles of Naval Architecture …* , Thos. Gordon, 1784.

1833, … : *Arrimage de Vaisseaux*, De Missiessy Quiés, 1789.

1833, … : *Du Transport de la Conservation et de la Force Des Bois …* , Duhamel du Monceau, 1767.

1833, … : *Essai Sur La Marine des Anciens …*, Deslandes, 1768.

1833, … : *Le Manoeuvre, ou, Essai sur La Théorie* … , Bourdé de Villehuet, 1814.

1834, Portsmouth: *An Introductory Outline of the Practice of Ship-Building* … , John Fincham, 1825.

No doubt shepherding a goodly number of stout trunks, John Lenthall sailed from Havre for New York in late January 1834. It was mid-winter and luck ran against him. His ship was forced into Portsmouth, of all places, for a delay long enough that Lenthall later complained of having to pay for his own board.[35] Sometime that spring he finally set foot again on U.S. soil.

Looking back on the flow of John Lenthall's European odyssey, it can be appreciated that while his tour included robust spells of dockyard inspections, it was also a journey of immersion into the cultures of the countries he visited. His extended dalliance with his English relatives demonstrated his abiding respect for his parents' homeland. And his lengthy stay in France, the real object of his travels, allowed him to become *au courant* with the naval technology, past and present, that flowed from the birthplace of the science of naval architecture. Lenthall's tour experience would remain indelibly imprinted on his soul for the remainder of his life.

* * *

BOOK TWO
Constructor

CHAPTER 8

Board of Navy Commissioners

John Lenthall's homecoming must have sparked intense joy in the hearts of his family. Aged twenty-six and sporting his trademark pair of side whiskers, a mature man of the world strode across the threshold of the Lenthall's venerable F Street dwelling. Greeting him was his mother Jane now aged fifty-three, his oldest sister Mary, just turned thirty-two and a confirmed spinster, and youngest sister Libby—Mrs. Stone—thirty years old and a mother of four. It was springtime in Washington City, a season of rebirth. The prodigal son had returned. Never again would he venture away for so long from his home town.[1]

Gainful employment must have been first and foremost on John Lenthall's mind. His tour of three long years, while self-fulfilling and intensely satisfying, was the means to the end of achieving his ultimate goal of serving his country as a naval constructor. And the path to an appointment to that office was through the Board of Navy Commissioners. In mid-1834, Commodore John Rodgers sat as the board's president; its other two members were Commodores Isaac Chauncey and Charles Morris.[2] All three were veterans of the War of 1812 and were familiar to Lenthall from his apprentice days. John Lenthall had returned from his travels, bringing heightened knowledge of the latest European naval developments, especially of steamships, but the fall-out from his alleged past 'indiscretion' must have still hung the air. It seems Lenthall's relations with Samuel Humphreys were never impaired and his collection of drawings no doubt erased any remaining qualms. But the board was another matter, a power beholden only to the secretary of the navy and whose authority must be treated by any supplicant with the utmost respect.

Lenthall made his opening move on 9 July 1834 by presenting the board with a list of the drawings he had brought back from Europe.[3] Perhaps a summer absence or recess intervened, but it wasn't until after a second, later prod by Samuel Humphreys on 4 October, recommending Lenthall as an assistant for mould loft duties, did the board finally respond to Lenthall:[4]

Navy Comm office
6th October 1834

The Navy Commissioners wish you to inform them if you are disposed to perform such services as they may require at the mould loft in the Navy Yard at this place, and perform such other duties as they may require, under the direction of Mr. Humphreys the Chief Naval Constructor, and if so at what rate of daily compensation for the time you may be employed. The Board having seen your plans of steam vessels recently constructed in France requests that you will inform them at what price you will furnish copies of such as they may select.

Respectfully,
John Rodgers

Mr. John Lenthall
Washington[5]

Taking Rodgers' reply at face value, it appeared to offer John Lenthall a promising opportunity—ready employment in his hometown and reimbursement for making copies of his precious drawings. But as events proved, both parties were bargaining at cross purposes. Lenthall was dangling access to his trove of drawings as bait for an offer of full employment as a naval constructor, while Rodgers was simply aiming to address Humphreys' request for an assistant and to obtain copies of those drawings the board found of interest. This and subsequent exchanges serve to demonstrate the extent to which the Board of Navy Commissioners attempted to regulate every detail of Navy business, in this case by directly stipulating the terms for and managing the offer of temporary mould loft employment.

Lenthall replied four days later, on 10 October, leaving the requested plans of the steam vessels (or possibly just a list of them) with the board.[6] It seems he also accepted their offer of mould loft work. The board promptly responded on 14 October, this time under the signature of Commodore Chauncey, instructing Lenthall to report to Humphreys and Commodore Hull, commandant of the Washington Navy Yard, and informing him he would be paid three dollars per day. They further reiterated their desire to obtain select copies of Lenthall's drawings "in compliance with the terms of your letter of the 10th inst as may be deemed just and proper."[7] So far, so good. Lenthall had secured temporary employment and ahead lay the prospect of further demonstrating his abilities to the august members of the board. Chauncey followed up two days later by sending a note to Humphreys confirming the board's intention to "engage Mr. Lenthall ... in the mould loft ...under your direction."[8]

But now things began to unravel. Humphreys, no doubt anticipating a positive outcome for his former apprentice, sent a brief note to Lenthall on the 17th telling him to report to the board the next morning and to "bring with you all the drafts of steam vessels which you obtained during your late residence in France & England."[9] What Humphreys hadn't reckoned with was Lenthall's bull-headed pride. To Lenthall's way of thinking, he had immeasurably improved his professional knowledge through three years of self-directed European studies. The drawings he returned with were merely a vehicle to demonstrate his abilities; he wanted to be a constructor! "I am respectfully awaiting the proposition of the Commissioners," Lenthall stiffly replied to Humphreys, "with respect to my plans, of which a list is before them."[10]

Three days later and with no response from the board, Lenthall took matters into his own hands and sent a letter to the commissioners dated 21 October, laying bare his true feelings:

> I have the honor to acknowledge the receipt of the letter of the Commissioners of the Navy of the 14th inst. and would respectfully beg leave to state that I had expected a definite determination of both the subjects mentioned ... in their letter, the plans of the Steam Vessels having been submitted to the inspection of the Commissioners as well as a list of the others before them, and as notice has been taken of this letter, I would beg leave to observe that it was not presented with any view to the disposition of my plans by sale or otherwise but solely with a view to show the diligence with which I had availed myself of the opportunities which were presented.
>
> This collection of plans, including the whole experience of the French Government, is greater perhaps than is in the possession of any other individual and which in justice to myself I could not think of separating, and as I have before had the honor of stating my object, which has been to introduce myself to the notice of the Government and to be permanently employed in my profession. Having learned that the Government is daily expecting the return of an agent employed abroad to procure information on this subject, under the circumstances, I must respectfully beg leave to withdraw my plans from the notice of the Commissioners.[11]

Predictably enough, John Lenthall's confrontational letter ended the month-long dance between him and board over permanent employment and his drawings. He had grossly overplayed his hand. In his final exchange, Lenthall exposed a stubbornness of character and a blinkered adherence to achieving his end at the expense of all else, a trait that would reappear later in his career. He was truly his father's son. And although blemished, his future still held promise. Lenthall had providentially accepted the offer of temporary mould loft work at Washington Navy Yard before issuing his peremptory withdrawal demand. So with his tail between his legs, the next day he reported for duty.

* * *

Back once more in the familiar surroundings of a navy yard, Lenthall quickly and efficiently got to work. It appears he was placed in charge of the loft's activities, for he was given the responsibility of recording entries in the pages of its daily work log. This was fortunate for these logs, which have survived, yield a rare glimpse into the functioning of a navy yard's mould loft.[12]

From his first day on the job, Lenthall and his assistants were fully occupied with the task of producing moulds to be sent to timber contractors, who in turn were charged with delivering frames shaped from the moulds to the navy yards listed below for construction of three different classes of warships:

- Boston Navy Yard: one frigate, one sloop, one schooner.
- New York Navy Yard: one frigate, one sloop, one schooner.
- Portsmouth Navy Yard: one frigate.

The log entries do not give the names of the vessels to be built, but there is little doubt the sloops were *Cyane* and *Levant*, laid down in 1837, and the schooners were *Dolphin* and *Porpoise*, laid down in 1836. The identity of the frigates (44-gun ships) is rather trickier, but the best indications are that the frames were for *Cumberland* at Boston, *Savannah* at New York and *Congress* at Portsmouth.[13]

Lenthall's scope of work was to produce complete sets of moulds for each ship class, marked with the rough moulding sizes, together with sets of bevelling boards. One selected set of moulds and bevelling boards was to be retained in the loft for each class, while the additional sets of moulds and bevelling boards, one for each ship at each yard, were to be boxed and dispatched to the timber contractors.

As for the products of the mould loft—moulds and bevelling boards—they were an integral element of the technology of wooden ship building. Moulds were large wooden templates that captured in full scale the shape, size and location of each piece of a hull's timber framing and are described by a contemporary source as follows:

> In the government yards a mould is made for the floor-timber, futtocks, top and half-timbers, each edge of each mould giving a timber and its opposite. These moulds are made of pine boards, well seasoned, having painted upon them the name, floor, futtock, top and half-top, and the frame to which it belongs; upon these moulds are marked the diagonals, which are the stations of the ribbands, heads, and heels, and at which places the bevellings of the timbers are given.[14]

The purpose of the bevelling boards, hinted at in the above description, is intimately connected to the geometry of a ship's hull. If the frame of a hull were to be erected consisting entirely of square-sectioned timbers, it would be impossible to snugly wrap a watertight layer of planking around it, especially at the ends of the vessel, unless the faces of the frames were angled to suit the hull's complex curvature. Thus the faces of the frames needed to be sloped or 'bevelled', more and more as each end of the ship was approached, the convention being to cut away the fore side of the frames of the forward half of the vessel and the aft side of the frames of the after part of the vessel. The inside face of each frame was also bevelled to match its outside surface. So instead of having the rectangular cross-section of a midship frame, a bevelled frame's cross-section resembled a parallelogram, one that gradually changed its shape from top to bottom. The frames' varying spatial geometry was the data captured on the bevelling boards:[15]

> Bevelling-boards are made usually ten inches in width—a separate set for each body. They should be marked in the following manner: first, name the board that it may be known; then mark a square line across just below the name, marking this set of bevels First Diagonal. The bevels will now be marked in regular succession; the first will be (circled) +, and whether in the fore or after body, we continue on until we reach the highest number or letter, as the case may be, in the alphabet, or in the numbered square-body. Thus we have all the bevels of the square-body at the first diagonal together. The same may be said of all the remaining diagonals, sirmarks, and sheer-lines or breadths. Two sets of bevelling boards are always

prepared, one set for the mould-loft, the duplicate for the use of the foreman in the shipyard.[16]

That John Lenthall was tapped by the Navy's chief constructor to superintend the highly specialized work of lofting moulds and bevelling boards for the nation's latest warships speaks volumes about Lenthall's ability to think in the arcane language of descriptive geometry and his mastery of the projection of solids in space, the bane of many modern-day engineering students. It seems that Humphreys, Lenthall's mentor of twelve years, was able to overlook quirks of his former apprentice's personality in favor of his peerless skill in the mould loft. And Humphreys did visit the loft from time to time. Lenthall's work log entry for Wednesday, 12 November reads "Laying down the schooner of which Mr. Humphreys brought down the draughts on Monday forenoon."[17] This entry has additional significance because it unambiguously demonstrates that in 1834 (and for many years before), navy yards were taking ships' lines directly from drawings rather than off half-models as was still common among builders of merchant ships.[18]

The mould loft's compliment of workers varied from day to day. For example, on 22 October, it consisted of three men, one apprentice and one boy in addition to Lenthall. Employee names and absences were recorded in the work log. Another of Lenthall's duties was to issue requisitions for material needed for the loft's work. An order placed on the 31st of October consisted of "1000 feet of best culling white pine boards, 6 lb weight 10 penny nails, 20 lb weight 12 penny nails and 6 hand files."[19]

Humphreys appears to have done his best to keep Lenthall's name before the board. On 19 November, the week after his visit to the yard, he informed Commodore Rodgers that he had made a rough drawing of a schooner of 230 tons and that "Mr. Lenthall is now engaged in laying down her lines on the mould loft floor." Humphreys then asked if in addition to the moulds for the timber contractors, whether "building moulds" should now be made or postponed to a future date (they were ordered). This letter demonstrates how closely the board regulated each step of a warship's production. It also indicates that separate sets of moulds were required for the different phases of a ship's construction, one set with rough moulding sizes for timber contractors and a second, more refined set of building moulds for the constructors.[20] Lenthall's mould loft assignment also serves to illustrate the degree to which lofting had been centralized by the Navy's chief constructor through the instrument of the Washington Navy Yard. The other yards—in this instance New York, Boston and Portsmouth—

were clearly the recipients of products emanating from Humphreys' scheme of mould distributions.

And in turn, the Navy's commodores kept their eyes on Lenthall. On 9 December Lenthall received a formal letter from the commandant of the Washington Navy Yard, Commodore Isaac Hull, directing him to report daily to the clerk of the yard, Edward Clark. Why Hull felt obliged to remind Lenthall of this, six weeks after the start of his mould loft work, is unclear, but it was a routine protocol required of yard employees. And for reasons that can only be attributed to orneriness, Lenthall penciled a note on this letter stating that "I would not go to Clark—and did not go."[21] The belligerence of youth!

Fall gave way to winter as Lenthall's mould loft team labored away to complete their assigned tasks. The work log entries tell that when it rained, the loft's roof leaked in many places, and that there was no work on Christmas day. Early February 1835 brought a dramatic plunge of temperatures which together with high winds, resulted in "the river quite frozen." Steadily but surely the moulds were completed, boxed up and placed under the timber shed to await shipment. After nearly four months' effort, the work was nearly done. [22]

John Lenthall wrote to Samuel Humphreys on 19 February, telling him that the loft work would be finished in a few days, adding "I would ask if there are more moulds to be made." He appended a summary of the moulds' production and where the boxes containing them were shipped. Four days later, Humphreys forwarded Lenthall's letter to the board.[23]

Meanwhile, Commodore Hull of the Washington Navy Yard instructed Lenthall to close the mould loft, which he did on 24 February. Lenthall's final wistful log entry recorded that he "had better bring the key to [the commodore's] office and then go, as when I would be again wanted could easily be hunted up and found." He informed Humphreys of the closure in a letter written on the 26th, which Humphreys again promptly forwarded to the board's attention.[24]

* * *

John Lenthall's temporary employment by the U.S. Navy had come to an end. Other commercial work was available to take its place, but he would have to find it. His old shipbuilding friend, John Murray, had been in touch the month before, asking to borrow a book on tonnage rules.[25] And Lenthall's mould loft assignment had brought him in contact with other like-minded men who were active in the local industry, one being James Owner, a noted master shipwright.

Samuel Humphreys remained steadfast in his support of Lenthall's efforts to gain a permanent position. Apart from his genuine appreciation of Lenthall's fitness as a constructor, the "Philadelphia fox" was likely motivated by another factor. Following his appointment in late 1826 as chief constructor, James Keen, a former master joiner at the Philadelphia Navy Yard, had been assigned as that yard's naval constructor. But around 1833, Keen left government service and the constructor's slot at Philadelphia remained unfilled. That placed a burden on Humphreys, who in addition to his chief constructor's duties, was obliged to mind the work at Philadelphia. [26] If Humphreys could get Lenthall, his trusted former apprentice, appointed to a position at Philadelphia, all parties would benefit. But there was a rub. Despite Lenthall's acknowledged aptitude and fitness to serve, he was too junior to be appointed a naval constructor. In spring of 1835, he was twenty-seven years old, but his last three years had been spent touring Europe, not at the actual work of building ships. Humphrey's appointment as a constructor came at age thirty-five, Samuel Hartt at New York had been thirty-three. Only Francis Grice, now at Norfolk, had made constructor at an age of less than thirty but he had been a shipwright ever since he was a teen.[27] What was needed to satisfy Humphrey's and Lenthall's ambitions was a specific job—new construction requiring a master builder's supervision but not significant enough to warrant a naval constructor. And to leverage such a situation, patience and an eye for the right opportunity were needed.

* * *

Two weeks after the mould loft's closure, Samuel Humphreys again wrote to the board. Evidently, moulds were now required for a sloop of war and John Lenthall had declined supervising the work unless there was "a certainty of employment."[28] This was a dissatisfying outcome for all—no trusted manager for Humphreys, no work for Lenthall and a continuation of the status quo with the board. One wonders if any residual mistrust over Lenthall's alleged indiscretion of four years before still lingered in Commodore Rodgers' mind, or even if the matter had been formally aired. The record is silent.

Two weeks later and with nothing more from the board, Lenthall played one of his few remaining cards. He took up his pen and addressed a letter directly to Commodore Rodgers. Referring to a communication of the previous summer on the "the application of camels to ships of war in Russia," he then wrote "I would herewith respectfully ask leave to present a paper and plans on that subject."[29] A clever move, possibly suggested by Humphreys, it again put Lenthall's name before the board, cast in the most favorable light.

More weeks of inertia followed with no recorded response from the board. But invisibly things began to shift in Lenthall's direction. The Navy had decided to divert a small portion of the funds approved by Congress for continuing the work on its fleet of unfinished frigates and liners toward the construction of a new store ship. This modest-sized vessel was to be allocated to the Philadelphia Navy Yard.[30] It was the perfect job for Lenthall.

Events now moved quickly. Commodore Rodgers wrote to Samuel Humphreys on 28 April 1835, requesting his opinion of "whether Mr. J. Lenthall is well qualified to superintend the building of the proposed store ship." Humphreys immediately responded in the affirmative.[31]

The commodore then wrote a second letter on the 28th, this one to John Lenthall. In the name of the board, Rodgers wished "to be informed if you are disposed to superintend the building of a store ship at the navy Yard Philadelphia ... and if so, at what compensation per day." Should he accept, Lenthall would "be expected to perform any other of the duties of a Master Builder." Finally, an offer of permanent employment! Lenthall must have been ecstatic. Writing the next day, he accepted the Navy's proposal and asked for $1,500 per year.[32] Two days later, after months of unceasing effort, John Lenthall received what must have been an enormously satisfying letter from the Board of Navy Commissioners' office:

Navy Comm Off
1st May 1835

Sir,
With the approval of the Secretary of the Navy, you will proceed to Philadelphia and report yourself to the commandant of the Navy Yard at that place for the purpose of superintending the building of the store ship about to be constructed there, and to perform such other duties usually performed by a Master Builder as he may assign to you. Your compensation while thus employed will be at the rate of fifteen hundred dollars a year.

I am very respectfully, &tc
Your obt serv.
/s/ Jno Rodgers

Mr John Lenthall
&tc, &tc Washington[33]

* * *

CHAPTER 9

Master Builder

What did John Lenthall's new appointment mean? The first and most obvious impact was that he would be returning to Philadelphia, the city where he had served most of his apprenticeship. His place of work, the navy yard, was quite familiar to Lenthall. Since he had last seen the yard, its facilities had been marginally improved, but during the intervening eight years, just one warship had been completed, the sloop of war *Vandalia.* The hull of the mighty *Pennsylvania* still loomed in the big ship house and *Raritan*'s frame graced the stocks of the smaller frigate house. Commodore James Barron, an ill-starred officer unpopular with many in the Navy, had been in command of the yard since 1831.[1]

John Lenthall had now entered the naval establishment. Navy records indicate he did so at the Washington Navy Yard and was then transferred to Philadelphia.[2] From the date of his appointment, he would begin to accrue the seniority so integral to the system of naval bureaucracy. But a master builder was too junior to rate inclusion in the prestigious *Navy Register*, for that Lenthall would need to wait until he was promoted to constructor.[3]

The vessel whose building he had been hired to supervise, a store ship to be named *Relief*, was at the bottom of the hierarchy of warship pedigree. Although not intended for combat, nonetheless, store ships served a vital role in support of the U.S. Navy's far-flung squadrons, similar to today's fleet auxiliaries. Their purpose was twofold: to bring supplies to distant stations and to serve as dispatch vessels bearing orders or as packets carrying personnel. Store ships had long been a fixture of the U.S. Navy's inventory but until *Relief*'s order, had typically been purchased from civilian owners.[4] *Relief* was the Navy's first purpose-built store ship, the need for which was an outgrowth of the mounting pressure for the Navy to dispatch an expedition to explore the uncharted reaches of the Pacific Ocean. In 1838, after much intrigue and delay, the Wilkes Expedition finally sailed in fulfillment of this vision, and was accompanied by *Relief.*

Relief's design came from the drawing board of Samuel Humphreys and followed contemporary merchant vessel practice. She was a handsome but bluff-bowed little ship of 108.9 ft length, 30.9 ft beam and 15.0 ft depth of hold, with a tonnage of 468 (old measure). Her one claim to uniqueness was in her ship rig, which featured spencer masts abaft all three of her square-rigged masts, a first for the U.S. Navy. They allowed *Relief* to set gaff-headed trysails when her square lower yards had been struck down on deck, a handy feature if she needed to maneuver in a crowded anchorage. For self-protection, she mounted six guns.[5]

* * *

Lenthall settled into his premises at the Philadelphia Navy Yard and quickly applied himself to the work of supervising *Relief*'s construction. A steady stream of documents soon flowed from his hand to the chief constructor in Washington, as evidenced by Humphreys' subsequent submittals to the board: 12 May, a bill of copper bolts, sheets, nails and spikes; 19 May, a bill of yellow pine beams; 21 May, instructions for building and iron required for the store ship and 22 May, a drawing of the location of beams, hatchways, &tc.[6] Of these documents, the instructions for building have survived and are reproduced in Appendix 1. Lenthall's original "Directions for building Store Ship" covered twelve pages of folio foolscap sized paper and has been transcribed in its entirety. The document is undated but contains comments received from Humphreys on 12 June 1835. This revised copy was signed by John Lenthall and bears John Rodgers' signature of approval.[7]

Lenthall's "Directions" provide a comprehensive guide for building a wooden ship. Each principal member of the ship's structure—the keel, stern post, frame and so on—is described as well as the member's component pieces, dimensions of the pieces, how the pieces' dimensions varied within the hull, the material the member was made of, and how it was to be trimmed and fastened. The "Directions" employed a standard format closely resembling the set of "General Instructions" that Lenthall marked-up in 1830 when he assisted Humphreys with designing the 'rebuilt' frigate *Macedonian.*[8]

An integral element of any ship's design are the drawings which describe her. A total of ten drawings of *Relief* are extant in the John Lenthall Collection, most if not all drawn by John Lenthall and attributed to the period 1835-36. Ship plans of this era did not carry title blocks which indicate who drafted the drawing and the date it was drawn. Unless the draftsman's initials were marked—JL in the case of Lenthall—or his lettering was recognizable, it is difficult to definitively assign authorship of such plans. The Collection's guide describes them as "detailed drawings, mostly ink-on-paper, of the hull sections, various deck plans, and the windlass. Also included are the sail and spar plan, fore and aft body plan, and the launching diagram."[9] A specification book is also listed. The sail and spar plan, which includes an outboard profile, is reproduced as Plan No. 2.

Sometime during his first months at Philadelphia, Lenthall began the intensive work of calculating *Relief*s hydrostatic properties. These calculations have also survived and cover almost fifty pages. They are complimented by a score of sheets containing tables of the store ship's offsets, frame sizes, sketches and supporting constructional data. The highlights of these calculations are presented in Appendix 2. Lenthall's summary of *Relief*'s hydrostatic properties were formatted in much the same way as those he performed for *Macedonian*, as discussed in Chapter 6. Similarly, his calculations of *Relief*'s metacenters, both transverse and longitudinal, employ formulae from the previously mentioned classic texts of Chapman and Atwood. Appendix 2 also reproduces Lenthall's original calculation of *Relief*s transverse metacentric height. This particular example was chosen because it represents, on a single page, a perfect example of how a naval architect should present his work: the object of the calculation is clearly stated, formulae applied are prominently posted, the data employed are well laid out, key assumptions are noted and the flow of Lenthall's numerical analyses can be easily followed.[10] The unexpected aspect of Lenthall's work is that he performed such exhaustive and precise analyses for a plebian, 6-gun store ship. But then *Relief* was his first project and he was clearly giving it his all.

* * *

While in the midst of documenting the many facets of *Relief*s design, John Lenthall opened a letter from his old mentor at the Washington Navy Yard, Master Builder William Easby. Dated 7 June 1835, Easby first complimented Lenthall on his new appointment, writing "I feel assured that you will prove an honor to your profession and a credit to your preceptor (I will not say master)," an oblique reference to Humphreys. Easby then got to the point, arrangements Lenthall had made at Philadelphia for his son John, then sixteen years old. Although not expressly stated, the implication is that Easby's son was to be an apprentice of Lenthall's. The son's accommodation and board with a Mr. Black is discussed and Lenthall is enjoined to "have a care of the boy's morals" and to "direct his reading to such books as will be most beneficial to his intended profession." Easby had asked that his boy be paid wages of $1.00 a day but would be satisfied with $0.75.[11] The son in question, John Ward Easby, later followed in Lenthall's footsteps: in 1866, he was appointed a naval constructor, finally rising in 1877 to the office of the chief of the Bureau of Construction and Repair (see Appendix 12). That

William Easby's son would be sent to learn his trade under Master Builder Lenthall's supervision makes perfect sense. There was no resident constructor then assigned to Philadelphia and the bonds connecting former apprentice John Lenthall to his mentor at the Washington Navy Yard clearly ran deep and strong.

* * *

In the first days of summer, the Board of Navy Commissioners were handed a letter from the office of the secretary of the navy. Under the date of 26 June 1835, Secretary Mahlon Dickerson requested that the board take immediate steps to build a "steam battery" capable of defending the nation's ports and harbors, and asked that plans of the vessel be submitted to the Navy Department for the approval of the president.[12] This order, invoking the higher authority of President Andrew Jackson, was a hesitant first nudge toward the resurrection of the U.S. Navy's long dormant interest in steam-powered warships.

The vehicle of this initiative, Mahlon Dickerson, was an unlikely herald of the future. A career politician for three decades, Dickerson was sixty-four and in ill health when he assumed the mantle of navy secretary. His loyalty to "King Andrew" had much to do with his appointment. Dickerson was characterized by a biographer as being "ignorant of naval affairs" and the steward of an indecisive Navy Department. He is credited with two main accomplishments during his four-year tenure: organizing the Wilkes Expedition and initiating the building of the Navy's long overdue war steamer.[13] The first of these achievements had motivated John Lenthall's being hired to superintend *Relief*'s construction and the second would soon indelibly impact his career.

The prodding of the Navy to grasp the nettle of steam propulsion ended a twenty-year hiatus. The Navy's first war steamer, Robert Fulton's *Demologos* of 1815, was now but a distant memory. She had never been commissioned, was quickly relegated to the role of a receiving ship and in 1829 was accidentally destroyed by an explosion. With the exception of the steamer *Sea Gull*, purchased in 1822 to help fight West Indian piracy, America's warships had remained wholly powered by their "grand wind muscles." And this was the maritime bulwark of a vast nation possessing some seven hundred steamers that regularly plied its lakes, rivers and coastal waters.[14]

European powers had been far more progressive in their embrace of steam technology. France commissioned its first naval steamer in 1819, *Voyageur*, built at Lorient, one of the yards Lenthall was known to have visited. In the year he attended the trials of the paddle aviso *Crocodile*,

1833, the French could boast of up to twelve steamers having entered naval service.[15] Britain was close on France's heels, ordering its first purpose-built steamer, *Comet,* in 1821. By the time Secretary Dickerson issued his order to the board, the Royal Navy had already procured nearly two dozen steamers, one of which was the 179 ft long, 835 ton *Medea,* the Woolwich-built side-wheeler whose plans Lenthall had traced.[16]

The board hurriedly restated Secretary Dickerson's specifications for the new steam battery and forwarded them to an ad hoc committee of constructors headed by Samuel Humphreys and including Samuel Hartt and John Lenthall. Humphreys and Lenthall happened to be at the New York Navy Yard in early July, examining the frigate *Constitution* then undergoing repairs supervised by the yard's resident constructor, Samuel Hartt.[17] It may have simply been expedience that motivated the board to assign Hartt and Lenthall to the new committee, so conveniently together in New York with Humphreys. As future events would prove, Samuel Hartt possessed an enduring interest in steam ships, and the board had certainly not forgotten about Lenthall's submittal of his many plans of British and French war steamers.[18]

Instructions to the committee expressed the board's desire that the new steamer be "of the least dimensions and of the least expense," a text book prescription for a cramped, marginally useful vessel.[19] Jotted down by John Lenthall on a page headed "Called for by Commissioners July 9th 1835," the board's other, more pragmatic specifications were:

- Armament to weigh with equipment, ammunition, &c about 65,000 lb.
- Provisions, water, spirits for 60 men, 20 days.
- 2 light lugger masts.
- Sufficient power to go 10 miles in ordinary weather with 2 engines.
- To be able to go with safety from one harbor to another, as from Newport to New York or Philadelphia and from the latter places to Norfolk.
- Re arm 4 Guns or [illegible]
- Our report date 14 July 1835.[20]

One glimpse into how the committee apportioned their work comes from a cost estimate prepared by Lenthall dated "July/35." As the junior member, Lenthall was tasked with the tedious job of calculating the costs of the steam battery's hull. His methodology is recognizably modern, first listing the shipyard trades' (carpenters, smiths, etc.) hours and rates then itemizing specific materials (masts, rigging, etc.). His bottom line was $126,007. A backup calculation using a different metric—length x breadth factors—is shown on the top right corner, with ten percent margins applied. The whole is very workmanlike.[21]

As if Lenthall needed to be reminded, on 13 July the board urged him, in concert with Humphreys and Hartt, to "report your opinions of the general dimensions and arrangements for the proposed steam vessel."[22] This Lenthall did and, after signing the committee's report, returned to the Philadelphia Navy Yard.

The committee's report, submitted as requested on 14 July 1835, largely reflected the views of its senior and most experienced member, Samuel Humphreys.[23] A long, narrow and sharp hull owing much to inland steamer proportions was advocated, powered by novel high-pressure, vibrating cylinder engines. The report's recommendations tempered by further directions from the board prompted Humphreys to revamp an earlier proposal for a steam battery and lengthen it by 55 feet to suit the new specifications. His plans featured a double-ended hull with a rudder at each extremity. Both of these unorthodox features traced directly back to Fulton's 1815 design, although now Humphreys placed the paddle wheels at the hull's sides rather than enclosed within. This unusual and uniquely configured warship would be laid down later that year at the New York Navy Yard, and two years later, enter naval service as *Fulton II*.[24]

John Lenthall must have relished his role as a member of a committee integral to the re-introduction of steamers into the U.S. Navy. During his European tour, he had made a special effort to familiarize himself with the new technology of steam and now the powers that be had sought his input. Master Builder Lenthall did his best to further encourage the board to take notice of his abilities. A lengthy response penned to Commodore Morris soon after his arrival at Philadelphia brimmed with aggressive confidence:

> It was only yesterday on my return from New York that I received your letter of the 30th of June in which you refer to the plans of steam vessels and would state, that the whole of these together with the plans of the other vessels I intended presenting to the Commissioners as I should have time to copy them, and therefore had no objection to submit them whenever they might be of service. Their correctness and identity cannot be questioned, having copied them all, myself, from the original plans. I am well

> aware they may not be of any real or positive value, but as being the experience of a scientific nation their comparative value may be much higher when an analysis of the elements of our ships of war may be made, as doubtless will be, when it is remembered the great attention this subject is receiving elsewhere.
>
> I fear in to trespass too much on your time but the following particulars with respect to the French steam vessel "Crocodile" may not be uninteresting. ...

Lenthall then presented a dense, two-page summary of *Crocodile*'s trials, copiously documented with tables of principal dimensions, hydrostatic data, drafts and displacements, a weight breakout as well as a complete account of the vessel's performance under steam. The sentiments of his final paragraph could well have been written by a modern-day engineer:

> I must again beg, Sir, you will not consider me as intruding officiously and you will excuse the length of this but I could not well compress in a lesser space.[25]

* * *

Occupied though he was by navy business, John Lenthall's scholarly interests still beckoned. An episode in his life-long pursuit of just the right book is documented by a letter he received in December 1835 from Octavius Longworth, a publisher and stationer based in Brooklyn, New York. There was a misunderstanding about a book Lenthall wanted (which was not identified), and the chatty nature of Longworth's letter made clear that the two men often corresponded.[26] As will be seen, Longworth would prove helpful to John Lenthall in other ways.

Closer to home in Philadelphia, Lenthall had not forgotten about the organization that had proven so beneficial to his education as an apprentice, the Franklin Institute. He decided to renew his ties, this time as a full member. The institute's records show that he made good on his intentions. During a board of directors' meeting held on 16 December 1835, "John Lenthall, Ship Builder, Navy Yard" was one of twenty-six candidates proposed for membership, in his case "by actuary." At its next board meeting on 26 January 1836, the institute's minutes recorded that "The candidates proposed at the last meeting were duly elected." John Lenthall's membership in the Franklin Institute would endure throughout his life and beyond, and was responsible in large part for the preservation of so many of his papers, books and drawings in today's John Lenthall Collection.[27]

John Lenthall continued his program of burnishing his reputation with the Board of Navy Commissioners. Early in 1836, he forwarded them a copy of one of the many plans he had brought back from Europe, that of a French frigate, to which the board responded with a note of thanks.[28] In March of that year, Lenthall opened what may have been the first of many letters he would receive from a member of Congress, inaugurating his private correspondence with those serving in another branch of the government. Such communications were (and still are) an integral element of the workings of Washington and John Lenthall, a true son of the nation's capital, now had the opportunity to spread his wings. The letter at hand came from Samuel P. Barton, a New York congressman who had previously worked as an agent for Cornelius Vanderbilt's steamship lines. Barton asked Lenthall for a concise comparison of the United States and British navies, as well as of their merchant marines. The information was for his private benefit, but as Barton sat on the House's Committee on Naval Affairs, it behooved Lenthall to give him his promptest attention. Perhaps Lenthall met Barton during his steamer committee work in New York of the previous year; how he replied is not known.[29]

* * *

As spring of 1836 waxed into summer, John Lenthall focused on completing his first big Navy project, the Store Ship *Relief*. The matter of her castings—for example, rudder pintles—were the subject of correspondence with the board in April, and later that month with the firm supplying them.[30] In May, Lenthall forwarded additional drawings of *Relief* to Humphreys, including those of her cabins, and again the board was promptly advised.[31]

Because both ship houses were occupied with unfinished hulls, *Relief*'s keel had been laid down on a slipway aligned between the houses. All phases of her construction and of Lenthall's supervision of her progress had been carried out in the open, exposed to the elements. That factor, together with the Navy's desire to get their new store ship in service, ensured that by fall of 1836, *Relief* was ready for launching. In comparison to the many years spent piecing together the still incomplete vessels occupying the ship houses—*Pennsylvania* was started in 1822 and *Raritan* in 1820—the pace of her construction had been downright brisk.

Relief slid into the waters of the Delaware on Wednesday, 14 September 1836. Her total building cost tallied $91,288.[32] One source suggests that the yard's commandant, Commodore Barron, pressed for a naval constructor to supervise her launching.[33] *Relief*'s launch would have been Master Builder Lenthall's first and it was not uncommon for constructors beyond those managing the site activities to attend such an important event.

The heir to a long but unspectacular career, for almost thirty years *Relief* supplied warships on every station the Navy maintained. She sailed with Wilkes Exploring Expedition to the Pacific in 1838, doubling Cape Horn over the course of a long cruise, a feat she repeated when later assigned to the Pacific squadron. During her life, she touched at many distant ports, including Sydney, Callao and Macao. She remained active throughout the Mexican and Civil Wars, after which she was placed in ordinary. She last served as a receiving ship at the Washington Navy Yard. Sturdy little *Relief* was finally sold in 1883, a year after John Lenthall's death.[34] *Vitam bene vixit.*

* * *

CHAPTER 10

Life in Philadelphia

While *Relief* may have absorbed the bulk of John Lenthall's attention during his first year in Philadelphia, she was not the only ship to claim his skills as a naval architect. In this era the pace of the navy yards' construction was dismally slow; *Relief*'s launch had been the first at Philadelphia since 1828. Supervising her building was not enough to fully occupy the active mind of someone like Lenthall. Compounding the situation, the job of designing the Navy's warships had been monopolized by its chief constructor, Samuel Humphreys, allowing the yards little initiative. One option that gave rein to a constructor's progressive bent was for him to accept outside commercial work. Such a path was not encouraged by the commandants who ruled their fiefdoms as if they were still afloat. But for those who had the character to accept a challenge and the capacity to handle the extra work, the rewards far outweighed the inevitable bureaucratic opprobrium and mental stagnation. John Lenthall was just such a man.[1]

By the mid-1830s, it is believed that Lenthall had designed a number of vessels, both sail and steam. The records are incomplete and adding to the uncertainty, then as now it was notoriously difficult to assign authorship of a design. As an illustration, consider the sequence of events when an owner ordered a ship. He first went to a builder and asked for an improved model of a successful vessel. Perhaps a naval architect drafted the ship's plans, calculated her displacement and hydrostatic properties, estimated her weights and specified her scantlings. The shipyard's master carpenter would then loft the ship's moulds, bevelling boards and other templates, and start building her hull. Soon enough the owner appointed the ship's prospective captain to superintend her construction, and he could be relied on to force his ideas on the naval architect and builder. When christening day arrived, the builder managed the launch, the naval architect checked his preparations and the superintendent took control once the ship was afloat. And all three could lay claim to being the designer, each with some credibility. So then, who designed the ship? The moral is that a healthy dose of skepticism should always be applied when someone is labeled a ship's 'designer'.

One of the earliest vessels Lenthall is thought to have designed is the Atlantic packet *Georgiana.*[2] With a length of 130 feet, breadth of 30 feet, tonnage of 554 and square rigged on her three masts, she resembled a lengthened *Relief.* She was launched in 1836 from the yard of Vogle & Pearson in Southwark, close to the navy yard. Her construction timeline would have easily allowed Lenthall's participation in her design. *Georgiana* was built for New York owners, and sailed out of that port on European routes for at least a decade.[3] In *Georgiana*'s case, however, caution is warranted if John Lenthall is assigned as her designer because his prime link to her is a single drawing.[4] Perhaps the restless master builder simply took off her lines while she was building, in the same way, he created a number of the other plans in the John Lenthall Collection.

* * *

The city that John Lenthall returned to in 1835 had become smokier, grittier and noisier than it was during his apprentice days. Industrialization's steady march, fueled by a local abundance of coal, iron and limestone, had steadily transformed Philadelphia and its environs into a sprawling center of manufacturing and mechanical enterprise. Lenthall's first brush with the city's new face came within days of his arrival when 20,000 workers went on strike, demanding a ten-hour work day and increased wages. It was the first of several large public disturbances he would witness during the next decade. The city's fast-growing labor force was a perennial source of protests, some of it driven by racial and ethnic animosity toward the many newly arrived immigrants.

The sinews of Philadelphia's changing economy manifested themselves in the form of brash, new factories springing up within the city. Matthias Baldwin's locomotive works was established in 1831 and since 1835, it had occupied a site at Broad and Hamilton Streets, where it would remain until the end of the century. Closer to the Philadelphia Navy Yard, Samuel Merrick's Southwark foundry began operations in 1836 at Washington Avenue and 5th Street. In time it would grow into a formidable engineering and machine works that supplied engines, boilers and armor to the Navy's war steamers.[5]

Under pressure from the forces of change, Philadelphia's shipyards had gradually consolidated over the first decades of the nineteenth century. By 1830 some fourteen major yards dotted the western shore of the Delaware River, stretching from their original core near the navy yard at Southwark, and now were increasingly clustered in the Kensington district, north of the city center. In that year, William Cramp, a boatbuilder whose family had long been settled on the Delaware, opened a shipyard at Kensington. Cramp would prosper over the coming years, and in partnership with his sons, expand his yard's capabilities to eventually include the fabrication of iron-hulled steamers.[6]

By the time Lenthall returned to Philadelphia, iron boats albeit small ones had already made their appearance. The product of local boilermakers, iron barges were increasingly found serving Pennsylvania's growing network of canals and interior waterways. Typically of twenty tons capacity, their durability and lightness compared to their wooden predecessors were much prized. By the end of the century, the forces of industrialization, steam power and iron shipbuilding would allow the Delaware to proudly boast of its nickname, the American Clyde.[7]

Under pressure from its merchants to keep the port of Philadelphia open the year round, in 1837, the city founded a Bureau of Ice Boats. The bureau's mandate was to "operate a vessel on the Delaware River which would be instrumental in breaking the ice during winter months and ensuring a free and open passage on the river." [8] To fulfill its mission, the bureau needed an 'ice boat' or what could be now called an icebreaker. Such a vessel, dubbed the *City Ice Boat* and one of the world's first icebreakers, was launched in August of that same year from Van Dusen & Birely's yard in Kensington. She was a side-wheel steamer of 170 ft length, 30 ft breadth and 12 ft depth of hold. Her engines were manufactured and installed by Matthias Baldwin. She was soon at work on the Delaware, crushing ice ridges up to five feet thick. [9]

Three drawings and a dozen pages of Lenthall's calculations and correspondence for this vessel are extant in the John Lenthall Collection.[10] These documents show that directions for building the ice boat's hull were drafted by Lewis Paleski, possibly a superintending captain, and that John Lenthall calculated her displacement, weights, scale of tonnage and launching conditions.[11] The *City Ice Boat* story yields a fine example of shared design responsibility. Digging into the documents reveals that Paleski provided Lenthall with a "model lift" made to a scale of ½ inch per foot. Such half models, fashioned of parallel layers of thin wooden 'lifts', were commonly used by commercial builders to capture a ship's hull form. Lenthall must have disassembled and measured this model's lifts at each station to create a table of offsets and lines plans that allowed him to apply his naval architect's formulae and calculate the hull's hydrostatic properties. It was just another day's work for a navy-trained master builder.

* * *

For all his dedication to his profession, John Lenthall managed to enjoy a personal life beyond the walls of the Philadelphia Navy Yard. It is not known where he lodged when he first arrived in the city, but by late 1836 his mailing address was 318 South Front Street. That put him on a major city road that ran parallel to the river and which formed the western boundary of the navy yard. It was also the same street Samuel Humphreys had lived on. But as Philadelphia's street numbering system was radically altered in 1856, it is difficult to pin down just where he lived. Presumably, it was close by the yard in Southwark. Today this address would place him further north, in the Society Hill neighborhood.

John Lenthall also attended to his spiritual needs. His family had practiced the rites of the Church of England and so it was logical that he chose an Episcopal church as his place of worship. Aiming to be a respectable member of his adopted town, he made enquiries about obtaining a suitable "sitting." They met with success. St. Paul's Episcopal Church on South 3rd Street offered him a "pleasantly situated" seat for an annual rent of $4.80, but that did not give him burying privileges or a vote in the church.[12] Never mind, he was young and unconcerned with such temporal matters.

One thing that John Lenthall was concerned about was meeting a life partner. When assigned to the Philadelphia Navy Yard, he was twenty-eight years old, already a mature age for such thoughts. Of importance to any prospective mate, he was the son of a distinguished family, had some means and was gainfully employed in a secure government job. By any measure, John Lenthall was a well-educated man with a promising future.

The dates are fuzzy, but not long after beginning his new career in Philadelphia, John Lenthall met his future wife, Mary Dugan Eck. One source says their introduction occurred in 1835 and family correspondence confirms they knew each other before 1838.[13] Mary Eck's background is also sketchy with only ephemeral anecdotes to flesh out a history. And regrettably no likeness of her or description of her appearance has come to light. Her birth year was 1812, which meant that she was about five years younger than Lenthall.[14] Mary Eck's father, John Joseph Eck, was of German descent, his family emigrating from Hanover for religious reasons.[15] Many German settlers immigrated to America through Philadelphia; their influence was especially strong during the eighteenth century. Her mother, Ann Maria Eck, née O'Connor or Connor, was by surname of Irish origins. Mary was a native of Philadelphia, so the Ecks must have been well settled in the city before the turn of the century. But their life was not without its trials. Mary's father died in 1824 when she was barely a teen, and one of her little brothers was "lost," tragedies that must have brought hardships to the family's survivors.[16]

One constant throughout the story of the Ecks was that they were a strongly Catholic family; both of Mary Eck's paternal grandparents and her father were buried in the Old St. Mary's Church graveyard. Mary Eck continued to practice her Catholic faith after marrying the Episcopalian John Lenthall in 1843 and did so for the remainder of her days.[17] Such differences of inter-family faith were unusual in that era and would remain visible during their years of married life. What is remarkable is that any religious differences they may have had were never aired in their or their family's voluminous correspondence.[18]

John Lenthall's twentieth-century descendants' recollections cast the Ecks in a somewhat frivolous light:

> The family was one he had met during his stay in Philadelphia, living on Chestnut St. They were apparently quite well to do, and I judge engaged in real estate and commerce although they never mention business, but clothes, parties and gossip.[19]

One document that provides an interesting glimpse into Mary Eck's character and her social status is a contract of indenture dated 24 February 1837. The indenture bound Elenor Daly to her new mistress, Mary Eck, for a period of four years, during which she was to learn the art, trade and mystery of a "housewife and a tailoress, a mantua maker or a milliner." In return, she was to be provided sufficient meat, drink, lodging, wearing apparel and washing appropriate for an apprentice and to be taught reading, writing and cyphering.[20] Mary Eck was then twenty-five years old and described as "of the district of Southwark," which is well removed from the Chestnut Street address suggested by Lenthall's descendants. It is also where the navy yard was situated and where Lenthall lived and worked.[21]

In 1837, Mary Eck's mother was alive and reasonably healthy at age forty-two. However, her only living brother, Joseph, three years her junior and newly married, had 'gone west' the year before to find his fortune. The Daly indenture together with her brother's departure thrust Mary into the role of responsible caretaker of the Eck family—now just herself, her mother and her servant. It was a quiet but determined woman that John Lenthall would choose to marry and share his life with.

* * *

Despite the many distractions of life and work, John Lenthall was a person who remained in touch with friends and acquaintances. Exemplifying this habit, one name that reappears within the trove of his letters preserved in the Ives Collection is Daniel Brent. Two letters were received by Lenthall from Brent, both written from Paris during Brent's tenure as the U.S.

consul in that city. Brent took over the post in 1833, right in the middle of Lenthall's stay in Paris. But it is likely that Lenthall knew Brent well before then, for Daniel Brent had already wrapped up a long career as chief clerk of the State Department in Washington before setting off for France at age sixty-three. Serving as chief clerk from 1817 through 1833, Brent must have known Lenthall's uncle, Robert King Jr., who had officed on the first floor of the State Department building. And Lenthall probably dealt with Brent in 1830 when obtaining letters of introduction from Martin Van Buren. Even in the early years of the Republic, Washington's clique of insider bureaucrats spread their web far and wide.[22]

Brent's latest letter to Lenthall, dated 22 November 1836, shines a light on the methods Lenthall used to keep up with the latest foreign naval developments. The subject of Consul Brent's correspondence was the French navy. He reported to Lenthall that he had been able to obtain the latest report of the Minister of Marine but had not yet been able to get the Department of the Marine's budget. He would do his best to take advantage of the first private opportunity to forward these documents to Lenthall's correspondent in New York.[23] From Brent's previous letter of March of the year before, this contact was named as none other than Octavius Longworth, stationer, one of Lenthall's regular correspondents.[24] John Lenthall's system was simple but effective. Using his network of known government officials, professional contacts, friends and colleagues, he was able to tap into sources of information that would have otherwise not been accessible. The benefits of his private network will reappear in later years and become increasingly valuable as Lenthall rose within the hierarchy of the U.S. Navy Department.

* * *

CHAPTER 11

Launch of Pennsylvania

One of the year-end rituals of the United States government's executive branch is for its department heads to submit annual reports to the president. Such reports are finely crafted political statements but they also shed light on the departments' achievements over the past twelve months and signaled their future intentions. Secretary of the Navy Mahlon Dickerson's December 1836 annual report touched on a number of subjects that must have been of intense interest to Master Builder John Lenthall:

> In presenting for your consideration at this time the condition of our navy for the past year … there has been an increased activity in the construction and equipment of vessels at our navy yards.
>
> The frigate *Macedonian,* of the second class, has been finished, launched and equipped for sea; and she is now receiving her crew, as the ship of the commanding officer of the South Sea exploring expedition.
>
> The store-ship *Relief* has been finished, launched, and equipped, and is now receiving her stores.
>
> The labor upon the ship of the line *Pennsylvania* has been resumed, with a view to her completion, and she will probably be ready for launching in the early part of next summer.
>
> The steam-vessel building at New York is so far completed as to be ready for the reception of her engines and machinery; in procuring which there has been some unavoidable delay … and the vessel will probably be ready for service in the course of the next summer.[1]

Macedonian, for which Lenthall had run calculations, was ready for sea as was his first big project, *Relief.* The Navy's newest steamer, *Fulton II*, was awaiting her machinery and her engines were delayed. But it was the decision to complete the mighty *Pennsylvania* in the coming year that would exert the greatest impact on John Lenthall. As the Philadelphia Navy Yard's master builder and protégé of her designer, Samuel Humphreys, it was he who was chosen to superintend this important task.[2]

Pennsylvania was a handful by any standard. At 210'-0" length, 56'-9" breadth, 23'-0" depth of hold and pierced for 138 guns, she was the world's largest ship, bigger than the most powerful British first rates then afloat, the vessels of the *Caledonia* class.[3] Framed of live oak and planked with white oak, *Pennsylvania* boasted four complete gun decks within her lofty and enormously strong hull. Designed to serve as a ship of the line, she was more of a massive gun platform intended to destroy any warships attempting to blockade America's ports. However, her very size meant that her operating costs would be more than the Navy's meager budget could bear, which helps to explain why she remained under construction for so many years.[4] Now the Navy had decided to complete *Pennsylvania* and preserve her afloat 'in ordinary'. But first, she had to be launched and that was to be John Lenthall's next big challenge.

The launching of a ship is a complex undertaking. Its success is wholly dependent on the meticulous completion of the many steps required to ensure that the ship will slide unhindered into her natural element. Much of the preparations lie more in the realm of civil and structural engineering than naval architecture. The slipway which hosts the ship's launch must rest on solid ground—piled and reinforced if necessary—inclined at just the proper angle and at just the right distance from a body of water deep enough to float the completed vessel. Prior to the ship's launch, the weight of her hull must be carefully transferred from the keel blocks on which she was built to pairs of longitudinal bilge ways, sliding structures of stout blocks and packing erected on each side of the keel and shaped to accept her curved bottom, which in turn rested on well-greased inclined ground ways leading straight and true into the waiting waters. Once free of the constraints of land, the vessel would hopefully be found to be watertight, stable and floating at her calculated drafts.[5] The climax of all these carefully orchestrated steps, the actual launching, played out under the expectant gaze of thousands of people—boisterous spectators, officious politicians, opinionated naval officers and the highest of the Navy Department's office holders. It is no surprise, then, that the superintendent of a ship's launch was under enormous stress. Being fully cognizant of the stakes involved and how it could affect his reputation and career, John Lenthall promptly asked the yard's commandant for a raise. The Board of Navy Commissioner's response to Commodore Barron reveals that Lenthall had learned something about dealing with his superiors since he was first hired. And more importantly, his request had gotten their attention:

Navy Comm. Off.
10th Febr. 1837

Sir,
In reply to your letter of the 6th inst. enclosing copy of a communication to you from Mr. Lenthall, the Board have to state, that they are perfectly sensible of the value of Mr. Lenthall's services, but they have it not in their power at this time to increase the amount of his compensation, but you may assure him that the subject will claim the early consideration of the Board.

I am, Very respectfully
Sir
Yr. Obt. Srv.
/s/ Jn. Rodgers[6]

Several years before, the secretary of the navy had estimated six months' work would be required before *Pennsylvania* could be launched.[7] That translated into a mid-summer launch date. As the days steadily lengthened, Master Builder Lenthall became a very busy man indeed.

* * *

Two documents residing in the John Lenthall Collection provide an exceptionally close look at the preparations put in hand to ensure *Pennsylvania*'s safe launch.[8] Both are reproduced in full in Appendix 3. The first is a brief set of "Orders to be Observed," which touches on the particulars of the launching and bilge ways, hull shoring and crowd control measures for the day of the launch—no more than 100 people on board the ship—and was signed by Samuel Humphreys, Samuel Hartt and John Lenthall. The second, far more detailed "In Describing the Launch" was written by John Lenthall, almost certainly after the event, and is thought to be the text of a paper he later presented on this subject. Lenthall relates in great depth the preparations made for the launch, the composition of the launching (ground) way and bilge (sliding) way structures and how they were erected, and the step-by-step actions taken during the hours that led up to the launching.

Lenthall's description explains that a largely invisible cause for delay of *Pennsylvania*'s launch was the decayed condition of the piled structures supporting her slipway. The renewal of the piles and the ground ways' structural underpinning, with *Pennsylvania*'s "considerably advanced" hull in place, and subsequent additions to the ways' length, some of it carried out under water, were in of themselves major feats of civil engineering.

Pennsylvania's preparations occupied a small army of men and required vast quantities of timber. Oak logs up to forty-five feet in length measuring three feet wide and one foot thick were laid down as the launching planks on each side of the ship, extending for more than twice her length, well into the Delaware. The surfaces of these planks were carefully planed smooth. Next, the bilge ways were assembled on top of the launching planks. These were made of yellow pine logs two and a half feet in width and pieced together to create cradles 147 feet long. Packing blocks were then shaped to snug up against *Pennsylvania*'s curved bottom and groups of upright shores fitted to each end to act as poppets. Once the bilge ways and their packing blocks were fitted up to Lenthall's satisfaction, they were disassembled and their surfaces rubbed with chalk to prevent any slippage. At this time, the launching planks were coated with 2400 pounds of tallow and 350 pounds of castile soap to ensure their lubricity. Then the bilge ways and packing blocks were re-assembled and their wedges, some three hundred per side, were inserted, ready to be driven home just before the launch. Ninety men on each side were required for this task. Surrounding the huge wooden battleship were a virtual forest of shores, stout oak logs jammed into the ground and against the hull to prevent it from tipping over.[9]

Lenthall's notes make it clear the tides of the Delaware were evaluated to determine the proper day and hour for *Pennsylvania*'s launching.[10] Philadelphia's average tidal range is about five feet, so knowledge of its timing was essential to success.[11] And the chosen launch date, 18 July 1837, was the day after the full moon, when the highest tides could be expected. The optimum time to schedule a ship's launch is a half an hour before high water, to allow for the inevitable delays. *Pennsylvania*'s launch was set for just after 2 p.m. which was near the ideal time.

Closer to the event, John Lenthall the naval architect documented his calculations of the forces at play during a launch. He first prepared an estimate of the weight of *Pennsylvania*'s completed hull. Using this weight of 2,696 long tons, the angle of inclination of the ways, 3° 31', and an assumed frictional coefficient of 0.04, he determined the net force that would "cause the ship to descend the plane" was 57.4 tons. His data are complete enough to allow a technical analysis of *Pennsylvania*'s launching conditions and a comparison to modern standards—and all of it passes muster.[12]

* * *

Soon enough it was launch day at the Philadelphia Navy Yard. The weather that morning was fine although warm. John Lenthall and his workmen started work at 5 o'clock, inside the dark vastness of the ship house. Standing in deep shadows under *Pennsylvania*'s enormous hull, nearly two hundred men wielding heavy hammers began 'setting up' the wedges. A score of guttering candles cast a feeble glow on the proceedings. Their job was to drive long, thin wedges between the bilge blocks and the packing above, which after repeated cycles of hammering, gradually transferred the ship's weight from its keel blocks to the bilge ways. A calculated rhythm marked their pace, with intervals of deafening blows spaced by long pauses to remove shores on each side of the vessel. In the last stages, battering rams were manned, their stout oak masses gaining the wedges' final inches. By 10 o'clock, the aftermost keel block was removed and an iron shoe fixed under the end of the keel. The rising tide was now coming in.

Outside the navy yard, "a huge, black living mass" of humanity choked the streets, covered nearby buildings and clung to every conceivable vantage point. For the past two days, the city's public conveyances had been packed and now the spectacle that had brought them to Southwark was about to unfold. The excited atmosphere of a national holiday enlivened the waiting throngs, both ashore and in boats crowding the Delaware. An eye-witness to the events recorded his impressions:

> Mr. Mahlon Dickerson, at that time the Secretary of the Navy, arrived at the yard about 11 o'clock, and inspected the preparations with great interest. The blocks from the keel were knocked away gradually, and by 2 o'clock every arrangement seemed to be complete; in ten minutes after, the salute was fired, and the flag from the top of the building was hauled down, as a signal to the boats in the river to beware. The sawing off the ways now commenced cheerily; when this was completed, she still hung for a few minutes, until some beams were brought into requisition manned by thirty men each; a few well-directed strokes from these put her in motion, and down the greasy ways she started, moving about as rapidly as a man could run, and just as she touched the water Commodore Biddle performed the christening ceremonies, Hercules the "figure head," grinned a savage smile, and the great leviathan moved a short distance out into the stream. As the noble Delaware received her, the shouts of many thousands went up

> mingled with the roar of cannon that reverberated from shore to shore, and were prolonged in the far-distant echoes.[13]

Pennsylvania's launch was a success! The world's biggest ship was safely afloat. No one could have been more delighted—and more relieved—than John Lenthall. All those weeks of focused preparation had paid off. A close examination of Lenthall's post-launch descriptions brings to light a number of valuable observations. First was the check he made when the last keel block had been knocked away—*Pennsylvania*'s keel was perfectly straight. This confirmed that her hull had suffered no structural distortion or racking after its transfer from the keel blocks to the bilge ways.

Second, although the ship refused to start when the ways had first been cut, Lenthall's judicious planning paid off. Awaiting rams quickly drove iron wedges across the way ends. Their extra horizontal forces supplied the final jolts the battleship needed to break free. Many a ship hung up on their ways for much longer, *Constitution* being a good example. Her launch succeeded on the third try and then only after her slipway was completely rebuilt.[14]

Third was Lenthall's comment that "the ship did not poise on her ways at all." By "poise" Lenthall meant that *Pennsylvania* did not visibly 'tip' her bow up due to insufficient buoyancy astern, which could easily have strained her back, or 'pivot' on her fore poppet, which might have locally over-stressed her hull.[15] She entered the water without any indication of the trauma that all too often deformed a wooden hull before it was fully afloat. Her floating drafts of 14'-10" forward and 18'-8" aft show she was trimmed by the stern, which probably contributed to her trouble-free entry into the water.

Finally, Lenthall reported that "the ship did not touch bottom" based on evidence from pulling up the ways the following day. This must have been very gratifying to him and to Samuel Humphreys, her designer, who although not mentioned in the accounts, almost certainly attended *Pennsylvania*'s launch. The first of the U.S. Navy's 44-gun frigates, *United States,* touched bottom during her 1797 launch from Samuel Humphreys' father's old yard just up the river.[16] The Delaware was an unforgiving place to launch a big, deep ship.

* * *

The story of Lenthall's supervision of *Pennsylvania*'s launch would be incomplete without mention of its satisfying postscript. Nearly six years after the event, in the year 1843, the American Philosophical Society "determined to celebrate the hundredth anniversary of its organization ...

on Thursday the twenty-fifth of May next." Elegant printed invitations were sent out to members and guests, one of which was directed to John Lenthall, naval constructor. On the invitation's blank side was written a message, part of which read "We respectfully urge your attendance at the meeting and ... further ask you to present a communication upon the subject which we have taken the liberty to indicate on the margin." The named subject was "Account of the Launch of the Pennsylvania."[17]

Two of the society's members signed the invitation, A. D. Bache and John Ludlow. Alexander Dallas Bache, a great-grandson of Benjamin Franklin and a West Point graduate, was a fellow member with John Lenthall at the Franklin Institute. He was also a highly regarded educator and a scientist of great ability. Before the end of the year, Bache would be appointed as the supervisor of the United States Coast Survey, then the nation's largest scientific establishment.[18] It must have been quite flattering for John Lenthall to have received such a personal request from the likes of Bache.

Lenthall accepted the society's invitation and submitted a "communication" for presentation at their centenary event in Philadelphia. The full title of his paper was "On the Launch of the Three-deck Ship the Pennsylvania in 1837" and it was read by Mr. J. C. Cresson in Lenthall's absence on the evening of 27 May 1843.[19] Cresson, another fellow member of the Franklin Institute, has been variously styled as a professor or a manager. Lenthall's "In Describing the Launch" reproduced in Appendix 3 is almost certainly an early draft of the paper presented by Cresson. While the "communication" published in the society's *Proceedings* covered little over a single page, careful reading makes it clear that it closely follows Lenthall's longer-winded draft. But Lenthall made one small but significant late change to his account. Perhaps in belated recognition that *Pennsylvania* had not easily started her launch and required an extra nudge, he increased his estimate of the ways' frictional coefficient from 1/25 to 1/20 of the pressure, or from 0.04 to 0.05, which reduced the calculated net horizontal force "causing the ship to descend the plane" by nearly half. Better to admit a fault late than never.

* * *

Lenthall had barely caught up with his sleep when on 20 July he again addressed the commandant of the Philadelphia Navy Yard on the subject of his compensation, no doubt emboldened by *Pennsylvania*'s successful launch. And in response to his persistence, he received a reply direct from the Board of Navy Commissioners dated 24 July which offered some grounds for optimism:

> The Board ... expect to be in Philadelphia on Wednesday next, and will see you at the yard, and upon the return of the Board to

> Washington, the subject will be duly considered and a fuller notice of your communication will be transmitted to you.[20]

No record of a "fuller notice" from the board has been found. Lenthall's hopes for advancement, or least for more pay, were once more unfulfilled. But he was too stubborn to let it go. In late September, he wrote the board asking about the matters raised in his letter of 20 July.[21] As Lenthall would eventually come to realize, he was butting his head against the Navy's bureaucracy and its entrenched barriers that offered little scope for individual initiative.

Meanwhile, the Navy's business both in Washington and its yards carried on. The matter of steamers had again claimed the board's attention and at the end of August, they wrote to Samuel Humphreys, then in Philadelphia. He was directed to consult with constructors Hartt and Lenthall, and to prepare a set of plans for "a sea steamer to work her engines perpendicularly." General dimensions proposed by the board were a length of 215 ft and a breadth of 36 ft. She should be armed with 8-inch pivoting shell guns fore and aft and carry fuel enough to last for twenty days.[22] It is noteworthy that the trio of naval architects named by the board were the same who had been appointed to advise on the arrangements of the last steamer, *Fulton II.* They diligently performed their assigned task and prepared the requested drawings. The vessel envisaged by the board and reflected on their plans was longer than anything the Navy had yet contemplated —33 ft more than *Fulton II,* longer than any of its frigates or liners, and 5 ft greater in length than the recently launched *Pennsylvania,* the world's largest ship. Although their work was shelved without further action, the seed planted by their labors would yet germinate into a successful 'sea steamer'.[23]

* * *

CHAPTER 12

Naval Constructor

The first chink in the wall of bureaucracy that had stifled Lenthall's advancement opened in the fall of 1837. Constructor William Doughty, a fixture at the Washington Navy yard since the turn of the century, submitted his resignation. Aged sixty-four, Doughty had become wealthy and with a score more years of life left in him, retired to join his son in the timber trade.[1] His resignation marked a passing of the old guard. William Doughty, the protégé of the Navy's first naval constructor, Joshua Humphreys, had been instrumental in the design of many of the nation's warships, the finest examples being the 74-gun liners *Delaware* and *North Carolina.*

But before the Navy Department and its bureaucrats could adjust to Doughty's departure, news reached Washington of an even more profound loss to the community of naval constructors, the death of Joshua Humphreys. Dying in Philadelphia on 12 January 1838 at age eighty-six, Humphreys' passing truly symbolized the end of an era. Joshua Humphreys merited more than any other the title of "father of the American Navy." It was he who was the progenitor of the super frigate, embodied for generations by the legendary Old Ironsides, the U.S.S. *Constitution.* His skill and design acumen quickly gained the infant U.S. Navy the respect and admiration of the world's naval powers. At his death, he was considered one of Philadelphia's most influential business leaders. And during his lifetime, he fathered eleven children, one of whom was still carrying his legacy forward, the Navy's chief constructor, Samuel Humphreys.[2]

Five days after Joshua Humphreys' death, the Board of Navy Commissioners summoned John Lenthall from the Philadelphia Navy Yard to their offices in Washington. Their purpose was not specified, but his services were needed "for some days." Lenthall was ordered to "repair to this place with Mr. Humphreys when he returns," tying his Washington summons to the chief constructor, who was then in Philadelphia dealing with the aftermath of his father's funeral.[3]

The precise sequence of events over the next two weeks is unknown, but what is clear is that John Lenthall submitted a formal application to the board for the naval constructor's position opened by Doughty's departure. Perhaps the idea was suggested to him by Samuel Humphreys while travelling to Washington, but then making an aggressive request was certainly within Lenthall's character. Soon enough, he heard back from the board:

> Navy comm. off.
> 2 February 1838
>
> Sir,
> The Board have received your application for the appointment of naval constructor to fill the vacancy produced by the resignation of Mr. Doughty. The Board deems it essential under ordinary circumstances, that no appointment of navy constructors should be made without a favorable report from a Board composed of at least three naval constructors; but from the fact of your having been employed as master builder at the Navy Yard Philadelphia for some time past, and during that time superintended the building of the Relief and completing the Pennsylvania in a manner which has been deemed satisfactory, they are willing in your case that your examination should be conducted by the Chief Naval Constructor Mr. Humphreys. If therefore you are disposed for such examination you will present yourself to him for that purpose and if he should report favorably upon your qualifications, the Board will recommend you to the Secretary of the Navy as a proper person to receive the appointment.
>
> I am Sir,
> Very respectfully
> Yr Obt Srv
> /s/ I. Chauncey
>
> Mr. John Lenthall
> Washington[4]

Chauncey's letter marks a watershed in John Lenthall's dealings with the board. Lenthall's persistent applications for recognition of his abilities had finally won him a fair hearing, in fact, more than fair. Given that Lenthall had been Humphreys' apprentice, that Humphreys had promoted Lenthall's interests through thick and thin, and that since Lenthall's hiring as a master builder the two had worked hand-in-hand, it was tacit approval for his promotion to naval constructor.

Under the same date of 2 February, Chauncey wrote Humphreys a letter mirroring the terms he had spelled out to Lenthall, the last paragraph of which read:

> Mr. Lenthall will therefore be authorized to present himself to you for that purpose, and you will, after carefully examining him upon all such points as you may deem essential to ascertain his qualifications for performing all the various duties of Naval Constructor in one of the Navy Yards, and report to the Board your opinion upon them.[5]

Lenthall's examination obviously passed without a hitch and the process of approving his appointment positively sped through the Navy Department. On 8 February 1838, less than a week after Chauncey composed his two letters, John Lenthall was appointed a U.S. Navy naval constructor.[6] For Lenthall, then thirty years old, it was the culmination of a quest for professional recognition and the beginning of an even longer journey of personal fulfillment.

* * *

The Navy's business that had prompted Lenthall's call to Washington in January kept him there for the remainder of February. He must have enjoyed having the chance to catch up with his family's affairs at the house on F Street, now occupied by just his mother and sister Mary. But soon enough, a letter from the board was handed to him. Dated 6 March, it was brief and to the point. "You will proceed to Philadelphia and report yourself to the commandant of the Navy Yard at that place as Naval Constructor at that yard."[7] What is remarkable about this order is that while Lenthall's promotion to naval constructor was actioned by a vacancy at the Washington Navy Yard, he was assigned to his former yard in Philadelphia. The board must have been comfortable with Samuel Humphreys temporarily covering for Washington.

Now a newly minted naval constructor, John Lenthall's first order of business was to come to grips with the Navy Department's hierarchy that defined—or more accurately, attempted to define—his place within a navy yard. As a resident constructor, he was under the administrative supervision of the yard's commandant and reported to him on the progress of new construction and on those technical issues and repair questions about which he had been consulted. He was acknowledged as the yard's master shipwright and in this role, he directed the activities of the foremen, loftsmen, draftsmen and apprentices under his control as well as the wide range of tradesmen—carpenters, joiners, caulkers, blacksmiths, coopers and so on—that made up the yard's workforce. In the case of a captain of a new or repairing ship, the constructor's role was rather hazier. While the constructor was an acknowledged authority on naval architecture, he was a civilian employee—deemed a 'civil officer'—and commissioned naval officers were not obliged to accept or even ask for his advice. Constructors could dispute a captain's decision but could not override it. Because of this diffusion of authority, the circumstances of a warship's arming, equipping, sparring and ballasting often varied, sometimes to the detriment of the vessel, depending on the personalities of her captain, the constructor and the commandant. It was an imperfect system and the wonder is that it worked as well as it did.[8]

John Lenthall's first year as a naval constructor was rapidly overtaken by the Navy's latest building project, a new class of sloops of war. Responding to an act of Congress from the previous year authorizing their construction, the board issued a request for design proposals from its constructors. The U.S. Navy's normal progression for nearly all of its men of war, from liners to frigates and sloops, had been to gradually increase their size and capability. However, in the case of the 1838 sloops, for reasons that are not fully understood or explicable, this trend was reversed. As follow-ons to the last built sloops of war, *Cyane* and *Levant*, they should have been at least as large as that class' dimensions of 132'-3" in length and 35'-3" in breath. But they were much smaller. The best consensus is that the new sloops were conceived as nostalgic reversions to the original *Peacock* of 1813, a fast and successful sloop renowned for her seaworthiness.[9]

Proposals submitted by the constructors in response to the board's requirements ranged in length from 111'-0" by Francis Grice to 114'-6" by both Josiah Barker and John Lenthall. After some internal debate about optimization of the new sloops' size, speed and armament, the board selected Lenthall's design, but with the stipulation that it be redrafted to match a length closer to the original *Peacock*'s. The final design for what were now designated 3rd class sloops featured a length of 117'-7", a beam of 32'-0" and depth of hold of 15'-0". Although Lenthall probably had some exchanges about these ships' features with Humphreys, the evidence is that the class' design came entirely from Lenthall's drafting board.[10] The drawing reproduced as Plan No. 4, bearing the notation "Sloop Proposed, actually built as 'Dale', Length was 114"6 JL" and clearly by his hand, further documents this claim. Ultimately known as the *Dale* class sloops, these warships would be the first of many designed for the U.S. Navy by Constructor John Lenthall.

Lenthall's *Dale* class were trim, compact ships with an entrance that was not too full or too sharp, a fine long run, and strong but straight deadrise ending in moderately rounded bilges. Her gradually increasing sweep of forward sheer together with her partially enclosed head would prove to be a signature of Lenthall's designs. The sloops were fitted with topgallant forecastles and short poops, both of which would contribute to their dryness. Although pierced for eighteen guns, they were typically armed with only sixteen—fourteen 32-pdr carronades and two 12-pdr long guns.

Plan Nos. 4 and 5 are worth a closer look, both for what they reveal about the *Dale* class and Lenthall's design methods. They were specifically chosen for inclusion because they illustrate features that are seldom shown on the more conventional drawings reproduced in scholarly works. As previously mentioned, Plan No. 4 offers a rare glimpse of a naval architect's working drawing. Drafted around a half breadth plan, the sheet is cluttered with tabulations, side notes and graphs hinting at the drawing's true function—the source of Lenthall's hydrostatic data for the class, some of which are plotted (center of gravity of waterplanes and metacenter). Comparison with a traditional lines plan for these ships, the best example being Chapelle's, reveals the very different character of Lenthall's working plan.[11]

Plan No. 5 is a more conventional drawing focusing on the *Dale*s' bow. The grace of Lenthall's lines and his balanced proportions are immediately evident. The inboard profile and half breadth plans were drafted in multi-color inks—black for the principal lines, red for hidden or section lines and blue for the 'floating' or design water line—again with many rough notations jotted throughout. The locations of the bolts piercing the bow's deadwood and breast hook structures are drawn in, as is Lenthall's evaluation on the half breadth plan of the reach of the fore yard over the ship's cathead, probably to demonstrate its utility for anchor handling. The note "'Dale' & 'Preble' by JLenthall" appears on the drawing's lower right corner.

The Navy apportioned construction of the *Dale* class between five of its principal yards, naming the sloops in harmony with their places of building: *Dale* to Philadelphia; *Decatur* to New York; *Marion* to Boston; *Preble* to Portsmouth and *Yorktown* to Norfolk. *Preble* was the first to be laid down in April of 1838 and curiously enough *Dale*, built under Lenthall's supervision at Philadelphia, was the last to have her keel laid. However, *Decatur* was the first to be launched and in March 1840, the first to commission.[12]

In service, the *Dale*s were popular with their officers and crews. They were seaworthy, handled well, steered easily and stiff under sail. As with many smaller sailing vessels, their motions and speed were sensitive to the rake and set of their masts, the amount of ballast they carried, and how much of their stores and water had been consumed. They also showed a surprising difference in speeds, *Dale* being demonstrated the fastest and *Yorktown* the slowest. It was in the matter of speed that they most failed to live up to expectations.[13] For a ship, all other things being equal, speed is a function of hull length; in choosing the sloops' reduced dimensions, the board had only itself to blame.

With the exception of *Yorktown* which was wrecked in 1850, the ships of this class had long and colorful careers. The four remaining sloops served mainly on the Brazil, African and Pacific stations and were active into the opening years of the Civil War. Philadelphia-built *Dale* was the longest lived, lasting well into the twentieth century as a training ship. She was finally sold in 1921. Given their small size, the class proved to be economical peacetime cruisers. But had a war erupted with a major European power, they would have been at a disadvantage in contests with larger foes. Overall, the *Dale* class sloops were remembered within the U.S. Navy as successful warships.[14]

* * *

On 31 July 1838, a merchant vessel by the name of *Clarion* was registered under the American flag at the port of Philadelphia. Joseph Vogels and John H. Young were listed as the owners, with Young also documented as the ship's master. Vogels or Vogle—spelling of names was fluid in that era—was also *Clarion*'s builder, the same whose Southwark yard had constructed *Georgiana* two years earlier. Reliable sources claim that, as he had with his previous new-building, Vogels asked John Lenthall to design his ship.[15]

Clarion was a small barque rigged vessel intended by her owners for the Havana-New Orleans trade. Her dimensions differ somewhat depending on the source, but using data later generated by John Lenthall, her length was 93 ft, breadth 24½ ft, depth of hold 14 ft and register tonnage about 220.[16] These dimensions taken together with the only existing drawing of her indicate *Clarion*'s hull was very small for a vessel rigged with three masts. That her lines plan was described as showing "a particularly attractive hull" provides some credibility for Lenthall's connection to her design.[17]

Little *Clarion* would probably have lived out her short life and passed into oblivion except for a singular circumstance: after serving her Philadelphia owners for two years, she was sold to New York interests who decided to fit her with a novel twin screw propulsion system then being zealously promoted by a newly arrived Swedish immigrant named John Ericsson.[18] In due course, *Clarion*'s journey into history will be told. And from this point on, the careers of the Swedish inventor and Constructor John Lenthall would become increasingly intertwined.

* * *

Placing a bookend on the theme of passing of the guard, Commodore John Rodgers died in mid-summer of 1838. As president of the Board of Navy Commissioners, Rodgers had been a fixture in young John Lenthall's early struggle to become a naval constructor, almost becoming his *bête noire* before finally reaching out and hiring him to build *Relief.* Failing health caused Rodgers to resign as president of the board on 1 May 1837, prompting his replacement by Isaac Chauncey. But Rodgers' health continued to decline, and exhausting his final hope at the Philadelphia Naval Asylum, he breathed his last a year later on 1 August.

It fell to the commandant of the navy yard, Charles Stewart, to organize Rodgers' funeral procession. All naval officers in Philadelphia on 3 August 1838 attended in full dress uniform. Assuming John Lenthall was then in the city, he would have taken his place in the long stream of subdued marchers who slowly wound their way to the Christ Church burying ground, their pace measured by minute guns booming from the navy yard. There, after full honors had been rendered, Commodore John Rodgers was laid to rest. One of the defining icons of the War of 1812 had now passed from the scene.[19]

* * *

In the fall of 1838, John Lenthall's mother was fifty-eight years old. Her son was now established in his profession, her youngest daughter married and a mother four times over and her oldest daughter, Mary, a confirmed but content spinster. Perhaps looking to her remaining years, Jane King Lenthall made the decision that many people often do at that phase of their lives: while still in good health, fit and strong, to return to the country of their birth and visit their remaining relatives. One source suggests that in October 1838, she and her daughter Mary embarked on that long journey—by steamer to Liverpool, then train and finally by coach—back to Yorkshire, England.[20]

It is known that Jane Lenthall, together with her daughter Mary, made such a journey. The one stalwart English King family correspondent whose letters dominate the Ives Collection was her older, unmarried sister Margaret King, a crusty school mistress who lived in the seaside town of Scarborough, Yorkshire. Margaret's letters are instantly recognizable due to her habit of writing in one plane then turning the paper ninety degrees and continuing her message over the first half of her 'aerogram' style folding letter forms. She once testily responded in defense of her economical habit that "with us any thing under ½ oz. is single postage, from that to an ounce double."[21] Writing to Mary Lenthall many years later, Aunt Margaret fondly reminisced "I often think over the days your dear Mother & you spent here but had I the happiness of seeing you, we could not walk as before, I have neither strength, energy nor breath ..."[22]

Margaret King's folding letters were always enlivened by small but bold engravings of Scarbro's dramatic seascapes. Jane and Mary Lenthall must have been refreshed by its sea air and invigorated by renewal of their links to the land from which the King family came. And for the dozen more years that she corresponded with her American kin, Margaret King never failed to express her thanks for the Lenthall family's many "kindnesses," small gifts they sent to their long-lived English relative.

* * *

CHAPTER 13

The Sea Steamers

The U.S. Navy's hesitating embrace of steamships was tested once again, this time by Congress when on 3 March 1839, it enacted a new directive within its annual appropriations bill:

> That it shall be the duty of the Secretary of the Navy, under the direction of the President, to make preparations for, and to commence, the construction of three steam vessels of war, on such models as shall be most approved, according to the best advices they can obtain.[1]

Implementation of the Congressional mandate for the 'sea steamers', as they became known, fell to the Board of Navy Commissioners. At this point in its twenty-four-year history, the board and its visible inefficiencies were beginning to lose favor with both Congress and public opinion. According to their custom and perhaps to demonstrate their diligence, the commissioners appointed two advisory boards to address their new task. One board, consisting of five senior line officers, was to advise on the general characteristics of the war steamers, and a second, composed of naval constructors and engineers, to develop the vessels' design. Navy Captain Matthew Perry, a steam enthusiast, also sat on the second board.[2]

Keeping to habit, the commissioners' choice of naval constructors again fixed on their favored trio of steamer specialists, Samuel Humphreys, Samuel Hartt and John Lenthall. New to their company were Charles Haswell, chief engineer of *Fulton II,* and William Kemble, one of the proprietors of the West Point Foundry of Cold Spring, New York. The inclusion of Kemble, a civilian and part owner of one of the nation's premier iron founders and engine builders, added a novel dimension to the second board, reinforcing its focus on the vessels' machinery.[3]

The boards began their deliberations in Washington during the first weeks of April. Soon the constructors had learned enough to start work on their drawings and specifications, and so they appealed for permission to retreat to the Philadelphia Navy Yard, which they suggested would "afford better accommodation for making the draft & model of the Sea Steamer, than can be furnished at this place." Commodore Chauncey approved their request, granting them the discretion "to proceed ... as early as a change to that place will in your opinion be advantageous."[4] They labored away in Philadelphia for the next month, developing their plans, calculations and supporting design documents. In mid-May orders arrived from the commissioners "to report yourself at this office on the 22nd instant, for the purpose of a conference with the Engineers & others, in relation to the Sea Steamers."[5]

John Lenthall made ready to obey the board's summons, but before leaving took time to conclude an agreement that would bind sixteen-year-old George Much to him for the next five years. His young apprentice would prove to be a willing and intelligent worker, and served him and the Navy well over a long and productive career (see Appendix 12).[6]

Back in Washington, the boards again met and stayed in session for nearly a week before adjourning *sine die.* It had been decided to build two steam vessels of war, with a consensus having been reached regarding "the model of the vessel, the size, form, and location of the engines and machinery."[7] Specifications for the two new sea steamers called for:

- Armament of two 8-inch and eight broadside guns.
- Provisions for two months for 200 men.
- Fuel for twenty days steaming.
- Speed under steam of 9 knots.
- The ability to cruise under sail alone.

These requirements would be expanded upon as the design progressed. One issue that the board couldn't agree on was the configuration of the steam machinery to drive the ships' side-wheels, its choices being engines featuring direct-acting inclined cylinders or side-lever engines, as were favored by the British. So it was decided to build one ship with each type to test the competing concepts. [8]

With the sea steamers' principal features chosen, the Navy had finally completed its convoluted 'design by committee' process for its new warships, which in time would enter service as the U.S. Steam Frigates

Mississippi and *Missouri.* Constructors Humphreys, Hartt and Lenthall were again set to work wrapping up details of the frigates' designs. What sort of vessels had they created?

To begin with their length set a record. At 220 ft between perpendiculars, they were the longest warships yet to be built by the U.S. Navy. The volumes of their steam machinery and coal, together with the provisions, stores and water needed for an efficient cruiser, forced the increase in size in order to keep their hulls within a well-proportioned envelope. A comparison with other Navy warships demonstrates the sea steamers' great length.

TABLE 13.1 *Comparison of Warship Dimensions* [9]

Name of Vessel:	*Raritan*	*Pennsylvania*	*Fulton II*	*Mississippi*
Year Launched:	1843	1837	1837	1841
Class:	Sailing Frigate	Sailing Liner	Steam Gunboat	Steam Frigate
Guns (nominal):	44	120	4	10
Length (LBP):	174'-10"	210'-0"	181'-6"	220'-0"
Breadth (molded):	45'-0"	56'-9"	34'-10"	39'-0"
Depth (of Hold):	14'-5"	23'-0"	12'-2"	23'-6"
Tonnage (BM):	1708	3100	720	1732

The frigates' hull form also broke new ground. While they retained a key characteristic of sailing cruisers—centers of displacement placed forward of midships—their features were strongly influenced by contemporary steamship developments. The frigates' straight moderately rising floors, low hard bilges and vertical sides with no trace of tumblehome were a distinct departure from sailing vessel hulls, as were their sharp entrances and hollow lower waterlines. Compare the lines of *Mississippi* (Plan No. 6) with those of the sailing frigate *Raritan* (Plan No. 11) and the differences are obvious.

Hidden inside their wooden hulls were a number of firsts for the U.S. Navy. Their keel, keelsons and frames were dimensioned to sustain the concentrated loads of the massive engines and heavy boilers placed within their hulls and to resist the pounding forces of their reciprocating machinery. Four iron watertight bulkheads subdivided their length to give them resistance to flooding from grounding or battle damage. And unlike any of their 'double-banked' sailing frigate predecessors, all of their guns—ten in number and each one a Paixhans-type shell gun—were placed on a single, open gun deck.[10]

The new sea steamers' great length forced the adoption of extraordinary measures to prevent their inherently weak wooden hulls from deforming under the stresses of their own weight and the actions of the sea. Diagonal iron strapping was applied to reinforce their hull structure. Straps of iron flat bar were laid on the inside of their frames at a forty-five degree angle to the vertical, from the head of the floors to the underside of the upper deck and spaced at intervals of about four feet. Riveted together and bolted into the ships' frame, the web of strapping vastly increased their hulls' shear strength and prevented the destructive working of the ceiling or hull planking that so weakened traditionally built hulls. It certainly contributed to the legendary strength and longevity exhibited by *Mississippi*, a hard-used ship that was Perry's flagship when he opened Japan, fought in two wars and twice circumnavigated the globe. While the frigates' incorporation of iron strapping was a first for the U.S. Navy, the system had been used before on commercial vessels and ships of the Royal Navy. Which of the three constructors responsible for designing these frigates proposed the use of diagonal strapping is not known, but as Lenthall was familiar with British developments and both he and Hartt had exposure to outside commercial design work, Lenthall may well have contributed to their application.[11]

One element of the sea steamers' design that garnered criticism was their awkward sail plan. Rigged as three-masted barques—an arrangement not often seen in the Navy—the steamers were distinctive in the placement of their main masts further aft than a balanced rig would demand. This was dictated by their machinery arrangement and in particular, the close proximity of their tall funnels. As a result, the frigates did not set a mainsail, giving the Navy's longest ships an unsymmetrical sail plan that was inimical to efficient cruising. In this choice, Lenthall could well have been the culprit for the sea steamers' arrangements bore an uncanny resemblance to those of *Crocodile*, the French *Sphinx* class paddle aviso whose steam trials he had attended just six years before. Naval architects promote ideas of successful ships they've been involved with and Lenthall's enthusiasm for French practice just might account for *Mississippi*'s ungainly profile.[12] The next generation of side-wheelers did not repeat this misstep.

* * *

The Navy sensibly allocated construction of the two new sea steamers to the yards of their contributing designers, *Mississippi* being assigned to Lenthall at Philadelphia and *Missouri* to Hartt at New York. Work on them commenced with uncharacteristic haste, *Mississippi*'s keel being laid on 10 August 1839 with *Missouri* also begun that same year.[13] And if Lenthall wasn't already busy enough, his sloop of war *Dale* was launched at Philadelphia little over two months later on 22 October.[14] *Mississippi*'s machinery was ordered from the nearby works of Merrick and Towne, and the contract for *Missouri*'s was awarded to Kemble's West Point Foundry. Chief Engineer John Faron, formerly of *Fulton II*, was detailed to Philadelphia to superintend the fabrication and installation of *Mississippi*'s boilers and engines.[15]

A reliable source claims that friction existed between Constructor Lenthall and the Philadelphia Navy Yard's commandant, Charles Stewart, due to Lenthall's willing embrace of steam power and Stewart's conservative distain of the new technology's dirt and noise.[16] This may have been so although it doesn't appear to have materially affected the progress of *Mississippi*'s construction.[17] Lenthall was temporarily pulled away from his work by the board in February of 1840 and ordered to Norfolk to complete a survey of the frigate *United States*, but such multi-tasking was common among naval constructors.[18]

One example of how John Lenthall managed his responsibilities comes from his search for skilled artisans. He received a response from local shipbuilders dated 12 October 1840 which opened with "When you were up here, you mentioned something about a master caulker. The bearer of this Mr Jacob Hill ... we are well acquainted with and we do recommend." Beneath this message were the signatures of fourteen noted Kensington shipbuilders. Lenthall's personal relations with these builders succeeded in getting him the right man for the job.[19]

By spring of the following year, John Lenthall was ready to launch the first steamship built by the Philadelphia Navy Yard. *Mississippi*'s long black hull slid into the Delaware on 5 May 1841 before a crowd estimated at 30,000.[20] Although she was the second of the Navy's new sea steamers to enter the water, she would be the first to commission. On 22 December 1841 the American flag was raised on a ship that would steam into a long and illustrious career.[21]

* * *

One month after *Mississippi*'s launching, John Lenthall found himself on the deck of the barque *Clarion*, a ship he had designed three years before. She had been recently converted into a steamer propelled by twin screw machinery designed by John Ericsson, and Lenthall was about to embark on an "experimental trip" across New York's harbor to test her engines. He spent the greater part of Tuesday, 8 June 1841, recording *Clarion*'s steam trial data, including her coal consumption, propeller slip and much else, perhaps the most important result being in that in four hours she covered a total of twenty-six miles. But one thing that cannot be found on Lenthall's two pages of meticulously recorded data is *why* he was there.[22] Perhaps he had been invited to attend because he had designed *Clarion*, or maybe to survey her before she began a U.S. government charter, or that the Navy wished to learn more about the first American flagged screw steamer to make regular ocean voyages. While creditable, these reasons pale before the most plausible explanation—John Lenthall was ordered there because of the Navy's recent commitment to build a war steamer powered by Ericsson's revolutionary new screw propeller.[23]

Captain Ericsson, as he was often addressed, had patented his novel screw concept in England five years before, but it wasn't until one of his early steam power trials was observed by an American naval officer that the trans-Atlantic dimension materialized which so boosted his fortunes. Lieutenant Robert F. Stockton, a native of New Jersey and scion of his family's wealth, status and political heritage, was then on leave seeking financial backing for his Delaware and Raritan Canal. Outspoken and forceful, Stockton was the perfect complement to the cerebral, calculating Swede. He quickly grasped the screw propeller's potential to enable a quantum leap forward in the realms of steam navigation and invulnerable war steamers.[24] Demonstrating his confidence in Ericsson, Stockton ordered a technologically advanced iron-hulled, steam screw tow boat from John Laird's Liverpool shipyard in 1838 for use on his New Jersey canal system. The tiny seventy-foot-long *Robert F. Stockton* was sailed to America, arriving at New York in April 1839. Soon after she was put to work and remained active for nearly thirty years. The little steamer was the first iron-hulled ship to cross the Atlantic and the first screw propelled commercial vessel.[25]

Promoted to captain in late 1838, Stockton next focused on advancing his vision of a screw propelled war steamer whose machinery "snug in the bottom of the vessel" would be protected from shot or shell. Drawings by Ericsson together with a model were dispatched from England to America, and then on to the Navy Department in fall of 1839, not long after Congress mandated building three sea steamers. John Ericsson soon followed, landing in New York City in November of that year, where he took residence and prospered before becoming a U.S. citizen nine years later. In 1841 Stockton, now on leave pursuing political objectives, kept up the pressure and sent another model of his proposed steamer to the secretary of the navy. His request for the Department's assistance to further develop his scheme was granted on 1 June.[26] And eight days later, John Lenthall found himself attending *Clarion*'s steam trials.

Stockton's next crucial step—securing a firm commitment from the Navy to build his visionary warship—occurred during an interregnum of President Tyler's navy secretaries. Short-timer George Badger resigned on 11 September 1841 and wasn't replaced by the energetic Abel Upshur until a month later—but only after Robert Stockton had refused the job.[27] On the 21st of September, Commodore Stewart was informed that a "steamer of six hundred tons on the plan proposed by Captain Stockton; steam to be the main propelling power upon Ericsson's plan" had been authorized for construction at the Philadelphia Navy Yard. The next day Stockton received orders to superintend the steamer's building.[28] This new vessel, which was destined to sail into history as the steam sloop *Princeton*—named for Stockton's hometown—would be the third of the sea steamers authorized by Congress in 1839.[29]

Stockton lost no time prodding John Ericsson into action. One request led to another, and Ericsson quickly created what would today be called a preliminary design package: "drawings of a ship with ... dimensions" showing "both bow and stern to her" and the "cost of hull, equipments, etc., etc., as well as for the engines, displacement, metacenter, centre of gravity, centre of floatation, five midship sections, etc." All these drawings and calculations were dispatched by Stockton to Washington and soon thereafter found their way to the Philadelphia Navy Yard, where they would have been eagerly examined by its resident constructor, John Lenthall.[30]

Immersion in Ericsson's work must have given John Lenthall a first-hand grasp, engineer to engineer, of Ericsson's true worth as a designer. Unknowingly, it also prepared Lenthall for a far more momentous confrontation twenty years later when Ericsson's plans for another innovative warship, a shot-proof ironclad steam battery named *Monitor*, would cross his desk. Ericsson later claimed he spent 113 days superintending *Princeton*'s progress, some of it in Philadelphia dealing with matters that directly involved Lenthall and the navy yard.[31] It would have been immensely valuable to historians if Lenthall had left a record of his thoughts about Ericsson's abilities, but unfortunately, the archives are silent.

For the present, Lenthall's responsibilities were rather more mundane—to convert Ericsson's plans into construction drawings, specifications and building instructions that would permit the navy yard to construct a 156 ft long steam sloop. And here is yet another example of obscured ship design attribution. While there is no doubt Captain Stockton was *Princeton*'s progenitor and that "Princeton was essentially the child of Ericsson's brain," there is equally no question that the man whose design acumen enabled her to actually be constructed was John Lenthall.[32] Yet he has rarely been granted recognition as one of *Princeton*'s 'designers'. Ericsson's few drawings were not finished plans and, as far as guiding a constructor's work, were limited to half breadth and body plans together with a midship section.[33] With these as a starting point, Lenthall drafted *Princeton*'s lines plans, calculated her hydrostatic data, and worked up all the construction drawings needed to build her, many of which bear his signature or initials.[34] Of special interest considering that *Princeton* has been credited with being the world's first warship to be designed and built with screw propulsion are the construction features of her stern that enabled Ericsson's propeller to efficiently function—the lines of its fine run, its tail shaft bearing foundations, propeller aperture, removable stern post and rudder—all of which were finalized on Lenthall's drawing board (see Plan No. 7).[35]

* * *

John Lenthall had more than Captain Robert Stockton's pet project to keep him occupied at the Philadelphia Navy Yard. After years of glacial progress, work was afoot to complete *Raritan*, the longtime inhabitant of the yard's frigate house. Originally laid down as one of William Doughty's "Gradual Increase" frigates and tweaked over time by Samuel Humphreys, Lenthall applied some of his own innovations to the 44-gun warship. The most striking was his treatment of her head structure. Instead of the old open rail system of earlier vessels, *Raritan* was completed with a fully enclosed head that seamlessly blended into the sweep of her bow. Enhancing the effect were planked-in hammock rails that gave the ship a clean, uninterrupted shear line from bow to her stern.[36] Similar hull profile treatments would reappear in later Lenthall designs. He also modified her lines, slightly filling them out between her light draft and load line and sharpening them below.[37]

Lenthall's pressure to complete *Raritan* brought him an unwelcomed intrusion from the now vigilant Captain Stockton, who on 12 March 1842 complained that workmen at a local shipyard repairing a steam boat of interest to him, were leaving for better opportunities at the navy yard. He begged Lenthall to allow them to remain until she was finished.[38] The role of a civilian constructor working for an organization controlled by uniformed naval officers was not an easy one, but presumably, Lenthall found the right balance. Sometime that same year, work on *Princeton* began in earnest and, no doubt even more satisfying to Captain Stockton, on 20 October 1842, her keel was laid.[39]

* * *

By the time *Princeton*'s construction was underway, momentous changes had been made to the very core of the Navy Department's administrative structure. Dissatisfaction with the Board of Navy Commissioners had been festering for some time and the impetus to substantially transform their responsibilities was finally realized by the activist navy secretary, Abel Upshur. The new secretary's intentions were clearly signaled in his first annual report:

> That *reform* is necessary, in every part of our naval establishment, is on all hands admitted; and it is a subject of general regret that it has been so long delayed. The delay has been in the highest degree injurious to the service, and is daily rendering reform more and more difficult, as it becomes more and more indispensable. Impressed with this truth, and anxious that no time should be lost in commencing this important work, I respectfully bring it to your notice at the earliest day.[40]

Embodied in an Act of Congress dated 31 August 1842, Upshur's reformist zeal resulted in the abolishing of the Board of Navy Commissioners and its replacement by the 'bureau system', a division of administrative responsibility based on grouping of functions. Each bureau was headed by a chief who reported directly to the secretary of the navy. The bureau chiefs were appointed by the president and confirmed by the Senate, making them political appointees. The five new bureaus, their first named chiefs and the chiefs' former positions were:

1. Bureau of Navy-Yards and Docks, Commodore Warrington, former board president.
2. Bureau of Construction, Equipment and Repairs, Commodore Conner, former board member.
3. Bureau of Provisions and Clothing, Charles Goldsborough, former secretary of the board.
4. Bureau of Ordnance and Hydrography, Commodore Crane, former board member.
5. Bureau of Medicine and Surgery, Dr. William Barton, navy surgeon.[41]

It can be seen that although the Board of Navy Commissioners was abolished, their members lived on as chiefs of four of the five bureaus. And while the law creating the bureau system mandated that the head of the Bureau of Construction, Equipment and Repairs (BCER) be a "skilful naval constructor," Secretary Upshur's judgement that no person was well enough qualified to build, equip and repair a warship caused him to disregard Congress' will and appoint a line navy officer as the bureau's first chief. How Samuel Humphreys and his fellow naval constructors reacted to their new boss' lack of confidence in them has yet to be discovered.[42]

Other aspects of the new bureau system are noteworthy. The bureau chiefs' terms of office were unspecified, which endowed future bureau chiefs, including John Lenthall, with an unintended longevity of tenure. Further, a last-minute Congressional compromise caused the 'equipment' function to be grafted on to the bureau of construction and repair. In practice this meant that the BCER chief had to manage the supply of many disparate items of equipment: anchors and their cables, rigging and tackle, sails, yeomen's supplies, and of greater consequence as the years went by, coal for steamers.[43]

Also enacted by Congress on 31 August 1842 was a statute authorizing the formation of a naval Corps of Engineers. Such a regularization of the increasing numbers of engineers—the engine room chiefs and their assistants—was overdue and allowed the establishment of their ranks, pay grades and position within the Navy's administrative hierarchy. The first nominated corps engineer-in-chief, an inept political hack named Gilbert Thompson, was soon replaced by the veteran engineer, Charles Haswell.[44]

In early 1843 Secretary Upshur's desire to shake up the navy establishment caused him to advise certain naval constructors of his intention to reassign them to different navy yards. The notice John Lenthall received from the secretary on 6 February 1843 was brief and to the point. "You will hold yourself in readiness for a transfer to another yard by the 1st of May next."[45] Rumors were that he was to be sent to take the place of Francis Grice in Norfolk. A few days later, Lenthall opened a private letter from George Read, commandant of the Philadelphia Navy Yard, asking if he knew more about the change and expressing Read's dismay at Lenthall's pending reassignment.[46] Lenthall, who was by now well established in Philadelphia, could only have been disheartened by the idea of being abruptly relocated to Virginia. But fortunately, the impetus behind Upshur's directive faded and Lenthall remained where he was.

* * *

The work of the Philadelphia Navy Yard progressed uncertainly in the immediate wake of the wholesale reorganization of the Navy Department, with its now changed lines of authority and newly empowered bureau chiefs gradually asserting themselves. Things slowly picked up and by late spring of 1843, the frigate *Raritan* was ready to be launched. Local steamboat proprietors had heavily promoted the event and by 2 p.m. of the appointed day, the 13th of June, great crowds packed a small fleet of excursion boats and thronged the banks of the Delaware. With all his preparations complete, John Lenthall ordered the bilge ways to be cut through and the big frigate briskly began her descent down the slipway. A little too briskly as it turned out. *Raritan* charged into water, parting her chain cable restraints and shot across the river, narrowly missing spectator boats. She was soon captured by a steamer and towed back to the yard, no worse for her adventure.[47] Oblivious to the drama, one press report later gushed "We never saw so beautiful a launch. It was indeed a perfect moment."[48]

Three months later, the navy yard was ready to try its hand at another launch, this one of *Princeton*, the second of the sea steamers built in Philadelphia. Captain Stockton officiated at the launch ceremonies conducted in early September 1843, and she was placed under his command soon afterwards.[49] Her screw propeller proved successful, which must have delighted John Ericsson although *Princeton* never attained the speed her projectors claimed, making only seven knots under steam. Early in the new year she received her two big guns, both 12-inch 225-pdr pivot-mounted pieces: *Peacemaker*, a Stockton designed, American made 'improved' version of Ericsson's *Oregon*, a British manufactured banded wrought iron gun. Then *Princeton* was ordered to Washington, where both the ship and her guns were enthusiastically received.

On 28 February 1844, Captain Stockton welcomed President Tyler, his cabinet and 200 guests on board for a cruise on the Potomac. At the end of a pleasant day demonstrating *Princeton*'s capabilities, one last firing of Stockton's gun was requested. Then tragedy struck. *Peacemaker*'s breach burst, instantly killing six onlookers, including Secretary of State Upshur, new Secretary of the Navy Gilmer, Chief of the BCER Kennon, and wounding twenty more including Stockton. President Tyler was spared. A subsequent court of enquiry exonerated Captain Stockton, his officers and crew of all blame, but Stockton was much less charitable to John Ericsson.[50] Insinuating that Ericsson was somehow responsible for the defects in Stockton's gun, the good captain refused to authorize payment of Ericsson's invoice for two years' work on *Princeton*. This snub of the man who owned key patents of screw propeller technology did not bode well for the Navy and contributed to a stasis in its introduction of screw-powered war steamers.[51] What all had failed to recognize was that "Princeton was in reality Ericsson's first monitor."[52] In time the Navy would come to regret its shabby treatment of the inventive Swede.

* * *

CHAPTER 14

Family and Marriage

During the years that the Navy's sea steamers were designed and built, John Lenthall's personal life began to crystalize as so often happens to men of a certain age. His interest in Mary Eck matured at a measured pace, he the only son of a distant Washington family of social prominence and she the well-to-do daughter of her widowed mother in Philadelphia.

By early 1840, when Lenthall was thirty-three years old and Mary in her late twenties, they were exchanging letters expressing a degree of intimacy. On being ordered to Norfolk in February of that year to survey the frigate *United States,* after his arrival, Lenthall wrote Mary a silly, frivolous message of the kind that young men think will impress a woman. After relating details of his steamboat journey and first day in Norfolk, he boldly declared "To those that behave in a proper manner ... you may give a kiss from me, which if they do not like, upon my return they may pay back to me." His exaggerated closing read "With magnificent respect, your gracious humble servant." Curiously, his letter's outside cover was marked with a note Lenthall probably wrote long after saying "Does not like salutes from the guns."[1]

Later that year, Mary made her first visit to Washington and her potential in-laws. Writing to her mother, she noted her safe arrival and told of her "travel on the water" to Baltimore, sightseeing while in transit and that she "was determined to see all that I could of Washington." Near the end, she remarked "I now must conclude as I hear the breakfast cups rattling."[2]

Recollections by a Lenthall descendant, who eighty years later still possessed the voluminous Ives Collection in her "papers trunk," add a distant relative's nuance to Mary Eck's correspondence. It was recalled that "Her letters to her mother are refreshing, conservative, devoid of struggle in any form."[3]

***

John Lenthall's personal life in Philadelphia embraced more than just the delightful Miss Eck. He had always maintained a lively interest in work outside the navy yard, designing merchant ships and attending surveys and trials on the behalf of owners. The records are sketchy about just what he did and who employed him, but names of prominent Philadelphia builders such Vogle and Pearson, John Vaughan and Son, James Keen and John Lynn have been cited as clients of Lenthall as well as his former mentor at the Washington Navy Yard, William Easby, who now ran his own yard. Lenthall's active years spanned the period between his 1835 return to Philadelphia, through to his departure in 1850.[4] Three of his earliest projects, *Georgiana*, the *City Ice Boat* and *Clarion* have already been explored.

The best-known vessels that Lenthall designed during this time were two large packets that began their lives plying the Philadelphia-Liverpool route. The first was *Shenandoah*, a 143 ft long, 738-ton three-master ordered by the Brown Brothers. She was built in the Kensington yard of John Vaughan and Sons and entered service in 1839. The second and perhaps the last of Lenthall's private designs was the magnificent *Tuscarora*, a 176 ft long, three decked, 1,231-ton packet that served Philadelphia's own Cope Line. She was also constructed by Vaughan at Kensington and first sailed in 1848.[5] Plans for both these packets may be accessed in the John Lenthall Collection.[6]

As the historian Howard Chapelle has observed, constructors such as John Lenthall who participated in private work were able to keep abreast of the latest developments in their profession at a time of rapidly changing technology.[7] It also allowed them to become much more closely involved in the everyday marine life of the ports they served. For this reason and because of Lenthall's life-long connection with the Franklin Institute, it is fitting that the John Lenthall Collection is now housed in Philadelphia's own Independence Seaport Museum.[8]

* * *

A second method used by John Lenthall to keep abreast of affairs affecting his profession, especially those pertaining to other navies, was his regular correspondence with foreign sources of intelligence. His time studying in France gave him a predilection for keeping up with developments of that country's navy. In this, he was well served by an acquaintance who had already been of great help earlier in Lenthall's career, Guillaume Tell Poussin. Prior to Lenthall's European dockyard tour, Poussin wrote two letters of introduction, one to a librarian and the other to a professor of mathematics. Since then, Poussin, a former soldier-émigré and naturalized American citizen who had risen to the rank of major in the U.S. Army's topographical engineers, returned to his native France. A republican at heart and a lover of the United States, Poussin was an intellectual who, in

1848, would take an active role in the establishment of Louis-Napoléon Bonaparte's French Second Republic.[9]

But for now, Poussin was an energetic and frequent correspondent of John Lenthall's. Two letters written by Poussin to Lenthall in early 1843 shed light on the nature of the exchanges between the two men, what documents each other desired and how they managed to forward packages. The first, dated 6 February, opens with Poussin's acknowledgement of the receipt of a 250 franc (about $50) payment from Lenthall which may be connected to the next subject, an "instrument" that Poussin had sent Lenthall. Just what the instrument was—a musical instrument or perhaps something to calculate or measure with—is not mentioned, but directions for its use were enclosed with a later package. Then Poussin wrote that he would obtain documents for Lenthall which are "of an administrative character and treat generally of the expenses of the Navy Department." He goes on to say that he has "not received any documents sent by you; would be glad of such which would give me a minute account of the Navy Department in all its breadth, the correct list of vessels, size, armaments, etc." In the next paragraph Poussin proudly announced he has "produced" a new book on "our dear United States" titled *De La Puissance Américaine …* [*American Power…*]. He ends his letter by enlarging on his favored method for avoiding usurious postage rates—placing the packages they exchanged in the care of trustworthy travelers and the captains of trans-Atlantic packets.[10]

The second letter of Poussin's also mentions a payment made by Lenthall, this time 450 francs (about $90), and again the "instrument" comes up and is described as a "first rate one." Poussin apologized for its maker, M. Desbordes, who had neglected to inscribe his name on it. Lenthall is told he will be sent the French navy budget for 1844, "the only printed document submitted by the Navy, and a navy register in exchange of the documents accompanying the President's message" which Lenthall had already forwarded. Then Poussin requested:

> a correct statement of … the state of the U.S. Navy, the strength and main dimensions of men of war … particularly in regard to steamers, but improvements in those vessels, engines, wheels, etc. Please be aware that I am publishing these information [sic] in the form of books under the title of American Puissance. Would be happy of all contributions … to make our United States better known on this side of the water.[11]

Some parting observations about these most revealing letters. First is that they were written entirely in English; although Lenthall could read and write in French, Poussin no doubt chose English because Lenthall was relatively more fluent in that language. Second is that Poussin made no secret that he meant to publish the requested information, which was all largely in the public domain. And finally, it is curious that Poussin the engineer writing to Lenthall the constructor sent documents that had so little to do with technology but were more focused on administrative affairs and budgets. Perhaps it was an indication of Lenthall's budding interest in the management tasks he would later face as a bureau chief.

* * *

By the year of *Raritan* and *Princeton*'s launchings, 1843, John Lenthall's family was still centered on his mother, aged sixty-three, who lived together with his spinster sister Mary King Lenthall in the heart of Washington. Their place of residence had changed, however, from the old King house on F Street to the city address of Lenthall's younger sister Libby, now Mrs. Stone, on Pennsylvania Avenue between 12th and 13th Streets.[12] The F Street home was still owned by the Lenthalls; it may have been temporarily rented to allow the mother and sister a more comfortable life with the Stones. From the limited extant correspondence, the impression is that Jane and Mary Lenthall were socially active, their days filled with visits to friends, shopping excursions and the unending chores of an urban household.

Sister Libby's husband, William Stone, retired from his engraving business at age forty and purchased a country home named Mount Pleasant. He then indulged in the pursuit of fine arts, his true passion being sculpture. The Stones were parents of four children. The oldest son, Robert King, now twenty-one, was studying to become a surgeon; second son William James, nineteen, had begun reading law; third son George Blagden, eighteen, was soon to take up medicine; and the youngest, daughter Jane, was sixteen and still at home. The Stones led lives blessed by affluence, but through their great energy and volunteer achievements, they considerably benefitted the welfare of the nation's capital.[13]

The sibling interest that dominated Mary Eck's life was her brother Joseph. By 1843 Joseph and his wife Ellen had settled down in distant St. Louis, Missouri. They had two healthy children, Ann Maria and her younger sister Caroline. Joseph was something of a speculator and, together with a business partner, pursued what opportunities presented themselves under the handle of Messrs. Clark & Eck.[14] The family's existence seemed to be financially precarious, its fortunes ebbing and flowing but always buoyed by hope.

* * *

Visits by Mary Eck to the Lenthalls in Washington became more frequent, the Lenthall family getting to better know the young woman who had captured their son's heart. The exchanges had, it seems, included the two mothers, Ann Maria Eck and Jane King Lenthall. But as so often happens with a prospective wife and her future in-laws, personality clashes began to surface. Friction between Mary Eck of Philadelphia, whose mother was born of Irish immigrants and her father a German Catholic, and the prim and proper Episcopalian Lenthalls of Washington developed soon enough. It came to a head in June 1843 and was graphically documented in a remarkable letter written by John Lenthall's sister, Mary King Lenthall, to Mary Eck. The immediate subject was a cancelled trip to Washington which was quickly followed by a visit by Lenthall's mother to Philadelphia—then the daggers flash:

> My dear Mary,
> On seeing my dear Mother, you will at once perceive that we return you good for evil and I hope you will so repentant as never to transgress in future. Sorry & disappointed I was that you would not come on, yet notwithstanding, send dear Mother to make you a nice long visit. She can tell you how hard I worked for some days to get things smartened up, fit for a 'Philadelphian' to see, yet after all you never came, & all was lost on John as he has no taste for these matters. I hope all this will weigh heavily on your conscience, and produce a sincere repentance and future amendment. ... Remember me affectionately to your Mother and believe me to be affectionately yours,
>
> M. K. Lenthall[15]

This was a stiff message to deliver to anyone, especially the fiancé of a brother. It evokes a mean and selfish caricature of Mary King Lenthall, who exhibited the strong hint of an inferiority complex. The implication was that John Lenthall, a third party to this blow-up, preferred to avoid dealing with a confrontation initiated by his holier-than-thou sister. In time relations between the two Marys healed, certainly enough for them to resume the outward appearance of harmony, but deep within the hurt must have lingered.

* * *

Perhaps it was for the best that John Lenthall remained at his naval constructor's post in Philadelphia, giving some distance between his immediate family and Mary Eck. The dust-up with his sister had little if any effect on their own growing relationship which continued to blossom. The records are frustratingly vague but the best information is that they were joined in holy matrimony on 21 November 1843.[16] The descendants' writings tell only that "They were married in Philadelphia" and that "No letters about the wedding ..." have been found.[17] On this date Mary was thirty-one years old and her husband John was thirty-six, making them both rather mature for a first marriage by the standards of the day. Just who attended their wedding, where in the city it occurred and under what ritual they exchanged vows are not known.

Soon after their marriage, the Lenthalls set up house on 27 Christian Street in Philadelphia's Southwark district.[18] Given that the street numbering system was later changed, it's difficult to pinpoint the location of their home, but today that address would place them just across the street and to the north of the Gloria Dei (Old Swedes') Church. Whatever the exact location, the Lenthalls lived not far from their former South Front Street addresses and only a few blocks from the entrance to the navy yard.

With the inevitable time lag of overseas post, in May 1844, the newly-wed John Lenthall received a congratulatory letter from his Aunt Margaret writing from Scarborough, England. She had been informed of his marriage through a letter from Sister Mary and expressed her joy at his "having chosen a partner calculated to make you happy. May every blessing attend your union!" Demonstrating that she kept up with news from America, she went on to remark:

> We had a sad account of a frightful accident on the Potomac. I hope it will prevent any future use being made of such a sad engine of destruction. It is to be expected when talent is thus employed instead of being exerted for the benefit of mankind.[19]

Aunt Margaret almost certainly wasn't aware that her talented nephew was the naval constructor responsible for building *Princeton*, the vessel that carried the "sad engine of destruction" she so abhorred.

* * *

Less than a year after Lenthall's marriage, the Stone side of his family hosted a wedding, this one in Washington. Sister Libby's daughter, Jane Lenthall Stone, and a young army officer by the name of James W. Abert were joined as husband and wife on 21 October 1844. She was seventeen years old and he was twenty-four, a marked contrast to the ages of John and Mary Lenthall at the time of their marriage.

Aunt Margaret's wish for blessings to brighten the Lenthalls' union was soon granted. Sometime during 1844, Mary Lenthall gave birth to a baby boy. The child was given the name John Lenthall, the third of his line. But his parents' joy was short lived. Their son John died shortly after his birth.[20] A mother and father's worst nightmare, it was an all-too-common occurrence in that century. The precise date and cause of death are unknown, and indeed, no mention of either the child's birth or death can be found in the otherwise informative Ives Collection. A letter from Mary to her mother in March of 1844 says nothing about being pregnant.[21] The only record of the baby's fate comes from a descendant of John Lenthall, who later remember that "His son John died when an infant."[22]

Tragedy had struck the Lenthalls, an unimaginable loss, so much hope gone forever. A child to bury, grief to share and an emptiness to confront. The Lenthalls were resilient and in time would recover from the death of baby John.

* * *

CHAPTER 15

Sloop of War Germantown

The most prominent casualty of *Princeton*'s burst gun, Abel Upshur, had resigned as navy secretary seven months before his untimely death, and taken the mantle of secretary of state. During his twenty-one months at the Navy Department, Upshur's crusade for reform significantly reconfigured the naval establishment. Abolishing the old board and instituting the bureau system were only a fraction of the many changes introduced by the energetic Virginian. Before his departure in July 1843, Secretary Upshur acted decisively to address widespread concern that many of the Navy's ships were reputed to be "dull sailors." In its last years of life, the Board of Navy Commissioners attempted to avoid responsibility for the performance of the warships it authorized by reliance on committees of constructors to approve the final designs—recall the boards convened to pass judgement on the sea steamers. The board's design by committee process, however, drew strong criticism from those who claimed it produced mediocre war vessels that failed to keep up with the latest trends in naval architecture. Abel Upshur believed that the reorganized Navy Department could do better. His solution, compared to what had been done before, was simple but radical—he ordered a program of six sloops of war to be designed and built by the naval constructors at the navy's different yards, each given wide discretion to model a vessel of his own creation, with the hope that their competition would deliver superior ships.[1]

The empowered constructors did not start with a clean sheet of paper. A template for their designs, *Saratoga,* was commissioned during Secretary Upshur's final month in office. Her plans came from the minds of Chief Constructor Humphreys and Samuel Pook, the resident constructor at the Portsmouth Navy Yard where she was built. *Saratoga* reintroduced the Navy's traditional emphasis on fielding the largest and most heavily armed ships of their class. At 146'-7" length and of 882 tons burden, she dwarfed Lenthall's *Dale* class sloops, and to increase her punch, she was given four Paixhans-type 8-inch 64-pdr shell guns to supplement her 32-pdrs.[2]

The six new sloops marked the next step of the design evolution the Navy had begun with *Saratoga.* They were apportioned between the various yards, with John Lenthall at Philadelphia assigned to build a vessel that would be named *Germantown.* He must have been delighted at being given the opportunity to produce a warship that was, compared to so many he had previously constructed, uniquely his own.

The ship that Lenthall created is illustrated by Plan Nos. 8 and 10, a hoisting plan and a lines plan drawing. *Germantown* was completed with dimensions of 150'-0" in length, 36'-8" of breadth, 16'-8" depth of hold and a tonnage of 939, all slightly larger than *Saratoga.*[3] She has been described by writers of naval history as "handsome" and "graceful," well deserved accolades for a ship that exhibited Lenthall's signature design elements: an uninterrupted, gently rising sheer line; a fully enclosed head; a moderately raked stem and sternpost; and a pleasingly balanced overall profile.[4] Externally she resembled a miniature, single-decked *Raritan.* Like *Dale,* however, she was given a small forecastle and poop deck in the interests of dryness but unlike several of the other competing sloops, had no spar deck. *Germantown* was also one of the first of the Navy's ships to be fitted with sidelights to help illuminate her berth deck.

Examining *Germantown*'s lines, a glance at the body plan reveals her strong, straight deadrise, firm bilges and moderate tumblehome. Her entrance was sharp, certainly on the lower waterlines, but flared more toward the load line to allow her to bear the weight of her guns, stores and anchors. She had a long and fine run, all of these features contributing to her reputation as being fast in light airs. *Germantown*'s sail plan showed a traditional ship rig setting royals, the one remarkable feature being that she carried spencers and trysails on all three masts, which were by now common on American sloops.

Plan No. 8 illustrates elements of naval warship design which are not usually covered by standard treatments. This hoisting plan demonstrates the attention constructors took to ensure the vessels they built were operationally functional. In this case, the drawing projects the range of the lower yards' coverage over the main deck, and in particular, their ability to hoist the heavy anchors stowed on the ship's side. This plan is the precursor of a modern offshore rig's crane load radius chart which serves a similar purpose. Further, the midsection inset on the drawing of *Raritan*'s lines, Plan No. 10, shows the location in *Germantown*'s hold of her iron water tanks, which had by this date completely replaced water casks. Boat stowage on main deck centerline cradles is also indicated.

The hoisting plan described above is but one of thirty-three plans of *Germantown* held in the John Lenthall Collection. Other drawings in this collection yield the first glimpse of the presence of draftsman Richard Powell, who would later become a fixture at the Bureau of Construction, Equipment and Repairs during Lenthall's tenure and beyond. Several of the drawings are signed by him, including a sail and spar plan and a lines plan, which bears both his and Lenthall's signatures.[5] Little is known about Powell other than that he was born in and was a citizen of Pennsylvania, and that Lenthall placed great trust in both his character and abilities.[6]

Germantown was laid down in the Philadelphia Navy Yard's frigate house on 7 September 1843, the same month that *Princeton* was launched.[7] As most of Lenthall's drawings, specifications and instructions for building *Germantown* would necessarily have been completed before then, the coincidence of dates well demonstrates Lenthall's ability to simultaneously manage multiple complex projects.

The inexorable march of technology decreed that *Germantown* was to be the last sailing warship built by the Philadelphia Navy Yard.[8] She would prove to be popular with squadron commanders, early in her career flying Commodore Matthew Perry's broad pennant during the Mexican War.

* * *

As an example of the variety of assignments that fell to John Lenthall, three urgent demands for his services materialized during the later phases of *Germantown*'s construction. The first came from Captain Stockton who, after the horrifying events on the Potomac, still commanded *Princeton*. Now at the Norfolk Navy Yard, on 10 March 1843 he wrote to Lenthall:

> I wish to take the rudder post of this ship down for the purpose of fitting a new propeller. I do not remember precisely the manner in which you had it secured at the upper end. Will you please send by <u>next mail</u> a drawing and such information as will enable us to take it down, and put it up with the least trouble.[9]

The unanswered question is why Stockton, then at a navy yard staffed by an experienced constructor, felt it necessary to make such a request of John Lenthall in Philadelphia. This would seem to indicate that Lenthall had as much to do with the design of *Princeton*'s removable false rudder post arrangement as did Ericsson (see Plan No. 7). Next came an order from the commandant of the Philadelphia Navy Yard, Jesse Elliott, dated 25 April:

> You will hold a survey on the ship "Robert G. Shaw" which has been offered to the Bureau of Provisions to carry about 4,000 barrels of Government stores to Rio de Janeiro, and make a report to me of

your opinions as to her capacity, and whether she is otherwise adapted to the service for which she has been offered.[10]

Yet one more ship survey for the busy constructor. And finally, the commandant of the New York Navy Yard, Silas Stringham, requested a report on the time, cost and expediency of converting the 2nd class frigate *Macedonian* into either a razee corvette or a steam frigate. Lenthall together with Humphreys and Hartt—the steamer constructors—as well as two others were copied Stringham's letter of 15 August 1845, and it was Lenthall who was tapped to draft their response.[11] It will be recalled that Lenthall had helped Humphreys with *Macedonian*'s original hydrostatic calculations, so he knew her properties well.

Following a brief evaluation, the constructors recommended that the frigate be converted into a steamer, the cost being estimated at $70,000 "ready for her engines" versus $17,500 to cut her down to a large corvette.[12] Predictably the Navy blanched at the steamer conversion's high price, and after several years of hesitation, chose to make a razee of her.

Of interest to the curious naval architect is the formulation that Lenthall devised during the constructors' review process to quickly establish the increase in *Macedonian*'s length, L, necessary for her conversion into a steamer. His goal was to calculate L knowing that at the section where her length was to be increased, *Macedonian*'s hull weighed 6.5 tons per foot and its displacement was 16.82 tons per foot. Lenthall then proposed the following algebraic expression to solve for L:

Weight of engines + increased length of hull = increased displacement + reductions in loading

$$E + (L \times 6.5) = (L \times 16.82) + R$$

where E is the weight of the engines and R is the sum of the reductions in loading—ballast, stores, water and armament—caused by the conversion. Rearranging terms yields the formula:

$$L = \frac{(E-R)}{10.32}\text{ ft}$$

Very neat and logical, typical of Lenthall's work, a simple method to speed up a repetitive analysis. Using the constructors' data, the increase in hull length was 66 ft.

* * *

The work in hand at the Philadelphia Navy Yard also exerted its pressure on John Lenthall. Constant requests came his way—for budget estimates of "stage plank," to inspect the steam tug *Water Witch*, and to dress out *Germantown*'s new gun carriages. These everyday tasks together with *Germantown*'s ongoing construction and the Navy's peremptory demands kept Lenthall busy through the end of 1845 and into the new year.

Early in February John Lenthall was forced to pause his work pace. But it was for the very best of reasons—his wife Mary gave birth to their second child, a girl. The baby was born on 4 February 1846.[13] After the heartbreak of losing their first child, unbounded joy must have surged through the Lenthall household on the baby's safe delivery. She was christened Jane but always called by her familiar name, Jenny (sometimes styled Jennie). Jenny instantly became the apple of her loving parents' eyes.

Scant documentation exists for Jenny's birth. Eighty years later, Lenthall descendants remembered only that there were "No letters about the … birth of Jane."[14] But Mary's brother Joseph in St Louis did not disappoint. After receiving word of the baby's arrival, he grabbed his pen and gushed "Congratulations and joy at the happy event and may Jane Lenthall be 'mighty in the land'…" Joseph's prompt acknowledgement was somewhat diminished by his flippant jest, "take care old boy, recollect this is only a daughter."[15] A daughter, yes, but it was John and Mary Lenthall's daughter. Little Jenny was a precious gift and her presence brought a radiant new dimension into their lives.

* * *

Just three months after Jenny's birth, Congress declared war on Mexico. The conflict with America's southern neighbor would rage on for almost two years and at its conclusion, resulted in vast new territories being annexed to the United States. While the war had a strong naval dimension, it was not fought at sea, the hostilities playing out almost entirely on the coasts and lands of Mexico. Its immediate effect on the Navy and the demand for services by the navy yards was shaped by the fact that the Navy already had in commission more large warships than it could readily man. The types of vessels most urgently needed for operations against Mexico were smaller, light draft schooners, brigs and especially steamers, which could be more expediently purchased than built. Of all the Navy's ships then under construction, only the sloops *Germantown* and *Albany*, building at New York, were deemed worthy of accelerated delivery.[16] Accordingly, on 21 May 1846, the Philadelphia Navy Yard's new commandant, Charles Stewart, ordered John Lenthall to "cause the sloop of war Germantown to be completed and launched without unnecessary delay, and …equip her for sea, as early as practicable."[17]

In the months that followed, Lenthall pressed ahead with the work on *Germantown.* Sometime during this period, he received a packet of information from France, possibly sent by Poussin, which contained "specifications of proposals for French steam engines" for propeller-driven ships. He deemed them of enough importance to forward a copy to the Chief of the Bureau of Construction, Equipment and Repairs, from whom he received a note of thanks. It was yet one more instance of Lenthall leveraging his access to foreign sources for self-promotion.[18]

With the nation mobilizing for war and its need for experienced personnel never greater, the unimaginable happened—Samuel Humphreys died. The chief constructor's death was "sudden" although he had been in poor health for years; it occurred at his Georgetown home on Sunday, 16 August 1846.[19] He was nearly sixty-eight. Humphreys' death marked the end of his twenty-year reign as the Navy's chief constructor.

Samuel Humphreys was buried in Washington's Congressional Cemetery. It is not known whether John Lenthall attended Humphreys' funeral, but it is hard to believe he would have missed the chance to bid a final farewell to his mentor of so many years. Assuming he did attend, it placed Lenthall in a real time bind as *Germantown* was slated for launching in Philadelphia on Saturday 22 August, just six days after Humphreys' passing. Sometimes life deals out awkward moments and this was one for John Lenthall. Being forced to concentrate on the mechanics of a ship's launch must have offered a welcomed mental diversion. As scheduled, *Germantown* slid down her ways into the Delaware. A war was on.

The question that must have resonated in the minds of each of the Navy's constructors was: who will be appointed as the new chief constructor? Francis Grice was the most senior constructor and so was presumed to be the obvious choice. But it was not so, at least for the moment, as an article in the *Alexandria Gazette* explained:

> Seizing the occasion presented by the recent vacancy, the Secretary of the Navy determined to leave the naval constructors on an equal footing, and not to continue a doubtful office. They will now be called on, as their services are needed, to report at Washington for such duty as may be required of them in the line of their profession. In pursuance of this arrangement, Mr. Grice has been called to Washington, not as chief naval constructor, but for temporary duty in connexion with his present office.[20]

The secretary's expressed sentiments may have been rung true in September but soon he changed his mind, for on 1 December 1846,

Francis Grice was appointed the Navy's chief constructor.[21] A new era had begun; it was now to Grice that John Lenthall and his fellow constructors reported.

* * *

Two of the casualties needing urgent attention that fall at the Philadelphia Navy Yard were caused not by acts of war but by a more ancient foe, the sea. The great hurricane of September 1846 dismasted and nearly sank the Coast Survey brig *Washington,* taking the lives of her captain and ten of her crew. Especially poignant for Philadelphians, her lost captain was the son of the city's prominent scientist, Alexander Dallas Bache, now chief of the Coast Survey. And not long after, the brig *Perry,* also dismasted and grounded by another fierce storm, limped into the yard. Still busy completing *Germantown,* Lenthall directed all the attention he could toward their soonest repair.[22]

But the fates decreed otherwise. As November ended, John Lenthall found himself consumed by a far more urgent war effort—constructing America's first purpose-built amphibious landing craft. Within days of Winfield Scott's appointment to command the U.S. Army's expedition to seize Veracruz, the general identified his need for 140 flat-bottom 'surf boats' capable of landing 5,000 men and eight guns on hostile shores. No such boats existed, certainly not in the quantities Scott demanded. To fill the void, an expedited procurement program sprang to life.[23]

Lenthall was "ordered to Washington by Lee of [the] Navy to make plans for [the] boats,"[24] where he met with Lieutenant George Totten, who is said to have 'designed' the surf boats. The best evidence is that Totten conceived the boats' functional specifications—craft of sizes that could be nested on a transport's deck, weighing no more than could be hoisted by a ship's tackle, carrying forty men or one gun each, propelled by banks of oars, and manned by eight sailors. The army's agent, Captain Richard Loper, quickly concluded contracts with Philadelphia-based firms to churn out 141 of the boats, all within one month.[25]

And that is where John Lenthall took over. He detailed the surf boats' material specifications, directions for building, tables of offsets and calculated their weights. It all happened in a tremendous rush and must have involved countless visits throughout the Philadelphia area to review builders' progress, then inspect and survey the boats. Lenthall's opening lines of his surf boat specifications and their principal particulars appear below:

> The boats to be built with both ends alike to steer with one oar at each end and store in nests of three each. To be built of the best seasoned materials in the most substantial manner and iron fastened ... The drawings of the boats will be furnished by the Department.[26]

TABLE 15.1 *Surf Boat Particulars*[27]

Surf Boat (nesting order):	1st	2nd	3rd
Length (between rabbets at top of gunwale):	40'-0"	37'-9"	35'-9"
Breadth (molded):	12'-0"	11'-0"	10'-2"
Depth (from rabbet of keel to top of gunwale):	4'-4 ½"	4'-0"	3'-9"
Weight (pounds, actual):	6522	5343	4132
Oars (number, of white ash):	16	14	12

Lenthall recorded results from weighing the boats on a sheet dated 31 December 1846, and General Scott's invading force employed them to seize Collado Beach on 9 March, evidence that the whole job progressed rapidly from beginning to end. There was no time that Christmas for a Lenthall family gathering other than a pause at the fireside with wife Mary and baby Jenny. And as for *Germantown*, to avoid being trapped by winter ice, she was spirited away to Norfolk early in December to complete her equipping for sea.[28]

* * *

The new year of 1847 saw John Lenthall again dealing with the backlog of work at the Philadelphia Navy Yard. Not for the first time he was vexed by inconsistent orders issued by well-meaning naval officers attached to the yard. At the end of January, he was reminded that "higher wages than ... given in private yards will not be authorized" but one month later was told by the same captain that "some extra and energetic efforts must be made to procure workmen to finish the Washington."[29] Wartime demand caused the gap in expectations. But as March of 1847 drew to a close, Lenthall was diverted from minding everyday yard activities and ordered to once again sit on another Navy Department board.

The ongoing war with Mexico had demonstrated beyond a doubt the great utility of steam propelled warships. Accordingly, Secretary of the

Navy John Y. Mason requested funding for four sea steamers which Congress promptly authorized. Following procedures largely unchanged from the days of the commissioners, the secretary convened a board on 22 March to evaluate the specifications for the new ships. Members of the board included Chief Constructor Grice, Constructors Hartt and Lenthall, Chief Engineer Haswell, civilian engineer Copeland, and bureau chiefs Morris (BCER), Smith (Yards and Docks) and Warrington (Ordnance and Hydrography). The points of reference for the board's deliberations were the steamers *Mississippi* and *Princeton,* both of which had been constructed by John Lenthall. *Mississippi* was regarded as a highly satisfactory steamer but lacked the capacity to carry all her assigned loads. *Princeton* was deemed underpowered and worries still persisted about the need to dock screw steamers should any access be required to their propellers or shafting.[30]

During the course of sessions that lasted, on and off, until early May, the board concluded that the Navy should build two first-class side-wheel steamers similar to *Mississippi* but with greater capacity, and two second-class steamers somewhat larger than *Princeton,* one a side-wheeler and the other screw propelled. All four vessels were to be wooden hulled. It was decided that Grice and Lenthall should each design a first-class side-wheeler; these would be named *Powhatan* and *Susquehanna,* respectively. Constructor Hartt was assigned the two-second class steamers, side-wheel and screw, which were to share a common hull design; their names were *Saranac* and *San Jacinto.* All the side-wheelers would be equipped with inclined, direct-acting engines. No decision was reached about the engines for the screw propelled *San Jacinto.* The Navy's desire to avoid Ericsson's patents was already beginning to cast its shadow over the *San Jacinto,* setting the stage for her machinery's ultimately chequered reputation. [31]

During the board's deliberations about the characteristics of the new vessels, the constructors had been asked "Shall the model of the *Mississippi* be retained for the new side-wheel steamers, and the required displacement be obtained by simple expansion, or shall a new model be adapted." Both Grice and Hart recommended a new model but John Lenthall held firm for a simple expansion of *Mississippi*'s lines.[32] Lenthall's decision was an early manifestation of his conservative approach to naval architecture. He had been part of the team that had created *Mississippi,* he had supervised her building and she proved successful in service, all motivations to improve rather than innovate.

Like her predecessor, John Lenthall's *Susquehanna* was the longest vessel yet built for the U.S. Navy. She was a full 250'-0" between perpendiculars, her beam was 44'-0" and she had a depth of 26'-6", all dimensions significantly greater than *Mississippi*'s. These increases were an attempt to overcome *Mississippi*'s inability to carry her full capacities, the goal being to gain more displacement on a lighter draft. Compared to Grice's *Powhatan*, whose hull featured a hint of a modern parallel mid-body, *Susquehanna*'s lines clearly displayed their sailing ship lineage with the hull's center of displacement placed forward of midship.[33] Both of these long wooden steamers required extraordinary measures to preserve their longitudinal strength: iron diagonal strapping, live oak frame, solid bottoms and white oak plank were all employed, as in *Mississippi*. They also both carried that ship's same barque rig but with a much-improved balance of masting made possible because of the funnel's placement forward of the paddle shaft. Their initial armament included three 10-inch pivoting shell guns and six 8-inch guns on broadside. *Susquehanna* proved to be a strong and reliable steamer although her engines were heavy consumers of coal. The big steam frigate was laid down at Philadelphia on 8 September 1847, just four months after the board finished its work. She accompanied Perry to Japan, served in the Mediterranean and then operated in home waters throughout the Civil War.[34]

The Navy's archives contain a curious statement about John Lenthall and *Susquehanna*. In response to a 1940s query about Lenthall's design credits, the Navy's director of history, Captain D. W. Knox, replied "The only vessel which our records show to have been definitely designed by Lenthall was the SUSQUEHANNA." Knox went on to mention Lenthall's service at Philadelphia and cited names of ships constructed there, saying that he "naturally was connected with any vessels which were built at that station."[35] This statement is perplexing on several levels (see Appendix 11) and illustrates the confusion so often associated with the term 'designer'. Unfortunately, Knox did not offer an explanation of the logic behind his assertion.

* * *

Despite his responsibilities for *Susquehanna*, Lenthall was on the move again, this time to New York with Francis Grice to inspect the French steamer *Union*.[36] His relatives' letters, especially those of his sister Mary, paint colorful accounts of his family's activities. Lenthall's younger sister, Libby, was visiting London that summer with her husband, who was studying sculpture with the expatriate American, Hiram Powers. This same letter, written to Lenthall's wife Mary, mentions the receipt of a daguerreotype of Mary and her child Jenny. It's a pity it hasn't come to light.[37] In October, Mary wrote again, telling of her excitement at the Stone family's return from England. Two other letters written the following month make it clear that a regular pattern of visits between Lenthall's mother and Sister Mary in Washington and John and Mary Lenthall's home in Philadelphia was now occurring. The newborn baby Jenny seems to have been the glue that brought them together. Sister Mary asked her sister-in-law to "give a thousand kisses to my precious girl. Remember me affectionately to your mother and my precious brother." She then rather possessively added, "He is a gem, Mary, you and I know it."[38]

Although it is not mentioned in any of the letters, the Mexican War was brought to a successful conclusion with the signing of the Treaty of Guadalupe-Hidalgo in February 1848. However, unbidden glimpses into the realities of mid-nineteenth-century health care pop out of the dry lines of family gossip. Mary King Lenthall expanded on the use of chloroform, then in vogue for relieving pain. "Sister had come to the conclusion to take it when all her remaining teeth were extracted." Sister Libby was only forty-four years old. Her family dissuaded her from using chloroform, but she still had all her teeth pulled "and as they were very loose, it caused her scarce a pain. She is going to have a complete set made by the dentist."[39]

John Lenthall proudly informed his sister Mary in October of that year that his dear girl "Jenny has commenced French." Jenny wasn't yet five but her father, a confirmed Francophile, wanted his daughter to appreciate the beauty of the country's language. And several months later, in March of 1849, Lenthall's St. Louis in-laws were writing to his wife about a proposal that had caught everyone's attention. They had heard that "Mr. Lenthall had an offer from the German government to build ships for them, and that he would decide in a few days. Do you think you will go with him if he goes?" This snippet is all that is known about this offer, presumably from the Kingdom of Prussia, other than that John Lenthall ultimately decided, like his mentor Samuel Humphreys had in a similar situation, to turn it down and stick with the country of his birth. An additional element of interest from this letter is that it documents the Lenthall's were now living on Lombard Street, near Second Street in downtown Philadelphia. [40] Later correspondence gave their address as No. 38, which today would put them a block south of Second Street and its historic New Market and Head House Square, a charming urban neighborhood.

The final jarring episode related by this stream of Lenthall family correspondence was the sad and unexpected death of Sister Libby's only daughter, Jane L. Stone Abert, on 17 August 1849.[41] Married five years before to young Army topographical officer James W. Abert, and recently the mother of their son Willie, Jane came down with an illness from which she was expected to recover. But it was not to be. The Lenthall legacy following from her death was that the little boy, William S. Abert, would inherit the letters written by Benjamin Latrobe to his grandfather, John

Lenthall Sr., Latrobe's clerk of the works. This priceless volume of correspondence was later cited by Glenn Brown as one of the sources used in writing his *History of the United States Capitol.*[42]

* * *

CHAPTER 16

Chief Constructor

John Lenthall's next promotion, his appointment to chief constructor, is conspicuously documented as having occurred on 1 November 1849.[1] What is less clear are the circumstances behind it. First, his appointment was known some time beforehand. Lenthall rather coyly wrote to his wife in September that "I will not be able to say anything about my ... title," and three weeks later, Joseph Eck in St. Louis wrote to his sister Mary that he was expecting to hear about the Lenthalls "removal" to Washington.[2]

The second question is why was the current chief constructor replaced? Francis Grice had been on the job for three years and although the oldest naval constructor, he was healthy enough to immediately step into Lenthall's shoes at Philadelphia. Perhaps Grice fell out of favor with the Navy Department's bureaucracy or maybe he tired of the ways of Washington. Chapelle, attuned to nuances of the constructors and their careers, is silent on the matter.[3] And then why wasn't Samuel Hartt, the next most senior constructor, appointed in Grice's place? The answer might be that he was invited but turned down the offer, echoing Doughty's declining the job that was given to Humphreys. Writing two years before to his wife, Lenthall observed that "Mr. Hartt has no wish to leave New York."[4]

Compared to his predecessors, Lenthall's rise to chief constructor was meteoric. Samuel Humphreys, first to hold the position, had been thirteen years between his appointments to constructor and chief constructor (see Appendix 12). Grice had been twenty-nine years by the same measure and Lenthall only eleven. But then John Lenthall's training, self-education, experience and achievements surely warranted his rapid ascension. Accompanying him to Washington was his trusted assistant, Richard Powell, who assumed the duties of draftsman at the Bureau of Construction, Equipment and Repairs on the same date of Lenthall's appointment.[5]

Lenthall's promotion relieved him of his responsibilities in Philadelphia and required that he move back to Washington. A native of the capital city,

Lenthall undoubtedly found this far easier to deal with than his wife, the "Philadelphian." Their 'removal' to Washington meant, of course, they would be living in the same city as Lenthall's mother and sisters. During his first years in Washington as chief constructor, John and Mary Lenthall made their home on the corner of 7th and I Streets NW.[6] This fourth ward address put them about nine blocks to the northeast of Lenthall's mother and sister Mary, who still lived on Pennsylvania Avenue between 12th and 13th Streets.

* * *

Early in 1850, two events of keen interest to Chief Constructor Lenthall took place, the launches of the new large sea steamers, *Powhatan* and *Susquehanna. Powhatan*'s launch came first at the Norfolk Navy Yard on 14 February.[7] The yard's Commodore John Sloat had expressly urged Lenthall's attendance, writing "I would be greatly gratified to have a person of your science and experience present on the occasion."[8] It is not known if Lenthall acceded to the commandant's request but regardless, one wonders what Francis Grice, *Powhatan*'s designer, thought of Sloat's preference.

Susquehanna was next into the water on 6 April. As the longest ship yet launched at Philadelphia, her sheer size presented a challenge. The river bottom opposite the big ship house was dredged out beforehand. At the appointed hour, *Susquehanna* successfully slid down her ways and into the Delaware, but created large waves that tipped several spectators into the water and swept a boat under a pier. Towed alongside for fitting out, work on the big side-wheeler progressed quickly and she was commissioned before the year was out.[9]

In that same year, a less satisfying task was assigned to the new chief constructor, sitting on yet another survey board. The board's purpose was to evaluate the steam bark *Allegheny* and pronounce on her fitness for naval service. *Allegheny* was the largest of three steamers built for the Navy employing the novel Hunter's wheel mode of propulsion. Patented by Navy Lieutenant William Hunter, the concept featured a pair of horizontally arranged paddle wheels which were placed below the water line and protruded from the vessel's hull. The wheels turned inside massive casings built into the bowels of the ship. The advantage of Hunter's wheels over conventional side-wheels was that they were immune from battle damage and, with the wheels removed from the warship's topsides, an unimpeded row of broadside guns could be mounted. But such advantages brought compromises. To allow a Hunter's wheel steamer to lie alongside a pier or another vessel without damaging its wheels, for example when coaling, it was necessary to configure the hull with an inverted bell cross-section to recess its sides in way of the wheels. Further, with the era's imperfect understanding of fluid dynamics and marine propulsion, the efficiency of the Hunter's wheels was difficult to correctly model. In practice, it was found that much of the power applied to the wheels was absorbed by the recirculation of enormous volumes of water through the hull casings, limiting vessel speeds to little more than five knots while boosting coal consumption compared to steamers of equal power.[10]

Allegheny also suffered from being one of the Navy's first iron-hulled ships. She was built by the Pittsburgh yard of Stackhouse & Tomlinson, whose experience was limited to constructing vessels for service on inland waters. *Allegheny*'s hull structure, inherently weak because of its unusual form, was ill-designed to resist the dynamic loads a ship encounters on the high seas.[11]

The board's report condemned not only *Allegheny* but also the Hunter's wheel concept, finally ending the Navy's many agonizing years of trials. Lenthall had already experienced some of these same frustrations when serving at the Philadelphia Navy Yard.[12] In late 1845 another iron-hulled Hunter's wheel-equipped steam tug, *Water Witch*, had been brought to the yard to be lengthened by thirty feet and refitted with side-wheel machinery. The first part of the conversion was carried out, but instead of side-wheels, she was fit with twin screws of a pattern developed by Richard Loper, the same who acted as the Army's agent during the surf boat mobilization. Subjected to trials overseen by the Franklin Institute, the scheme was rejected and *Water Witch* was again re-engined, this time with side-wheels.[13] Lenthall would, in the not-too-distant future, be obliged to deal with this hapless steamer's final reincarnation.

At the risk of speculation, it must be wondered if John Lenthall's unsatisfactory experience with *Allegheny* and *Water Witch* contributed to a skeptical attitude on his part regarding iron's suitability as a building material for warships. *Water Witch* had been constructed at the Washington Navy Yard and although *Allegheny* was a product of an inland yard, her building had also been supervised by a Navy-appointed constructor.[14] Yet both ships were ultimately condemned for naval service. For Lenthall, it was hardly an auspicious introduction to iron.

* * *

The spring of 1850 witnessed the gathering of forces that, over time, would cause Chief Constructor Lenthall's return to the realm of merchant ship construction in an altogether different manner than he had previously experienced. The vast new American territories acquired during the course of the Mexican War spurred United States authorities to dramatically expand the reach of federally subsidized mail service, both on domestic and trans-Atlantic routes. This impetus resulted in the awarding of numerous contracts to operators of mail steamers. However, in the process of give and take implicit in any government subsidy, the steamship owners were required to do more than just carry the mail to earn their money.

One of the more controversial contract proposals was that received from Edward Knight Collins on 6 March 1846 for carrying mail between New York and Liverpool. A year later and after much debate, an act of Congress was passed on 3 March 1847 that sought to define the scope of mail contracts with Collins and other steamship operators. It included provisions that touched on the design, construction and operation of federally subsidized mail steamers. A principal argument aired by Congressional supporters of the act was that in return for its subsidies, the nation would obtain a ready reserve of steamers which, with only a modest expenditure, would be capable of serving as warships.[15] To achieve this end, the act stipulated:

> The steamships to be employed by the said E. K. Collins ... shall be constructed under the inspection of a naval constructor in the employ of the Navy Department, and shall be so constructed as to render them convertible, at the least possible cost, into war steamers of the first class.[16]

Collins' proposal envisaged the building of five ships in all, four of which were to be ready in eighteen months and to be of not less than 2,000 tons and 1,000 horsepower. And now, in accordance with Congressional dictates, these very large mail steamers were to be built under the supervision of the Navy Department. But the issue that would be of the greatest concern to John Lenthall was that they should also be "war steamers of the first class."

The U.S. Navy was generally supportive of the mail steamer-to-warship conversion scenario. An added benefit was that the mail steamer contracts required the posting of naval officers on the ships, which provided those officers with valuable experience operating steamers. Most naval officers viewed *any* large steamer as having, for all intents, the pedigree of a war steamer. Back in 1849, two days before the launch of Collins' first mail liners, *Atlantic* and *Pacific*, the Navy's most vocal proponent of steam, Commodore Perry, reported to the Navy Department:

> As the contract with Mr. Collins does not refer to any particular vessel as a guide for the model or manner of construction of his ships, he has availed himself of the best materials at command, and of his well-known judgement and experience as a ship-builder, in producing two very superior sea steamers.[17]

Even Lenthall's predecessor as chief constructor, Francis Grice, had accepted that the big mail steamers could be easily converted into first class war steamers, and had approved the specifications of Collins' ships as meeting the requirements of the act of 3 March 1846.[18]

But John Lenthall was unconvinced by his peers' arguments. He had surveyed the first of the Collins line steamers, *Atlantic*, on 5 April 1850 and had submitted his evaluation to Commodore Perry.[19] And three years before, Lenthall together with Samuel Hartt had reviewed the steamers' specifications and finding them poorly conceived, submitted numerous proposals to ensure their hulls would be strongly built. With a length of 284 ft, a breadth of nearly 46 ft, a depth of 32 ft and a tonnage of 2,845, *Atlantic* was bigger than the largest Navy war steamer, Lenthall's *Susquehanna*.[20] Conceived of as a fast passenger-carrying mail liner, *Atlantic*'s hull boasted sharp entry lines, three continuous decks, massive engines and an auxiliary sailing rig. All of these features militated against her qualities as a war steamer. Her fine lines could not provide the necessary buoyancy for her to carry heavy guns forward or to easily rise to the sea—she was designed to cleave through the waves. *Atlantic*'s upper deck was too weak to support big pivot guns and if it was cut down, it exposed her machinery to a dangerous extent. Her powerful engines consumed coal at a prodigious rate which, in combination with her light barque rig, disqualified her as an efficient cruiser. Lenthall had no hesitation in pronouncing *Atlantic* and her sisters as mail steamers of the first class, but beyond that he refused to budge. They could never be first-class war steamers.[21]

By the spring of 1850, a number of senators, led by southern Democrats, were also expressing their concerns over the mail contracts with Collins and others. Their numerous questions prompted the passage of a Senate resolution on 27 May to:

> inquire and report to the Senate the facts in relation to the respective contracts for building mail steam-ships ... ; whether said ships have been completed in the manner and at the time stipulated in the contracts ... ; whether any of said ships have been increased in their tonnage, dimensions and machinery, and, consequently, in their value and effectiveness for naval and mail purposes.[22]

The investigation carried on until September, produced reams of paper but did not find any evidence of malfeasance. [23] The opinions of numerous naval officers and of Lenthall's predecessor, Francis Grice, were aired during the course of its hearings. Lenthall's sole exposure was a terse statement regarding the fitness of the mail steamer *Georgia*. "I can concur ... as to her ability to carry the mail on her destined route."[24] All of it served as a valuable lesson to John Lenthall. As the U.S. Navy's chief constructor, he was now cast on a stage with far more visibility than that which he had previously occupied as a resident naval constructor. He was acting not only before the Navy Department's Washington establishment, but on occasions such as the Senate hearings, his audience was now potentially national. As a capital city native and the son of a father who was once a federal employee, Lenthall had been raised in an environment that allowed him to quickly grasp the consequences of his new exposure. With each step up in the navy's bureaucracy, the pressure would only increase.

* * *

Throughout John Lenthall's first year as chief constructor, the makings of a confrontation with Francis Grice had been slowly simmering. Lenthall had replaced Grice, the most senior of the constructors, as the chief constructor in Washington. On the occasion of the launching of *Powhatan,* a ship designed by Grice, Lenthall's presence had been requested by the yard's commandant. And it came out during the recent Senate hearings that Grice, while serving as chief constructor, had agreed that the Collins mail steamers could be first-class war steamers, a stance rejected by Lenthall. In January of 1851, a "plan" proposed by Grice, now the Philadelphia Navy Yard's constructor, brought their differences to a boil.

Grice's proposal, presented to the secretary of the navy in a letter dated 21 January, was to convert the Navy's sailing frigates of the first class—the 44-gun *St. Lawrence* served as the template—into propeller-driven steam frigates. On the surface, it appeared to offer a relatively inexpensive way to upgrade the frigates without materially altering them, for example, by lengthening their hulls. At a cost of only $70,000, Grice claimed that engines of 700 hp driving a 12 ft diameter propeller could be installed, and that the converted ships, with only modest adjustments to their internal arrangements and capacities, would be capable of thirty days endurance and speeds of 10 to 13 knots.[25]

Grice's proposals soon made their way to John Lenthall's desk. The chief constructor quickly determined that Grice's proposal was seriously flawed. First, the speed Grice predicted for the 700 hp steam frigate conversions was hopelessly optimistic. Lenthall compared them to *Mississippi* and *Princeton,* and readily demonstrated the mismatch in Grice's claims. Next, he evaluated the volume occupied by the new machinery and found that Grice had underestimated the extent to which it, together with 300 tons of coal, would fill the frigate's hold. Working backwards, he then systematically itemized the impairments to the frigates' efficiency resulting from the necessary reductions in stores, water, outfit, accommodation and armament. As

Lenthall sagely observed, "For a mechanical or mathematical question to be true, all its parts must be true." And John Lenthall's calculations demonstrated that every aspect of Francis Grice's proposal was wanting. Adding veracity to his rejection of Grice's proposal, Lenthall could cite his evaluation, together with Humphreys, of a request by Captain Stockton in 1840 to similarly alter the frigate *Raritan* into a screw steamer. In both cases, the result was the same—a marginally effective warship. [26]

Lenthall's critique of Grice's plan, submitted to the chief of the Bureau of Construction, Equipment and Repairs on 6 February 1851, was surprisingly mild. Perhaps hoping the matter would be easily deflected, his response outlined the plan's principal weaknesses but avoided a harsh point-by-point assault. He concluded by remarking "I am inclined to the opinion that this plan cannot be satisfactorily carried out."[27]

But Grice was undeterred. Again addressing the secretary of the navy, Grice wrote back on 28 March, reiterating the soundness of his original proposal. Grice's reply was handed to Lenthall who answered with a lengthy endorsement on the back of the letter. Here matters are somewhat confused by file copies of Lenthall's responses marked "not sent." These drafts consist of half a dozen pages of his detailed analyses. But it is sufficiently clear that Lenthall's second formal reply to Grice's plan laid bare its fundamental flaws. He ended by warning "that the plan will result in much expense and disappointment."[28]

Still Grice refused to let go. He next resorted to the media to advance his scheme. On 3 June, a most flattering article titled "Important and Valuable Application of a Propeller" appeared in a Philadelphia paper. It told of a model of *St Lawrence* that Grice had built and displayed at the navy yard, which showed all "objections ... are entirely overcome" and would soon "create ... a great sensation in Washington."[29]

The final documented salvo in this heated exchange between naval constructors appeared in the form of a letter written on 27 September by John Lenthall to Commodore Stewart. The commodore favored Grice's plan, and so Lenthall used his letter to convey every detailed calculation he had performed to demonstrate the plan's irredeemable faults. Lenthall further revealed that "the model they had made was exactly the same as the draft for which I made my calculations... [and] is exactly the same as that proposed by Mr. Humphreys ...the plans of which are still in that office," subtlety suggesting that Grice may have purloined Lenthall's and Humphreys' prior analyses and used them to craft his 'new' plan.[30]

Just how the matter of Grice's proposal played out in detail is not entirely clear—both he and Lenthall continued in their current positions and over the coming years, for all appearances, amicably pursued their work as constructors. But what is known is that, unlike its European rivals, the U.S. Navy did not convert any of its sailing frigates or sloops into war steamers.[31] Its reluctance to innovate was caused by factors beyond John Lenthall's singular intransigence. In fact, five years later, he proposed rebuilding an old liner into a steam frigate. However, Lenthall's stubborn exposition of the pitfalls of ill-conceived conversions stood as both a caution and a yardstick for any future attempts. As will be seen, when he did turn his mind to providing the Navy with first-class propeller-driven steam frigates, the resulting *Merrimack* class were far grander than anything yet conceived.

* * *

Lenthall's correspondence with Commodore Stewart ended with small talk about the dire illness that had beset Commodore Lewis Warrington, one of the dwindling brotherhood of War of 1812 veterans. Early next month Lenthall's mother-in-law, who was living with his family in Washington, wrote to her daughter in Philadelphia and told of venturing out "to see the funeral of Commodore Warrington."[32] It was no ordinary procession, including President Millard Filmore, cabinet members and many dignitaries, and must have offered a splendid spectacle. Her daughter Mary was soon to reply, telling of her own adventure:

> I was very anxious to get my teeth fixed … I took a very early start … Dr. Harris says I must be very careful and not to take cold. He has done them beautifully and with little or no pain, as they were taken out before the roots had time to decay.[33]

John Lenthall's wife Mary, only thirty-eight, was the second of his close female relatives to suffer full teeth extraction. Her ordeal makes one truly appreciative of modern advances in dental care.

John Lenthall's household during this period consisted of his wife Mary, daughter Jane, mother-in-law Ann Maria Eck, a young girl also named Mary Eck, and a female Irish servant.[34] They still lived in a house on the corner of 7th and I Streets, but that was soon to change. Perhaps sensing her mortality and realizing son John's family needed a more permanent home, in March 1852 Lenthall's mother Jane and his two sisters conveyed their interest in the old King house on F Street to John Lenthall. This was the same house in which the Lenthall children were born and it would remain Constructor John Lenthall's home for the rest of his life. According to family accounts, not long after the transaction, Lenthall had the house "rebuilt or enlarged."[35] The 1818 F Street NW location (using new street numbering), lying just two blocks to the west of the Navy Department building, could not have been more convenient to Lenthall's place of work.

In the last days of spring 1852, the Church of the Epiphany's new sanctuary was officially consecrated. This Episcopalian parish, which had been organized ten years before, had become the center of spiritual life for the Protestant worshipers of the Lenthall family and would continue in that role over the years to come.[36] Located on G Street between 13th and 14th Streets, the Church of the Epiphany was only two blocks behind the Pennsylvania Avenue residence of Lenthall's mother and Sister Mary. It still stands today and graciously welcomes all worshipers.

Summer of 1852 witnessed the passing of two of the women closest to John Lenthall. First to go was his mother-in-law, Ann Maria Eck, who died at age sixty-four on 9 July 1852. The cause of death is not known. Her grave is presently in Mount Olivet Cemetery, a Roman Catholic graveyard established in 1858, which suggests she was originally interred in one of Washington's older Catholic burial grounds.[37]

Second to pass was Lenthall's mother, Jane King Lenthall. She died one month later at age seventy-one, and was buried next to her husband at Rock Creek Cemetery.[38] John Lenthall Sr.'s remains had been reinterred many years before in this newer cemetery, and now forty-four years after his death, she joined him and her brothers, Nicholas King and Robert King Jr., who were buried nearby. Jane King Lenthall's headstone recalled her storied heritage:

JANE wife of John Lenthall
and daughter of Robert King
Born at Pickering, Yorkshire
England October 11th 1780
and departed this life Washington
August 9th 1852

These two deaths irrevocably affected John Lenthall's family. Both John and his wife, Mary, buried their mothers within a month of each other. And daughter Jenny lost her only grandparents. Patterns of the past would in time adjust to the Lenthalls' new realities. The coming distraction of moving into a new home must have now seemed a welcome comfort.

* * *

In the wake of his dealings with Grice's steam frigate plan, John Lenthall turned his attention to a pair of new ship designs, each a one-of-a-kind and both historically obscured by the Navy's artifice of administrative 'rebuilding'. The first was a throwback to his recent experience with the former Hunter's wheel steamer *Water Witch.* Her new side-wheel machinery proved capable but her weakened iron-hull did not, hopelessly failing during a coastal voyage.[39] The Navy's solution was to discard the hull—it was used for target practice—and construct a new vessel of wood to accept her engines. To this end, Lenthall drafted the lines of a handsome steamer somewhat larger than the original *Water Witch.* She was laid down and launched at the Washington Navy Yard in 1852, and was the first U.S. Navy side-wheeler to be fitted with more efficient feathering floats, courtesy of an up-and-coming engineer named Benjamin Franklin Isherwood. Little *Water Witch* proved to be a robust steamer, venturing the length of the Atlantic and up the Rio de la Plata as far as Paraguay, but she did not survive the traumas of the Civil War.[40]

Lenthall's second design project marked the last hurrah of the American sailing navy. The 1797 vintage frigate *Constellation* had been laid up for years, obsolete and worn out. Although funds were available for her repair, the navy had no need of another frigate but it could readily find employment for a sloop of war. Several older frigates, the 'rebuilt' *Macedonian* among, them, had been recently razeed into what were now being called spar deck corvettes. Accordingly, John Lenthall drafted plans for a 22-gun sloop larger than *Saratoga, Germantown* or any of the 1842 sloops and nearly the size of a 44-gun frigate. The new ship's lines displayed the hallmarks of a Lenthall design—an elegant sheer line, gracefully rising to an enclosed head (see Plan No. 9). The old *Constellation* was quietly dismantled and on a nearby slip in the Norfolk Navy Yard, the new sloop laid down. Commissioned in 1855, the spar deck corvette *Constellation* was the last sailing man-of-war designed and built by the U.S. Navy—the age of steam had finally prevailed.[41] Because she was officially a rebuild of the older frigate, some confusion has persisted over the origins of this splendid vessel, which has been preserved in Baltimore's inner harbor. *Constellation* is the sole surviving warship to have served during the Civil War and the only remaining example of John Lenthall's handiwork.

* * *

IMAGES

No. 1 *Constructor John Lenthall*

John Lenthall posed for Mathew Brady in this undated photograph taken sometime between 1860-65. His handsome and somewhat stern face captures the viewer's attention. In his late fifties, Lenthall still has a full head of hair (Image 527130, courtesy of the National Archives and Records Administration).

No. 2 *Old Supreme Court Chamber*

It was here that John Lenthall's father was killed when the ceiling vaults collapsed after removal of their supports. Baby John was only one year old. The intricate structure of the chamber's ribbed semi-dome ceiling can be readily appreciated. This magnificent room is in the north wing of the Capitol under the old Senate chamber (Photo from survey HABS-DC-38-B, control number dc1045, courtesy of the Library of Congress).

No. 3 *City of Washington from Beyond the Navy Yard*

This painting circa 1833 provides an indelible impression of how sparsely populated Washington City was during the early days of the Republic. The navy yard and Capitol are at center with the President's House to the left. (Painting by George Cooke, Digital ID pga-00192, courtesy of the Library of Congress).

No. 4 *Launching of the Pennsylvania*

A view of the 120-gun *Pennsylvania* being launched from the ship house of the Philadelphia Navy Yard. The Delaware is crammed full of boats, their passengers watching what was said to be the world's largest vessel take the water. A holiday atmosphere is evident among the many spectators (Lithograph by Lehman & Duval, Federal Street Navy Yard Collection, gift of J. Welles

Henderson, Image 1992.035.028, courtesy of the Independence Seaport Museum, Philadelphia, PA).

No. 5 *U.S. Steamer Mississippi*

A dramatically rendered illustration of the U.S. Steam Frigate *Mississippi* going to the relief of vessels off Veracruz. The first of the Navy's successful sea steamers, *Mississippi* was legendary for both her durability and as Commodore Perry's flagship, first off Mexico and then opening Japan. Note the awkward placement of her main mast aft of the funnel. Although rated a frigate, she carried guns on only her main deck (Print rendering by LT H. Walke, USN, Digital ID pga 04094, courtesy of the Library of Congress).

No. 6 *Sloop of War at Charlestown Navy Yard*

This photograph provides a wonderfully detailed view of the stern of a *Dale* class sloop of war sitting in the graving dock at the Charlestown (Boston) Navy Yard. The vessels of this class were the first warships designed by John Lenthall. Note the hull's compact size as indicated by the height of the workmen (Negative 23977, Courtesy of the Peabody Essex Museum).

No. 7 *Launch of the U.S. Steam Propeller Princeton*

A contemporary print picturing the moment *Princeton* emerged from the Philadelphia Navy Yard's ship house. Note her rudder post and propeller have not yet been installed; compare with the details of her stern post arrangements as shown on Plan No. 7 (Federal Street Navy Yard Collection, gift of J. Welles Henderson, Image 1992.035.038, courtesy of the Independence Seaport Museum, Philadelphia, PA).

No. 8 *Scene on the Delaware at Philadelphia*

The severe winter of 1856 is remembered by this atmospheric print taken from the frozen Delaware River, looking toward the Philadelphia Navy Yard. Clearly illustrated in superb detail are the huge ship houses that dominate the skyline. Also note the two sheers for hoisting in guns or tall masts. Tied up in front of the ship houses is a side-wheel steam frigate, possibly *Susquehanna*

(Lithograph by James Queen, Digital ID ppmsca19644, courtesy of the Library of Congress).

No. 9 *United States "Auxiliary Screw" Steam Frigate "Merrimac"*

Shown in this lithograph off the entrance to New York harbor is Lenthall's masterpiece, the steam frigate *Merrimack*. Her size and towering full ship rig are emphasized by this illustration. When commissioned in 1856, she was one of the earliest large men of war to carry a battery of all shell-firing guns (Image LC-03650, courtesy of the Library of Congress).

No. 10 *Admiral Samuel Francis Du Pont*

A painting of John Lenthall's fast friend and frequent correspondent, Captain (and later Admiral) Samuel Francis Du Pont. In March 1863 Du Pont confided to his journal that "Mr. Lenthall ... has more brains than any civilian in the Navy Department ..." (Painting by Daniel Huntingdon, Object No. 56G22/P19-1, courtesy of the Hagley Museum and Library).

No. 11 *Engineer-in-Chief Benjamin Franklin Isherwood*

Isherwood served as John Lenthall's engineer-in-chief at the Bureau of Construction, Equipment and Repairs, and then after the bureaus were reorganized in 1862, as the first chief of the Bureau of Steam Engineering. Throughout their bureau careers, the two had closely compatible ideas on the Navy's future trajectory and neither were fans of Ericsson or his monitors. In later life, they kept up a vigorous correspondence (Digital ID cwpbh 03238, courtesy of the Library of Congress).

No. 12 *Ironclad Roanoke*

The first of Lenthall and Isherwood's ironclads to get afloat was *Roanoke*, a converted *Merrimack* class steam frigate. She has been derided for her shortcomings—excess rolling and structural weakness—but *Roanoke*'s ship-shape hull, triple turrets and greater freeboard set her apart as a first attempt by the U.S. Navy to field a powerful ocean going ironclad (Image NH 60891, courtesy of the Naval History and Heritage Command).

No. 13 *The Old Navy Department Building*

Shown in this photo is the old Navy Department building. It faced out on 17th Street and was just across from the Winder Building, which still stands. This view was taken after the Civil War and shows the building with its two additional stories that were added during the war. Bureau Chief Lenthall officed in this building, which was only two blocks away from his F Street home (Image NH 1527, courtesy of the Naval History and Heritage Command).

No. 14 *Miantonomoh at Malaga*

One of four *Monadnock* class ironclads specified by John Lenthall, *Miantonomoh* was designed by B. F. Delano and built at the New York Navy Yard. She took Assistant Secretary Fox on a show-the-flag voyage to Europe in 1866 and is pictured here at Malaga, Spain, in late December 1866. Note her relatively high freeboard, the prominent hurricane deck and the enthusiastic crowd of visitors thronging her decks (Image NH 46260, courtesy of the Naval History and Heritage Command).

No. 15 *Lenthall and his Granddaughter*

No apologies are needed for presenting these two low-resolution but historically significant photos. John Lenthall is shown in the upper left, perhaps at age forty. (Cameo portrait by Mathew Brady, courtesy navsource.org). On the lower right is Anny, Lenthall's favorite grandchild, at close to the same age. Prior to her passing in 1951, Anny—then Mrs. Eugene Semmes Ives—donated her collection of Lenthall's private papers to the U.S. Naval Academy Museum (Courtesy of Lillie Riney, findagrave.org Memorial ID 5401730, image retouched by R. Thorp).

* * *

No. 1 *Constructor John Lenthall*

No. 2 *Old Supreme Court Chamber*

No. 3 *City of Washington from Beyond the Navy Yard*

No. 4 *Launching of the Pennsylvania*

No. 5 *U.S. Steamer Mississippi*

No. 6 *Sloop of War at Charlestown Navy Yard*

No. 7 *Launch of the U.S. Steam Propeller Princeton*

No. 8 *Scene on the Delaware at Philadelphia*

No. 9 *United States "Auxiliary Screw" Steam Frigate "Merrimac"*

No. 10 *Admiral Samuel Francis Du Pont*

No. 11 *Engineer-in-Chief Benjamin Franklin Isherwood*

No. 12 *Ironclad Roanoke*

No. 13 *The Old Navy Department Building*

No. 14 *Miantonomoh at Malaga*

No. 15 *Lenthall and his Granddaughter*

PLANS

No. 1 *Brig, "First draws made by JL"*

John Lenthall's first formal ship drawing was apparently this lines plan of an 85½ ft long brig. If so, it represented a very creditable effort from the sixteen-year-old apprentice. Shown are the standard sheer, half breadth and body plans, with the latter being unconventionally turned ninety degrees. Buttock lines are drawn in aft with some reworking of the waterlines. Good but not perfect line control techniques are in evidence. Scale: 4 ft = 1 inch (John Lenthall Collection, Ship Plan FI L90.43.59, courtesy of the Independence Seaport Museum, Philadelphia, PA for the Franklin Institute).

No. 2 *Relief, Outboard Profile and Sail Plan*

Circa 1835, this drawing shows the outboard profile and sail plan of the store ship *Relief,* the first vessel John Lenthall built for the Navy. He has marked in each sail's center of effort, and also the hull's center of displacement, the center of the floating line (LCF), the longitudinal center of effort of the full sail plan and the height of the longitudinal metacenter, all evidence of intense numerical analysis. Drawings of this era were, unfortunately, absent proper title blocks with all the helpful information they provide. Scale: 5 ft = 1 inch (John Lenthall Collection, Ship Plan FI L90.43.82, courtesy of the Independence Seaport Museum, Philadelphia, PA for the Franklin Institute).

No. 3A *Pennsylvania, Inboard Profile (Forward)*

No. 3B *Pennsylvania, Inboard Profile (Aft)*

This detailed inboard profile is of the U.S. Navy's only four-decked ship of the line, *Pennsylvania.* Interior arrangements and compartment names are inked in together with pencil notes on what is clearly a working drawing. Weights of the ship's displacement at a 25 ft draft are calculated for each frame station interval and written in between station numbers. Table summaries are presented fore and aft, and at the extreme lower right (forward plan) a port sill height calculation has been penciled in. Scale: 5 ft = 1 inch (John Lenthall Collection, Ship Plan FI L90.43.48, courtesy of the Independence Seaport Museum, Philadelphia, PA for the Franklin Institute).

No. 4 *Dale, Half Breadth Plan*

Dale's half breadth plan is much more complex than first meets the eye. A profile forward is penciled in as are numerous graphs and other calculations on what is essentially a naval architect's working plan. Areas and centers of gravity of the water planes are graphed (fore, aft and combined) and presented in tabular format. The floating line(s) and heights of the transverse metacenter and the center of gravity of the hull's displacement are also indicated. Alternate frame station spacings have been penciled in, probably to facilitate volume-CG calculations. Scale: 2 ft = 1 inch (John Lenthall Collection, Ship Plan FI L90.43.105, courtesy of the Independence Seaport Museum, Philadelphia, PA for the Franklin Institute).

No. 5 *Dale, Bow Profile*

This handsome drawing circa 1838 is a fine example of the art of the naval architect. Lenthall's skill as a draftsman is on full display, with sections identified by red ink and floating line in blue. Location, size and materials of bolts are shown—copper below the "copper" line, iron above. The bow's structure of breast hooks and deadwood is drawn in as are its hawse holes and cat heads. The lower plan shows the reach of the foreyard and what appears to be a whisker boom for the fore tack. Scale 2 ft = 1 inch (John Lenthall Collection, Ship Plan FI L90.43.107, courtesy of the Independence Seaport Museum, Philadelphia, PA for the Franklin Institute).

No. 6A *Mississippi, Lines Plan (Forward)*

No. 6B *Mississippi, Lines Plan (Aft)*

The steam frigate *Mississippi*'s lines plan is more conventional than the previous Lenthall drawings with its standard sheer, half breadth and body plan views. Note the indications of where diagonal iron strapping was let into the frames to stiffen the hull, a first for a U.S. Navy vessel. Plots of *Mississippi*'s hydrostatic data are drawn in as is the outline of her side-lever machinery. The location of her midship section 'dead flat' is marked in on the three frame stations aft of the paddle shaft center. (John Lenthall Collection, Ship Plan FI L90.43.132, courtesy of the Independence Seaport Museum, Philadelphia, PA for the Franklin Institute).

No. 7 *Princeton, Aft Inboard Profile*

John Ericsson is usually credited as *Princeton*'s designer, but this drawing confirms that Lenthall drafted her working plans; note his initials "JL" just below her rudder. Details of her stern post, removable rudder and rudder post, shafting and stern tube arrangement and iron diagonal bracing also show clearly on this drawing of the first warship *designed* with a screw propeller. And it was drafted by Constructor John Lenthall. Scale: ½ inch = 1 foot (John Lenthall Collection, Ship Plan FI L90.43.193, courtesy of the Independence Seaport Museum, Philadelphia, PA for the Franklin Institute).

No. 8 *Germantown, Hoisting Plan*

An unusual drawing demonstrating attention to the operational need for a crew to move weights about a ship. The lower yards of each mast are shown in their extreme braced-up positions to prove that they can reach loads along the sweep of their coverage. It can be seen how the foreyard can readily shift the sheet anchor forward to anywhere alongside the forecastle. This plan is akin to a modern drilling rig's crane loading diagram. Scale 6 ft = 1 inch (John Lenthall Collection, Ship Plan FI L90.43.165, courtesy of the Independence Seaport Museum, Philadelphia, PA for the Franklin Institute).

No. 9 *Constellation, Lines Plan*

No excuse is necessary for including this drawing. The spar deck sloop of war *Constellation* was the last sailing warship built for the U.S. Navy and her lines were drawn by Chief Constructor John Lenthall. A restored *Constellation* is afloat today in Baltimore's inner harbor, the only surviving example of Lenthall's handiwork. Scale: 5 ft = 1 inch (John Lenthall Collection, Ship Plan FI

L90.43.257, courtesy of the Independence Seaport Museum, Philadelphia, PA for the Franklin Institute).

No. 10 *Germantown, Lines Plan*

The next two plans are from the drawing board of Howard I. Chapelle, former curator of transportation at the Smithsonian Institute. He was a professional naval architect and a first-class draftsman, which lends great authority to his work. Presented here is his reconstruction of *Germantown*'s lines plan and the features of her interior and deck arrangements. It appears as Plan 28 in his book, *The History of the American Sailing Navy.* (Plan WS-38a, courtesy of the Division of Work & Industry, National Museum of American History, Smithsonian Institute).

No. 11 *Raritan, Lines Plan*

Raritan was one of the "Gradual Increase" frigates whose design was tweaked by Samuel Humphreys and altered in detail by Constructor John Lenthall before she was launched in 1843. Of special note is her distinctive enclosed head. Chapelle's drawing of *Raritan* presents a more traditional set of lines compared to those of *Germantown.* It appears in his book as Plan 29 (Plan WS-40, courtesy of the Division of Work & Industry, National Museum of American History, Smithsonian Institute).

No. 12 *Navy Department Ironclad, Midship Section*

One of the six extant drawings of Lenthall and Isherwood's Navy Department designed ironclad, this one displays her hull structure to good advantage. Note the three heavy bilge keelsons to support the boiler, and also the coal bunkers arranged outboard and the wing passageway inboard of the armor belt. This later feature was probably intended for fore and aft access, and to check for shot damage (Image ID No. 98045d, General Plan of Machinery for U.S. Iron-Plated Steam Batteries, Naval History Collection, Gustavus Vasa Fox Collection, courtesy of the New-York Historical Society).

* * *

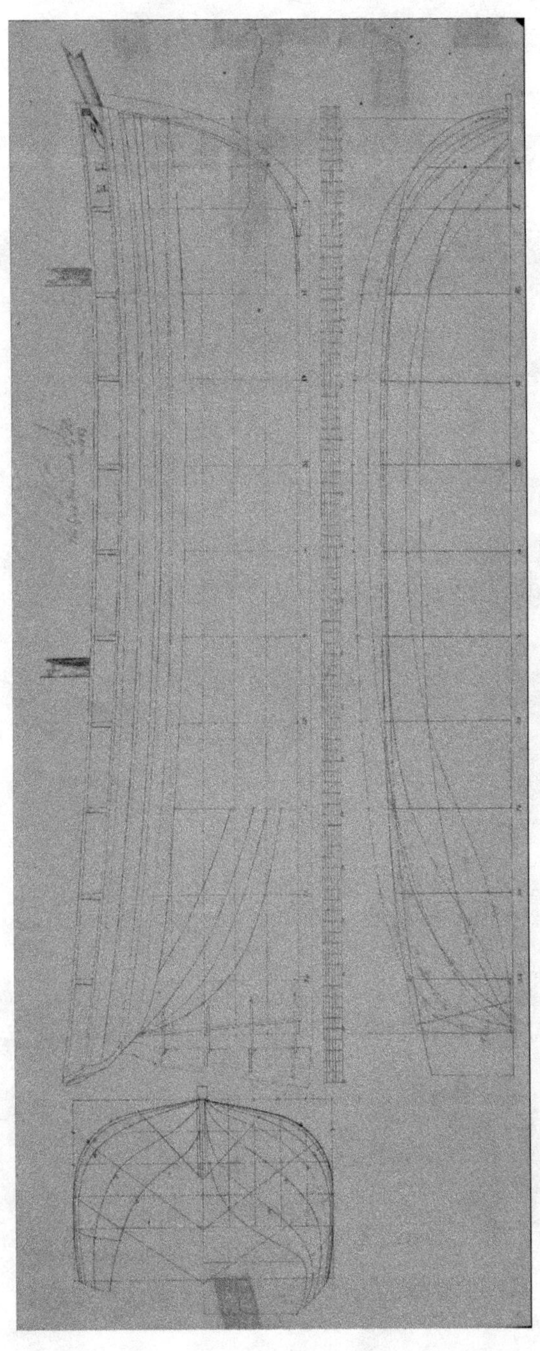

No. 1 *Brig, "First draws made by JL"*

No. 2 *Relief, Outboard Profile and Sail Plan*

No. 3A *Pennsylvania, Inboard Profile (Forward)*

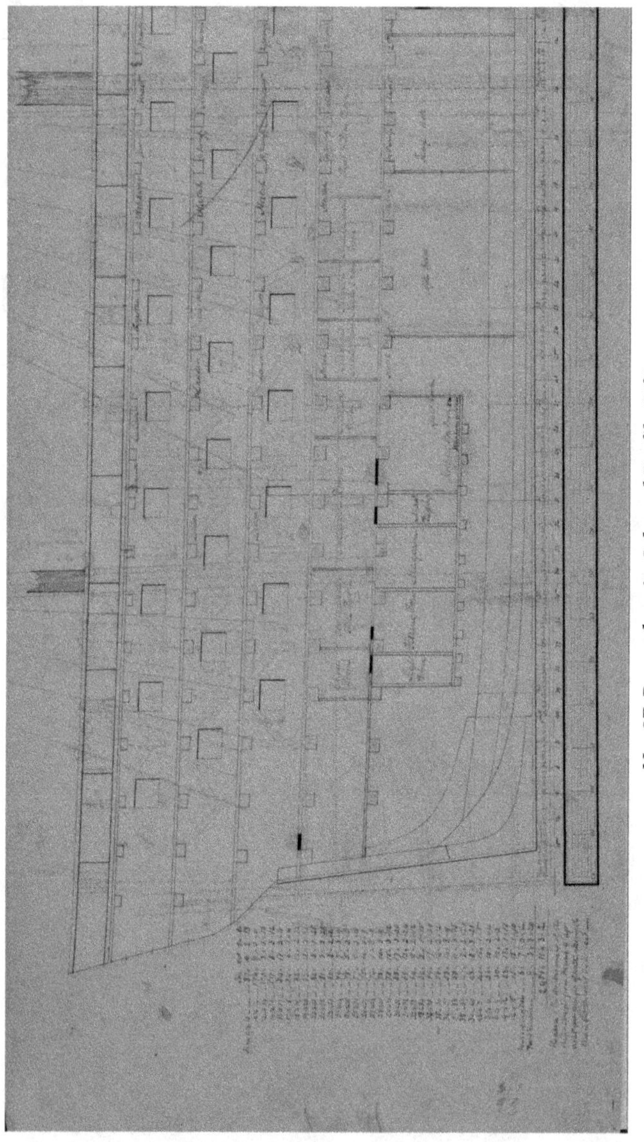

No. 3B *Pennsylvania*, Inboard Profile (Aft)

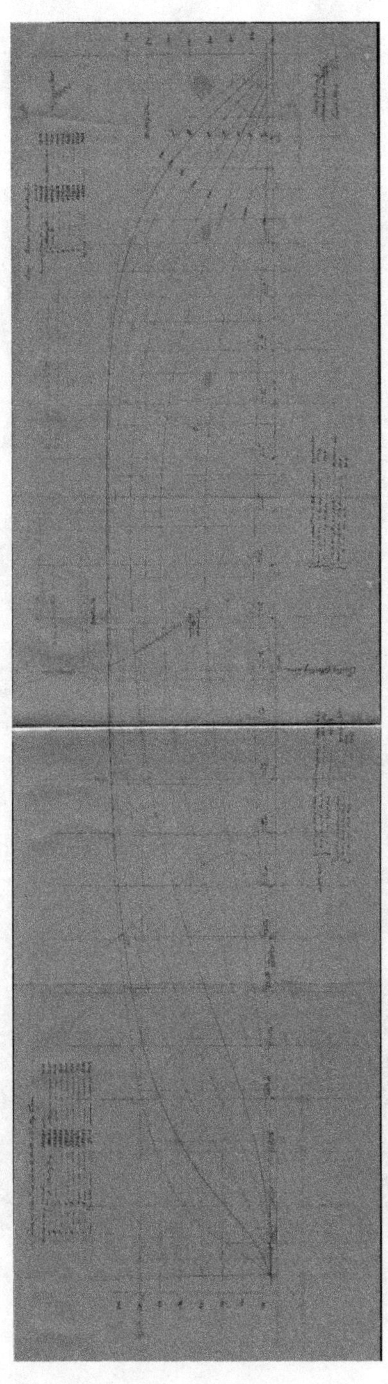

No. 4 *Dale, Half Breadth Plan*

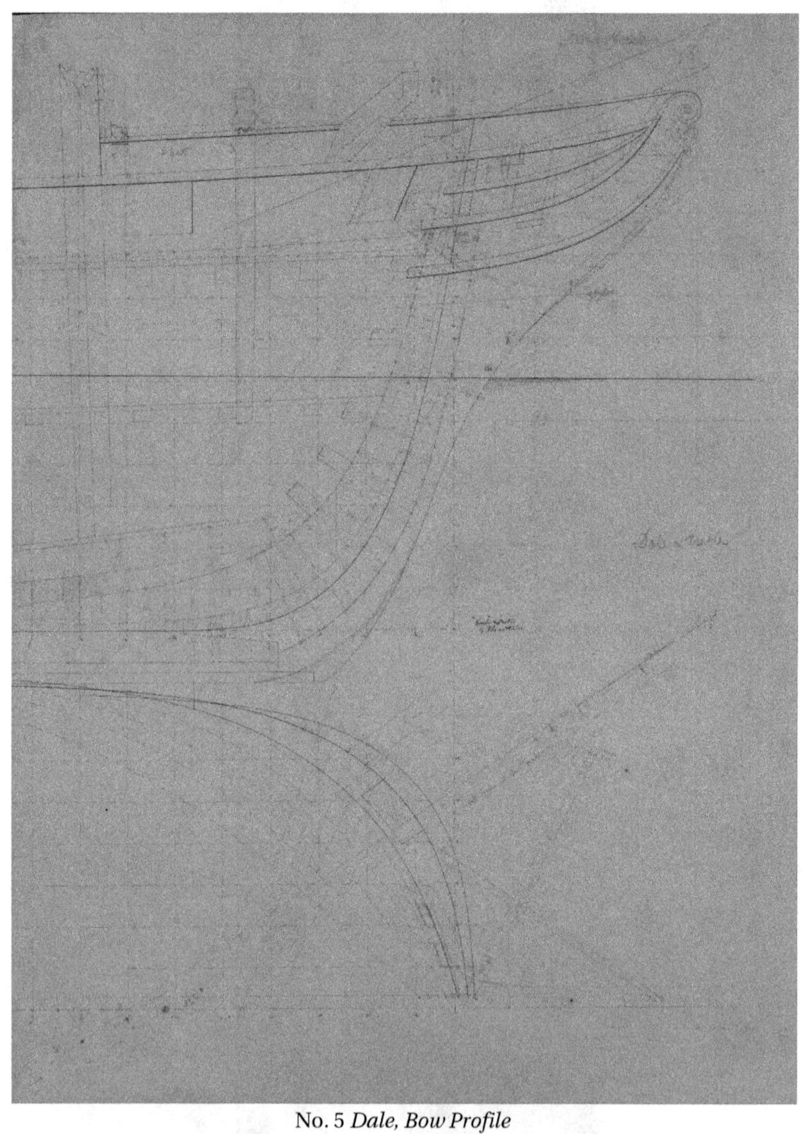

No. 5 *Dale, Bow Profile*

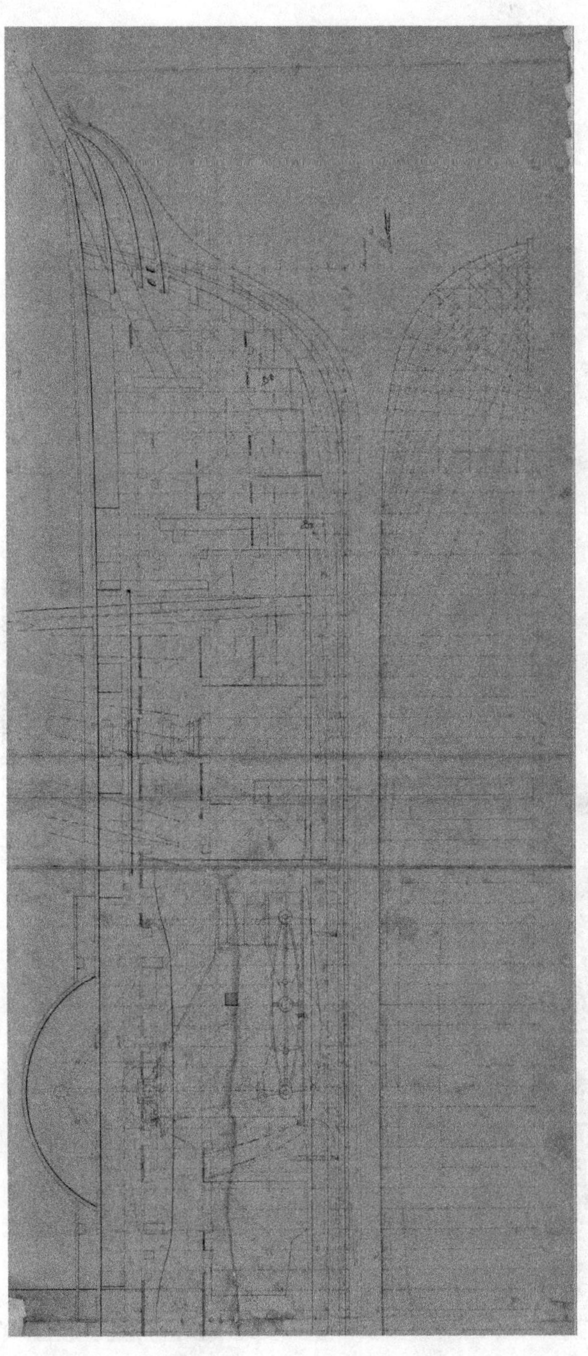

No. 6A *Mississippi, Lines Plan (Forward)*

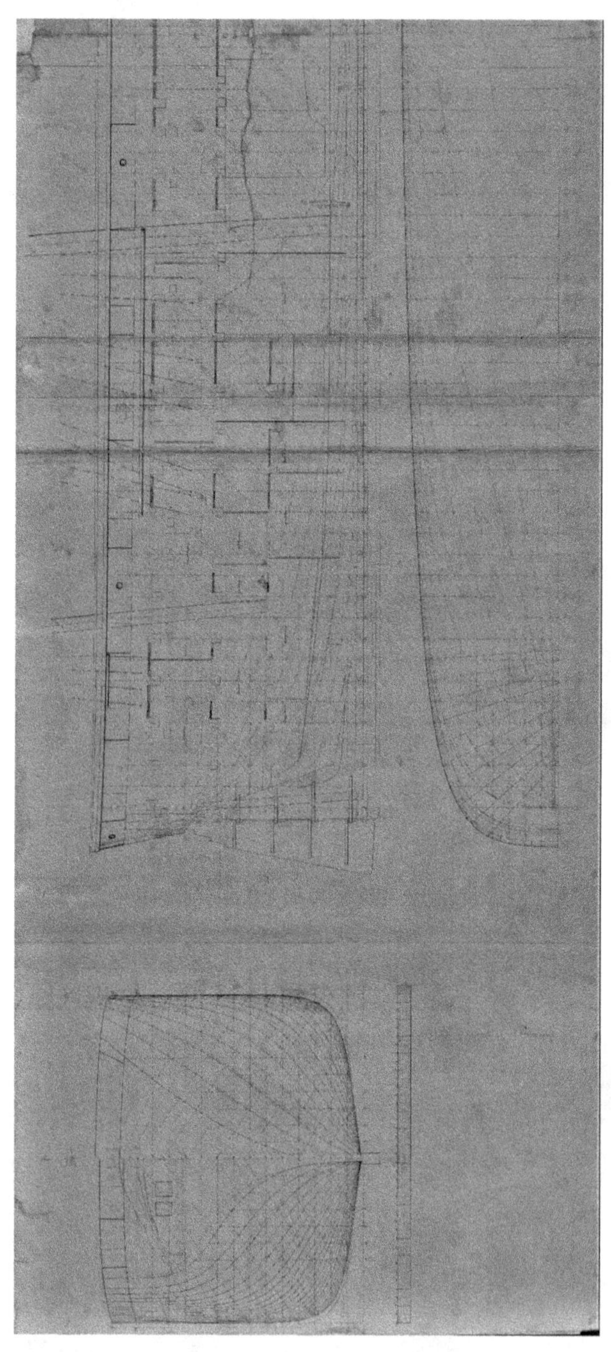

No. 6B *Mississippi*, Lines Plan (Aft)

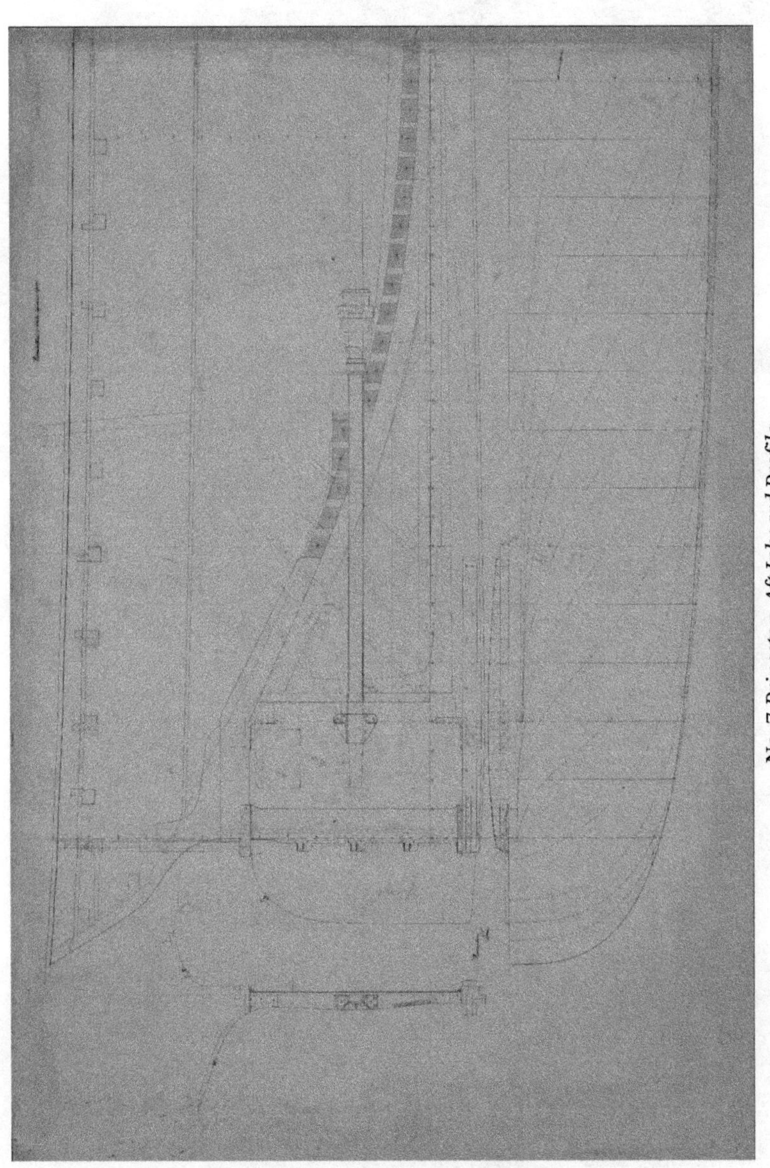

No. 7 *Princeton, Aft Inboard Profile*

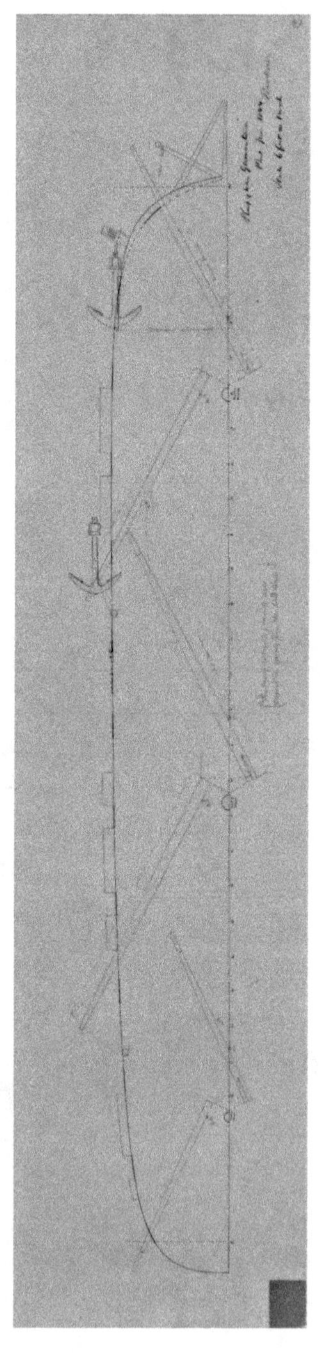

No. 8 *Germantown, Hoisting Plan*

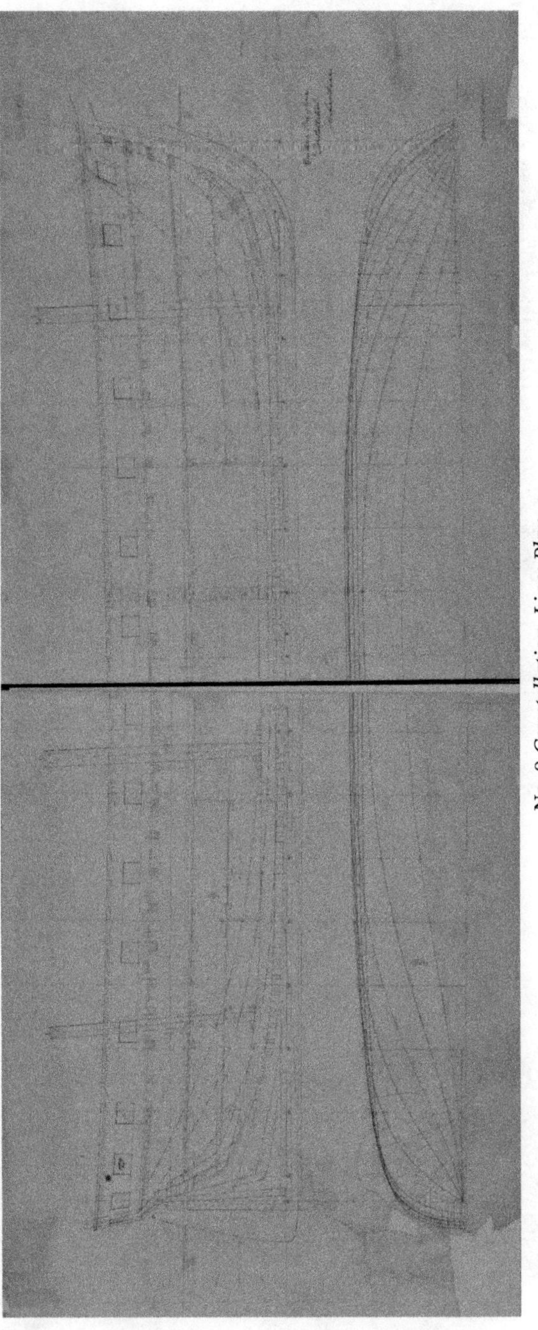

No. 9 *Constellation, Lines Plan*

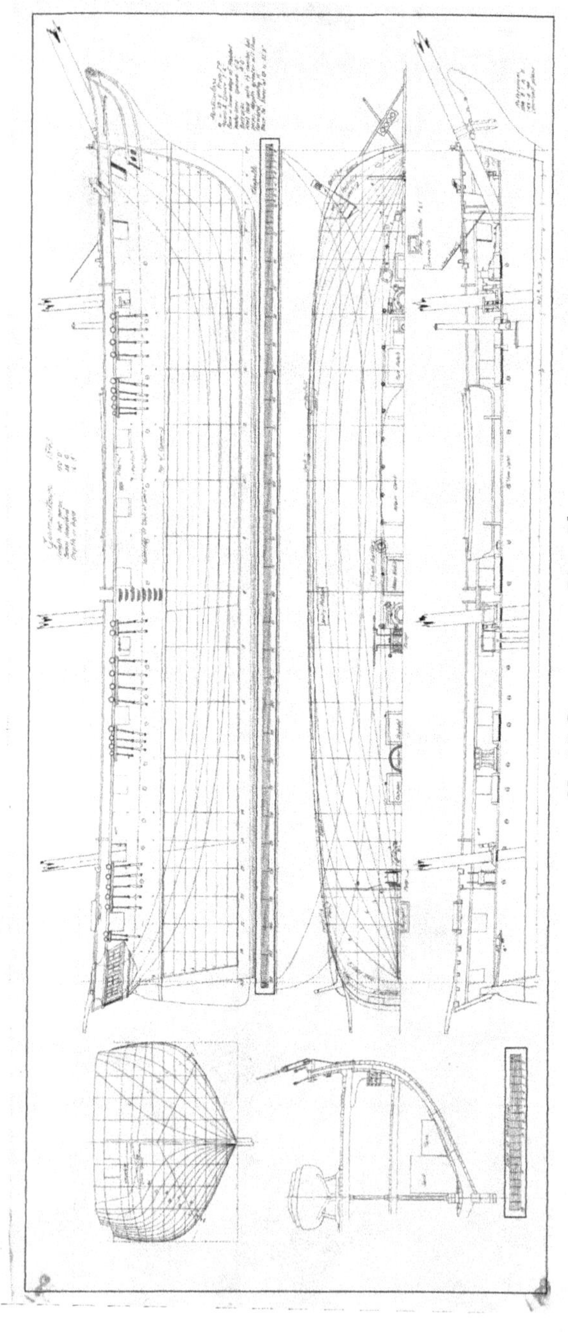

No. 10 *Germantown*, Lines Plan

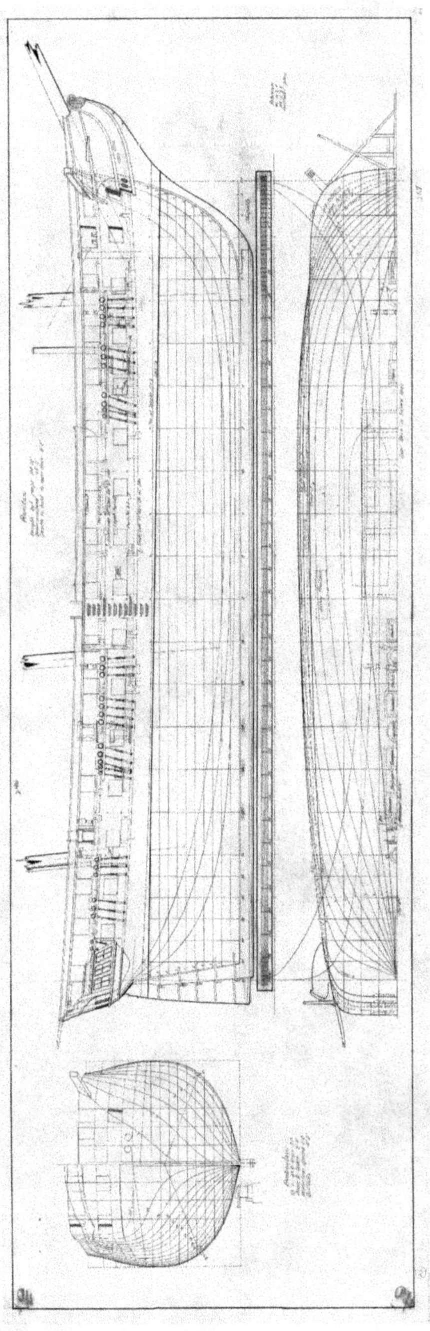

No. 11 *Raritan, Lines Plan*

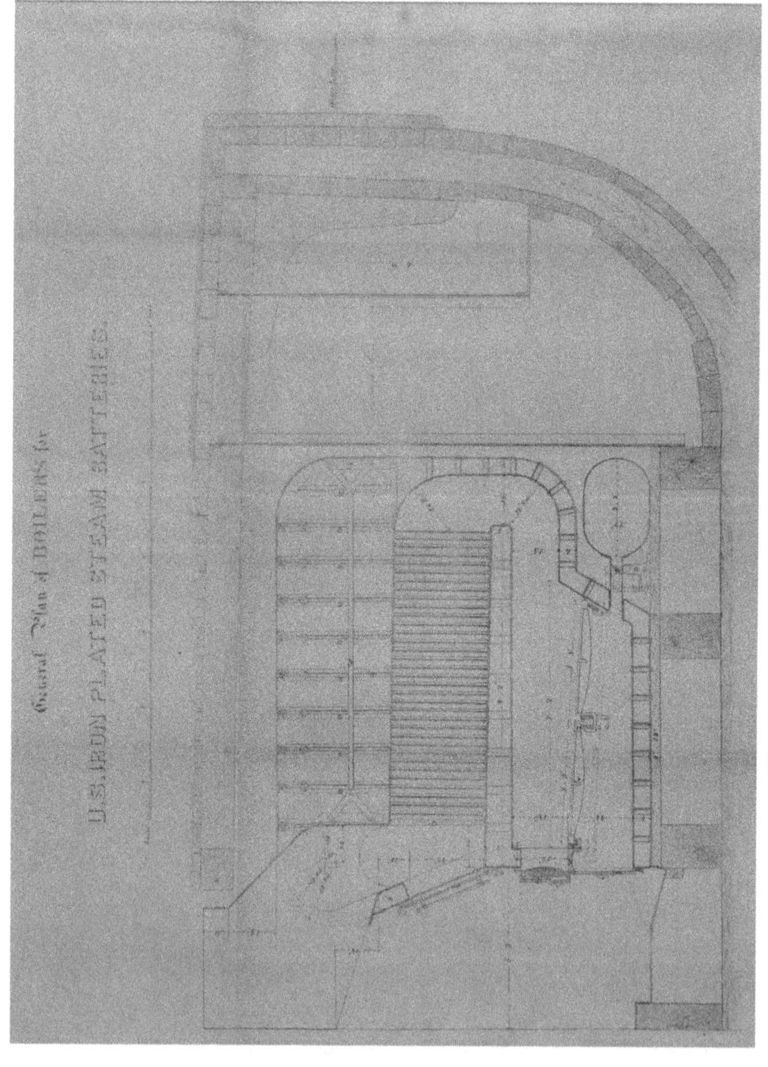

No. 12 *Navy Department Ironclad, Midship Section*

BOOK THREE
Bureau Chief

CHAPTER 17

Promotion to Bureau Chief

The election of 1852 brought Franklin Pierce to Washington as president of the United States. A dark-horse Democrat candidate from New Hampshire, Pierce came to his high office with mixed expectations of success. But the underlying forces that propelled him into power gave momentum to his party's muscular platform that encouraged the "full expansion of the energies of this great and progressive people." At this time in the nation's history—four years after the Mexican War and the California gold rush that followed—the Young America movement was at its full-throated peak. It envisaged an expansionist country; a young giant yearning to challenge the enfeebled European powers and claim America's rightful place on the world's stage. Heir to vast new conquered territories that made it a Pacific as well as an Atlantic power, the United States also had ambitions on Cuba and hungered for control of the Central American isthmus' strategically vital 'Panama Route'. The expansion of America's seaborne commerce during this period fully mirrored the nation's territorial growth, its merchant marine nearly doubling its registered tonnage. Whaling ships now dotted the far-flung stretches of the Pacific, mail steamers plied the east and west coasts, and Yankee clippers raced across the ocean blue in pursuit of trade.[1]

America's vigorous ambitions, growing international presence and enlarged merchant fleet spoke to the need for a strong navy capable of defending its interests and pursuing its national goals. But the U.S. Navy had not kept pace with the country's accelerating demands. As the year 1853 dawned, it could count only seventy vessels of war in its inventory. A good number of these were obsolete ships of the line still 'on the stocks' and others were vessels 'in ordinary' and unfit for service. Its five active steam frigates mounted but forty guns between them, and beyond these, only a handful of miscellaneous steamers, some of them 'rebuilt', could put to sea. A score of sloops and a handful of frigates, all of them sailing vessels, formed the backbone of the Navy's fleet.[2]

Considering the preceding decade's incoherent program of naval administration, the real surprise is that the U.S. Navy was as capable as it was. In the nearly ten years since Abel Upshur's departure, no fewer than seven men had assumed the office of navy secretary, one of them twice, and the longest any had continuously served was two and a half years. None had the time to make an impact. And on 8 March 1853, when Franklin Pierce's appointed secretary of the navy, James Cochrane Dobbin, assumed his office, it was easy to assume he would be of the same mold.[3]

A North Carolina politician with no prior military experience, J. C. Dobbin was not an obvious harbinger of naval reform. A lawyer by training, the thirty-nine-year-old navy secretary did have the advantage of being an honest and intelligent man and, perhaps most important of all, he possessed the full confidence of President Pierce and his administration. In the months ahead, he would need to muster all the support he could and focus his considerable energy on his latest challenge, managing the Navy Department.[4]

* * *

The organization that Dobbin aspired to reinvigorate inhabited the old Navy Department building, which after decades of continuous tenancy "was by now well-worn and somewhat dilapidated." Fifty years later historian Oscar Paullin wrote this description of it:

> The only Navy Department building was about two hundred yards west of the White House. It was built of brick, and was one hundred and sixty feet long and forty-five feet wide. It was originally two stories high, with a basement and an attic. It was divided throughout its length by a broad passage; and in the center of the building was a "spacious staircase."[5]

In early 1853 the entire personnel of the Navy Department, including the navy secretary, the bureau chiefs, all their respective clerks, messengers and draftsmen, and those attached to bureaus totaled sixty-one.[6] Most but not all were housed in the Navy Department building. The Bureau of Ordnance and Hydrography had occupied their own nearby quarters since 1844 and the attached personnel of the Bureau of Construction, Equipment and Repairs (BCER) were housed in rented rooms in "Winder's Building," just across 17th Street from the Navy Department. Still standing today (circa 2019) and home of the U.S. Trade Representative, the Winder Building was first opened for business in 1848 and at the time, was the largest and tallest office building in Washington. Later purchased by the federal government, it is one of the capital's few surviving antebellum office structures and has been faithfully restored by the General Services Administration to its nineteenth-century appearance.[7]

It was in the Winder Building that Chief Constructor John Lenthall kept his office. Also sitting there were other BCER attached personnel including Engineer-in-Chief Charles B. Stuart and Chief Engineer Benjamin Isherwood. The same Washington directory that confirmed Lenthall's office location also documented that by the year 1853, he was again living in the old King house on F Street, a block away from the Winder Building.[8] What an easy commute!

Lenthall's boss and Chief of the BCER, Commodore William Shubrick, was officed together with most of the other bureau chiefs on the Navy Department building's second floor. Shubrick had served as chief since March of 1852 but that was about to change. Congress' act of 1842 creating the bureau system had stipulated that the chief of the BCER must be a "skilful naval constructor," but the navy secretaries ignored the mandate and continued appointing senior captains—commodores—in their place. But finally, eleven years later, Congress inserted specific language in its general appropriation bill that reiterated the 1842 act's original intent together with the qualifier "instead of a Navy captain" to ensure compliance.[9]

In mid-May 1853, John Lenthall received a private letter from an old acquaintance at the Philadelphia Navy Yard, William Knowles, thanking him for exerting his influence to restore several colleagues to their former positions. Knowles casually mentioned that Francis Grice, the yard's constructor, had the idea that he would be called to Washington as the new bureau chief. Lenthall's friend ended his letter-writing "my sincere wish is to see you there at the head of the bureau, and I cannot think that it will be otherwise."[10]

Motivated by Congress' caveat, Secretary Dobbin moved to appoint a replacement chief. His choice was Samuel Hartt, the resident constructor at the New York Navy Yard. Although Grice was senior by twenty months, whatever forces that had motivated his resignation as chief constructor four years before must have still been in play. Hartt was a good choice. Of all the constructors he had consistently displayed the most interest in the steamers so integral to the Navy's future. Together with Humphreys and Lenthall, Samuel Hartt had been a consistent pick for the boards assigned to advise on the arrangements and specifications of sea steamers. He had designed the Navy's first iron-hulled steamer, *Michigan*, which saw long service on the Great Lakes, and had been intimately involved with the designs of *Fulton II, Mississippi, Missouri, Saranac* and *San Jacinto.* Curiously he had no sailing warships to his credit, but in the mind of a progressive navy secretary like Dobbin, that may have been to his advantage.[11] Hartt assumed his new duties on 1 July 1853, the first naval constructor to become head of the Bureau of Construction, Equipment and Repairs.[12]

One of Hartt's earliest charges from Secretary Dobbin was the 'rebuilding' of the old liner *Franklin*. Using his authority to repair war vessels, Dobbin authorized the recasting of the 1815 vintage 74-gun battleship into a new steam frigate. But the work proposed by the Navy Department was no mere razeeing of an aged liner's hull, it was a wholesale replacement of a ship of one class with another of an entirely different character.[13] On the last day of August 1853, Samuel Hartt, together with Joseph Smith, chief of the Bureau of Yards and Docks, Charles Morris, chief of the Bureau of Ordnance and Hydrography, Chief Constructor John Lenthall and Charles Copeland, a civilian engineer, reported back to Dobbin.

As a substitute for the old *Franklin*, they had "agreed upon a frigate built ship of war, which shall have in addition to her sails an auxiliary steam power to be applied to a propeller." The new frigate would mount twenty-eight 9-inch guns on her gun deck and twenty 8-inch guns, supplemented by up to three pivot guns, on her spar deck. Although not stated, all of these cannons would be capable of firing shells. She would be sized to carry provisions for six months for a compliment of 620 men. Her "auxiliary steam power" was intended to give her a speed of seven knots using a screw propeller that could be "taken above the water when not required for use" so as not to harm her "best possible sailing and working qualities."[14] Although John Lenthall hadn't yet begun drafting the vessel's plans, the scope of this audacious proposal can be grasped by comparing the 'rebuilt' *Franklin*'s final dimensions to those of the old liner. The new frigate would be 265 ft long, 53 ft in breadth, 27 ft in depth and of 3,173 tons burden compared to the original *Franklin*'s 188 ft length, 50 ft breadth, 20 ft depth and tonnage of 2,257.[15] The new ship was a steam-powered super frigate, larger and more heavily armed than any vessel yet built for the U.S. Navy. Because *Franklin*'s rebuilding was tied to the availability of repair funding, her construction progress at the Portsmouth Navy Yard would be painfully slow; she didn't enter service until after the Civil War. But her design would exert an outsize influence on the Navy's next generation of warships, the six steam frigates of 1854.

* * *

During this mid-1853 period, two letters to John Lenthall provide a glimpse into his standing amongst his peers. The first was a brief message from John Dahlgren, then a lieutenant in charge of ordnance testing at the Washington Navy Yard. Dahlgren asked Lenthall to tell him the English terms for a list of four "French technicalities," such as *serrebauquiéres.* Lenthall dutifully wrote in the answers, in this case, "clamps," strakes fastened to the inside of a ship's side.[16] It is clear that John Lenthall was regarded as the resident authority on the French language. The second communication was of greater significance. In early October, Commander W. L. Hudson, stationed at the New York Navy Yard, wrote a private and confidential letter with the authorization of a "friend" to solicit Lenthall's interest in providing "a full complete and perfect specification" for a 90-gun propeller-driven battleship "to be sent abroad." All of Lenthall's expenses would be met by the unnamed client and the work must be completed before the end of the month. This unsolicited invitation harkened back to Lenthall's earlier days of accepting commercial assignments. It is not known how Lenthall responded to Hudson's query, but given his capacity for work, it is entirely possible that he took the assignment.[17]

Adding to Lenthall's workload that fall was his assignment to a board formed at Congress' request to investigate the recent spate of engine failures. Dobbin appointed the new engineer-in-chief, Daniel B. Martin, Chief Engineer Henry Hunt and engineer Charles Copeland, to determine the reasons for the poor performance of the machinery installed in *Allegheny,* the rebuilt *Princeton* and most recently, *San Jacinto.* Lenthall was directed to advise the board's engineers in his area of expertise.[18]

Continuing his efforts to come to grips with the current state of his department, Secretary Dobbin next solicited the advice of his bureau chiefs about the future directions of the Navy. Two of the chiefs, Joseph Smith of Yards and Docks and Samuel Hartt of BCER, gave him the benefit of their many years of accumulated experience. Smith, whose bureau managed the facilities that actually built the Navy's ships, unhesitatingly promoted the concept of his yards acquiring the capability to manufacture and repair steam machinery rather than, as at present, being forced to rely on the workshops of private contractors. Given Dobbin's directive to the newly appointed board to investigate machinery failures, his point was well received.

Samuel Hartt, chief of the BCER, expressed his desire to fully harness the latest technology—steam power, the screw propeller and shell firing guns—to modernize the Navy by constructing more new ships rather than wasting scarce funds repairing old ones. Taking his cue from the bureau's efforts to design *Franklin*'s replacement, he suggested the building of "six first-class steam propellers" as an initial installment. Hartt had the estimated costs for his new program at his fingertips, calculating their total at $4½ million, of which a third could be met by existing material on hand. Given the navy yards' capacities to undertake such work, about one million dollars would be needed for the next fiscal year's appropriation.[19] Hartt's forthright proposal carried the credibility of his bureau's recent experience.

Dobbin digested his bureau chiefs' wisdom and went to work preparing a draft of the secretary of the navy's annual report to the president. But little more than two weeks before Dobbin's address was due, Bureau Chief Samuel Hartt submitted his resignation. In a letter dated 17 November 1853 that was both apologetic and thankful, Hartt expressed his deep emotions:

> In consequence of an exceedingly severe and frustrating illness, under which I have been a great sufferer, my friends have advised that I should ask for relief from the duties and responsibilities of the office and by doing so, to tender the resignation of the Commission I had the honor to receive from your hands with so much heart felt satisfaction, with so much hope of promise, with so much devotedness to the cause of the Naval Service.[20]

It is clear that the sixty-seven-year-old Samuel Hartt had been ailing for some time and that he had consulted with a number of "friends" in reaching his decision. His resignation was probably not unexpected. Hartt would live for seven more years and continue, in a limited fashion, to serve the Navy. But with his resignation in hand, Secretary Dobbin needed a new bureau chief. It is no surprise that he chose John Lenthall. And he did so without a pause. Bureau chiefs were formally appointed by the president and confirmed by the Senate; in Lenthall's case his appointment was officially dated the day after Hartt's letter. On 18 November 1853, John Lenthall became the chief of the Bureau of Construction, Equipment and Repairs, the second naval constructor to hold that position. He was forty-six years old. The records also show that Samuel Hartt assumed Lenthall's former position, chief constructor, on the date of his resignation.[21] In essence, with the approval of the navy secretary, Hartt and Lenthall exchanged their positions. Although no one could have foreseen it at the time, over seventeen years would pass before Lenthall stepped down as bureau chief. A very long and productive phase of John Lenthall's life had begun.

* * *

A vast new administrative responsibility now rested on John Lenthall's shoulders. As chief constructor, he had fulfilled his ambition to be the Navy's senior naval architect, but as bureau chief he was now expected to manage the affairs, functions and employees of one of the Navy Department's five bureaus. The Bureau of Construction, Equipment and Repairs, as its name implies, was in charge of the designing, building, repairing and fitting out of all the nation's warships. The facilities where this work was carried out were the responsibility of another bureau, Yards and Docks, but the BCER's corps of civil officers, its naval constructors, superintended every detail of this wide-ranging work. In addition, the BCER was entrusted with procuring all the equipment necessary for a ship's construction. This included an enormous variety of material, from the timber to build a hull, the iron and copper work to fasten it, the anchors, sails, rigging and spars to outfit and complete the vessel, and even the coal to power its steamships. The Navy's timber and hemp agents, scattered throughout the southern states, reported to the bureau as did a staff of attached engineers who were charged with overseeing the manufacture, installation and, increasingly, the design of all steam engines and their dependencies.[22]

In the first full year of Lenthall's stewardship of the BCER, he directly managed the activities of a chief clerk, seven subordinate clerks, a draftsman—the stalwart Richard Powell—and a messenger. Lenthall's salary was the same he had earned as chief constructor, $3,000 per annum. His chief clerk drew a salary of $1,800, the clerks and draftsman $1,200 and the messenger $700. Additionally, the chief constructor, now Samuel Hartt, as well as the attached engineer-in-chief, Daniel Martin, and three other Navy engineers all reported to him.[23]

A fuller understanding of the activities managed by the BCER can be gained by examining the responsibilities of those who performed the bureau's administrative work, its clerks. Many years later, John Lenthall described their precise duties in response to a query from the secretary of the navy, and although only five clerks were then employed, their assigned work scopes had not substantially changed:

> Chief Clerk – has charge of the correspondence of the Bureau, supervises, under the direction of the Chief of the Bureau, the duties of the other clerks, prepares the correspondence in conformity with the drafts and memoranda received from the Chief, &c.
>
> Clerk 1 – has charge of all contracts, and transfer accounts between the Bureaus; keeps bill-book for entry of all charges requiring the approval of the Bureau, assists in preparing answers to Resolutions of Congress, &c.
>
> Clerk 2 – assists in the daily general correspondence, prepares schedules for proposals under contracts, verifies calculations connected with proposals, has charge of all records connected with

> apprentices in Navy Yards, keeps the Key Books of correspondence, and performs miscellaneous duties.
>
> Clerk 3 – has general charge of all money accounts under contracts and open purchases; of all accounts of sale of vessels and other property, keeps the accounts of Paymasters, contractors and others, &c.
>
> Clerk 4 – has general charge of all property accounts, and of the monthly and quarterly accounts & returns of stores from the Navy Yards and from all U.S. vessels in commission.
>
> Clerk 5 – keeps the record books of the Bureau, and copies all letters and reports in appropriate books.
>
> Draftsman – prepares all the drawings of the construction and fittings of vessels, and has charge of all the drafts connected with the building and repair of naval vessels. [24]

In addition to managing a bureau, John Lenthall was also responsible for resolving any quarrels or disagreements with the other four bureaus or from the Navy's many opinionated line officers. And with his tenure subject to Senate confirmation, he was now a political appointee. As such Lenthall's exposure to personal criticism, Congressional oversight and the hostile commentary of the press was greater than ever before.

* * *

His administrative distractions behind him, Secretary Dobbin could again focus on the details of his first annual report. His address, which was presented to Congress on 5 December 1853, was the Navy Department's major policy statement for the year and he had a lot of ground to cover. After making the usual introductions, Dobbin pointed out that the number of readily available warships, especially steamers, were inadequate for an expanded nation's needs, stating that the Navy should "at least be large enough to command our own seas and coasts." The solution was not just more ships but demanded a Navy improved by the "inventive genius of the architects of our own and other countries." Here the secretary indulged in a brief diversion.

> Steam is unquestionably the great agent to be used on the ocean, as well for purposes of war as of commerce. The improved system of screw propellers, instead of side-wheels, is one of the grand desiderata to render the use of steam effective in naval warfare, the

> one being exposed to the shot of the enemy, the other submerged, and comparatively secure. When the bayonet was added to the musket, the invention was applauded for placing in the hands of the soldier, at one time, two engines of *destruction*; and the introduction of the screw propeller has been similarly appreciated, as combining without confusion two elements of *progress*—the sail and the steam-engine.[25]

The way of the future was clear. All new vessels of significance constructed for the U.S. Navy would be steamships driven by propellers. Since it was unlikely that ships of the line would ever be built again, the secretary's technical mandate applied to the Navy's future frigates and sloops of war. Secretary Dobbin now focused on the principal object of his address:

> I recommend, therefore, that the Department be authorized to have constructed at least six first-class steam frigate propellers. The opinion is entertained that that number may be built in our several yards, in addition to the work now going on .... It is estimated that they will cost between four and five millions of dollars, and can be built in about twenty months. With the exception of some deficiency in the supply of white-oak and yellow-pine, ... we have on hand, at the various yards, ample material to accomplish what is recommended.
>
> There are two frigates ... on the stocks [which] ...can be altered and ... be most useful substitutes for two frigates of the same class withdrawn as worthless. I recommend that they be thus reconstructed and launched. ... The old ship-of-the-line, the Franklin, is being repaired at Kittery, and her model much changed, with a view of converting her into a first-class steam frigate.[26]

The secretary had proposed a bold plan to build the Navy's next generation of warships and put them into service in less than two years. The kernel had been planted that would ripen into the *Merrimack* class steam frigates. Dobbin also broached the matter of *Franklin*'s "repair," the ready template that would underpin his ambitious plan. Assuming Congress authorized Dobbin's new building program, a major transformation of the U.S. Navy was about to begin.

The House of Representatives sprang into action and reported on a bill furthering the secretary's goals before Christmas. But then the bill languished, not gaining any traction until 21 February when the Senate took up a similar bill and passed it three days later. Notified of the Senate's action, the House debated the bill but then progress stalled.[27]

Just over a week later, the startling news broke, decrying the seizure of the U.S.-flagged mail steamer *Black Warrior* by Cuban authorities in Havana.[28] Strident Young America advocates howled for Spanish blood. At times of foreign provocation, a nation's eyes turned to its navy. In a letter almost certainly inspired by the crisis, three days after *Black Warrior*'s seizure Secretary Dobbin requested bureau chief John Lenthall's views "as to whether ... the steam ships employed in the ocean mail service of the United States are of proper construction to be converted into vessels of war ... and if so, how many and which of them." Lenthall's opinions on this subject had remained unchanged since he first evaluated mail steamers' potential as warships. He briefly laid out his earlier rationale, referring to previous correspondence on the matter, and unhesitatingly stated his conclusion. "Upon these grounds, I am of the opinion that the ocean and mail steamers are not of proper construction to be converted into vessels of war."[29] The full text of Lenthall's response is transcribed in Appendix 4.

Secretary Dobbin was coming to know his new bureau chief's immovable character.

* * *

CHAPTER 18

The Steam Frigates

The *Black Warrior* affair and its implications for national defense motivated Congress to again take up its moribund naval appropriations bill. After additional debate, on the last day of March, the bill passed the House. In its final form dated 6 April 1854, the act of Congress' most significant passage read:

> That the Secretary of the Navy be ... authorized to cause to be constructed for the United States navy, at as early a day as practicable, consistently with a due regard for economy and efficiency, six first-class steam-frigates, to be provided with screw propellers, and properly armed and equipped for service; said vessels and machinery to be built by contract, or in the government navy-yards, as the Secretary of the Navy may think most advisable for the public interest.[1]

Secretary Dobbin's ambitious plan to rejuvenate the Navy had been approved by Congress. The act appropriated a total of $3 million to begin the construction of six steam frigates and for completing two older sailing frigates, *Santee* and *Sabine*. The importance of this act cannot be overstated. It marked a turning point in the development of the United States' steam navy. It not only committed the Navy to a future fleet of propeller-driven war steamers, but it also signaled the end of sailing vessels as effective men of war. Sailing ships would still dominate the Navy's lists for the near future and find employment on remote stations, but they would increasingly be relegated to roles secondary to the all-powerful steamers.[2]

Now that Dobbin's wish list had been granted, the Navy Department was under pressure to perform. And there were risks, big ones. Handed the authority to begin an aggressive program of new building, it had yet to answer for its recent missteps implementing the same new technology that was so integral to its future. The recent spate of steam machinery failures still begged full explanations of their cause. Presumably, the board which Lenthall had been asked to advise would provide guidance. But the Navy's task was clear. It had to convincingly demonstrate to Congress and the public that it was an able steward of public funds and that it could successfully administer its daunting new construction project.[3]

The Congressional act also brought immediate challenges to John Lenthall, who on the date of its passage had been chief of the BCER for just four and a half months. The first was their truncated construction periods, pegged by Secretary Dobbin at "about twenty months." To build a 44-gun sailing frigate in such a short period was feasible, but to construct the larger, more complex steam frigates within the same time frame would be exponentially more difficult. One saving grace was the existence of the nearly complete design of the very similar *Franklin.*

Lenthall's second challenge was that Dobbin had sold the new building program on the premise that "we have on hand, at the various yards, ample material to accomplish what is recommended." By this, he meant the precut, live oak frames for sailing frigates like *Congress* and her sisters. But these ships' hulls were 179 ft long and 46½ ft in breadth; the new steam frigates would closely match *Franklin*'s 265 ft length and 53 ft breadth. Since the existing frames had been trimmed to moulds lofted for the sailing frigates, their use in a larger vessel required that the new steam frigates' hulls must closely conform to the old frigates' lines and that great care be taken when laying out the new frigates' frames to ensure no waste or want.[4]

His third challenge was that while the new steam frigates would not be the first propeller-driven war vessels constructed by the U.S. Navy—*Princeton* and *San Jacinto* preceded them—they were the first class of large warships to be designed and built as 'propellers'. The Navy still had a lot to learn about screw propeller technology, and the engineer-in-chief and his staff were attached to Lenthall's bureau. As chief of the BCER, that meant that the frigates' machinery was his ultimate responsibility.

Lenthall's fourth and perhaps more manageable challenge was that the steam frigates would carry a battery composed entirely of shell-firing guns, placing them among the earliest large warships of any nation to do so. This brought two issues to the fore of supreme importance to naval architects—weight and space. The new shell-firing guns developed by the indefatigable Lieutenant John Dahlgren, the same who queried Lenthall about French technicalities, were both heavier and required larger gun port spacing than did the older 32-pdr broadside guns they replaced.[5]

And finally, John Lenthall, together with the chief of the Bureau of Yards and Docks, Commodore Joseph Smith, was expected to complete a class of six large, technologically sophisticated steam frigates within a fixed budget. This would require a continual, rigid discipline to be exerted over all aspects of the ships' building costs.

Chief Lenthall had his work cut out for him.

* * *

Warships are never built in a vacuum. Their characteristics are driven by perceptions of foreign contemporaries' capabilities, and so it is fair to ask what John Lenthall knew of similar British and French men of war before he began to design the Navy's new steam frigates. He was certainly well informed about the Royal Navy's long experience with steam power, the early stages of which he had witnessed during his European dockyard tour. Since then, Britain had fielded its first prototype screw frigate, *Amphion,* a sailing vessel converted to steam in 1847, and in the years following began vigorous programs of conversions and new buildings, of both two and three-deckers, all to produce a fleet of propeller-driven ships of the line. The Royal Navy's first purpose-built screw line of battle ship, the 91-gun *Agamemnon,* ordered in 1849 and completed by early 1853, proved to be a successful template for future two-decked steam liners.[6] The English naval architect credited with refining her final design, Isaac Watts, was well acquainted with John Lenthall from his tours of British dockyards.[7] In 1852 the British launched another innovative newbuild, *Imperieuse,* the first of a class of powerful 51-gun steam frigates. The French navy had also pushed their line of battle ships into the steam age. One of its notable successes was the 90-gun *Napoléon* which created a sensation by reaching 13 knots during her trials in late 1852. She was designed by young *sous-ingénieur de 1re classe* Dupuy de Lôme who had very recently completed his drawings for the first of a new class of 60-gun screw steam frigates, *Imperatrice Eugénie,* which were part of a group of six ships ordered by the Minister of Marine on 10 October 1853.[8] More will be heard from Dupuy de Lôme in the future. The timing of the French navy's order and Secretary Dobbin's proposal two months later, both for six screw steam frigates, makes for an uncanny coincidence. With his embedded sources of intelligence, John Lenthall may well have heard of the French initiative prior to Dobbin's address to Congress. That Lenthall was familiar with the specifications of the latest European war steamers was documented in a December 1853 exchange of his with Secretary Dobbin regarding *Franklin*:

> The present length of the Franklin is 36 feet more than that of the 90 gun ships built and building for screw propellers in the English and French navies and is 54 feet longer than the 50 gun frigates with screw propellers building in the British Navy.[9]

Recalling *Franklin*'s length was tentatively set at 265 ft, Lenthall was referring to liners of about 229 ft in length and frigates 211 ft long or looking at the table below, the liners *Agamemnon* and *Austerlitz* and the frigate *Imperieuse.* The short answer to the question of just how much John Lenthall knew of foreign practice is quite a lot.

TABLE 18.1 *Steam Frigate Franklin Compared to British and French Contemporaries* [10]

Name of Ship:	*Franklin*	*Imperieuse*	*Agamemnon*	*Imperatrice Eugénie*	*Austerlitz*
Nation:	U.S.A.	Britain	Britain	France	France
Year Launched:	1864	1852	1852	1856	1852
Class:	Frigate	Frigate	Two-Deck Liner	Frigate	Two-Deck Liner
Guns (nominal):	60	51	91	60	90
Speed under Steam (knots):	10.25	9.85	11.24	12.5	10.2
Length (LBP):	265'-0"	212'-0"	230'-0"	245.3'	231.7'
Breadth (molded):	53'-0"	50'-2"	55'-4"	47.1'	55.1'
Depth (of hold):	27'-3"	16'-9"	24'-6"	22.3'	27.0'
Displacement (tons):	5298	3345	4614	3797	4467

* * *

Soon after the act of Congress passed on 6 April, John Lenthall together with his fellow bureau chiefs Morris and Smith as well as Engineer-in-Chief Martin were verbally informed by Secretary Dobbin of the new steam frigates' principal specifications. Time was short and the Navy Department had much to do if the frigates were to be delivered as promised. The precise technical criteria were later spelled out in a letter by Dobbin to Lenthall written on 10 June 1854, two months after the fact.[11] The central portions of this letter, which could only have been drafted by a naval constructor, were likely composed by Lenthall and inserted into Dobbin's directive to ensure the steam frigates' design basis was properly documented going forward.

Compared to *Franklin*'s design, the frigates' specifications were largely the same but incorporated a number of significant changes. Unchanged was that the new ships were to be auxiliary steam frigates of the first class. They would carry the full spar plan of sailing frigates while their machinery was considered a secondary mode of propulsion. Like *Franklin* they would be fitted with lifting screw propellers so as to not spoil their sailing qualities. But it also meant that they would be relatively underpowered, capable of barely nine knots under steam—*Franklin*'s speed given in the above table was achieved with later steam machinery of twice the power of the engines installed in the new steam frigates. At the time, the auxiliary nature of their engines seemed quite progressive, but in hindsight and as compared to their European peers, it would prove to be their greatest weakness.

The new steam frigates' armament was the same as that planned for *Franklin*. In the matter of stores and manning, however, the new ships were to carry provisions for only five months, not six, and be crewed by 560 men rather than 620. These reductions, which implied savings in water tankage, meant the new frigates would be burdened with less deadweight than *Franklin* and could therefore be slightly smaller.

It is widely accepted that Lenthall used the lines plan for *Franklin*, which had been completed in February 1854, as the basis for the new steam frigates' lines. The first of the class, *Merrimack*, was nearly eight feet shorter and three feet less in breadth than *Franklin*, probably reflecting a desire to take advantage of reduced deadweight. She was the first to have her keel laid, on 11 July at the Boston Navy Yard.[12] The subsequent four vessels, *Wabash*, *Minnesota*, *Colorado* and *Roanoke*, were somewhat longer, nearly matching *Franklin*'s 265 ft, with the latter two ships being a foot greater in breadth than their sisters. These four frigates, also named after American rivers, were assigned, respectively, to the Philadelphia, Washington and the Norfolk Navy Yards, with Norfolk building the last two. The sixth steam frigate, *Niagara*, was a different beast altogether. George Steers, the creator of the cup-winning yacht *America*, was engaged to design her and the resulting ship, a huge steam sloop, bore little resemblance to the double-banked frigates that came from John Lenthall's drawing board.[13]

The ships' great length meant that Lenthall was faced with a familiar challenge, that of designing a wooden hull strong enough to resist the inevitable hogging stresses. As he had done before, he specified that two sets of iron diagonal strapping, crossed on the inside, be bolted into the hull's oak framing, running from below the turn of bilge, up to the spar deck clamps.[14] That two of these vessels lasted into the next century demonstrated the efficacy of his solution.

How did Lenthall model the frigates' hulls? He was constrained, as naval architects always are, by the specifications of the ships he was creating—their capacities, overall dimensions, service requirements and so on. But more invisibly, he was tightly bound by the mandate that he use the precut live oak frames, and nowhere did this show itself more than in the frigates' lines. Their resemblance to the last sailing frigate laid down, *Congress*, is striking. The frigates' hulls displayed significant deadrise, easy bilges, pronounced tumblehome and full waterlines with a slight hollow fore and aft. Aft under their counters, Lenthall arranged a rectangular well above the propeller aperture to allow their lifting screws to be hoisted clear of the water. Aside from this feature, the latest trends exhibited by steamer hulls—flat floors, hard bilges, straight sides and sharp ends—were notably absent. For this, he would be roundly criticized by his rivals. But all things considered, John Lenthall designed a magnificent class of warships. They were truly his masterpiece. With their gradually increasing sheer and enclosed heads, these handsome steam frigates were widely admired. They also marked the end of an evolutionary line, that of the American super frigate, which had begun sixty years before with Joshua Humphreys' *United States*. It is fitting that John Lenthall, who had served as an apprentice to Humphreys' son, Samuel, was the constructor who created the last of their kind.

* * *

During the summer of 1854, John Lenthall suffered the passing of two people particularly close to him. On the 29th of July Captain William Easby died of bilious fever at the age of sixty-three. His death was particularly wrenching as it came just a month after his only daughter's wedding. Easby, a self-made, self-educated entrepreneur in the mold of the father Lenthall hardly knew, had been a mentor to young John. After leaving the Washington Navy Yard, Easby went on to manage his own nearby shipyard and was a willing public servant, his last position being commissioner of public buildings. Easby's son, John Ward, had begun his apprenticeship under John Lenthall's supervision at Philadelphia; years later, he would become a naval constructor and ultimately, chief of the Bureau of Construction and Repair (see Appendix 12). Captain Easby remains were interred in Washington's Congressional Cemetery.[15]

Just a month later, the Lenthall family was rocked by an even more intimate death. Joseph Eck, the brother of Lenthall's wife Mary, died suddenly at the age of thirty-nine. His wife Ellen survived him together with their five children, aged six to eighteen. Living in distant St. Louis, the fatherless Eck family would be of constant concern in the years to come to both Mary and John Lenthall.[16]

* * *

But the workings of the Navy Department refused to pause for anyone. A week after Joseph Eck's death, on 6 September 1854, John Lenthall was appointed to a board to examine plans and proposals for steam machinery intended for the new steam frigates. The board also included Engineer-in-Chief Daniel Martin and four other engineers.[17] As bureau chief supervising the engineers' work, Lenthall bore responsibility for their decisions. The story of these ships' machinery is a complex tale in itself—the frustrating and hesitating development of early marine steam engines—but is regrettably beyond the scope of this book.[18]

During the antebellum years, navy yards built many of the lightships so necessary for the safe navigation of America's coastal waters. Acting on recommendations from the lighthouse board, orders for the little vessels were placed with the BCER which designed them and supervised their construction. Once completed, the Treasury Department reimbursed the Navy for their costs, placed them in service and operated them.[19] Accordingly, on 13 September 1854, John Lenthall received orders from the Navy Department to issue instructions for the building and equipping of a second class (150 ton) light vessel at the Philadelphia Navy Yard.[20] Eleven months later, Lenthall reported back to Secretary Dobbin, advising him that *Light Ship No. 2* had been completed, "the whole cost of which, for materials and labor, is 16,194.07, which I respectfully request may be refunded from the Treasury Department ..."[21]

The seemingly dry papers that recorded the lightship's expense data provide an unexpected glimpse into how John Lenthall, with little more than a year under his belt as chief of his bureau, exerted constant vigilance over the costs reported by his constructors. Lenthall's quoted costs were filed in his personal papers folder "Light Ships 1854-55," which also contain tables of mould loft dimensions, cost calculations and other papers related to lightships built at Philadelphia, all under the watchful eye of constructor Francis Grice.[22] A companion folder, "Nantucket Shoals Lightship 1855-56," holds similar documents for lightships built at the Portsmouth Navy Yard by its resident constructor, William Hanscom.[23] And here is where it gets interesting. Portsmouth completed the lightship *Nantucket Shoals* on 22 December 1855 and Constructor Hanscom duly submitted his tally of her costs, which totaled $48,550.36. But six months before, Grice had completed a sister vessel at Philadelphia, *Light Ship No. 1*. His total cost was $26,956.07, almost half of Hanscom's. Lenthall pounced on the gross discrepancy and scribbled a note of complaint on the cost estimate's final page, immediately under Hanscom's signature. "The cost of this vessel is outrageous, as will be seen by examining the cost of exactly similar vessels built in Philadelphia Navy Yard. /s/ JL." Just how Lenthall relayed his displeasure to the constructor is not known, but more will be heard from William Hanscom in the coming decade.

* * *

Progress with the first of the new steam frigates, *Merrimack*, kept pace with the Navy's aggressive schedule. On 14 June 1855, she was successfully launched before a huge crowd of enthusiastic citizens at the Boston Navy Yard. Over the following months, her boilers, engines and shafting were hoisted into her belly while workmen swarmed the decks above to complete her outfitting. After a strenuous final push, on 20 February 1856, *Merrimack* was commissioned as a U.S. warship by her recently appointed commander, Captain Garrett J. Pendergrast. Then she was hurriedly prepared for sea trials.

Five days after her commissioning, America's first screw-propelled steam frigate slipped her fasts and nosed her way through Boston's harbor. *Merrimack* was deeply laden, drawing seven inches more than her designed draft of 23 ft. Amongst those on board was her constructor, Edward Delano, Engineer-in-Chief Daniel Martin and Mr. Lawson, a representative of the company that manufactured her machinery. After a promising burst of speed in smooth water, she paused to drop off day passengers, then under sail and steam, she disappeared over the Atlantic's eastern horizon.[24]

Engineer Martin, who was attached to Lenthall's bureau, managed to hastily compose a brief report to his chief and pass it on to a debarking passenger:

> The ship is exceeding all expectations ... I have just had the Log hove twice, the first 9"6, the second 9"4 ... Revs 43. Engines working well and plenty of steam ... She will I think exceed all our expectations, but you must make allowances for the excitement everybody appears agreeably disappointed.[25]

Four days later, *Merrimack* still at sea on her trials, Lenthall received what must have been an unexpected letter from Captain Pendergrast's wife, Virginia:

> If you have not already seen the Boston Post, pray get it. I see the pleasing account of your noble ship—It is indeed most flattering & I trust my dear husband knows how to take care of so fine a ship.[26]

Meanwhile, *Merrimack* plunged eastward through the wintery ocean, her deck log recording speeds between ten and twelve knots. But her trials program allowed for only one week at sea—a key contract requirement for her engine builders—and so late on the second day out, Captain Pendergrast altered course towards the Virginia Capes. It was shortly after she changed her heading that *Merrimack*, under steam and sail, experienced a burst of fifteen knots, the highest speed yet, and then began to roll heavily in a cross sea.[27] As she drove south, the weather gradually moderated and after several days under easy steam, she anchored in Hampton Roads on the afternoon of 3 March. Later that evening, Captain Pendergrast took up his pen, informing Secretary Dobbin of *Merrimack*'s safe arrival and that he found her to be "eminently successful in all respects."[28] He also dashed off a message to John Lenthall, opening with the flattering words, "Make yourself easy about this ship—she will prove a monument to your fame."[29]

And following soon on the heels of Pendergrast's letter, came a missive from Captain Francis Gregory who, until he fell ill, was originally slated to be *Merrimack*'s captain. "I believe she will, with proper management, astonish the naval world and I shall never be satisfied until she has a chance to exhibit her qualities fully."[30]

But the many detractors of the Navy's big frigates had been sharpening their knives. Following the spread of rumors about *Merrimack*'s trial performance, in late March a derogatory article appeared in the popular journal, *The Scientific American*:

> We have been informed, in a private manner, for the correctness of which we will not vouch, that the machinery of the *Merrimac* proved, on the late trial, to be a miserable failure; that the highest speed obtained was nine miles per hours, and forty-five revolutions of the propeller per minute, while the average speed was given as only seven miles per hour. If this is so, she is a disgrace rather than a credit to the country, and the treasury has been robbed for her construction more than it ever ought to be again for such a purpose.
>
> It is a singular fact that no public statement of the speed of *Merrimack* has heretofore been given. What does it all mean?[31]

The anonymous author was almost certainly John W. Griffiths, a talented naval architect renowned as the designer of the clipper *Sea Witch.* He was also the publisher of an influential monthly magazine, *The U.S. Nautical Magazine and Naval Journal,* and an ardent critic of the Navy's failure to embrace more progressive design practices.[32] Like so many other characters in Lenthall's story, more will be heard again from John Griffiths. And seemingly in anticipation of his unanswered question, a well-timed response appeared in the April 1856 issue of the highly regarded *Journal of the Franklin Institute.* The article began by acknowledging the significance attached to *Merrimack*'s performance:

> The recent successful trial trip of this vessel of a week at sea, is of more than usual importance, from the fact that she is the first of five vessels (almost identical in size and having the same power and armament), now building by the Navy Department, all of which will be in service during the year 1856.

Having opened by describing the trials as "successful," the article offered a positive assessment of the speeds achieved by *Merrimack*:

> On the trial trip she easily made under steam and sail, 15 knots per hour, and 9½ knots under steam alone in smooth water, having a full complement of men, stores, &c., on board and 600 tons of coal. When it is considered that this vessel is 700 tons larger than any of the Collins' steamers, is 6 feet wider, and draws 2 feet more water, and that she has a little more than half the power, her performance is one with which the Navy Department may well be pleased.[33]

In all, the *Journal of the Franklin Institute*'s article robustly defended *Merrimack*'s trial results. However, recall that John Lenthall was a Franklin Institute life member and that the article presented trials data recorded by Martin and in the ship's deck log that was invisible to the public, raising the possibility that the Navy may have been behind it. One area of vessel performance not yet addressed by media critics was that of *Merrimack*'s hull form and its motion responses. But true to form, John Griffiths could be relied on to weigh in on that subject:

> We observe that mention is made in the log that *Merrimac* rolled very deeply—rolled badly, &tc.; we inferred as much from the model when the ship was first in frame. The bottom of the body of the ship is too sharp for the position of the center of gravity, and the proportion of breadth given. Great deadrise, or sharpness of floor is

> a bane of the naval service, whence it found its way into merchant shipping where it has been thoroughly exploded. A vessel with great deadrise will not carry a deck load of merchandise with ease and safety in rough weather, and a battery of guns carried on the sides is infinitely more detrimental and dangerous to such a ship. ... It would not surprise us if the model ... should be found altogether antiquated for success.[34]

The great deadrise Griffiths described was a direct consequence of Constructor Lenthall's conundrum of how to model a large steam frigate using frames cut for sailing frigates of an older vintage. *Merrimack*'s deep rolling occurred when she was unable to change course and caught in "the trough of the sea." According to Pendergrast she rolled no more than a sailing frigate.[35] A warship's primary mission is to accurately aim and quickly fire her guns. The subsequent service records of *Merrimack* and her sisters leave little to suggest that excessive motions, roll or otherwise, prevented them from fulfilling this most basic function.

* * *

As a class, *Merrimack* and her sisters ably met the requirements of their auxiliary screw steam frigate design specifications. They were powerful, staunch capital ships but were hobbled by a lack of speed caused by the secondary role assigned to their steam propulsion. The big frigates had varied antebellum careers, three serving as foreign squadron flagships. They sailed and steamed far and wide, winning praise and admiration. But they were soon taken out of commission because of their high maintenance costs and the Navy's dearth of enlisted men.[36] As magnificent as they were, the steam frigates were an evolutionary dead end. The Navy's next class of new-buildings, the smaller, more versatile steam sloops, could perform their same tasks and do so far more economically.

The Civil War fates of two of the steam frigates would, in a manner unforeseen when they were originally conceived, exert a profound influence on John Lenthall's career. *Merrimack*, the lead ship of the class, was early in the war converted by her Rebel captors into an imperfect but powerful next-generation ironclad ram. Her dramatic success at Hampton Roads forced Lenthall to come to grips with the dawning of a new era of naval warfare. And her sister *Roanoke*, third of the class to commission, would serve as a vehicle for Lenthall to field an ironclad of his own conception. *Merrimack* has been described by some historians as a "ship of destiny." [37] This was so true, not only for the steam frigate but also for her designer, John Lenthall.

* * *

CHAPTER 19

The Steam Sloops

In the wake of the excitement over *Merrimack*'s trial voyage, Secretary Dobbin requested John Lenthall to report on the strength of the Navy's fleet and measures in hand to ensure a ready supply of seasoned timber. Securing funding for the six new steam frigates was a vital first step in rebuilding the Navy, but Dobbin was convinced that there was more to be done.

Writing on 18 March 1856, Chief John Lenthall began by listing the numbers of ships in service as well as those on the stocks or in ordinary that could be repaired at a reasonable cost:

There will then be	5 Ships of the Line mounting		420 guns as
at present rated,	9 Frigates	"	456 "
	18 Sloops of War	"	362 "
	2 Brigs	"	10 "
	7 Steam Frigates	"	202 "
	11 Small Steamers	"	82 "

> Of these vessels three of the ships of the line, and two of the steam frigates are on the stocks; of those afloat four of the frigates, nine of the sloops of war, and five of the small steamers will require costly repairs but they cannot be abandoned until there are other ships to take their places.

Lenthall also confirmed that ample supplies of seasoned live oak were available, enough to build at least eight sailing sloops of war and eleven frigates, two sea steamers and a number of smaller classes. Contracts were in hand to ensure their timely replenishment.[1]

Over the past two years, Secretary Dobbin had tirelessly campaigned for Congressional authorization of a new class of screw steam sloops to compliment the Navy's steam frigates. Lenthall's response reconfirmed his judgement. Apart from the alarming state of the Navy's existing sloops of war—all were sailing vessels and half of them unfit for service—it had become increasingly clear that more sloops—steam powered and drawing less water than the big frigates—were necessary to defend the nation's coasts. This was especially true for the shallow southern ports and harbors. America's greatly expanding maritime commerce, now flung across all of the globe's oceans, was also woefully short of protection. The big frigates were too few and too expensive to fill this role, but steam sloops with their smaller crews and lower costs could ably perform this vital mission.[2]

Following his second annual report to the president in 1854, Secretary Dobbin responded to Congressional queries by spelling out just the sort of vessels he believed the Navy needed: seven well-armed lighter draft steam sloops. He even tried to leverage the availability of live oak frames as a cost-reducing factor, much as he had done with the steam frigates. But Congress failed to bite.[3] Had the funds been forthcoming, the Navy's idea of what it wanted to build were steam-powered versions of its large sailing corvettes, like the razeed *Macedonian* and Lenthall's new *Constellation.* Gun calibers and weights had steadily increased and with the introduction of shell-firing guns, any new sloop's gun deck needed more room than ever, wider gun port spacing and clear areas fore and aft for pivot-mounted chase guns. All these features, together with a steam power plant meant a bigger ship.[4]

Other forces were at play, demanding new types of steam war vessels with minimal drafts. American merchantmen sailing off the coasts of China had for years been harassed by pirates. With even more U.S.-flagged vessels now at sea, their owners clamored for protection. Stephen Mallory, chairman of the Senate Committee on Naval Affairs, asked the Navy Department to advise of the costs for a light draft steamer capable of operating against the Chinese pirates. John Lenthall composed the Department's response; it was dated 5 February 1857:

> The lightest draft of water for an efficient armed vessel for this purpose would be about 9 feet, mounting a long 24^{pd} on a pivot, with two 24^{pd} howitzers and two 12^{pd} boat howitzers for landing. The estimated cost of such a vessel completed is 120 thousand dollars.
>
> It is respectfully suggested that if a draft of water of 12½ to 13 feet can be permitted such a vessel could be armed with a long 32^{pd} on a pivot and with 4 light 32^{pd} in carriages and boat howitzers for landing. The estimated cost for this vessel is 193 thousand dollars.[5]

Nothing came of Lenthall's proposals although vessels resembling those envisaged by his second suggestion would materialize in the not too distant future. But other cross-currents were at play in the minds of the government and especially Congress. In the preceding fall, the Pierce Administration had been voted out of office and Secretary Dobbin would soon be replaced. His entreaties to rejuvenate the Navy, spurred by recent threats to American interests in the Caribbean, finally found traction during the last days of the 34th Congress. On 3 March 1857, it authorized the expenditure of one million dollars for the construction of five large screw steam sloops of war.[6] It was a triumph for Secretary Dobbin although he had no time to savor it. He retired from his office three days later and returned home to North Carolina, only to die in August from tuberculosis.[7]

* * *

Unlike the steam frigate appropriation three years before, the Navy had the gift of time to consider just what sort of ships it wished to build with its unexpected windfall. Contributing to its inertia, March also brought a fresh administration to Washington, that of President James Buchanan. It also meant that John Lenthall now had a new boss. The incoming secretary of the navy, Isaac Toucey, was a Connecticut native and a veteran politician. On the surface he appeared to be as well qualified for the office as was James Dobbin, but he was the servant of an indecisive president and so, lacking a passion for naval matters, he ably performed his duties but without the creative zeal of his predecessor.[8] Bureau Chief Lenthall must have felt some anxiety over the change of administration but he came through it unscathed.

Three months after passage of the act authorizing the steam sloops, the following excerpt from a letter by John Lenthall to Secretary Toucey made it clear that the Navy had yet to firm up its specifications for the new ships:

> It is respectfully requested that the Naval Bureaux connected with the Department may furnish the following statements, viz., the gross weight of the guns and ordnance equipment of all kinds for the 16 9-inch guns with which it has been proposed to arm the steam propeller sloops of war; the height of the lowest port sill above the load line and the draft of water the sloops ought to have for the most advantageous military services and purposes of the navy, also the total compliment such armed cruizing vessels should have together with the length of time for which they should carry provisions and water.[9]

Apart from the number and caliber of the main battery's guns, the principal criteria driving the sloops' hull size were still undecided and required extensive input from naval officers. Stymied for the moment with the steam sloops, Lenthall pressed ahead with schemes to better utilize the Navy's existing assets. That same day he presented Secretary Toucey with an aggressive plan to razee the old frigate *Savannah*, one of the Navy's many ships in urgent need of extensive repairs:

> By removing the bulwarks and ports on the spar deck and taking off the light guns carried on it, the ship can be made to mount 22 9-inch guns carried on the main deck with 2 10-inch chase guns on the weather deck, which is a more formidable armament than she now carries; the increased distance between the ports gives a greater facility for working the guns, a less number of men will be required, being thus much more comfortable, and the provisions and stores will last for a proportionally longer time; the reduction of the top hamper and the lowering of the boats will enable her to carry sail longer and to be more weatherly; the draft of water will not be increased, and in all respects it is considered the vessel will be more efficient.[10]

Lenthall's plan would result in a more formidable, efficient and seaworthy vessel that required a smaller crew. It represented a well thought out scheme to leverage the capabilities of Commander Dahlgren's technologically advanced shell guns that were now entering service. It also embodied core elements of the Navy's vision for a powerful single-decked fighting ship that would surface again in the five new steam sloops. Lenthall's proposal was accepted by the Navy although the converted *Savannah* carried a weaker main battery than that outlined by Lenthall.[11]

Two months later, Chief Lenthall floated another proposal, this one to convert the old 74-gun *Columbus* into an auxiliary steam frigate "as has been done with many such vessels in the English and French navies." Again, Lenthall had a ship on his hands that needed extensive repairs but which was now obsolete. His scheme employed much of the same persuasive logic that underpinned his proposal for razeeing *Savannah*, the result being a useful steam frigate of the largest class. As a selling point, Lenthall noted that all the work could be done at the Norfolk Navy Yard, where *Columbus* now lay, "and the steam machinery can be made in that yard, bringing the expenditure altogether under control."[12] Lenthall's proposal demonstrates he was not against converting sailing vessels into steamers *per se*, but that he opposed doing so, as in the case of Grice's steam frigates, if the resulting vessel would not prove to be an efficient and capable addition to the fleet. As for *Columbus*, the Navy declined to act on Lenthall's plan.

* * *

The Navy had won Congressional approval to build its five new steam sloops, but it couldn't have foreseen that the nation would fall hostage to a crisis that brought its banking system to a standstill, the Panic of 1857. The government's reluctance to press on with new spending gave the Navy additional breathing space to gather its thoughts on how to proceed with the sloops. In the fall of 1857, a board was appointed to consider the matter consisting of bureau chiefs Joseph Smith, Yards and Docks; John Lenthall, BCER; Duncan Ingraham, Ordnance and Hydrography; and Engineer-in-Chief Samuel Archbold.[13]

The Navy apparently decided to design the steam sloops using an approach similar to that employed by Upshur for the sailing sloops of 1842. One of the vessels was to be awarded to a commercial shipyard "to incite a healthful rivalry between the naval constructors and civilian shipbuilders."[14] And as will be seen, the remaining four would be designed by three different naval constructors, producing a class of ships in name only, each exhibiting significant dimensional differences. Before the board could issue its final opinion, a contract had been signed with Jacob Westervelt of New York, for construction of a steam sloop that would be named *Brooklyn.*[15] She was the first major American fighting ship built outside of a navy yard since the years following the War of 1812.

Of the remaining four steam sloops, the board recommended that the Navy build three 14-gun flush deck vessels and one 18-gun spar decked (or covered deck) sloop. Drafts should range from a minimum of 16 ft to a maximum of just over 18¼ ft.[16] Two of the three smaller flush decked sloops were assigned to the Boston and Norfolk Navy Yards and named *Hartford* and *Richmond*, respectively. *Hartford* was built to plans prepared by Constructor Benjamin F. Delano and *Richmond* was designed by Constructor Samuel T. Hartt, a relative of the former bureau chief. These two sloops were the closest to being moulded sisters, having lengths of 225 ft and breadths of 44 ft and 42 ft, respectively.[17] Although the smallest of the five new steam sloops, these ships were twice as long as Lenthall's *Dale* class of 1838, nearly fifty feet longer than the Navy's last sailing sloop, *Constellation*, and five feet longer than the pioneering steam frigate *Mississippi.*

The remaining two sloops, soon to be named *Lancaster* and *Pensacola*, were both designed by John Lenthall. How he managed to find time to draft their plans given the constant burden of his bureau responsibilities is a credit to his stamina. *Lancaster*, the only one to be completed with a full spar deck, was built at the Philadelphia Navy Yard. She was also the largest of the class, with a length of 235'-8" and a breadth of 46'-0". Her slightly smaller sister, *Pensacola,* was built as her name suggests at the Pensacola Navy Yard. At 230'-8" long and 44'-6" in breadth, she had the greatest displacement of the flush decked sloops.[18]

Lenthall's lines for *Lancaster* reveal a steady progression toward contemporary steamer models, displaying characteristics that might have won a nod from John Griffiths. Her floors, while not flat, now showed only moderate deadrise; her bilges were much harder; her sides nearly vertical until reaching the gun deck elevation, then having noticeable tumblehome. Outboard she resembled a miniature *Merrimack,* with gentle rising sheer and an enclosed head. *Pensacola* was comparable to *Lancaster,* with a slightly greater deadrise and fuller entry lines. The five steam sloops of 1857, known as the *Hartford* class, had not yet fully shed their auxiliary steamer origins, all having a full ship rig and capable of little more than ten knots under steam alone. But as one authority has concluded, these sloops were probably the best warships produced by the antebellum Navy. *Hartford* became a national icon as Farragut's flagship, and they all rendered yeoman service during the Civil War and for many years beyond.[19]

* * *

Following in the footsteps of his predecessors, Secretary of the Navy Isaac Toucey prepared his first annual report to the president. Dated 3 December 1857, he began as usual sketching out the activities of the Navy's forward-deployed squadrons. Locations of special concern included China's coasts and rivers, where England was engaged in hostilities against rebellious forces and American warships had been fired upon by the outlaws' barrier forts. Unrest in the Caribbean littoral and General Walker's filibustering also received mention as did the Navy's efforts to explore South America's Paraná and Paraguay Rivers. He then reported on the Navy's progress implementing the construction of the five new steam sloops, but reminded his audience that the act authorizing them "did not admit of the construction of small steamers of light draught, which are very much wanted in the public service." Leaving aside the foreign areas of conflict, the Navy had few war vessels "that could enter most of the harbors south of Norfolk." To redress this glaring national vulnerability, the secretary urged consideration of a "class of steamers, of light draught, great speed, and heavy guns." Toucey concluded that "economy, efficiency, and utility, combine to recommend them as almost indispensable. Ten of them would be of incalculable advantage to the naval service, and would cost $2,300,000."[20]

As the calendar turned over to a new year and members of Congress began to mull Secretary Toucey's proposal, John Lenthall found himself confronted with a request unlike any other he had received from the Navy Department. It concerned the specifications for a new warship, but not for a steam sloop or a light draft steamer, but something altogether different—a 131-gun ship of the line for the Ottoman Empire. How did *that* happen?

It seems the Turkish sultan, in his enthusiasm to bring advanced technology to his sprawling realm, desired that his navy possess an American-built ship of the line. His appeal was transmitted through the U.S. resident minister, James Spence, then back to Washington where it was favorably received by members of Congress. And so, in spring of 1858, John Lenthall was ordered to confer with Rear Admiral Mehmet Pasha of the Ottoman Navy and to respond to his queries. The admiral wanted an outline specification for building a battleship that could be used to facilitate the preparation of bids by American yards.[21]

Chief Lenthall ably replied to his request and on 23 April 1858 forwarded the completed specification to Secretary Toucey. Compared with the sloops he had recently dealt with, the vessel outlined in Lenthall's letter was, quite literally, enormously different. She was a giant 4,700 ton three-decker stretching 283 ft in length, 60 ft in breadth and drawing 25 ft of water. Armed with a combination of 8-inch shell guns and 32-pdrs, she would be manned by a crew of 1,200 and powered by steam engines producing up to 1,000 horsepower. Lenthall calculated the quantity of live oak needed to frame her massive hull to be 70,000 cubic feet, which he wryly remarked "may require the most time to collect." The ship's overall cost, ready for sea, was estimated at $1,600,000.[22]

No such colossal ship of the line was ever built in the United States. What use the Ottoman Navy made of John Lenthall's specification is not known. It was but one more ship design that sprang from the desk of a very busy bureau chief.

* * *

Spurred by indignation over British enforcement of its 'right of search' of suspected U.S.-flagged slavers, on 12 June 1858 Congress coalesced over terms for the coming year's naval appropriations. Their act's final section allowed $1,200,000 for the construction of:

> seven steam screw sloops of war, with full steam power, whose greatest draught of water shall not exceed fourteen feet, which ships shall combine the heaviest armament and greatest speed compatible with their character and tonnage; and one side-wheel

war steamer, whose greatest draught shall not exceed eight feet, armed and provided for service in the China seas.[23]

Navy Secretary Toucey's request for light draft steamers had been honored, but for eight rather than the ten he proposed. Congress also stipulated that they be given "full steam power" and one of them should be a side-wheeler of very shallow draft. Coming on the heels of the five steam sloops authorized the year before, the latest act represented a significant and much needed expansion of the nation's steam navy.

The Navy Department responded quickly to its new remit, giving the strong impression of advance preparation. Echoing Lenthall's proposals to Senator Mallory of the year before, it chose to build the seven screw sloops with drafts even less than the fourteen feet mandated by Congress: four were specified to draw no more than thirteen feet of water and three not to exceed ten feet. All of the class were built by navy yards and the resident constructor at each yard was given responsibility for his ship's design. Chief John Lenthall does not appear to have drawn up the new sloops' plans although he must have been involved with developing their specifications. In contrast to the bureau's handling of the previous class of sloops, much tighter control was exerted over the dimensions of the completed vessels. Their finished lengths and breadths differed only by inches, hardly more than the building tolerances of that era, resulting in a much more homogeneous class of war steamers.[24]

The four sloops with thirteen-foot drafts were assigned as follows:
Mohican to the Portsmouth Navy Yard, supervised by Constructor William Hanscom.
Iroquois to the New York Navy Yard, supervised by Constructor Benjamin F. Delano.
Wyoming to the Philadelphia Navy Yard, supervised by Constructor Francis Grice.
Dacotah to the Norfolk Navy Yard, supervised by Constructor Samuel T. Hartt.

These ships' lengths ranged from 198'-5" to 198'-10½" and their breadths from 32'-2" to 33'-10". Two of the ten foot draft sloops were assigned as follows:

Narragansett to the Boston Navy Yard, supervised by Constructor Edward H. Delano.
Seminole to the Pensacola Navy Yard, supervised by Constructor John L. Porter.

Their lengths varied from 188'-0" to 188'-6" and their breadths were both 30'-6".[25]

The third sloop of ten foot draft was built to a design radically different than any of its six near sisters. Naval architect John Griffiths, the same who had repeatedly disparaged the *Merrimack* class steam frigates and their designer, had proposed to build a twin-screw steamer capable of carrying four 11-inch guns on a draft of less than ten feet. The Navy accepted Griffiths' offer and gave him a temporary appointment as a constructor at the Philadelphia Navy Yard to supervise the vessel's building. She was subsequently named *Pawnee*. To achieve the necessary buoyancy to float her great weight of ordnance, Griffiths' shallow-draft sloop was much larger than any of the other steam sloops, her length reaching 221'-6" with a breadth of 47'. *Pawnee*'s bent frame construction and concave bottom rendered her hull unlike any other built for the Navy.[26]

The eighth steam sloop, a small side-wheeler, was named *Saginaw* and assigned to the new Mare Island Navy Yard, to be built under the supervision of Constructor Isaiah Hanscom.[27] Giving weight to the suggestion that the Navy had prepared itself for Congress' approval of these vessels, all were laid down before the end of the year, a remarkably fast reaction by the bureau and its constructors.[28]

Seven of the steam sloops of 1858 gained high marks for innovation, not from their hull forms or light drafts but because of their armament. Each of the sloops was designed to carry the newly developed 11-inch Dahlgren smoothbore shell gun, the thirteen-foot draft *Mohican* group being armed with two, the smaller *Narragansett* group one, and as originally conceived, the one-of-a-kind *Pawnee* with four. These huge weapons were typically supplemented by four 32-pdr guns mounted on conventional carriages. But what branded this class of war vessels as a paradigm shift was that they abandoned reliance on traditional broadside batteries in favor of a distinctly modern arrangement of centerline-mounted pivot guns.[29]

This fundamental change of how a warship carried her weapons was the result of a revolution in naval ordnance. Starting with Henri-Joseph Paixhans' development of the shell gun in the 1820s, it progressed within the U.S. Navy under the aegis of Commander John Dahlgren. His 9-inch weapons populated the gun decks of the big steam frigates, all mounted on the newer Marsilly-style carriages. But the larger calibers, starting at 10-inch, were too large and heavy for a conventional trucked carriage. The 11-inch Dahlgren that armed the new steam sloops boasted a gun tube weighing 15,700 pounds and fired a shell of 135 pounds. To efficiently handle such a weapon on the moving deck of a ship required a more complex carriage fixed on a pivoting slide structure, one that used compression devices to absorb its recoil. With a gun of over thirteen feet in length and a pivoting slide assembly measuring more than seventeen feet long, such a mounting would simply not fit inside a traditional broadside gun port.[30] It had to be stowed on the vessel's centerline and, because of its weight, close to midship where the hull's buoyancy could support it. When needed for action, the slide was swung to either port or starboard, repositioned and pinned, then aimed out of a specially elongated opening in the ship's side. The size of the new pivot guns meant fewer could be carried, but in theory, that was not a drawback: one 11-inch gun could throw the same weight of metal as four 32-pdr guns. So, whereas the preceding *Hartford* class of sloops carried twenty or more 9-inch broadside guns, the new light draft steam sloops of only marginally less length mounted just six guns.[31] An irony of this class' conception is that the naval appropriations bill authorizing their construction contained language formally codifying the names of the Navy's classes of war steamers according to the number of guns they carried.[32] The lead ship of the class, the 6-gun *Mohican,* could have handily destroyed any of the Navy's existing 44-gun frigates. The era where numbers of guns alone determined a ship's power was rapidly passing into history.

Through its focused efforts to meet Secretary Toucey's call for sloops "of light draught, great speed, and heavy guns," Chief John Lenthall's Bureau of Construction, Equipment and Repairs produced a new class of war steamers with a recognizably modern main battery configuration. Capable of operations in shallow waters, endowed with full steam power and armed with the heaviest guns yet afloat, these steam sloops marked a significant step toward the next generation of warship, turreted ironclads (see Appendix 7). Their evolution was far from complete, however. But it would soon accelerate faster than anyone could have predicted.

* * *

CHAPTER 20

Gloire and Warrior

While the Navy Department's bureau chiefs strove to breathe life into their windfall of new warships, the family of John Lenthall carried on with the everyday chores of a Washington household. Firmly settled into the old F Street homestead, wife Mary was now forty-six and daughter Jenny fourteen. At about this time, John Lenthall's oldest sister, Mary King Lenthall, began occupying a dwelling just next door to his family's 1818 F Street house.[1] When she moved there is uncertain, but it was probably not long after the death of her mother in 1852.

Jenny Lenthall was now enrolled at the Academy of Visitation, a Roman Catholic preparatory school for girls in nearby Georgetown.[2] The attendance of John Lenthall's daughter at this school was, no doubt, due to the will of his very Catholic wife, Mary. In contrast, his sister Mary King Lenthall was firmly established at the Episcopal Church of the Epiphany, across the grounds of the President's House from the Lenthalls' F Street dwellings. She was the church's first organist, and in 1857 she organized their infant class as a separate Sunday school. Affectionately known as "Aunt Mary Lenthall," it is said that mothers brought their children to her "that they might come under the gracious influence of the gentle teacher."[3] John Lenthall and his younger married sister, Mrs. Elizabeth Stone, were also active members of the Church of the Epiphany. Exactly how the various Lenthall clans managed their Sunday morning logistics has not been discovered.

Since late 1857, Lenthall's wife Mary had been engulfed in an evolving crisis three years in the making. After the death of her brother, Joseph Eck, his wife Ellen's health had dramatically worsened. Adding to Ellen Eck's anxiety over her fate and that of her children, amplified no doubt by her isolation in faraway St. Louis, was the decline and death of her own mother. In July 1858, Mary Lenthall received a heart-rending letter from Ellen, its uneven script and ink blots attesting to her infirmity. In it, she darkly wrote "My own health is no good ... it will not be long before I follow mother ... If you will only promise to take care of the children I will die perfectly satisfied."[4] Ellen Eck recovered and lived for ten more years. But the anguish caused by her family's strained circumstances weighed heavily on their kin in Washington, Mary and John Lenthall.

* * *

As 1858 drew to a close and the new year dawned, the Navy Department bent its best efforts toward completing the mass of new construction unleashed by Congress' largess. But as it so labored and with its insular eyes focused on American concerns, events had been unfolding in Europe that would soon exert a profound influence on naval thinking in the United States.

Stepping back five years to 30 November 1853—just six days before Secretary Dobbin made his pitch for the new steam frigates—a fleet of Russian battleships attacked a squadron of Turkish frigates at the Black Sea port of Sinope. In the first real test of their effectiveness, the Russian's Paixhans shell guns utterly annihilated the Ottoman warships. The widely reported action brought shock waves to European naval powers, whose strengths were measured by numbers of 'wooden walls'. And well it should have, for these same major powers, Britain, France and the Ottoman Empire, soon found themselves fighting against Russia in a conflict known as the Crimean War.[5]

Alarmed at the apparent vulnerability of his navy's wooden battleships, the French Emperor Napoleon III requested proposals for shell-proof floating batteries to confront Russian coastal fortresses armed with Paixhans guns.[6] Trials of armor soon followed, leading to the construction of a class of five squat, flat-bottomed ironclad batteries. Hardly proper warships, they were protected by 4-inch thick wrought iron plates and designed to be towed to the theater of conflict, then steam to the battle site and fight while anchored. Despite their shortcomings, three of these batteries went into action on 17 October 1855 against a Russian fort at Kinburn, on the estuary of the Bug and Dnieper Rivers. While their contribution to the fort's reduction has been debated, the batteries withstood four hours of fierce 24-pdr gunfire at ranges of less than 1,000 m with no loss of combat efficiency. The allies' taking of Kinburn did more than demonstrate the batteries' effectiveness; it provoked European powers to embrace the next logical step, an ocean-going ironclad.[7]

But the U.S. Navy, for reasons that are not entirely clear, took little notice of the Crimean War's fast march of technology. True, it had some prior experience with shot-proof ironclads, courtesy of the inventor Robert

Stevens and his futuristic steam battery for which appropriations were first authorized in 1842. However, following his death in 1856, the project lost what little coherence it had and the Stevens Battery's giant hulk was left to rust in Hoboken, New Jersey, unfinished and largely out of mind.[8]

Of all the European powers, France was the quickest to digest the lessons of Kinburn. From that year on it laid down no more new wooden liners, merely completing the older sailing vessel conversions already in hand. Although the war was now over, Napoleon's will to further experiment with armor plating continued unabated. And unheralded at the time, France moved one step closer toward realizing its inchoate vision of a sea-going ironclad by the appointment of constructor Dupuy de Lôme as its navy's *directeur du matériel*, the equivalent of John Lenthall's position as the chief of the Bureau of Construction, Equipment and Repairs.[9] A bold genius of only forty, Dupuy de Lôme had already gained renown as the designer of the highly successful steam liner *Napoléon*, and again with the *Imperatrice Eugénie* class frigates. For the past decade he had promoted the concept of a fast iron-hulled, ironclad steam frigate, capable of withstanding gunfire from any existing battleship. Now the heir to years of armor plate tests, encouraged by the Emperor and superbly prepared by his own experience, Dupuy de Lôme set to work designing just such a war vessel.

One obstacle Dupuy de Lôme was forced to confront was the immature state of France's iron industrial infrastructure. Long a proponent of iron, he had published a set rules for building iron ships following a dockyard tour of England during which he had surveyed Brunel's trendsetting screw steamer *Great Britain*. He was also an advocate, as are most naval architects, of using proven concepts and changing only what was necessary. And so, although he started his design with a clean sheet of paper, he was influenced by his previous creations and sought to improve upon them, striving to do so within the capabilities of France's naval dockyards.[10]

The result of Dupuy de Lôme's labors was a large, wooden-hulled 36-gun steam frigate 77.89 m (255.5 ft) long, 17.0 m (55.78 ft) in breadth and of 7.26 m (23.82 ft) depth of hold. Her dimensions, with the addition of 6 m (19.5 ft) on the waterline, largely mirrored those of his fast battleship *Napoléon*. However, the big frigate had only a single gun deck to protect and was armored from her spar deck to below her waterline with iron plates of 11 to 12 cm (4.3 to 4.7 inch) thickness. She was given engines of 900 nominal horsepower which drove her at a maximum speed of thirteen knots. In the matter of size, the French warship was very close to the U.S. Navy's *Merrimack* class, but she was a fully powered steamer and significantly faster. Dupuy de Lôme's ironclad frigate design formed the basis for three ironclads ordered by the French Navy on 4 March 1858. The first of the class was named *Gloire*. She would steam into history as the world's first ocean-going ironclad battleship.[11]

* * *

Although far away in Washington and busy with his own navy's new building programs, Chief John Lenthall determinedly kept abreast of the latest French naval developments. In his most private of papers, those of the Ives Collection, six pages of technical information on *Gloire* exist. All of their text is in Lenthall's hand and all of it in French. The sheets consist of one page of vessel particulars, a page with a scale of displacement, three pages of weight breakouts and a final page documenting *Gloire*'s horsepower and speed.[12] Lenthall did not date any of the six pages nor did he cite a reference. So, where did he get his data, and how accurate was it?

Since no letters have been found in the Lenthall archives that shed light on these questions, some speculation is in order. The classic work by James Phinney Baxter, *The Introduction of the Ironclad Warship,* offers a clue. Baxter did most of his research in the 1920s and used it to write his Ph.D. dissertation, eventually publishing his book in 1933. He was also fluent in French and made extensive use of France's naval archives. What is striking when comparing Lenthall's six pages of data to page 110 of Baxter's work is that both document the same key vessel data, to the last decimal point, for *Gloire*'s displacement (5617.936 tons), length on the waterline (77.89 m), beam (17 m) and mean draft (7.758 m). Baxter provides a list of the best contemporary publications that issued accounts of *Gloire*, first appearing in 1860, which would have been eagerly sought by a large audience of navalists. But he also says that they were "all, more or less, inaccurate."[13] In answer to the last question above, Lenthall's data is very accurate, conforming to Baxter's summary culled from French navy archives some sixty years after *Gloire* first appeared and to other authoritative sources. He may well have copied his six pages of data from published documents, but if he did, Lenthall was able to sort the wheat from the chaff. Even so some of it, especially the scale of displacement table, presented data seldom published by authoritative sources. So the question of where he got it still lingers. But recall that in the past, John Lenthall had sources of his own fully capable of supplying him with the latest intelligence from France.

* * *

Tidings of the French ironclad building program reached London in May of 1858. The British greeted the news with unease and dismay. Since the Crimean War, France's battle fleet had been allowed to reach near parity with that of the Royal Navy, a disturbing development for an island nation dependent on command of the seas. The additional twist of an ironclad dimension to the threat was even more ominous. As the world's largest navy, Britain had the most to lose by the introduction of revolutionary new technology—the instant obsolescence of her dominant fleet of wooden battleships. By June of that year, Surveyor of the Navy Sir Baldwin Walker admitted Britain's moment of crisis was at hand. In his oft-quoted report to the Admiralty, he stated that the need to counter the French threat had become "a matter not only of expediency but of absolute necessity."[14]

Britain's ability to react was tempered by a number of divergent considerations. Similar to France, her naval dockyards could construct only with wood. However, concentrated within her realm were the world's most capable builders of iron ships. On the Thames, Mersey, Clyde and many other estuaries, shipyards had been fabricating advanced iron vessels of all kinds for decades. Although possessing such a reservoir of experience, the problem of fouling of iron hulls and their need for frequent dry-docking still remained. And with its extensive overseas colonial commitments, the Royal Navy could not afford the luxury, as could the French, of limiting its war steamers to operations in European waters. On the positive side of the ledger, Britain had also conducted its own gunnery versus armor trials and determined the best combination of iron plate and wooden backing. Designs of ironclad war steamers had been considered by the Royal Navy, but absent the need to seize the initiative, such ships existed only on paper. But now, it was imperative that Britain respond "without a moment's delay."[15]

If Britain was to have an ironclad to counter *Gloire,* Surveyor of the Navy Walker had a firm idea what she should look like—an armored version of *Mersey,* the Royal Navy's longest and most powerful frigate to date. *Mersey* and her sister *Orlando* marked the final development of a heterogeneous class of fast war steamers dubbed the big "Walker Frigates" which had been inspired by John Lenthall's *Merrimack* class. In fixing on a single deck frigate configuration for his first ironclad, Walker's thinking paralleled that of his rival, Dupuy de Lôme, although the two men's visions of how their ships should fight differed markedly: the French viewed ironclads as units of a battle line while Walker saw his armored frigate as a tactical addition to Britain's wooden walls.[16]

Integral to Walker's concept was that the gun ports of his powerful vessel should be spaced fifteen feet apart to facilitate handling of her weapons. Given that nearly all the frigate's guns would be mounted on her main deck, this meant a very long vessel. And that in turn, due to hull strength considerations, implied England's first ironclad must be built of iron rather than wood.[17]

Under the Surveyor of the Navy's direction, Chief Constructor Isaac Watts, assisted by Chief Engineer Thomas Lloyd, began work developing a design for the new ship. On 27 January 1859, Walker issued an outline specification for a "Frigate of 36 guns cased with Wrought Iron Plates." It was submitted to eight private yards and seven Royal dockyards with a request for proposals. In the end, none of the designs received, either with wooden or iron hulls, were deemed acceptable. On 11 May the Admiralty awarded a contract for its first ironclad warship, based on Constructor Watts' design, to the Thames Iron Works.[18]

What were the features of the ship Britain had just ordered? Soon to be named *Warrior*, the cased frigate's iron hull was built to a length of 380 ft, a breadth of 58 ft 4 in and a depth of hull of 21 ft 1 in. Externally she was a handsome, graceful vessel, strongly reminiscent of her wooden predecessor, *Mersey*, with a traditional head structure and a frigate's stern. At a draft of 26 ft she displaced 9,137 tons and her compliment totaled 707. She was given engines producing 5,267 horsepower and equipped with a lifting screw propeller and telescoping funnels. *Warrior* was credited with the remarkable speed of over fourteen knots. And despite her being a powerful steamer, she was masted and rigged as an 80-gun ship to facilitate oceanic cruising. Now rated at 40-guns, *Warrior* carried a battery of 68-pdr smoothbores supplemented by the new breech-loading 110-pdr Armstrong rifles.[19]

The novel approach adopted by the Royal Navy to protect its first ironclad from hostile gunfire can only be fully appreciated by examination of her internal arrangements. Of her hull's 380 foot length, only its central 213 feet was covered by 4½ inch wrought iron plates. Transverse armored bulkheads were fitted at each end, creating a citadel enclosing most of *Warrior*'s battery. The unprotected extremities of her hull were minutely compartmented to guard against flooding from battle damage. This arrangement allowed for the concentration of *Warrior*'s iron cladding over her machinery and most of her gun deck, relieving her ends from excess weight. It was a complete departure from *Gloire*'s stem to stern belt of armor, and only feasible because *Warrior*'s hull was constructed of iron and capable of effective watertight subdivision.[20]

In responding to the French ironclad challenge, the Royal Navy countered with a warship superior in every way. *Warrior*'s iron hull was the most technically advanced of any war steamer yet built. She was 125 feet longer than her French rival, with the fine lines and power to steam one knot faster. In battle, she could have picked her range and with her heavier guns, dominated *Gloire*. Her greater capacities, lifting screw and full sailing rig gave her a worldwide potential denied to Dupuy de Lôme's shorter-legged ironclad. And in the matter of durability, *Warrior* takes the palm; she is still afloat and beautifully restored to her Victorian splendor.[21]

* * *

As with *Gloire,* it is instructive to examine just what Bureau Chief John Lenthall knew about Britain's first ironclad. A partial answer lies, once again, within his papers archived in the Ives Collection. Lenthall possessed a document titled "No. 211, An Account of the Quantity and Weight of the Various Articles of Stores, Provisions, &c &c Received on Board Her Majesty's Ship Warrior."[22] This was a four-page standard form tallying all of the weights and stores on board a Royal Navy warship, and was used for the central administration of the Navy Board and its victualling establishment.[23] Lenthall also had 211 forms for four other British warships: *Agamemnon,* a 91-gun screw liner; *Diadem,* a 32-gun screw frigate; *Liffey,* a 51-gun screw frigate; and *Neptune,* an 89-gun screw liner. But the information on a 211 form was confined to a summary of the vessel's deadweight; they contained no design data. Further, as all five of these No. 211 forms were almost certainly sent to Lenthall in 1865 by Donald McKay, they add little to the question of what John Lenthall knew about *Warrior* in the months surrounding her creation.[24] However, McKay's transmittal letter also mentioned how Isaac Watts, *Warrior*'s designer, had been previously acquainted with Lenthall, leaving open the possibility of later contact between the two. Other papers in the Ives Collection give abundant evidence of Lenthall's keen interest in the Royal Navy's iron ships, developing technology and shore establishment particulars.

Did Lenthall ever have the opportunity to inspect *Gloire* or *Warrior*? The answer is "no." He never journeyed back to Europe and neither ironclad visited the United States, although *Gloire*'s sister *Normandie* sailed to Mexico in July 1862, the first ironclad to cross the Atlantic.[25] Lenthall did survey foreign warships when possible and other vessels of interest; he was ordered to New York by Secretary Toucey to examine Brunel's masterpiece, the steamship *Great Eastern,* and to "notice any improvement adapted to the Naval service of the United States."[26]

Beyond what John Lenthall may have known about France and England's first ironclads, the broader question is what trends of importance to world navies were signaled during the course of their escalating rivalry? An obvious starting point was that the introduction of ironclads accelerated the dominance of war steamers with fewer and fewer guns, the corollary being a fighting ship's power could no longer be effectively gauged by her number of weapons. In France, Dupuy de Lôme's 36-gun *Gloire* supplanted his 90-gun battleship *Napoléon,* and in Britain, Isaac Watts' 91-gun *Agamemnon* was rendered obsolete by his 40-gun *Warrior.* The United

States Navy also experienced this progression; its 20-gun *Hartford* class sloops were followed by the powerful 6-gun *Mohican* and her near sisters. As will be seen, this trend became even more embedded as the race between gun and armor intensified.

In turn, European navies' fielding of larger protected ships with fewer guns—ironclad frigates in particular—hastened the erasure of age-old boundaries between the different classes of fighting ships. The navies of the Napoleonic Wars could have conceivably embraced, with a dollop of imagination, an ironclad ship of the line or even a fast steam frigate. But an armored steam frigate that dwarfed a battleship had no place in any fleet's tactical doctrine. Thus, with the addition of each new ironclad, navies were forced to reimagine how they should be used in combat.[27]

A final lesson was the crucial impact each country's infrastructure exerted on its ability to deliver an ironclad. In the case of France, Dupuy de Lôme's conceptual leap of the imagination was hobbled by French naval dockyards' limited ability to construct iron ships. France's first effort, a wooden-hulled fast ironclad, was an instant sensation but an evolutionary dead end.[28] On the other hand, Great Britain faced a similar constraint—its naval dockyards could not build large iron ships—but its technologically advanced private shipyards allowed it to grasp the full potential of a metal hull. Within a very short time, it commissioned the world's first iron-hulled ironclad war steamer.

For those in the United States paying attention to Europe's recent experience, a sobering message would have emerged. None of its navy yards had the ability to construct iron warships. And although its private sector counted a number of shipyards that could build in iron, their capabilities lagged far behind Britain's. The limits of American infrastructure would, as it had with France, constrain the nation's ability to effectively respond to its impending crisis.

* * *

During the same month that Sir Baldwin Walker issued *Warrior*'s design specifications, John Lenthall was obliged to answer a query from the House Ways and Means Committee about the bureau's estimates for the fiscal year ending 30 June 1860. The core question raised was: could he submit detailed estimates for the equipment and repairs parts of his budget.[29] Lenthall's response yields a glimpse into the state of the U.S. Navy during the last of the antebellum years.

First, Lenthall patiently explained to Congress that it was impossible to make a detailed estimate for repairs, which were often unpredictable and varied ship by ship with each year. But he was able to submit an estimate predicated on the previous year's expenditures, which he trusted would be satisfactory. He then ticked off the size of the fleet subject to repairs: nine ships of the line, ten frigates, twenty-two sloops, four brigs, eight receiving vessels and store ships, and thirty-two steamers. Lenthall reminded Congress that appropriations for new building covered only a warship's first cost and not its subsequent maintenance, neatly avoiding the Navy's pernicious habit of 'rebuilding' new ships using repair funds. He further clarified that his figures did not include costs for the ships' armament, which were covered by the Bureau of Ordnance and Hydrography's budget. Then he dove into his assumptions. Lenthall calculated the Navy's steamers were under power a quarter of their time, which meant they consumed a total of 56,000 tons of coal a year. The cost of coal, including freight, lighterage and storage, was fifteen dollars per ton. Add to that 800 tons of hemp (for rope-making) per year at a cost of 250 dollars per ton. Recapitulating his cost data:

For Repairs, Equip^{t}, Stores and Wear & Tear	$2,060,000
" Coal for Steamers	840,000
" Hemp	200,000
Amounting in all to	$3,100,000

The above table concisely summarizes Chief John Lenthall's estimate for the equipment and repairs components of his bureau's expenditures for the fiscal year ending 30 June 1860.[30] Circumstances beyond his control would cause them to dramatically increase during the years that followed.

* * *

CHAPTER 21

War of the Rebellion

As the first year of the new decade began, correspondence covering many familiar issues crossed the desk of Chief John Lenthall. Captains frequently sent private letters to Lenthall, sometimes paying compliments to their commands but often lamenting their poor performance. Captain Thomas Dornin of the screw sloop *San Jacinto* fell into the latter column, writing under the date of 4 September 1860. "The wind on this African coast, where our principal cruising is done, is nearly always very light, and this vessel is good for nothing in light winds ... and we have the necessity to resort to our steam power."[1] Lenthall likely shook his head at this one. There was little he could do about a vessel's dull sailing. And the man who designed *San Jacinto*, Samuel Hartt, was long retired and ill; three months later, he would shed his mortal coil.

But Lenthall had recently heard from another constructor who was very much alive, William Hanscom, resident at the Boston Navy Yard. Hanscom, it will be recalled, was the constructor who submitted inflated costs for his lightship; now, he had lots to say about repairing the old side-wheeler *Mississippi* and the even more ancient sloop of war *Vincennes*. Hanscom ended his letter with a bit of gossip concerning the steam trials of *Pawnee*, one of the new light draft sloops. "The real truth may not appear in the papers. I do not think Griffiths will ask to go out in his ship again. I would not advise him to."[2] The unclarified "truth" was likely connected with the poor performance of *Pawnee*'s novel twin screw propulsion system.

One of Lenthall's escapes from the endless flow of correspondence was his need to sit on yet another board. Richmond's *Daily Dispatch* of 15 September supplied the details:

> In pursuance of a proviso in the naval appropriation act of 22nd of June 1860, the Secretary of the Navy has appointed a board of "naval officers, engineers, and constructors to examine into the condition of

> the sailing vessels of the navy, and the cost of giving them, or any of them, full steam power, together with the expediency of making such changes, in view of the cost, condition, model, and general character of such vessels so altered."[3]

Toucey's new board actually surveyed *all* the Navy's sailing vessels, but concluded it was expedient to convert only the big liners, in which case they would need to be razeed to a lesser rating. This conformed with Lenthall's thinking three years before when he recommended much the same treatment of the 74-gun *Columbus.* By making the recommended conversions, the Navy could get steam frigates to sea that were nearly as powerful as *Merrimack* but cost half as much.[4] European navies were pursuing similar projects and in fall of 1860, the new generation of ironclad warships had only begun to alter the balance: *Gloire* had just completed her sea trials and *Warrior* was scheduled to be launched at the end of December. But rapidly unfolding domestic events would cause the Navy to cast aside any thoughts of upgrading its liners.

* * *

The federal elections of 1860 brought political upheaval unlike anything before experienced in America. On the morning after balloting, the nation awoke to the news that it would soon be led by a president who had won by twenty-seven electoral votes but who was opposed by sixty-one percent of the voters. That new president, a Republican named Abraham Lincoln, had unequivocally voiced his view that slavery was headed toward "ultimate extinction."[5]

South Carolina, long a champion of states' rights, quickly reacted and on 20 December approved an ordinance of secession. Other southern states soon followed. By early February 1861, a constitution for the new Confederate States of America had been adopted and on the 18th, Jefferson Davis was sworn in as its president. Just sixty days after South Carolina's action, the Union was sundered and a nation had been born. America was now a "house divided" and Abraham Lincoln had yet to be inaugurated.[6]

The Navy's constructors were all too aware of the crisis that had overtaken their homeland. Writing from the New York Navy Yard on the 1st of January 1861, Constructor Benjamin F. Delano first wished Lenthall, his wife and daughter Jenny a happy new year, and then got down to business. But after only a page, he changed the subject. "I feel sad in regard to the appearance of things in this country. They seem deplorable and uncalled for." Delano expressed heartfelt sentiments of kindness and moderation, and concluded on a positive note. "I think if you and myself had this trouble to settle there would not be much difficulty in bring[ing] about a good state of things."[7]

The Navy Department's other B. F., Chief Engineer Benjamin Franklin Isherwood, wrote to Lenthall later that month. His ostensible purpose was to ask if Chief Lenthall could help him obtain a new posting by "giving my boat a friendly push." But Isherwood soon veered into current events, expressing a rather darker outlook than Delano. "I hope the political squabble will soon blow over though I confidently expect a civil war sooner or later. No mere patched-up, hollow compromise can cure the disease—it is radical."[8]

* * *

Meanwhile in the nation's capital, members of Congress uneasy about the growing domestic discord expressed their concern over the latest European naval developments. On 19 January Senator Grimes of Iowa tabled a resolution, requesting "that the Secretary of the Navy be ... directed to furnish ... a detailed estimate of the expense of building and equipping a sloop or iron-cased gunboat of the capacity and armament of the U.S. gun-boat 'Iroquois'."[9]

Toucey tasked John Lenthall with addressing the resolution. On 1 February, Lenthall replied to the secretary, first outlining *Iroquois*' specifications then stating that "the least thickness of iron plating that should be put on, is thought to be 3 inches." Because of the plating's great weight and height, "a larger vessel than the 'Iroquois' will be required to carry the same equipment and armament." Lenthall's calculations showed that a single decked vessel drawing 15 ft of water and measuring 1500 tons was needed, the total cost of which would be $558,000.[10] Placing his estimates in perspective, *Iroquois* drew 13 ft, measured 1061 tons and originally cost $323,830.[11]

Secretary Toucey wasn't the only one Lenthall wrote to about the Senate resolution; two days later he penned a reply to an earlier note from his fast friend and frequent correspondent, Captain Samuel Francis Du Pont, then commandant of the Philadelphia Navy Yard.[12] Du Pont would later be tapped to command the Navy's "Great Southern Expedition" which went on to capture Port Royal, but for now, he was just a sympathetic ear.

At the beginning of his letter's second paragraph, the full text of which is transcribed in Appendix 5, Lenthall launched into a discussion about his analysis of an ironclad *Iroquois*. He expressed surprisingly defensive sentiments—namely that "some of those young, smart, modern improvement, spirit of the age fellows should take hold of it"—which would be later misconstrued by others who branded him a hopelessly out-of-touch reactionary. His thoughts were further infected by the possibility he might soon be replaced by the incoming Lincoln administration, a concern clearly expressed at the end of his letter. And he exposed to Du Pont his very human fear of being tainted with failure and overwhelmed by events. Lenthall rationally concluded that absent firsthand experience designing an ironclad warship, he would "prefer to decline combat." In his decidedly pessimistic assessment, we hear the voice of an eminently practical man. He well knew the gravity of the task. But then Lenthall shrugged off his doubts and delved into an engineering analysis of the principal weaknesses of an armored *Iroquois*—insufficient size, excessive roll and extravagant cost. She would be a failure that would smear the reputation of her designer. Lenthall further concluded that because any such armored vessel "should have a covered gun deck," only the largest class would answer. To make *Iroquois* work with the admittedly thin belt of 3 inch thick iron, something bigger than the one-of-a-kind *Pawnee* would be necessary. It was, indeed, "not a matter a prudent person would like to jump into with his eyes shut." Despite his innate caution, Lenthall's dialogue demonstrated that he *had* begun to grapple with issues central to the design of an ironclad.

Lenthall wrapped up his letter with the frank admission that he had packed up his office in the expectation of being replaced by the new administration. His fears were understandable. Such partisan changes were always possible and by this date, Lenthall had been chief of the Bureau of Construction, Equipment and Repairs for over seven years. Events would prove Lenthall to be correct regarding the pitfalls of ironclad design but wrong about the Lincoln administration's intentions; he would retain his position as bureau chief.

Du Pont responded to Lenthall two weeks later, urging him to pursue the matter of an ironclad warship. "Can you not get the seven-sloop bill so amended in the House as to permit the dimensions of one of them to be sufficiently extended to make a proper experiment of iron plating?" But on the day when the bill "was got up and passed," 21 February, Lenthall was at home ill. Du Pont's suggestion sheds a glimpse into the potential reach of Congressional intervention available to a successful appeal. Beyond that, one wonders at how the birth of the Navy's first ironclad might have evolved had John Lenthall been able to exert the influence urged by Du Pont.[13]

* * *

The "seven-sloop bill" mentioned by Du Pont was actually an amendment to the naval appropriations bill for the fiscal year ending 30 June 1862, an act that was hurriedly passed during the final days of the 36th Congress. The amendment's language was identical to that authorizing the seven

1858 light draft screw sloops.[14] Given the turmoil enveloping Washington that spring, it wasn't until closer to the start of the next fiscal year that the Navy Department issued orders to prepare plans for its new sloops.[15] To expedite the ships' construction, it chose to order three of the thirteen-foot draft sloops as repeats of the *Mohican* class. The remaining four screw sloops would be built to a new and larger hull design created by John Lenthall which became the *Ossipee* class, and included *Housatonic, Adirondack* and *Juniata.*[16]

In the waning days of the Buchanan administration an atmosphere of unreality cloaked Washington. By mid-February, the seven deep South states had seceded and formed the Confederacy. Throughout this time of disunion, Secretary of the Navy Isaac Toucey issued no orders to either the navy yards or ships at sea, to place them in readiness for resisting the rebellion. Furthermore, the resignations of officers from seceded states began to arrive on the secretary's desk, all of which were accepted without delay or question. In hindsight, it is easy to fault Toucey's inaction, but he was only following the example of President Buchanan who, although he disapproved of secession, felt his office lacked the constitutional authority to respond.[17]

During this tense period, John Lenthall kept his head down and awaited the changing of the guard, hoping for the best but prepared for the worst. On Monday 4 March 1861, Abraham Lincoln was inaugurated as the nation's sixteenth president. The following day, Lincoln's newly appointed secretary of the navy, Gideon Welles, assumed his duties.[18] By the end of the week, John Lenthall, still sitting at his same desk in the old Navy Department building, opened a letter from Captain Du Pont in Philadelphia. Its post script asked the question on everyone's mind: "Tell me what kind of man is the new chief?"[19]

A native of Connecticut, Gideon Welles was a man of many parts. He was trained as a lawyer but had been the proprietor and editor of a newspaper, a member of his state's legislature and the former postmaster of Hartford. Politics ran in his blood. Welles' appointment had much to do with his being a New Englander and the necessity for Lincoln to have a sectionally balanced cabinet. But what clinched Welles' choice was his stint from 1846-49 as the chief of the Navy's Bureau of Clothing and Provisions. While he claimed no special naval aptitude, his three years' service as a bureau chief ensured he was conversant with the ways of the Navy and of the Washington establishment. This endowed the fifty-nine-year-old Gideon Welles with an incalculable advantage over his predecessors who had lacked such experience. Although presenting a rather outlandish appearance, sporting a full wig and luxuriant beard that gave rise to the nickname "the Old Man of the Sea," Welles was fair and honest, a shrewd judge of character, a tireless worker and a gifted writer. He would prove to be one of the more enduring of the nineteenth-century navy secretaries.[20]

Sensing the growing threat to the Union, citizens of all stripes sent numerous proposals for ironclad warships to the Navy Department. One such suggestion received during the first week of the Lincoln administration was from an aggressive Navy lieutenant named David Dixon Porter, who doubted the efficacy of steel plates but promoted a protective scheme of evenly spaced longitudinal iron bars. The well-known East Boston builder of clipper ships, Donald McKay, wrote on multiple occasions, offering to construct iron-cased corvettes and frigates. Even Welles' confidant, Commodore Paulding endorsed an ironclad proposed for river service.[21]

Early in April, Secretary Welles instructed John Lenthall to prepare the sloop of war *Plymouth*, then laid up at Norfolk, for the annual summer midshipman cruise, further adding to the air of unreality.[22] Naval Constructor Isaiah Hanscom at Portsmouth, brother of William in Boston, contributed his perspective, cautioning Lenthall about Porter's "scheme for an Assistant Secretary to be filled by an old Commodore. I hope it will be prevented."[23] Hanscom's Porter was the same lieutenant who had proposed the dubious method of ironclading; more will be heard from him and of the plan for an assistant secretary of the navy.

A spring of false hopes was abruptly shattered early on 12 April when Southern gunners in Charleston opened fire on Fort Sumter. Beauregard's cannonade blew away any chance for a peaceful preservation of the United States. Hostilities had commenced. The nation would be at war for the next four years. And largely invisible to the public or even to most in government, a forty-year-old ex-Navy lieutenant named Gustavus Fox was foiled in his bold attempt to relieve Fort Sumter. Its defenders lowered their flag the next morning.[24] Fox's patriotic zeal would not be forgotten by President Lincoln.

* * *

But Lincoln's attention was now focused elsewhere. During the week that followed Fort Sumter's surrender, the president and his administration were forced to respond to increasingly grave threats to the Union. On the 15th Lincoln called up 75,000 state militia to aid in suppressing the rebellion. Four days later, against the advice of Navy Secretary Welles, Lincoln's cabinet issued a proclamation declaring a blockade of Southern ports. Welles, who by now knew that his navy had only twenty-four steamers in commission, argued that the government should instead *close* the ports. To declare a blockade without the warships to enforce it would invite the European powers to recognize the Confederacy as a belligerent—which Britain did less than a month later.[25] But Welles lost the argument and so the Navy's war at sea began. In a blink, it was charged with maintaining a blockade of Southern ports scattered along 3,500 miles of coastline.[26]

But the most dramatic catastrophe was yet to come. Distracted by blunders surrounding the confused attempts to relieve Fort Sumter and its Florida counterpart, Fort Pickens, Lincoln had allowed his attention to wander from the biggest prize of all, the Norfolk Navy Yard. Afraid of rousing Virginia's secessionist sentiments, he rebuffed Secretary Welles' urgings to better protect the yard. At stake was the Navy's premier dockyard and ten of its warships, all laid up in ordinary, including the steam frigate *Merrimack*. Then came the news on the 17th of April—Virginia had adopted a secession ordinance. Realizing too much discretion had been left in the hands of the yard's commandant, Commodore Charles McCauley, a man later characterized as "feeble and incompetent," Welles hurriedly dispatched Commodore Paulding and *Pawnee* to the rescue ... but it was too late.[27]

Alarmed by increasingly hostile threats from Virginia militia gathered outside the walls of the Norfolk Navy Yard, McCauley ordered the scuttling of the most valuable warships within its waters—the steam frigate *Merrimack*, the sloops *Germantown* and *Plymouth*, and the brig *Dolphin*—as well as the demolition of the yard's machinery, masting shears and the spiking of its guns. By the time Paulding arrived, the evidence of destruction was everywhere. Quickly concluding that the yard could not be defended, Paulding made the fateful decision to finish the job that McCauley had begun. Before departing early the next morning, he put the torch to all but one of the yard's ships, its store houses, workshops and huge ship houses, and attempted to blow up its graving dock.[28]

The destruction of the Norfolk Navy Yard shocked the nation much as the attack on Pearl Harbor did eighty years later. The U.S. Navy had lost its most capable shipyard, had been forced to burn nine of its warships and surrendered vast quantities of war matériel, including more than a thousand guns, many of them the newest Dahlgren types. All those in the Navy were stunned by the tragic turn of events. The constructor in John Lenthall must have mourned the loss of so many fine ships he had breathed life into: the mighty *Pennsylvania*, his handsome sloop *Germantown*, the powerful frigate *Raritan* and his magnificent *Merrimack*. And at a personal level, the disgraced commandant, Charles McCauley had been a close F Street neighbor of his, living with his family but a few doors away.[29] A small world had gotten even smaller.

* * *

During the tumultuous first months of the Lincoln presidency, John Lenthall and his fellow bureau chiefs anxiously took the measure of their new boss, Secretary of the Navy Gideon Welles. Four of them had been chiefs through two different administrations and Commodore Smith of Yards and Docks even more, his tenure stretching back to 1846.[30] The first surprise to the Navy Department's closely-knit world arrived on the day following the Norfolk debacle—the newest bureau chief, Captain George Magruder of Ordinance and Hydrography, resigned from the service. He and most of his staff joined the Confederacy. Departures of other employees bred uncertainty and caution among those who remained, further impairing the Department's efficiency. [31] But an even bigger disruption soon followed.

In early May, the Navy Department's chief clerkship became vacant. This position, the navy secretary's chief of staff, had traditionally been awarded to a confidant of the secretary. Welles planned to install a close friend and fellow newspaperman from Hartford, William Faxon, as his chief clerk. But he hadn't reckoned on the political force behind an aspirant for the yet to be created slot of assistant secretary of the navy, Gustavus Vasa Fox. The former Navy lieutenant and leader of Fort Sumter's relief effort was a favorite of Lincoln, who pressed Welles for Fox's interim appointment to the clerkship until Congress could create the assistant secretary position. Gideon Welles understood better than anyone that he needed such an assistant—his workload was crushing and increased with each day—and so after interviewing Fox, he acquiesced to Lincoln's request. But all parties agreed the appointment was temporary until Congress returned in July, and then Faxon would have his promised clerkship.[32]

What did the bureau chiefs think of this new development? Fox was by all accounts an extrovert and most genial, a real storyteller who well knew the business of the Navy. But the chiefs, by law, were individually responsible to the secretary of the navy, not his newly appointed assistant. As Paullin observed, "The only unifying factor in the Department was the Secretary."[33] Now a political favorite of Lincoln's was positioned on the path between them and the man they reported to. Even after Congress later authorized Fox's position, he was described by a confidant as Welles' "able assistant" and the secretary as being the "responsible head to whom all under him owned proper obedience."[34] The evidence is that the bureau chiefs adjusted to Fox and the new organization, but it must have involved a conscious effort by all parties. As for John Lenthall, he had just passed through the experience of replacing his own bureau's chief clerk with the appointment to that position of A. B. Farwell of Maine on 20 April 1861.[35]

The first month of war was not an easy one for the Navy Department. To the natural hurdles of coping with a new administration were added the emotional stresses arising from an armed conflict. The imperative of mobilizing the Navy's resources was amplified by the urgent necessity of buying or building war vessels to enforce a blockade of a magnitude never before attempted. And into the charged atmosphere of a Department struggling with a crisis, yet more schemes of ironclads were received. As before, they were sent on to Chief John Lenthall for comment. Excerpts of his endorsements noted on two such proposals read as follows:

> ... the necessarily large size, the cost and the time required for building an iron cased steam vessel is such that it is not recommended to adopt any plan at present.
>
> The subject of iron clad vessels ... has been freely discussed in European ... journals, but their draft, cost and the time required in the introduction of a new system render it inexpedient at this time to commence such vessels which will require very careful consideration.[36]

Lenthall's views, which were made on 11 May, are best understood as a continuation of those he had previously shared with Captain Du Pont. By that date, one month after the outbreak of hostilities, it was not clear what foe a U.S. Navy ironclad would face. The threat of European intervention was nearly as real as any that could be conceived of arising from a disorganized Confederacy. Should the ironclad be ocean-going or designed to storm Southern harbors? It was also widely believed that the war that had just begun would be of short duration. With the Navy Department overwhelmed by so many immediate demands—getting its warships to sea, building new sloops, converting vessels for blockade duty, expanding its facilities and increasing numbers of personnel—thoughts of leaping into a new ironclad program were chimerical. Lenthall's opinions would be tempered by the changing fortunes of war but for now, he who knew the consequences better than anyone else was amply justified in declaring it "inexpedient."

* * *

CHAPTER 22

The Ninety-Day Gunboats

The Navy's priority during the war's first month was to get more ships at sea to enforce President Lincoln's blockade. But its sailing ships were nearly useless, its steam sloops too few and converted merchant vessels at best imperfect. It is to the Navy's credit that so early on it recognized the urgent need for large numbers of relatively inexpensive, light draft, well-armed war steamers. The steps it took to satisfy that demand epitomized the Union's capacity to swiftly marshal its industrial might to crush the Southern rebellion. Its methods also illustrated how the Navy's insular family of constructors so ably responded to the challenge.

John Lenthall had a clear idea of what the Navy needed and by early May, he had already developed sketches and preliminary arrangements for the new vessel. Historians attribute Lenthall's inspiration to the second class sloop *Pocahontas*, a screw gunboat of 154 ft length, 30 ft 4 in breadth and of 694 tons that was the product of an 1859 administrative 'rebuilding' at the Norfolk Navy Yard. Constructor Samuel Moore Pook had worked up her plans; it was his son, Samuel Hartt Pook, a thirty-four-year-old Boston-based naval architect renowned for designing the clippers *Challenger* and *Red Jacket*, who was summoned to Washington to assist Lenthall in completing the new gunboats' detail drawings.[1]

Representatives of Northern shipbuilders travelled with Pook to Washington to make the case for responding to the Southern crisis with an ironclad. Secretary Welles sensed that at this moment, it would be a step too far. However, Lenthall's scheme to field a fleet of gunboats offered a swift answer. But with both Norfolk and Pensacola occupied, the Navy's remaining yards had little spare capacity. Private builders were the only alternative. So great was the sense of emergency that the Navy decided to begin the acquisition process without prior Congressional authorization.[2] By late May Lenthall's new engineer-in-chief, Benjamin F. Isherwood, had drafted specifications and contract provisions for their machinery, aided by his recent work on a pair of Russian gunboats.[3] Advertisements for them soon appeared in national newspapers.[4]

Meanwhile, Samuel H. Pook beavered away under Lenthall's direction, producing drawings and building instructions for the new gunboats. The vessel he designed was a wooden-hulled screw steamer with a length of 158 ft 4 in, breadth of 28 ft, draft of 9 ft 6 in and displacing 691 tons, equipped with 400 horsepower engines capable of ten knots, and armed with a pivot mounted 11-inch Dahlgren, two 24-pdrs in broadside and a 20-pdr rifle chase gun. The gunboats stepped two masts and were rigged as topsail schooners. While characterized as "small" these warships were of nearly the same length and breadth as the Navy's first screw steamer, the sloop of war *Princeton.*[5] Although hurriedly designed and built, they presented a jaunty appearance with a raked funnel, pronounced sheer and a short bowsprit.

By late June, the Bureau of Construction, Equipment and Repairs was ready to execute contracts for its latest class of war steamers. Over the next two weeks, twenty-three contacts were signed, each with a different shipyard. Legend has it that the number built was governed by the quantity of available slipways. Terms of the first four contracts required completion within ninety days, hence the popular moniker of 'ninety-day gunboats'. The first one finished and class namesake, *Unadilla,* took ninety-three days to commission. Of the twenty-three gunboats ordered, a total of seventeen entered service before the year was out.[6] This remarkable achievement was a testament to the organizational skills and technical prowess of John Lenthall's bureau, the Navy Department and American shipbuilders.

On the date the last gunboat contract was signed, 10 July 1861, Secretary Welles appointed Commodore Francis H. Gregory to oversee their building and equipping. As the shipyards were scattered along the Atlantic seaboard, Gregory was authorized to establish his headquarters in New York City and was assigned four principal inspectors, each covering a different region. The formerly retired Gregory, a seventy-one-year-old veteran of the War of 1812, now had the prime responsibility for supervising progress on the Navy's new gunboats. His General Superintendent's office would gain even greater importance as the war progressed.[7]

* * *

May of 1861 had been a busy month for John Lenthall, and he had more than just the ninety-day gunboats to occupy his attention. On 6 May, Secretary Welles ordered him to prepare plans for the seven screw sloops authorized in late February by the outgoing 36th Congress.[8] As the Department had already decided to handle three of the new ships by repeating earlier designs, Welles' latest directive spurred Lenthall to complete the drawings for the final four sloops which would later be known as the *Ossipee* class. Improved versions of *Mohican* and her sisters, the new sloops measured 205 ft long, 38 ft in breadth and 16 ft 9 in depth of hold, their fuller lines yielding a displacement of 1,934 tons. They carried the same basic six-gun armament centered on two pivot mounted 11-inch Dahlgrens.[9] Before the month was out, Lenthall had been ordered to issue directions for building the seven sloops at four navy yards, two each at Portsmouth, Boston and Philadelphia and one at New York, the latter yard alone in not receiving a repeat *Mohican*.[10] A week later, Welles assigned names to the seven sloops, the repeat sloops being named *Kearsarge, Wachusett* and *Tuscarora*, and the class of larger sloops *Ossipee, Housatonic, Adirondack* and *Juniata*.[11] Curiously Welles' letter spelled the name of what would become the most famous of these ships, *Kearsarge,* as *Kearsage* ... but spelling was fungible in those days. Progress with the seven sloops reflected the exigencies of war: *Kearsarge*'s keel was laid before May was out and all but two of them were laid down before the end of June.[12]

As May closed out, Secretary Welles took steps to tighten the rules governing the Navy Department's office. Its new hours ran from 9 a.m. to 4 p.m. (instead of 3 p.m.), no absences were permitted without approval, only visitors on public business were allowed in the office and clerks who were behind in their work had to stay late until it was finished.[13] New Chief Clerk Gustavus Fox was unimpressed with the Department's protocols, remarking "that a private concern would be ruined by conducting business as it is carried on here."[14] Two days later, in further recognition of the war emergency and its effect on the Department's outdated budget, Welles requested his bureau chiefs to prepare supplemental estimates for his submittal to Congress, both for the current and upcoming fiscal years.[15] The chiefs' work never ended.

Bureau Chief John Lenthall's expertise was sought not only by the Navy but also by the U.S. Army. Its campaign to suppress the rebellion along America's vast inland system of rivers prompted the Army's chief engineer, General Joseph G. Totten, to ask for his advice. In a memorandum written on 1 June 1861, Lenthall provided design guidance for a war steamer suitable for Mississippi River service. His response was remarkably detailed and included building directions, specifications and a sketch for a 170 ft long side-wheel steamer configured with "both ends of the vessel to be alike, and a rudder at each end." This was a harbinger of what would later be called a 'double-ender', the focus of the Navy's next new building program. Lenthall was astute enough to identify the biggest problem facing any designer of a shallow draft river steamer—obtaining adequate hull strength to resist longitudinal bending moments. Lenthall offered an honest assessment:

> It is difficult for anyone practiced in sea-going shipping to give precise instructions for river boats, as no doubt the experience of persons engaged in this kind of work has led them to many things that are not to be reached in any other way.

In closing, he recommended the services of one of his constructors then on the Ohio, Samuel M. Pook, father of the naval architect drafting plans for the ninety-day gunboats. Lenthall described Pook as "an industrious man, and to be relied on."[16] The steamer proposed by John Lenthall never materialized, but Pook later designed an ironclad on similar principles, known as "Pook's Turtles," that formed the basis of St. Louis boat builder James Eads' successful city class river ironclads.[17]

Requests began to flow in from others seeking to tap Lenthall's influence. Delaware native Captain Samuel Du Pont, still at his post in the Philadelphia Navy Yard, asked "if we could not have one or two of those Gun Boats built on the Delaware."[18] A colleague from many Navy boards, engineer Charles Copeland, wrote from New York offering to sell the Department two steamers.[19] And Rosina Easby, the wife of Lenthall's former apprentice, John Ward Easby, sent letters seeking for her husband "an appointment under government … as he desires and is fitted for." She stated that he could be reached at their Washington home, on G Street between 20th and 21st Streets, which she and her daughters had been compelled to leave because of "our immediate neighborhood being occupied by the soldiery."[20] The Easbys' address was only two blocks north-west of Lenthall's F Street home and very close to where the old Lenthall houses stood.

* * *

The stress of war creates surprising alliances and exposes hidden animosities. By mid-1861, John Lenthall had been an employee of the Navy for twenty-six years and dealt with innumerable active-duty naval officers. Some like Captain Du Pont became long-lasting friends while others harbored bitter grudges. Falling into the latter category was a newly promoted commander whose name has been previously mentioned, David Dixon Porter. Now captain of the steamer *Powhatan* on blockade duty off the mouth of the Mississippi, on 5 July 1861, Porter addressed a private letter to a former naval officer and old colleague who had been recently elevated to a position of power and influence, Gustavus Fox.[21]

David Porter came from a distinguished naval family, was esteemed as an aggressive war-fighter and served the Navy well during the Civil War. In the years that followed, he was promoted to admiral and briefly reigned as the *de facto* secretary of the navy. Given this perspective, what he had to say about John Lenthall is all the more shocking:

> I see by the papers that Lenthall, Chief Naval Constructor, has issued bids for building the new steamers [ninety-day gunboats]. I don't wish to do any man an injury, and when I do it, I do it openly and don't care a snap of my finger who knows it. That man Lenthall has been an incubus upon the Navy for the last ten years. ... Now this man Lenthall is a creature of Mallory; Mallory got him there, Mallory kept him there in spite of all his miserable doings. Mallory and Lenthall had their heads together months before these difficulties took place, and they were plotting at the time to throw as much of the Navy as possible into the hands of traitors— When it was proposed to Lenthall to have the Merrimac towed up from Norfolk, he said it was impossible to move her, and he delayed the work on her ... If any one will go into an investigation of those matters, he will find that there has been a regular system in the Bureau of Construction to embarrass the Navy, when the time should come for action— Lenthall was moving heaven and earth to have Navy Yards put under the control of Constructors, and get the Navy Officers put out, for his own ends and those of traitors,— ... Get Delano, now at New York, put in the Bureau (and you can do it), and everything will go right. ... And then too we are hampered with that little fellow Isherwood, who will take all the signs in Algebra to prove how many ten penny nails it will take to shingle a bird's nest ... and yet can't make an engine— He was an engineer with me 9 months. I took him out of the engine room for incapacity, he may have improved since—pity that a country like ours with so much talent in it, can't produce better results in the Navy.[22]

Porter was generous with his bile—he defamed not only Lenthall but Isherwood too. His hateful accusations were unsubstantiated but contained just enough truth to give them the cloak of plausibility. As chief of the Bureau of Construction, Equipment and Repairs, John Lenthall was necessarily in touch with Florida's Senator Stephen R. Mallory, who until the war broke out was the chairman of the Senate's Committee on Naval Affairs. Immediately after the Confederacy was formed, Mallory was appointed as its secretary of the navy. He was reviled ever after throughout the Union but especially by naval officers.[23] And John Lenthall, civilian bureau chief of a department dominated by line Navy officers, was frequently at odds with them especially over matters of concern to a naval constructor. His advancement to chief was undeniably aided by Congressional pressure to "get the Navy officers put out" and replaced by constructors. But he always conducted himself as a dedicated and loyal public servant.

After he retired, Porter penned a well-received book titled *Naval History of the Civil War.* His handling of John Lenthall on those pages adopted a tone entirely different from that he had used writing to Fox:

> The chief constructor of the navy, Mr. John Lenthall, ... was at that time the ablest naval architect in any country having built some of the most effective ships afloat. ... Mr. Lenthall, a constructor of the highest order, was always ready, with his practical skill and science, for any emergency. He had planned the great frigates ... "Merrimac" ... which had elicited the applause of the world. He planned the "90-day gun-boats" ... and their value could not be over-estimated.[24]

More could be quoted, all of it flattering. Perhaps in belated recognition of his excesses, Porter did offer a *mea culpa.* "Time is a great promoter of good feeling and softener-down of asperities, enabling a writer of the present day to view things in a different light from what he did twenty years ago."[25] A final observation from a biographer of Porter's places his villainous accusations in context. "Porter fired words like grapeshot, indiscriminately and in haste, often regretting rash comments."[26] As the war progressed, more harsh criticism would be hurled at Bureau Chief John Lenthall but none was so personally vindictive as Porter's.

* * *

In early July, Secretary Welles requested John Lenthall to provide a summary of all the contracts his bureau had entered into since 4 March, the start of the Lincoln administration. The specifics of Lenthall's response yields an interesting snapshot of the bureau's volume of activity which was just beginning to ramp up in response to the war:

- Four charters for shipments of coal, totaling 4,675 tons, ranging from $7 to $12 per ton depending on the destination.
- Four contracts for steam machinery for the repeat *Mohican* class steam sloops (by this date a fourth sloop, *Oneida,* had been added), at a total cost of $412,000, or about $103,000 for each engine.

- Twenty-one contracts for as many ninety-day gunboat hulls, totaling $1,121,500, or about $53,500 for each hull.
- Ten contracts for seventeen of the gunboats' steam engines, totaling $776,000, or about $45,500 for each engine.[27]

Of the coal shipments, three were to foreign squadrons and only the fourth, dated on 5 July, was to the Gulf of Mexico littoral. Most but not all of the ninety-day gunboats' hulls and machinery had been contracted but the engines for the *Ossipee* class steam sloops had yet to be ordered. Lenthall's summary represents a total of thirty-nine separate contracts, each of which had to be drafted, negotiated and signed, all within a space of four months. It was a blistering pace and would continue to accelerate.

The Navy Department's next big project was its 'double-ender' class of steam gunboats. As the name suggests, this class of vessels was designed with light draft hulls featuring nearly identical lines fore and aft, with a rudder at each end and their side-wheel machinery arranged amidships. Drawing their inspiration from harbor ferries that never needed to turn around, they were intended to bring the war to the shallow rivers and estuaries of the South. John Lenthall's first participation in a Navy steamer design was with Samuel Humphreys on *Fulton II*, which was conceived of as a double-ender, so he was familiar with the concept and had only recently suggested it for use on the western rivers.

The ordering pattern and design methodology employed by the Bureau of Construction, Equipment and Repairs for this class was markedly different from that used for the ninety-day gunboats. Although the first class of double-enders totaled twelve vessels, they were a mix of nine similar but not identical designs. Further, nine of the so-called *Octorara* class were constructed in four different navy yards with the remaining three contracted to private builders. And while their plans and building directions were prepared under the direction of John Lenthall, each vessel was designed by the constructors or civilian naval architects at their different construction sites.[28]

The namesake and smallest of the class, *Octorara*, was 205 ft long, 34 ft 6 in breadth, 12 ft depth of hull and displaced 981 tons. Drafts among the twelve hulls ranged from 8 ft to 10 ft. Their dimensions made these inland waters war steamers longer and beamier than the *Mohican* class sloops; the increases were necessary for them to float on much lighter drafts. *Octorara* mounted an 80-pdr at one end and a 9-inch gun at the other, with four 24-pdrs in broadside. The double-enders were powered by inclined direct-acting engines, which gave them a speed of 11 knots. Although fitted with two masts and a fore and aft rig, their shallow hulls made them poor sea boats and even worse sailing vessels. The gunboats' "double-bowed" configuration did not lend itself to a pleasing profile, Gustavus Fox describing them as clumsy and ugly. Newspaper advertisements for their construction appeared in August; all of them were laid down and five of them had been launched before the end of the year.[29]

In that same August, a board was convened to look into the matter of a new class of "fast screw propeller steamers." Its goal was to implement Congress' latest authorization for an extra seven steam sloops. The board's focus on speed was "in consequence of the representations of many persons that much faster vessels than those in the naval service" were needed. To this end, the Department had advertised in mid-July for ships capable of fourteen knots under steam alone, but John Lenthall and his engineer-in-chief, Benjamin Isherwood, subsequently found that none of the submitted proposals were satisfactory.[30] This board was one of the first on which the newly installed assistant secretary of the navy, Gustavus Fox, exerted his opinions over vessel design; they were largely directed at the class' armament and appearance. The sloops arising from its deliberations, known as the *Sacramento* class, were essentially repeat *Ossipees* with an extra 20 to 27 ft added to their midship sections, having lengths of between 225 and 232 ft, breadths of 38 ft and depths of hold of 17 ft. The sloops' extra length was used to add a third centerline pivot-mounted gun, a 150-pdr Parrott rifle, forward of their two 11-inch Dahlgrens, a culmination of a trend first seen on the *Mohican* class. Further accentuating their unconventional armament, these ships were initially given no broadside guns, although this decision was soon changed. And despite the board's original emphasis on speed, none of the class achieved better than twelve knots. As for Fox's influence on the sloops' appearance, several of this class featured a near plumb stem with no traditional knee or bowsprit which, together with their minimal barquentine rig, gave them a severe, futuristic profile.[31] One wonders how Lenthall and the other Navy traditionalist felt about the assistant secretary's design preferences...or that he chose to interfere.

The Department reverted to its light draft steam sloop protocol to build *Sacramento* and her near sisters—all were designed under the direction of John Lenthall and all were constructed in navy yards. *Monongahela* and *Shenandoah* were assigned to Philadelphia and their plans came from the hands of Constructor Henry Hoover; *Lackawanna* and *Ticonderoga* were given to New York and designed by the capable B. F. Delano; *Canandaigua* was built at Boston according to drawings produced by William Hanscom; and *Sacramento* was assigned to Portsmouth and Constructor Isaiah Hanscom. Despite the navy yards' heavy workloads, three of this class were laid down in 1861 but only one, *Canandaigua*, was in commission before the end of 1862.[32] And to round out the Congressional authorization, a seventh sloop, a repeat *Mohican* named *Oneida*, was assigned to New York.

* * *

Chief John Lenthall's first year at war was his busiest yet. Looking back at his bureau's accomplishments since the formation of the Confederacy, its record was nothing short of astonishing. Starting in February 1861, the following classes of war steamers had been authorized, designed and assigned for construction, either in navy yards or private shipyards, twelve of which were in commission by 31 December of that year:

- Four *Mohican* class screw sloop repeats, all to navy yards.
- Four newly designed *Ossipee* class screw sloops, all to navy yards.
- Twenty-three newly designed *Unadilla* class ninety-day gunboats, all to private shipyards.
- Twelve newly designed *Octorara* class double-enders, nine to navy yards, three to private builders.
- Six newly designed *Sacramento* class screw sloops, all to navy yards.

All forty-nine of these ships were substantial vessels, adding an aggregate of 238 guns to the fleet. The fourteen screw sloops, many of which served for decades after the war was over, ranged in size from 1,500 to 2,500 tons. Even the smallest, the ninety-day gunboats, rendered invaluable service during four hard years of blockade duty, several of them later venturing as far as China and Japan. Each one of these warships were either designed by or under the direction of John Lenthall. And he managed to do it all during a period when his bureau was confronted with countless other strenuous demands—repairing the Navy's existing vessels, refitting many of the seventy-nine purchased merchant steamers, chartering shipments of coal, acquiring shipbuilding timber and more, and as will be seen, learning how to design an ironclad.

Once it had recovered from its initial stumbles, the Navy Department's performance during its first year of war was commendable. Considering that two of its six Atlantic coast yards were lost to the enemy, it ably ramped up production at its remaining facilities and before the year was out, had started construction of all nine of its double-enders and most of the fourteen first-class steam sloops. But all of the forty-nine new vessels authorized in 1861 were built of wood, including those assigned to civilian yards. This put an intolerable strain on supplies of shipbuilding timber, especially seasoned oak. Lenthall was already addressing concerns about availability of white oak in July of that year.[33] The shortages would become worse as the war continued, the remedies being the use of green timber or building with iron—and only private shipyards could do that.

On 7 November 1861, Flag Officer Samuel Du Pont led a large fleet of U.S. Navy war steamers in an assault on the Confederate forts guarding Port Royal, South Carolina. His flag flew from the *Merrimack* class steam frigate *Wabash*, and his flotilla included four recently commissioned ninety-day gunboats, *Unadilla*, *Ottawa*, *Pembina* and *Seneca*.[34] Two weeks after his successful action, Du Pont took up his pen and addressed a five-page letter to John Lenthall. After describing his ships' battle damage and much else, he closed with the following mellow thoughts which stood in stark contrast to those of another active-duty naval officer, David Porter:

> One word now about your gunboats, they have now been tried every way, and they have come out nobly ... It is strange I should have had so much to do with your naval architectural creations—first on the Minnesota, then the Wabash, and the gunboats. You remember the armament in the East place an emblem or symbol of profession on a man's tombstone. Your head board shall be a model of this ship or the Minnesota, and I would put an Ottawa or Seneca for the foot stone. But long may these honors be deferred my friend; besides you must give us an iron clad ship, which if relatively equal to the above, you will be ready yourself to depart in peace.
>
> Yours faithfully,
> S. F. Du Pont[35]

* * *

CHAPTER 23

The Ironclad Board

During the same mid-summer special session of Congress that authorized the extra *Sacramento* class steam sloops, Secretary of the Navy Welles was directed to appoint "a board of three skilful naval officers" to evaluate proposals for armored steam batteries. Further, should the board report favorably $1,500,000 was appropriated to build one or more of them. The motivation for this legislation, which was championed by the same Senator Grimes of Iowa who in January had enquired about an iron-cased *Iroquois,* was to protect American harbors in the event that "a conflict with some foreign Power might grow out of our present complications." Although Grimes' bill was introduced on 19 July 1861, eight days after Confederate Secretary of the Navy Stephen Mallory approved the conversion of *Merrimack*'s charred hull into a shot-proof steamer, the North was at best only dimly aware of the potential threat that she would represent. But the menace of Britain and France's recent *de facto* recognition of Jefferson Davis' government coupled with the might of their sea-going ironclads was all too real.[1]

The Congressional directive, which was enacted on 3 August, could not have come at a worse time for Secretary Welles. Congress' special session had also voted to boost his Department's budget from $13.1 to $43.6 million in recognition of its urgent need to build, purchase and equip a massive expansion of the Navy.[2] Welles had suggested as much in his opening address to Congress when he urged their consideration of a process for acquiring ironclads:

> The period is perhaps not one best adapted to heavy expenditures by way of experiment and the time and attention of some of those who are most competent to investigate and form correct conclusions on this subject are otherwise employed.[3]

All of his bureau chiefs were overworked and the Navy was fighting a war. And perhaps remembering the clumsy steam batteries of the Crimean era, there was little passion in the Navy for the harbor defense ironclads that the board would be evaluating.[4] John Lenthall, who would seem an obvious board candidate, was not a naval officer as stipulated by Congress. Besides, he was consumed with supervising the designs of the new screw sloops and double-enders, not to mention the building of twenty-three gunboats. His previous declaration that consideration of ironclads would be "inexpedient" may have lingered in Welles' mind. But there were plenty of naval officers, busy or not, who satisfied Congress' mandate and on 8 August Secretary Welles chose the three who he felt best qualified: Commodore Joseph Smith, Chief of the Bureau of Yards and Docks; Commodore Hiram Paulding, chief of the Office of Detail; and Commander John Dahlgren, the Navy's reigning gunnery expert. But curiously, Dahlgren requested to be replaced and so Commander Charles Davis, a scientifically minded officer who had managed the editing of the *Nautical Almanac*, was substituted.[5]

Welles had already advertised for proposals by parties interested in building "iron-clad steam vessels of war...for sea or river service," requesting that their propositions be submitted within twenty-five days. The specifications embedded in this advertisement indicate that the Navy had already given previous thought to what sort of ship it wanted. A draft range (10 to 16 ft) was called out as were the weight of armament to be carried (80 to 120 tons), crew size (165 to 300 persons), endurance for provisions and stores (60 days) and coal (8 days), and that the vessel should be rigged with two masts. The qualities of the warship so described were similar to but an improvement on those called out for the Navy's second war steamer, *Fulton II*. However, the vessels' most radical feature—their armor plating—was left wholly unspecified.[6]

The ironclad board tackled its assignment with vigor. On 16 September 1861, two weeks after the request for proposal due date, it submitted to Secretary Welles a twenty-page summary which included seven pages of tabular technical detail.[7] Although the board's letter presented an intelligently reasoned overview of ironclad technology and well-conceived suggestions for the Navy's way forward, it opened on a down note. "Distrustful of our ability to discharge this duty ... we approach the subject with diffidence." The three skillful naval officers had hoped to remedy their "scanty knowledge in this branch of naval architecture" by applying for the help of a naval constructor, but were informed that they were "all so employed on important service that none could be assigned to this duty." This is a telling point—it wasn't only Lenthall who was overloaded, but at that moment in time *all* of the Navy's constructors were too busy to be disturbed. But one board member recalled events differently. Commodore Paulding later claimed John Lenthall was consulted about the proposed ironclad models, the bureau chief declaring "it was not his trade and refused by his silence to give either opinion or advice."[8] The truth of the matter probably lay somewhere in between; it's hard to believe Lenthall was never asked for his opinions. And Paulding's account does undeniably invoke the image of Lenthall's father's reticent personality.

Their excuses made, the board tabled multiple objections as to why ironclads, as they perceived them, would not make efficient sea-going cruisers. But the board considered "iron-clad vessels of light-draught ... as very important, and we feel at this moment the necessity of them on some of our rivers and inlets to enforce obedience to the laws." Looking more closely at the range of proposed vessels, which featured both wooden and iron hulls, the board was of the opinion that "it would be well to try a specimen of each, as both have distinguished advocates."

In the pages following its general remarks, the board focused on the plans and offers it had received. But first, it veered into territory beyond evaluation of the recently solicited proposals by suggesting the most expedient way for the Navy to obtain an ironclad warship was to simply buy one from England, noting that "we are assured that parties there are ready to engage in such an enterprise." This was a subtle reference to back-channel communications about the possible supply of an ironclad that had occurred between Lairds, a leading British builder of iron ships, and the Navy Department. Although Welles had "turned them off," his new assistant Gustavus Fox kept the contact alive, surreptitiously encouraging them to bid on a floating battery in the hope "of obtaining something tangible to force Lenthall to work out our greatest want."[9] But Lenthall marched to his own drummer and the board shrank from the potential risks of a foreign contract, observing that "every people or nation who can maintain a navy should be capable of constructing it themselves." Narrowing its scope to choosing from the proposals at hand, the board concluded:

> Our immediate demands seem to require first ... vessels invulnerable to shot, of light draught of water to penetrate our shoal harbors, rivers and bayous; we therefore favor the construction of this class of vessel before going into a more perfect system of larger iron-clad sea-going vessels of war.

In making its final selection, the board admitted the difficulty of striking a balance between a well-armored war vessel and one capable of operating in shallow water. Its three choices, all considered experimental at the time, covered a sensible range of ironclad steam batteries which adhered to its stated general principles. In the order presented by the board and using the names these famous ships would later bear, the highlights of their proposals can be summarized as follows:

Galena, a medium-sized wooden-hulled steamer clad by a "rail and plate system" of armor, was offered for $235,250 in four months' time by C. S. Bushnell & Co. of New Haven, Connecticut. Originally proposed with a length of 180 ft, breadth of 36 ft and draft of 10 ft, this vessel was designed by Samuel H. Pook, the same naval architect who drafted the ninety-day gunboat plans. Despite his credentials, the board expressed their fear that "she will not float her armor & load sufficiently high & have stability enough for a sea-vessel." *Galena* represented an economical solution for an armored steam sloop capable of coastal operations as well as harbor defense. Unfortunately, her system of armor would prove to be a total failure.

New Ironsides, a large wooden-hulled steamer clad by a conventional side belt of armor, was offered for $780,000 in nine months' time by Merrick & Sons, of Philadelphia. Merrick and its predecessor had manufactured steam machinery for many of the Navy's warships, starting with *Mississippi*, and planned to subcontract the ship's hull to Cramp & Sons, also of Philadelphia. The board considered their proposal as "the most practicable one for heavy armor," their main concern being that her contract should ensure she "comply with the specifications." *New Ironsides* was the most expensive selection, but offered a large frigate-sized vessel pierced for sixteen heavy guns and was capable of ocean-going service as well as harbor defense. She most resembled the European approach to ironclads and has been likened to France's *Gloire*. For all her faults, *New Ironsides* would gain the reputation as the most powerful and hard-fought battleship in the Union fleet.

Monitor, an iron and wooden-hulled steamer protected by conventional side and turret armor, was offered for $275,000 in 100 days' time by John Ericsson of New York. Ericsson's steam battery, featuring a revolving turret housing only two guns and mounted on a raft-like hull, was the most controversial of the board's selections. Her designer, known to the Navy from his previous work on the screw sloop *Princeton*, intended to subcontract *Monitor*'s hull, machinery and armor to a handful of experienced New York ironworking firms. The board was "somewhat apprehensive that her properties for sea are not such as a sea-going vessel should possess." Surprisingly, the board committed to the experiment she represented, but only with a contract "guarantee & forfeiture in case of failure of the properties ... of the vessel." Ericsson's proposed steam battery, a radical concept with questionable seaworthiness, was aimed at the shallow water harbor defense role. What must not be overlooked is that *Monitor* offered a relatively low-cost answer to the Navy's need for an ironclad, one that could be delivered in the least possible time.

Finally, mention should be made of a proposal that was not recommended, one from Donald McKay of Boston. The famous clipper ship designer offered a 227 ft long ironclad of 3,100 tons displacement, in essence, a large armored steam sloop. However, her high cost of $1 million, or two-thirds of the Congressional appropriation, precluded further consideration by the board.

* * *

The Navy moved quickly to implement the ironclad board's recommendations. On 21 September, John Ericsson was given verbal instructions to start construction and told a contract would soon follow.[10] Less than a week later, after receiving assurances about her ability to float her armor, the Navy signed a contract with Bushnell for *Galena*.[11] And within a month of the board reporting its findings, Merrick & Sons concluded an agreement to build *New Ironsides*. Throughout, Secretary Welles continued Commodore Smith's oversight of the Navy's first foray into ironclads, vesting in him the responsibility for negotiating their contracts, a function that would normally have been carried out by John Lenthall's Bureau of Construction, Equipment and Repairs.[12]

It wasn't until 4 October 1861 that John Ericsson signed the Navy's contract, which contained the onerous performance guarantees sought by the board. On that date, he submitted amended specifications for his steam battery to Commodore Smith for review.[13] The next day Smith requested the services of Chief Engineer Alban C. Stimers to "superintend the vessel, machinery &c. now rapidly progressing under contract with Mr. J. Ericsson at New York."[14] By his choice of Stimers, who had the reputation of being "a very clever and intelligent man in his calling," Smith set the Navy up for a future store of triumph and tragedy.

It was on or about this time and probably at Commodore Smith's request that the Navy took steps to check John Ericsson's steam battery displacement calculations. Of all the ironclad proposals, Ericsson's merited the closest scrutiny from a naval architect's perspective because of *Monitor*'s uniquely low freeboard, just eighteen inches. Freeboard is the height above a vessel's waterline to the first deck or opening through which water could enter and result in its loss. For a conventional ship, say a sloop of war, the first down flooding point was typically the lowest gunport sill, some eight or more feet above water. But in the case of *Monitor*'s raft-like hull, trouble would begin the instant its top deck became awash. Her minimal freeboard was a feature Ericsson touted as making her impregnable—a hull offering only a low, flat target—but it was also one that worried the skillful naval officers who had staked their reputations by recommending a vessel so vulnerable to loss of buoyancy.

Documents in the Bureau of Construction, Equipment and Repairs' files bear evidence that calculations of the freeboard of Ericsson's ironclad were performed, almost certainly by John Lenthall. The weight of Ericsson's vessel was determined to be 171 tons greater than claimed. Such a calculation would have entailed a tedious compilation of *Monitor*'s lightship weight as well as all the loads normally on board—stores, crew and effects, coal, guns and ammunition. A displacement curve covering the vessel's range of drafts also needed to be calculated. Both of these evaluations were of the sort naval constructors had performed countless times before. Together they showed that the ironclad's excess weight had the effect of "increasing the draft 12⅜ inches, and leaving the *deck only 5⅝ inches above water-line.*" Further, Ericsson's displacement calculations did not take into account an additional 70 tons for masts, spars, rigging, boats, davits and other outfitting items required by his contract. This extra weight ate up nearly all the already too-low remaining freeboard of 5⅝ inches.[15] A naval architect reviewing such calculations would be inclined to conclude that Ericsson's *Monitor*, if delivered in accordance with her designer's specifications, possessed insufficient buoyancy to remain afloat.

At the time and in later accounts of this period, John Lenthall was widely derided for his doubts about Ericsson's ironclad. Admiral David Porter, hardly an unbiased observer, wrote that "Mr. Lenthall, at first condemned the 'Monitor' *in toto*" and "he did not hesitate to say, while she was building, that she would go down as soon as she was launched."[16] Assistant Secretary Fox stated during a Congressional investigation that "Lenthall said the monitors would go to the bottom, and Isherwood had no confidence."[17] But Lenthall, who knew John Ericsson all too well from their cooperation eighteen years before during *Princeton*'s building, had sound reasons for questioning whether the Swedish inventor's latest creation possessed adequate buoyancy.

On 11 October, Commodore Smith informed Ericsson that, based on calculations by expert naval architects, his vessel "will not float with the load you propose and if she would she could not stand upright for want of stability" and reiterated his misgivings about the hull's pronounced overhang. Annoyed by Smith's complaints, Ericsson snapped back at his "absurd statements in relation to the battery" and promised to send clarifying explanations. He later penned his oft-quoted boast that "there is no living man who has tripped me in my calculations or proved my figures wrong."[18]

A copy of the Navy Department's evaluation of *Monitor*'s freeboard was received by Ericsson on 17 October; two days later, he submitted revised specifications for his ironclad. The thickness of her deck plate had been decreased from two inches to one, and the hull's side belt went from six inches to five at the gunwale, tapering down to three inches. Once again, the "expert naval architect" at Lenthall's bureau went to work and quickly calculated that Ericsson had reduced his armor's weight by 172 tons, almost exactly the overweight first identified. Smith accepted Ericsson's changes but only under the proviso that he stood by his guarantee that his ironclad was still shot-proof.[19]

By now Ericsson knew it was Lenthall who was behind checking his figures, and he lost little time in ridiculing Lenthall's calculations as "erroneous from beginning to end." He cited the fact that the thickness of one-inch plate was actually 15/16 inch and that there were many vessel details which had been altered or weren't shown on the drawings. [20] Ericsson took particular glee in calling out Lenthall for having assumed the steam battery was floating in fresh rather than salt water, the difference accounting for two inches of Lenthall's calculated reduction in freeboard.[21] This was a foolish accusation. Salt water is denser than fresh water; its specific gravity is 1.025 and a vessel's draft will be proportionately less in salt water than fresh. But if a naval architect were asked to perform freeboard calculations for a vessel intended to operate in the waters of harbors, rivers and estuaries, whose densities ranged from fresh to salt, the most conservative assumption he could make would be to assume the vessel floated in fresh water, which is what Lenthall did. This second-hand distanced duel between two proud and stubborn naval architects may well have been what crystallized the distrust that became so evident in Ericsson and Lenthall's later relations.

* * *

Despite the ironclad board's good work, it was clear to all that the Navy would need more armored ships. The first three—*New Ironsides, Galena* and *Monitor*—were hurriedly ordered experiments of widely varying designs that had yet to prove their value. Neither John Lenthall or his engineer-in-chief, Benjamin Isherwood, were impressed with *Monitor*. She was not intended for ocean transits, had very poor sea-keeping characteristics and her sole means of offense—a single turret—lacked redundancy. U.S naval constructors, bred in a service largely devoted to cruising on remote foreign stations, would have approached the design of a coast defense ironclad in a very different way. And that is just what happened. John Lenthall together with his engineer-in-chief—under constant pressure from Assistant Secretary Fox—digested the latest developments, evaluated the new technology and returned to their drawing boards.

By November 1861, they had worked up a concept that took advantage of their own considerable experience and drew what they could from *Monitor* and her ironclad cohorts.[22] Lenthall based their new design on a conventional wooden hull with substantial scantlings. Such a hull could be built in a navy yard or by a contractor and was a reliable choice for quick delivery. Its length and breadth were close to Griffiths' *Pawnee* but the hull's depth was slightly less. The need to provide longitudinal strength for a vessel intended to operate in very shallow water was balanced by Lenthall's desire to minimize the height of the hull's armored topsides. Here he found a way out of his perceived need for a covered gun deck from the example of Ericsson's *Monitor*. In lieu of exposed pivoting carriages, armored towers (turrets) now enclosed the ship's guns. But even so, he couldn't avoid the inherent weaknesses of a wooden structure, its susceptibility to rot and that its iron cladding could give "no strength, but is a great tax on that of the ship." Lenthall's path of design evolution, from an iron-cased *Iroquois* to his and Isherwood's new armored steamer, both armed with large centerline mounted guns, is traced in further detail in Appendix 7.

The Navy Department's ironclad was powered by twin screw propellers driven by gearing from a single engine. Coal bunkers were conventionally arranged but featured a distinctive access trunk inboard of the hull's side armor (see Plan No. 12). The flush deck vessel was armed with two guns, 11-inch Dahlgren smoothbores, each mounted inside armored revolving "Cole towers," one forward and one aft, based on the principles of English inventor Cowper Coles, RN. Again, his earlier analysis of *Iroquois* showed itself, for both the steam sloop and the Navy Department's ironclad were designed to carry the same guns arranged in the same positions on their hulls. An armored pilot house was located on each end of the vessel. Taken as a whole, Lenthall and Isherwood's design offered a more ship-like solution as compared to Ericsson's, closer to *New Ironsides* and *Galena*, incorporating arrangements and vessel management features better aligned with conventional U.S. Navy practice.[23]

Lenthall again took up his pen on 18 November and dashed off a private letter to his friend, Captain Du Pont. He had much to discuss for Du Pont's 'Great Southern Expedition' had recently captured the strategic harbor of Port Royal. Matters of fleet logistics and repairs filled his first pages, then Lenthall turned the conversation to the latest happenings in Washington:

> He [Goldsborough[24]] has got Fox and the Navy Department worked up to the boiling point on iron clad vessels, and then he had the hot metal poured over me. I say it is a pretty hard case when in England and France they have been at it for years to set me to work to bring it out in a week or two. Great geniuses may do things in a hurry, but a prudent ordinary man likes a little time to turn it over in his mind, not to make a start where others started, but if possible to start where they left off and use their experience, not buy it new.
>
> Being for harbor use only, the vessel need only be about 3 feet above the water and have two towers on the deck a gun in each. To make such a vessel of wood I find requires a displacement of 2400 tons to get a draft of 12 feet water. The iron on the sides and deck amounts to so much—on the sides 4½ inches, the deck 1½ to 2 inches and the tower about 26 ft diam. at the base weighing from 100 tons each. The iron for the sides, say 5 feet deep or 2 feet under water will be a cube of 10 feet only think of it. That for the decks a cube of 11 ft of wrought iron.
>
> Can any one blame me for not wanting to have to do with such business. It will be the ruin of me. After a thing is done any one can tell how it might have been better. If I ask any one, nobody knows, it is my pidgeon not theirs; then as though I was a balloon, they begin to inflate me, but I see the danger all the same. [25]

Unremarked but hovering in the background, outliers of the *Trent* affair had just appeared in Northern papers. The possibility of British intervention was now a reality, adding to the stress of war. And it is abundantly clear that Lenthall was under great pressure to quickly deliver what the European powers had been working on for years. Lenthall's structured thinking, methodical approach and unease at being rushed are on full display. But then as before, his complaints aired, the engineer took over. Lenthall quickly outlined his design for the Navy Department's new ironclads. His graphic visualizations of the side and deck armor's weight—that of an equivalent iron cube—are both brilliant and effective. But Lenthall's concern with failure again surfaced; the metaphor of being pumped up like a balloon is all too familiar. Within Washington's insular bureaucracy, the long knives were poised and ready for him to stumble.

As the end of 1861 drew near, the Navy Department prepared to construct its self-designed ironclads. Secretary Welles' annual report, delivered on 2 December, requested the incredible sum of $12 million for twenty of them.[26] Building instructions and specifications for the ships' armor and machinery had been issued. House Bill HR 153 authorizing the construction of up to twenty ironclads to plans which had been "perfected" was quickly passed in mid-December and referred to the Senate.[27] In the first days of January 1862, Lenthall instructed the New York Navy Yard to begin the vessels' mould loft work.[28] And on 5 January, he again addressed a letter to Captain Du Pont. First greetings for the new year, then a discussion of coal shipments and floating workshops. At the top of the fourth page, he delved into his new design:

> I have been busy trying to get up the plans for the iron clad steamers. They want them to draw about 12½ feet water and to save the weight, the deck will only be about 2½ feet above the water, having two iron "Cole" towers in each of which will be an 11 inch gun.
>
> The vessel to bear the weight must necessarily be very flat and full and will have two propellers of 10 feet diameter. The side for 5½ feet plated with 4¼ inch, the deck with 1½ inch iron. This requires a vessel of 216 feet long and 48 feet beam. There is a great deal about such a thing that requires careful thinking (at least for me), but it is required to do it at once and right too; no excuses. At this season of the year no one has the materials and men cannot work half the time. Then there are few if any who can manufacture the iron, some can make it in straight plates, but it is a great work to bend it to the vessel. The Department (Mr. Fox) was in a great hurry in the commencement but there seems to be a calming down just at this time, the reason of which is not yet known to me. The shearlatin [charlatan] and sharp men are on hand, and I sometimes think they have bullied them to a halt. ...
>
> Mr. Martin (the former engineer-in-chief) has gone to England and France and Belgium to see if the plates can be had there, which is doubtful at this time.[29]

Lenthall's account repeated a description of the ironclad's features which were little changed since November. The hull's length and breadth were now fixed. A realization that the coming of winter would slow down the work in shipyards is expressed as well as his admission that it was nearly impossible to obtain the ironclads' thick wrought iron plates, either domestically or abroad. Lenthall wanted to clad his vessel with superior single thickness armor as opposed the laminated construction used by Ericsson, but the plates simply could not be manufactured soon enough, especially if they had to be shaped to fit a hull's curvature. And Lenthall's suspicions were well founded. The “calming down at just this time” was because John Ericsson had recently proposed the building of six improved monitors, and his backers—the “sharp men”—were now chasing after Fox and Welles. Ericsson’s offer to deliver the ironclads for $325,000 each and within four to five months’ time had seriously disrupted the Navy Department’s plans. [30] Just how much would soon become apparent.

But by early February, the momentum to build the Navy Department ironclads had most certainly ebbed. Ericsson’s *Monitor* had been successfully launched on 30 January and the Senate was still debating Bill HR 153, which finally passed on 7 February 1862.[31] Secretary Welles was now reluctant to make a commitment. Pressed by the powerful Monitor lobby and concerned about the suitability of its own ironclad program, Welles opined that the Navy Department wished to avail itself of her experience before moving ahead.[32] He would not have long to wait.

* * *

CHAPTER 24

Monitor Fever

On late Saturday morning of 8 March 1862, the Union fleet blockading at Hampton Roads was surprised by *Virginia,* the much-anticipated ironclad resurrected from *Merrimack*'s burned-out hulk. Within a few violent hours, the Southern goliath had rammed and sunk the sloop of war *Cumberland* and set afire the frigate *Congress.* 250 men's lives had been lost in a vivid confirmation of what navies had long known, that shell-firing guns could destroy wooden warships, especially immobile sailing vessels. It was an unmitigated disaster, one that had befallen a navy mortified less than a year before by the humiliating loss of its premier dockyard, just ten miles away. Hours later, Ericsson's *Monitor* arrived from New York, her crew thankful to have survived a near sinking, largely through the efforts of Engineer Alban Stimers. Early the next morning, she was confronted by *Virginia.* During the course of four hours' fierce but inconclusive combat, the two ironclads demonstrated the latest truism of military science, that armor could defeat guns. A new era of naval warfare had begun.

The consequences of the Battle of Hampton Roads, the second day of which was witnessed by Assistant Secretary Gustavus Fox, indelibly shaped the U.S. Navy for decades to come. *Monitor*'s tactical superiority and ease of maneuver in shallow waters stood in stark contrast to the clumsy handling of the frigate-sized *Virginia.* Further, the 9-inch Dahlgrens of *Cumberland* had no visible effect on *Virginia*'s armor, and apparently, *Monitor*'s 11-inch guns caused little damage. Even eye witness Fox admitted "Whether she is injured or not is impossible to say."[1] The logical conclusions were that light draft monitors armed with but two heavy guns could successfully challenge much larger, conventional broadside ironclads and that even bigger guns were needed to defeat armor. But above all else, the inescapable message broadcast to an anxious nation panicked by *Virginia*'s first day of rampage was that John Ericsson's *Monitor* had saved the day.

***

An uneasy stalemate reigned at Hampton Roads. *Virginia* licked her wounds and *Monitor* anxiously stood watch. Accounts of the battle soon appeared in the newspapers, agonizing over the Navy's loss but ebullient at its apparent salvation by the plucky *Monitor*. Largely invisible to the public but wrenching to the Navy Department was the death of Lieutenant Joseph Smith, *Congress*' acting captain. When the news came that *Congress* had surrendered, his father, Commodore Joseph Smith, knew the worst had happened. "If the flag's down, then Joe is dead."[2] It was a cruel reward for a man who, apart from John Ericsson, had done more than anyone else to ensure *Monitor*'s success.

As time went on, the Battle of Hampton Roads underwent a metamorphosis in the popular imagination. The same people who derided the Navy Department for indulging in "Ericsson's folly" were all too eager to heap abuse on it for not having more monitors to confront the Southern menace. "Monitor fever" had infected the nation, many believing that the Union's ironclad, now cherished as a uniquely American creation, was somehow "conceived of ... by the people themselves." [3] The public's eagerness to assign blame for the Navy's shortcomings was captured by an article that appeared in the New England press:

> Hardly had the present Secretary of the Navy been confirmed, when several of the most eminent mechanics urged upon him to have iron-clad vessels built with which to reduce the Southern forts; but the "power" behind him sneered at vessels of this class, pronounced them all wrong upon scientific principles, and not until the fifth or sixth month of the war, did he have sufficient light upon the subject to act. The vessels now under contract will not be finished to be of any use against the rebels, for the war will be finished before they are completed. The Stevens' Battery lies uncompleted because she is iron-clad.
>
> A year ago Mr. Donald McKay submitted the model and specifications for an iron-clad vessel, to be finished in ten months; yet, like others, he was treated with indifference. We state these facts to show that the people have not been slow to appreciate the importance of using every known means to quell the rebellion, but their servants, for want of knowledge, have been guided by the advice of those who are rebels in their sympathies. If this were not so, why were not the Minnesota and Colorado, and vessels of this class, covered with iron to meet the Merrimac? If the rebels could raise a wreck, cover her with iron, and send her down the river in a few months, surely we, who know what was the object of her equipment,

> could in the same time have sent a dozen vessels, all iron-plated, to resist her. Why not rough-plate a dozen at once—why wait to have them cased scientifically?
>
> The publication of Mr. Lenthall's opinion of iron-cased ships of war, would probably show the advice upon which the Secretary of the Navy has relied. It would be of special interest at this time. Mr. Lenthall is the prime Naval Architect at Washington. [4]

If John Lenthall had been so inclined to air his opinion of ironclads, he could not have done better than to publish his 13 March letter to Secretary Welles, written just four days after *Monitor*'s apparent success:

> The Bureau of Construction having in November last, with the sanction of the Department, proposed a plan for an iron plated steam vessel, it is respectfully submitted and requested that in justice to the Bureau there may be a vessel built on the principles of the plan then prepared ... .[5]

Outside of the public eye, and in spite of his many other responsibilities, Lenthall had been hard at work perfecting his and Isherwood's Navy Department ironclad design. The "plan" he referred to represented a considerable body of engineering: "printed specifications of hull, plating, towers and machinery accompanied by photographic working drawings." [6] Lenthall's letter closed by citing details of a proposal from the Novelty Iron Works of New York, which offered to build a vessel to the Department's plan for $530,000 and deliver it in 5½ months' time. The contractor had even "suggested modifications in the plating" which would have overcome the vexing thick plate delivery problem. But the reality was that Lenthall's ironclad would cost more and take longer to deliver than the now-proven Ericsson-designed monitors offered in December—a classic example of advanced technology's ability to deliver a new product more quickly and at a lower cost. Setting aside its feasibility, the extraordinary aspect of Lenthall's plea to Welles was that it marked a rare instance of a Bureau chief begging his superior for permission to build a warship of his own design. He was clearly driven by the emotions of the moment. And this was the "prime naval architect at Washington" who was pictured as "sneering" at iron-cased vessels. In hindsight, it is hard to escape the feeling that Lenthall sensed the inevitable outcome of Hampton Roads and Monitor fever—sidelining the Department's ironclad design in favor of Ericsson's. But being the person he was, John Lenthall refused to concede the field without a struggle.

* * *

Assistant Secretary Fox arrived back in Washington on Thursday, 13 March. Although exhausted from his excursion to Hampton Roads, he was aglow with visions of how the victorious *Monitor* could be made even more formidable. Early the next day, President Lincoln personally requested that he travel to New York to confer with Ericsson and enquire about hiring a steamer that could, if necessary, run down *Virginia*.[7] On the morning of 15 March, a Saturday, Gustavus Fox and John Ericsson met; their discussions would have a far-ranging impact on "the future shape of the Union's ironclad Navy for the rest of the Civil War and beyond." [8]

Improvements to Ericsson's recently proposed batch of new monitors—the future *Passaic* class—were quickly agreed upon. They included a relocation of the pilot house, permanent smoke pipes and bigger guns. But woven into the two men's dialogue was Fox's tacit approval of features that defined the Swedish inventor's next generation of "swift turret carriers," ironclads that would eventually see the light as the mighty *Dictator* and *Puritan*. *Monitor*'s original hallmarks, a single turret armed with the heaviest available guns carried by a low freeboard hull, had been taken to their extremes. For the U.S. Navy, however, to adopt Ericsson's vision all but ensured it would spawn a fleet of impregnable but barely habitable, unseaworthy warships. Despite their thick armor and huge guns—only two by design—they lacked offensive hitting power. Further, monitors could only be efficiently used for harbor and coastal defense; their defining features rendered them incapable of sustaining oceanic operations. [9] By trusting its fate to a fleet of such vessels, the Navy would find itself without the means to command the seas or to challenge its foreign adversaries where it mattered most, far from America's shores.

On the first work day of the new week, Monday 17 March, Lenthall delivered a letter to Secretary Welles that was even more remarkable than the one he had written just four days before. Although no connection between it and Fox's Saturday meeting with Ericsson has been discovered, after reading Lenthall's words one can hardly believe that he didn't fully grasp the threat Fox's accord represented to his beloved Navy. Signed by both Lenthall and his engineer-in-chief, Benjamin Isherwood, their letter laid out a clear-eyed understanding of the strategic underpinnings of a blue-water navy. That they felt the necessity of presenting such thoughts in writing to the Secretary of the Navy speaks volumes: about the magnitude of the Navy's challenge, about its significance to the nation and about the willingness of their superiors to address it. Their letter's full text is reproduced in Appendix 6; a summary of its highlights is offered in the following paragraphs.[10]

Lenthall and Isherwood opened with a discourse on the problems plaguing the Navy's attempts to obtain armor plate from the nation's rolling mills and forges. By the end of their second page, they proposed as a solution "the absolute necessity of the Government at once preparing a factory to make for itself the most important and costly parts, both for the iron hulls and for the armature." They then described such a facility, insisting it should be a "storehouse and workshop, and not a military establishment," and that it should be situated on deep water but "secure from the possibility of attack by foreign foes."

Having outlined the need for and the features of their proposed factory, Lenthall and Isherwood subtly shifted their focus by evoking the image of how a navy so strengthened by such a facility would be able to "secure a country like ours from foreign aggression..." Grasping the importance of this nexus was, they respectfully submitted, a "national question second to none."

The way was now open for the true object of Lenthall and Isherwood's letter. The sudden rise of ironclads had rendered Europe's existing fleets of wooden warships obsolete and had handed the United States a golden opportunity to "start equal with the first powers of the world in a new race for the supremacy of the Ocean." To win such a race would require America to field "a fleet of first class invincible ocean ships" and sustain a larger navy than before, one of a very different character than the antebellum Navy. Lenthall boldly suggested that such a fleet should consist of powerful frigate-built ironclad steamers, leavened by lighter draft armored corvettes. It was a "system" readily recognizable to any informed observer. The European maritime powers had adopted it—witness France's *Gloire* and Britain's *Warrior*—and were now hurriedly replacing their obsolete wooden walls with ironclads. Now was the right time for the United States to do the same, thereby maintaining "command of the open sea with all the power it gives..." rather than relying on "any system of harbor defence."

The core of Lenthall and Isherwood's argument was clear. Monitors were brilliant solutions for harbor and riverine warfare but were wholly unsuited to maintain control of the high seas. To compete with other powers who were now rapidly introducing ocean-going ironclad battleships, the United States must do the same. Failure to do so would forfeit its ability to control its oceanic destiny. "Harbor defences are indeed valuable adjuncts...but cannot constitute a navy or perform its proper function." In a final, Mahanian flourish, they concluded their letter with the admonition of "how much better it is to fight at the threshold than upon the hearthstone."

Victorian naval authority Sir Thomas Brassey was so enamored of Lenthall and Isherwood's strategic insight that he quoted an edited version of their last two paragraphs in the introduction to the third volume of his influential series, *The British Navy: Its Strengths, Resources, and Administration.*[11]

* * *

Now back in his Washington office, Assistant Secretary Fox lost no time activating his interpretation of Ericsson's visions for the Navy's future monitors. To arm them, Commander Dahlgren was instructed to immediately begin work developing new models of 15-inch and 20-inch guns.[12] And on 18 March, in a shadow riposte to Lenthall and Isherwood's initiative of the day before, Fox wrote to Ericsson:

> Ever since my connection with the Department, I have used every proper opportunity to awaken an interest in iron-clad vessels and very many ... especially the Secretary, have felt an awakening.
>
> We ought to have a dozen monitors at least instead of six. How many can be made in the country, including your fast boat?[13]

But John Lenthall and his engineer-in-chief refused to relax their efforts to prevent the Department's retreat from the Navy's blue water heritage. On 19 March they sent yet another memorandum to Secretary Welles, this one proposing a specific vessel conversion to achieve that end.[14] The object of their scheme was the *Merrimack* class steam frigate *Roanoke*; perhaps they were spurred in part by that biting newspaper piece which had asked "why not rough-plate a dozen at once?" One wag later suggested that *Roanoke* had been chosen over her other sisters, each named for a river, because she alone honored a Southern river.[15]

Lenthall and Isherwood began their proposal by stating they now held the opinion that future ironclads should have iron hulls; however economic considerations suggested that wooden ships could be converted into efficient iron-plated sea-going vessels "as practiced in England and France." Their calculations showed that by cutting *Roanoke* down "to the top of the gun deck plank," she could be clad with iron and equipped with four Coles-type turrets, each armed with two 12 or 15-inch guns. The resulting war steamer would have freeboard of six feet and draw 22 ft 9 in of water. Observe that while Lenthall and Isherwood were proposing an ironclad armed with turrets, she was fundamentally different than an Ericsson-style monitor because of her greater freeboard and multiple turrets of a competing design, which gave her a broadside of eight guns. Further, her compliment of 250 men berthed in traditional accommodations, stowage of stores and provisions for 40 days and a bunker capacity of 600 tons had the potential of rendering *Roanoke* into a formidable ironclad capable of ocean cruising. Their estimated costs totaled $495,000, still more than a monitor but yielding a vessel with real hitting power and a significantly greater range.

Assistant Secretary Fox endorsed Lenthall's letter of proposal with the dismissive remark "I am afraid she will be useless." His comment was keyed to her draft, which he compared to *Merrimack*'s, an observation that rang true for harbor defense or river warfare but not for a sea steamer. The Navy Department sanctioned *Roanoke*'s conversion, which began the next month at the New York Navy Yard. But due to inevitable wartime delays, she wasn't completed until mid-1863, rather longer than the three and a half months forecast by Lenthall and Isherwood.

In the end, Fox was right; *Roanoke* was not a success. Her hull was strained by the weight of her turrets and she rolled too heavily to safely handle her guns in a seaway.[16] She was the Navy's only warship to be converted into an ironclad and the experiment was not repeated. But for all her faults, *Roanoke* represented a constructive effort by Lenthall's bureau to address the nation's need for sea-going armored war steamers. She was the world's first sea steamer to carry more than two centerline mounted turrets and as such, was a precursor of the modern battleship. Perhaps if she had been built new rather than converted, and of iron like Britain's *Prince Albert*, history might have judged her more kindly. As it was, *Roanoke* bore an uncanny resemblance to the Royal Navy's only conversion of a liner into a turreted ironclad, *Royal Sovereign*, a vessel also ordered in the immediate aftermath of the Battle of Hampton Roads.

* * *

Other issues beyond those wrapped around monitors were causing friction between the Navy and John Lenthall, one of the most acute being the supply of coal. The equipment function of Lenthall's bureau meant that it was responsible for delivering fuel to the Navy's far-flung blockading squadrons. This would change with the major reorganization of bureaus that occurred in the summer of 1862, but for the moment, coal logistics rested squarely on John Lenthall's shoulders. And with the wartime shortage of shipping, labor and much else, it was a thankless task.

An early note of discontent was sounded by Lenthall's arch critic, Commander David Porter. Writing directly to Assistant Secretary Fox on 11 March 1862, he quipped that "it will be a blessing to the country when the coal arrangements are placed in a 'bureau of equipment' under a competent man."[17] Two weeks later, even Lenthall's friend, Captain

Samuel Du Pont, sounded a plaintive note in a private letter to his wife. "My squadron is crippled for want of it. I am almost crazy, for a steam fleet without coal is like a sailing squadron dismasted."[18] Du Pont later quantified his squadron's coal requirements: 1,000 tons per week.[19] Writing to "My dear Commodore" Du Pont, Fox later made it clear who he thought was to blame. "The deficiency of coal is entirely Lenthall's fault, for on the impression gathered from your notes, I have spoken to him daily for sixty days."[20] Forward deployed officers not only complained about coal shortages but also griped when it arrived in large steamers. They were then forced to pay demurrage while the costly vessels waited their turns to offload. Smaller, more frequent loads shipped in handier-sized schooners were the desired alternative. But then Lenthall was under constant pressure to send coal as soon as possible, creating an impossible conundrum.

* * *

The momentum of Monitor fever proved to be irresistible; neither Lenthall nor Isherwood nor any of the Navy's traditionalists could hold it in check. By the end of March, Secretary Welles had agreed to accept Ericsson's offer for six improved *Monitors*, the new batch being named the *Passaic* class. Thoughts of building twenty ironclads to the Navy Department's own design were brushed aside, thwarted by a convergence of circumstances: the *Passaics*' lower costs, faster delivery, combat-proven features and the relentless pressure of the Monitor lobby, urged on by the enthusiasm of Assistant Secretary Fox. One of the minor heroes of Hampton Roads, Chief Engineer Alban Stimers, was promptly ordered to New York, to serve under Commodore Gregory as the general inspector for their construction. [21]

The *Passaics*, expanded to a class of ten through contracts with other builders, were just the beginning. In late July, two of Ericsson's very large, high-powered "fast boats," the future *Dictator* and *Puritan,* were ordered. The former was a 312 ft long, 4,400-ton monster completed with but 16 inches of freeboard, although she had been expressly configured to challenge European ironclads on the high seas. She displaced more than any other iron vessel yet built in the United States and her cost, $1,150,000, reflected her designer's outsized ambitions.[22] Then followed in September orders for nine *Canonicus* class monitors, much-enhanced *Passaics* carrying two 15-inch guns. And finally, in spring of 1863, contracts were let for twenty *Casco* class light-draft monitors.[23] Within a single year, forty-one Ericsson-designed monitors intended for saltwater service had been ordered by the U.S. Navy, thirty-four of which would be either commissioned or completed by the end of the war's final year. Other ironclads, especially those for western river operations, had also been placed in service during this period, but no one group was so functionally dominant as Ericsson's monitors. In that same interval, just one casemate broadside sea-going ironclad, William Webb's gigantic *Dunderberg*, was contracted for but she was finished too late for the war and never accepted into service.[24] To be sure, a diversity of opinion on desirable ironclad features was still alive within the Navy, as would be witnessed by the next ironclad board's findings, but a significant portion of it had already been spoken for. John Ericsson's vision, aided and abetted by Gustavus Fox, had not only triumphed over traditionalists like Lenthall, it was destined to transform the U.S. Navy.

Monitors gave the nation the ironclads it needed at its moment of crisis, but fixation on *only* them marginalized the Navy during the decades that followed.[25] Lenthall and his constructors were still performing miracles churning out gunboats, steam sloops and, in time, fast frigates, and while their wooden hulls and smoothbore guns would serve to protect commerce and show the flag, they were increasingly unable to wage modern naval warfare. Only iron-hulled, armored steamers capable of commanding the seas could do that. But the Navy wasn't building vessels of that kind. And Secretary of the Navy Gideon Welles, who acknowledged their necessity, failed to actively promote a sustained program to implement their construction.[26]

There was also the Fox factor. The influence of Assistant Secretary Gustavus Fox in creating a Navy focused on monitors cannot be overstated. Ericsson's biographer, recounting the days before Ericsson's offer for the *Passaic*s was accepted, wrote "Fortunately, Assistant-Secretary Fox was by this time a complete convert to the monitor system." [27] That he also contributed enormously to the Navy's success during the Civil War is also undeniable. By taking a great burden off Welles' shoulders and employing his mind to intelligently manage the operational side of the Navy, Fox did the country great service. Paullin deftly characterized their interaction: "The brilliancy of Fox has somewhat obscured the deeper colors of Welles." [28]

However, if the relations between Fox and Lenthall are brought into the equation, a favorable verdict on their mutual synergy is not so readily reached. To start with, the two men had completely different personalities. Fox was progressive and genial, a back-slapping former naval officer buoyed by political interest; Lenthall was conservative and reserved, a cerebral engineer shaped by years of practical experience. Without doubt they approached their departmental duties from very different perspectives. Their correspondence suggested a cordial, respectful relationship, but the same was said of Dahlgren and Fox. Years after the war, Dahlgren remembered him most unfavorably, writing that Fox exerted:

> an insufferable tyranny over the Navy—and has entirely deranged it in fastening his notions upon everything. ... absorbing every function of the Depart[ment]—filling the Bureaus with his own creatures, and spending money in every fancy that entered his pate. ... Nothing could exceed the insolent tyranny of Fox.[29]

Lenthall and Fox no doubt butted head over many issues, the monitors forming the most obvious point of disagreement. Not being an Ericsson acolyte tangibly diminished Lenthall's standing, as observers have attested.[30] Although Fox respected Lenthall's competence as a constructor, some of Fox's pronouncements about him were disparaging. And he took counsel from those like Porter who actively campaigned against Lenthall. Did John Lenthall care? Probably. But at heart he was a realist. He dealt with Fox and the others as best he could, and carried on with the business of a bureau chief. A war was on and there was much to do.

* * *

CHAPTER 25

Naval Expansion

Lenthall's ongoing struggle to shape the course of the new ironclad Navy again surfaced, the latest episode documented in a letter dated 11 May 1862, written to Captain Du Pont who was then onboard his flagship *Wabash* at Port Royal.[1] Explanations about shipments of stores and fitting out the ex-liner *Vermont* filled the first page. He then aired a disagreement with Fox over how to forward coal: "No statement I could make was considered satisfactory." But Lenthall saved the main point of his letter until the end—thoughts arising from the latest ironclad board appointed by Secretary Welles:[2]

> Commodore Smith, Isherwood, Mr. Martin, Mr. Hartt, and myself are on a board examining all the models offered for ironclad vessels, rams and all such matters. My opinion is men-of-war for war times must now be of iron; this may be against my personal interests, but it is in the interest of my employers. Wooden vessels covered with iron, when wanted, will be found to be rotten, and unless for temporary immediate use ought not to be. Congress has appropriated twenty-three millions for ironclad vessels, and the impression seems to be it must be spent at once, but surely so great a thing as reconstructing the Navy at such an immense expense is not to be hurried quite so fast. Well, I suppose I am slow, and there are plenty of fast ones ready to jump in the boat. The commodore will not agree to the report I proposed, so he makes his own. I will send you a copy.[3]

Several important points are revealed in Lenthall's letter. First was that he, together with other engineers and a constructor, had been appointed to the ironclad board in lieu of only "skilful naval officers." This was a sensible selection by Secretary Welles, now unconstrained by Congressional dictates. Second, Lenthall portrayed himself as the methodical, measured naval architect of before, admitting "I am slow" but citing convincing rationale for adapting such an attitude toward "so great a thing as reconstructing the Navy." But most important, Lenthall was convinced that "men of war ...must now be of iron." This marked a profound shift in his thinking, as he readily admitted. It was due, in part, to nearly a year's exposure to ironclad fighting vessels. But another factor was at play—the government's stock of seasoned timber was nearly exhausted. Future wooden ships could only be constructed of green timber. John Lenthall's long experience told him that such hull structures would rapidly decay into a mass of rot. So, he reasoned, why build short-lived wooden-hulled ironclads at enormous cost if a viable alternative existed—iron ships.

Two days later, on 13 May 1862, Lenthall forwarded the ironclad board's majority report to Secretary Welles.[4] Its full text is presented in Appendix 8 and its principal points are summarized in the following paragraphs.

The board began with a brief review of the rapid pace of ironclad development since the outbreak of hostilities, citing the Department's satisfaction with *Monitor*'s performance in combat. While the American experience and the latest European warship trends had demonstrated the supremacy of ironclads, the board's majority still envisaged a role for unarmored wooden vessels as economical cruisers on distant stations.

With the stage thus set, the majority opinion rejected wooden-hulled ironclads in favor of iron because of the expected rapid deterioration of structures built of wood. It is on this point that Commodore Smith differed from the board's majority, particularly regarding large, sea-going ironclads. Smith proposed building one of wood and another of iron, as insurance to guard against failure of either "experiment." [5]

For river and harbor defense, Lenthall and his colleagues recommended the use of towers (turrets) as opposed to a casemate, two in number, on a vessel propelled by twin screws, each powered by independent engines. Further, ironclads should be armored with plates of a single thickness rather than a lamina of thinner plates. A ten-knot speed, a four-day coal endurance and a maximum draft of thirteen feet were also stipulated. The only proposal that met these criteria—and the only one recommended by the majority—was that offered by G. W. Quintard of the Morgan Iron Works. His vessel was subsequently ordered and will be separately examined.

The majority opinion also held that if the Department needed additional harbor defense ironclads beyond those already under contract—the *Passaic* class—it should order more of the same rather than vessels of an inferior design. This statement confirms the acceptance of monitors as useful warships; some credit is owed to Lenthall for this admission. As for the larger sea-going ironclads intended for coastal defense, the majority opinion was firm on two interrelated points. First, such vessels should be designed and specified by the Navy Department rather than by interested contractors and second, their designs should receive "much more study before a practical solution is attempted" and be "prepared with great deliberation and care." John Lenthall's voice can be heard behind the board's clearly expressed desire that "more mature consideration" be given before the Navy committed itself to such expensive and potentially controversial ocean-going warships.

* * *

The Navy acted with celerity on the board's report. Less than two weeks later it placed a contract for George W. Quintard's proposed vessel, which subsequently bore the name *Onondaga*.[6] It is easy to see why she was recommended by the board. Not only did her design meet their list of desired features, but of all the proposals, she conformed closest to the specifications advertised by the Navy on 20 February, which in turn were based on Lenthall and Isherwood's aborted ironclad design. For these reasons, although she was built to plans submitted by a contractor, *Onondaga* can be thought of as the first ironclad designed by the Navy Department.[7] Her particulars are listed in Appendix 7.

Onondaga's most characteristic feature was her two turrets. She was the Navy's first warship to be so equipped. Her hull was equally unique—it was fabricated exclusively of iron and conventionally modeled, without the overhangs of an Ericsson monitor. As the board's report also noted: her dimensions were sufficient, she was driven by twin screws powered by machinery of a familiar plan, and her time of completion was satisfactory. Typical of monitor-like vessels configured for harbor or river service, she operated with only fourteen inches of freeboard. And her coal capacity was restricted due to a lack of buoyancy. It would be interesting to learn whether Lenthall checked Quintard's calculations as closely as he did Ericsson's. However, she proved to be quite durable. After the war, she was sold to France, crossed the Atlantic and remained in active service until stricken in 1904.[8]

In early July 1862, two months after the ironclad board had spoken, the Navy placed in train orders for five more ironclads, all of them very large. The first was the "ocean-going ironclad frigate ram" *Dunderberg*, contracted on 3 July from William Webb's New York shipyard, closely followed by the *Monadnock* class of four coastal ironclads, the first armored ships to be built in navy yards.[9] The aggregate displacement of these five war steamers was just over 20,000 tons, greater than the combined tonnage of the ten *Passaic* class monitors and twice that of Ericsson's two "fast boats," *Dictator* and

Puritan.[10] And all five were wooden-hulled. Why such a dramatic naval expansion based on vessels of a kind Lenthall's majority had recently cautioned against? His board opined "Only the most pressing necessity can justify construction from such materials." Secretary Welles' memoirs identified the pressing necessity:

> At the time this decision was made and the vessel [*Dunderberg*] commenced, a foreign war was feared. We had a large defensive force, but not as many and formidable vessels as we should need in the event of a war with a maritime power.[11]

The maritime power of concern was Great Britain, and in the wake of the *Trent* affair, an uneasy stasis prevailed between it and the United States. The federal blockade of the South was beginning to hurt Britain's cotton-dependent textile mills, but was still viewed as a short-term disruption rather than a permanent condition. And the British knew that if they moved to break the blockade, a war with the Northern states would inevitably result. Further, tensions were rising over the imminent sailing from Liverpool of No. 290, a British-built steamer that before the summer was out, would reappear as the Confederate raider *Alabama.* In early July, the U.S Steam Sloop *Tuscarora* was lying in Southampton Water, waiting to intercept the Southern "pirate." Even more dire news soon reached American ears. On 1 July, Confederate naval agent James D. Bulloch signed a contract with Lairds of Birkenhead, the builders of No. 290, for two powerful, double turreted sea-going armored war steamers—the infamous Birkenhead rams. [12] Secretary Welles' fears were amply justified.

* * *

The first of the five large, ocean-going ironclads ordered by the Navy, William Webb's *Dunderberg* or Thunder Mountain was an extraordinary vessel by any measure. Her overall length of 377 ft set a record for a wooden warship, and she was constructed with structurally distinct inner and outer hulls that tapered into a massive fifty-foot-long solid oak ram. *Dunderberg*'s armor scheme was centered on a sloped casemate like *Virginia*'s, which was designed to carry two turrets on its top, but Webb was forced to abandon this enhancement due to structural and weight problems. Lenthall had strongly objected to the turrets and had predicted such an outcome. It was planned that she would be armed with a combination of 15-inch and 11-inch guns. Her single screw was intended to give her fifteen knots but she never made this speed during her trials.[13]

One point must be clarified about *Dunderberg*'s design. She has often been attributed to John Lenthall. But in fact, she was the creation of her builder, a gifted naval architect in his own right, William H. Webb.[14]

Building a 7,000-ton vessel in New York City during a time of war was bound to be attended with delays, and *Dunderberg* suffered accordingly, not being launched until July 1865. By the time she was ready to commission, the Navy no longer needed such a huge ironclad and so, by an act of Congress, William Webb was allowed to sell her foreign. The French bought *Dunderberg* and renamed her *Rochambeau*; she flew the Tricolor until she was broken up in 1874.[15]

Of the other four large ironclads authorized in July of 1862, there is no confusion over who was in charge of their design. John Lenthall was probably tickled to finally get the chance to build the ironclad steamers that he and Isherwood had championed for so long. Although he had been a recent convert to the advantages of iron hulls, constructing the ironclads of wood made it feasible to build them in navy yards. On 9 July 1862, he issued instructions to the four east coast yards to start the work of laying down their keels.[16]

Lenthall's bureau followed the format previously employed with the steam sloops: each ironclad was designed under his direction by the building yard's resident constructor. Using the names they would later be assigned, *Agamenticus* was built at Portsmouth and designed by Isaiah Hanscom; *Monadnock* at Boston by William Hanscom; *Miantonomoh* at New York by Benjamin Delano and *Tonawanda* at Philadelphia by Henry Hoover. Although conforming to the same general specifications, each ship was completed with slightly different dimensions and hull forms, their lengths ranging from 250 to 256 ft and their breadths from 52 ft to 53 ft 8 inches. This has led to them being referred to by varying class names but for consistency's sake, they will be described herein as the *Monadnock* class, after the first of them to enter service. See Appendix 7 for their particulars and how they completed the evolution of the Navy's double turreted ironclads.

The varying moulded properties of the *Monadnock*s highlight the differences between the art of building a wooden ship and the emerging technology of the iron shipbuilder. Lenthall's ironclads were the product of long-established traditions which permitted significant interpretations of a general design by the constructor actually building the wooden hull. A hull's lines as well as its final dimensions and details of arrangements varied between the yards. A good example is the Philadelphia-built *Tonawanda*. She featured a hull five feet longer than that of her next longest sister, had modest deadrise rather than the flat floors of her sisters, measured less depth of hull and carried turrets spaced conspicuously closer together than the others of her class. In sharp contrast, the dimensions and locations of every plate, frame and rivet for an Ericsson-designed monitor was predetermined on a drawing produced by a draftsman far distant from the vessel's building site. The wooden shipwright had his well-thumbed booklet of mould loft offsets and a dozen pages of building directions to guide his labors whereas the iron shipbuilder was issued stacks of oversized drawings and books of printed specifications to ensure his fabricated product turned out precisely as the designer intended. The cult of the artisan was now overshadowed by that of the engineer.[17]

The *Monadnocks*, while inspired by the abortive Navy Department designed ironclads, represented a fresh approach incorporating lessons learned from the Battle of Hampton Roads and experience with the monitors. Features they borrowed from the earlier design included double turrets, twin screws and, in comparison with Ericsson's monitors, ship-shaped hulls with relatively higher freeboard. But now, the turrets mounted a pair of 15-inch guns rather than a single 11-inch gun and were of the Ericsson type, not the Coles pattern. The turrets were also sized two feet greater in diameter than those specified for the *Passaics*, giving more room for handling the big Dahlgrens they would contain. Also following Ericsson's lead, their armor was built up of layers of thin iron rather than being made from the superior but unavailable single thickness wrought iron plates.[18]

Three of the *Monadnocks* were laid down before 1862 was out, but only the class namesake was commissioned before hostilities had ended. Although their fighting exposure was brief, John Lenthall's ironclads soon gained a reputation throughout the Navy as the best of the monitors.[19] Even the cross-grained David Porter was forced to admit that "Mr. Lenthall ... produced vessels of the Monitor type that had not their equals at that time in any European navy."[20] Adding to their luster, two of the class successfully undertook significant ocean voyages: In late 1865, *Monadnock* sailed from the east coast around South America to San Francisco, and in the following year, *Miantonomoh* crossed the Atlantic and showed the flag throughout Europe, venturing as far as the Russian stronghold of Kronstadt. Both were escorted by other vessels, and *Miantonomoh* was under tow for a portion of her cruise. That John Lenthall's ironclads were able to accomplish their blue-water passages without injury was a testament to their sound design. All of these favorable factors coalesced into the Navy's later decision to 'rebuild' this class, a story told in a coming chapter.[21]

* * *

Not only were the shape and fabric of its ships altered by the crucible of combat, but the organization of the Navy Department was forced to adapt to the new environment in which it now operated. Defects in its system of administration largely invisible during times of peace became all too apparent under the pressures of war. As historian Oscar Paullin suggested, the Department was unresponsive to its secretary's "executive touch." Appointment of an assistant secretary was meant to strengthen Welles' hand, but more tools were needed. High on the list was a more focused delineation of its bureaus' fundamental responsibilities.[22] After months of Congressional debate, an Act to reorganize the Navy Department was finally passed on 5 July 1862.[23] Its first section addressed this priority by adding three new bureaus to the original five, two of which were significantly altered. The eight bureaus and their first chiefs were as follows:

1. Bureau of Yards and Docks, Rear Admiral Joseph Smith, former chief.
2. Bureau of Equipment and Recruiting (new), Rear Admiral Andrew Foote.
3. Bureau of Navigation (new), Captain James Gilliss.
4. Bureau of Ordnance (altered), Commodore A. A. Harwood.
5. Bureau of Construction and Repair (altered), John Lenthall, former chief of BCER.
6. Bureau of Steam Engineering (new), Engineer-in-Chief Benjamin Isherwood.
7. Bureau of Provisions and Clothing, Paymaster Horatio Bridge, former chief.
8. Bureau of Medicine and Surgery, Dr. William Whelan, former chief.

Note that the ranks of Smith, Foote and Harwood reflect their status as set by the Act to establish and equalize the grade of the Navy's line officers, which became law on 16 July and created the new ranks of rear admiral, commodore, lieutenant-commander and ensign.[24] Together these two acts profoundly reshaped the U. S. Navy.

Of the five bureaus first established in 1842, none was more affected by the reorganization than John Lenthall's former Bureau of Construction, Equipment and Repairs. Most visibly it lost its equipment function, which would soon free Lenthall from the thankless task of chartering coal shipments.[25] Less obvious was the transfer of the Navy's engineers attached to his bureau to a new bureau of their own, Steam Engineering, under his colleague Benjamin Isherwood. Lenthall's revamped Bureau of Construction and Repair would remain unchanged until the eve of World War II when it was absorbed into the Bureau of Ships.

The Act to reorganize the Navy strengthened the secretary of the navy's authority to assign duties to the bureau chiefs, and established the number and grade of employees allowed each bureau, Lenthall's being assigned a chief clerk, five clerks, a draftsman, a messenger and a laborer. But it also introduced a term limit for bureau chiefs—four years—who were to be appointed by the president and confirmed by the Senate. This last provision set off a chain of unintended consequences for both John Lenthall and Benjamin Isherwood who, for all appearances, were simply assuming their former management roles under new bureau names.

President Lincoln duly nominated Lenthall and Isherwood as chiefs of bureaus on 11 July, but their smooth confirmations quickly fell afoul of a cabal of opponents—rivals from within the Navy and commercial interests who clamored for their replacement.[26] Typical of many line officers, Commander David Porter wished both men gone and John W. Griffiths, designer of the steam sloop *Pawnee* and author of numerous articles denouncing Lenthall, actively conspired to supplant Lenthall's authority.[27] Eight days later, Washington's *National Republican* brought the unwanted news. "Within the last day of adjournment of Congress, the Senate confirmed upwards of 300 nominations. A number failed of confirmation, including ... B. F. Isherwood ... and John Lenthall."[28]

Despite the Senate's inaction, Secretary Welles notified Lenthall on 25 July of his appointment by the president as bureau chief, which Lenthall acknowledged that same day, closing with a note of assurance. "By strict attention to the interests of the Government I hope to show that the trust reposed in me has not been misplaced."[29] Here matters rested uneasily until 1 December when President Lincoln renominated Lenthall and Isherwood as chiefs of bureaus. Vigorous debate in the Senate ensued, in response to which Lenthall's friend and now a rear admiral, Samuel Du Pont, took up his pen and wrote an unsolicited memorial to Senator James W. Grimes. The admiral quickly got to the point—his estimation of John Lenthall:

> He is the most able man we have ever had in the Navy in his line and, besides, he has saved the Government more money than any individual that could be named—no contactor could ever bribe him, no Southern lumber merchant could ever bully him. ...

> He is a man of science, of method and of administrative capacity. In England he would have been knighted ... In France, Louis Napoleon would have given him a red ribbon every time he visited a dockyard. ...
>
> The ostensible fault found with him is that he is not progressive enough—the real objection being that he has stood all his life in the way of jobbers and plunderers.
>
> In my judgement his removal from his present place, and more especially during this war, would be a serious injury to the public service and ... a cruel injustice to one of the most faithful of public servants. ...[30]

After enduring seven months of uncertainty, John Lenthall was finally confirmed by the Senate on 21 February 1863 as chief of the Bureau of Construction and Repair.[31] His patience was rewarded a month later when the Navy Department issued a general order which separated naval officers into line and staff—naval constructors were considered staff—and realigned the staff officers' relative ranks.[32] As students of naval history are keenly aware, rank is a matter of supreme importance to naval officers. The portion of the order applicable to Lenthall read:

> Chief of Bureaux of the Staff Corps to rank with Commodores, and to take precedence of each other according to their dates of commission as Surgeons, Paymasters, Naval Constructors and Engineers, and not according to the date of appointment as Fleet Officer, or Chief of Bureau.[33]

Bureau Chief Lenthall was now ranked as a commodore. The young apprentice who had aspired to become a naval constructor had come a long way.

* * *

Throughout the turmoil of bureau reorganization and the heartburn of his nomination, John Lenthall doggedly pursued his prime responsibility, the construction and repair of the Navy's hundreds of ships. One of his less publicized directives was contained in an official letter written to Rear Admiral Du Pont enclosing a sample paint color card with instructions for its use "in painting the outside of iron vessels, and also the vessels in the blockading squadrons ... including the inside of port shutters, heads of masts, and all parts exposed to distant observation."[34]

Instead of the squadron's blockaders being easily identified by their standard black and white livery, they would now adopt the blueish gray hues of the blockade runners. It was one of the earliest instances of the Navy ordering the application of a camouflage paint scheme to significant numbers of its warships.[35]

Bigger and better war steamers were demanded by the Navy and John Lenthall did his utmost to oblige. The popular ninety-day gunboats had by now garnered criticism as being too small and too slow, so Lenthall drafted plans for a "fast cruising gunboat." Two of the new *Kansas* class were laid down before the end of 1862, and ultimately eight would be launched, all from navy yards. With lengths of 179 ft 6 in and breadths of 30 ft, they were some twenty-one feet longer and two feet greater in breadth than their quickly built predecessors.[36]

Operations on the South's shallow rivers and estuaries demonstrated the merits of the original double-ender design. Taking the plans for what was considered the best of the first batch, *Port Royal*, Lenthall's bureau advertised for proposals and by September 1862, had signed a significant number of construction contracts. The trend toward increased size resulted in the new *Sassacus* class, measuring 236 ft long, 35 ft in breadth and 12 ft depth of hull. In all, twenty-eight of them were completed, most built by private yards, the largest class of warships turned out by the U.S. Navy until World War I. They would be followed in 1863 by orders for seven, 255 ft long iron-hulled double-enders of an improved design, the *Mohongo* class.[37]

Overseeing a second turbulent year of naval expansion, John Lenthall's bureau had begun or authorized the construction of six enormous ironclads (beyond those awarded for Ericsson designed monitors and the one-of-a-kind ironclad, *Keokuk*), eight large gunboats and nearly thirty enhanced double-enders. These numbers were complimented by steady increases in the ironclads constructed on the western rivers. It was another blistering year for the Bureau of Construction and Repair. Chief Lenthall must have been very proud indeed.

* * *

CHAPTER 26

The Light-Draft Monitors

In early August 1862 Assistant Secretary Fox, frustrated that Confederate ironclads so dominated the inland waterways, vented his frustration in a letter to John Ericsson. "I wish somebody with brains could give us a six foot draught boat of great velocity ... for the Western waters, impregnable like your boats."[1] Later that month Fox dropped by at Ericsson's New York office and urged the Swedish inventor to "make a plan" for river monitors, this one of four feet draft. After a lively exchange over the design of ironclads—Ericsson held that six feet was the minimum possible—Fox took his leave and Ericsson "commenced reflecting on the subject."[2]

But John Ericsson had no time for thinking. The coming weeks proved to be very busy for him and his associates. Throughout September 1862, the U.S. Navy signed one contract after the other for monitors of a new class incorporating major improvements over the preceding *Passaic*s. Designed with twenty-five feet more length and enhancements promising greater speed, nine *Canonicus* class monitors were soon placed on order. Counting the original *Monitor,* within the space of a year the Navy had committed itself to twenty-two Ericsson-designed ironclads. However, the pace of its appetite had outrun the monitors' combat experience. None of the *Passaic*s had yet been commissioned, and their baptism of fire would prompt many alterations to the follow-on *Canonicus* class, all of which kept their designer fully occupied.[3]

Sparked by the Navy's recent spate of new buildings, on 8 September Secretary Welles sent a letter to Bureau Chief John Lenthall assigning official names to thirty-eight of its latest war vessels: twenty-one *Sassacus* class double-enders, four *Kansas* class screw gunboats, seven of the new *Canonicus* class monitors, a renamed *Passaic,* all four of the *Monadnock*s and Webb's *Dunderberg.* In recognition of the increased responsibility given to its regionally based general superintendents, Commodore Hull in

St. Louis and Admiral Gregory in New York City, Welles concluded his letter with the following directive:

> The western boats will be superintended by an organization of which Commodore Hull will be the head. All vessels building on the Atlantic coast outside of Navy Yards will be under the superintendence of Rear Admiral Gregory with such assistance as the Bureau of Construction and Steam Engineering consider necessary.[4]

Admiral Gregory's office, first established in June 1861 to oversee the ninety-day gun boat program, had since been expanded far beyond its original staff of four inspectors to cover the greatly extended and more complex scope of construction supervision outlined by Welles' letter. Of the vessels named by Welles, most of *Sassacus* class, all of *Passaic* and *Canonicus* classes, the turrets for the *Monadnock*s and the massive *Dunderberg* were being built under the supervision of Gregory's organization. Due to the preponderance of Ericsson designed products it inspected—ironclads, turrets and machinery—his office had gained the nickname "Monitor bureau." Its principal inspector was the ambitious Chief Engineer Alban Stimers, a protégé of both Gustavus Fox and John Ericsson, who had been attached to the bureau for nearly a year.

Vesting such authority in Gregory's office, however, created a discontinuity in the Navy Department's established system for supervising new construction based on the bureaus headed by John Lenthall and Benjamin Isherwood. The final phrase of Welles' order was a clumsy attempt to close the gap. Traditionally navy yards built the Navy's ships, but its rapid expansion and the increasing dominance of iron now placed most of its advanced war steamers—and all those *not* designed by Lenthall's bureau—in the hands of private contractors. And by order of the Secretary of the Navy, any vessels on Atlantic coast slipways were Gregory's to supervise "with such assistance as the bureaus ... consider necessary." Welles' imprecise language, which avoided assigning responsibility beyond the superintendence for these vessels' construction, would over time create enormous problems for the Navy.[5]

* * *

After additional prodding by Fox delivered through Stimers, Ericsson snapped to the task of designing a light-draft monitor. On 9 October 1862, he forwarded an outline plan and specifications to the Secretary of the Navy. The simple vessel he proposed was intended to be constructed on a Mississippi riverbank with a minimum of supporting infrastructure:

> I conceived the idea of building a plain, oval tank with a flat bottom and upright sides ... Around this I attached a raft made of timber, the idea being to give stability and impregnability to this wooden raft. The engine itself I proposed to be on the simplest, high-pressure principle ... such as they were in the habit of using out west.[6]

Assistant Secretary Fox must have been delighted. The concept he had long championed had now been brought to life by the man who created the *Monitor*. But Ericsson's plans needed their details fleshed out before they could be advertised for proposals and the Swedish inventor was much too busy to do that. However, the ever-accommodating Alban Stimers could manage the job. And so, in Fox's words, "The elaboration of the plan of Captain Ericsson and preparation of the drawings and specifications were confided to Chief Engineer Stimers, who was instructed to consult with and follow the directions of that gentleman."[7] So far, so good. All should have proceeded as planned but for Stimers' over-confidence in his abilities as a "constructing engineer" of iron ships and the Navy Department's failure to exert any sort of management control over Stimers' activities.

In all of the exchanges related above between Fox, Ericsson and Stimers, mention of the Navy Department's organizations that normally managed the design, construction and steam engineering of its warships, John Lenthall and Benjamin Isherwood's bureaus, was conspicuously absent. This pattern was a characteristic of both chiefs' alienation from the Navy's acquisition of Ericsson-designed monitors. Although Lenthall was vested with the responsibility of preparing and managing the contracts for such ironclads and participated in reviews pertaining to construction progress payments, he and Isherwood were often bypassed during the design development stages. Charles Cramp, son of the founder of the Philadelphia shipyard bearing his name, later recalled their plight:

> Mr. Lenthall, the Chief Constructor of the Navy, and Mr. Isherwood, who was on his staff as engineer, were entirely set aside, and practically disappeared from the scene as far as new constructions were concerned. ... [they] had no power to antagonize the monitor craze successfully ...[8]

A clique of monitor acolytes had arisen within the Navy Department, headed by Assistant Secretary Fox, willfully encouraged by Commander David Porter, dutifully enabled by Admiral Joseph Smith, chief of Yards and Docks, and shamelessly exploited by Chief Engineer Alban Stimers. John Lenthall and Benjamin Isherwood, both of whom had long opposed the Navy's wholesale embrace of the monitors, inhabited uncomfortable positions within the close-knit department. This bred an unhealthy willingness in both of these loyal bureau chiefs to avoid, when possible, direct involvement with issues related to Ericsson's monitors. They had been denigrated, rebuffed and minimized all too often and had learned their lesson. It was easy for Lenthall and Isherwood to not *consider* it *necessary* for them to intrude into matters related to Fox's latest project. This conflict of personalities would cost the Navy dearly.

* * *

Stimers did as instructed by Fox but with an important exception. While he diligently prepared the necessary detailed plans and consulted with Ericsson, he selectively chose what elements of Ericsson's advice he would follow. After seeking input from Bureau Chief Isherwood, Stimers reengineered the monitor's boilers, engines and propeller shaft arrangements, adopting a mix of his own thinking and Isherwood's. When Stimers described to Ericsson what changes he was contemplating, Ericsson objected and after that, heard nothing further from the chief engineer. Later in this process, Admiral Joseph Smith pressed Stimers to arrange water tanks around the perimeter of the iron inner hull to permit partially submerged operations and to deballast the monitor should she run aground. Stimers eagerly sketched in Smith's proposed changes—and all the necessary extra iron structure, bracing, piping and pumps.[9] When Ericsson was informed of this latest improvement, the crusty Swede thoroughly protested, pointing out that the benefit gained was not worth the complication. But Stimers refused to admit any doubts and so the water tanks remained. And during this entire period, Stimers' office was next door to Ericsson's. [10]

As any naval architect can attest, making decisions about what vessel system to add or modify is an integral part of the design process, but when the work is done, the finished product is reviewed and approved by a higher authority. That vital element of project control was signally absent from Stimers' development of the light-draft monitor plans. Fox thought Ericsson was performing the review function. But Ericsson, who sensed things were getting out of control and was blind to Stimers' changes, found it a "delicate subject for me to meddle with," and remained quiet. He was reluctant to confront Fox, his most ardent patron, with his suspicions "because no information had been asked; I had simply advised the engineer strongly against what he was doing."

What involvement did the bureau chiefs have? Later testimony in Congress on the subject of the light-draft monitors—all 120 pages of it—is rife with conflicting statements.[11] Both Lenthall and Isherwood's statements suggest they only had casual knowledge of Stimers' elaborations on Ericsson's design and, except for brief conversations, dealt with him through his superior, Admiral Gregory.[12] Recall that at this time, October 1862 through February 1863, both Lenthall and Isherwood were still awaiting confirmation of their appointments as chiefs by the Senate, and had little inclination to intrude on matters that would inflame the Monitor lobby.

Stimers' work was sufficiently advanced by 10 February 1863 for the Navy Department to publicly advertise for proposals from interested contractors. Bids were requested to be submitted in two weeks' time.[13] It was at this juncture that Assistant Secretary Fox finally reached out to John Ericsson to confirm that he fully approved of Stimers' drawings. The telegraphed reply he received must have come as a shock. "Permit me to say the leading principle has been completely frittered away ... and much regret that I have had only a few hours to investigate a subject of great national importance."[14] Ericsson followed up with a longer written explanation in which he repudiated all responsibility for Stimers' work.[15]

A major fault in the Navy's program to build a fleet of river monitors had now been exposed. The timing could not have been worse. Ericsson's message arrived on the same day, 24 February, that bids from the contractors were due to be opened. In an effort to salvage the situation, one week later, Ericsson and his associates submitted an unsolicited proposal to build six of them for $375,000 each.[16] What to do? For reasons that are difficult to fathom, the Navy decided to decline his offer and proceed with contract awards based on the bids it had received. Stimers had by this date produced a package of "general plans and specifications" adequate for contractors to evaluate their scope of work.[17] According to Fox, "Stimers' plan was elaborate and full, and in the opinion of Lenthall and Isherwood, was better than Captain Ericsson's."[18] The two bureau chiefs' views, as recollected by Fox, were understandable. In comparison to Ericsson's original sketch, Stimers' drawings *were* more "elaborate and full." But that didn't mean they had been independently reviewed and checked. All acknowledged that they needed to be developed into much more detailed working plans before they could be used for construction. Fox was by now far too vested in promoting the light-draft monitors to think of backing down. And so, Secretary Welles, largely unaware of the program's embedded conflicts, allowed the contract awards to go ahead. He later revealed in his diary that he had "trusted too much to Fox and Stimers" who "had taken the whole into their hands." [19]

Between March and May of 1863, the Navy Department signed contracts for twenty light-draft monitors with builders throughout the east coast and western rivers. The *Casco* class, as they became known, represented the largest ironclad acquisition to date. Costing just under $400,000 each, their aggregate expense of nearly $8 million dwarfed the prewar Navy's annual budgets. That they all were ordered so quickly would seem to indicate any misgivings about their design had evaporated, a view further reinforced by how the Navy chose to manage its new program:

> Mr. Stimers was placed in charge of their construction, and the contractors were directed to look to him for instructions. He was ordered to consult with Mr. Ericsson in preparing his plans and drawings for contractors, and at his own request, was authorized to establish an office and employ assistants in New York city, where he could have facilities for frequent and easy consultation with Mr. Ericsson.[20]

* * *

Secretary Welles' support for Bureau Chief Lenthall's efforts to persuade the Navy to build more ocean-going ironclads waxed and waned with the threat of foreign intervention. However, the political risks of ending the Department's pursuit of such vessels meant that proposals for large armored ships continued to be sought and evaluated. Advertisements for vessels similar to *Dunderberg* but with iron hulls had been placed in October 1862, and again in March of the following year, this time with an option for smaller 3,500 ton versions. Welles ordered a board consisting of Lenthall, Isherwood and Admiral Davis, chief of the Bureau of Navigation, to review the latest batch of proposals. Their report dated 23 July 1863 provides an interesting snapshot of America's rapidly evolving technology of the iron fighting ship.

Seven different proposals had been received, and that from Merrick & Sons of Philadelphia, the prime contractor for *New Ironsides*, was deemed the best in terms of cost per size of vessel. Their 5,700-ton ironclad was priced at $1,950,000 and measured 325 ft long, 54 feet in breadth and a 21 ft depth of hold, had twin screws and an iron hull. A small armored casemate housed four 15-inch Dahlgren guns and its turtle-backed hull ended in a ram. The board's twelve-page analysis also included extensive descriptions of the features deemed most desirable for machinery, hull construction and armor. In conclusion, it recommended three of the proposals, from Merrick, Tufts of Boston and Rowland of New York, but none of their designs was accepted as submitted. [21]

Nothing concrete came of the board's recommendations, although further exchanges with Merrick continued and a modified ironclad design was apparently "accepted" by the Navy.[22] In April of the following year, John Lenthall alone answered the secretary's request for an evaluation of six estimates for "a sea-going vessel of about 7,000 tons." Indicative of changing priorities, Lenthall's reply was compressed into a single page and simply repeated the cost and delivery quotes, which now ranged from $4.3 to $6.95 million and up to three years.[23]

As time marched on, John Lenthall must have known he was swimming against an increasing tide. With each month that the Union's armies continued to prevail, Secretary Welles' willingness to commit to building such large and expensive warships visibly diminished. By the time the war ended, he considered one *Dunderberg* more than enough, as his diary makes clear. "Could I have the money which she costs, I should prefer it to the vessel."[24] And beyond Secretary Welles stood the ultimate arbiter, Congress. During a February 1865 exchange in the Senate, its member best informed on naval affairs, Senator Grimes of Iowa, expressed that august body's sentiments. In answer to the question of why more large war vessels like those of England and France had not been built, he replied:

> Because the Senate and House of Representatives very wisely refused to do it. ... All we want is the monitors to protect our harbors, and then fast vessels to destroy the commerce of a hostile power. It is utter folly for us to undertake to build a navy with which we can compete with France and England ... That is not our policy. Our true policy is to protect ourselves at home ... and the system that has been pursued by the Navy Department during the last four years ... is calculated to accomplish that purpose.[25]

The will of Congress was clear, enunciated by one of the Navy's most vocal supporters. A mix of monitors and commerce destroyers were all that the nation needed.

The second component mentioned by Grimes, fast cruisers to destroy a hostile power's commerce, had been addressed by the Navy's 1863 program for three new classes of ocean-going cruisers. Secretary Welles' motivation for this initiative sprang from the alarming success of the first British-built raiders fielded by the South, *Florida* and *Alabama.* As described in Welles' 1863 annual report, the Navy had that year placed under construction a total of twenty-seven "steamers of high speed... with which to sweep the ocean, and chase and hunt down the enemy."[26] But due to crowded shipyards, shortages of labor, a dearth of seasoned wood and masses of projects already in hand, Welles' words were largely smoke and mirrors for political consumption. The fates of these three classes speak for themselves.

The first class listed in Welles' report, the "clipper screw-sloops," were the twelve ships (later ten) of the *Contoocook* class designed by John Lenthall. These steamers were specified, as were the other two classes, to emphasize higher speed and increased size compared to their predecessors. Their outsize dimensions were also necessitated by the Navy's reversion to broadside batteries in lieu of large centerline-mounted pivot guns. The *Contoocooks* were 290 ft long, 41 ft in breadth and powered to achieve speeds of thirteen knots. Although the ships of this class were officially named by the Navy on 5 November 1863—just before Welles issued his report—the first four weren't formally ordered until mid-1864 and the class namesake wasn't commissioned until 1868.[27] David Porter loved these sloops, claiming that they were "the most efficient kind of ships we have had in the navy."[28] However, the four *Contoocooks* actually completed were all built of unseasoned white oak and, as a result, very short-lived.[29]

"Screw-sloops, spar deck" comprised the second group listed by Welles, the eight vessels of the *Guerriere* class. These oversized sloops were designed by Constructor Delano of the New York Navy Yard, and measured 312 ft 6 in long, 46 ft in breadth and were rated at twenty guns, making them the most heavily armed of the three classes. Like the *Contoocooks*, none were actually laid down until 1864 and only three were ever commissioned, the first in 1867. Constructed of green timber, all three had been sold by 1877.[30]

The third group, the "screw-sloops of great speed," are the best known of the ocean-going cruisers. The heterogeneous *Wampanoag* class were built to be the Navy's fastest steamers, but at the exclusion of most other warship qualities. Also designed by Delano, their hulls were elongated *Guerrieres* and measured 335 ft long with breadths ranging from 44 to 48 ft. Five of the seven were commissioned but none before 1866. However, *Wampanoag* of this class achieved enduring fame. During her February 1868 steam trials and powered by engines designed by Bureau Chief Benjamin Isherwood, she sustained the record speed of 17¼ knots, making her the fastest ship in the world. The British did take notice, which might partially excuse *Wampanoag*'s whooping cost of $1.5 million. While her trial performance vindicated Isherwood's machinery design philosophy, it didn't save *Wampanoag* from being laid up soon thereafter. Her lesser-known sister was reengined, given a spar deck and renamed *Tennessee*, under which guise she served as flagship of the Asiatic squadron before being decommissioned.[31]

The ocean-going cruisers left behind a mixed legacy. Despite being advertised by Welles in late 1863, none were completed until long after the war was over. *Wampanoag*'s stunning achievement was offset by the three classes' rapid structural deterioration and abbreviated service lives. Although he saw it coming, John Lenthall must have been greatly disappointed. He had predicted just this outcome in an October 1864 report to Secretary Welles:

> Could the new vessels have remained on the stocks for a year or eighteen months, their durability would have been much increased; but that could not be permitted by the necessities of the case, and in a year or two will be felt the full weight of this evil, for they will decay with great rapidity.[32]

* * *

Throughout the summer and fall of 1863, construction of the light-draft monitors progressed under Chief Engineer Stimers, although more slowly than planned. Testimony from the later Congressional hearings about the failures of this class implied that Bureau Chief Lenthall had no direct contact with Stimers and little with his superior, Admiral Gregory, but that was not the case. Lenthall had a voluminous correspondence with Gregory and others of his staff, all to manage the tremendous amount of Navy's business that funneled through the general superintendent's office. To begin with, Lenthall was the "agent" of the Navy Department for *all* contracts, including those for the Ericsson-designed ironclads.[33] Further, as the Navy's chief constructor, he was responsible for design issues related to its other ironclads—*Onondaga, Dunderberg* and turrets for the *Monadnocks*—as well as for the many vessels being built or converted, such as the double-enders, all handled through Gregory's office. In addition, he was in regular receipt of bi-weekly reports issued by the general superintendent.[34]

John Lenthall had a number of exchanges with Gregory and Stimers that specifically addressed the light-draft monitors. For example, on 14 August 1863, Gregory transmitted a copy of Stimers' proposals dated the 12th for alterations to them. Lenthall's hand-written note at the letter's top reads: "Mr. Stimers was verbally informed that these changes would not be made."[35] And in September Stimers wrote directly to Lenthall about proposed enhancements to the design of the *Tippecanoe* (*Canonicus*) class anchor well arrangements which, because they would likely result in charges beyond the contract price, required a response from Lenthall.

It was from this perspective and the receipt of numerous bills for change orders to both the *Canonicus* and *Casco* class monitors that Chief Lenthall was finally obliged to raise a red flag. Writing to Secretary Welles on 7 October 1863, he warned:

> The accounts against these vessels arising from these changes have become very complex, and the contract will soon be no guide in the settlement, and their cost will much exceed the sum stated in the contracts.[36]

Lenthall cited examples of egregious charges already presented and urged that Admiral Gregory be asked to examine and report on the extent of the government's liabilities. Welles shot back the next day and approved Lenthall's recommendations. He further ordered Lenthall to give directions that no charges would be allowed without "an approval of the Bureau" and that the general superintendent be directed to so notify each contractor.[37]

This exchange sparked further transmittals from the Monitor bureau. Stimers sent Lenthall a copy of his specification for the light-draft monitors and two days later, through Gregory, a listing of all thirty-six draftsmen employed at his New York City office.[38]

On 14 November, Secretary Welles clarified Gregory's full control over all contract work outside of navy yards, and directed that all reports must flow through Gregory.[39] And as if to demonstrate the immensity of the Navy's current order book for "vessels, armor plates, turrets and materials," in January 1864, John Lenthall transmitted to Welles ninety-three original contracts covering such work. The list accompanying his letter filled five full pages, which he closed by noting "Press of business has prevented an earlier compliance with this duty."[40]

The first of the *Casco* class light-draft monitors, *Chimo* built by Aquila Adams of Boston, was launched on 5 May 1864. Stimers attended the event, and after she was afloat, her drafts and trim were measured to confirm whether her lightship weight and centers matched their estimated values. One week later, Admiral Gregory broke the bad news to John Lenthall:

> Chief Engineer Stimers' report ... stated that the mean draft of water was 5 feet 8 inches, if that be so, it will be impossible for her to float the great weights of turret, armament, etc. which it was intended she should carry when completed. ... and so much of the weight will come so far aft as to render it impossible to trim her without a counterpoise forward which will increase the difficulty.[41]

On the back of the National Archives' copy of Gregory's letter, jotted down in Lenthall's unmistakable hand, are a series of focused calculations. They reveal John Lenthall's intuitive grasp of Gregory's problem, and his familiarity with the monitors' design. First, knowing *Chimo*'s waterplane area and the density of water, he calculated her tons per inch immersion

(TPI); it was 17.7. Then, from the mean draft Gregory had reported, he determined the freeboard remaining "to top of deck in side of vessel," or 7'-2" less 5'-8", which equaled 18".[42] Multiplying *Chimo*'s freeboard remaining by her TPI yielded the weight "to immerse vents & decks," which was 318.6 tons. Finally, he added up all the weights he knew "she should carry when complete" (water in boilers, turret, equipment, armament and coal) and the answer, 342 tons, exceeded that which she could sustain. Adding 140 tons for "water in compartments" to balance her trim, made things even worse. Lenthall had confirmed that *Chimo* was grossly overweight and floated much deeper than she should have.[43] And the Navy was building nineteen more ironclads to the same design. Stimers, Gregory and now Lenthall—soon to be joined by Fox and Welles—had a colossal crisis on their hands.

What had caused a blunder of such magnitude? Stimers' initial lightship calculations may have contained errors and were apparently never independently checked.[44] But the greatest source of extra weight was the numerous changes to the monitors' design that were introduced throughout their building process. Starting with his hull tank ballasting system, larger boilers and altered machinery shown on the bid documents, Stimers subsequently added enhancements such as a glacis ring at the turret base, two extra inches of pilot house armor, cast iron engine frames, a larger condenser and pumps, iron bulkheads, heavier floor frames and countless other items of 'gold plating'.[45] The oft-cited misunderstanding of the hull raft's white oak density—seasoned versus unseasoned—has been exaggerated; Stimers used a reasonably correct value (55 lb/ft^3) and Lenthall later confirmed he did, noting that at the most, any variation of density might have caused a draft difference of one inch.[46]

How did such a failure in basic project controls occur? Two major causes can be cited, both of which were foreshadowed during the monitors' preliminary design phase. At some point during their construction period, Stimers and Ericsson's relation suffered a "rupture," after which the proud Swede only marginally participated in the drawing review process.[47] Second, Stimers was "led away by his ambition" in supposing he could carry on without Ericsson's guidance and design the monitors himself.[48] Stimers' deceit cloaked his break with Ericsson which, astonishingly, remained unappreciated by Welles, Fox or Gregory, or at a greater remove, by Bureau Chiefs Lenthall and Isherwood, until the scope of *Chimo*'s disaster became public.

Who was responsible? Perhaps best placed to assign blame was Secretary Welles, who bore the brunt of Congressional criticism that soon followed. Welles confided to his diary that Fox "was probably more in fault than any other. It was his specialty. ... Stimers was implicated about as deeply." He further observed that "the bureau officers failed in their duty in not informing me" and "Lenthall and Isherwood culpably withheld from me information of what was being done." On matters of such importance, Welles expected Lenthall to come directly to him.[49] But Lenthall *had* pushed back on Gregory about Stimers' numerous alterations to the light-draft monitors, and raised an early warning about the monitors' excessive contract change orders, to which Welles promptly responded. As for the design documents, Lenthall testified:

> I was not asked to examine or approve these plans, nor had I reason to suppose any such action was expected of me in this case any more than in those of the preceding nine monitor vessels, or of the Dictator and Puritan, for which I have been directed to execute their contracts.[50]

Further, it has been suggested that Lenthall should have checked the monitors' weight calculations handed to him by Stimers. However, both parties' testimony makes it clear that Stimers' calculations were those provided "for the information of bidders" and as such, would have shed little light on the principal cause for the monitors' failure, Stimers' subsequent alterations to Ericsson's original design and the accumulation of undocumented weight.[51]

Welles' diary is silent about someone else who carries a share of the blame for the light-draft monitor fiasco, John Ericsson. No one knew better what travesties Stimers was perpetrating to his designs than him. Ericsson had disowned Stimers' excessive modifications to them not once but twice, had access to all that he was doing and remained in frequent contact with those in the Navy Department able to decisively respond, especially Welles and Fox.[52]

What remedies could be adopted? A commission was appointed on 11 June 1864 to examine the monitors' defects and on 9 July, it rendered its opinion. Five of the monitors were designated "torpedo boats" and completed without their turrets and armed with a single, open gun and a spar torpedo. The remaining fifteen had their decks raised by 22 inches, which although increasing their drafts by six inches, provided them with about 16 inches of freeboard and rendered them useful river ironclads. The cost of these alterations ranged from $55,275 to $115,500. As a result, the deliveries of all of the light-draft monitors suffered. Only two were commissioned in 1864 and just three more before Appomattox. They never fulfilled their original purpose and by 1875, all twenty had been sold or scrapped.[53]

On 29 June 1864, Congress passed a resolution instructing its Joint Committee on the Conduct of the War to investigate the light-draft monitors. Their work began in December and concluded five months later; a 120-page report was subsequently issued. While declining to blame any one person, the Committee did fault the Navy's decision to order so many monitors of the same design "without first testing the questions involved by the construction of one or two."[54]

A letter written by John Lenthall to the *Boston Daily Advertiser* condemning Stimers' handling of the light-draft monitors was published in March 1865; it appears in Appendix 9.

The toll on the careers of those bearing responsibility for the light-draft monitors' failure was surprisingly light. Stimers was assigned to service afloat and, once the war was over, resigned on 3 August 1865. Fox was chastened but uninjured by his involvement, and Ericsson successfully managed to keep his reputation intact. Gregory remained unscathed but died a year later. As for John Lenthall and his fellow chief, Benjamin Isherwood, they were undeniably linked to this sorry affair. Their decision to avoid active involvement with the light-draft monitors, although understandable, contributed to the failure of one the Navy's largest procurement programs of the war. Perhaps, in hindsight, even the self-assured John Lenthall must have realized that he might have handled things differently.[55]

* * *

CHAPTER 27

A Time for Economy

While the light-draft monitor saga played out, John Lenthall's role as bureau chief required that he attend to an enormous variety of matters, both big and small. Of distinctly the latter variety, he received a private letter on 6 March 1864 from Admiral S. P. Lee, then in command of the North Atlantic Blockading Squadron and at the recaptured Norfolk Navy Yard. Lee was responding to Lenthall's request that pieces of the wrecked ironclad *Merrimack* and brig *Dolphin*, both burned and sunk when the yard changed hands, be retrieved and sent to Assistant Secretary Fox. [1] *Dolphin* was Lieutenant Fox's last assignment during his active U.S. Navy career.[2] Lee willingly obliged but there is no record to indicate whether he was successful.

Even during times of war, bureau chiefs were forced to defend their turf. Lenthall's push-back on an attempt by the Bureau of Yards and Docks to shift budgetary responsibility for building wharfs and foundations to his account "as it is for constructing a ship" is a true gem. His reply: "All the wharves, foundations, launching-slips, ship-houses, timber sheds, workshops, etc., are ultimately for the construction of ships; indeed, the main object of a Navy Yard is for that purpose." End of argument.[3]

One of John Lenthall's less visible duties was managing the vast purchases of materials necessary for the Navy's expanded construction activities, especially timber, iron, copper and lead. While Lenthall's bureau had shed its equipment function, it still had to provide stores for the five active navy yards and its shore establishments. These articles were obtained by contract and, when those quantities fell short, from the open market. As Lenthall had made clear to Secretary Welles, "repairs and fitting out of vessels would admit of no delay." The press of war meant the bureau often had no option other than resorting to open purchases to make up its deficiencies. By the third year of hostilities, funds spent on open purchases, $2,262,012, actually exceeded the $1,964,546 disbursed for materials bought under contract, a stunning reversal of prewar magnitudes.[4]

The unpleasant truth was that open purchases gave rise to corruption, which was hardly surprising when considering the large amounts of money in play. During peacetime, the quantity of materials bought varied little from those obtained by contract, allowing navy yard commandants the opportunity to check the few open purchase invoices that crossed their desks and ample time for inspectors to do their jobs. But all that had changed. Navy agents, inspectors and storekeepers were now ripe targets for skillful traders, sharpened by practice and with but one objective—defrauding the government. In an unaddressed memo dated May 1864, penned in response to statements received from a Mr. Wilson about suspicious happenings in New York, Lenthall opined "No system of securing honesty in the purchases of stores can be devised that cannot be eluded by dishonest men." As for those it hired to supervise its purchasing, he wrote "It is of especial importance that those positions should be filled by honest and competent men whose interest is that of the government."[5]

But Lenthall's theories of human behavior didn't always work out in practice. Witness the private letter he received from A. B. Farwell, dated 4 October 1864. A confidant of Lenthall's, Farwell had served as chief clerk at the Bureau of Construction and Repair until his return to Maine in 1863 to recuperate from a serious illness:

> I cannot forego the pleasure of telling you a word about a letter of F. W. Smith to his brother, written from Washington after he got the extra allowance on the lead. He speaks of your stern integrity and the manner in which he had induced the Secretary to override you, and then tells his brother that "something must be done to tip you out, because ... you are in the way." [6]

Here was a confession by a loathsome "sharp" that as long as Lenthall remained bureau chief, opportunities to steal from the Navy would be few and far between. Lenthall's immunity to corruption was a quality that Secretary Welles recognized and prized. Welles confided to his diary his private thoughts about John Lenthall's honesty:

> He has not much pliability or affability, but, though attacked and denounced as corrupt and dishonest, I have never detected any obliquity or wrong in him. His sternness and uprightness disappointed the jobbers and the corrupt, and his unaffected manner has offended others.[7]

Although Welles had faulted Lenthall for his handling of the light-draft monitors, he well understood that John Lenthall was a man of integrity. Indeed, as will be seen, the two men continued to work together in close harmony for another five years.

Welles' trust was evidenced by Lenthall's long-standing participation in contract change order technical issues, including those applying to Ericsson's most prestigious monitors, *Dictator* and *Puritan*. This was demonstrated in a letter written by Admiral Charles Davis and Lenthall to Secretary Welles, dated 20 October 1864, the continuation of a saga that had begun back in February and was still unresolved. The familiar names of Stimers and Gregory also formed part of the background. And even though fresh entreaties by Ericsson associates Griswold and Bushnell had been introduced, both Lenthall and Davis refused to approve payment of the bills in question. An enormous amount of Bureau Chief Lenthall's time was consumed by the continuous flow of such contract change orders—it is unsurprising that he did all he could to identify and halt their root causes.[8]

* * *

On 8 November 1864, President Abraham Lincoln was convincingly reelected to a second term. By then, Admiral Farragut had prevailed at Mobile Bay and Union forces had swept away Atlanta's defenders. After nearly four years of war, the beginning of the end was in sight.

The demands of a peace-time Navy were anticipated by Secretary Welles' directive of 23 November that "all vessels building at the Navy Yards, or intended for permanent existence in the Navy, should have their spars and rigging so arranged that they would be efficient cruisers at sea."[9] During the war, the supremacy of steam had been accepted to the extent that the Navy's newest sloops and gunboats were designed and built with much reduced sail plans, and the spars and upper masts fitted to many older vessels had been unshipped and sent ashore. Now, with an eye to economizing on the consumption of coal, that trend would be reversed.

John Lenthall, who was a master at calculating a sail plan's optimum balance, saw at once that Welles' order was impossible to fully implement:

> It is not practicable to combine in one vessel steam power lying wholly below the water line and sufficient to give great speed and such a distribution of sail as to make the steamer as efficient under sail alone as though it was a purely sailing vessel.

What was needed to transform these powerful war steamers into handy sailing cruisers, Lenthall patiently lectured, was to ensure that "the proper portion" of their sail plan was "distributed as headsail on a bowsprit and its attendant spars."[10] Many of the Navy's latest steam sloops—the *Sacramento* class is a good example—were built with plumb stems and no head knees or bowsprits. Now the prewar appendages would make their reappearance on the Navy's cruisers. Blame it on Lenthall.

As a further confirmation that the end of war was near, the Navy's struggle to capture Fort Fisher, guardian of Wilmington, the last major Confederate port open to blockade runners, drew to its violent climax. After a failed first attempt, Union forces prevailed on 15 January 1865. John Lenthall must have taken particular delight in learning that the first of his Navy Department-designed ironclads, *Monadnock*, had been at the front and center of Fort Fisher's naval bombardment and acquitted herself well.[11] And he probably suppressed his amusement when he heard John Ericsson's vaunted ruler of the ocean, *Dictator*, had suffered a shaft bearing failure on her way to the battle site and was forced to turn back.[12]

With Fort Fisher's fall, the Confederacy was doomed to an inexorable strangulation and its demise was now only a matter of time. While the armies continued to fight on land, the Navy's four-year campaign to enforce the blockade and exert control over the South's coastline was largely at an end. The much-expanded U.S. Navy had successfully accomplished its mission, but like the rebellion it had helped to crush, it too was living on borrowed time.

Two days after the fall of Fort Fisher, William James Stone, the husband of John Lenthall's sister Libby, died at his Washington home. He was sixty-six years old and his widow sixty. A gifted engraver, Stone had turned to sculpture during his twenty-five years of retirement, his epic final work of a noble Indian chief remaining unfinished. Of the Stone's four children, two had predeceased their father—daughter Jane, the wife of James Abert, at age twenty-three followed just months later by her younger brother, George. The surviving two sons, Robert King Stone, "the dean of Washington's medical community" and William James Stone, Jr., a prominent lawyer, carried forward the Stone family's lineage. The elder Stone was laid to rest in the family crypt within Rock Creek Cemetery, and his wife—Mrs. Elizabeth J. Stone—began her twenty-seven years of widowhood.[13]

* * *

As winter melded into spring, the war that had convulsed the nation drew to an untidy closure. On the morning of 9 April 1865, at Appomattox Court House General Robert E. Lee surrendered his Army of Northern Virginia to Union General Ulysses S. Grant. Lee's capitulation signaled the end of the

Confederacy's armed resistance. Together with all his fellow Americans, John Lenthall must have digested the news with feelings of joy mixed with disbelief: the sectional struggle that had for four long years so completely ruled his life was nearly over.

An even greater shock followed. Five days later, President Abraham Lincoln was assassinated. John Wilkes Booth fired the fatal shot at 10:20 p.m. and soon after, the president's prostrate body was carried from Ford's Theatre to a private home across the street. There he was attended to by a trio of doctors who had been at the theater. Minutes later, the Lincoln family's personal physician arrived, summoned by the president's distraught wife. Doctor Robert King Stone, the nephew of John Lenthall, later described his initial examination:

> I proceeded then to examine him, and instantly found that the President had received a gun shot wound in the back part of his head, into which I carried immediately my finger. I at once informed those around that the case was a hopeless one; that the President would die.[14]

Of the many who rushed to Lincoln's death bed that grim night were Secretary Gideon Welles and his opposite, Edwin Stanton, the secretary of war. And true to the prediction of Doctor Stone, Abraham Lincoln died early the next morning. It later came to light that Lincoln's murder was but one piece of a plot to decapitate the federal government; attempts had also been made on Secretary of State William Seward and Vice President Andrew Johnson.

President Lincoln's assassination personally affected John Lenthall at many levels. First and most obviously, the president of the United States, his ultimate superior as a Navy Department bureau chief, had been killed, leaving the nation rudderless at an unusually turbulent moment in time. On a more visceral level, he must undoubtedly have paled at hearing his nephew's eyewitness account of Lincoln's slow death from a head wound and the hemorrhaging that followed. On another plane was the certainty that Lincoln was someone Lenthall had actually met. Lenthall must have talked with the president during his many, unannounced visits to the old Navy Department building, plodding across from the White House in his carpet slippers and shawl.[15] And it appears Lenthall may have had a final, perhaps even more emotional encounter, marching in the president's funeral procession.

One of more remarkable documents in the Ives Collection is a black-bordered message to William Faxon, the chief clerk of the Navy Department, from the assistant secretary of the treasury dated 19 April 1865. Although he was not named, the note was from George R. Harrington, the man who organized every facet of Lincoln's Washington, D.C. funeral ceremonies.[16] The message simply enquired "Will the Bureau officers of your Department meet those of this Department here at 10 O'clock ... to proceed together to the Executive Mansion or will they prefer to go by themselves?" On the opposite page was Faxon's endorsement, "To introduce Mr. Lenthal Chief of the Bureau of Construction & Repair."[17]

This document strongly suggests that John Lenthall was one of the Navy Department's representatives who attended the first public event of Lincoln's two-week-long funeral observances. Beginning with religious services in the East Room, Lincoln's remains were escorted by an honor guard, pallbearers and civilian dignitaries the length of Pennsylvania Avenue and into the Capitol's Rotunda. There Lincoln's body lay in state until the morning of 21 April when it began its long journey across the Northern states to his final resting place in Springfield, Illinois. Secretary Welles escorted Lincoln's coffin to Washington's railway depot and Admiral Charles Davis, chief of the Bureau of Navigation and a colleague of Lenthall's, formed part of the honor guard who rode the funeral train. For John Lenthall and the entire nation, those days immediately following Lincoln's assassination remained forever seared in their memories.

But a navy waits on no man; its business must proceed. On 4 May 1865, Secretary Welles wrote a letter to Chief Lenthall, and its contents were probably not unexpected. Orders had gone out to trim the Navy's blockading squadrons by half and it was now the bureaus' turn:[18]

> The time has arrived when the naval establishment can be largely reduced, and the extraordinary expenses incident to the war can have a corresponding reduction. Measures for this end have been for some time in progress by the Department and the Chiefs of the Bureaus are now directed without delay to institute rigid economies and initiate such measures as will materially reduce the expenses of the service.[19]

Welles' directive outlined specific measures: all night work in the navy yards was suspended, further purchases of additional supplies were halted, all other work was to be put on the most economical footing, the rapid completion of new work was discouraged, and the Department was to be consulted prior to making any contract proposals or before beginning the construction of new vessels. And finally, "the greatest economy consistent with the efficiency of the service is enjoined upon all officers of the Department." Welles' orders were followed by another in June which forbade new requisitions for naval stores as long as those taken from decommissioned vessels remained available.[20] The time for the Navy to tighten its belt had arrived.

* * *

While he endeavored to restore his bureau to a peacetime footing, John Lenthall received a private letter from Donald McKay, the well-known shipbuilder.[21] Writing from East Boston, McKay's ostensible purpose was to forward five "tables of weights of stores, provisions, coal, etc. put on board British warships" that he thought might be of interest to Lenthall. These "tables" were undoubtedly the five previously mentioned No. 211 forms that documented all of the items of deadweight carried by the Royal Navy's ships (see Chapter 20). As the forms were official documents issued by the Surveyor of the Navy's office, the unanswered question arises: how did an American civilian obtain them? McKay then suggested he would send Lenthall "the detailed plans of their last 52 gun class of sloops … trial speed of over 14 knots … designed by Isaac Watts, Esq, formerly Chief Constructor of H.M. Navy." He conspiratorially assured Lenthall that these plans had "never been out of my office, nor handed to any parties."[22] McKay then further related some observations and reminiscences of interest:

> I consider Mr. Watts the ablest naval constructor in Great Britain, though through some friendship Mr. Reed has superseded him but not in talent & ability. I have had many interviews with Mr. Watts, in which he often mentioned your name—he said he remembered you well when in England on your persevering tour through foreign Dockyards.

McKay's letter was cast in a friendly way and transmitted technical documents of value to a chief of the Bureau of Construction and Repair. But in the not-so-distant past, McKay had published harsh public ridicule of Lenthall in one of his many public letters. Writing from Britain on 24 January 1862—after the U.S. Navy's first three ironclads had been ordered but before *Monitor*'s trial by fire at Hampton Roads—Donald McKay opened by describing Britain and France's new "system" of ironclad warships. He then referred to his failed, over-priced tender for an ironclad which McKay claimed was "declined under the pretext that the new system had not been sufficiently tried." Next, he attacked Lenthall, his criticism focused on the many other proposals solicited by the first ironclad board:

> On the heads of our bureau of naval construction falls, therefore, all the blame, that they had not earlier made themselves masters of a subject which entirely belongs to the province of the naval constructor. ... The real purpose to be obtained by these tenders appeared to be to *furnish the chief of our bureau of naval construction with ideas and information on the new system,* which he failed and neglected to obtain himself in time to serve his country...[23]

The Boston shipbuilder's accusations echoed those raised by others during that stressful summer of 1861 and must have made Lenthall bristle. McKay's later public letters shifted their tone, adjusting to the increased potency of the U.S. Navy's fleet of ironclads, and by the end of the war, had become downright complimentary. Indeed, by then, he had acquired the competence to construct in iron, and built two vessels for the Navy, the light-draft monitor *Nausett* and the *Mohongo* class double-ender *Ashuelot.*[24] But one theme of Donald McKay's public essays remained ever constant, his admiration for the Royal Navy and its advanced warship designs.[25]

* * *

In the last week of June, the sad news reached John Lenthall of the untimely death of a good friend and staunch supporter, Admiral Samuel Francis Du Pont. He died in Philadelphia on the morning of 23 June 1865 at the age of sixty-one, and was buried in the Du Pont family plot near Louviers, his beloved home. The Navy was not officially represented at his funeral and there is no evidence that Lenthall was present. In July 1863, Admiral Du Pont had been relieved of command of the South Atlantic Blockading Squadron in the aftermath of his failed attack against the forts of Charleston, the first-ever naval assault by a fleet of ironclads. His dismissal was blamed on his lack of aggression during the battle and Welles' subsequent loss of confidence in him, but its roots go much deeper. In a parallel to Lenthall's marginalization, Du Pont had questioned the Navy Department's over-reliance on monitors and the conviction of Secretary Welles, reinforced by his assistant Gustavus Fox, that they were capable of overcoming any obstacle. That Charleston resisted all further naval assaults until war's closing ultimately vindicated Du Pont. But by then, his career was in tatters and he died soon after hostilities ended, largely forgotten by a navy he served for forty-nine years.[26]

Unfortunately, Lenthall was not quite done with funerals. Six weeks after Du Pont's passing, Captain Percival Drayton, the recently appointed chief of the Bureau of Navigation and Office of Detail suddenly died. At Admiral Porter's invitation John Lenthall, together with several other bureau chiefs, was requested to act as one of Drayton's twelve pallbearers. Drayton, a less well-remembered Civil War fighting captain, was a South Carolinian who remained faithful to the Union. He commanded the monitor *Passaic* under Du Pont at the attack on Charleston and served as Farragut's fleet captain on *Hartford* at the Battle of Mobile Bay. Captain Drayton had been one of Admiral Du Pont's clique of officers and it is ironic that Du Pont's final letter, written the night before he died, was to Percival Drayton. And now they had both passed from the scene.[27]

* * *

On 15 August 1865, Secretary Welles ordered John Lenthall to "visit the several navy yards on the Atlantic coast and the naval station at Cairo, Illinois."[28] Welles' directive was undoubtedly motivated by the Navy's massive demobilization. Soon after its May cutbacks had been announced, a new goal was set to reduce the total number of active vessels in domestic waters to less than one hundred; by early July, the blockading squadrons were down to thirty. At the end of July, the Potomac flotilla had been disbanded and on the day before Welles issued his order to Lenthall, the Mississippi flotilla met the same fate. The downward trajectory was staggering—the Navy had begun the year with 471 ships on blockade duty and by December, the number was less than thirty. But not all of Secretary Welles' readjustments were negative. Starting in spring of 1865, vessels were dispatched to repopulate the Navy's long-neglected foreign squadrons. After a four-year hiatus, the cruising navy was again showing the flag and protecting American interests abroad. [29]

Lenthall dutifully turned in budget estimates for the beginning of the 1866 fiscal year and, on 5 September, notified Assistant Secretary Fox that in his absence, Admiral Smith had agreed to act for him.[30] Then he was off on his inspection tour of the navy yards. One clue to his initial routing is that two days later, his daughter Jenny, now a young woman of nineteen, wrote a letter to her mother from Niagara, New York, having just arrived at the Cataract House hotel after an exhausting all-day journey from Albany which had been preceded by an enjoyable run up the Hudson.[31] Perhaps John Lenthall escorted his daughter as far as New York City before parting ways, her to upstate New York and he to New England.

Lenthall's itinerary is not known in detail, but he certainly travelled as far north as Portsmouth, New Hampshire and made the long journey west to Cairo, Illinois, at the junction of the Ohio and Mississippi Rivers, probably stopping in Boston, New York and Philadelphia in between. Perhaps he had time to visit his Eck family in-laws in nearby St. Louis, Missouri. Of interest to the historian are a paymaster's notations on the original letter that ordered him to make the trip, recording his travel cost reimbursements.

Dated 16 November 1865, they read: Paid $299.44 Mileage, to Portsmouth and back $99.56, to Cairo, Ill. and back $199.88.

By early October, John Lenthall had returned to Washington, as evidenced by a letter he wrote to Secretary Welles. Back in his familiar Navy Department office, he recommended breaking up or selling the old sailing sloop *John Adams.*[32] Her story is typical of the Navy's constant outlays to keep its decaying fleet of wooden ships afloat. *John Adams* was an 1831 administrative 'rebuilding' of an even older frigate of the same name.[33] By 1865 her cumulative repairs had absorbed nearly four times her original building cost and, in that year, the Navy had more ships on its hands than it knew what to do with. It was an easy decision to let her go.

* * *

CHAPTER 28

Postwar Years

The first full year of peace brought a strange game of musical chairs to the Navy Department and its source came from a land far from Washington. Assistant Secretary Fox relished his official duties but aspired to a change, possibly a European posting. Meanwhile, in distant Russia, Emperor Alexander II, who in the earliest days of the American Civil War voiced his strong support for the Union, had survived an assassination attempt. As an expression of its heart-felt relief on hearing of the czar's escape, on 16 May 1866, the U.S. Congress passed a joint resolution of congratulations. But how to ceremoniously deliver it in the hands of a personage of high standing who represented a restored United States, and do so in a way that showcased American power? The answer—give the job to Gustavus Fox and send him to Russia in one of the Navy's powerful new ironclads.[1]

From Bureau Chief Lenthall's viewpoint, the government's solution had a big impact. The post of assistant secretary of the navy remained—it was filled by former Department Chief Clerk William Faxon whose position, in turn, was taken by Gideon Welles' son, Edgar—but Fox had resigned and accepted the temporary sinecure created especially for him by Congress.[2] By June, he was gone from the Navy Department and, indeed, for the next six months from the United States. Instead of contending with Fox's demanding personality, Lenthall now had only to deal with the administratively-minded Faxon.

The powerful warship chosen to convey Fox to Russia was, ironically, one of the Navy Department-designed ironclads that sprang from the minds of John Lenthall and Benjamin Isherwood, *Miantonomoh.* Curiously, the U.S. Navy's most advanced armored war steamer was accompanied by two side-wheelers: *Augusta,* a William Webb-built former coastal packet dating from 1852 and *Ashuelot,* the iron-hulled double-ender constructed by Donald McKay.[3] *Miantonomoh* successfully crossed the Atlantic Ocean, making her the first American armored vessel and first monitor to do so. Although she was towed for part of the distance, she behaved well on the high seas, helped no doubt by her relatively large 2½ feet of freeboard. *Miantonomoh*'s six-month tour of European ports created exactly the impression the Navy desired, awe and respect for its double turreted ironclad.

Congress wasn't yet finished with tinkering into the Navy's affairs. Largely to address the plights of the many capable volunteers who served during the war but were now threatened with dismissal, on 25 July 1866 an act was passed that created new positions within the ranks of naval officers. This same act also contained the language "that naval constructors ... in the Navy shall be appointed by the President and confirmed by the Senate, and shall have the naval rank of officers of the Navy," thus inaugurating the formal birth of the U.S. Navy's Construction Corps.[4] Naval constructors had long been considered to be civil officers who, since 1862, had been assigned relative ranks within the line-staff officer hierarchy. But from this date on, constructors were commissioned officers of the U.S. Navy and given the rank of "naval constructor." The former relative ranks still applied, a senior constructor being equivalent to a captain and one serving as a bureau chief, a commodore. So, by an act of Congress, John Lenthall was now ranked as a naval constructor—the most senior of all—and thus appeared as such on official records.[5]

This enhancement of naval constructors' status was not applauded by many of the Navy's line officers. They were resentful that staff officers, who never served afloat in harm's way, were accorded rank, the all-important mark of status that governed so many rituals of the service and determined the hierarchy, place and order of everything important to a naval officer.

The Congressional act of July 1866 also coincided with the expiration of John Lenthall's four-year term as chief of the Bureau of Construction and Repair. Accordingly, on 28 July 1866, Secretary Welles reappointed the fifty-eight-year-old John Lenthall as bureau chief. Lenthall responded on 6 August with a letter in which he acknowledged receipt of his enclosed new commission "and respectfully ask leave to thank the Department for the trust it has been pleased to continue to repose in me."[6] By this date, John Lenthall had served as bureau chief for almost thirteen years.

Word of Lenthall's new status and continuation as bureau chief travelled quickly. From Augusta, Maine, his former chief clerk and now political savant, A. B. Farwell, wrote:

> I was greatly rejoiced at your re-appointment as Ch. of the Bureau for four more years. More so to learn that you had been commissioned as the ranking naval constructor ... I watched with the most friendly

> anxiety the passage of the bill which for more than two years met the most determined opposition from Mr. Hale & Mr. Fox.... the latter it is quite possible on his return may fail to be an object of concern.[7]

Senator John Hale, of New Hampshire, had long been a thorn in Secretary Welles' side And Gustavus Fox, a former line officer, was by now on his way to Russia.

Another actor from the past who had become firmly embedded in the postwar naval establishment was David D. Porter. Now a vice admiral, he had been recently appointed as superintendent of the United States Naval Academy.[8] In his efforts to "make the seamanship department of the academy as respectable as possible," on 16 December 1866, Porter addressed a letter of appeal to Bureau Chief Lenthall. "Dear Sir, I am looking up models of all kinds, and among them I should like to get models of some of the beautiful vessels you have constructed ... I write purely unofficially and desire it as a matter of good will on your part."[9] It is not known how Lenthall responded to Porter's subtlety intimidating request, but given the admiral's position and power, it is likely that some of the bureau's models made their way to Annapolis.

* * *

Although a high bureau chief, John Lenthall still got his hands dirty, tramping through navy yards and climbing inside the Navy's warships. In early March 1867, at the request of Secretary Welles, he conducted an examination of the steam sloop *Richmond* then tied up at the Washington Navy Yard. The summary of his findings, which dissented from the majority report of other officers participating in the same survey, makes an interesting read especially for naval architects.[10] *Richmond* had a poor reputation for motions, not an unusual occurrence in an era of idiosyncratic ship designs. She pitched excessively and had an uneasy roll; twelve years after Lenthall's examination she was fitted with bilge keels in an attempt to dampen her rolling.[11] Recall that *Richmond* was one of the class of five screw steam sloops authorized in 1857 (see Chapter 19) and built at the Norfolk Navy Yard by Constructor Samuel T. Hartt. First commissioned in late 1860, she had a remarkably active war career. It was this veteran warship that was the subject of John Lenthall's submitted opinions:

> It is represented by officers who have sailed in this vessel, that she is uneasy, and rolls heavily: this is to be expected when there is an undue proportion between the draught of water, and the breadth of the vessel. When this ship was built, the instructions were to have a draught of water that could enter any Southern port, and the naval

constructor who built her, was highly complimented for having attained such a satisfactory result; this also shows, that an excess of one quality can only be obtained at the sacrifice of some other.

Lenthall's last phrase encapsulates a designer's eternal conundrum. *Richmond*'s beam of 42 ft was two feet less than that of her near sister, *Hartford.* Hartt also gave her little deadrise, hard bilges and minimal tumblehome, all to increase her midship section area, thereby obtaining the relatively light draft of 15 ft 6 in while keeping her ends moderately sharp. But he paid for that gain with less than optimal hull motion characteristics:[12]

In order to change the period of oscillation, or rolling, the distance between the points on which this quality depends, or the length of the representative pendulums, must be reduced and the radius of gyration increased; this has been done by placing the coal on the berth deck [discussed earlier in Lenthall's letter], and in winging it out, and in my opinion, these bunkers should not be removed, as the quantity of coal they contain is indispensable to the efficiency of the vessel, in addition to which, the weight in that part tends materially to ameliorate the defect of rolling.

John Lenthall had correctly analyzed *Richmond*'s problem. Reducing a ship's roll to simple harmonic motion allows use of the following formula to calculate her roll period:

$$T = \frac{1.108\,k}{\sqrt{GM}}$$

where k is the radius of gyration, GM the metacentric height above the center of gravity and T is the period of motion in seconds.[13]

The solutions proposed by Lenthall, reducing the "representative pendulum," GM, and increasing the radius of gyration, k, both had the effect of increasing the period of motion, T, which would result in an easier roll with less snap. Retaining *Richmond*'s berth deck level coal bunkers achieved this goal. Chief Lenthall had not lost touch with the theory and practice of naval architecture.

* * *

The postwar years brought with them the need for more travel and John Lenthall dutifully complied. In late 1866 he made another round of visits to the navy yards, some in the company of other constructors, followed always by proposals for the maintenance or disposition of the Navy's dwindling inventory of warships.[14] And the demands kept coming. Not long after completing his examination of *Richmond,* Secretary Welles again tapped Lenthall, this time for a trip south. Dated 26 April 1867, he issued the following instructions:

> Proceed to Pensacola, Florida and New Orleans, La. and examine the Naval Stations & Naval property at each point and upon your return make report of the conditions with your recommendation for their future improvement and care.
>
> Incidentally extend your enquiries to the conditions of the Live Oak Plantations.[15]

At just this moment, John Lenthall suffered a severe health crisis. Its cause was "a fatty degeneration of the heart" that so impaired his blood circulation he could only walk "at a snail's pace." The slightest exertion left him exhausted.[16] Benjamin Isherwood feared for his life and Constructor Isaiah Hanscom opined "Our present Chief ... is very much out of health ... it is doubtful if he does any more duty..."[17] Lenthall's close friend, A. B. Farwell, alarmed at his near total breakdown, wrote "Knowing as I do that you rarely complain and never unless you are really sick, let me beg you not to return to that table and room which for twenty years has sapped your very life ..."[18] Approaching his sixtieth birthday, John Lenthall had borne a bureau chief's unceasing stress throughout the four long years of war. The strain had clearly taken its toll.

Lenthall sought help from his nephew, Doctor Robert King Stone. On his first visit, Stone prescribed five remedies, the first of which was mustard plasters with instructions to "continue as before," suggesting Lenthall's ailment was the worsening of an existing condition. He also recommended that Lenthall, together with his family, embark on a restorative sea cruise. Two days later, on 1 May, a second round of eight prescriptions followed under the heading "For the Trip." Topping the list was the importance of a midship cabin, to avoid motion and nausea. Instructions for using aromatic spirits of ammonia, chloroform, tincture of red pepper, Brown's shaken extract from Jamaican ginger and more followed, with a caution to avoid fatty food and eat plenty of meat and fish. Stone's final admonition was to "Live simply but well."[19]

With his doctor's instructions in hand, John Lenthall, his wife Mary and daughter Jenny hurriedly took their leave of Washington. But where to go? One popular destination in those days was the coastal voyage from New York to Havana. Eight years earlier, the author of *Two Years Before the Mast,* Richard Henry Dana, had written a lively account of just such a journey titled *To Cuba and Back: A Vacation Voyage.*[20]

It appears the Lenthalls did exactly that: they booked cabins for the six-day passage to Havana, and with only a brief pause, returned to New York. The warmer waters of the Gulf Stream and tropical airs of Cuba must have worked wonders on Lenthall's health, for once back in the United States, he decided to fulfil Secretary Welles' orders to visit Pensacola and New Orleans, but to do so at a leisurely pace in the company of his family. And so, the Lenthalls promptly reembarked for Charleston on the steamer *Champion*, arriving on 22 May 1867.[21] They then caught trains to Savannah, across Georgia, finally ending their journey in Mobile. From there, the Navy took over, the commandant at Pensacola having placed the steamer *Estrella* at the Lenthalls' disposal, and brought them by sea to the navy yard.

In mid-1867, the Pensacola Navy Yard was still recovering from its destruction by evacuating Confederate forces, and many of its facilities were temporary war-built structures.[22] But the Lenthalls were warmly greeted by the resident assistant constructor, Theodore Wilson, who gave them rooms in his house.[23] The twenty-seven-year-old Wilson, a native of New York and a former apprentice of B. F. Delano, must have made a favorable impression on Lenthall. Later that year Wilson was transferred to the Philadelphia Navy Yard, a more prestigious posting, and in 1869 Lenthall's influence ensured his appointment as an instructor at Annapolis.[24] Wilson went on to publish a textbook in 1873, *An Outline of Ship Building, Theoretical and Practical*, and eventually rose to become chief of the Bureau of Construction and Repair (see Appendix 12).[25] And it all began with a late spring visit from his ailing boss.

Next, the Lenthalls were whisked across the warm waters of the Gulf of Mexico to New Orleans on *Estrella*, a former British-built blockade runner. There bureau chief Lenthall inspected a number of decommissioned ironclads before he and his family journeyed up the Mississippi to Memphis. Now on their way home, the Lenthalls spent a night at Lookout Mountain House, Chattanooga, where Jenny scribbled a note to her Aunt Mary in Washington:

> Father has been very well, he walks about quite nicely, not fast, of course, but he does far better than when he left home. ... Mother has had a severe "boil" on her face and nose ... the bite of some poisonous insect in Pensacola. No body takes us for Yankees, all think we are French or else German.[26]

Once home, there are indications that John Lenthall and his family extended their rest and relaxation to a stay at Cape May on the New Jersey shore. If so, it would be the first of many visits.[27] But by late August, in a still hot and muggy Washington, the chief was back at his desk, his health apparently restored.

* * *

The postwar years brought abruptly declining levels of naval expenditures, plummeting from $123 million in 1865 to just $31 million in 1867, and even less in the years that followed. When Congress met in December of 1867, Secretary Welles' efforts to maintain a functional navy ran into the lawmakers' demands for further reductions, and he was forced to take strong measures as indicated by orders he issued on the 12th to Bureau Chief Lenthall:[28]

> You will limit the new work, under your direction in the several Navy Yards, to the completion of the 'Contoocook', and the construction of the 'Algoma', 'Alaska', 'Kenosha' and 'Omaha'.
>
> If work is being done upon any others of the new vessels, you will have it brought to a close as soon as it can be done, with proper protection to the vessels.[29]

Welles' directive allowed completion of the most advanced of the *Contoocook* "clipper screw sloops" and authorized building of four new "fast vessels of a small class." These *Algoma* class steam sloops were conceived as less expensive alternatives to the larger *Contoocooks* and *Guerrieres* for service on the reactivated foreign cruising stations. At 250 ft in length and 38 ft breath, they also embodied the Navy's reversion to a traditional broadside battery rather than relying on a few large pivot guns. Designed by John Lenthall, these ships were regarded as a particularly handsome class, with their distinctive twin funnels and graceful sheer lines.[30]

Congressional efforts to reduce naval expenditures continued to squeeze hard. In answer to a House resolution enquiring about green and seasoned timber held by the navy yards, Lenthall responded "There is no timber on hand that can be considered seasoned except Live Oak," adding that "annual contracts only provide for the wants of ... the current year."[31] Further pressure came from a 3 February 1868 Congressional joint resolution authorizing the sale of all ironclads other than those of the *Passaic, Dictator, Monadnock* and *Kalamazoo* classes, unless demands of the service warranted their retention.[32] Not yet three years after Appomattox, the rush to liquidate a navy created so quickly at such a great cost is sobering; on the block were the latest monitors of the *Canonicus* and *Casco* classes, twenty-eight in all. Two months later, John Lenthall notified Secretary Welles of the receipt of funds for the purchase of

Catawba and *Oneota*; never commissioned in the U.S. Navy, they were bought by Peru for $755,000, little more than half their original cost.[33] They would be the first of many ironclads to be discarded.

Queries about the number of men employed by the several navy yards, with a view to their potential "proper reduction," were answered by Bureau Chief Lenthall in late February.[34] His list forms a valuable overview of the yards' status in the aftermath of the Civil War:

Portsmouth	325	persons
Boston	417	"
New York	463	"
Philadelphia	334	"
Washington	96	"
Norfolk	130	"
Pensacola	26	"

With the warmth of spring nearly at hand, John Lenthall suffered another round of visits to his physician, Robert King Stone. Two lengthy prescriptions in Doctor Stone's distinctive underlining style of handwriting documented a new ailment: "excess secretion of oxalic acid" or the agony of kidney stones. Recommendations followed for a nourishing diet, plenty of fresh air, exercise "in the cars (until you have your carriage)" and multiple drops of patent medicines.[35]

However, Chief Lenthall's health was robust enough in June for Secretary Welles to order him to New York to examine "the Spanish iron-clad frigate in the dock of the navy yard."[36] The vessel was not named but she was one of the five armored frigates then active in the Spanish Navy.[37] Constructors, then as now, were always curious about the competition.

* * *

The national elections of November 1868 brought the administration of Ulysses S. Grant into office and that meant Secretary Welles' days were numbered. His tenure at the Navy Department was already unprecedented—two full presidential terms—and by spring of 1869 he would have been nearly sixty-seven. One of the greatest navy secretaries ever, Gideon Welles' patient guidance and wisdom would be sorely missed, especially by his bureau chiefs.[38] Just how much they would soon learn.

It was no secret that President Grant wished he could have appointed Vice Admiral David Porter to be his secretary of the navy, but tradition required that a civilian fill the position. Grant's workaround was to appoint a compliant figurehead who would allow Porter to control the Navy on his behalf and the man he chose was the "proper Philadelphian," Adolph Borie. During the new secretary's first day at the Navy Department, 9 March 1869, Porter personally escorted the fifty-nine-year-old Borie through the building, flaunting his new authority. Instructions quickly followed that all business of the bureaus was to be first routed through Admiral Porter. On his second day, Porter acted on his visceral dislike of Benjamin Isherwood—a staff officer who had worked tirelessly to improve the Navy's steam machinery and pushed hard for ranking engineers as equals to line officers—and removed him from office as chief of the Bureau of Steam Engineering. It is no surprise that Porter also ensured Isherwood's triumphs—the super cruisers *Wampanoag* and her speedy sisters—met similar fates and, with one exception, were permanently laid up, consigned to oblivion.[39]

John Lenthall must have been appalled at Isherwood's treatment. They had served together in the Navy Department since the earliest days of the war and were of the same mind on many controversial issues, the most significant being the primacy of monitors. But now Lenthall could see the handwriting on the wall and must have realized that his career, too, was living on borrowed time. And just when he thought things couldn't get worse, Porter struck again.

On April fool's day of 1869, Secretary Borie issued his infamous General Order 120, which struck down Welles' directive of 13 March 1863 that had expanded relative rank to, among others, naval constructors. President Grant's attorney general had determined that Welles' order was invalid because only Congress had the authority to grant rank, and Porter took full advantage of his ruling to further humiliate staff officers. At the stroke of a pen, the relative ranks of all staff officers reverted to their pre-1863 status, which for surgeons meant a "degradation" of rank but for naval constructors, chaplains and professors of mathematics, caused the loss of their relative ranks altogether. Bureau Chief John Lenthall, together with his peers at the Bureaus of Medicine and Surgery, Provisions and Clothing and Steam Engineering, were commodores no longer.[40]

More general orders followed, driven by Porter's single-minded ambition to push the Navy back into the era of canvas and hemp. Directives were issued ordering "constant exercises … with sails and spars" and banning the use of steaming save for "the most urgent circumstances." Transgressors were warned that the cost of wastefully expended coal might be "charged to their account." And to firmly embed his reactionary motive power preferences, a board was appointed which tabled proposals to replace more efficient four-bladed propellers with the older two-bladed style in a misguided effort to improve ships' performance under sail.[41] The new program had the opposite effect to that intended and increased the coal consumption of every vessel so refitted. Years passed before the harm was made good.[42]

* * *

John Lenthall must have been thankful for a brief but welcome distraction from the oppression of Porter: his daughter's marriage. Jenny Lenthall, now a young woman of twenty-three, became engaged that year to Thomas Ennalls Waggaman, a thirty-year-old Washingtonian. Waggaman had attended Georgetown University and was now a wealthy real estate broker. One of the links between Jenny and "Ennals," as she fondly called him, was their shared Roman Catholic faith which may also explain how they first met.[43] Waggaman was a noted connoisseur of art and his growing collection of Dutch masters and Oriental porcelains would in time be recognized as one of the finest in Washington.[44] Photographs of him reveal a handsome, lean-faced man sporting a prodigious moustache. Regrettably, no images have been found of the bride, Jenny Lenthall. They were married on 16 June 1869.[45] It must have been a memorable day for her father, John Lenthall, and his wife Mary. Their only surviving child had now truly begun her own life.

* * *

Less than a week after Jenny's wedding, Secretary Borie resigned. Given his lack of interest for the office he held and his constant intimidation by Admiral Porter, it is not surprising that he chose to retire to his former life in Philadelphia. President Grant must have anticipated Borie's departure for the next day he nominated George M. Robeson, the forty-year-old attorney general of New Jersey, to fill the position. Possessing a greater aptitude for the responsibilities of a navy secretary than Borie, Robeson was his own man and once installed, Porter's absolute stranglehold on the Navy began to wane.[46] A month later, on 19 July, Porter was still issuing orders to the bureau chiefs in his own name but his grip was loosening.[47]

16 September 1869 brought John Lenthall to his sixty-second birthday. That event triggered another silent push toward the door. By an act of Congress passed on 21 December 1862, all serving officers who reached that age were required to be placed on the retired list. Official Navy records show that on 28 September, he was so entered, dating from the sixteenth.[48] Lenthall had nearly one more year remaining from his reappointment as bureau chief in 1866, and Secretary Robeson was content, for the moment, to allow him to continue on in that role. Earlier that year his long-time colleague, Admiral Joseph Smith of the Bureau of Yards and Docks, had been eased out of office, replaced by Captain Daniel Ammen. Indeed,

seven of the original chiefs appointed to office when the bureau system was reorganized in 1862 were gone, leaving John Lenthall as the sole holdout. His tenure of over fifteen years was, save for Smith's, the longest of any of them. Lenthall, the stalwart survivor, must have savored his achievement. But for how much longer could he last?

* * *

CHAPTER 29

Moved Aside

On the retired list he might have been, but John Lenthall kept as active as his body allowed. In early October, he submitted a proposal to Rear Admiral Gordon at the New York Navy Yard for systematizing the dimensions of each type of ships' boats carried by the different classes of warships, which included two tables of detailed data.[1] And in early October, "for the purpose of making a personal inspection of all the matters under the cognizance of the Bureau of Construction and Repair," Lenthall was ordered by Admiral Porter to visit the several navy yards on the upper east coast.[2]

Lenthall must have forewarned his former chief clerk and friend, A. B. Farwell, of a shipyard tour which might afford the chance to pay him a visit in Augusta. Farwell, now firmly entrenched in Maine politics, was quick to respond, writing that he would leverage his influence with Maine's Senator Morrill to "relieve the naval staff from the manifest oppression from which they now labor," adding that "Porter is a tyrant if he is a great man in other respects." A visit to Maine, Farwell reassured, would be "excellent for your health."[3]

In early October, John Lenthall began his navy yard tour starting with Philadelphia, and then in the company of Benjamin Delano, the resident constructor at New York, went on toward Maine. A Boston newspaper snippet dated 19 October recorded that they had "been at Augusta, Me., the guests of Hon. A. B. Farwell. They leave for the Charlestown Navy Yard to-day."[4] Once finished with their official business, on their way home Lenthall and Delano stopped off at Hartford, Connecticut to call on their former boss, Gideon Welles. Much had changed at the Navy Department since Welles' departure in March and there would have been plenty to talk about. Unfortunately, Welles was out of town. But soon after Lenthall's return to Washington, a 'private' letter arrived from Welles dated 8 November 1869. Opening with "My Worthy Friend," Welles first explained how he had tried to catch up with Lenthall and Delano, then dove into an ironic commentary:

> I wanted to see you, and to congratulate you on those wonderful expenditures, of which we learn so much in almost daily bulletins. I had supposed we had managed affairs with some degree of economy, but the newspapers and correspondents hint at, and tell a different story. They have doubtless examined the books or learned the facts from somebody.
>
> I had also supposed that you and Mr. Delano understood your profession, and had done as well for the country as any two men could during the war and subsequently that you had intelligently and skillfully assisted in building up a great Navy, and faithfully aided in reducing it when hostilities ceased, but I learn that there have been one or two boards of line officers appointed to examine the naval vessels, and criticize the work of our naval constructors, whose conclusions are different from mine. The papers say also, that Vice Admiral Porter had entirely reorganized the Navy, and naval vessels, on some economic plan by which immense saving has been, or will be made and the vessels rendered vastly more efficient. This has been his own <u>personal</u> effort and handy work ... Perhaps there is some leak in the Department by which all these astonishing <u>facts</u> get out.
>
> Now, I wished some information on these and other interesting subjects, and you, one of my official family, could have enlightened me. Perhaps you may find time to whisper to me by letter—for I suppose it must be a great secret how to repair and refit the vessels and re-organize them and the Navy without cost.
>
> I am incredulous on these subjects, and do not believe the vessels can be repaired without money, which Congress refused to appropriate—nor do I believe that Selfridge or Porter can instruct you and Delano in the art and mystery of ship-building or improve your designs.
>
> The schemes and intrigues to defame those who gave their time, and minds, and energies with unsparing devotion to their country and service, are ungenerous and wicked. No enduring fame or lasting honor can be acquired by such means, nor do men ever succeed in building for themselves a good reputation by injustice to others.

> But great changes have been made in the Department, Isherwood was the first victim, and others have followed. You are a special monument of those, who during the war, wrought out the grand work which gave the officers the means, by which they acquired immortal renown, and long may you be spared in life, health and position … The severe labor which you underwent for about six years, when the country demanded so much, was exacting and exhaustive—few constitutions could have stood it. I shall always be glad to hear from and see you, and be posted in a quiet way, on what is being done. [5]

Almost as satisfying as Welles' letter were the orders Lenthall received one week later from Secretary Robeson. He had been appointed to a board to "take into consideration the subject of assimilated rank between line and civil officers of the Navy."[6] Hopefully, the board could right the wrong of Borie's demoralizing general order. Lenthall was encouraged to seize the opportunity to express his long-held views about naval constructors and how they fit into the Navy's hierarchy:

> The number of Naval Constructors is not now determined by any laws, but in making a law for that purpose, regard should be had to the probable wants of the service, that is one for each Yard, and to so small a number as would be required by this arrangement, there should be one in addition, for special duty, in aid in this Bureau, where much useful information is obtained as to the manner in which the business of the Navy is transacted.
>
> Naval Constructors, in the line of their duty are mainly brought in direct connection with the officers of the Navy stations at Navy Yards, and have little or nothing to do with any others, nor can their duties, which are wholly mechanical, conflict with those of any other department. Much the largest portion of the expenditures of the Navy is made under their immediate supervision; Naval officers at Yards are continually being changed, and with this change there is a consequent change of duties, but if a Naval Constructor is removed, it is to perform exactly the same duties at another yard, and thus much of the permanence and constancy of the administration of the Navy Yards, devolve on them. …
>
> I would respectfully ask that the number of Naval Constructors assimilated or having precedence with Captains be increased, and that the Constructors of that grade be not less in number than two

> thirds of the whole number allowed, and that of the Assistant Naval Constructors not more than one third have assimilated rank with Lieutenant Commanders.[7]

* * *

The old year turned over into 1870, and John Lenthall promptly responded to Secretary Robeson's requests for, among other things, accounts of his bureau's monthly expenditures and a statement of the names and duties of his office employees. On 25 February, however, his work ground to a halt as he, half of the Navy Department and many other Congressmen and high officials, caught an early train to Annapolis. The purpose of their all-day excursion—a tour of the very latest British ironclad battleship, H.M.S. *Monarch.*[8]

Why was the pride of the Royal Navy lying just off Annapolis? The recent death of the American philanthropist, George Peabody, had spurred the British government, in a gesture of peace and harmony, to make her available to carry his remains back to his homeland. Winter of 1870 was also the moment of Britain and America's final stages of sparring over how to settle the vexing *Alabama* claims, so *Monarch*'s timely arrival might also be viewed as a riposte to *Miantonomoh*'s 1866 appearance on the Thames. Whatever her visit's true purpose, it served as a stunning exhibition of a state-of-the-art ocean-going turreted ironclad. She was one of two such vessels recently commissioned by the Royal Navy, the other being Captain Cowper Coles' ill-fated *Captain. Monarch* was 330 feet long, carried two turrets each mounting a pair of 12-inch rifled guns, and was fully rigged for ocean cruising. During her voyage across the Atlantic, *Monarch* sailed in company with the U.S.S. *Plymouth,* one of Lenthall's *Algoma* class steam sloops, which she handily outpaced.[9] Not only was *Monarch* a powerful battleship, she was faster than America's latest cruiser.

The party from Washington, some 150 in all, included Secretary Robeson, Admiral Porter, Bureau Chief Lenthall, many members of the U.S. government and numerous foreign emissaries. They were treated to a full demonstration of *Monarch*'s capabilities. Once all were on board, she steamed down the bay and fired off rounds from her 12-inch guns and then returned to Annapolis in time for her guests to catch a late train back to Washington.

One can only imagine the thoughts going through John Lenthall's head on that late February day. *Monarch* was just the sort of war steamer he and Isherwood had urged the U.S. Navy to build, only to see their beloved service overwhelmed by Monitor fever. Even if only costs were considered, she was by far the better bargain. Britain built *Monarch* for £350,000, or less than a fifth of what the Navy spent on the twenty useless *Casco* class light-draft monitors, or only slightly more than the cost of Ericsson's great *Dictator*—with but one turret and sixteen *inches* of freeboard.[10] Thoughts of all that lost treasure and opportunity must have made Lenthall shake his head, dreaming of what might have been. Here, at Annapolis, was evidence that such ships *could* be built, but only by a country with a clear vision of its strategic destiny.[11]

* * *

Back at the Navy Department, Lenthall teamed up with his seven fellow bureau chiefs on the last day of February to sign a memorial to the members of Congress. The issue was their salaries, which they sincerely believed were too small for their stations and respectfully requested that they be made equivalent to the sea pay of a commodore.[12] Their appeal was an outgrowth of the recently appointed board to consider relative rank. The 1870 naval appropriations bill conceded to the bureau chiefs the pay of a commodore, but only for shore duty, the difference being $1,000 per annum.[13] Lenthall and his colleagues would not regain their coveted relative ranks until the following year's appropriation bill, when Congress formally restored the rank of commodore to the chiefs of the Bureaus of Medicine and Surgery, Provisions and Clothing, Steam Engineering and Construction and Repair.[14] It took nearly two years before Porter's disparagement was finally blotted away, but its memory lingered on.

Recent happenings at the Navy Department were directed at more than just matters of rank and reporting expenses. An effort was afoot to reinstate naval constructor William Hanscom, who in January 1866 had abruptly resigned under a cloud of suspected dishonesty.[15] Hanscom, it will be recalled, was the constructor at Portsmouth whose submitted costs for building a lightship had so outraged John Lenthall. He was next assigned to the Boston Navy Yard where he constructed the double turreted ironclad *Monadnock*, but suspicions about his character continued to grow. His younger brother, Isaiah, was an up-and-coming constructor who had also served in those same yards.[16] And in early March, John Lenthall received a letter about William Hanscom from, of all people, Gustavus Fox. The former assistant secretary, now privately employed, expressed his concern at hearing the House Naval Affairs Committee was considering allowing Hanscom to withdraw his resignation. Fox reminded Lenthall of why Hanscom had been originally forced out, then added "he is probably now a Grant man but you may be very sure of one thing that he never can be trusted."[17] Now he had Lenthall's attention.

Fox's tag of a "Grant man" reflected the new and unsettling morals of President Grant's administration. The ethos of many federal officers hired by the president and his underlings were questionable at best and at worst, tainted with corruption. Grant's secretary of the navy and Lenthall's immediate superior, George Robeson, would at the end of his nearly eight years in office go down as the most comprehensively investigated of any of the navy secretaries.[18] And his opposite at the war office, Secretary William Belknap, was eventually forced to resign, then impeached on charges of malfeasance. Both men were never found guilty of wrongdoing but, especially in Belknap's case, it was a close-run thing. The opportunities for dishonest officeholders to exploit the system were, as Lenthall well knew, endless. He was a witness to Robeson's preference for open purchases and the shameless influence peddling he tolerated from contractors bent on winning lucrative work. And as Lenthall had recently advised the secretary, the largest portion of the Navy's expenditures were made under the immediate supervision of naval constructors, which is why Hanscom's possible reinstatement was so worrying. The Navy Department had no immediate need for such a man, and if it did, why employ a constructor with such a questionable past? Any conclusions Lenthall could draw about motives were, at the least, very troubling.

* * *

Joyous news greeted the Lenthall family later that spring—the birth of their first grandchild. On 23 May 1870, Jane Lenthall Waggaman delivered a baby girl, who was given the name Ann Marie in honor of her maternal grandmother. Naval historians have good reason to mark the date, for this tiny infant would grow up to be Mrs. Eugene Semmes Ives, donor to the U.S. Naval Academy Museum of the invaluable trove of John Lenthall's correspondence known as the Ives Collection.[19] But for the moment, her delighted grandfather was simply thankful that his daughter Jenny had safely given birth to a healthy child.

Two months later on 8 July, federal census takers provided a fresh snapshot of the Lenthall household on 1818 F Street NW.[20] John Lenthall now aged sixty-two, a "naval constructor," headed the listing, followed by his wife Mary D., aged fifty-six (actually fifty-eight) and "keeping house," then his sister Mary K., aged sixty-one (actually sixty-eight) and finally two Irish-born female servants. Lenthall's sister Mary, the spinster, had by now moved into the family's F Street home. Also living with them was their niece from St. Louis, Ellen Eck, aged twenty-one, who had probably been taken in several years earlier following the death of her namesake mother. Sadly, Ellen did not survive the month, dying from unknown causes. She was buried in the Catholic Mount Olivet Cemetery next to her paternal grandmother, Ann Marie Eck.

The census data shows that, relative to their neighbors, the Lenthalls were very wealthy. Of the eight households listed on the page documenting the Lenthalls, the aggregate value of real estate owned was $38,600 of which the Lenthalls accounted for $20,000. As for the value of personal estates the picture is even more overwhelming. The page total was $37,700 and the Lenthalls' share accounted for $35,000, or nearly all of it.[21] And these were the figures they reported to an anonymous census taker; the actual values of their "real estate owned" were probably greater. Many years of full employment—John Lenthall was making $3,500 per year by 1870—a restrained lifestyle, wise investments and the accumulation of inherited property were behind these impressive totals.[22]

* * *

Following Admiral David Farragut's death in August, David Dixon Porter rose to assume the mantle of the highest-ranking admiral in the U.S. Navy. It was from his new position that he wrote to John Lenthall on 16 November 1870, introducing him to the American polar explorer, Charles F. Hall. Congress had authorized the funding of Hall's third expedition into the frozen north, and as Porter informed Lenthall, Hall was to be "provided with a naval vessel for use in the exploration of the arctic regions." Further, Lenthall was asked to "discuss with him the fitness of the Periwinkle for the service in question and give him the benefit of your suggestions on the matter."[23] The incongruously named *Periwinkle* was a small, schooner-rigged steamer acquired in 1864. Rechristened *Polaris*, in 1871, she would take Hall to the northern-most position yet reached by a ship, 81° 11' N; the unfortunate Hall died soon after under suspicious circumstances.[24] But John Lenthall had done his best to get him off to a good start.

One week later, on 22 November, Lenthall advised Secretary Robeson of the results of a recent survey of the steam sloop *Kearsarge*, then lying off the Mare Island Navy Yard. The nine-year-old warship was "in a very decayed condition" and her repairs were estimated at "$195,000, being about thirty-two percent more than the original cost of the vessel." Lenthall recommended that she be "condemned and sold." Perhaps realizing the trophy value of *Kearsarge*, whose guns had sunk the Confederate raider *Alabama*, Secretary Robeson endorsed Lenthall's letter, "Let her be laid up."[25] The doughty old steamer was rebuilt and served on the Asiatic, North Atlantic, Mediterranean and West Indies stations until she was wrecked on Roncador Reef in 1894.[26]

* * *

John Lenthall's four-year term as chief of the Bureau of Construction and Repair had expired in July 1870, and as the months ticked over, no clarification of his status had been voiced by Secretary Robeson. What discussions occurred between the two during this period are not known, but that his situation remained unresolved must have made Lenthall anxious.

As an indicator of what might be expected of him in the months to come, Lenthall had been instructed by Secretary Robeson to sign two bills for "extra pay on their contracts" for old monitor work by Secor, builders of iron ships, totaling some $93,000. These were invoices that Lenthall recalled had been settled during Secretary Welles' tenure, but now, by written order of the Secretary of the Navy, he was being asked to disburse funds for them out of current appropriations funding. John Lenthall did so but it left him with a sense of disquiet.[27]

The new year had come and gone and still no word from Secretary Robeson. Then on Thursday, 19 January 1871, the dreaded letter arrived on John Lenthall's desk:

> Dear Sir,
> After a great deal of consideration, I have been constrained by what I consider my duty to advise the President to nominate a younger person to the position of Chief of the Bureau of Construction and Repair made vacant by the expiration of your term. This, I assure you is not done by reason of any want of confidence in you or appreciation of your ability and services. The records of the Department and history of our Navy will remain lasting memorials of those. But to nominate a retired officer for a fixed term to the head of a Bureau is, in my opinion, contrary to the spirit if not the letter of the law ... Neither do I wish that you should retire at present from active duty, but I shall be glad if the service can have the benefit still of your ability and experience. I shall therefore, if you are willing, designate you as a general inspector and detail you for such duty as may be most agreeable.
>
> Very respectfully,
> /s/ Geo. M. Robeson
> Secretary of the Navy[28]

Not unexpectedly, Secretary Robeson had leveraged Lenthall's retired status to remove him, a reasonably fit sixty-three-year-old man with over seventeen years of unparalleled experience, as the sitting bureau chief. On the surface, it was reasonable, but then Admiral Smith, who had survived the horrendous war years as did Lenthall, was eighty and still going strong when he was eased out. And as he learned on the following Monday, 23

January, his successor had been chosen, Isaiah Hanscom, the fifty-six-year-old resident constructor at Boston and a brother of the ousted William.[29] The other logical heir, Benjamin F. Delano, was sixty-two that year and so would also be considered officially retired although he was still actively serving.

The official records show that John Lenthall was formally relieved of his duties as bureau chief on 28 January 1871, and confirmed the next day as a "general inspector of ships." Isaiah Hanscom was commissioned as chief of the Bureau of Construction and Repair on the 28th.[30] It was the end of the Lenthall era, the longest ever for a serving bureau chief.

No record has been found of John Lenthall's thoughts or feelings about being moved aside. He was now faced with the age-old problem of any man who chooses a calling, gives it his all, with every moment alive with purpose—then it comes crashing to a halt. Was he glad that his many years of stressful duties were over? Almost certainly not. Lenthall loved his work and thrived on its multi-faceted demands. Was he glad to be parting ways with Secretary Robeson and his morally fluid methods of conducting the Department's business? Perhaps yes. But Lenthall must have been saddened by the prospects of what might follow at the hands of Robeson. That such possibilities could materialize was confirmed by his descendants' recollections, who leave no doubt as to why they thought John Lenthall had been moved aside. "He was retired and the shipyard graft was put through without him."[31]

Confirming Lenthall's misgivings, two weeks after he was relieved of his duties, Isaiah Hanscom's brother William was, by an act of Congress, allowed to withdraw his resignation and on 17 April 1871, officially reinstated as a naval constructor.[32] Secretary Robeson now had his own hand-picked team in place. As *The Sun*'s exposé on "Robeson's Mighty Frauds" insinuated, especially in connection to impending naval appropriations bills, "This is where the milk in the Hanscom coconut appears."[33]

* * *

BOOK FOUR
Inspector

CHAPTER 30

Cape May

The final days of January 1871 must have felt hollow to John Lenthall. For the first time in over thirty-five years his life was not brimming with the Navy's work. Restless in his home on F Street, less than two blocks from an office—*his office*—that no longer demanded his presence, he struggled to adapt to a new routine. But what routine? His family beckoned and a wide circle of friends welcomed him. He was free to do as he wished, to travel and to indulge those interests which had lain dormant for so long. Like many others who have been forcibly retired, it took time to find that new path, but time was a commodity he now had in abundance.

Even though he had been retired by the Navy, it still had uses for him. One of John Lenthall's first such calls as general inspector came in mid-April with a summons by Secretary Robeson. The request seemed straightforward: proceed to New York for "duty as a member of a board to examine into the condition of the U.S.S. Tennessee on her late trip to Santo Domingo."[1] However, as Lenthall and anyone else who read newspapers knew, this board's purpose was entirely political. During February's House debates over whether to allow William Hanscom to be restored as a naval constructor, one of his more ardent supporters, former Union General Nathanial Banks, now a Massachusetts representative and an enemy of Admiral Porter, had insinuated that *Tennessee* was unseaworthy. Even worse, he suggested she had been ordered to sea by Porter who knew of her condition, and that the newly installed bureau chief, Isaiah Hanscom, had failed to step forward and proclaim "Do not send that ship."[2] The Navy Department had no choice but to correct the public record. Lenthall made the journey to New York from 21 to 24 April, and not surprisingly, the board unanimously concluded that *Tennessee* was seaworthy, staunch and as fit for her mission as any of the Navy's war steamers.[3]

The following month, Lenthall was tapped for duty as one of a thirteen-man board of visitors convened to examine midshipmen at the U.S. Naval Academy. Other naval officers called for this duty were Rear Admiral Selfridge and Chief Engineer Wood.[4] It seems there were plenty of boards to fill the former bureau chief's days and, for the first time in his career, he probably welcomed such assignments.

* * *

On 27 October 1871, John Lenthall and his wife Mary were grandparents once again. Daughter Jenny delivered a baby boy who was named John Lenthall in honor of both his grandfather and great-grandfather. Young John would live a relatively long life, well into the next century, finally passing away at age sixty-seven in Tampa, Florida.[5]

Grandfather Lenthall's joy was soon trampled later that winter by the untimely death of his wife of twenty-eight years, Mary Dugan Lenthall. She was sixty years old and her passing was rendered even more cruel because of its date—4 February 1872—her daughter's twenty-sixth birthday.[6] John Lenthall's faith and internal strength must have been sorely tested during the grief-filled days that followed. It was a blessing that his two sisters, Mary and Elizabeth, and daughter Jane were so close at hand and could offer the comfort he so needed.

For the second time in eighteen months, members of the Lenthall family and their close friends assembled at the by now familiar gravesite at Mount Olivet Cemetery. Mary was laid to rest beside her mother and niece, her headstone reading:

HIS
Sacred
in the memory of
Mary D. Lenthall
who departed this life
Feb 4th 1872 Aged 60 Years
May she rest in peace[7]

Her place of burial, one of Washington's newer Catholic cemeteries, was over a mile to the southeast of the Lenthall and Stone families' established plots at the Protestant Rock Creek Cemetery, which held the remains of John Lenthall's father, mother and King uncles. Although it was the custom of that era to segregate burial grounds by religious denomination, it must have been very wrenching for surviving family members to bury their loved ones so far from where they knew they would finally be interred.

Of the sympathy letters received by John Lenthall, the one that most stands out was from Admiral David D. Porter. It is remarkable that Porter reached out in such a personal way considering the treasonous bile he hurled at

Lenthall just twelve years before. Dated 10 February and addressed to "My Dear Mr. Lenthall," it read in part:

> I know how your warm heart suffers from the loss of your best friend but you must not sit down and brood over what cannot now be helped. ...
>
> You have many years of usefulness in you yet and I am afraid our country is about to be involved in a contest that will require all the ability and ingenuity from our best men.
>
> You may rest assured that no one feels for you more that I do for no one knows better than myself your true character and how much you feel this loss. ...[8]

Time heals all ... but another factor may have been in play. With the Navy Department so firmly in Robeson's hands, Porter sensed his interests were now more closely aligned with Lenthall's. The "contest" suggested by Porter was one with Great Britain, whose government he had long demonized; the *Alabama* claims between Britain and the United States were then in their final throes of adjudication in Geneva by an international tribunal.

* * *

Only a month later, the newspapers flashed lurid headlines proclaiming "Robeson's Mighty Frauds" followed soon after by "The Robeson Investigation." And now John Lenthall's name was caught up in the mess. *The Sun*'s editor, Charles Dana, a fervent Democrat and foe of President Grant, had declared war on his administration. Dana's weapons of choice were lurid exposés on Secretary Robeson and his alleged wrong-doings at the Navy Department. A former assistant secretary of war, Dana well knew the ways of Washington and his blasts spared no one. His highly sensational style of attack initially focused on Robeson's efforts to oust "honest John Lenthall" and replace him with the compliant Hanscom brothers. It was claimed that "with this class of men for constructors, Robeson has a sure thing should Congress decide to increase the navy." The secretary could then milk naval appropriations for all they were worth. *The Sun*'s articles painted an indelible image of Robeson scheming to subsidize favored contractors with Navy funds, who would then reward him and his cronies with kickbacks and financial favors.[9]

One of Dana's more specific accusations, that of the "Secor steal," motivated Congress to call John Lenthall in late March 1872 as a witness to aid their investigations into Robeson's behavior. Lenthall testified that, yes, he had signed the two bills in question, one to Secor & Co. for $62,605 and the other to Perrine, Secor & Co. for $30,450, both for "extra pay" on their contracts. There was no concealment; the bills were processed like any other. Further, Lenthall said that he did not protest against making the payments but that he only paid them after receipt of a written order.[10] Although he had done Robeson's bidding, albeit with reservations, Dana's exposé made it clear that John Lenthall's "doom was ... sealed. He had to go." And in turn, that led to *The Sun*'s lengthy recapitulation of Representatives Banks and Butler's fierce efforts to reinstate constructor William Hanscom, all of which come to pass.

After his experience of giving testimony about the Secor claims, which Congress determined were a "somewhat dangerous stretch of official authority," Lenthall may well have concluded that perhaps it *was* best he had been pushed aside. He left the Department with his reputation intact and was spared the indignity of attempting to perform the duties of a bureau chief under a compromised navy secretary.

* * *

As the spring of 1872 warmed the capital city, John Lenthall and his sister, Mary King Lenthall, must have felt rather alone in their F Street home. Niece Ellen Eck had passed out of their lives over a year before, as had so recently John's dear wife Mary. One or both of them may have needed constant bedside attention during their final months, but that was all behind John and Sister Mary. Ahead they found their attention increasingly captured by John's infant granddaughter, Anny (also styled Annie). And Jenny was pregnant with her third child. The Lord giveth and He taketh. The Lenthalls adjusted as best they could to their altered world.

A new destination began its regular appearance in the Lenthalls' changed landscape—Cape May, New Jersey. At about this time, the Lenthall family correspondence documents their annual summer pilgrimages to the popular seaside resort.[11] They may have visited it before, possibly during John Lenthall's recovery from his heart problems in mid-1867. But starting in 1873 and extending reliably to the end of the decade, an increasing number of letters were written to and from members of the Lenthall clan vacationing in Cape May.

Cape May sits at the south-eastern tip of New Jersey, boldly jutting into the waters where Delaware Bay empties into the Atlantic Ocean. Originally called Cape Island because of its isolation from the mainland, by 1850, Cape May was the most famous of America's seaside resorts. Its biggest attraction was an endless expanse of white sand beaches that gradually sloped into the ocean's surf and which provided a near-perfect setting for bathing in the sea. At the beginning of the nineteenth century Cape May was easily accessible by water, a day trip from Philadelphia or less from New Castle, Delaware. The same journey on land took a full two days over execrable roads, but that all changed during the Civil War when the railroad finally reached Cape May. Travel times from Philadelphia were cut to only three and a half hours. The city of Cape May consisted of an eclectic mix of grand, brightly-painted wooden hotels with sweeping verandahs, all of which faced the beach and its boardwalk, and a collection of smaller homes and buildings sprinkled in between. Vacation season began at the end of June and carried on until the beginning of September. With water on both sides of Cape Island, cool breezes ensured temperate conditions throughout the year. That feature, together with its fine beaches, drew a never-ending stream of visitors, only too happy to escape an urban summer's stifling heat.[12]

Just where the Lenthalls stayed in Cape May is not entirely clear. Best evidence from sifting the contents of various letters suggests that Sister Libby either owned or leased one of the island's many spacious cottages which were then quite the fashion for summer visitors. Imposing Victorian-style structures of three stories, they were typically surrounded with wide-open porches that admitted refreshing breezes and allowed unobstructed views. Accommodations at her place always seemed available to late-arriving guests, and a coach or hack was available for family outings.[13] Sister Libby even arranged for her "help" to accompany the family to Cape May.[14] Of Lenthall's two sisters, however, it seems that the oldest, Mary King, almost always chose to remain in Washington and eschew the lures of the beach.

Perhaps giving a pause to the Lenthalls' early departure for the New Jersey shore in 1873 was the birth of Jenny's third child. The Waggamans' second boy was delivered on 6 May and named after his father, Thomas Ennalls. Young Thomas would outlive his grandfather but only by a year, passing at age ten in 1883.

On the last day of June, John Lenthall received a letter that put his further employment as a general inspector on hold. Issued by the Navy's Office of Detail and signed by its chief, Commodore Daniel Ammen, he was informed "You will regard yourself detached from special duty and waiting orders."[15] Now officially idled, John Lenthall could allow himself to depart for the pleasures of Cape May with a clear conscience.

Rather than travel that summer, Daughter Jenny decided to recover from her recent birth and nurse her newborn. Her letters to her Aunt Mary Lenthall project the image of an increasingly ill woman. On 22 August, over three months after her delivery, she wrote "I am much stronger and better, but the past two days the pain in my stomach has not been so better [?]. ... Little baby is sick. ... I have not been able to walk much since Ennals returned, but feel much better today."[16] Jenny's health would become a growing worry in the coming months. Four days later, she cheerfully wrote she was glad "that Cape May folks are well."[17]

* * *

At a certain stage in life, some men are gripped by the urge to give away possessions that were once central to them. John Lenthall was so affected during the spring of 1874 and it provoked him to make two donations, one small and one very big. In fact, huge would be an understatement. But first, the smaller.

To the Smithsonian Institution, John Lenthall donated "a funeral vase and ... a medallion in marble, both taken from a Roman tomb in Baiae in the presence of Capt. Geo. S. Blake, U.S. Navy." Baiae was an ancient Roman town on the northern shore of the Gulf of Naples and Captain Blake a familiar correspondent of Lenthall's. A letter of acknowledgement and thanks dated 13 May 1874 was signed by Joseph Henry, the Smithsonian's first secretary and, incidentally, the scientist responsible for the first practical electro-magnet.[18]

Lenthall's second donation was breathtaking in its scope and quality—his collection of books, drawings and memorandums (personal papers)—all of which was initially 'on deposit' at the Franklin Institute in Philadelphia, and became a gift on his death. Whether some very private motivation caused him to make such a generous offer is not known; perhaps it was simply that the realization he would not be returning to the Navy Department had finally sunk in. But the year of his bequest, 1874, was also the fiftieth anniversary of the Franklin Institute's founding and Lenthall had been a life member since 1850.[19]

John Lenthall's book collection was one of the best and most complete of its kind in private hands, featuring many rare tomes on shipbuilding and naval architecture, of both English and French origins (See Appendix 10 for more details). Its size alone is staggering, over 360 books, pamphlets and government publications, and its chronological scope is equally dazzling, ranging back as far as 1707. The drawings that Lenthall also donated include an unparalleled selection of U.S. Navy ship plans, dating from the early 1800s through the Civil War period. As a man who rose through all the levels of a naval constructor's hierarchy, from apprentice to bureau chief, John Lenthall had his hands on vast numbers of drawings over his decades of active service, and it is clear he retained copies of the ones that were most important to him. A total of 518 individual drawings, illustrations and specification books are extant from his original 1874 deposit. Finally, John Lenthall's donation included what has been organized (circa 2018) into eighty-three indexed folders of his "memorandums" or papers on different subjects, ranging from individual ship calculations and notes to specialized topics such as surf boats for the Mexican War, his correspondence regarding propellers, and much more. All of these three main groupings—books, drawings and personal papers, in aggregate called the John Lenthall Collection—are today housed at Philadelphia's Independence Seaport Museum.[20]

Today's Franklin Institute archives offer only the briefest outline of Lenthall's donation. However, Lenthall's cover letter transmitting the first four boxes of his collection, dated 20 June 1874 and addressed to the Franklin Institute's secretary, William Wahl, yields more details:

> The drawings are all vessels that have been built for the navy in which, if not the whole, I have had a large hand.
>
> They will be found assorted (after a fashion) but many of them have not been disturbed for years, and knowing exactly what I had and where to find it I never took time to make copies, and arrange them in better form.
>
> I have yet to send about one third more of books being my best on ship building, and two or three times more of drawings of foreign ships, and our own navy and memorandums, all by my own hands (not over nicely done because I had not time) but they are accurate ....
>
> I wish it distinctly understood that all my books, drawings and papers are to be considered and treated as of the class which are not loaned out of or from the building of the Institute, and I would like as far as practical for them to be kept together.
>
> Should it at any time happen that I desired the use of any of the books, drawings or notes, I am allowed to take them from the Institute ...[21]

* * *

Ten days after Adams Express whisked his boxes off to Philadelphia, John Lenthall was in Cape May. Writing to his sister Mary, who was happily minding their home on F street, he described how he spent the day with his younger sister Libby. By then Libby was nearly blind:

> Sister has been stirring about ... I see for her and help her in all ways. We rode down in her coach and back again so she had all her strength for the sand beach. I took the same hack down Broadway to the sea, then up past Congress Hall and as far as Dr. Marcy's—all took an ice cream and then went home.[22]

Everyone was enjoying life at the shore, the only discordant note being Lenthall's concern about his ailing daughter Jenny, who he opined "must not upset her heart to get well at once, for it will only do so very slowly." Jenny and her husband "Mr. W" were expected to arrive the following weekend for a brief visit to escape the heat of a July in Washington. The Waggamans duly arrived on Saturday, 11 July, and Lenthall met them at the steamboat landing. As he told his distant Sister Mary, with whom both he and Libby constantly corresponded during the days that followed, "Jenny does not look so well." But he chose not to dwell on her health and filled his letter's final page with explanations of an F Street lease issue.[23]

However, Libby was shocked at her niece's appearance, writing "I had no idea of her serious condition. ... Mr. W told me ... that the doctor said there was no hope and said I was not to mention it to John."[24] This was an era when relatives were shielded from knowledge of a loved one's life-threatening illness, and so Lenthall was kept in the dark. Two days later, Libby wrote that Jenny had been persuaded to stay on to avoid fatiguing herself traveling back to hot Washington; Mr. W caught a late train out that afternoon, promising to soon return. Libby cautiously observed, "John does not appear to be aware of Jenny's serious condition."[25]

So far, John Lenthall had not grasped the gravity of Jenny's illness. On Thursday, the 23rd he remarked that "Jenny ... does not feel so well as when she came," suggesting to Mary that when "when Jenny leaves here, she will go to you."[26] And on Monday the 27th he wrote that Mr. W had returned and "Jenny was much better that day." But then, unannounced family friends appeared at the door and the Lenthalls were forced to rearrange bedrooms to accommodate everyone. Unsurprisingly, that night was a bad one for Jenny but, as John informed Mary, Jenny was planning to return to Washington on Wednesday. The weather at Cape May was cool and pleasant, and the Lenthalls "went to our usual wading place and all had a wade in the water."[27]

Two days later, Wednesday 29 July 1874, John Lenthall at last realized his only child's life was in danger. The pain in her lungs was so intense it was difficult for her to breathe much less travel; she couldn't be moved. A doctor summoned that morning told Lenthall that it must be cancer spreading in her lungs, and that the disease had … reached her breast. Then a clergyman came to offer spiritual comfort. Opium was administered to dull her senses, and ease her cries and moans. The doctor cautioned that with consciousness, her pain would be unendurable. Throughout the family's ordeal, John Lenthall penned a running dialogue of his daughter's downward spiral, his handwriting becoming visibly worse as the nightmare unfolded. Jenny's visit, so cheerfully anticipated two weeks before, had turned into a death watch. Near midnight Lenthall despaired "Poor dear Jenny—and there is no help or hope, it cannot be long."[28]

Jane Lenthall Waggaman died early on Thursday morning, 30 July 1874.[29] She was twenty-eight years old, the mother of three and John Lenthall's only surviving child. Little over two years before he had buried his wife; now he faced burying his daughter. On that bleak Cape May morning, John Lenthall must have felt more alone than he had ever been in his entire life.

The Lenthall family, stunned and grief-stricken by the tragic turn of events, hurriedly regrouped. John and his son-in-law returned to Washington late that same day together with Jenny's lifeless body—packed in ice to preserve it from the heat—arriving early Friday morning. Sister Libby, it seems, remained at Cape May. Once home, Mary Lenthall took over with her usual efficiency and directed the preparation of Jenny's remains for burial. The evening before the funeral, the Lenthalls hosted a viewing at their F Street home. Jenny's many acquaintances made it a tiring night for all. Mr. Waggaman brought their little boy Johnnie, then two years and ten months old, for a final goodbye. Johnnie "knew her at once and exclaimed, why don't she get up." Mary could only sympathize, "Poor dear children! What a loss they have had."[30]

On Monday, 3 August, a large crowd of people gathered for Jenny's funeral service at St. Stephen's.[31] The Waggaman's oldest child, Anny aged four, attended silent and staring; she did not cry. "A eulogy on her character" was delivered by the pastor. Later Jenny was laid to rest in the same grave as her mother at Mount Olivet Cemetery. Before parting, Mary Lenthall urged little Anny "to throw into the grave a bunch of white flowers." As the emotional day drew to its close, Sister Mary described her brother John as "exhausted by his sorrow" but now seeming "more composed."[32] Two days later, Mary wrote to Libby "At night when I lie awake, I can hear dear John's low moans of sorrow, yet he is more calm …"[33]

* * *

A death in the family often causes the survivors to reflect on their own mortality, and so it was with John Lenthall. On 5 October 1874, two months after his daughter's funeral, he signed his last will and testament, a document drafted in his own hand. First, he directed that on his death $1,000 be given to each of the Eck family children, two nephews and a niece. Second, that his house on F street, its furniture and all his personal property were to be placed in a trust administered by his son-in-law, Thomas E. Waggaman. Third, when his granddaughter, Ann Maria Waggaman came of lawful age, she was to inherit the house and its furniture. Meanwhile, his personal property was to be invested in bonds, and its income used to pay for maintenance, taxes and insurance on the house and for his grandchildren's education and support. Then as each grandchild came of age, one third of the investment was to be given to them. [34]

As for witnesses to his will, Lenthall relied on his home's proximity to the Navy Department and his former fiefdom, the Bureau of Construction and Repair. By this date, construction of the new State, War and Navy Building had begun on the site of the old Navy Department building, but John Lenthall knew where to find the three men he sought.[35] His signature was witnessed by Hugh A. Goldsborough, chief clerk of the bureau, and two of its clerks, Charles S. Hughes and Rudolph A. Knapp.[36]

* * *

CHAPTER 31

Monitor Rebuilds

John Lenthall's brief visit with his former colleagues brought him face-to-face with a Navy he had been absent from for over three years. It was a Navy that had changed since his departure and vastly so since the end of the Civil War. By numbers alone, it was in steep decline, going from 203 ships in 1869 to 146 at the middle of the next decade, of which only seventy-five were in actual service.[1] With Congress' attention claimed by the Reconstruction and westward expansion, lawmakers hesitated to fund new warships, especially after the excesses of the war. During Secretary Robeson's eight years of administration, only ten vessels were authorized—two torpedo boats and eight small steam sloops.[2] Lenthall must have wistfully recalled the heady months of the early 1860s when many times that number had been ordered of just *one class*.

The U.S. Navy of the 1870s was also becoming an old navy, and as John Lenthall well knew, an old navy was one that constantly needed expensive repairs. The ships built during the Civil War, especially those laid down in its final years, had been constructed of unseasoned white oak and often fitted with defective machinery. Many had already been laid up, soon to be sold. The one bright spot was that while Congress was loath to authorize new ships, they provided ample funding for the fleet's maintenance, especially at politically important navy yard districts. That in turn caused a relentless squeeze—faced with the natural loss of its ships and no replacements, the only way to sustain the Navy's number of active vessels was to keep repairing its ageing assets. The apotheosis of this trend was the large screw sloop *Tennessee.* Originally a sister to the record-setting *Wampanoag* and costing $1.856 million, she had been refitted to make her into a more practical cruising flagship for $576,800. After her worrisome voyage to Santo Domingo, she was again repaired over a span of three years for $801,713. Before she was finally sold in 1887, she had cost the government a total of $3.8 million! As it was said, "She had a short life, but as a consumer of money, a brilliant one."[3]

One trend that must have made John Lenthall smile was the restoration of the Navy's traditional cruising stations. Indeed, ten years after the end of the Civil War, many of the same war steamers that he had either designed or were built under his supervision still served as squadron flagships—the steam frigates *Franklin* and *Colorado* and steam sloops *Brooklyn, Hartford, Richmond* and *Pensacola*.[4] With the crush of war-time monitor building a fading memory, the vessels that now protected America's worldwide interests were the wooden-hulled ship-rigged steamers of his earlier years. Of true ocean-going ironclads the U.S. Navy had none: the first of its fully rigged armored frigates, *New Ironsides*, had accidentally burned in late 1866 and Webb's mighty *Dunderberg* now flew French colors.[5] Perhaps Lenthall thought back to that letter he and Isherwood had written in 1862 to Gideon Welles, ending with the words "how much better it is to fight at the threshold than upon the hearthstone." But no one listened.

A still unfolding confrontation that had begun the year before must have caused some to wish they had heeded his warning—the *Virginius* affair. This seemingly trivial incident involving the seizure of an American-flagged steamer attempting to run guns into Cuba had quickly escalated into a major international crisis after Spain summarily executed fifty-three of her men. War threatened between the United States and Spain, and late in 1873, Secretary Robeson hurriedly assembled a squadron of the Navy's war vessels. The motley collection of aged monitors and wooden-hulled auxiliary steamers that gathered at Key West embarrassingly revealed what John Lenthall had known all along—the monitors that were so useful defending harbors could not be relied on to exert their power beyond sight of land.[6] Even more threatening, one of Spain's ironclads, the 5,700-ton frigate *Arapiles*, was then at the New York Navy Yard undergoing repairs.[7] The realization dawned that if war broke out, this one ironclad could have shelled New York City virtually at will. The U.S. Navy had nothing to match her. Spain, regarded as a second-rate power, possessed six other equally powerful war vessels including the formidable frigate *Numancia*, the first ironclad to circumnavigate the world.[8] It was the good fortune of both nations that a diplomatic solution to the crisis was soon found. But the U.S. Navy had been exposed as totally unprepared to fight a war at sea, even against Spain.

* * *

Chastened by the *Virginius* affair, on 23 June 1874 Congress authorized the expenditure of $849,045 for "completing repairs of such double turreted monitors as the Secretary of the Navy should select."[9] By the year's end, Secretary Robeson reported on his progress placing the Navy in a "good and effective condition:"

> The whole of our fleet of single-turreted monitors has been thoroughly overhauled and repaired, their sides raised up, their rotten wooden beams and decks replaced by iron, and their turrets and machinery put in complete order, so that they are now efficient to their utmost capacity ... Four of our powerful double-turreted monitors, viz, the Terror, the Miantonomoh, the Monadnock, and the Amphitrite (by far the most formidable vessels ever in our Navy,) are also now in hand undergoing repairs, and the plans are also being matured for the repair of the Puritan ...[10]

Any rational person reading the secretary's report would sensibly conclude that the Navy was planning to repair its double turreted monitors in much the same way as it overhauled its single turreted monitors. However, the *Monadnocks*' hull structures were so greatly decayed—unseasoned wood was the culprit—that any repairs would have been, at best, a temporary fix. And so, adopting a device the Navy had employed before, Secretary Robeson decided on a program of administrative 'rebuilding'. This scheme entailed the construction of entirely new ships under the guise of repairing old ones: the ironclads' wooden hulls would be replaced by iron, their five inches of laminated armor upgraded to seven inches of solid plate, and efficient compound steam engines fitted in place of their old simple expansion machinery.[11] It was an ambitious undertaking which clearly skirted the will of Congress. And although he had no say in the matter, it must have pleased John Lenthall that four of the five ironclads selected for rebuilding—described as the most formidable in our Navy—had been built to designs he and Isherwood had so vigorously championed against those of the Ericsson lobby.

Although navy yards had built the original four *Monadnock* class ironclads, they were still incapable of constructing large, iron-hulled war steamers, so it was necessary to look to private builders. This was a troublesome complication but Robeson rose to the challenge. The largest contract he awarded was to John Roach of Chester, Pennsylvania for both *Miantonomoh* and *Puritan*. The other three contracts were given to Harlan & Hollingsworth, Wilmington, Delaware for *Amphitrite* (ex-*Tonawanda*); to William Cramp & Sons, Philadelphia, for *Terror* (ex-*Agamenticus*); and to Phineas Burgess and Continental Iron Works, Vallejo, California, for *Monadnock*. Because funding for the secretary's irregular program was outside of the usual naval appropriations channel, contracts for each vessel were awarded in phases: a first contract to put the vessel in frame, a second to plate the hull, and a third to build and install her machinery.[12]

But soon, Secretary Robeson ran out of money. Congress' original allocation might have covered the reconstruction of one ship but not five. Current appropriations for "repairs and preservation of vessels" and for "steam-machinery" had been exhausted by costs incurred from the hasty *Virginius* crisis mobilizations. Undeterred by the questionable legality of his methods, Robeson resorted to bartering old, obsolete war vessels as partial payments for the five new double turreted ironclads. John Roach, who had contracts for two vessels and his own steel processing facilities, absorbed the majority of the scrapped warships, consuming the original *Puritan,* seven light-draft monitors and two decrepit cruisers. William Cramp accepted the old *Terror* and three light-drafts, and Harlan & Hollingsworth the original *Amphitrite* and one light-draft monitor. The Department's normal procedure for naval vessels sold or broken up was for any funds received from their sale to be refunded to the Treasury. But instead, Robeson traded their valuations against new work; it was this practice that later raised so many questions. The light-draft monitors, each costing up to $600,000 were valued for scrap at between $7,000 and $20,000, and Ericsson's *Puritan,* on which the Navy had spent $1.9 million before suspending work, went to Roach for a $43,000 credit.[13] It wasn't long before chants of "Roach, Robeson, Robbers!" began to appear in the headlines. With such a large volume of unsanctioned transactions funneled through Isaiah Hanscom's Bureau of Construction and Repair and his chosen agents, the scope for irregularities was vast. Thus were sown the seeds of many years of Congressional investigations which would fill several thousand pages of testimony and reports.[14]

By 1876 even Robeson's sleights of hand were insufficient to keep pace with payments on the monitors' construction contracts. In his final annual report given late that year, he admitted more money was needed. "I beg to suggest that the sum of [$2,300,000] ... be made available at once in order that the repairs of our five double-turreted ironclads ... may continue." In typical Robeson fashion, he didn't request additional funding for this purpose, "but only that a portion of the regular appropriations be made available for it now," knowing full well that within four months, the incoming Hayes administration and its new navy secretary would be in office.[15]

In fairness to Secretary Robeson, his goal was laudatory—to provide the Navy with modern war vessels at a time when Congress refused to appropriate funds for them. It was his methods, tinged with favoritism, corruption and graft, that got him in trouble. That they did not result in criminal convictions of Robeson or his bureau chiefs was largely because of Congress' difficulty assembling creditable evidence. Whatever good intentions Robeson may have had were ultimately thwarted by his 'ways and means' which caused extraordinarily long construction times for warships that, when finally commissioned, bordered on obsolescence.[16]

* * *

At the beginning of Secretary Robeson's final full year in office, an event occurred which must have caused John Lenthall a nostalgic twinge—the closure of the old Philadelphia Navy Yard. For many years the yard's limited size and its inability to grow within the by-now congested urban confines of Southwark had been readily apparent. The Civil War, which caused it to be worked harder than ever before, especially after the loss of Norfolk, had confirmed what the Navy already knew. After considerable evaluation of alternative sites, the decision was made to move the yard to nearby League Island, just south of Philadelphia at the mouth of the Schuylkill River. Of course, with Secretary Robeson in charge, motives of favoritism and profits were indistinguishably mixed with the more practical business of relocating a navy yard. But finally the sad day came on 7 January 1876, when after three-quarters of a century of naval presence in the heart of Philadelphia, Old Glory was lowered for the last time at the navy yard. Adding to the irony, the last ship repaired at the Southwark site was the venerable frigate *Constitution*, whose sister and first of her class, the 44-gun *United States*, had been built by Joshua Humphreys at his nearby yard.[17]

* * *

Like the changing seasons, the administration of President Rutherford Hayes came to Washington in March 1877, thus ending Robeson's reign over the Navy and ushering in a new secretary, Richard Thompson. He was the first secretary of the navy from west of the Appalachians and had no affinity for the business of running a navy, but unlike his predecessor he was content to conform to the will of Congress. Thompson was shocked to discover the indebtedness to which Robeson had committed the Navy, absent Congressional appropriations, for completion of the monitors and so suspended work on their construction.[18] By this date, John Roach had launched *Miantonomoh*'s hull but the other four were still on the stocks.

In May 1877, Lenthall received a four-page letter hurriedly scribbled in pencil by the hand of W. J. Powell. Young Powell was the son of draftsman Richard Powell, a protégé of Lenthall's and employed by the Bureau of Construction and Repair since 1849. At this time of administrative uncertainty, the younger Powell, also a draftsman who had evidently been seconded to Roach's site, turned to the one man he knew he could trust—John Lenthall:

> Things look a little queer to me:—those plans of Miantonomoh and Puritan which I have been making were taken down today to Washington by Mr. Farron (Roach's superintendent) what he will do with them of course I don't know exactly ... The fact is John Roach is a sharp man, he is well acquainted with the president (Mr. Hayes) ... And I don't know what these plans may be some of the ammunition to fire at the new secretary to get further contracts, or to finish what is in hand here.[19]

Powell's message was probably not a surprise to Lenthall. It had been widely reported that the new navy secretary had appointed a board to determine the cost of completing Roach's *Puritan.* It was, in fact, the first of many boards Thompson would assemble to gain a clearer understanding of the monitors' status. The first board found that the work to finish *Puritan* would cost $1.4 million, which, if compared to Robeson's estimate of $2.3 to complete all five, was hardly encouraging. The second board, convened to examine *Puritan*'s plans and report on her condition, delivered even worse news. Echoing the light-draft monitor fiasco, the board found she was grossly overweight and would not float if completed as designed. The magnitude of the miscalculation was 1,095 tons, enough to submerge her thirty inches of freeboard.[20]

The second board's findings, issued on 21 August 1877, were soon known to John Lenthall. The younger Powell had copied them, together with their supporting calculations, and sent them to him.[21] Both documents by W. J. Powell were just two of many accumulated by John Lenthall over the course of the next three years on the double turreted monitors. As will be seen, Lenthall was later officially connected with Congress' and the Navy's investigations into Robeson, which helps to explain their provenance. At this stage of his life, he had already shipped off his naval memorandum folders to the Franklin Institute. Any post-1874 technical documents remained in his possession and so formed a substantial portion of the future Ives Collection. They include forty-six items on *Puritan,* forty on *Miantonomoh,* fifteen on *Terror,* one each on *Amphitrite* and *Monadnock,* and fifteen on general categories applicable to all of the monitors. Some items contain information on more than one vessel. These documents present mostly weight and cost data related to the monitor rebuilds, but also general particulars, armor details, payment invoices and various memos or notes, the majority of which are undated. They are truly a treasure trove for anyone studying the convoluted evolution of these warships.

* * *

The long arms of Congressional investigators finally reached out to former bureau chiefs John Lenthall and Benjamin Isherwood. On 13 May 1878, W. C. Whitthorne, chairman of the House Committee on Naval Affairs, requested that both Lenthall and Isherwood review *Puritan*'s plans and Hanscom's statements regarding quantities of live oak at the navy yards.[22] Whitthorne, a Tennessee Democrat and former CSA adjutant general, was a longstanding member of the House of Representatives who would manage the Robeson investigations for the next three years. Soon after Lenthall received a letter from Secretary Thompson, stating that Whitthorne had "expressed his desire that your valuable services be availed of as a member of a board" to assist with their queries.[23] Lenthall agreed to participate and four days later, Thompson sent a second letter, directing that he and Isherwood "examine plans and specifications of Puritan in compliance with the wishes" of the House Committee.[24]

John Lenthall was now formally involved with the investigations into the 'rebuilt' double turreted monitors and the dealings of Robeson and Hanscom. He quickly found that "neither plans nor specifications" had been drawn up for *Puritan* and that the builder, John Roach, had free reign to deliver an "undescribed vessel."[25] And the closer he looked, the worse it got. Three pages of what are believed to be his written report confirm that he found much about *Puritan* that needed changing, all related to her excess lightship weight:

> ... with regard to the "Puritan" the examination made in 1877-78 was sufficient to show there could be no doubt that the vessel would have been a miserable failure if completed in the manner originally proposed notwithstanding the depth of the vessel has been increased while she was building. ... Keeping in view the weight of the hull, the armament should be reduced to one turret having a thickness of 18 inches of iron ... for 2-40 ton guns; maintaining the armor on the hull at 12 inches ... reducing the weight of the entire steam department to 770 tons excluding 500 tons of coal. ... If the vessel is completed in the inefficient manner of reducing all the weights except that of her steam machinery, her speed will only be available to flee from an enemy of far inferior size ... a mortifying position for any naval officer ... [26]

Lenthall's suggestions clearly display his willingness to trade speed and fire-power for greater protection. Two months later, he received a letter from his fellow board member, Benjamin Isherwood, offering equally negative observations about other aspects of *Puritan*'s construction. The Easby that Isherwood mentions is John W. Easby, a former apprentice of

Lenthall who had replaced Isaiah Hanscom as the chief of the Bureau of Construction and Repair. As is typical of Isherwood, his mind ranged far and wide:

> Easby said she was miserably built, and that he would have to put in a number of bulkheads and other things to strengthen her. … There are to be two wretched turrets, 10 inches thick, 9 feet high, and about 21 feet in diameter. … No backing in the turrets, but the plates tongue and grooved together as we saw in the drawing. Such work will hardly hold together of itself, much less endure the impact of shot. Webb admitted that weights calculated by the 1st board were a minimum and might easily be exceeded between 100 & 200 tons. …
>
> I imagine Whitthorne will make another little rumpus next session, about Robeson, Hanscom &tc, but it will amount to nothing, and those thieves will laugh in their sleeves and keep their 'swag'.
>
> Reed has returned to England via Japan, China, the Mediterranean, etc. He stays so few hours in any place that he sees nothing anywhere … I hope he saw none of your ancient colleagues, Webb especially, if he did, what must he think of us, and of a Navy with such constructors.[27]

Reed was, of course, Edward Reed, the former Royal Navy director of naval construction who designed H.M.S. *Monarch*, the turreted ironclad that Lenthall had inspected eight years before. It would seem that Reed must have met Isherwood in New York. Thomas Webb was a naval constructor then on duty at the New York Navy Yard (see Appendix 12).

In February 1879, Secretary Thompson again wrote to John Lenthall in compliance with a request by Chairman Whitthorne about testimony from former Chief Hanscom, asking that he "examine it and make such statements in regard to its correctness as you may think proper."[28] A newspaper article appearing a week later clarified the subject of the query:

> But perhaps the greatest loss is in the purchase of live oak timber. It appears from the report of Lenthall & Isherwood and the proof of chief of bureau, Easby, that large quantities of inferior oak have been purchased and allowed to rot from exposure. This could not have happened if a report of the contract had been made to Congress, as required by law.[29]

Congressional investigations continued into the next year and John Lenthall's work in support of them was far from done. On 6 April 1880, Secretary Thompson requested Lenthall, now seventy-two years old, to report to Admiral Preble in Philadelphia and sit on a board to examine the monitors *Terror* and *Amphitrite*.[30] Similar boards were also appointed to look into *Monadnock* and, once again, *Puritan*. Only *Miantonomoh*, now afloat, was spared scrutiny by a board, but Lenthall evidently surveyed her and wrote a report for the House committee.[31]

Lenthall apparently found himself at odds with Admiral Preble's board; a week later he received a reply from Isherwood to a letter he had written the engineer—Lenthall requested that it be burned—and to which Isherwood responded "no upright man should lend his name to any document that his conscience does not fully approve."[32] Excerpts from Lenthall's report on *Terror* and *Amphitrite* hint at potential differences of opinions:

> In compliance with the instructions of the Dept. of the 6th inst, the hulls of turret vessel Terror ... and the Amphitrite ... have been examined: ...
>
> These new vessels are ... relatively worthless, when compared with foreign vessels of the present time, whereas the old vessels built 18 years ago were much more powerful than any foreign vessels of their time. ...
>
> If these vessels were intended to be more efficient than the old ones of the same names, which preceded them so many years ago, that end does not seem to have been attained.
>
> These vessels can only be made efficient by a radical change, by increasing the thickness of the side armor to the greatest extent possible. ...
>
> In place of the two 10 5/8 inch turrets, it is proposed to substitute a single turret of 15 inches with an oak backing of 12 inches and an inner lining of 1 inch, the internal diameter to be 24 feet. Such a turret would give room sufficient for the heaviest armament the vessels can carry ...
>
> If steel faced armor is used and if it has the advantages claimed for it, the compound armor will be equivalent to a thickness of 11 inches for the side armor of the hull, and the turret to 18 inches. ...

To complete them as originally proposed, would be wasting more than double the amount that has been expended on them ...

It is not considered in the interest of the government to break up or abandon these two expensive vessels, on which 580 thousand dollars has been expended for labor alone, but from the vicious system of trading in old iron, the absolute cost to the government cannot be obtained. This system of peddling is discreditable to the government, and may be made to cover gross frauds. ...[33]

Once again, Lenthall pressed his scheme of increasing the vessels' armor protection and reverting to a single turret carrying the most powerful guns. Given his knowledge of the British naval establishment's trends, he may have been inspired by similar configurations embodied in the Royal Navy's ironclad rams *Hotspur* and *Rupert*, which were echoed in their final form by the larger battleship *Conqueror*.[34] But regardless of how his opinions may have diverged from those of his fellow board members, the several boards could not agree among themselves on the way ahead, differing mainly on the issues of compound armor and breech-loading rifles versus smoothbore guns.[35] And so no progress could be made completing the monitors.

Whitthorne wrote again to Lenthall, twice in early June 1880, first urging that he speak with a Mr. McPherson and then requesting he read an enclosure and "give me your opinion. You will see that the Double-Turrets won't get through."[36] Two weeks later, Whitthorne must have again sent Lenthall another message, this one containing criticism of his weight take-offs of *Miantonomoh*. Lenthall was by that time vacationing at Cape May and away from his files, but he was more than capable of addressing his accuser's key points:

I do not know by whom the calculations of Miantonomoh may have been made, but I have no doubt as to the accuracy of my own, as regards the displacement and draft of water. The writer ... is in error. ... which may be correct as far as Monadnock is concerned. ...

Lenthall then touched on arguments made about the vessel's weight and remaining freeboard, and reiterated his position that the best plan to produce an efficient warship was to increase the thickness of her armor and to replace the two original turrets with a single larger turret. He also admitted that objections had been made to his proposals and concluded his dialogue with a metaphor evoking the bigger picture that only an engineer could make:

> In a quadratic equation there are two roots which will answer the equation; the one positive and the other negative. Now in this case I am not sure that I was right in taking the + or positive one, and as far as the real interests of the navy is concerned, perhaps I should have taken the – or negative one and condemned the vessels.[37]

The satisfying conclusion to this drama was the unmasking of Lenthall's critic, who a month later responded to Whitthorne regarding the calculations. "I am also convinced that Mr. Lenthall's are correct as such estimates can be made ... ask him to accept my apology. I have always ... mentioned him as far superior to any other naval constructor in the U.S. Navy."[38]

* * *

The endless saga of the double turreted monitors continued well past John Lenthall's time on earth. It was concluded that the 1880 boards hadn't spent sufficient time evaluating the monitors. The four that were still on the stocks were finally launched by 1883 and towed away to navy yards. It wouldn't be until 1891 that the first of them, *Miantonomoh,* was commissioned. And *Puritan* waited another five years before she was finally accepted by the Navy, logging some twenty-two years from her conception to completion.[39] Lengthy vessel gestations were common during the era of wooden-hulled frigates but adhering to such a schedule in the age of steel and shellfire was a terrible way to produce a modern warship: they were obsolete when launched and even more so when commissioned. All five monitors were active during the Spanish American War of 1898, and survived well into the twentieth century.

The monitors' fundamental problem was, as Lenthall relentlessly pointed out, that they were too small to achieve their lofty design ambitions—well armored, double turreted coastal defense vessels with a fair turn of speed. This was largely due to their being the spawn of a shadowy vessel rebuilding scheme—"bad copies of old models"—rather than an officially sanctioned program of new construction.[40] In the zero-sum world of naval architecture, one must make big compromises when attempting to squeeze a quart of warship into a pint pot. That these ships were spared from Lenthall's proposed reduction to one turret was possible only because each was completed to specifications that, in sum, accepted the necessary compromises to their armor, guns, turrets, engines, boilers and superstructures, all of which were different from ship to ship. The double turreted monitors saga forms a melancholy postscript to the U.S. Navy's remarkable Civil War achievements. But one good came from their turmoil: the experience gained during their troubled evolution contributed to the success of the new American Steel Navy that followed.

* * *

CHAPTER 32

Twilight

In the years that followed the death of his daughter, John Lenthall's household underwent several subtle but important changes, all reflecting a new balance in his life. Most significant was the raising of Jenny's children. To be sure, Mr. Waggaman was often present, taking the children for outings and birthday excursions, but the day-to-day care of Anny, Johnnie and little Thomas fell to Grandfather John and Grand Aunt Mary Lenthall. Mary's skills as an activities organizer and household manager came into their own in this latest phase of her life, as her many letters amply attest. Her script was invariably neat and legible, her line of thinking always crisp and direct. She was an inveterate planner and projected far ahead to coordinate life's messy details.

The third Lenthall sibling, their sister Elizabeth or Mrs. Stone as she was formally called, lived nearby in her 14th Street town house.[1] There she was right around the corner from the center of the Lenthalls' spiritual life, the Church of the Epiphany. By the mid-1870s, Sister Libby was nearly blind and unable to pen a comprehensible letter or write a bank cheque. Mary often dropped by to help with such tasks or to take her out for appointments. While Mary was described in the Epiphany's archives as the church's first organist and Sunday school teacher—a talented doer and organizer—Elizabeth was remembered for her "unobtrusive piety, her boundless sympathy for the unfortunate and the sorrowful and her countless works of charity and mercy." [2] John Lenthall was recalled, too, by the church's records and complimented for his lengthy career in the service of his country.

The three Waggaman children were brought up as Catholics. That was the legacy of both their father and mother, and of their families' ancestors, a circumstance which the Lenthalls fully respected. One can imagine Mr. W showing up on Sunday mornings to whisk the children off to Saint

Stephen's while John and Mary Lenthall strolled by the grounds of the White House to join their sister in the Church of the Epiphany.

Despite the fact that his daughter Jenny died at Cape May, that sad memory did not stop John Lenthall from vacationing there. He continued to do so through the end of the decade. The Lenthall family's pattern became well entrenched. John would travel to the shore with his sister Libby, typically in June, often with granddaughter Anny in tow, while Mary Lenthall usually stayed in Washington to take care of the F Street house and any remaining children. Out-of-town guests often enlivened their routine. During the summer of 1876, the daughter of an Eck niece, Susie Hunter, came to Washington for an extended visit.[3] That year also marked the Centennial Exhibition in Philadelphia, which drew nearly ten million visitors, including Anny Waggaman and Susie Hunter in the company of John Lenthall. Left to her own devices, Mary organized daily outings for the children that often included the Washington Monument, the Smithsonian Institution's museum and the Capitol building. On occasion, she allowed the children to choose whether they wished to walk home or ride the "cars." The cars always won.[4]

* * *

Living in Washington and having spent his entire life working in government service, it was impossible for John Lenthall to escape participating in the semi-official events that occurred around him. Funerals captured an increasing amount of his time. His former bureau chief colleague of many years, Admiral Joseph Smith, died on 17 January 1877 at the age of eighty-six. Lenthall was honored to be one of his pallbearers, standing in the august company of General Sherman, two other generals, three admirals and the solicitor general. The funeral services were held at St. John's Episcopal Church; Secretary Robeson and Admiral Porter attended along with many others from the Navy Department. Smith's remains were interred in his family vault at Oak Hill Cemetery. At noon that day, thirteen-minute guns boomed in his memory from the navy yard.[5]

Early in the summer of 1877, John Lenthall again became seriously ill. The cause is not known but it may have been heart problems again. Once the word got out, those who knew him were quick to respond. Samuel Archbold, one of Lenthall's former engineers-in-chief, wrote from Philadelphia "Sorry to hear of your being taken sick and hope this will find you recovering. ... I sent you per 'Adams' express ... two gallons of whiskey, Gibson's best old Rye..."[6] As Lenthall was then at Cape May, his sister Mary must have been amused by the unexpected express delivery. Constructor Edward Hartt posted a letter to Lenthall at Cape May, writing "I hope you will soon regain your strength." Hartt then brought up the possibility he might be moved into a posting not to his liking, stating "I don't think I have been treated very well any time since you left the Dept." He ended by asking Lenthall to "again urge my case."[7]

It was almost like the old days when Lenthall had been chief; his subordinates came to him if a problem demanded attention or to find a sympathetic ear. And now, even a former superior of his turned to Lenthall for a favor. In the midst of his health problems, a letter arrived from Gustavus Fox. The two had kept in touch since Fox's departure from the Department; in company with Constructor Delano, Lenthall had paid him a visit years before at his Massachusetts home. The matter now concerning Fox was a report Benjamin Isherwood was preparing that summarized his findings following an eighteen-month tour of dockyards throughout Britain and France.[8] That Fox took an interest in Isherwood's report was evident from his message to Lenthall:

> I know his intellectual value—no one can equal him—but a square old head like yours ought to go over it with him, page by page. This will ... increase its value and add to his own reputation. For eight years he has been ignored and unfairly treated by scamps & rogues ... Something must be said to right himself and here he will say too much unless some friend takes the helm until those chapters are passed.[9]

It is not known how Lenthall responded to Fox's suggestion; he was severely ill at the time. But given his deep friendship with Isherwood, he probably did what he could to help.

John Lenthall soon recovered his health and was, by October, off on a trip to Philadelphia and, among other places, Hartford, Connecticut. Sister Mary wrote him and included a shopping list for a set of teaspoons, stockings and other household goods, and named stores where each item could be found. Such requests were frequent features of Mary's missives to her brother. There were also a pair of former acquaintances—Christie Marshall and Mary Cavanaugh in Philadelphia—that she sent her best wishes to.[10] The level of intimate socialization embodied in her correspondence casts Mary as a fully engaged, gregarious woman.

Early in the following year, on 11 February 1878, former Secretary of the Navy Gideon Welles died at the age of seventy-six.[11] There is no indication that Lenthall attended his funeral, and it may have been only a coincidence that he traveled to Welles' hometown just four months before his passing. But if he did visit his old boss, he must have been gratified that he was given one final opportunity to share a few last words.

* * *

In spring of 1879, John Lenthall, together with his granddaughter Anny, then aged eight, made a trip to Florida. The purpose of their journey is not clear but its highlight was a "cordial reception at Daly Grove," which from parsing clues in their letters, was "remote from the thoroughfare," perhaps close to modern Palm Coast, Florida. The event may have been connected with Anny's schooling or religious education. On their way there, they passed through Jacksonville and St. Augustine. Homeward bound, Lenthall expressed his hope to "obtain conveyance to Matansas, where ... [he] could catch a steamer to St. Augustine." Sister Mary informed her distant brother that he had received a pamphlet from the U.S. Naval Institute containing their prize essay for 1879. It had been sent by Secretary J. C. Soley, and invited members to submit "such criticism as they desire to have read." But, she curtly informed him, "You being absent have lost the chance, as also, your being photographed." [12]

Not long after John Lenthall's return to Washington, he received a warm message from his old apprentice, George Much, then the resident constructor at Mare Island Navy Yard. Much's letter demonstrated that his protégés paid close attention to their former master's performance in the public arena and were forever grateful of his guiding hand:

> Your trip to Florida proved, I trust both beneficial to yourself and grand daughter. ... I hear but little from, or about the constructors, occasionally receive a letter from Hichborn, who has a brother in the yard, and from Fernald, but from no others ... I have read the testimony taken by the Committee on Naval Affairs particularly in reference to the "Puritan" and your reply to the strictures of Mr. Hanscom in your report on that vessel of June 4/1878, and think you completely annihilated that Gentleman ... I strive to do right and to establish a record, at least for honesty and purity of purpose, that you who took me from among the hewers of wood and aveners of water and to whom I am so much indebted for my position in life, shall have no cause for regret.[13]

Lenthall was again in Cape May for the summer and so missed a visit to his F Street home by Benjamin Isherwood in late June. Sister Mary did the honors in his absence, and "Mr. Isherwood ... took tea and sat with us until 9, when he left." Mary introduced him to Mrs. Chubb, the daughter of Commodore Warrington, whom Isherwood had known well and that sparked a lively conversation.[14] With John Lenthall's home so near the Navy Department, such visits by close colleagues must have been a common occurrence.

* * *

The tenth federal census was taken in June of 1880 and the named inhabitants of the Lenthalls' 1818 F Street property showed few surprises. Listed were John Lenthall, aged seventy-four (actually seventy-three), shipbuilder; his sister Mary, seventy-eight (actually seventy-seven), housekeeper; granddaughter Ann Maria Waggaman, ten; grandsons John L. Waggaman, eight, and Thomas E. Waggaman, seven; and two female servants. Two 'boarders' were also recorded, both family acquaintances from Philadelphia, Christina Marshall, aged thirty, and Mary Cavanaugh, sixty-two. Whether they were simply paying an extended summer visit or were long-term residents is not known.[15]

Old memories coming to the surface infused a chatty letter from Gustavus Fox, vacationing that summer with his wife at Jordan Alum Springs. Arriving in August of 1880 when John Lenthall was still at Cape May, it was probably forwarded to him by the ever-attentive Mary. Fox mentioned that he had read the House executive documents covering their investigations into the double turreted monitors and reminisced about his days at the Department and of Secretary Welles, now departed. He then broached the subject of another bigger-than-life personality from those times, Admiral Porter:

> Porter is returning to his loyalties and faith in those who controlled his actions and expenditures during the war. If he had delicate sensibilities he would mourn over his short reign. I knew him so well and had so high an opinion of his fighting capabilities that I forgave him.[16]

Welles, Fox and Porter would, it seems, remain indelibly entwined with John Lenthall's life. Less than a month later, Mary again wrote to her brother on a rather more somber subject, the death of an acquaintance:

> I was able to attend the funeral of the mother of my friend, Mrs. Burnside, to whom I gave the permission to use a site in our lot at Rock Creek. I have not been there for a long time, and was pleased to see how very neat all the grounds are.[17]

Rock Creek was, of course, the cemetery that held the graves of so many Lenthall, King and Stone family members. The Mrs. Burnside cited in

Mary's letter—Helen Waldo Burnside—thirteen years later published a brief account of the life of a woman she greatly admired, John and Mary Lenthall's sister.[18] Under the title of *Mrs. Elizabeth J. Stone, Sketch,* her thirty-five-page biography proved most helpful in the preparation of this account of John Lenthall's life.

* * *

With the coming of spring 1881, the James Garfield administration took its place inside Washington's corridors of power. It wasn't long before the new secretary of the navy, William H. Hunt, fully grasped the pitiful state into which his service had fallen. At the urging of a still influential Admiral Porter, Hunt appointed a naval advisory board to guide his efforts obtaining Congressional support for an expanded Navy.[19] The board first met on 11 July under the presidency of Admiral John Rodgers, and included an unusual range of seniorities within its total of nine line and six staff officers. Two of the latter were retired Constructor John Lenthall and Engineer-in-Chief Benjamin Isherwood.[20]

On 7 November, the board presented its findings. While it could easily agree that an increase in the Navy was needed, the board's opinions regarding the numbers, types and qualities of any new warships sharply diverged. A majority favored building sixty-eight vessels, including thirty-eight unarmored cruisers, supplemented by thirty torpedo boats and rams. Of the new cruisers, a full twenty were to be of wood while the remaining eighteen would feature steel hulls. Steel was just then becoming accepted as a shipbuilding material and had weight and strength advantages over iron, but as yet the United States did not possess a single mill that could roll the steel plates required to construct a ship nor did it have the facilities to forge the large guns needed to arm them.[21]

The board's minority, consisting of Isherwood, Lenthall and its other two naval constructors, Wilson and Hichborn, submitted an alternate report. They felt that given the state of American technology, steel was an impractical choice for such an ambitious program of new building; iron was their preferred material. Further, they held that rather than large numbers of unarmored small cruisers, the Navy needed high-powered, well-armed ironclads that could keep the sea and decisively engage an enemy.[22] Their formula echoed Lenthall and Isherwood's letter to Secretary Welles of March 1862 with its similar Mahanian arguments (see Appendix 6). While the minority's preference for iron over steel has been characterized as conservative, even reactionary, it is of significance that its choice was endorsed by *all* the board's naval constructors, or in other words, by those who would have to live with the consequences.

Adapting a more progressive tilt, the minority declared that a "modern navy must consist essentially of powerful ironclads; and the constant tendency in their design has been to depart farther and farther from the ships of the unarmored type."[23] This statement of a minority led by John Lenthall and Benjamin Isherwood, in opposition to the board's line officer establishment viewpoint, is arresting in its irony. It almost reads like a description of Ericsson's original *Monitor*. And recall early in the Civil War, Fox groused that "Isherwood thought ironclads a humbug and Lenthall shrank from touching the subject."[24] The tables were now turned.

The extravagant proposals of the board's majority coupled with the vocal dissent of its minority encouraged Congressional naval opponents to dig in their heels. The House leadership, despite strenuous efforts by Secretary Hunt to promote the board's findings, held back from decisive action. A second advisory board, led by Commodore Shufeldt, was convened in November 1882. The core of its proposals became enshrined in Congress' landmark act of 3 March 1883, which appropriated funds for the construction of the three cruisers and a dispatch vessel that became popularly known as the ABCD ships.[25] They marked the beginning of the new Steel Navy, and although John Lenthall wasn't there to savor the moment, in a very real way, he participated in the regeneration of his beloved U.S. Navy.

* * *

One month after the first advisory board rendered its mixed findings, the current chief of the Bureau of Construction and Repair, John W. Easby, relinquished his office. His sixty-second birthday fell on 13 December 1881, and on that date he retired.[26] For reasons that are unclear, Easby left the bureau before his successor was named, and it wasn't until 3 March of the following year that Theodore D. Wilson was named as bureau chief. Both Easby and Wilson had been protégés of John Lenthall and, not by coincidence, the hints of impropriety that clung to the Bureau of Construction and Repair in the Robeson years did not reappear during their terms.

John Lenthall, then aged seventy-four and suffering bouts of illness that kept him housebound, must have felt a twinge of pride on hearing of Wilson's appointment.[27] Many years before, Lenthall had been impressed with young Wilson and managed to get him installed as an instructor at Annapolis. Theodore Wilson acknowledged Lenthall's help with a heartfelt letter of thanks: "I will never be able to repay you for the great kindness you have shown to me in using your influence to give me this great chance to improve my mind."[28] And Wilson lived up to Lenthall's expectations, later publishing a textbook on naval architecture, excelling as a constructor and now assuming the role of Bureau chief.

* * *

Early Tuesday morning of 11 April 1882, John Lenthall together with one of his grandsons, either Johnnie or Thomas, left his F Street home to catch a train to Philadelphia. He was feeling stronger and was looking forward to the journey. They arrived at the old Baltimore & Ohio depot at New Jersey Avenue and C Street and purchased their tickets. In time the train was ready, they boarded their car, took their seats and began to make themselves comfortable. Then Lenthall "suddenly threw up his hands and making a spasmodic movement, fell forward on his face and was dead before he could be lifted." [29] So ended the life of John Lenthall.

His body was removed to the baggage room and his son-in-law, Thomas Waggaman, was summoned. After arriving, Waggaman gave instructions for Lenthall's body to be brought to his F Street home. The cause of death was variously reported as apoplexy—a stroke—or heart disease; most accounts mention "his heath had been failing for some time." [30]

His sisters Mary and Elizabeth must have been stunned and heartbroken. The trauma suffered by his grandson who witnessed his death can only be imagined. His three grandchildren to whom he was so close, especially Anny of nearly twelve years, had lost their loving grandfather. An undertaker was called and Lenthall's body prepared for burial. His funeral was scheduled for Thursday 13 April at 2 o'clock p.m.[31]

Services were held in the Church of the Epiphany, officiated by Assistant Minister Charles H. Mead.[32] All five of his known pallbearers had Navy connections:

- Rear Admiral C. R. P. Rodgers, Chief of the Bureau of Yards and Docks and grandson of Commodore Rodgers who first hired Lenthall in 1835.
- Rear Admiral John J. Almy, retired in 1877 and a parishioner of Church of the Epiphany.
- Hugh A. Goldsborough, Lenthall's chief clerk at the Bureau of Construction and Repair and witness to his will.
- Samuel H. Pook, naval constructor, designer of clipper ships and the 90-day gunboats.
- John W. Easby, apprentice of Lenthall and recently retired chief of the Bureau of Construction and Repair.[33]

John Lenthall's remains were buried later that day at the Lenthall family's site in the Rock Creek Cemetery. His headstone is a simple dark grey slab and bears the inscription:

JOHN LENTHALL
CONSTRUCTOR
U.S. NAVY
BORN SEPTEMBER 16, 1807
DIED APRIL 11, 1882[34]

Secretary of the Navy William Hunt issued a general order on the day of Lenthall's funeral. It opened with an announcement of Lenthall's death and was preceded by a comprehensive summary of Naval Constructor Lenthall's career, noting he was retired with the rank of commodore. The general order concluded with the following paragraphs acknowledging the Navy's high esteem for John Lenthall:

> His ability, probity, zeal and patriotism in the discharge of his duties, manifested during a long period and for a time amidst unusual trials, and the virtues which characterized him in private life, earned for him the respect and confidence of the Navy and the country.
>
> … As a mark of respect to his memory, the flags of the Navy Yards and Stations and vessels in commission will be displayed at half-mast from sunrise to sunset, and eleven minute guns will be fired at noon from the Navy Yards and Stations on the day after the receipt of this order.[35]

* * *

Soon after his death, John Lenthall's will was submitted to the cognizant court authorities, presumably by his executor, Thomas E. Waggaman. On 28 April, it was fully proved and admitted to the probate record of the Supreme Court of the District of Columbia.[36] The biggest beneficiary of Lenthall's estate was his favorite grandchild, Ann Marie Waggaman, although it would be nearly ten more years before she came of age and could realize her generous legacy.

In the year following her brother's death, Elizabeth Lenthall Stone acted on her long-standing desire to establish a home for widows of little means. A plot of undeveloped land inherited from her father at the corner of G and 19th Streets NW together with twenty-five thousand dollars was given to found The Lenthall Home, named in her father's memory. The rector and vestry of the Church of the Epiphany were designated as the home's trustees.[37]

By 1886 Mary K. Lenthall, now eighty-five years old and increasingly feeble, left the old house on F Street and moved into the home of her sister Libby. In this year, Ann Maria Waggaman was sixteen and John Waggaman fifteen. The youngest of the Waggaman children, Thomas, died at age ten the year after John Lenthall's passing.

Three years later, momentous news surprised the Lenthall and Waggaman families—Anny's marriage. How it happened reads like a fairy tale:

> Annie ... spent much of her life behind the seclusion and security of a convent walls and planned to become a nun. She was sitting in a drawing room when she met Eugene Ives. He engaged her in a game of twenty questions, and she gave the correct answers. Not knowing that she had passed the test, she boarded a train to take her to the convent where she planned to enter the order. As steam clouds enveloped the railway car, the senator came bounding into the train. He proposed to her on her way to the convent. She changed her mind and gave up the life of cloistered nun to become Mrs. Senator Eugene S. Ives of New York.[38]

The mother of Anny's husband, Cora Semmes Ives, was a family acquaintance of the Lenthalls and the daughter of Raphael Semmes, an uncle of the captain of the same name who won fame commanding the legendary Confederate cruiser *Alabama.*[39]

On 3 May 1892, Mary King Lenthall died at the age of eighty-nine and was buried in the same plot as her brother. Brother and sister share a common headstone.[40] Three months later, Elizabeth Lenthall Stone, aged eighty-eight, followed her sister in death. Her remains were interred in the Stone family crypt at Rock Creek Cemetery.[41]

Returning to Anny, now Mrs. Ives, she bore the senator eight children and lived the last decades of her long life in California, her husband dying in 1917.[42] One of her daughters, Annette, exchanged a number of letters with Maud Burr Morris in 1926; Annette's anecdotes about the Lenthall family were used throughout Morris' seminal article, "The Lenthall Houses and Their Owners," first presented in 1927 and published in 1930.[43] Another equally tenacious researcher, Thomas Hornsby of Pennsylvania, made contact with Mrs. Ives' children over twenty years later in search of John Lenthall's personal papers. Mrs. Ives' daughter Cora responded to one of Hornsby's first enquiries in 1949, her letter yielding a fleeting glimpse into young Anny Waggaman's earliest years:

> Mrs. Ives was very close to her grandfather, John Lenthall. As a tiny child until the time he died, she went with him on many of his inspection trips, and to this day has his love of boats and construction. Mrs. Ives wishes to thank you for your interest in her grandfather, a living and very dear person to her ...[44]

Hornsby's continued correspondence in pursuit of John Lenthall's letters and documents possessed by the Ives family brought him a message that must have been frustrating but was to the immeasurable benefit of future researchers: "In view of the fact that the Navy is very anxious to have that correspondence, we are going to send all the letters to Annapolis and donate them to the Naval Academy."[45]

In 1951, Mrs. Eugene Semmes Ives bequeathed the family's archive of Lenthall letters and documents, in care of her grandson, Lieutenant Commander Eugene I. Malone, to the United States Naval Academy Museum, where they are now conserved as the Ives Collection.[46] Mrs. Ives—little Anny—died later that year.

Constructor John Lenthall would have been very proud of his granddaughter.

* * *

LENTHALL'S LEGACY

History has not forgotten John Lenthall but what it does remember reflects only an incomplete picture of this most important naval constructor. Lenthall's achievements, and in many cases *how* he realized those feats that comprise his legacy, are the historical gems meriting closer attention. Each phase of his career had its own unique cast which lends a ready format for subdividing an overview of Lenthall's place in history.

Lenthall as an Apprentice

It was John Lenthall's good fortune to be a student of the prolific constructor, Samuel Humphreys, son of the iconic Joshua Humphreys. To say Lenthall carried forward their legacy is too simplistic, but he did carry forward a deeply imbibed knowledge of their profession—the art, trade and mystery of the shipwright—that he gained during his apprenticeship. Lenthall's earliest drawings, calculations and other extant documents give us a glimpse into the arcane schooling of the naval constructor. Perhaps most revealing are his calculations of the metacenters of the frigate *Macedonian* performed in 1830, making them the earliest known example of stability calculations performed on a U.S. Navy warship. And it is not just his focus on those particular properties of *Macedonian*'s hull, but his methodical and orderly calculation of *all* of her hydrostatic properties that merits attention. If twenty-three-year-old John Lenthall was performing such exemplary work, then others were too. Perhaps further research will reveal whether it was Humphreys or someone else who first instructed Lenthall.

The early formative experience that set John Lenthall apart from his fellow constructors was his European dockyard tour. It was a naval architect's equivalent of the grand tour of antiquities that a young gentleman of that era undertook to complete his education. Becoming fluent in French and immersing himself in France's culture and technology stamped its lasting influence on the young American ship carpenter from Washington City. There is still nothing like gaining a foreign perspective to stimulate one's awareness of the full range of a subject, whether it be ship design or the theory of war. And Lenthall made the conscious choice to study in France over England for reasons that should make scholars take notice—thirty years after Nelson's smashing victory at Trafalgar, France still held the reputation of being the most scientific of nations when it came to naval architecture.

All these threads coalesced in a continuum of self-education practiced by John Lenthall. He listened carefully to what his mentors said, he took advantage of all available opportunities to learn, and he read and absorbed the lessons contained in the hundreds of books that filled his library. And he never forgot his foreign connections, so valuable in his youth and doubly so during his career. In all these senses, he was a true renaissance man of his profession.

Lenthall as a Constructor

As a master builder then a constructor, the direction of Lenthall's achievements took a new trajectory. In his earliest years, he was responsible for building ships, then, in time, for designing them. His first project, the store ship *Relief*, is one of the best documented of his creations and the subject of perhaps the most extensive set of calculations performed on a ship of that era (see Appendices 1 and 2). Next was his supervision of the launch of the 120-gun ship of the line *Pennsylvania*. This assignment was the definition of high-profile. Launchings can be make-or-break accidents waiting to happen if not handled perfectly and, in this case, the ship to be launched was the world's largest (see Appendix 3). But Lenthall brought it off flawlessly and he later presented a paper about his experience to the American Philosophical Society.

John Lenthall's innate understanding of sailing warship design was on full display with his sloops of war *Dale* and *Germantown*. The first was rather small for her class and the last a typically over-sized American warship; both were praiseworthy in their own ways. *Dale* and her sisters were weatherly, safe ships, well-liked by their crews and *Germantown* was one of the fastest and most admired of the Navy's sailing sloops.

It was John Lenthall's fate to be in the right place at the right time when it came to the Navy's early embrace of steam. In the year he was hired by Commodore Rodgers, 1835, the Navy was tasked with developing plans for a steam battery capable of defending the nation's harbors. Together with the Chief Constructor Samuel Humphreys—his master while an apprentice—and Constructor Samuel Hartt, John Lenthall was selected to sit on the board that drew up plans for the war steamer *Fulton II*. This same trio of constructors went on to design the Navy's first sea steamers, the frigates *Mississippi* and her ill-fated sister, *Missouri*. These were the longest ships yet launched by the Navy and its first to employ diagonal iron strapping to stiffen their wooden hulls. *Mississippi* would steam into history with Commodore Perry, and twice circle the globe during her long career.

Lenthall's ability to construct the immensely stout hulls demanded by steamers was put to the test with Captain Robert Stockton's sloop *Princeton*, the first warship to be designed with a screw propeller. John Ericsson, a protégé of Stockton, was responsible for this vessel's machinery and has been also credited with her hull design. But it was John Lenthall who drew the plans for *Princeton*'s hull and supervised her construction. He devised the stern and rudder post arrangements that allowed Ericsson's novel screw propeller to successfully function. It also gave Lenthall the chance to take the measure of the Swedish inventor who would later bring to the Navy his unique creation, the ironclad *Monitor*.

Largely overlooked by official accounts, John Lenthall had prepared well for his Navy steamer work through two separate bodies of experience, one prior and the other concurrent. While a resident in France, Lenthall absorbed the latest of the new technology of steam propulsion. He even managed to wrangle his way on board the French Navy's side-wheel dispatch vessel *Crocodile* and witness her steam trials. And once relocated in Philadelphia, newly appointed Master Builder John Lenthall took on private commissions that gave him exposure to the latest trends in steam propulsion. Especially noteworthy was his design work on Philadelphia's *City Ice Boat*, and his attending the steam trials of one of John Ericsson's early twin-screw installations in *Clarion*, a sailing barque Lenthall had designed.

Also in the realm of overlooked if not forgotten was Constructor John Lenthall's involvement in what was the U.S. Navy's first purpose-built class of amphibious landing craft, the surf boats that allowed General Scott's army to be swiftly landed prior to his assault on Veracruz. Boats of three different sizes to permit nesting were designed and their specifications drawn up by Lenthall, who also supervised their hurried construction in Philadelphia shipyards.

Lenthall as a Bureau Chief

John Lenthall's baptism as bureau chief was delivered by Secretary Dobbin's signature proposal for six screw propelled frigates. What had begun as a hull for the 'rebuilt' liner *Franklin* morphed into the magnificent *Merrimack* class steam frigates. These warships were widely admired when first commissioned and sparked a reply from the Royal Navy. Carrying formidable batteries of all shell-firing guns, the *Merrimacks* were in effect pocket battleships of their day. Their weakness was their underpowered machinery which stemmed from the Navy's mindset that they must be auxiliary steamers. The ships of this class that survived the Civil War rendered yeoman service, the hulls of three of them lasting into the twentieth century. Lenthall did all that he was asked to do and he did it well.

The two classes of steam sloops that followed proved to be workhorses of the Union fleet, their proportions yielding a much better, more economical solution for the U.S. Navy's cruising needs. John Lenthall drafted the plans for some of them but supervised the design and construction for all. The second class of sloops, the light draft *Mohicans*, initiated an unheralded evolution from broadside batteries to centerline-mounted heavy pivot guns (see Appendix 7), an arrangement of weapons that became the hallmark of the modern warship.

The production of the ninety-day gunboats and the iconic double-enders displayed the ability of Lenthall's Bureau of Construction, Equipment and Repairs to swiftly deliver much needed very light draft steamers, a type of vessel largely absent from the antebellum cruising navy's fleet. When President Lincoln came to office, the U.S. Navy numbered only ninety warships of all classes, both in and out of commission. By the end of his first term and at the peak of its strength, the Navy's inventory of vessels had swollen to 671 of which nearly 500 were bought by or transferred to the Navy. The volume of administrative activity necessary to create a fleet of this size, much of which fell on the shoulders of John Lenthall's bureau, was simply staggering. But he, his handful of staff and his overworked constructors somehow managed to get the job done.

The sloops and frigates launched during or in the wake of the war were reiterations of the earlier successful classes, the exception being the over-powered fast cruisers inspired by the Southern commerce raiders. Most of these war-built ships were constructed of unseasoned wood and relatively short lived, consequentially they exerted little lasting influence.

The same could not be said of the Navy's embrace of the ironclad. Driven by the apparent success of Ericsson's *Monitor* at Hampton Roads, the U.S. Navy embarked on a headlong rush to build monitors to the detriment of a balanced cruising fleet. To be sure, monitors were inexpensive, proven solutions to an immediate problem, but by focusing on them to the exclusion of other classes of ironclads, especially ocean-going types capable of countering European built armored cruisers, the Navy locked itself into a brown water, defensive mindset that hobbled it for decades. It was to John Lenthall's everlasting credit that he, together with his engineer-in-chief, Benjamin Isherwood, recognized the pitfall and voiced his concerns (see Appendix 6). But a polarized Navy Department, swayed by Gustavus Fox's infatuation with Ericsson's inventions, turned a deaf ear to their entreaties. A parallel development confirming that the Navy had lost its way came with the embarrassing exposure of its mismanaged light-draft monitor program, a blunder that cost the nation dearly.

Pressing against the might of the powerful Monitor lobby, Lenthall and Isherwood pioneered ironclads configured more like the Navy's traditional warships. Belying his vilification as an old fogey, Lenthall proposed an ironclad design incorporating twin-screws and double turrets, advanced features rejected by John Ericsson. Plans to build these warships were cancelled in the wake of Hampton Roads but their specifications resurfaced when the Navy contracted for *Onondaga* and, even more substantially, in the *Monadnock* class of heavy ironclads built in navy yards. These later vessels were deemed by officers who served on them as the best of the war's ironclads. In a confirmation of their superior qualities, their designs were copied by the 'rebuilt' monitors of the Robeson era.

Mention of Secretary Robeson's administration and its taint of corruption places the many years served by Chief John Lenthall in a clearer perspective. Considering the vast amounts of public money that funneled through the Navy Department during the war years, no example of financial malfeasance was ever attributed to "honest John Lenthall". The nation was lucky to have been served by such a dedicated chief of the Bureau of Construction and Repair.

Following his forced departure as chief in 1871, Lenthall served sporadically as a general inspector until he caught the attention of the House Committee on Naval Affairs. His testimony about the sorry state of Robeson's rebuilt monitors led to his being appointed as a member of Secretary Hunt's first naval advisory board. It was Lenthall's final act of public service. John Lenthall's first year as a master builder saw him placed on a board whose mission was to bring the Navy into the age of steam. And so it is fitting that the capstone of his career, during which he designed many fine sailing warships, was to again be a member of a board that led the Navy into a future he had anticipated—the creation of the new Steel Navy.

Lenthall's Legacy and his Donations

It would be remiss to end a section on Lenthall's place in history without mentioning the magnitude of his donations to naval history, both direct and indirect. His decision in 1874 to deposit his collection of drawings, memoranda and books at the Franklin Institute gave researchers of naval history an archive of incalculable value. Seventy-seven years later, Lenthall's favorite grandchild, Anny, who later become Mrs. Eugene Semmes Ives, made a second installment on Lenthall's first gift by giving her collection of his personal papers to the United States Naval Academy Museum. Together these two donations have endowed future generations with a stunningly clear window into the life of the U.S. Navy's greatest naval constructor of his time, John Lenthall.

* * *

APPENDIX 1

Directions for Building a Store Ship [1]

Master Builder John Lenthall's first project for the U.S. Navy was to superintend the Store Ship *Relief*s construction at the Philadelphia Navy Yard. These directions, which follow a generalized format, specify how the named vessel was to be constructed and what materials were to be used. The original document covered twelve pages of foolscap folio-sized paper. *Relief* was built of live oak, white oak and yellow pine, and fastened by treenails, spikes and bolts. Iron or copper fasteners were specified depending on the part of the ship they were used in, iron for above the waterline and copper below.

These set of directions are undated but they must have been drafted shortly after Lenthall received his appointment on 1 May 1835 as master builder at the Philadelphia Navy Yard. Corrections received from "Mr. Humphreys" on 12 June 1835 are marked up on the copy in Lenthall's hand, as shown in *italic font.*

Regarding dimensions in feet and inches, Lenthall's original format has been preserved throughout. Thus, for a dimension of one foot two inches, which in modern form would be styled 1'-2", Lenthall writes it as 1"2. For definitions of the terms and structural member names, the reader is referred to *The Oxford Companion to Ships & The Sea.*

* * *

Store Ship Relief of Philadelphia {468 tons old measure}

Directions for building Store Ship		No	feet inch
Keel	Of white oak, number of pieces	3	
	To be sided		1"1½
	Scarphs in length not more than		10
	nor less than		9
	Scarpfs to be fastened with copper bolts in diam.		⅞
	In number (to be kept clear of floor & keelson bolts) about	5	
	In the nibs of each scarpf drive two copper bolts in diam.		¾
	in length		1"2
	Nibs of scarpfs in depth		5
	The scarpfs to be plain without jogs, and six coaks in two rows let in / coaks of seasoned white oak in width		3
	in depth		3
	The scarpfs of keel will have two stirrups to each. The heel of Stem post and lower piece of Stem will have two dove tail plates to each, bolts in diameter		¾
	Depth of keel & false keel clear of the rabbet		1"6
	False keel to be put on after the floor, keelson & deadwood bolts are drove and riveted in length about		14
	The lengths of false keel will depend on the position of the scarpfs of the main keel.		
	To be fastened to main keel with copper bolts in diam.		⅝
	The bottom & sides of false keel as well as the bottom of main keel to be coppered before they are fastened together.		
Deadwood	Amidships & Aft to side		1"1½
	Bolts or scarphs of deadwood to be placed clear of the scarphs of main keel. The midship deadwood to be white oak; the fore & aft deadwoods to be Live oak. The stern post knee (of Live oak) to be fayed on the Keel & to the fore side of inner post, and over this knee the deadwood is to be built agreeably to the mould keeping the shortest piece below. When the knee and deadwood are in their places, mark off the number & direction of the deadwood bolts; then mark off the number & direction of the bolts to be drove through the knee. This precaution is necessary as the knee will be bolted first & the danger of the bolts of this piece & those of the deadwood from coming in contact will be avoided.		
	Bolts in Stern post knee in diam.		1⅛
	Bolts in deadwood abaft after square frame		1⅜
	The bolts for deadwood where it is not more than 7 inches deep will be in diameter		⅝
	gradually increasing in diameter as the depth enlarges but they are not in any case between the foremost & aftermost square frame, to be of greater diameter than		1
	No more bolts are to be used in the deadwood than a sufficiency to draw it to the keel.		
	The bolts for drawing the deadwood to the Keel will be short ones of copper & the proportion of the length will be about twice & one third the depth of the piece through which they are first drove. When twice & one third the depth of deadwood is equal to the depth of keel & deadwood less 4 inches let the bolts be through bolts & rivet on the under side of the keel.		

Stern Post	-of Live oak sided	1"1½
	Moulded at cross seam clear of rabbet	11
	Do at keel	2"4
	To keep its full siding on aft side down to cross seam from thence to taper at keel to	7½
Inner Stern Post	of Live oak sided at head & lower transom (if to be had)	1"6
	Moulded at under side of main transom	6
	At lower Transom & keel	9
	Let the head of inner Stern post jog into the main Transom about two inches to prevent it splitting.	
	Temporary fastenings only will be required for this piece as the bolts of Transom, deadwood & Stern post knee will sufficiently secure it.	
Main Transom	to side & Mould	1"3
	Cross seam to be lined down from the top	7
	The remaining transom to side	10
	The main transom to be bolted to stern post with two bolts in diam.	1⅛
	The second Transom to be bolted to Stern post with two bolts - Do	1⅛
	The remaining Transoms to have one bolt in diameter	1⅛
	The fashion pieces to be bolted into the sides of each Transom with one iron bolt in diameter	⅞
Stern	Of Live oak to side	1"1½
	Scarphs to be jogged	1½
	The jogs to be left open and a well seasoned Live oak key to be drown in to set the nibs close.	
	Nibs of upper scarph	4½
	In the nibs drive two copper bolts in diameter	⅝
	in length	10
	The scarph to have two through bolts (riveted) in diameter	⅞
	& an apron bolt must go through in the middle of the scarph only avoiding the Key.	
Apron & Fore	of Live oak to side	1"8
Deadwood	Apron moulded at head	9
	fastened to the Stern with bolts in diameter	1
	To be drove asunder about	1"8
	In marking the apron bolts, attention must be paid to the position of the Breasthooks in order that the apron bolts may come clear of the throat bolts of Breasthooks.	
	Bolts in fore deadwoods before the fore most square frame	1
Frame	-The floor timber, futtocks, top timbers, Half top timbers, & counter timbers to side	9
	The square frames to be kept apart 1½ inches, & the pieces to knocked out for salting.	
	Moulded in the Throat at ¤	1"3
	Do at floor heads	10
	Do at under side of plank sheer	6
	The immediate sizes, and at rail, to be ascertained by a diminishing line. There are two sizes the timbers are to hold when dubbed off ready for planking. The cant timbers in the fore body will increase ¼ of an inch in each frame the moulding way from the square frames the cant frame ... being the fourth & last cant frame will be one inch larger than the moulding size of the square frames. The cant frames in the after Body will increase ⅛ of an inch in each frame the moulding way from the aftermost square frame. This cant frame 32 will be ½ an inch longer than the	

	moulding size of the square frame excepting at the under side of plank sheer where they will be the same size as the square frames.		
Cant Timbers	The heels to Cant timbers to have 1½ inches left on their insides to jog that much into the deadwood, the jog about 12 inches (or half the distance between bearding line & top of deadwood) from their heels & when fairly dubbed off, the heels are to be secured by a copper bolt in each pair in diameter		1
Keelson	of Live oak sided		1"1½
	Made of 3 six inch plank coaked together with dry Live oak coaks in two rows square	3	
	The throat of every other floor timber will be bolted before the keelson is fayed with the copper bolt in diam.		1⅛
	And after the Keelson is fayed the alternate floors will be bolted through the Keelson with one copper bolt in diam.		1¼
	All the floors & keelson bolts to be riveted.		
	The Keelson to be bolted abaft the aftermost square frame & before the foremost square frame into the Deadwoods and apron with copper bolts in diam.		1
	Number of iron bolts in each scarph of the frames	2	
	In diameter		1
Knight Heads	To side		1
	Knight heads moulded at head		8½
	to be bolted to the apron & to each other with iron bolts in diam.		1
	Bolts asunder about (to be kept clear of Hause Holes)		4–
	Let there be an iron bolt drove through the Heels of each Knight Head & Hause piece into the foremost square frame in diam.		⅞
Counter Timbers	of Live oak sided		9
	The corner timber to be secured by a Live oak Knee faying on the inside & on the top of Main Transom, bolted with bolts in diam.		⅞
	The heels of Counter timbers will be dovetailed in the main Transom, depth of tail		2
	The space of two inches left on the side of Counter timber will be filled by a well seasoned Live oak Key for the purpose of setting the heels well home.		
	The heels of Counter timbers will then be bolted through the main Transom fore & aft with one bolt in each in diam.		1
	After the Counter timbers are dubbed off a false Transom of Live oak will be fitted to the top of the Transom in depth		8
	Jogged over the heels of Counter timbers & the Counter timbers will be bolted through the piece with one bolt in diam.		1
	The false transom will be bolted to the main Transom with bolts in diam.		1
Hause Holes	Two on each side, one on each side to be fitted for Hemp cables, diameter of pipes in the clear		1"
	The other two will be fitted for chain cables.		
Running planks	for bottom of white oak to be in thickness		3
	To be fastened with composition spikes in length		8
	Though a portion of the spikes say one fourth will be		8½
Wales	of white oak, the thickest wale to be		5½
	The upper edge of upper wale to be		4½

The thickest part of the wale will be at or near the lower edge of fifth wale from aloft, from his point they will gradually and fairly diminish downwards until they fall in with the thickness of the remaining plank of the bottom, & upwards they will also gradually & fairly diminish to the upper edge which will be in thickness — 4½

The fastening of planks where it is more than 3½ inches thick will be bolts in diam. — ⅝

The Short fastenings for wales & other thick stuff will be in length about twice & one third the thickness of the strake through which they are drove—Thus a 3½ inch plank will require a bolt in length 8½ inches or nearly & this will [sic] the length of the short bolts for Strings & Drifts.

The bright work will be yellow pine in Strakes of 4½ inches wide full 3 inches Thick at the lower edge & 2¾ inches thick at the upper edge. These strakes will only be cross fastened, that is one fastening only in each strake on each timber. All the rest of the plank will be square fastened, that is two fastenings in each strake to every timber. The heads of spikes in bright work will be plugged.

Length of spikes (of iron) in bright work lower edge — 7–

upper edge — 6½

Treenails will not be used. Bolts in diam. — ¾

will be substituted—There will be one through bolt & one short fastening to each strake in every timber excepting where a knee bolt will answer for the through bolt & if near the Bow where the strakes will be narrow, where one fastening will be sufficient.

The copper fastening will be continued up to a water line 17 feet 6 inches from the bottom of the keel. *June 12th 1835/18 feet aft – 17 feet fwd.*

Strings & Drifts of white oak in thickness — 3½

Widths per draught

To be fastened with short bolts in diameter — ⅝

in length about — 8½

Plank sheer in thickness — 3¼

Bolts through plank sheer & half top timbers — ⅝

The waist outside from plank sheer to rail will be narrow strakes of pine in thickness — 1¼

Excepting round the Bow from Frame O forward where it will be 2 inches in thickness of white oak. Inside plank 2 inches—Inside & outside to be caulked. All the timbers, knight heads and Hause pieces will run up to the rail from frame O & forward of frame O. Abaft frame O—the half timbers only will run up. The ports will be formed by the Half top timbers. Those half top timbers that form the aft side of the ports will have to be shifted a few inches forward so as to bring the ports to the width of — 2"10

Half Top timbers that run up to Rail abaft frame O. N, L, J, H, F, D, B, ¤, 2, 4, 6, 8, 10, 12, 14, 16, 18, 20, 22, 24, 26, 28, 30, 32

Butt Bolts To be drove through the frame next on each side. The one which the strake butts on (to be riveted on the inside) in diam. — ¾

In shifting the butts for planking let there be six feet between each and let there be three strakes between every two butts on the same timber

Bilge Strakes Inside at floor heads in number on each side — 3

	In thickness		4½
	To be fastened with bolts in diam.		⅝
	Bolts in length about		10½
Lower Deck Clamps	of white oak number of Strakes	3	
	in thickness		4
	Hooked together		
	To be fastened with iron bolts in diam.		⅝
	In length about		9½
	At the lower edge of Clamps there will be an air strake in width		6
	The ceiling will be white oak plank in thickness		3
	Fastened with spikes in length		8
Breasthooks	of Live oak—There are to be 3 Breasthooks in the Hold besides the Lower deck Breasthook sided		10
	To be bolted with bolts in diam.		1⅛
Steps of Masts	The steps of masts & all the Breasthooks are to fay to the timbers. *Mr. Humphreys' letter of June 12th 1835—Steps of Masts of Live oak jogging over Keelsons and resting on two fore & aft pieces of Live oak on each side, fayed to the timbers, in thickness 5 inches*		
Lower Deck Beams	Of yellow pine sided		1"0½
	moulded		11
	The longest Beam to spring		5
	Beams shaped at the ends to		9½
	Let down into the clamps		1
	To be kneed at each end with the one Lodge & one Dagger knee sided		7
	To be bolted with bolts in diameter		1
	There will be half an inch trimmed off from the upper edge Clamps under the Lodge knee to admit air, leaving a jog of about 4 inches in length next the Beam for the knee to rest on. After the Beams are cut off to their proper length let there be holes bored about 4 feet into the beam with a two inch auger to be well filled with salt & plugged up.		
	Let the ends of each knee be nailed to the Beams & Ceiling with two 5 inch spikes.		
Carlings	or fore & aft pieces of heart yellow pine in two ranges-square		7
Ledges	of heart yellow pine square		5
	Not to be more than two feet four inches asunder.		
Planks	Heart yellow pine in thickness		3
	Average width amidship about		10
	Fastened with composition spikes to the Beams in length		7½
	to the Ledges in length		6½
	The following remarks will apply to the upper as well as to the Lower decks.		
	In driving spikes in deck plank let the spike be placed two inches from the nearest edge, two in each beam & ledge until the plank is reduced to 6 inches* (*June 12th Say 7 inches*) in width & less when there will be one spike only in each beam & ledge to be drove on the alternate edges, two inches from the nearest edge. When the plank is reduced to 4 inches in width & less, the spike will be drove in the middle.		
Partners	of Fore & Main Mast of Live oak in width	1	
	in depth		9
	With one lodge & one lap knee to each piece sided		6
	Bolted with bolts in diameter		¾
	To be framed so far apart as to receive wedges in thickness		3½

Partners	of Mizzen Mast of Live oak in width		10
	in depth		8
	With one lodge & one lap knee to each piece sided		5
	Bolted with bolts in diameter		¾
	To be framed so far apart as to receive wedges in thickness		3
Coamings	of white oak in width		1"4
	sided first to		6½
	Chined in 1½ inches 7 inches from below		
	Height above decks		6
	Headledges sided		5
	Bolted with bolts in diam.		⅞
Waterways	of heart yellow pine deck edge in thickness		3
	side edge in thickness		4
	The edge next the deck will be chined on two inches: the wood taken off in a straight line across as per figure in the margin. There will be primings out or stops for salt—one near floor head one at the upper edge of air Strake below Lower deck, & one at the upper edge of air strake above Lower deck.		
Spirketting	of white oak, one strake in thickness		4
	At the upper edge of this spirketting there will be an air Strake in width		6
Transom Knees	The arms faying against Main Transom—Body in length	7	
	Arms Do	5	
	Sided		8
	Bolted with bolts in diameter		1
Pumps	In number	2	
	Placed between the first & second Beams next abaft the main mast. To be chambered pumps—diameter of the chamber		7
Breasthooks	There will be one Breasthook between Lower and upper decks, one to the upper deck, and one above the Bowsprit sided & bolted the same as those below--		
Stantions	under lower deck square		6
	fitted with caps under the Beams and into shoes at heel fastened to keelson.		
Upper Deck	of white oak in thickness		3½
Clamps	Made of two strakes hooked into each other		
	To be fastened with short bolts in diameter		⅝
	in length about		8½
	The planks between the clamps and air strake next below will be white oak in thickness		3
	Fastened with spikes in length		8
Beams of Upper	of heart yellow pine sided		11
Deck	moulded		9½
	To be shaped at the ends to		8
	Beams abaft the main mast (excepting the Mast Beams) to mould		8
	To be bored & salted as those below		
	Knees to be sided		6½
	To have one Lodge & one dagger knee to the end of each Beam except the cabin Beam which will have Lap & Lodge knees.		
	To be bolted with bolts in diam.		⅞
	Note the knee bolts that come between the lower edge of String & upper edge of wales to be drove before the bright work is put on.		

Carlings	or fore & aft pieces of heart yellow pine in two ranges square		7
Ledges	of heart yellow pine square		5
Coamings	of Hatchways of white oak in depth		1"8½
	To be clinched in as those below 7 inches from below		7
	Height above deck		10
	To be bolted as those below		
	Headledges sided		5
Plank	for upper deck of heart yellow pine in thickness		3¼
	Width amidships not to exceed		8
	To be fastened to the Beams with composition spikes in length		8
	Ledges		6½
Waterways	Of heart yellow pine to be worked with a faint hollow square		10
	Spirkettings of white oak		3
	There will be a narrow Spriketting above the waterway		
Partners	Of heart yellow pine square		7
	Framed up so far apart that the mast shall be 4 inches clear all round		4
Cat heads	of tough white oak or Live oak sided		11
	in depth		11
	The cat heads are to run out about the height of plank sheer		
	The bed to be covered with Sheet lead		
	Two bolts in the heel of each in diam. with plates above & below		1⅛
Rudder	To have a crooked head rudder, diameter of head *June 12th 1"3 in place of*		1"2
	To be bolted with bolts in diameter		1
	Braces pintle straps, dove tail plates & stirrups to be fastened with bolts in diam.		¾
Coppering *To be coppered to a line 17"6 aft 17" forward*	to be coppered with 30 & 28 oz copper equal quantities of each to a water line 17 feet, Copper to be put on over felt. Two strakes of 30 oz will be put on each side from the Stem to mizen chains. There are to be two upper strakes. False keel & main keel to have 30 oz copper & the Bilge from Stem to frame 16 will have 30 oz & so will the rudder. The remaining part of the 30 oz copper will be expended forward from keel to water line as far as it will go.		
Channels	of white oak of width sufficient for the shrouds to clear the Rail at the fore end of fore channel. All the channels will be the same width, in thickness next the side of Ship		3½
	Do at outer edge		3¼
	Bolted with bolts in diameter		⅞
	Number of Shrouds to Foremast one each side	5	
	Topmast Back Stays	2	
	Number of Shrouds to main mast on each side	6	
	Topmast Back Stays	2	
Fore & Main Chains	Made of the best American iron in diam.		1¼
	Chain bolts & preventer bolts in diameter		1⅜
	The foot link bolts to be drove in the first or upper wale		
	The preventer bolts to be drove in the third strake of wales		
	Number of Shrouds to the mizen mast	4	
Mizen Chains	made of the best American iron in diam.		1⅛
	Chain bolts in diameter		1¼
	Topmast Back Stay	1	
Bowsprit & Bitts	of tough white oak to run down & be secured on Lower deck Beams square		10

	Distance asunder so as to admit jogs on each side of Bowsprit	3
	Tapered at heel to	8
	Each Bitt to be bolted with 4 bolts 2 in each beam in diam.	⅞
	Heel of Bowsprit to have 2 bolts drove through an iron plate on top in diameter	1¼
	Rivetted or forelocked underneath.	
Pall Bitt	of tough white oak square	1"3
	To run down & be secured in Lower deck	
	Tapered at heel to	1"0
	Bolted with four bolts 2 in each beam in diameter	1
Windlass Bitts	of tough white oak in width	1"6
	in depth	8
	dove tailed in white oak partners resting on three beams in depth	1"
	in width	1"6
	Jogged down below top of Beam	7
Knees for	Windlass Bitts sided	8
	To have a patent windlass abaft Foremast and a Capstan on quarter deck.	
Scuppers	To have Three Scuppers on each side—size of Scupper pipes 3 inches by 5 inches in the clear.	
Rudder Braces	& pintle straps to have thin plates of Copper sheets let in behind them.	
Rudder Bolts	in diameter	1
Cutwater Bolts	of Copper in diameter	1
	Do of iron from 1 inch to 1⅜ inches—the three upper ones to go through & forelock on apron.	
Cheeks for Head	to be bolted with bolts in diam.	⅞
Hood end bolts	To be drove on the upper corners of fore & after Hoods—Those for the lower after hoods will be drove through from one side & riveted on the other.	¾
Ring & Eye Bolts	for Ports—2 ring & 2 eye bolts to each in diam.	⅞
Ring Bolts	on upper decks in diameter	1⅛
	The after Bolt to be drove through the Beam at fore side of main Hatchway, and the foremost bolt to be drove in the beam next abaft the windlass—	
	Each intermediate Beam to have one ring bolt on drove in the second strake from coamings of main Hatchway.	

Approved
/s/ Jn Rodgers
/s/ John Lenthall

* * *

APPENDIX 2

Relief Calculations, Summary and Metacenter [1]

In addition to writing directions for building the Store Ship *Relief,* Master Builder Lenthall performed a very complete set of calculations to determine her hydrostatic properties. Close to fifty pages of his calculations exist, all in his tight hand, displaying Lenthall's fluid application of numerical analysis to derive *Relief*s sectional and waterplane areas, volumes of displacement, centers of floatation and of gravity, coefficients of form, and of her transverse and longitudinal metacenters. Half again as many pages containing tables of mould loft dimensions, frame sizes and other calculations necessary to erect the ship's timbers compliment his purely naval architectural evaluations. That such a mass of meticulous analyses was performed during the design of a lowly store ship speaks volumes about both Lenthall's grasp of mathematics and of the abilities of his fellow naval constructors in the 1830s.

First presented in this Appendix is a single sheet facsimile summary of *Relief*'s key data as calculated by John Lenthall. [2] His presentation is recognizably modern and surprisingly detailed, carrying his numbers to a two-decimal accuracy, all of it performed by hand. Notes [in square brackets] are definitions and units provided by the author.

* * *

Calculations on Store Ship "Relief" built at Phil^{a} 1836

Length of mean load floating line from fore side of rabbet of Stem to aft side of rabbet of Post	108.875 ft [LBP]
Extreme Breadth of load line	30.916 ft [B]
Depth from mean load line to lower edge of rabbet of keel [BL]	15.00 ft [D]
Content of circ. parallelepiped	50489.68 cft [LBP x B x D]
Hull displacement to outside of planking including stem, keel, post, rudder	33,313.08 cft [V w/appendages]
" " " " " " " before ¤	13361.77 cft
" " " " " " " abaft ¤	19951.31 cft
Displacement exclusive of stem, keel, post, rudder	33040.33 cft [V w/planking]
" in proportion to circ. paral^{d}	.6544 [C_B]
Displacement before the middle of the length of mean load line	17886.89 cft [V fwd]
" abaft the middle of the length of mean load line	15426.19 cft [V aft]
Ratio of displacement before middle to that abaft	1: .8624
Distance of ¤ before the middle of the length of mean load line	11.395 ft
Center of Gravity of Displacement <u>abaft</u> ¤	9.047 ft [LCB]
do do <u>Before</u> middle of length of mean load line	2.348 ft [LCB]
do do Below mean load floating line	6.1 ft [VCB]
Area of mean load floating line	3054 sft [A_{WP}]
Area of cir. Parallelogram	3365.98 sft [LBP x B]
Area of mean load line in proportion to circ. par^{m}	.907 [C_{WP}]
Area of greatest immersed transverse section at ¤	396.6 sft [A_M]
Area of cir. Par^{m}	463.74 sft [B x D]
Area of ¤ in proportion of circ. parall^{m}	.855 [C_M]
Height of Latitudinal metacenter above center of displacement	6.54 ft [BM_T]
" Longitudinal metacenter above center of displacement	77 feet [BM_L]
Area of rudder	47.33 sft
Center of gravity of rudder abaft center of gravity of displ	56.735 feet
Surface of the 10 sails	8880.4 sft
Moment of Sails Fwd to Moment of Sails Aft	1:81

Calculation of Metacenter

With the summary of calculations on *Relief* digested, Lenthall's determination of *Relief*'s metacentric height can now be examined.[3] Of all the numerical analyses he performed on this small store ship, calculation of her metacentric height was the most complex because of its use of a cubic integral function to determine the waterplane's moments of inertia. But first, what is a metacenter? The metacenter, designated by the symbol M, is the point on the ship's vertical centerline (CL) through which its center of buoyancy (B) acts when the vessel is heeled. If this point of intersection is above the ship's center of gravity (G), then the vessel possesses a positive righting moment and is stable; if M and G coincide, then the vessel is neutrally stable; and if M is below G, the vessel is unstable and will tend to capsize. Thus, a ship's transverse metacentric height is a fundamental measure of its inherent stability. In the longitudinal axis, a conventionally configured hull's metacentric height provides less a measure of stability than of its resistance to pitching, which significantly affects a ship's behavior in a seaway. Lenthall calculated both *Relief*s transverse and longitudinal metacentric heights. The calculations examined here are for her transverse metacenter, or BM_T, and so relate to her stability.

Lenthall's calculation of *Relief*'s transverse metacenter covered a single sheet of foolscap folio-sized paper, headed "Calculation of Metacenter." What appears to be a later pencil note tells us that this sheet applies to the Store Ship *Relief* and gives the date of 1835. Lenthall's work is performed in ink and, like any good engineer, he makes note of formulas used, properly heads his columns of numbers and defines the key constants. At the top of the page, he references the two principal equations used in his calculation of metacenter:

- Atwood's 2nd Rule, or what would now be called Simpson's First Rule.[4] Atwood and Simpson were contemporaries; perhaps Lenthall cites Atwood because he owned a copy of his "Disquisition." Atwood's Rule II, which is used to determine the area under a curve as defined by known ordinates, is written in red ink above the title word "Metacenter" (modern brackets substituted for overhead line):

  (S + 4P + 2Q) x ⅓ r – must be odd [must use an odd number of ordinates].

  Where S = 1" & last [or the 1st and last ordinates].

  P = 2, 4, 6 [or the sum of the even numbered ordinates].

  Q = 3, 5, 7 [or the sum of the odd numbered ordinates].

In the case of Lenthall's calculation of *Relief*s metacenter, the curve of interest is the half-breadth of the plane of the waterline at the draft being analyzed.

- per Chapman, or use of the integral formula proposed by Swedish naval architect Fredrik Hendrik af Chapman to solve for the metacentric height.[5] Lenthall writes this equation most prominently in the middle of the page, next to the vertical border:

  $$\frac{2}{3} \int y^3 dx \,/ D$$

  Where y^3dx = the function of the cube of ordinates describing the waterplane's half-breadth.

  D = the volume of displacement of the hull at the draft being analyzed.

  Lenthall owned an English translation of Chapman's *Tractat.* By 1835, Chapman's integral formula was commonly referenced by other sources, e.g., Clairbois, mentioned in Atwood's "Disquisition," had published a French translation of it.

One fact Lenthall doesn't explicitly define is the draft of the ship being evaluated for its metacenter. The answer is given by the volume of displacement noted at the very bottom of the page (he's converting it into $\log_{10}$ for later use): 33,313.087 cubic feet. From his summary of calculations, this we know is *Relief*s hull's volume with appendages at a mean load line of 15 feet (molded), which makes perfect sense—he is analyzing her stability at her maximum design draft. If the depth of the keel was considered, *Relief*s extreme draft in this condition would be 16'-6".

The starting point of Lenthall's calculation is his list of half-breadth ordinates for the 15 ft waterline, shown in the column on the left margin headed "Ordinates", with their defining frame station numbers written just to their left. Ordinates were taken from tables of offsets Lenthall produced and are measured to "the outside of plank." The accompanying table titled "Water Lines in After Body of Store Ship" is the source of Lenthall's offsets for *Relief*'s aft waterplane (a similar table supplied the forward waterplane offsets).[6] Confusingly, the offsets for the 15 ft (molded) waterline are in the table's bottom row, which is labeled "1" in black ink. Also observe that Lenthall has prominently marked his table in red ink with the symbols S, P and Q as well as numerical series to facilitate the application of Atwood's 3rd Rule (Simpson's Second Rule) for separate analyses, all of which tends to obscure the true frame station and waterline designations written in black ink.

Returning to the metacenter calculations, *Relief*s frame stations start with the foremost, T, and run down to midship (¤), then continue down, or aft, using numbered stations through to 32. This station designation, alpha before and numeric aft of midships, is typical of this era. The station spacing, "r = 4 feet," is written in red ink just below Station 32's label.

To the right of the column of ordinates, a second column is filled in, this one of the ordinates cubed (the y^3 function). Lenthall has written the Atwood Rule multipliers to the right of each cubed ordinate and to the left, a mark indicating whether it belongs to the P series, both entries using red ink.

Moving to the center top of the page, Lenthall lays out his method of multiplying the Atwood multipliers and summing them up to calculate the (S + 4P + 2Q) function. Here he displays the art of a calculator seeking to minimize the burden of multiplication—he organizes the cubed ordinates into three columns, headed S, P and Q, adds them first and *then* multiplies their summations by their multipliers, 4 for the P column and 2 for the Q column. Next, he adds the results of this exercise for the S and Q columns to the result for the P or center column. The summation 244630.89 is the (S + 4P + 2Q) function. Lenthall then applies another mathematical simplification. To multiply this function by ⅓ r, which he has already noted as equal to 1⅓, he simply adds one third of the (S + 4P + 2Q) function to itself, achieving the same end. Neat!

To complete his summation of the y^3dx function, Lenthall adds corrections to account for the small portion of the waterplane outside of stations T and 32. The forward triangle's moment of inertia is equal to 293.60 ft^4 and the after triangle's is 218.62 ft^4. Their calculation is shown below the ordinate and ordinate cubed columns. Adding these corrections to the much larger (S + 4P + 2Q) function yields the "Moment" or the waterplane's transverse moment of inertia in ft^4.

Now Lenthall is ready to apply Chapman's formula, $⅔ \int y^3dx / D$. First, he multiplies the Moment by 2 then divides it by 3. The result is $⅔ \int y^3dx$, the symbol of which he writes next to the number. To complete his calculation of the metacenter, this result must be divided by the volume of displacement, D in ft^3. Both numbers are large, $⅔ \int y^3dx$ is on the order of 10^5 and D on the order of 10^4. To ease his work and maintain accuracy, Lenthall uses logarithms; the log to base 10 of both the numerator and denominator are written below the $⅔ \int y^3dx$ = 6.5377 result: 5.3380399 and 4.5226147. The anti-log of their difference, 0.8154252, is equal to the height of the metacenter, 6.5377, as measured in feet above the center of displacement (VCB). A pencil note converts this to feet and inches, 6"6⅜. Also in a later penciled calculation, Lenthall adjusts this result to the hull's baseline (BL) reference, by adding 9.0472 ft to it, yielding 15.5849 ft above BL. Here we have a bit of mystery, for the VCB is given in the summary of calculations as 6.1 ft *below* the mean floating line (15.0 molded draft), yet Lenthall's later correction implies it is now 6.2472 ft below. Yes, it's very small difference of 0.1472 feet, but Lenthall's calculations were always very precise.

The sheet's final tabulations, in the lower right-hand block, are simply a check of the $\frac{2}{3}\int y^3 dx$ calculated on the upper part of the page. Compare the 217041.58 with the top number of 217791.16.

In conclusion, Lenthall's calculation of metacenter demonstrates his mastery of numerical analysis and his ability to clearly present his assumptions and methodology. And it was all for the humble store ship *Relief*.

* * *

Store Ship "Relief"
Mid 1831

Calculation of Metacentre (in Chapman

By Atwood's 2nd Rule

TT	7.125	362,47	1
R	11.6249	1573,04	4
P	13.5416	2487,81	2
N	14.5	3054,94	4
L	14.9582	3348,07	2
J	15.1666	3491,05	4
H	15.3125	3595,64	2
F	15.3955	3652,26	4
D	15.4374	3680,80	2
B	15.4582	3695,12	4
⊗	15.4582	3695,12	2
2	15.4582	3695,12	4
4	15.4582	3695,12	2
6	15.4582	3695,12	4
8	15.4374	3687,95	2
10	15.3756	3638,05	4
12	15.3125	3595,64	2
14	15.2291	3532,64	4
16	15.125	3463,51	2
18	14.9791	3361,52	4
20	14.8125	3254,95	2
22	14.6041	3118,53	4
24	14.2916	2924,21	2
26	13.9166	2697,23	4
28	13.3333	2373,93	2
30	12.7708	1851,80	4
32	7.5533	437,24	1

Moment = 326686.7½ $\int y^3 dx$

3)653373.48

217791.16 $\frac{2}{3}\int y^3 dx$

$\frac{\frac{2}{3}\int y^3 dx}{D}$ = 6.5397 above centre of displacement

6.6½

forward Δ = 362.47 × .81 = 293.60

after triangle = 437.24 × .49

Displacement = 33.313,087 cubic feet = 4.5226147

Lenthall's Calculation of Relief's Metacenter

area = S + 2P + 3Q × 3r/8 a + 3b + 3c − d × 3/8 r

Water Lines in After Body of Store Ship to Outside of Plank — 12 inches asunder commencing at Lower Edge of Rabbet

r = 4 feet r = 2 feet r = 1⅓ feet

	S	Q	Q	P	Q	Q	P	Q	Q	S	Q	Q	P	Q	Q	P	Q	Q	P	Q	Q	S	Q	Q	S	
	1	2	3	4	5	6	7	8	9	10/1	2	3	4	5	6	7	8	9	10	11	12	13/1	2	3	4	
Frame	⊗	2	4	6	8	10	12	14	16	18	19	20	21	22	23	24	25	26	27	28	29	30			32	
S 1 W	,5625	,5625	,5625	,5625	,5625	,5625	,5625	,5625	,5625	,5625	,5625	,5625	,5625	,5625	,5625	,5625	,5625	,5625	,5625	,5625	,5625	,5625	,5625	,5625	,5625	1 S
2 Q	5,0416	5.0416	4,9582	4,7708	4.4791	4,0833	3,6041	3,0833	2,5625	2,0625	1.8333	1.6249	1.466	1.25	1.125	,9791	,8749	.7916	.7082	,666	,6249	,5833	,5730	,5625	,5625	2 Q
3 Q	9,125	9,125	9.—	8,7082	8,2082	7.5625	6.75	5.8333	4,9166	3,9791	3.5208	3,1041	2.6666	2,2916	1,9374	1,6249	1,3528	1.1458	,9582	,8333	,7291	,6458	,6041	,5625	,5625	3 Q
P 4	11,7291	11.7291	11,6249	11.4166	10,9791	10,3756	9,5208	8.5	7,3756	6,125	4.5	4,8333	4,2082	3,6041	3,0416	2.5	2,0416	1.6458	1.330	1,0833	,8958	,75	,666	,5833	,5625	4 P
5 Q	13,1666	13,1666	13,0833	12,9166	12,6666	12.25	11,6249	10,7916	9,6666	8.333	7,5833	6,8125	6,0208	5,2082	4,3538	3,6874	3.—	2,3955	1,8958	1,4791	1,1666	,9166	,7708	,666	,5833	5 Q
6 Q	14.—	14.—	13,9582	13,8749	13.6666	13,3955	12,9791	12,3756	11.5	10,2916	9,0625	8.75	7,8749	6,9582	6,0416	5,0833	4.1875	3,3756	2,6249	2.—	1.5	1,1041	,8958	,7291	,6041	6 Q
P 7	14,5416	14.5416	14,5416	14,4582	14,3233	14,1458	13,8333	13,4166	12,7708	11,8541	11.25	10.5416	9.7082	8.75	7.75	6,6666	5,6041	4.5416	3,5833	2,7082	2.—	1,2955	1.0833	,8333	,6458	7 P
8 Q	14,8958	14,8958	14,8958	14,8541	14,7708	14,6249	14,3955	14,0833	13,6249	12,9374	12.5	11,9374	11.25	10,4166	9.4582	8.3756	7,2082	6.—	4,7916	3.666	2.1666	1.8125	1,3538	,9791	,7082	8 Q
9 Q	15,1041	15,1041	15,1041	15,0833	15,0208	14,9166	14.75	14.5	14,125	13,6249	13,2916	12,8749	12,2538	11,7082	10,8958	9,9166	8,8125	7,5625	6,2082	4,8333	3,5416	2,4166	1.75	1,2291	,8125	9 Q
P 10	15,25	15.25	15.25	15,2082	15,1458	15,0625	14,9374	14.75	14,4582	14,0833	13,8333	13,5208	13.125	12.666	12.0625	11,3125	10,3538	9.2082	7.8125	6,2916	4.75	3,2082	2.333	1,5833	,9791	10 P
11 Q	15,3333	15,3333	15.3333	15,3125	15,25	15,1666	15,0625	14,9166	14,7082	14,3955	14,2291	14.—	13,7082	13.3538	12,9166	12.3333	11,6041	10.666	9.4791	8.—	6.25	4.333	3,1458	2,0833	1,2291	11 Q
12 Q	15,3955	15,3955	15.3955	15,3756	15,3125	15.25	15,1666	15,0208	14,8749	14,6249	14,4791	14,2916	14,0833	13,7916	13,4791	13,0416	12,5416	11,8541	10,9374	9,6874	8,0208	5,8749	4,3125	2,8749	1,6249	12 Q
P 13	15,4166	15,4166	15.4166	15,3955	15,3538	15,2916	15,2291	15,125	15.—	14,7916	14.6666	14,5208	14,3333	14.125	13,8749	13,5625	13,2082	12,7082	12,0416	11.1041	9.75	7,7082	5,9582	4,0416	2,2291	13 P
14 Q	15,4582	15,4582	15,4582	15,4374	15,3955	15,3333	15,2708	15.1666	15,0416	14,8541	14,7916	14,6666	14,5208	14,3756	14,1666	13,9374	13,6458	13,2916	12,8125	12,1666	11,2082	9,6249	8,0208	5.75	3,2291	14 Q
15 Q	15,4582	15.4582	15.4582	15,4582	15,4374	15,3756	15,3125	15,2082	15,1041	14,9582	14,8749	14,7708	14,6249	14.5	14,3538	14,1666	13,9582	13,6874	13,333	12,8749	12.25	11,2291	10,125	8,125	4,9166	15 Q
S 16	15,4582	15.4582	15.4582	15.4582	15,4374	15,3756	15,3125	15,2291	15,125	14,9791	14,9166	14,8125	14,7082	14,6041	14,4582	14,2916	14,125	13,9166	13.6666	13.333	12,9166	12,2708	11,6249	10,4582	7,5833	16 S
Launching Line [illegible]	15,0833	15,1041	15.1041	15.0833	15.0416	14.9582	14.8125	14.6458	14.3756	13.9791	13.7291	13.4374	13.0833	12,6249	12.0833	11.3756	10.5	11.4374	8,1666	6.7082	5.125	3,0416	2.6041	1.75	1,0625	

Distance from ⊗ to 18 is 36 feet Distance from ⊗ to 30 is 60 feet Distance from ⊗ to 32 is 64 feet

3/8 r = 1.5 = 1½ 3/8 r = .75 = 3/4 3/8 r = .5 = ½

Table of Offsets for the Aft Body of the Store Ship Relief

APPENDIX 3

Orders for the Launch of the U.S. Ship Pennsylvania [1]

Tucked inside Lenthall's personal papers folder for the U.S.S. *Pennsylvania*, subtitled "Orders for Launching," are copies of two documents written on foolscap folio sized paper detailing preparations for the ship's 1837 launch. These documents are of great significance because at that time, the 120-gun Ship of the Line *Pennsylvania* was the largest vessel to be launched in the United States, if not in the world. With a length (LBP) of 210'-0", breadth (molded) of 56'-9", depth in hold of 23'-0" and a displacement when launched of nearly 2,700 tons, she was gigantic by early nineteenth-century standards. That *Pennsylvania* would also be the figurative flagship of the U.S. Navy gave her launching a high visibility that ensured a consuming public interest in its every aspect. And the man supervising each detail of her launch was John Lenthall.

The first document, "Orders to be Observed," is a two page set of orders for launch preparations, dated 7 June 1837, nearly six weeks before *Pennsylvania* slid down the ways at the Philadelphia Navy Yard on the afternoon of the 18th of July. This document is signed by three civilian naval constructors: Samuel Humphreys, the Navy's chief naval constructor; Samuel Hartt, the naval constructor assigned to the New York Navy Yard, and John Lenthall, the master builder at the Philadelphia Navy Yard. Their "Orders" or instructions are general in nature, and give only the briefest particulars of the launching ways, bilgeways and other structures and procedures required for the ship's successful launch.

The second, "In Describing the Launch,' is in Lenthall's own hand and is a rather different document. Over its seven densely written pages, replete with original cross-outs, smudges and later corrections, John Lenthall provides an insider's narrative of the exhaustive preparations for *Pennsylvania*'s launching and a chronology of the key events on the day of her launch. It is almost certain that this document was written sometime after the event, and most probable that it formed the basis of a paper by

Lenthall on this same subject that was presented six years later before the American Philosophical Society.[2]

Of interest to the naval architect, Lenthall's account presents his calculations of the ship's launching conditions—her estimated weight (2,696 long tons) and its resolution into (1) the force that would propel her down the launching ways and (2) her weight normal to the plane. He documents the ways' inclination (3° 31' or 0.738 inch per foot), assumed way friction (0.04 or 1/25), spread of the launching ways (20'-4" at the upper end, widening to 20'-8" at the lower end), and the dimensions of the bilge ways. These technological snapshots indicate that the slope of *Pennsylvania*'s launching or ground ways was in the upper range of current practice (0.55 to 0.85 inches per foot) and her bilge way bearing pressure of 2 ½ tons/ft² was at the top of the accepted range (1½ to 2½ tons/ft²).[3] But her launch arrangements proved to be soundly conceived. After some initial hesitation, the ship glided down the ways and gracefully entered the Delaware's waters, all without mishap. Master Builder Lenthall could hardly have hoped for more.

Below is a sketch drawn by Lenthall showing the launching way, bilge way, blocking or packing arrangement and wedge system applied to each side of *Pennsylvania*'s hull.[4] The dimensions marked on the sketch compare favorably to his description of the solid bilge way blocking, packing and wedges. Hull centerline is to the left; the launching way is the largest plank on the bottom, with its ribband attached to its right side.

* * *

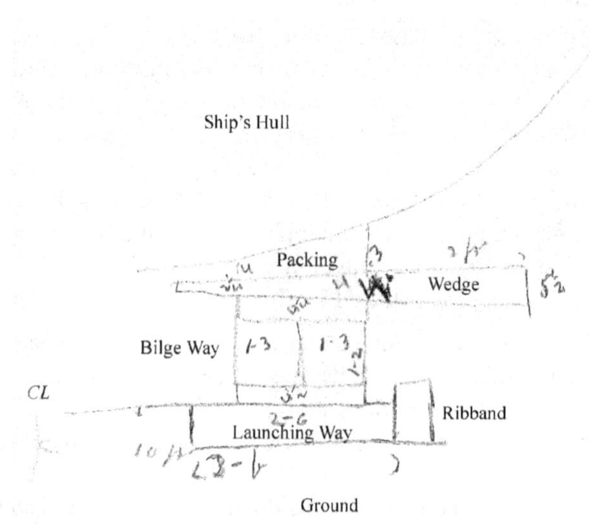

Section through Pennsylvania's Bilge Way

Philada June 7, 1837

Orders to be observed on the preparation for the launch of the U.S. Ship *Pennsylvania.*

The spreads of the launching ways for the length of the ship to be 20 feet 4 inches, the width at the lower end to be 20 feet 8 inches. The spread of the Bilgeways to be 20 feet giving 2 inches play on each side for the length of the ship and 4 inches on each side at the lower end.

The solid Blocking or packing on the Bilgeways to terminate aft 40 feet before the after end of the keel. Abaft the after Blocking there will be 9 upright shores on each side (the aftermost one placed 16 feet before the after end of the keel) resting on the Bilgeways, the upper end fitted to the bottom and secured at the head by a thick plank bolted to the Bottom. These shores will be about 20 inches asunder and 12 inches square placed perpendicularly, each shore to have a wedge placed under the heel.

The Blocking or packing forward will terminate 8 feet abaft the fore end of the keel. Before this Blocking there will be 3 upright shores (the forward to be abreast the fore end of the keel) of the same size and distance asunder as those abaft and secured in the same manner.

The after Blocking will be secured with 6 frappings and the forward Blocking with 4 frappings of 4 inch white rope.

The Bilgeways will have a cross piece at the aft side of the piece to be fitted to the aft side of the sternpost to protect the crowns of the rudder Braces from injury. This crosspiece may be 10 or 12 inches thickness and 14 inches wide jogged three inches over the Bilgeways and bolted to them. On this piece are to be placed two shores, one on each side, reaching nearly up to the cross-seam and secured there by a cleat large enough to receive the head of the shore.

Inside the Ship to be shored up directly over the Bilgeways, one shore to each beam up as high as the upper gun deck.

A shoe shod with iron to be placed under the after end of the keel and the Bottom of the river in the range of the keel ought to be examined for the distance of 250 feet from the end of the wharf.

As this ship is the largest ever built in this country and of great weight it is respectfully proposed that not more than 100 persons exclusive of those necessary to take care of her be admitted on board on the day of the launch.

It is also respectfully proposed that the number of persons to be admitted inside the house on that occasion be limited. The workmen will require all the room of the lower passages to take down the shores, and the galleries on each side the house are not sufficiently strong to bear-up the weight of the number of persons they would contain.

	(	Saml. Humphreys
Signed	(	S. Hartt
	(	John Lenthall

* * *

In describing the launch of the *Pennsylvania,* it will be necessary to say a few words respecting the foundation. The new wharf upon which the ship was built, was found, some years after her commencement & when the ship was considerably advanced, to be decayed, and nearly all that portion above high water line, required to be renewed. Piles had been driven in the line of the keel and also in the line of the Launching ways, which it was found necessary to cut off, at about low-water line and upon these pile heads substantial stone walls were built reaching to within 50 ft of the stern of the ship, from which point, to the end of the Wharf, there were cross logs as usual, laid on the pile heads. Upon the center wall, the blocks of the keel were replaced, the Ship during the operation being supported by the Shores.

An additional length of 75 feet of wharf was sunk at the stern of the Ship, over which she had likewise to pass, and into this wharf at a later period while the Ship was completing, upwards of 700 piles were driven, being of white oak, yellow pine and hemlock, the bays of the wharf in the range of the launching or ground ways being completely filled with piles—many of these piles had to be cut off under water, which from the usual height of the tides, caused by the almost constant succession of east winds, occasioned considerable delay in the time of launching

The building of the ship was commenced in the latter part of the Year 1822, and she was launched in July 1837 leaving Phila. November of the same year.

The weight of the Timber of the Hull was estimated at	2426 tons
" Metals of various kinds, as Iron, Copper, lead	230 "
Other materials and extra weights	20 "
	2676 "
Spectators on Board	20 "
Total weight when launched	2696 "

The inclination of the Ship's keel was 3° 31' from which the force down the plane is 165.24 tons and the pressure on the plane 2694.92 tons, allowing the friction to be .04 or 1/25 the pressure, there will be a tendency of 57.4 tons to cause the ship to descend the plane.

The blocking upon which the permanent or launching ways were laid were pieces about 8 feet in length which were put close together, making the foundation solid for a length of 325 feet. The pieces were laid in a transverse direction to the line of the Ship's motion. Where the height made it necessary at the fore end, this blocking was built of alternately fore and aft and cross blocking, the upper surface being entirely of cross blocks. The distance from the fore end of the false keel, to the end of the wharf was 305 feet, but as the inclination of the Slip or wharf was less than that of the keel the height of this blocking gradually diminished & at some distance from the lower end, the cross logs of the wharf were trimmed and the ways were laid on them. There was 25 feet at the Lower end of the wharf which had been built up solid from the bottom of the river, of this solid part it was necessary to take off the two upper courses, and the line of the top of the blocking of the launching ways at the water and of the wharf was about 15 inches below the lowest tide. It was in preparing this part of the foundation that the greatest delay was experienced.

When the upper surface was made perfectly fair and level across or athwartship, the launching plank or ways were laid over the center of this blocking.

These launching planks were made in lengths of from 40 to 45 feet scarfing on each other 18 inches, in thickness 12 inches and in width 3 feet except the two lower pieces, which were in width 3 feet 3 inches. The pieces were each formed by bolting 3 oak logs together with 1¼ inch bolts, about 5 feet asunder and when in their place on the cross blocking the scarphs were likewise bolted. To each piece there were two diagonal or spur shores, let into the blocking, and the after pieces were bolted into the cross logs and pile heads, with 9 bolts in each piece, all the holes being bored deep enough to allow of punching the bolts through, whenever it became necessary to take the pieces up. Against the edge of the launching plank for the whole length there were pieces bolted called technically "ribands", the object of which is to prevent the Ship in her motion down the plane from slipping on either side or to keep her in her track. These ribbands were made from oak plank 6 inches thick and 12 inches wide and projected 6 inches above the top of the launching plank and were bolted to their places after the launching planks has set [sic] perfectly fair and secure, except the two lower pieces upon which the ribbands were bolted before the [sic] were put in place. The width of the launching ways as given above are in the clear or independent of the ribband.

Against the ribband for the whole length, shores were placed about 2½ ft. asunder, the heads having a small inclination forward and the heels secured against the side of the wharf. The launching plank being of a parallel thickness and laid level athwartship there was consequently no horizontal stress or tendency to run against the ribband and upon when examining the ribband after the ship was launched, the appearance of the tallow showed that the bilge ways had not touched the ribband in any part on either side. The top or upper side of the launching plank was kept fair with the lower side or bottom of the false keel; there was thus in the nearest point 12 inches between the bottom of the keel and the cross logs of the wharf.

The spread of the launching ways of distance between the ribbands was 20"4 from the upper end to within 20 feet of the stern of the ship, from which point to the outer end of the wharf they gradually widened to 20 feet 8 inches. These launching planks and ribbands were very carefully planed and otherwise made smooth and while exposed for several days to a hot sun, had several coats of oil and tallow.

The bilge ways were in length 211 feet extending from 11 feet 6 inches before the fore ends of the keel to 4 feet 6 inches abaft the aft side of the stern post, in width 2 feet 6 in and in thickness 1 foot 11½ inches. The Bilge ways were formed by oak logs from 40 to 45 feet in length passing each other half their length; 14 inches thick or deep and 15 inches wide, the two logs making up the width of the ways. The upper side was covered with 4 inch oak plank, 10 in wide, the lower side, with 5½ inch oak plank. The plank on the lower side or the shoe, was left at the fore end about 20 feet longer than the Bilge ways and that part which was under the bilge way was very securely coaked & bolted to the ways. The object of this excess of the length of the Shoe beyond the bilge way was that when the bilge ways are under the ship in their place, they may be bolted to the solid foundation or launching plank and the bilge way can only be separated from the launching plank, when the ship is ready to go, by sawing off the plank or shoe. By this arrangement, both bilge ways can be let loose at the same instant and doing away with all dog shores or lashings.

The spread of the Bilge way was 20 feet, and they were kept parallel to the keel; there was thus 2 inch play on each side in the whole length of the Ship and 4 inches play on each side at the end of the wharf. The solid blocking on the bilge ways, was 2 feet, 6 inches, in width, extending from 8 feet abaft the fore end of the keel, to 40 feet before the aft side of the Stern Post, a length of 147 feet, and was formed by Yellow pine logs laid fore & aft upon which at the forward and after ends, was cross blocking of oak, and where the height required, fore and aft pieces, here again laid athwartships the packing on the Bilge way at the outer edge was 3½ in thick and on the inner edge 4½ inches, against this part shores were placed against the keel, so that by the first setting up of the wedges it might not be forced in from its place. Under this packing or blocking that is between it & the top of the Bilge ways the wedges were placed—these wedges were 5 feet 6 in long and 4 in wide. 1½ in thick at the point and 5 inches thick at the head and were placed about 4 inches asunder—there being about 300 on each side—abaft the after end of the solid blocking, were placed 9 perpendicular shores, directly over the centre of the Bilge ways, the after support or shores was at 16 feet from the after end of the Keel. These shores were of oak from 16 to 18 inches square and about 20 inches asunder. The upper ends were fitted close to the bottom and against their outer sides, a 5-inch oak plank 12 inches wide was bolted with inch [sic] copper to the bottom of the ship, the shores were let or jogged into this plank about 1½ inches—as this plank was not considered sufficient to secure the heads of the uprights or poppets when the pressure of the after part of the ship came upon them, a cleat of 5 in. oak plank, 5 feet in length was fastened to the bottom opposite the 5 after shores against the fore and aft piece. Under the heel of each shore was a shoe of 6 in plank and 3 wedges similar to those under the solid blocking. On the outer sides of these shores at 2 feet parallel to the Bilge ways and likewise another at 18 inches parallel to the bottom of the Ship, were oak Braces 18 inches thick, 12 inches wide, which were let over each poppet 2 inches and also having 2 bolts in each, connecting all the poppets together. At the fore-end of the forward blocking were 3 upright shores, the foremost one opposite to the fore-end [sic] of the Keel, of the same dimensions as those aft and arranged in the same manner. A piece of oak was fitted up the aft side of the stern post to protect the crown of the rudder braces and close against this on the top of the Bilge ways there was a cross piece 18 inches square, extending 2 feet beyond the Bilge ways on each side over which it was jogged 2½ inches. Upon this cross piece was place [sic] one shore on each side of Yellow pine 12 in square, reaching from over the centre of the Bilge ways to the head of the stern post where the upper ends were secured with cleats—the heels of these shores were placed upon the cross piece so as not to cause the after ends of the ways to spread. Under the bottom of the false keel was placed a shoe of 2 in oak plank covered with ¾ in iron which was fastened to the piece that had been let over the crown of the braces—this shore was put in its place after the after block was split out—In the solid blocking aft there were six lashings and forward there were 4 lashings of 4 in white rope of 5 turns each—The forward and after lashings were at one foot from the end of the solid blocking the remaining lashings were about 4½ feet asunder. These lashings passed round toggles of oak 6 by 8 inches, on the outside of the packing long enough to have a hold of 9 inches against the side of the Bilge way and reaching to within 3 inches of the bottom, Scores being cut in the blocking through which the lashing passed. The after and forward toggle had 2 lashings of 6 turns each, the lower turns being on the top of the Bilge way and the after turns about 18 inches below the bottom. In the other lashings, the turns passed between the bilge ways and the blocking, the latter being cut sufficiently to allow the rope to pass. The after ends of the Bilge ways, were lashed to the toggle in the stern post, with six or eight parts of 4 in. turned rope to confine them to the bottom. After the blocking was fitted & in every respect ready to launch, it was all taken apart and the surfaces were rubbed with chalk to prevent as far as possible any tendency to slip from grease or pitch, and while thus preparing, the ways were covered with a mixture of tallow and castile soap, the amount used being 2400 lbs tallow and 350 lbs soap. The lower ends of the ways at low water, were scorched with hot irons and the tallow put on—the thickness of the tallow was about half an inch. The ways and blocking were all put in place and the lashing set up the day before the ship was to be launched. While the blocking was preparing, men were employed in the hold and between decks, in placing a range of temporary shores or stanchions, directly over the center of the Bilge ways under each beam, from the ceiling to the upper Gun Deck.

On Tuesday, the 18th of July, at ¼ past 5 o'clock in the morning, commenced setting up the wedges with 90 under on each side, gave around 5 minutes, then took down the lower tier of shores, caulked the treenails and at 6 o'clock gave another set up of 8 minutes; after which, took down another tier of shores, plugged up the holes and at 7 o'clock, set up again for 10 minutes when the men when to breakfast. On returning to work at 8 o'clock, the wedges were set up with battering rams for the space of 8 minutes. These rams were made of 5 in. oak plank, about 8 in. wide and 8 ft. long, worked by hand with six men each. By this time, the wedges were driven in about a foot. When this was done, one half the entire number of blocks were taken from under the keel—those blocks which were to be taken out the last before the ship went off, had been sawed down close to the side of the keel the day before, the twenty blocks which were first taken out were knocked out by the malls alone; the ship having been eased from off them. When the false keel was put on free grain pieces, about 4 inches thick were put next the keel and the blocks below had a taper about ½ inch, but on shifting them, these all come out.

It being very dark under the bottom, about 20 tin candleholders were nailed against the bilge ways on each side, and the candle lighted, while the blocks were being taken out. Several men were constantly employed throwing water on the ways in advance of the tide, in order to prevent the tallow from dissolving. There yet remained 2 tier of shores, beside the wale shores—every other or alternate shore of the lower tier was now taken down and at 10 o'clock took out the after block and put on the shoe under the after end of the keel. The 5 blocks next to the after one were taken out as the tide had made some advance. Men now all rested, and indeed but a very few had any thing to do for the last 3 hours. At 12 o'clock, took down all the shores except the wale shores, pugging up holes and took out the blocks as the tide came up, at 2 o'clock took up the joggle wedges and oakum from between the ribband and bilge ways, took down the way shores and all the wale shores except 2 amidships. There was at this time 14 blocks under the ship forward, being every alternate block, the others having taken out in the morning. About 30 men went under the bottom and took out the remaining blocks, all of which were knocked out by a mall except the forward one to which wedges alone were used. The 2 remaining wale shores on each side were taken down at the same time—while the forward block was splitting out, the plank of the Bilge way which was bolted down, was sawed in 2 inches, the whole being 5½ inches thick. The remainder of the plank was sawed through and the ship was entirely free. On looking along the keel it was observed that the lower side was perfectly straight. As the ship did not start, another piece of a wedge shape was sawed from the plank and an iron wedge of 3½ feet long 4 inches wide and 2 in. thick at 2 ½ feet from the point, having been previously prepared was driven between two plates of iron, in driving the wedge, the tendency was to force the Bilge ways down. These wedges were struck with the hand rams—the end of the ways were struck with heavy pieces of timber suspended from the house and levers were placed against the side of the ways which were all worked when it was found the ship did not start. At 20 minutes past 2 o'clock she started, the ship did not poise on her ways at all, nor did the Bilge ways touch the ribband on either side. The shores which were against the post fell down as soon as the after end of the ship was immersed in the water; the poppets forward and aft and also the Bilge ways came out from under the ship as she was afloat, the toggles had slipped as was desired and let them loose. The ship did not touch the bottom as the tallow was fresh on the ends of the ways when they were hauled up the next day.

s/ John Lenthall

* * *

APPENDIX 4

Suitability of Mail Steamers as Ships of War

Two letters are evaluated in this appendix. The first, dated 18 March 1852, is from Chief Naval Constructor John Lenthall to Captain Charles Skinner, chief of the Bureau of Construction, Equipment and Repairs.[1] In it, Lenthall provides a workmanlike naval architect's assessment of the features of contemporary mail steamers and considerations for their conversion into efficient war vessels. His measured evaluation was more than just idle opinion in response to a superior's request; it was required by law. Recent government mail contracts for the transportation of mails by ocean-going steamships contained language that required just such a judgement as to their suitability as war vessels.

Lenthall is in full command of the technicalities of the issue, citing baseline data for comparison, such as the throw weight of a frigate's broadside and its sail area per ton of measurement. He is also visibly conditional in his views, citing his lack of experience with mail steamers, the limited "province of a ship builder to decide" on such matters, and his ultimate deference to those who were empowered to answer "military" questions.

Two years later and himself now a bureau chief, John Lenthall's response to the same question, no doubt motivated by the *Black Warrior* seizure a week before, adopts a rather different tone. Lenthall's letter to Navy Secretary J. C. Dobbin, dated 6 March 1854 and which references his first letter, employs noticeably less technological jargon but displays far greater confidence in his opinions.[2] While the substance of the two letters is broadly similar, Lenthall's conclusions have now crystallized. The persistent and unshakable recitation of hard facts emerging from his pen constitute a Lenthall trademark: this was a man who "says it like it is."

The specific detail of Lenthall's discourse regarding the requisite properties of ships of war should be borne in mind when, seven years later, he was confronted with a host of new and untested schemes for ironclad steam batteries, chief among them being John Ericsson's *Monitor*.

* * *

Washington Feb 18th 1852

Sir,

The letter from the Hon. Sec of the Navy (of 10th inst) to the Chief of the Bureau of Construction "requests him to direct me to furnish my views as to whether the steamships employed in the transportation of the foreign mails are in all respects suitable for immediate conversion into steamers for war purposes, capable of carrying the armament appropriate to the class specified in the contracts; and if not suitable for such immediate conversion whether they can be altered to make them efficient war steamers, and if so, what alterations would be necessary to be made at what expense to make them war steamers of the first class."

I would in the first place state that there is some doubt whether a side-wheel steamer can be made into a war steamer of the first class. The machinery of such a steamer should be placed below the level of common danger from shot, and to enable her to become a cruizer, requires that she should be a perfect sailing vessel in all respects, not only in the power of sail but also in its position. The fullness of the extremities should be such that the motions of pitching and scending may be within moderate limits, and they should be able to support the heavy guns at their extremities which are deemed essential to their armament. It is desirable that they should be fast vessels but they must be capable of using as well as carrying their armament, and as no other quality can compensate for a deficiency in this it becomes a primary consideration. The sharpness of the bow of a war steamer is not however restricted to such a degree as to prevent a speed but little short of the average of sea-going merchant steamers, which do not require the weights with which they are loaded to be distributed in the same manner.

The sharp bow does not rise to the waves so well as the full bow, but it divides them with greater felicity.

In a mechanical and economical point of view they should possess the necessary strength and power of endurance, as well after several years of service as when new; to attain which they must be built of the best materials and fastened in the most thorough manner.

I know but little of the steamers employed in the transportation of foreign mails, and those which I have seen were built under the superintendence of distinguished officers of the Navy and a Naval Architect appointed for that purpose.

A few days before these steamers sailed, I was ordered on their final survey, but in consequence of the highly finished state in which they were, it was scarcely possible to form any just opinion as to the manner and the materials of which they were built. Finding them ready for sea and fitted as mail and passenger vessels, I had under the circumstances and so far as such an examination permitted, no hesitation in pronouncing them mail steamers of the first class.

This explanation is necessary to show that it is upon a very slight observation that I can give any opinion upon the questions proposed and by no means to compare with that of the officers who superintended their building.

The words "suitable for immediate conversion into steamers for war purposes" I understand to mean the state in which an actual ship of war would be if temporarily employed in carrying the mail or passengers.

From the superficial examination, I had the opportunity of making these ships appeared in about the same degree of readiness for immediate conversion into steamers for war purposes, as Merchant Ships according to their size and speed are into Frigates or other classes of ships of war: possessing the advantages common to large vessels of a capacity permitting, if required, the additional materials necessary and the armament and equipment required to be placed on board to make them war vessels.

The Steam Frigates of the first class of other nations we find represented as throwing $1\frac{8}{100}$ lbs [1.08 pounds] of metal at each discharge and carrying 12½ square feet of sail per ton of our measurement.

Assuming the largest of these mail vessels to be armed in similar proportion to their size, as the first-class Steam Frigates of the nations with which it is presumed they are to cope, they should throw about 3,050 lb of metal, equal in amount to 44 guns of 8 inches, and have a surface of sail not less than that of a ship of line.

Whether space for such an armament could be found upon their decks, or is necessary, or was contemplated, or whether not a measure of power is to be considered a war steamer of the first class, I presume does not lay within the province of a shipbuilder to decide.

The impression left with me is, that to make these vessels into steamers for war purposes the upper deck was too light to bear an armament, and if heavy pivot guns were to be used it must be removed. The part of the engine thus left exposed would require protection and arrangement must be made for the proper accommodation of the officers and men and the convenient stowage of the stores and provisions.

These together with the other equipment I think could not be safely estimated at less than from 70 to 80 thousand dollars, in addition to which will be the destruction of materials and labour and highly finished work that has probably cost not less than 100 thousand dollars.

Such an estimate must of necessity be but an approximation, yet the amount may be exceeded, depending upon what may be deemed necessary by the many officers when they have possession of the ship; upon the quality of the materials used and the manner of construction; upon the extent to which beams and knees may be considered necessary if the decks are cut by the machinery; upon the age of the vessel; upon the degree to which she may be strained by the great work they have performed and also in anticipation of that which any unusual or heavy armament other than stowage, may cause to be brought upon them.

Many of the points above stated it is evident can only be determined by those who built them and have their plans.

In conclusion I would say, that as I understand being suitable for immediate conversion, they are not in that state, for much has to be done to them; their great size permits almost any addition that may be required to make them into steamers for war purposes, but whether great speed or powerful armament, or ability to keep at sea for [sic] long time under sail, or a shorter time under steam are to constitute a war steamer of the 1st class, are military qualities upon which I have very slight grounds, if any, upon which to base an opinion.

Rspt,
/s/ JL

To Captn. Skinner

* * *

Navy Department
Bureau of Constr. &c.
March 6th 1854

Sir,

In reply to your letter of the 3rd inst. as to whether in my opinion the steam ships employed in the ocean mail service of the United States are of proper construction to be converted into vessels of war in the event of requiring them for such purposes, and if so, how many and which of them, I would respectfully state as follows.

These ships are all paddle or side-wheel steamers, built under similar circumstances and for the same purposes.

They have been planned or modelled with a view to speed under steam alone, shown also by the great steam power with which they are provided; and all their internal arrangements have reference to comfort and accommodation as mail and passenger steamers.

But the height between decks, so necessary to obtain favor in the competition in which they were engaged, elevates the weight of the top sides, the decks and all that will be placed on them, and their sharpness reduces the room on the deck, particularly forward.

The reduction of the space on the deck is in the part where it is most essential and necessary for a proper arrangement of an armament.

A want of stability and uneasiness of motion which proceed from such causes would seriously affect, if not destroy, their military efficiency. With the top hamper that a war equipment would put upon them and their coal consumed, my impression is they would be very deficient in stability.

In ships of war, on the other hand, it is considered important to reduce the height above the water and have sufficient room for working the guns at the extremities.

In the largest of these ships, the shaft is so far above the main deck that it would be impractical to transport a heavy gun fore and aft; this height shows their machinery to be in a more than usual degree unprotected.

In ships of war, the shaft is under the main deck and the boilers are under the lower deck, thereby permitting the use of many more beams to that part.

In these ships, the number of beams and their distance asunder, forward and abaft the part occupied by the machinery, seemed to have reference to the length of the state rooms, cabins, skylights and companionways.

In ships of war, these most important pieces, upon which depend the connection of the sides and the ability of the ship to withstand the continued action of a heavy armament, are much closer together and are placed wholly with reference to the guns and the masts, to which all other considerations are subservient.

The upper deck of the largest of these ships is too slight for an armament, and to strengthen it would add greatly to the weight, to remove it would still further expose the machinery.

To enable these steam ships to cruise as ships of war they must be properly masted; for under steam alone they could not long keep at sea or extend their sphere of action far, if at all, beyond our shores. Their large wheel houses and surface above the water would make a great surface of sail necessary, but with the machinery they have it is impossible to place the main mast in a proper position, which is of the first importance in working under sail.

The large proportion of the capacity and of the length taken up by the machinery and coal, leaves only the sharp extremities for the stowage of the things which would be placed in a hold, and for which there must not only be sufficient space, but it must be convenient.

These extremities appear to me insufficient for that purpose, and many things would have to be placed on the decks, thereby elevating the weights and injuriously affecting the quality of the ships.

The impediment which the necessary masts and rigging would offer, their weight and that of the tanks, casks, cables, anchors, shot, shells, powder, water, provisions, boats, guns and stores which a ship of war of such magnitude should carry would more deeply immerse these vessels, and their reputation would fall very far below that for which they now have credit.

The cost of these ships and the expense of the alterations for converting them for temporary use, even when new, would be much out of proportion with the armament they could carry and the service they could render could not be compared with that which an equal expenditure would obtain if applied directly with the view of building a ship of war.

The consideration of the subject seems rather to turn upon the general principles of their construction, and usefulness when converted, than upon the manner in which they are built, or the nature of the materials used, or their present condition.

Upon these grounds then, I am of the opinion that the ocean and mail steamers are not of proper construction to be converted into vessels of war, which in substance agrees with the views in my letter to the Chief of the Bureau of Construction &c of date of February 18th 1852. I would further observe that as a member of the board for the reception of several of these ships, the certificate as to their being convertible into ships of war was not signed by me and my present opinion is based on the opportunities for observation offered on these occasions.

I have the honor to be,
Respectfully Your Obt Srt,
/s/ John Lenthall
Chief of the Bureau

* * *

APPENDIX 5

Young, Smart, Spirit of the Age Fellows[1]

John Lenthall and Captain Samuel Francis Du Pont, a rising star of the U.S. Navy, were fast friends. That circumstance, together with this letter's date—after the secession of most Southern states but before the Lincoln administration took office—sets the stage for an extraordinary glimpse into Lenthall's mind.

The letter opens with Lenthall responding to Du Pont's note about the dismissal of Smith, probably a draftsman or carpenter at the Philadelphia Navy yard of which Du Pont was then the commandant. Lenthall had helped restore both Smith and the latter mentioned Knowles to their positions at the yard eight years earlier. But soon, Lenthall segues into a discourse about a Senate request for the Navy Department to report on the feasibility of building an ironclad version of the light draft steam sloop *Iroquois.*[2] Here Lenthall displays his deeply rooted sentiments that would be later misconstrued by others who sought to brand him a hopelessly out of touch reactionary. His thoughts are also clearly infected by the possibility that he might soon be replaced. Lenthall rationally concludes that absent any experience with such a great leap of technology—designing a successful ironclad warship—he would prefer to "decline combat." But then Lenthall quickly shrugs off his doubts and delves into an engineering analysis of the principal weaknesses of such an armored sloop—insufficient size, excessive roll and extravagant cost. She would be a costly failure that would smear the reputation of her designer. To do anything useful would require a much larger ship.

In a prescient nod to the future, the Steam Sloop *Iroquois* and her light draft near sister sloops authorized by Congress on 12 June 1858 were the first to feature guns firing the majority of the vessel's throw-weight mounted exclusively on centerline pivoting carriages. Previous classes of steam sloops had been armed with broadside batteries of up to twenty-four guns. In *Iroquois*' case, her principal armament consisted of two 11-

inch Dahlgren smoothbores, one forward and one aft of her machinery spaces. Lenthall's evaluation of the many issues connected with iron-cladding a war steamer carrying her principal weapons on her centerline marked the starting point for his Navy Department designed ironclads proposed at the year's end (see Appendix 7).

Lenthall wrapped up his letter by unambiguously stating that he has packed up his office in the expectation of being dismissed by the new administration. His fears are not unreasonable. Such partisan sweeps of civil servants were not uncommon in that era, and by this date, Lenthall had been chief of the Bureau of Construction, Equipment and Repairs for seven and a half years. History would prove Lenthall to be correct regarding the complexities of ironclad design but wrong about the Lincoln administration's intentions. He would go on to serve as chief of the bureau for ten more years.

* * *

Washington
Feb 3/61

D Sir,

I can assure you it gives me much pleasure to receive your note concerning Smith. I have always thought he was one of the most industrious, persevering men in carrying on work and in my opinion, the Sec of the Navy made a mistake when he removed him—the present man I do not know, but he can scarcely be a better man. I had intended to write to you about him but am much more gratified that you anticipated me. You can do nothing for him now and I fear the next administration will have some friend to put before him, but if they want the most work for the least money then Smith is the man. If Commodore Armstrong had had a few men like Smith about him he need not have given up the yard. By referring to Captain Lardner's letter about Smith and the answer you will see, that you will employ him in any way that may be advantageous until the coal shipping commences. Having heard on good authority that the Boatswain on several occasions had treated him with indignity, which the man did not deserve it was just to ask you to show in some little way that you respected him in his position, which he would not take advantage of … . You have other clever men Knowles and Hoffman and as far as I know or have seen their equals, for equals are not in any other Navy Yard. It is only fair for me to say that the credit I have been floating on is mainly due to Hoover, Knowles, Smith and Hoffman. They did the work and I get most of the credit.

You have seen by the papers a resolution of the Senate calling for information about "iron cased" vessels. Much to my regret the Secretary sent it to me, for this is the age of Boards hoped it would be sent to another party and I might escape. The change from sailing to steam vessels was not so great as this with iron cased or iron war steamers. In sailing ship matters, we know almost to exactness as to what can be done, and now in steam or auxiliary steamers of war we have also picked up many of the correct principles, but in this new matter I at least have no facts, no data, very little to go on, and like a courageous man, if practical, would prefer to decline combat. The first trials must be failures in many respects and they will be most costly ships and I should much prefer that my successor or some of those young, smart, modern improvement, spirit of the age fellows should take hold of it. The resolution says the vessel to be of the armament and compliments of the "Iroquois." It is very clear however that a vessel of her size cannot be plated. The "Iroquois" and other vessels of her class roll very heavy, which is occasioned by the Congress limiting draft of water and the Department insisting on a heavy armament and great steam power. The natural result was there was very little of the vessel in the water, and the great weight was very high above the water—so they roll and will roll—had its beam been exaggerated to mend this then they should have jerked themselves to pieces. The "Pawnee" will be of this class. It is in the nature of things and great names will not prevent it, neither Mr. Griffiths, nor Mr. Toucey, nor Mr. Mallory can change it.

Now, a wooden ship to be cased with iron must be much stronger and therefore heavier, many more materials in it, for the iron plating gives no strength, but it is a great tax on that of the ship. Then this iron plating extending for some 2 ft below the water to the rail will weigh about 300 tons if only 3 inches thick, and then the great height at which this extra weight is placed diminishes the stability very rapidly and for these reasons you will find it hard to make a seagoing vessel of that kind. They can only be made of the very largest class as they should have a covered gun deck. Well, the "Iroquois," as you know, is a single deck and measures 1061 tons and after adding the extra weights and making the proper alterations of all kinds, I came to the conclusion that the vessel desired cannot be less than 1500 tons and should draw 15 ft water. You will tell me I have not given you much information at least for the tonnage of a ship amounts to nothing being very indefinite. But you will see by the mention of 15 ft that I had something. There is no use in tying up our hands and feet. The plating on such a vessel will weigh not less than 300 tons at 3 inches, whilst in England they say 4½–a small vessel with such topsides would roll even the "Pawnee." I have estimated the cost of this iron at 200k for the hull but I question if it will not cost more, and you will see from all this that it is not a matter a prudent person would like to jump into with his eyes shut.

There is one thing about the employment of men which I hope the Secretary of the Navy will mend. It is that when the Master workman refuses to name a good man, the naval constructor in his department shall have the authority to name him and the Commandant to direct his employment in spite of the opposition of a prejudiced Master workman.

You may remember on one occasion coming into my room in [sic] Winder Building and finding me packing up my books and papers. Well, I have just got through it again and this time sent them home, and am now ready for anything that may turn up. The new administration will doubtless make changes, and they may even be greater than they would be disposed to make.

If all the Southern states will not come back, which will be the doom of slavery—the politicians have got such a hold of all the forms of the Government with concurring primary elections that they are in a great measure a separate class from its people and they are not willing to sacrifice themselves.

Your Servant
/s/ J Lenthall

Capt Du Pont,
U.S.N.

* * *

APPENDIX 6

Better to Fight at the Threshold than Upon the Hearthstone[1]

John Lenthall's letter to Gideon Welles dated 17 March 1862 and co-signed by Engineer-in-Chief Benjamin Isherwood, ranks as one of the most profound articulations of the fundamentals of sea power ever penned by a U.S. Navy bureau chief. Even more extraordinary is that it was submitted to the secretary of the navy barely a week after news of the Battle of Hampton Roads reached Washington. John Ericsson's *Monitor* had saved the day and its upward trajectory as an icon of American sea power had just begun.

Lenthall and Isherwood opened with a discourse on the problems plaguing the Navy's efforts to obtain armor plate from the nation's rolling mills and forges, circumstances they were all too familiar with from their efforts to design an ironclad. By the end of their second page they proposed as a solution "the advantage if not the absolute necessity of the Government at once preparing a factory to make for itself the most important and costly parts, both for the iron hulls and for the armature." They then described such a facility, insisting it should be a "storehouse and workshop, and not a military establishment," and that it should be situated on deep water but "secure from the possibility of attack by foreign foes."

Having outlined the need for and the features of their proposed factory, Lenthall and Isherwood subtly shifted their focus by evoking the image of how a navy so strengthened by such a facility would be able to "secure a country like ours from foreign aggression …" Grasping the importance of this nexus, they respectfully submitted, was a "national question second to none."

Now the way was open for the true object of Lenthall and Isherwood's letter. The sudden rise of ironclads had rendered Europe's existing fleets of wooden warships obsolete and had handed the United States a golden opportunity to "start equal with the first powers of the world in a new race for the supremacy of the Ocean." To win such a race would require America to field "a fleet of first class invincible ocean ships" and sustain a larger navy than before, one of very different character than the antebellum Navy. Lenthall boldly suggested that such a fleet should consist of powerful frigate-built ironclad steamers, leavened by lighter draft armored corvettes. It was a "system" readily recognizable to any informed observer. The European maritime powers had adopted it—witness France's *Gloire* and Britain's *Warrior*—and were now hurriedly replacing their obsolete wooden walls with ironclads. Now was the right time for the United States to do the same, thereby maintaining "command of the open sea with all the power it gives ..." rather than relying on "any system of harbor defence."

The core of Lenthall and Isherwood's argument was now clear. Monitors were brilliant solutions for harbor and riverine warfare but were wholly unsuited to maintain control of the high seas. To compete with other powers which were now rapidly introducing ocean-going ironclad battleships, the United States must do the same. Failure to do so would forfeit its ability to control its oceanic destiny. "Harbor defences are indeed valuable adjuncts...but cannot constitute a navy or perform its proper function." In a final, Mahanian flourish, they conclude their letter with the admonition of "how much better it is to fight at the threshold than upon the hearthstone."

Victorian naval authority Sir Thomas Brassey was so enamored of Lenthall and Isherwood's insight, that he quoted an edited version of their last two paragraphs in the introduction to the third volume of his influential series, *The British Navy: Its Strengths, Resources, and Administration.*[2] And in 1890, eight years after Lenthall's death, Alfred Thayer Mahan published his epochal work, *The Influence of Sea Power upon History.*

While Lenthall and Isherwood's advice was superficially accepted by Secretary Welles, its tenets were imperfectly implemented and only a handful of inefficient sea-going ironclads emerged by the war's end. The nation and the Navy's hierarchy remained in the thrall of Monitor fever. But it was a false dawn. Reliance on a national strategy of harbor defense enforced by a fleet of single turreted, low freeboard ironclads barely capable of coastal transits would hobble the U.S. Navy for a generation.[3]

* * *

Navy Department
Bureau of Construction
March 17th 1862

Sir,

The subject of the design and construction of Naval Vessels of War, under the new conditions which recent progress has imposed, having for sometime occupied our attention, we take the liberty of briefly submitting the following considerations in relation thereto.

After the preparation of drawings and specifications for Iron Plated Steam Batteries, we were brought into communication during the last few months in consequence of submitting them for proposals to construct, with the principal establishments engaged in the manufacture of iron. We found there was but little reason to suppose that such plates as it was desirable to have could be obtained in the quantity and time required. There were but few forges prepared to undertake them, and the Rolling Mills would need new and expensive machinery before they could produce a plate, as such masses of rolled iron are not used in private business. Indeed, although we found both forges and mills willing to undertake portions of the work and hopeful of success, yet doubtless great disappointment and delay would have resulted: no means of bending were in existence, and many of the details of manufacture had still to be contrived. Some forged plates could have been commenced at once but, after the rolling mills were once prepared, would obviously require more time and money for their production than the rolled ones, and it appears judging from our own and foreign experience, that rolled plates, in consequence of their greater cheapness & rapidity of production, must be mainly relied on for such construction.

The propositions of the principal rolling mills embodied the conditions of a large order, a long time, and the advance of a very considerable sum of money. These terms, in effect, were: that the Government should be at [bear] all the expense of the necessary machinery, and have no right to the final ownership, thus assuming the risk of a large loan, and establishing a monopoly for the benefit of individuals. Nor could the mill, with safety, accept a less objectionable arrangement; for the appliances and machinery sufficient for the manufacture of the plates used in the construction of ordinary iron vessels are wholly inadequate to the production of those necessary for iron-plated ships of war, and no private establishment can be expected to provide them unless assured of constant employment by the Government.

Considering these facts in connection with the state of transition in which the methods of naval war now are, and with the inevitable tendency to the substitution of iron in place of wood for the hulls of armed vessels, and the certainty that iron plating must be used on all such vessels, whether of wood or iron, we are lead [sic] to respectfully suggest the advantage if not the absolute necessity of the Government at once preparing a factory to make for itself the most important and costly parts, both for the iron hulls and for the armature. Having an efficient establishment of its own of this kind, it can, in an emergency, receive much aid in those parts which are similar to what are used in merchant iron steamers from private parties without diverting them from their usual course of manufacture, and thus moderate prices only will be charged.

The establishment that we suggest ought to contain all the tools, facilities & machinery for the complete preparation of the materials for iron ships of the largest size and for their construction; also, for the rolling and bending of their armor plates; and for the building of the Steam Machinery for their propulsion. It should be altogether a Storehouse and workshop, and not a Military establishment. It should be situated upon deep water and have a large waterfront, and the location should be convenient for coal and iron, and secure from the possibility of attack by foreign foe.

We do not consider any of the Navy Yards suitable for this purpose, and the whole of these resources will be required for some years to come for the current wants of the present Navy.

The necessity and importance of an establishment that is to provide a future Navy sufficient for securing a country like ours from foreign aggression, for owing to our transoceanic position to the great powers of the world, our security must be sought in a Navy, is, we respectfully submit, a national question second to none, and as such we strongly urge it for consideration. No time could be more favorable than the present for the creation of such an establishment. The recent change in the Construction of Naval vessels has rendered nearly useless the formidable wooden ships composing the Navies of Europe, and the few we possess will soon be worn out. Under such circumstances we shall, with an establishment in operation of the magnitude and efficiency we propose, start equal with the first powers of the world in a new race for the supremacy of the Ocean. We shall start with the advantage of no loss of old stock and workshops: with material plans embodying all the improvements and appliances of modern science, gained at the expense & all the dear-bought experience of our competitors.

Every dollar will be fruitfully spent, and a few years will, and at the least practicable cost, put the nation in possession of a fleet of first-class invincible ocean ships which will prove not only the efficient protector of its honor and interests, but the best preventive against their being assailed. There seems no doubt that the country must hereafter maintain not only a larger navy than it has hitherto done, but of essentially a different character, and we are of opinion that the cruising vessels on which alone reliance must be placed for offensive war, and the preservation of our ports from the losses and inconveniences of blockades, should be frigate built iron Steam Ships of sufficient strength to be used as rams, clad with invulnerable armor plates, furnished with maximum steam power, and of a size larger than any vessel we now possess. Such a vessel could be adapted to and carry any armament deemed the most efficient. Subordinate to these, there should be a class of corvettes of the same character but having a less draft of water.

The first maritime nations of Europe have, for some years past, been gradually initiating this system, and if their experience is to profit us now is the time to introduce it. It is obviously cheaper, more effective, and more sustaining of the national honor to preserve our coasts from the presence of an enemy naval force by keeping the command of the open sea with all the power it gives of aggression upon his own shores and commerce, than to rely on any system of harbor defence which requires every point to be protected that may be assailed by any enemy having, in that case, the choice of time and place, and the advantages of perfect security for his own ports and commerce. In addition to these considerations, a clear coast is manifestly essential to any effective system of privateering. Though harbor defences might prevent an enemy's entrance to a port, they could not drive him from its gates, and if blockaded by his large iron-plated steamships no privateer could either get out himself or send in a prize.

The harbor defences are indeed valuable adjuncts and should not be neglected, but they cannot constitute a navy or perform its proper functions.

Wealth, victory and empire are to those who command the Ocean, the toll gate as well as the highway of Nations; and if ever assailed by a powerful maritime foe, we shall find it to our prosperity, if ready, how much better it is to fight at the threshold than upon the hearthstone.

With Great Respect,
We have the honor to be
Sir
Your Obedient Servants,
/s/ John Lenthall
/s/ B. F. Isherwood

Hon. Gideon Welles
Sec'y of Navy

* * *

APPENDIX 7

Evolution of the Double Turreted Ironclad

Presented in this Appendix is a detailed table of particulars for war steamers, some of which were built and others designs only, tracing the evolution of the U.S. Navy's development of ironclads to a recognizably modern double turreted ironclad. At its mid-point, this evolutionary path was parallel to but not directly coupled to John Ericsson's well-known monitors that so dominated Civil War naval accounts. It represents an alternate and largely unheralded line of development, occurring under the direction of the chief of the Bureau of Construction, Equipment and Repairs (BCER), John Lenthall, and his engineer-in-chief, Benjamin Isherwood.

The evolutionary starting point was a Senate resolution of 19 January 1861, proposed by Senator James Grimes of Iowa, requesting the secretary of the navy to furnish "a detailed estimate of the expense of building and equipping a steel or iron-cased gun boat of the capacity and armament of the United States gun-boat Iroquois."[1] Lenthall dutifully reported his findings to Secretary Toucey in a letter dated 1 February 1861, with further comments on this same subject outlined in a private letter written two days later to his close friend, Captain Samuel Du Pont (see Appendix 5).

Of direct interest to ironclad design evolution, this was one of the earliest instances—the never finished Stevens Battery excepted—of the chief of the BCER formally estimating the characteristics of an armored war steamer proposed for U.S. Navy service. The class of ship so examined, one of the light draft steam sloops authorized by Congress in 1858, marked the beginning of an independent but complimentary trend, that of positioning the heaviest guns—those firing the overwhelming mass of the vessel's throw-weight—on centerline pivot mountings. The short step separating this development from the logical end-point, guns mounted in rotating centerline turrets, can be readily visualized.

Lenthall's 3 February letter to Du Pont suggested that a more suitably sized ship than that proposed by the Senate, *Iroquois,* would be the recently completed very light draft steam sloop *Pawnee*. Even this vessel, with the snap roll that could be expected of its shallow draft hull, was not optimal. But *Pawnee*'s increased length and breadth would allow her, with suitable modification, to serve as a sounder basis for a coastal ironclad. These three designs—the *Iroquois* and *Pawnee* as-built configurations and the iron-cased *Iroquois*—are documented in the three left hand columns of the accompanying table.

The period between Lenthall's initial evaluation of *Iroquois* and the Navy Department issuing its first internally developed ironclad proposal later that year, was highlighted by the Navy's placing an order for John Ericsson's impregnable floating battery. This ingeniously designed vessel would steam into history as the U.S.S. *Monitor*. She was, according to the astute observation of Assistant Secretary of the Navy Gustavus Fox's wife, "not a ship—only a machine for carrying & working *two* immense guns."[2] *Monitor*'s basic concept, as emphasized by her inventor, was that of an armored raft surmounted by a rotating ironclad single turret. She was not intended for ocean transits, had very poor sea-keeping characteristics, and her sole means of offense—a single turret—lacked redundancy. U.S. naval constructors, bred in a service that was largely devoted to cruising on remote foreign stations, would have approached the design of coast defense ironclad in a different way. And that is just what happened.

When the rush of the Navy's hurried orders for its first three ironclads—all of widely varying designs—had subsided, Lenthall's BCER took stock of the situation. Neither Lenthall or his engineer-in-chief Isherwood were impressed by Ericsson's *Monitor*. Lenthall doubted her ability to float her armor, and Isherwood thought ironclads were a humbug. However, in light of the Navy's recent ironclad orders, both Lenthall and Isherwood digested the latest developments, evaluated what they could of the applied ironclad technology, and returned to their drawing boards. By the end of 1861, they had worked up a new design that took advantage of their own considerable experience and drew what they could from *Monitor* and her armored cohorts. The results are listed in the table's fourth column, the Navy Department ironclad.

Lenthall based the new design on a conventional wooden hull with substantial scantlings, which included three white oak bilge keelsons per side to firmly support the ironclad's machinery. Such a hull could be built in any navy yard or by a contractor and was a reliable choice for quick delivery. Its length and breadth were very close to *Pawnee*'s but the hull's depth was slightly less. The need to provide longitudinal strength for a vessel intended to operate in very shallow water was balanced by Lenthall's desire to minimize the height of the hull's armored topsides. But even so, he couldn't avoid the inherent weaknesses of a wooden structure, its susceptibility to rot and that its iron cladding would give "no strength, but is a great tax on that of the ship."

The Navy Department ironclad was powered by twin screw propellers driven by gearing from a single engine. Coal bunkers were conventionally arranged but featured a distinctive access trunk inboard of the hull's side armor. The flush deck vessel was armed with but two guns, 11-inch Dahlgren smoothbores, each mounted inside armored revolving "towers," one forward and one aft, based on the principles of English inventor Cowper Coles, RN. Here the similarity to *Iroquois* showed itself, for both the steam sloop and the Navy Department's ironclad were designed to carry the same guns arranged in the same positions on their hulls. Lenthall's use of Coles towers avoided the need to protect the guns behind armored sides or beneath a protective deck. The towers, or turrets, were to be protected at their bases by a surrounding iron glacis and featured substantial wood backing of their armor. Neither of these features were incorporated in Ericsson's *Monitor*. An armored pilot house was located on each end of the vessel. Taken as a whole, Lenthall and Isherwood's design offered a more ship-like solution as compared to Ericsson's, incorporating arrangements and vessel management features better aligned with conventional U.S. Navy practice.

Spurred by the threat of war with England over the *Trent* affair, the Navy Department prepared to construct its self-designed ironclads. Building instructions and specifications for the ships' armor and machinery were issued before the end of 1861. House Bill HR 153 authorizing the construction of up to twenty ironclads was quickly passed in mid-December and sent to the Senate. In early January 1862, Lenthall instructed navy yards to begin the vessels' mould loft work. But by early February, the prospect of war had diminished and the momentum to build ebbed. Ericsson's *Monitor* had been successfully launched on 30 January and the Senate was still debating Bill HR 153. Secretary Welles was now reluctant to move ahead so quickly. Pressed by the powerful Monitor lobby, Welles opined that the Navy Department wished to "avail itself of her experience" before placing a new bet on a different design.

Then the Battle of Hampton Roads changed everything. *Monitor*'s tactical success, witnessed by her most ardent advocate, Assistant Secretary Gustavus Fox, decided the matter. The course was now set for the U.S. Navy's ironclad program, not only for the duration of the Civil War but for decades to come. On the last day of March 1862, barely three weeks after *Monitor*'s victory, John Ericsson was given an order for six improved

Passaic class monitors. All thoughts of building the Navy Department's self-designed ironclad had now evaporated.

However, with the march of time, the Navy recognized it needed more than just the Ericsson monitors. In response to a navy board review of the latest batch of proposals for ironclad steamers for harbor defense (see Appendix 8), a design submitted by G. W. Quintard's Morgan Iron Works was recommended. This vessel, which was subsequently built and named *Onondaga*, incorporated many of the features of Lenthall and Isherwood's Navy Department ironclad, namely double turrets, twin screws and a conventional hull form. And in a technological leap forward, she was built entirely of iron.

Later in 1862, as building ways became available in navy yards, work was begun on the *Monadnock* class of double turreted ironclads. This group of four warships, specified by John Lenthall, adopted many of the features of his and Isherwood's Navy Department design, and can be considered improved models of their stillborn first effort. Their wooden hulls were significantly longer and better armored. In contrast to the earlier vessels, they were fitted with turrets of Ericsson's design—subcontracted from private fabricators—each mounting two 15-inch Dahlgren guns. While they were only commissioned at the end of the war, many navy officers considered them the best of monitor-type ironclads. They were certainly the most seaworthy; one of them crossed the Atlantic and another rounded South America for service on America's Pacific coast.

The *Monadnock* class marked the end of a circuitous line of evolution that began with the Senate's request for the Navy Department to evaluate an ironclad *Iroquois* class steam sloop. Within a period of less than a year, the Navy leapfrogged from concentrating its heavy guns on centerline pivot mountings to enclosing them in revolving armored turrets. Its final step, taken many years in the future, saw the 'rebuilding' of the *Monadnock* class into recognizably modern, iron-hulled turret ships which, in turn, heralded the era of the new Steel Navy and its pre-dreadnought battleships.

* * *

Table A7-1 *Evolution of the Double Turreted Ironclad*

Ship Name or Design	*Iroquois* Class Light Draft Steam Sloop [1]	*Pawnee* Very Light Draft Steam Sloop [2]	*Iroquois* Light Draft Steam Sloop Iron-cased Proposal [3]	Lenthall-Isherwood Navy Dept Ironclad Design [4]	*Onondaga* G.W.Quintard Harbor Defense Ironclad [5]	*Monadnock* Class Navy Department Ironclad [6]
Date Launch or Design	April 1859 L	Oct 1859 L	Jan 1861 D	Dec 1861 D	July 1863 L	March 1863 L
Length	198'-10 ½"	221'-6"	198'-10 ½"	216'-2"	226'	250'
Breadth	33'-10"	47'	33'-10"	48'	51'-5"	52'-6"
Depth	16'	15'	16'	13'-11"	13'-2"	14'-6"
Draft	13'	10'	15'	12 ½'	12'	12'-6"
Tonnage	1061	1533	1500	2400	2592	3298
Pivot Arrgt or Turret	CL Pivot	P&S Pivots	CL Pivot	2 Coles	2 Ericsson	2 Ericsson
Main Guns	2 x 11"	4 x 11"	2 x 11"	2 x 11"	2 x 15",150 pdr	4 x 15"
Armor, Hull & Turret	none	none	H 3"	H 4¼" T 5"	H 4½" T 11"	H 3-5" T 11"
Screws	One	Two	One	Two	Two	Two
Cost	$323,830	$457,151	$558,000	$540,000	$759,673	$981,439

NOTES:

1. First U.S. Navy major warship designed with main guns on centerline versus a broadside battery.[3]

2. Variant of *Iroquois* with lighter draft and twice the main battery. Mentioned by Lenthall (see 3. below) as a candidate for an armored sloop.

3. Proposal by Lenthall for iron-cased *Iroquois*, in response to Sen Grimes' resolution of 19 January 1861; never built. Breadth and depth were probably increased. *Pawnee* cited by Lenthall as large enough to carry the armor. How either ship's guns were to be protected wasn't specified.[4]

4. Building instructions for an ironclad steam battery, never built.[5] Compare dimensions and armament, respectively, to *Pawnee* and iron-cased *Iroquois*.

5. Only ironclad design accepted by board's majority opinion, signed by Lenthall. Basis for *Onondaga*.[6] Because she was specified by the Navy's RFP, *Onondaga* was considered the first Department-designed monitor.[7]

6. Navy department design, developed from earlier Lenthall-Isherwood ironclad. Considered by many USN officers as best of the Civil War-era ironclads. Later 'rebuilt' by Robeson et al. into recognizably modern coastal battleships.

Deck Plans of Evolutionary Ships
(drawn to scale)

Light Draft Steam Sloop *Iroquois*:
Iroquios' two 11-inch Dahlgren guns were both mounted on centerline pivot carriages, one before the machinery spaces and the other abaft. The gun positions are clearly indicated by the semi-circular racer tracks.

Very Light Draft Steam Sloop *Pawnee*:
Pawnee initially carried four 11-inch Dahlgren guns, mounted on pivoting carriages adjacent to one another to either side of the vessel's centerline. Their racers indicate how they were swung into action on each beam.

Navy Department Ironclad Design:
The Lenthall and Isherwood designed Navy Department ironclads would have carried two 11-inch Dahlgrens, one in each of its two turrets. Their main battery arrangement was but one step removed from *Iroquois*.

Monadnock Class Ironclad:
The *Monadnock* class of double turreted ironclads displayed the final evolutionary step—two guns per turret, in this case 15-inch Dahlgrens. Their main battery arrangement was that of a pre-dreadnought battleship.

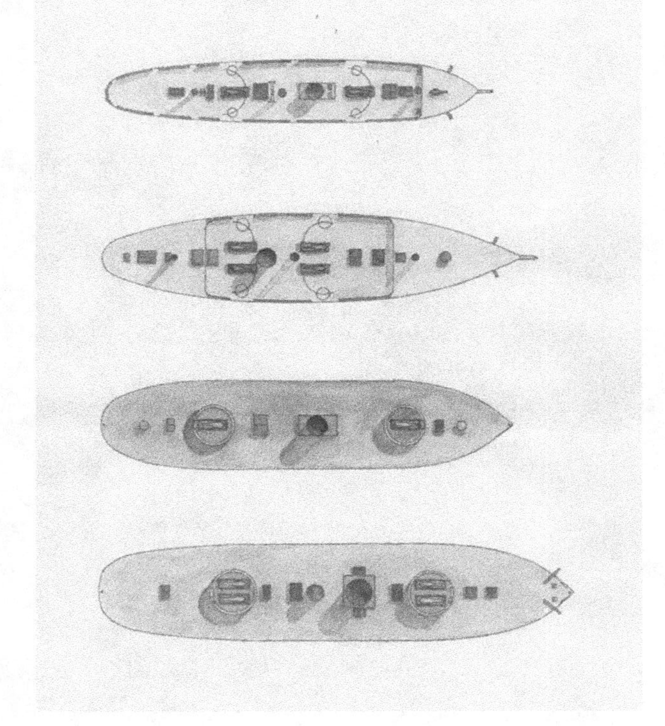

APPENDIX 8

Ironclad Steamers for Harbor and Coast Defense [1]

John Lenthall's letter to Gideon Welles, dated 13 May 1862 and co-signed by Engineer-in-Chief Benjamin F. Isherwood, Naval Constructor Edward Hartt and former Engineer-in-Chief Daniel B. Martin, provided a reasoned rationale for the desired characteristics of ironclad steamers intended for harbor and coast defense. Their opinions were meant to apply not only to the twenty proposals received in response to an earlier advertisement, but to the Department's future new buildings. This letter represented the majority opinion of a board convened to evaluate ironclad proposals; Commodore Joseph Smith, the board's chairman and its only line officer, issued a minority opinion in a letter dated 10 May 1862. [2]

Lenthall's letter began with a brief review of the rapid pace of ironclad development since the outbreak of hostilities, citing the Department's satisfaction with *Monitor*'s performance in combat. While the American experience and the latest European warships trends had demonstrated the superiority of ironclads, the board's majority still envisaged a role for wooden vessels as economical cruisers on distant stations.

With the stage thus set, the majority opinion emphatically rejected wooden hulled ironclads in favor of iron hulled vessels. The majority's logic was shaped by the much greater durability of iron—seasoned shipbuilding timber was by then unobtainable—making an expensive ironclad a far more sensible investment if its hull was fabricated from iron. Lenthall and his colleagues also recommended the use of "towers" (turrets) as opposed to a casemate, two in number, on a vessel propelled by twin screws, each powered by independent engines. The ironclads should be armored with plates of a single thickness rather than a lamina of thinner plates. A ten-knot speed, a four-day coal endurance and a maximum draft of thirteen feet were also stipulated. The only proposal that met these criteria—and the only one recommended by the majority—was that offered by G. W. Quintard of the Morgan Iron Works. This vessel was subsequently ordered and built, and served as the U.S.S. *Onondaga.*

The majority opinion also said that if the Department believed more harbor defense ironclads were immediately needed beyond those already under construction—the improved "Monitor" class—it should order more of the same rather than vessels of an inferior design. Where the board's majority differed from the minority opinion concerned "shot-proof ships ... for sea service." Smith suggested building a wooden ironclad as insurance in the event the iron-hulled version proved to be a failure.

As for the larger, more complex sea-going ironclads intended for coastal defense, the majority opinion was firm on two interrelated points. First, such vessels should be designed and specified by the Navy Department rather than by interested contractors and second, their designs should receive "much more study before a practical solution is attempted" and be "prepared with great deliberation and care."

* * *

Navy Department
Bureau of Construction, &tc.
May 13th 1862

Sir,

In obedience to your order of the 26th March we have carefully examined and analysed the plans of iron-clad steamers for harbor and coast defence, submitted by their projectors in answer to the advertisement issued by the Department on the 1st March last and have the honor to respectfully report here that:

The various plans proposed for the harbor vessels may be divided into two classes, one having the "Monitor" for its type and to be, like that vessel, an entirely iron construction protected by a series of thin plates, having one revolving tower and being propelled by a single screw; the other having for its type the thick plated iron-clad wooden vessel of the usual form, with two revolving towers, and two propellers, of which the complete printed specifications of hull plating, towers, and machinery, accompanied by photographic working drawings—prepared by order of the Department—have been for a long time widely circulated.

Of each of these types, the originals have been, in several instances, reproduced without modification; in others, there are attempts to combine them; while in some, an effort to modify one or the other in unimportant particulars appears to have been made; but no new solution of the problem has been presented. In fact, the above two types seem thus far to cover the entire field on this subject, and, respecting them, whatever may originally have been matter of opinion as to relative merits, an actual experiment with the "Monitor" has given a result satisfactory to the Department. No vessels afloat of the other type have been constructed, and, it is proper here to add that, at the period the original was designed so many were intended and so little time could be afforded for their construction, that the adoption of wood for the hulls instead of iron was not a matter of choice: the wooden vessels could have been obtained in the stipulated time, the iron ones could not.

Recent events, long since foreshadowed by the maritime authorities of the principal European navies, show the problem of the superiority of iron-clad vessels-of-war practically solved in so conclusive a manner as to render the reconstruction of our Navy a universally admitted necessity; and this reconstruction—whether in wood or iron—must be at several times its original cost, true economy requires it should be done with the most durable materials.

Although unprotected vessels of wood cannot be opposed in battle to those clad with iron armor, yet, as the navies of the world are of this description, and as the change will require both much time and money, and as the problem of cruising armored vessels—particularly of [sic] small class—has not yet been solved, the unarmored wooden vessel of small or moderate size will still be found useful, especially in times of general peace for the protection of commerce in distant seas, and for war purposes against half-civilized or barbarian nations, and others not having the means of obtaining armored vessels. The present wooden vessels are not only of greatly cheaper construction, but they have seagoing qualities and afford comforts to their crews not to be found with armored ones.

Although the rapid deterioration of our wooden steamers, even when constructed of the best seasoned and the most carefully selected materials, is very rapid and will be greatly accelerated by the iron plating, nonetheless, under actual conditions, it may be found to be sound economy to utilize some of them by giving them this protection, but it is only on large vessels, such as our steam frigates, that the experiment can be hopefully made, for it is only constructions of their magnitude which can carry iron plates of the thickness required to resist the artillery now in use. For the smooth water of harbors and the periods of fine weather along the coast, it is not important there should be much of the vessel above the waterline, and the nature of the service requires but a small crew which need not be on board for very long periods of time. The displacement, for the iron plates, can be obtained in our large vessels by reducing that part of the hull which is above the water and forms so large a portion of the total displacement. In this view, the Department has already commenced razeeing, fitting with towers, and plating one of our largest steam frigates, the "Roanoke," and the experiment will determine the question of the practicability and economy of the conversion of vessels of this class.

In the construction of unplated vessels, whether of wood or iron, equal strength requires very nearly equal weights of materials, but if the vessel is to be iron-clad this equality no longer exists, for the additional strength now required must be given in the case of the wooden vessel by the use of larger materials, for no strength whatever is derived from the iron plating which is altogether sustained simply as a load by the wooden hull; the larger materials, too, have the further disadvantage of increased liability for decay. In iron vessels, on the contrary, the strength of the armor plate can, to a very great extent, be incorporated in the hull which is thus rendered considerably lighter than the wooden vessel and yet have equal strength.

The government has no seasoned white oak or yellow pine timber, and it is not known that there is any in the hands of private parties, on the contrary, it is well understood that all our recent constructions have been, as our future ones must be, of green timber, which in a few years at furthest will be a mass of decay. If seasoned timber be used, two years, at least will be required to obtain it. To construct short-lived iron-plated steamers of green timber at their enormous cost will entail not only great pecuniary loss, but leave the country without their protection at some future period of sudden need. Only the most pressing necessity can justify construction from such materials, and in the event of less time being required.

For the foregoing, among other reasons, we are of opinion that no wooden vessels should be built for iron plating; and that no wood, except, perhaps, for the deck plank and backing of armor, should be used in the construction of armored iron hulls. We, therefore, cannot recommend the acceptance of any proposition on this material.

As regards the composition of the iron plating, we are of opinion it should be in a single thickness, and not in laminae, both on account of the far greater resistance that equal thickness offers to shot, and of its greater freedom from corrosion. The alternate presence of salt water and of air between the laminae must speedily rust both plates and fastenings, and thus not only impair the durability but reduce the strength; further, other things equal, the thinner the plate the more rapid the oxidation. The laminated armor can only be considered a make shift justified by the impossibility of obtaining solid plates in the time allowed.

Upon the question of the relative merits of casemates and revolving towers for the protection of the guns, we are of opinion that, for river and harbor defence, the advantage is in favor of the latter. We are, also, of opinion that harbor vessels should carry two towers: this number is practicable with the size of vessel adopted to such service, and the arrangement not only doubles the battery at, comparatively, a small additional cost, but divides it, and leaves one tower effective after the other may have become disabled, it, also, gives the ability to fire in opposite directions at the same instant, which may be of the first consequence in repelling a simultaneous attack on both sides. For equal efficiency of battery, the casemate requires more guns, and exposes more surface and of less resisting efficiency, and more and larger ports for the admission of shot or shell. As regards the risks and danger from the explosion of a gun, we are of the opinion such an accident would not be more calamitous in a tower than in a casemate containing several guns. The casemate has the advantage of greater cheapness and rapidity of construction, and of freedom from the risks inseparable to the revolving machinery of the tower; this machinery, however, is so simple that the probability of accident to it is very slight. For sea service there may still exist some indecision as to the superiority of the tower owing to the doubt of its ability to be efficiently worked in the undulations of the sea, independent of any rolling or plunging of the ships.

The vessel for harbor defence should be propelled by two screws working independently, one of the other, by means of a separate pair of engines. We regard this as essential, as it enables the vessel to be maneuvered in the limited space of a harbor without the rudder and to be turned on her own axis by going ahead with one screw while backing with the other. The rudder, screws and anchor should be protected by overhanging portions of the hull, the deck of which need not exceed two feet above the water level.

A speed of ten knots per hour, we are of opinion, will be found sufficient for any vessel to be maneuvered in a harbor, and the draught of water should not exceed twelve to thirteen feet with four days supply of coal for maximum steaming.

Among the numerous proposals submitted for vessels of harbor defence, the plan which embraces most of the foregoing requisites is the one offered by the "Morgan Iron Works" [G. W. Quintard] of New York City. The dimensions of the vessel are sufficient, the material is exclusively of iron, and the dimensions of the parts are large, the armor plates are four and a half inches thick and incorporated into the structure, the towers are two in number composed of two layers of plate each four and a half inches thick. The screws are two in number, and propelled by independent pairs of engines. The machinery is of known power and appropriate construction; the time of completion is one hundred and eighty (180) days. We believe the vessel would be satisfactory when finished and recommend the offer to be accepted.

From the unsatisfactory nature of the remaining proposals, and presuming that the number of vessels of the "Monitor" class, recently contracted for by the Department, are sufficient to satisfy the immediate wants of the government, we believe the public interest will be best sub-served, both pecuniarily and in efficiency, by the Department itself preparing the plans and specifications of a harbor defence vessel that will best suit its purposes, and then, by advertisement, receive proposals to construct a number of them from all who chose to compete for the contracts. Such plans and specifications should be prepared with great deliberation and care, both on account of the immense public interests at stake on the efficiency of the vessel, and its great money cost. The officers of the naval service in the several branches are necessarily familiar with the wants and necessities of the navy; and we are led to think, from the fact that many of the parties proposing have not hesitated to adopt the designs of others with a disposition to assist the government, that the method we have suggested of the Department preparing its own plans and specifications and receiving offers on them, would give more satisfaction to the mechanical establishments of the country than any other. They would be under no risk and penalty contingent on the performance of the vessel, which, indeed, amount to but little as protections to the government, but for which a very large price has to be paid.

In the event of the government having such immediate need of more vessels for harbor defence as to render further delay inexpedient, we suggest they could be built of the improved "Monitor" class from the designs of her projector, as this vessel has been approved by and given satisfactory results to the Department.

From an examination of the specifications and details of construction of the iron vessels presented, it will be perceived that no uniform system for the distribution of the material has been adopted, and the vessels built from them would have widely varying strengths and qualities. From the limited experience in this country in the construction of iron ships such a result might have been expected, and it furnishes a weighty argument in favor of the method we have suggested, which would put all parties in the possession of the same information, obtain the vessels at less price, and more certainly insure uniformity and a satisfactory result.

In connection with this object, it is proper here to express a doubt as to the efficiency of these or any small vessels for the defence of the harbors, as it is obvious they could not prevent the entrance of a large seagoing iron-plated steamer. Such an enemy need not reply to the fire of the harbor vessels, but could receive it with impunity and return unharmed after accomplishing the destruction of all the wooden vessels and land property within its reach. The successful defence of harbors will, probably, be found to consist in a combination of forts with a temporary obstruction in the channel commanded by their guns and removable at will.

The preceding remarks, although intended for the harbor defence vessels, applies in all assential [sic] features to the large sea-going steamers for coast defence; the problem, however, for vessels of this class is of greatly more difficult execution owing to provision having to be made for working the ordnance and keeping the sea in heavy weather, and for comparatively long periods of time. We are of opinion this question should receive much more study before a practical solution is attempted than appears in the various plans submitted, none of which do we feel willing to recommend. The cost of such vessels is so enormous, and the interests to be confided to their protection are so great that the most mature consideration should procede [sic] the adoption of any designs or system of construction; and we are, therefore, of opinion that the most judicious course, in this case as in that for vessels of harbor defence, will be for the Department to have plans and specifications prepared by a Board of Naval Officers with which might be associated, if the Department deems necessary, other persons of reputation and experience in the building of iron vessels, and upon such plans and specifications advantageous offers to construct will be proposed by contractors in competition on equal terms.

The same diversity of opinion in regard to materials and their distribution noticed in the plans of harbor defence vessels, is found also in those for the seagoing vessels, and furnishes, as in that case, a weighty argument for more mature consideration, especially as it is certain that vessels of this description cannot be obtained in less fifteen (15) or eighteen (18) months.

Accompanying will be found a tabular statement of the propositions received to which have been added a brief synopsis of their most characteristic features.

Very respectfully,
Your Obedient Servants,
/s/ John Lenthall
/s/ B. F. Isherwood
/s/ Edward Hartt
/s/ Dan. B. Martin

Hon. Gideon Welles
Secretary of the Navy

* * *

APPENDIX 9

The Light-Draught Monitors [1]

Bureau Chief Lenthall's open letter, addressing the "light-draught monitor" design fiasco and the role played by Chief Engineer Alban Stimers, represents perhaps the harshest condemnation of a U.S. Navy officer to flow from his pen. A letter of similar tenor written the following day by the chief of the Bureau of Steam Engineering, Benjamin Isherwood, was also published; both were annexed to the "Report of the Joint Committee on the Conduct of the War" on the subject of the light-draught monitors.[2]

The failure of the twenty *Casco* class monitors was a major embarrassment to the U.S. Navy; none of these vessels saw active service in their original guise. Divided responsibilities for warship design and construction within the Navy Department, combined with the ego of competing personalities, permitted the earliest of this class to be launched with inadequate freeboard to carry her turrets, guns, coal or stores. Lenthall's letter makes clear his view of who was responsible; the question of why the Navy Department's mechanical bureaus' oversight was not applied to the light-draft monitors makes for a far more complex tale.

As a postscript, in Lenthall's rush to vilify Stimers he told a little fib. Although he may never have been "asked to make any calculations of the weight or draught of water ... of the monitor vessels," he was most certainly involved with checking those of *Monitor*, the first of her class.

* * *

Washington, March 1, 1865

To the Editors of the *Boston Daily Advertiser*–

In your issue of the 20th ult., I find a letter from Chief Engineer A. C. Stimers, U.S.N., in relation to what are popularly known as the "Light-draught Monitors," which contains statements so utterly at variance with the truth, and so calculated to convey erroneous impressions, that I must ask a small portion of your space to correct them.

The original design of these vessels was made by Mr. Ericsson, who furnished, so far as I am aware, merely an outline plan, no details and no specifications; and had this sketch been filled up with ordinary ability, the vessels would probably have had the contemplated draught of water.

But Chief Engineer Stimers, to whom the immediate supervision of their construction was committed by the department, not content with carrying out Mr. Ericsson's idea, and furnishing working drawings upon his plan, undertook many and expensive alterations. Neither the working drawings containing these departures from the original plan, nor any other working plan were ever submitted to either of the mechanical bureaus of the Navy Department, and they first learned of the alterations through the contractors, who complained that after they had completed portions of their work, the plans had been withdrawn and others widely different substituted.

On the discovery of this system, or rather want of system, Chief Engineer Stimers was informed that these alterations, involving large expense, must not be made; but he still persisted in them, and it was only when a letter was written to each of the builders directing them not to make further alterations without the consent of the bureaus and an agreement beforehand as to the cost, that the department was enabled in the last degree to control the construction of the vessels. It is these unauthorized, and at the time unknown, changes and additions, more than anything else that necessitated the enlargement of the vessels.

So far was this carried, that patented inventions were inserted in the drawings, with the knowledge of Chief Engineer Stimers, by persons employed in his office, and claims were afterward made for patent fees upon the contractors.

When the advertisement was issued in order to place the work under contract, Chief Engineer Stimers deposited in the Bureau of Construction an outline plan and some general specifications, accompanied by his estimate of the weights of the vessel and machinery, which weights, he stated in it, corresponded to a draught of water 6 feet 5½ inches. Most, if not all of the contractors, have a copy of his paper containing these weights, and on them, they based their bids. Had these weights been adhered to by him, the vessels would not have required enlargement.

I was never asked to make any calculations of the weight or draught of water of the "light-draught," or any other of the "monitor vessels." I never approved plans, as Chief Engineer Stimers states, in relation to them, and was never asked to do so; and the statements in my letter to the Hon. Mr. Grimes, read to him in the Senate, are strictly true in every respect, both in the spirit and the letter.

There were never any plans submitted to me on which I or any other person could give an opinion, or make a calculation, and Chief Engineer Stimers's assertion that "when the plans were finally completed "they were examined by the two Bureaus of Construction and Engineering," is without the slightest color of truth.

Chief Engineer Stimers further states that "his superintendent of draughtsmen, Mr. Crabb, had orders from him, from first to last, to take all drawings to Captain Ericsson for approval,"—conveying the impression that Captain Ericsson did approve them, whereas it appears he protested against them in writing.

During the progress of the construction of the "light-draught monitors," Chief Engineer Stimers assumed the entire credit of them, and it is a ludicrous surprise to the hundreds of persons who recollect his pretensions then, that he is now endeavoring to shift the responsibility of his errors to others. He seems to shrink as abjectly from accepting the results of his own acts when failures, as he was eager and bold to assume credit for labors not his own when he thought they would render him famous.

So far from submitting to be instructed by Mr. Ericsson, he assumed to be his rival, and in the endeavor to imitate him underwent the fate of the frog who attempted to expand himself to the bulk of the ox.

All the facts herein stated, and much more, are well known to hundreds, and, in the endeavor to avoid the responsibility which belongs to him, and him alone, he forfeits the charity which might be extended to his ignorance as an engineer.

JOHN LENTHALL.

* * *

APPENDIX 10

Lenthall's Book and Pamphlet Collection [1]

It is well known that John Lenthall was a bibliophile. What isn't so widely known is the magnitude of his book collection, both in sheer quantity and in breadth of titles. But before delving further into details of his collection, a few words about its origins are in order.

Three years after stepping down as the chief of the Bureau of Construction and Repair, Lenthall deposited the majority of his book and pamphlet collection in the Franklin Institute's library. The year was 1874, the fiftieth anniversary of the founding of the Franklin Institute, of which Lenthall was a life member. A surviving letter from Lenthall to the Institute's secretary, William H. Wahl, dated 20 June 1874, describes Lenthall's intent and, in general terms, what the Institute could soon expect to receive. The deposit was conditional: the collection was to be kept in one place as much as practical, the books were not to be loaned out, and if requested, the Institute would allow Lenthall to take them for his own use with the understanding they would be promptly returned. After Lenthall's death in 1882, his deposit became a gift.[2]

Lenthall wrote that he intended to supply Wahl with a list of the books he sent, but such a list has not been found. The best source for the specifics of Lenthall's donation is the compilation provided in the cited reference, Farr and Bostwick's *A Guide to Plans and Drawings...* . But it must be remembered that Farr and Bostwick's *Guide* is only a snapshot of the collection's scope in 1991. In the years after Lenthall first donated his collection, the Franklin Institute moved to new, larger premises (1932), and then determined to "dismantle and sell" its library (1986). Fortunately, the Philadelphia Maritime Museum (now the Independence Seaport Museum) intervened and bought the collection with funds raised for that purpose. The collection they acquired, with the addition of five subsequently donated items, was professionally conserved and cataloged, and is now available to researchers at the Independence Seaport Museum's J. Welles Henderson Archives and Library.

However, there are good reasons to believe that Lenthall's book collection, in its present form, differs from that originally donated by John Lenthall. A year after Lenthall's death, a short piece appeared in the *Journal of the Franklin Institute* which listed books added to the Institute's library during the second quarter of 1883.[3] Of the forty-eight titles documented in the listing as "Presented by the late John Lenthall"—a small fraction of his original donation—twenty-two of them were *not* called out in Farr and Bostwick's *Guide*. These twenty-two volumes must have been sold or otherwise removed from Lenthall's original collection before 1991. One of them was an 1820 English translation of a book from which Lenthall often cited equations, Fredrik af Chapman's classic *Treatise on Ship-Building*, commonly known as *Architectura Navalis Mercatoria*. And if these were missing, there may well be others—we'll probably never know for certain.

* * *

What remains of Lenthall's book collection is a fabulously rich treasure trove. The two tables in this appendix present an analysis of 360 books in his collection; only titles published before his death were included. Table 1 presents a compilation of the languages of his books—English, French, German, Italian and Spanish—broken out by the decade of their publication. Table 2 presents a compilation of the subjects of his books, again broken out into the same chronological structure.

These tables yield a clearer understanding of John Lenthall. First, Table 1 documents that of the books in Lenthall's collection published prior to 1830—a year before he began his European dockyard tour—sixty-two were published in French against fifty-seven in English. This helps to explain why Lenthall chose to study in Paris rather than London—France was where he could access the best historical reservoir of naval architecture technology. Table 2 documents that Lenthall's collection was, unsurprisingly, heavily concentrated in subjects related to his profession—books on naval architecture, shipbuilding and naval warfare constitute over a third of the total. Given that he was employed by the U.S. Navy for his entire life, it is also entirely predictable that a quarter of his collection consisted of government publications, speeches or presentations and laws and regulations.

Lenthall the bibliophile regularly 'signed-in' the books he bought. Below is a list of selected books examined by the author that were annotated by Lenthall with the date and, in some cases, the location where he acquired them. In two instances, the price was marked inside. The books are arranged in the chronological order of acquisition:

1822, ... : Encyclopédie Méthodique: Marine, 1783.

1822, Washington City: Vocabulaire des Termes de Marine ... , Lescallier, 1799.

1825, Washington City: The Elements and Practice of Naval Architecture, Steel, 1805.

1827, Washington: Naval Architecture ... , Stalkartt, 1781. Price $25.

1830, ... : Élémens de L'Architecture Navale ... , Duhamel du Monceau, 1758. Price $12.

1830, Washington City: L'Art de la Marine ... , Romme, 1787.

1830, ... : Recherches sur la Construction La Plus Advantageuse Des Digues ... , Bossut and Viallet, 1764.

1830, ... : Traité Élémentaire de la Construction des Vaisseaux ... , Vail du Clairbois, 1805.

1832, ... : Philosophical Transactions, "The Construction and Analysis of Geometric Properties ... ," George Atwood, 1796.

1832, Paris: Principles of Naval Architecture ... , Thos. Gordon, 1784.

1833, ... : Arrimage de Vaisseaux, De Missiessy Quiés, 1789.

1833, ... : Du Transport de la Conservation et de la Force Des Bois ... , Duhamel du Monceau, 1767.

1833, ... : Essai Sur La Marine des Anciens ... , Deslandes, 1768.

1833, ... : Le Manoeuvre, ou, Essai sur La Théorie ... , Bourdé de Villehuet, 1814.

1834, Portsmouth: An Introductory Outline of the Practice of Ship-Building ... , John Fincham, 1825.

1835, ... : Mémoires de L'Academie Royale de Marine, 1773.

1845, ... : Mémoire ... Batiments en Fer ... , Dupuy de Lôme, 1844.

By the standards of the day, all of these books were expensive. Stalkartt's *Naval Architecture* cost young John Lenthall $25 in 1827; his daily wages as a first-year apprentice ship carpenter were fifty cents. And it tells much about Lenthall's desire to master his subject that the first two volumes listed, bought the year he began his apprenticeship, were an encyclopedia and a dictionary, both in French. He was keen to learn!

If the measure of one's character can be gauged by his book collection, John Lenthall comes off as an extraordinarily literate naval constructor who constantly sought to immerse himself in all aspects of his profession.

* * *

Lenthall's Book and Pamphlet Collection

Table A10-1 *Languages v. Dates of Publication*

Language	1700-1710	1730-1739	1740-1749	1750-1759	1760-1769	1770-1779	1780-1789	1790-1799	1800-1809	1810-1819	1820-1829	1830-1839	1840-1849	1850-1859	1860-1869	1870-1879	Totals
English		3			2		3	12	5	5	27	14	34	59	58	21	243 (67%)
French	1			2	5	3	5	4	6	16	20	15	18	4	13	2	114 (32%)
German									1								1 (<1%)
Italian			1														1 (<1%)
Spanish											1						1 (<1%)
TOTALS	1	3	1	2	7	3	8	16	12	21	48	29	52	63	71	23	360

Notes (both tables):

1. Translations of books are entered under the language of the book's original publication.
2. Books with multiple dates of publication are entered under the first date of publication.
3. Books published in the year of Lenthall's death (1882) or later are not listed.

Lenthall's Book and Pamphlet Collection

Table A10-2 *Subjects v. Dates of Publication*

Subject	1700-1710	1730-1739	1740-1749	1750-1759	1760-1769	1770-1779	1780-1789	1790-1799	1800-1809	1810-1819	1820-1829	1830-1839	1840-1849	1850-1859	1860-1869	1870-1879	Totals
Naval Architecture				1			2	5	3	5	8	7	3	4	5	1	44 (12%)
Shipbuilding, Outfitting					1	1	2	2	3	6	6	3	9	3	8	2	46 (13%)
Ships, Navy, Warfare		1			1	1		2		3	3	3	5	3	8	2	32 (9%)
Naval Ops, Tactics							2	1	1	1	2		1		1	1	10 (3%)
Marine Eng, Machinery									2		3	2	6	9	4	1	27 (8%)
Civil Engr, Forts, Guns				1	2	1				2	5	5	9	2	7	3	37 (10%)
Timber, Dry Rot					1			1		1	2				2		7 (2%)
Science, Mathematics	1		1		1		1		1	2	9	3	2		1	1	23 (6%)
General Maritime		1			1		1	2	1	1	3	2	4	16	1	1	34 (9%)
Navigation, Compasses		1						3			1	1		2	2		10 (3%)
Laws & Regulations											2		1		3		6 (2%)
Government Publications									1		3	2	9	16	20	8	59 (16%)
Speeches and Presentations											1	1	3	8	9	3	25 (7%)
TOTALS	1	3	1	2	7	3	8	16	12	21	48	29	52	63	71	23	360

APPENDIX 11

Ships Constructed, Designed and Specified by John Lenthall[1]

This appendix attempts to document the charged subject of just what ships were constructed, designed and specified by John Lenthall. In the world of naval architects, the question of ship design ownership can quickly get personal, as the credit for a truly noble design accrues great fame to its author. However, the complex and multi-faceted processes of designing and constructing a vessel ensures that the paternity of the finished product is rarely attributable to a single individual but is more a shared endeavor. To say one is the designer of a twelve-foot dingy is easy; to claim design ownership of a 235-foot long steam sloop is exponentially more difficult. With this caveat firmly in mind, the matter of Lenthall's ownership of 'design' can now begin.

The following tables are structured into groups documenting Lenthall's range of ownership, first for those ships he constructed, or more accurately, those whose construction he substantially supervised either as a master builder or a naval constructor. Second is a group of ships, both naval and merchant, for which creditable evidence documents that John Lenthall was responsible for their design. In these cases, the premise is that the design drawings for each listed ship came from Lenthall's own hand or that significant agreement amongst sources merits a design credit. And finally, there is a third, more ambiguous category, that of ships specified by Lenthall. The discerning eye will quickly detect that this later group includes nearly all U.S. Navy warships ordered during the Civil War. By specify, it is meant the definition of the ship's principal characteristics, instructions for building and main features such as hull form, general arrangements and sail plan. A good example of this process at work is the *Unadilla* class ninety-day gunboats. It is generally accepted that Lenthall oversaw the work of specifying and designing these ships, but that the drawings for them were drafted by naval architect Samuel H. Pook.

As the author of these tables, I would willingly alter the "specified by" categorization of a particular ship or class to "designed by" if further documentation indicated Lenthall's closer involvement. However, even here one must be careful. Many of the design drawings on record for the 1843 steam sloop *Princeton* are drafted by Lenthall, but most sources credit the design of this warship's hull to the Swedish inventor John Ericsson.

The post-war monitor rebuilds are neither fish nor fowl, and are listed for reference only. *Puritan* was originally designed by John Ericsson and the remainder, *Monadnock* class double turreted ironclads, were specified by Lenthall and their hulls were designed by the resident constructors in the navy yards that built them. The 'rebuilt' monitors were entirely new ships constructed in private shipyards, their murky "Roach, Robeson, Robbers" paternity exposed by investigations launched by Congressional hearings.

Sources used to create the following tables were principally the previously cited works by Chapelle, Canney, Silverstone, Bennett, Bauer & Roberts and Cutler. The author is also indebted to the prior research of the Philadelphia ship model maker Thomas Hornsby, especially for merchant ship design attributions. And there is the ultimate resource, the 518 ship plans and eighty-three memorandum folders John Lenthall left to the Franklin Institute which are now accessible at the Independence Seaport Museum. Plans or design material for all the merchant ships and most of the warships whose design is attributed to John Lenthall may be found in this invaluable collection.

* * *

Table A11-1 *Warships Constructed by John Lenthall*

Name (Number in Class)	*Type (Propulsion)*	*Date*	*Length x Breadth x Depth*	*Comments*
Relief (1)	6-g Store Ship (Sail)	1835 LD, 1836 L	109' x 30' x 12'	Designed by Samuel Humphreys, building supervised by Lenthall. *
Pennsylvania (1)	120-g Ship of the Line (Sail)	1822 LD, 1837 L	210' x 56'-9" x 23'	Completed and launched under Lenthall's superintendence. *
Mississippi (2)	10-g Frigate (Steam Sidewheel)	1839 LD, 1841 L	220' x 39' x 23'-6"	Designed together with Humphreys and Hartt. *
Princeton (1)	20-g Sloop (Steam Screw)	1842 LD, 1843 L	156' x 30'-6" x 21'-6"	Lines and dimensions by Ericsson, working drawings by Lenthall. *
Raritan (1)	50-g Frigate (Sail)	1820 LD, 1843 L	174'-10" x 45' x 14'-5"	Modified original design. *

Date key: L = launched, LD = laid down

*Mentioned in letter dated 5 May 1942, D. W. Knox, Captain USN, to Thomas Hornsby.[2]

Table A11-2 *Warships Designed by John Lenthall*

Name (Number in Class)	*Type (Propulsion)*	*Date*	*Length x Breadth x Depth*	*Comments*
Dale (5)	16-g Sloop (Sail)	1839 LD, 1840 L	117'-7' x 32' x 15'	Built under Lenthall's superintendence.
Germantown (1)	22-g Sloop (Sail)	1843 LD, 1846 L	150' x 36' x 16'8"	Built under Lenthall's superintendence.
Susquehanna (1)	15-g Frigate (Steam Sidewheel)	1847 LD, 1850 L	250' x 44' x 26'-6"	Only vessel definitely designed by Lenthall per ZB file letter. *
Water Witch (1)	3-g Sloop (Steam Sidewheel)	1852 LD, 1852 L	150' x 22' x 11'-6"	Second ship of name. Built at Washington NY.
Constellation (1)	22-g Sloop (Sail)	1853 LD, 1854 L	176' x 41' x 21'	'Rebuilt' 1797 frigate, design assist by B. F. Delano.
Franklin (1)	40-g Frigate (Steam Screw)	1853 LD, 1864 L	265' x 53' x 27'-3"	'Rebuilt' 74-g liner.
Merrimack (5)	40-g Frigate (Steam Screw)	1854 LD, 1855 L	256'10" x 50'-2" x 26'-2"	Half model at Portsmouth SH Museum notes "by John Lenthall."
Lancaster (1)	18-g Sloop (Steam Screw)	1857 LD, 1858 L	235'-8" x 46' x 22'-3"	Large spar decked sloop from 1857 program.
Pensacola (1)	16-g Sloop (Steam Screw)	1858 LD, 1859 L	230'-8" x 44'-5" x 18'-7"	Large sloop from 1857 program.
Ossipee (4)	10-g Sloop (Steam Screw)	1861 LD, 1861 L	205' x 38' x 16'-7"	Drawings & specs for Hulls...made in this Bureau.
Contoocook (4)	20-g Sloop (Steam Screw)	1864 LD, 1864 L	290' x 41' x 20'-8"	Lines similar to *Swatara.*
Algoma (4)	12-g Sloop (Steam Screw)	1867 LD, 1868 L	250'-6" x 38' x 19'-2"	Larger Versions of *Swatara* for foreign cruising.

Date key: L = launched, LD = laid down.

* Mentioned in letter dated 5 May 1942, D. W. Knox, Captain USN, to Thomas Hornsby. Lenthall "connected" with vessels built after November 1853 when he became chief of the Bureau of Construction, Equipment and Repairs.[3]

Table A11-3 *Warships Specified by John Lenthall*

Name (Number in Class)	*Type (Propulsion)*	*Date*	*Length x Breadth x Depth*	*Comments*
Mohican (4 + 4)	6-g Sloop (Steam Screw)	1858 LD 1859 L	198'-8" x 32'-2" x 16'	Light draft sloop class of 1858, later repeated.
Unadilla (23)	4-g Gunboat (Steam Screw)	1861 LD, 1861 L	156'4" x 28' x 12'	Ninety-day gunboats. S. H. Pook drafted plans.
Sacramento (6)	10-g Sloop (Steam Screw)	1861 LD, 1862 L	229'x 38' x 17'	Lengthened *Ossipees*. Differing hull dimensions, etc.
Octorara (12)	6-g Gunboat (Steam Sidewheel)	1861 LD, 1861 L	205'x 34'-6" x 12'	Double Enders, first batch dims varied.
Sassacus (28)	6-g Gunboat (Steam Sidewheel)	1862 LD, 1862 L	236' x 35' x 12'	Double Enders, largest class of USN vessels till WWI.
Kansas (6 of 8)	6-g Sloop (Steam Screw)	1863 LD, 1863 L	179'-6" x 30' x 12'	Successors of ninety-day gunboats, two others to a different design.
Roanoke (1)	Ocean Going Ironclad (Steam Screw)	1863 C	263'-8" x 51'-4" x 26'-2"	Triple turret conversion of steam frigate. Original frigate dimensions.
Monadnock (4)	Ocean-Going Ironclad (Steam Screw)	1862 LD, 1864 L	250' x 53' x 16'	Double turrets, see notes on rebuilds below.
Swatara (4)	10-g Sloop (Steam Screw)	1864 LD, 1865 L	216' x 30' x 13'-3"	Extensions of *Kansas* class. Includes *Resacas*.

Date key: L = launched, LD = laid down, C = conversion.

Table A11-4 *Post-War Monitor Rebuilds*

Original Name	*New Name*	*Hull No.*	*Monitor class*
Puritan	Original name retained	BM1	Large Ericsson single turret
Tonawanda	*Amphitrite*	BM2	*Monadnock* double turret
Monadnock	Original name retained	BM3	do.
Agamenticus	*Terror*	BM4	do.
Miantonomoh	Original name retained	BM5	do.

Table A11-5 *Merchant Ships Designed by John Lenthall*

Name (Number in Class)	*Type (Propulsion)*	*Date*	*Length x Breadth x Depth*	*Comments*
Georgiana	Vessel owned by NY merchant family (Sail)	1836	130' x 30 'x 15'* 554 tons	Built by Vogle and Pearson. +
City Ice Boat (No. 1)	Icebreaker for City of Philadelphia (Steam)	1837	170' x 26' x 12' 359 tons at launching	Built by Van Dusen and Birely, Phila, engines by Matthias Baldwin.
Clarion	Barque 1st owned by Vogels and Young (Sail-Steam)	1838	93' x 24'-6" x 14'* 220 tons	Converted with twin screw Ericsson propellers. +
Shenandoah	Packet for 3 Brown Bros. Phila-Liverpool Svce (Sail)	1839	143' x 32' x 21'* 738 tons gross	Built by John Vaughan & Sons, Phila. +
Tuscarora	Packet for Cope Line, Phila-Liverpool Service (Sail)	1848	176' x 38' x 22'* 1231 tons	Built by John Vaughan & Sons, Phila. +

* Hornsby MS p. 5 footnote dimensions from Philadelphia customs house records differ. +Mentioned in Carl Cutler, *Queens of the Western Ocean*, 1961.

APPENDIX 12

Naval Constructors Active During Lenthall's Career [1]

This appendix provides a concise listing of service data for naval constructors active during the span of John Lenthall's long career, until his retirement as Bureau Chief in January 1871. Constructors are listed in chronological order, based on the date of their "Original entry into service"—their appointment as full-fledged naval constructors. That event initiated the appearance of their names in the *Navy Register*, time spent as an apprentice or master builder was not recorded. After the Civil War, assistant naval constructors (ANC) began to be listed.

Ship design credits are according to the sources as noted with the by now familiar caveat—it is rare then and now that one person was fully responsible for any ship's design, the responsibility being distributed between the constructor who drafted her original plans and the constructor who built her. Sometimes other intermediaries, such as yard commandants, were involved. Credits are generally confined to the lead ship of the class; the date given is of the ship's launch. Where a constructor is strongly associated with a vessel building but didn't produce her design, the entry is styled "Constructed," e.g., Edward Hartt Delano, Constructed Steam Frigate *Merrimack* 1855. Merchant ship credits are not comprehensive and are only intended to represent the constructor's commercial involvement.

The longevity of certain of the constructors is remarkable, Doughty and Grice standing out in addition to Lenthall's lengthy tenure. A dynastic theme is also evident among the earlier constructors, particularly the families of Humphreys, Hartt, Pook, Delano and Hanscom. The families of Hartt, Pook and Delano were very closely intertwined; perhaps future research will shed more light on the achievements of the gifted naval architects they produced. According to federal law, constructors were forced to retire at age sixty-two unless officially authorized to serve longer. Lenthall was one of the few to have been granted this privilege.

Not included in the tables are two early giants of the naval constructor world, Joshua Humphreys and Josiah Fox. Both had left Navy service long before Lenthall began his apprenticeship.

An illuminating glimpse into the challenges faced by budding naval constructors, including a focus on Lenthall's own experience, is provided by this excerpt from a letter of his to Secretary of the Navy George Robeson:

> The Naval Constructors now in the service, have all passed through the various grades of Apprentice, Journeyman, Quarterman, Draughtsman, and Foreman, and were well advanced in life before their names appeared in the Naval Register, their whole time, without intermission, having been devoted to the study and practice of their profession; they are all competent to design a ship of war, in all its parts, and if necessary, to execute the work with their own hands. In my own case, which from fortuitous circumstances, was much more favorable than that of any of the Constructors now in the service, I was nearly 30 years of age before I was entered on the Navy Register, having then already built a ship, and finished and launched the "Pennsylvania," said at the time to have been the largest ship in any Navy. [2]

The primary source for constructor service dates and duty locations was the *Navy Register* with input for the post-Civil War constructors from Lewis R. Hamersly's *The Records of Living Officers ....* and NARA, RG 24, Abstracts of Service Records of Naval Officers. For ship design credits, works extensively consulted were: Howard I. Chapelle's *The History of the American Sailing Navy* and *The Search for Speed Under Sail, 1700-1855;* Donald L. Canney's *The Old Steam Navy, Volume One, Frigates, Sloops and Gunboats, 1815-1885; The Old Steam Navy, Volume Two, The Ironclads, 1842-1885* and *Sailing Warships of the U.S. Navy;* Paul Silverstone's *The Sailing Navy, 1775-1854* and *Warships of the Civil War Navies;* Frank M. Bennett's *The Steam Navy of the United States* and K. Jack Bauer and Stephen S. Roberts *Register of Ships of the U.S. Navy 1775-1990, Major Combatants.*

Please note the data listed in this appendix may include some unintentional errors or omissions, especially regarding the chronology of the constructors' service. This circumstance is due to gaps in availability of the most reliable of the primary documentation sources, the *Navy Register.*

* * *

Name	State Where Born	State of which Citizen	Original Entry into Service	Date of Present Comm	Duty or Station
William Doughty	Penn	DC	12 April 1804	...	Washington
do. constructor				1837	Resigned

Born 1773, Died 1859. Protégé of Joshua Humphreys. Originally appointed 'head carpenter' at Washington Navy Yard. After Samuel Humphreys' appointment as chief constructor, he ceased to be active in naval design.

Ship design credits: Frigate *Brandywine* 1825, Sloop *Wasp* 1813, Sloop *Erie* 1813, Liner *Columbus* 1819, Liner *North Carolina* 1824.

Name	State Where Born	State of which Citizen	Original Entry into Service	Date of Present Comm	Duty or Station
Samuel Humphreys	Penn	Penn	13 Apr 1813	...	Philadelphia
do. chief constructor				25 Nov 1826	Washington City

Born in Philadelphia 23 Nov 1778, Died in Georgetown 16 Aug 1846. Son of Joshua Humphreys. He was the first appointed chief constructor. Offered a constructor's position in Russia in 1824 but declined.

Ship design credits: Merchant Ship *William Penn* 1803, Pilot Schooner *Nimble* 1806, Liner *Franklin* 1815, Sloop *Boston* 1825, Frigate *Macedonian* 1829, Schooner *Enterprise* 1831, Store Ship *Relief* 1836, Brig *Dolphin* 1836, Liner *Pennsylvania* 1837, Sloop *Cyane* 1837, Frigate *Congress* 1839, Sloop *Saratoga* 1842.

Name	State Where Born	State of which Citizen	Original Entry into Service	Date of Present Comm	Duty or Station
Francis Grice	NJ	VA	7 May 1817	...	Gosport (Norfolk)
do. constructor				May 1843	New York
do. chief constructor				1 Dec 1846	Washington
do. constructor				1850	Philadelphia
do. constructor				1860	Leave of absence

Born 1789, Died 1865. Son of Joseph Grice and grandson of his namesake, both eminent shipbuilders of Philadelphia.

Ship design credits: Privateer Clipper Schooner *Transit* 1812, Constructed Frigate *Guerriere* 1814, Constructed Liner *Delaware* 1820, Pilot Schooner *Lafayette* 1824, Brig *Perry* 1843, Sloop *Albany* 1846, Steamer *Powhatan* 1850, Steam Sloop *Wyoming* 1859.

Name	State Where Born	State of which Citizen	Original Entry into Service	Date of Present Comm	Duty or Station
Henry Eckford	Scot	NY	13 July 1817	...	New York
do. constructor				1 June 1820	Resigned

Born 17 March 1775, Died Constantinople 12 November 1832. Noted New York shipbuilder. Directed construction of American fleet at Sackett's Harbor, NY 1812-14. Emigrated to Constantinople and built ships for the Turks.

Ship design credits: Constructed Brig *Oneida* 1808, Schooners *Sylph* and *Lady of the Lake* 1813, Brigs *Jefferson* and *Jones* 1814, Corvettes *Madison* and *General Pike*, Frigates *Superior* and *Mohawk* 1814, Liner *Ohio* 1820, Corvettes *Kensington* 1828 and *Mesir-i Ferah* ex-*United States* 1830.

Name	State Where Born	State of which Citizen	Original Entry into Service	Date of Present Comm	Duty or Station
Josiah Barker	Mass	Mass	mid 1817	...	Boston
do. constructor				9 July 1846	Dismissed

Ship design credits: Sloop *Falmouth* 1828, Sloop *Portsmouth* 1843.

Name	State Where Born	State of which Citizen	Original Entry into Service	Date of Present Comm	Duty or Station
Samuel Hartt	Mass	Mass	1 Jan 1819	...	New York
do. constructor				1842	Erie, PA
do. constructor				1846	New York
do. constructor				1852	Portsmouth
do. chief of BCER				1 July 1853	Washington
do. chief constructor				17 Nov 1853	Resigned bureau chief
do. chief constructor				1855	Not on duty

Born 4 April 1786, Died in Plymouth, Mass 16 Dec 1860. Tenure as Chief of BCER abruptly ended by ill health. He was the last appointed chief constructor.

Ship design credits: Steamers *Michigan* 1842, *Saranac* 1848, and *San Jacinto* 1850.

Name	State Where Born	State of which Citizen	Original Entry into Service	Date of Present Comm	Duty or Station
John Floyd	Mass	Maine	late 1820	...	New York
do. constructor				1826	
do. constructor				1836	after which not listed as active

Eckford's assistant, recommended by him as his replacement.

Ship design credits: Constructed Frigate *Savannah* 1842.

Name	State Where Born	State of which Citizen	Original Entry into Service	Date of Present Comm	Duty or Station
Charles D. Brodie	VA	VA	13 Jan 1826	...	Pensacola
do. constructor				1833	after which not listed as active
do. constructor				3 Sept 1842	Pensacola
do. constructor				1844	after which not listed as active

Died 14 October 1845.

Ship design credits: Sloop *St Mary's* 1844.

Name	State Where Born	State of which Citizen	Original Entry into Service	Date of Present Comm	Duty or Station
James Keen	...	...	12 Dec 1826	...	Philadelphia
do. constructor				1833	after which not listed as active

Master joiner at Philadelphia Navy Yard. "Last appearance" 8 February 1831.

Ship design credits: Constructed Sloop Vandalia 1828.

Name	State Where Born	State of which Citizen	Original Entry into Service	Date of Present Comm	Duty or Station
John Lenthall	DC	Penn*	8 Feb 1838	...	Philadelphia
do. chief constructor				1 Nov 1849	Washington
do. chief of BCER				18 Nov 1853	Washington
do. chief of BCR				16 Sept 1869	On Retired List
do. general inspector of ships				29 Jan 1871	Washington
do. detached from special duty				30 June 1873	Washington, w.o.

Born 16 Sept 1807, Died 11 April 1882. *From 1854 on, resident of DC.

Ship design credits: see Appendix 11.

Name	State Where Born	State of which Citizen	Original Entry into Service	Date of Present Comm	Duty or Station
Samuel Moore Pook	Mass	NH	1 Jan 1841	...	Portsmouth
do. constructor				1848	Boston
do. constructor				1855	Washington
do. constructor				1858	Special Duty, NY
do. constructor				1860	Norfolk
do. constructor				1862	Special Duty, NY
do. constructor				1864	Portsmouth
do. constructor				15 Aug 1866	On Retired List
do. constructor				1867	Philadelphia
do. constructor				1869	Boston, Portsmouth
do. constructor				26 Sept 1869	Retired

Born 1804, Died 1878. Author of *A Method of Comparing the Lines and Draughting Vessels, Propelled by Sail or Steam, Including a Chapter on Laying off on the Mould Loft Floor*, 1866.

Ship design credits: Sloop *Plymouth*, Steamer *Princeton II* 1851, Steamer *Pocahontas* 1859, City Class Ironclads 1861.

Name	State Where Born	State of which Citizen	Original Entry into Service	Date of Present Comm	Duty or Station
Foster Rhodes	NY	NY	3 Mar 1841	...	Washington
do. constructor				1842	New York
do. constructor				1846	after which not listed as active

Died 7 November 1846.

Ship design credits: Sloop *Jamestown* 1844.

Name	State Where Born	State of which Citizen	Original Entry into Service	Date of Present Comm	Duty or Station
Benjamin Franklin Delano	Mass	NH	14 Aug 1846	...	Portsmouth
do. constructor				1852	New York
do. constructor				17 Sept 1871	Retired

Born Scituate MA 1809, Died New York 30 April 1882. Apprenticed to his uncle, Samuel Hartt.

Ship design credits: Steam Sloops *Hartford* 1858, *Iroquois* 1859, *Ticonderoga* 1862, Commerce Destroyer *Wampanoag* 1864, Turret Ironclad *Miantonomoh* 1865.

Name	State Where Born	State of which Citizen	Original Entry into Service	Date of Present Comm	Duty or Station
Christopher G. Selfridge	Mass	Mass	15 July 1847	...	Pensacola
do. constructor				1848	after which not listed as active

Died 1855, uncle of ADM Thomas O. Selfridge, Jr.

Ship design credits: n.a.

Name	State Where Born	State of which Citizen	Original Entry into Service	Date of Present Comm	Duty or Station
Samuel T. Hartt	Mass	VA	15 July 1847	...	Norfolk
do. constructor				1852	Pensacola

do. constructor				1855	Norfolk
do. constructor				1859	after which not listed as active

Carpenter at New York Navy Yard 1840.

Ship design credits: Steam Sloops *Dacotah* 1859, *Richmond* 1860.

Name	State Where Born	State of which Citizen	Original Entry into Service	Date of Present Comm	Duty or Station
Edward Hartt Delano	Mass	Mass	19 June 1848	...	Pensacola
do. constructor				1852	Norfolk
do. constructor				1855	Boston
do. constructor				1859	after which not listed as active

Died 12 Sept 1875. Brother of Benjamin F. Delano.

Ship design credits: Constructed Steam Frigate *Merrimack* 1855, Constructed Steam Sloops *Hartford* 1858, *Narragansett* 1859.

Name	State Where Born	State of which Citizen	Original Entry into Service	Date of Present Comm	Duty or Station
William Leighton Hanscom	Maine	Maine	15 Oct 1853	...	Portsmouth
do. constructor				1860	Boston
do. constructor				4 Feb 1866	Resigned
do. constructor				17 April 1871	Restored to duty
do. constructor				1871	Mare Is, Boston
do. constructor				1873	New York
do. constructor				5 Aug 1874	Retired at age 62

Born Eliot 3 Aug 1812, Died Malden, MA 3 September 1881. Brother of Isaiah. 1866 resignation motivated by suspicions of dishonesty.

Ship design credits: Steam Sloop *Mohican* 1859, Turret Ironclad *Monadnock* 1864.

Name	State Where Born	State of which Citizen	Original Entry into Service	Date of Present Comm	Duty or Station
George Steers (temporary)	...	...	...	12 May 1854	New York

Born 15 Aug 1819, Died 25 Sept 1856. Served for two years during construction of *Niagara*.

Ship design credits: Yacht *America* 1851, Clipper Ship *Sunny South* 1854, Steam Sloop *Niagara* 1855.

Name	State Where Born	State of which Citizen	Original Entry into Service	Date of Present Comm	Duty or Station
Isaiah Hanscom	Maine	Calif	14 Mar 1856	...	Portsmouth
do. constructor				1858	Mare Island
do. constructor				1861	Portsmouth
do. constructor				1864	Norfolk
do. constructor				1868	Portsmouth
do. constructor				1869	Boston
do. chief of BCR				23 Jan 1871	Washington
do. chief of BCR				27 Apr 1877	Resigned

Born Eliot 29 June 1815, Died Washington, DC 5 March 1880. Brother of William. Tainted by Robeson affair; assimilated rank reduced upon retirement.

Ship design credits: Steamer *Saginaw* 1859, Constructed Steam Sloop *Kearsarge* 1861, Turret Ironclad *Agamenticus* 1865.

Name	State Where Born	State of which Citizen	Original Entry into Service	Date of Present Comm	Duty or Station
John W. Griffiths (temporary)	NY	NY	...	July 1858	Philadelphia
do. sup't of gunboats				Oct 1862	NY under S. M. Pook

Born 6 Oct 1809, Died 30 March 1882. Temporarily served during construction of *Pawnee* and western river gunboats. Prolific writer of naval architecture commentary, especially in the *U.S. Nautical Magazine and Naval Journal*. Authored *Treatise of Marine and Naval Architecture*, 1854.

Ship design credits: Clipper Ship *Sea Witch* 1846, Steam Sloop *Pawnee* 1859.

Name	State Where Born	State of which Citizen	Original Entry into Service	Date of Present Comm	Duty or Station
Henry Hoover	Penn	Penn	4 June 1859	...	Philadelphia
do. constructor				1865	Under suspension
do. constructor				1867	Not listed

Ship design credits: Steam Sloop *Monongahela* and *Shenandoah* 1862, Turret Ironclad *Tonawanda* 1865.

Name	State Where Born	State of which Citizen	Original Entry into Service	Date of Present Comm	Duty or Station
John Luke Porter	VA	VA	1 Oct 1859	...	Pensacola
do. constructor				Jan 1861	Washington
do. constructor				mid Apr 1861	Norfolk
do. constructor				22 Apr 1861	Resigned, joined CSN

Born 19 Sept 1813, Died 14 Dec 1893.

Ship design credits: Constructed Iron Steamer *Allegheny* 1847, Steam Sloop *Seminole* 1859, CSN Ironclad *Virginia* 1862.

Name	State Where Born	State of which Citizen	Original Entry into Service	Date of Present Comm	Duty or Station
Melvin Simmons	Mass	Mass	11 June 1860	...	Mare Island
do. constructor				15 June 1868	On Retired List
do. constructor				1869	Portsmouth
do. constructor				1870	Philadelphia

Died at Charlestown, MA 13 May 1871.

Ship design credits: Master carpenter, built Steam Frigate *Merrimack* 1855.

Name	State Where Born	State of which Citizen	Original Entry into Service	Date of Present Comm	Duty or Station
Edward Hartt	NH	NH	27 Nov 1861	...	Washington
do. constructor				1862	Special Duty, St Louis
do. constructor				1865	Philadelphia
do. constructor				1867	Boston
do. constructor				1869	Mare Island
do. constructor				1871	Pensacola, w. o.
do. constructor				1873	Philadelphia

Ship design credits: n.a

Name	State Where Born	State of which Citizen	Original Entry into Service	Date of Present Comm	Duty or Station
Thomas Davidson, jr.	England	Penn	4 May 1863	...	New York
do. constructor				1867	Portsmouth
do. constructor				1868	BCR
do. constructor				1871	Boston, Phila.
do. constructor				1872	USNA
do. constructor				1873	Not listed

Directed refloating of Steam Sloop *Monongahela* at St. Croix, W.I., in 1868 after she was washed ashore by a tidal wave.

Ship design credits: n.a.

Name	State Where Born	State of which Citizen	Original Entry into Service	Date of Present Comm	Duty or Station
Thomas E. Webb, ANC	NY	NY	27 Feb 1865	...	New York
do. constructor				1868	Norfolk
do. constructor				1871	Portsmouth
do. constructor				1874	Washington

do. constructor	1877	NY, Special duty
do. constructor	1886	Boston
do. constructor	18 June 1888	Retired

Served as an apprentice at New York under Samuel Hartt and B. F. Delano. Not well regarded by Benjamin Isherwood.

Ship design credits: n.a.

Name	State Where Born	State of which Citizen	Original Entry into Service	Date of Present Comm	Duty or Station
John Ward Easby, ANC	Penn	DC	17 May 1866	...	Philadelphia
do. constructor				17 June 1870	Washington
do. constructor				1870	Portsmouth, Washington
do. constructor				1871	Norfolk
do. constructor				1874	Boston
do. chief of BCR				28 April 1877	Washington
do. chief of BCR				13 Dec 1881	Retired at age 62

Born 13 Dec 1819, Died 17 June 1894. Son of Captain William Easby, protégé of Lenthall. Pallbearer at Lenthall's funeral.

Ship design credits: n.a.

Name	State Where Born	State of which Citizen	Original Entry into Service	Date of Present Comm	Duty or Station
George W. Much, ANC	Penn	Penn	17 May 1866	...	Boston
do. constructor				15 April 1871	Philadelphia
do. constructor				1871	Washington
do. constructor				1873	Mare Island
do. constructor				1879	Japan, China
do. constructor				1881	Mare Island

do. constructor				1885	Wash, Special duty
do. constructor				1886	Morgan I.W., NY
do. constructor				22 June 1887	Retired at age 62

Born Philadelphia 22 June 1825, apprenticed to John Lenthall at Philadelphia on 20 May 1839 until age 21, then served as shipwright, quarterman; appointed master carpenter 7 May 1863.

Ship design credits: n.a.

Name	State Where Born	State of which Citizen	Original Entry into Service	Date of Present Comm	Duty or Station
Samuel Hartt Pook, ANC	NY	NH	17 May 1866	…	Portsmouth
do. assist naval constructor				1867	Philadelphia
do. assist naval constructor				1869	Boston
do. constructor				15 April 1871	BCR
do. constructor				1871	Boston
do. constructor				1875	New York
do. constructor				1881	Washington NY
do. constructor				1886	New York
do. constructor				17 Jan 1889	On Retired List

Born 17 Jan 1827, Died 30 March 1901, Son of Samuel M. Pook. Prior to Civil War he was an independent naval architect in Boston. Pallbearer at Lenthall's funeral.

Ship design credits: Clipper Ships *Challenger, Red Jacket*, etc., 1850s, Drafted plans for 90-day Gunboat *Unadilla* 1861, Ironclad *Galena* 1862, Torpedo Boat *Spuyten Duyvel* 1864.

Name	State Where Born	State of which Citizen	Original Entry into Service	Date of Present Comm	Duty or Station
Theodore D. Wilson, ANC	NY	NY	17 May 1866	...	Pensacola
do. assist naval constructor				Dec 1867	Philadelphia
do. assist naval constructor				3 July 1869	USNA instructor
do. constructor				1 July 1873	Washington NY
do. constructor				1 June 1874	Portsmouth
do. chief of BCR				3 Mar 1882	Washington
do. chief of BCR				7 July 1893	Resigned, ill health
do. constructor				1895	Boston

Born 11 May 1840, Died at work in Boston NY 29 June 1896. Served as an apprentice at New York under B. F. Delano, protégé of Lenthall. 1870 tour of European dockyards.

Ship design credits: Supervised the designs of many warships of the new Steel Navy. Author of *An Outline of Ship Building, Theoretical and Practical*, 1873.

* * *

NOTES

ABBREVIATIONS

ANJ	*The United States Army and Navy Journal and Gazette,*
Appleton's	*Appleton's Cyclopedia of American Biography*
ARSN	Annual Report of the Secretary of the Navy
DAB	*Dictionary of American Biography*
DANFS	*Dictionary of American Naval Fighting Ships*
FI	Franklin Institute
JFI	*Journal of the Franklin Institute*
LOC	Library of Congress
NARA	National Archives and Records Administration
NCAB	*National Cyclopedia of American Biography*
ORA	*The War of the Rebellion: A Compilation of Official Records of the Union and Confederate Armies.*
ORN	*Official Records of the Union and Confederate Navies in the War of the Rebellion*
OSN1	*The Old Steam Navy, Volume One, Frigates, Sloops and Gunboats, 1815-1885,* Canney
OSN2	*The Old Steam Navy, Volume Two, The Ironclads, 1842-1885,* Canney
PNY	*The Philadelphia Navy Yard,* Dorwart
WNY	*The Washington Navy Yard, An Illustrated History,* Marolda

BOOK ONE *Apprentice*

CHAPTER 1 *Washington City*

[1] Ralph E. Ehrenberg, "Mapping the Nation's Capital, The Surveyors Office," *The Quarterly Journal of the Library of Congress,* 36 No. 3 (1979): 279-319. Hereinafter cited as Ehrenberg, "Mapping."

[2] Constance McLaughlin Green, *Washington Village and Capital, 1800-1878* (Princeton: Princeton University Press, 1962), 12. Hereinafter cited as Green, *Washington.*

[3] Talbot Hamlin, *Benjamin Henry Latrobe* (New York: Oxford University Press, 1955), 231, 259. Hereinafter cited as Hamlin, *Latrobe.*

[4] Pennsylvania Septennial Census, 1779-1863. In the year 1793 a John Lenthall was recorded as living in Philadelphia's north ward.

[5] Maud Burr Morris, "The Lenthall Houses and Their Owners," *Records of the Columbia Historical Society, Washington, D.C.*, 31/32 (1930): 1-35. Hereinafter cited as Morris, "Owners." An outstanding source of information on the Lenthall and King families and their impact on early Washington.

[6] Ibid., 20.

[7] Find A Grave, "John Lenthall," https://www.findagrave.com/memorial/142599741/john-lenthall, accessed February 2018.

[8] Morris, "Owners," 33.

[9] Stephen A. Hansen, "The Lenthall Houses: A Moving Tale of Historic Preservation," *TheInTowner* (November 2012).

[10] Independence Seaport Museum, John Lenthall Collection, Thomas Hornsby Collection, Manuscript Documents, transcribed letter, Annette Ives to Miss Morris, 11 October 1926. Hereinafter cited as Hornsby MS Docs. Annette Ives was the great-great-granddaughter of John Lenthall Sr.

[11] Taylor Peck, *Round-Shot to Rockets, A History of the Washington Navy Yard and U.S. Naval Gun Factory* (Annapolis: United States Naval Institute, 1949), 9. Hereinafter cited as Peck, *Round-Shot.*

[12] Morris, "Owners," 20.

[13] Green, *Washington,* 21-23.

[14] Ehrenberg, "Mapping," 304.

[15] Family relations data from the Ancestry and Find A Grave website entries listed in the bibliography. Also see Morris, "Owners," 10-11.

[16] Ehrenberg, "Mapping," 309.

[17] Ibid., p. 304. Also see Wilhelmus Bogart Bryan, *A History of the National Capital* (New York: The Macmillan Company, 1914), 1:300. Hereinafter cited as Bryan, *A History.*

[18] Ehrenberg, "Mapping," 298.

[19] Bryan, *A History,* 1:300; Morris, "Owners," 10; Ehrenberg, "Mapping," 304.

[20] Morris, "Owners," 10; Bryan, *A History,* 1:300.

[21] Morris, "Owners," 11.

[22] Ibid., 14-16.

[23] Ibid., 14. Morris makes it clear that many other instances were documented in early Washington of owners erecting their homes prior to completing their lot purchases and receiving their deed. John Lenthall Sr.'s purchase of his 19th Street houses occurred in this same manner.

[24] Hornsby MS Docs, transcribed letter, Annette Ives to Miss Morris, 11 October 1926.

[25] Ibid., transcribed letter, Annette Ives to Miss Morris, 14 November 1926, in re: Estate of Mary K. Lenthall with a family tree.

[26] Morris, "Owners," 14.

[27] Ibid., 15.

CHAPTER 2 *Father and Son*

[1] Morris, "Owners,"16.

[2] Ibid., 24.

[3] Bryan, *A History,* 1:300; Morris, "Owners," 10; Ehrenberg, "Mapping," 304.

[4] Morris, "Owners," 15.

[5] Hamlin, *Latrobe,* 296.

[6] Ibid., 130, 230-31, 257-58.

[7] Ibid., 13, 16-17, 27, 53.

[8] Ibid., 259.

[9] California State Library, California History Section, Vault Gen F 353 Jr, Proclamation appointing Nicholas King Surveyor of the City of Washington, dated 4 March 1803.

[10] LOC, Thomas Jefferson papers, Series 3, District of Columbia Miscellany. The papers include regularly submitted receipts and statements documenting the Capitol's construction progress, signed by John Lenthall on behalf of B. H. Latrobe.

[11] Glenn Brown, *History of the United States Capitol* (Washington: Government Printing Office, 1900), 96. Hereinafter cited as Brown, *History.*

[12] Ibid., 33; Morris, "Owners," 8; Hamlin, *Latrobe,* 260.

[13] Edward C. Carter II, "Benjamin Henry Latrobe and the Growth and Development of Washington, 1798-1818," *Records of the Columbia Historical Society, Washington, D.C.,* 71/72 (1971/72): 128-149.

[14] Brown, *History,* 96.

[15] Morris, "Owners," 20.

[16] Helen Waldo Burnside, *Mrs. Elizabeth J. Stone, Sketch* (Washington, D.C.: Gibson Bros., Printers and Bookbinders, 1893), 3. Hereinafter cited as Burnside, *Sketch.*

[17] Peck, *Round-Shot,* 19, 31.

[18] Hamlin, *Latrobe,* 260, 275-76.

[19] *DAB,* 11:173; Morris, "Owners," 25.

[20] Hornsby MS Docs, transcribed letter, Annette Ives to Miss Morris, 21 September 1926.

[21] Morris, "Owners," 18-20.

[22] Hamlin, *Latrobe,* 276-277, 561. Hamlin reproduced a sketch from Latrobe's letter to Jefferson, showing a section and plan of the Supreme Court vaults to better explain how the altered structural load paths led to their failure.

[23] Brown, *History,* 42.

[24] Hornsby MS Docs, transcribed letter, Annette Ives to Miss Morris, 21 September 1926. Also see Morris, "Owners," 21; Washington *The Evening Star,* 22 November 1884, "An Old Burying Ground." Many years later, John Lenthall Sr.'s body was reinterred in Rock Creek Cemetery where it rests today.

[25] Morris, "Owners," 11, 12; Ehrenberg, "Mapping," 298, 308.

[26] Bryan, *A History,* 1:300.

[27] Ehrenberg, "Mapping," 307-310.

[28] Morris, "Owners," 23.

[29] Fourth Census of the United States (1820), Washington, D.C. Robert King is listed under "Heads of Families" together with entries which, by age and sex, include Widow Jane Lenthall, daughters Mary and Elizabeth, son John and an unidentified girl under ten.

CHAPTER 3 *The War of 1812*

[1] Green, *Washington,* 21, 49.

[2] Brown, *History,* 47.

[3] Virginia Places, "Before the Pentagon, Where Were the Military Headquarters," http://www.virginiaplaces.org/military/beforethepentagon.html, accessed February 2019.

[4] Brown, *History,* 46.

[5] Edward J. Marolda, *The Washington Navy Yard, An Illustrated History* (Washington: The Naval Historical Center, 1999), 3. Hereinafter cited as Marolda, *WNY;* Peck, *Round-Shot,* plate "First Steam Engine in Yard" between 12 and 13, 21.

[6] Donald L. Canney, *Sailing Warships of the U.S. Navy* (Annapolis: Naval Institute Press, 2001), 120-21, 201. Hereinafter cited as Canney, *Sailing Warships.*

[7] Peck, *Round-Shot,* 32-33; Spencer C. Tucker and Frank T. Reuter, *Injured Honor, The Chesapeake-Leopard Affair, 22 June 1807* (Annapolis: Naval Institute Press, 1996), 1-17.

[8] Robert Gardiner, Ed., *The Naval War of 1812* (London: Chatham Publishing, 1998), 9-11. Hereinafter cited as Gardiner, *War of 1812.*

[9] Mark Collins Jenkins and David A. Taylor, *The War of 1812 and the Rise of the U.S. Navy* (Washington, D.C.: National Geographic, 2012), 20-25. Hereinafter cited as Jenkins, *Rise of the USN.*

[10] Donald R. Hickey, *The War of 1812* (Urbana and Chicago: University of Illinois Press, 1989), 46.

[11] Gardiner, *War of 1812,* 22.

[12] Howard I. Chapelle, *The History of the American Sailing Navy* (New York: W. W. Norton & Company, Inc., 1949),118-19. Hereinafter cited as Chapelle, *American Sailing Navy.*

[13] Canney, *Sailing Warships,* 26.

[14] Ibid., 26-29.

[15] Robert Gardiner, *The Heavy Frigate, Eighteen-Pounder Frigates: 1778-1800* (London: Conway Maritime Press, 1994), 61-63. Hereinafter cited as Gardiner, *Heavy Frigate.*

[16] Gardiner, *War of 1812,* 40-43; Andrew Lambert, *The Challenge, Britain Against America in the Naval War of 1812* (London: Faber and Faber Limited, 2012), 75-78. Hereinafter cited as Lambert, *The Challenge.* Also see Jenkins, *Rise of the USN,* 34-41.

[17] Chapelle, *American Sailing Navy,* 252.

[18] Gardiner, *War of 1812,* 46-9; Lambert, *The Challenge,* 94-96; Jenkins, *Rise of the USN,* 42-46.

[19] Gardiner, *War of 1812*, 57-61; Lambert, *The Challenge*, 168-77; Jenkins, *Rise of the USN*, 77-83.

[20] Gardiner, *Heavy Frigate*, 54-57; Larrie D. Ferreiro, *Ships and Science, The Birth of Naval Architecture and the Scientific Revolution, 1600-1800* (Cambridge and London: The MIT Press, 2007), 35. Hereinafter cited as Ferreiro, *Ships and Science*.

[21] Gardiner, *War of 1812*, 141-45.

[22] Anthony S. Pitch, *The Burning of Washington, The British Invasion of 1814* (Annapolis: Naval Institute Press, 1998), 30-85. Hereinafter cited as Pitch, *Burning of Washington*.

[23] Burnside, *Sketch*, 12.

[24] Pitch, *Burning of Washington*, 124-25.

[25] Ibid., 110.

[26] Green, *Washington*, 64-68.

[27] Peck, *Round-Shot*, 66-68; Hamlin, *Latrobe*, 439. This statement must be taken with a healthy grain of salt as the estimates behind it were considered very conservative (for the navy yard) or absurd (for the Capitol and President's House).

[28] Chapelle, *American Sailing Navy*, 303.

[29] Canney, *Sailing Navy*, 87.

[30] Donald L. Canney, *The Old Steam Navy, Volume One, The Frigates, Sloops and Gunboats, 1815-1885* (Annapolis: Naval Institute Press, 1990), 3. Hereinafter cited as Canney, *OSN1*.

[31] Charles Oscar Paullin, *Paullin's History of Naval Administration, 1775-1911* (Annapolis: U.S. Naval Institute, 1968), 165-171. Hereinafter cited as Paullin, *History*. Also see Chapelle, *American Sailing Navy*, 305-307.

[32] Paullin, *History*, 159.

[33] Ibid., 176.

CHAPTER 4 *Apprentice Ship Carpenter*

[1] Burnside, *Sketch*, 7, 12-13.

[2] Ehrenberg, "Mapping," 310.

[3] Hamlin, *Latrobe*, 436, 442, 445.

[4] *Appleton's*, Poussin.

[5] Peck, *Round-Shot*, 11; Hamlin, *Latrobe*, 230.

[6] Genealogy Trails, Washington, D.C., "Captain William Easby, 1791-1854," http://www.genealogytrails.com/washdc/biographies/bio5.html, accessed October 2019. Hereinafter cited as Easby Biography.

[7] Canney, *Sailing Navy*, 95.

[8] Paullin, *History*, 174.

[9] Hamlin, *Latrobe*, 453, 477.

[10] Ehrenberg, "Mapping," 313-16.

[11] Green, *Washington*, 21.

[12] Morris, "Owners," 29-31; Burnside, *Sketch,* 16.

[13] NARA, RG 181, Entry 70, Philadelphia Navy Yard, Payroll of Mechanics and Laborers for April 1823. Also see Independence Seaport Museum, John Lenthall Collection, Thomas Hornsby Collection, Biography of John Lenthall, 1958, 2. An unpublished but well researched manuscript. Hereinafter cited as Hornsby MS.

[14] Chapelle, *American Sailing Navy,* 338-39.

[15] *NCAB,* 26: 387-88.

[16] Independence Seaport Museum, John Lenthall Collection, John Lenthall Library of Books. Hereinafter cited as John Lenthall Collection Books.

[17] Historical Manuscripts, Navy Department Library, ZB folder for John Lenthall, Memorandum for Captain Bennett, 23 May 1923, headed "Army and Navy Register April 1882." The library's introductory biography of Lenthall states that he "learned the trade of ship carpenter at the Washington Navy Yard" which is repeated in a number of folder documents. Hereinafter cited as ZB Folder.

[18] Wilhelmina M. Easby-Smith, "Personal Recollections of Early Washington with a Sketch of the Life of Captain William Easby," *The Association of the Oldest Inhabitants of the District of Columbia* (1913): 10-28. Hereinafter cited as Easby-Smith, "Recollections."

[19] U.S. Naval Academy Museum, Ives Collection, FICm.008.0370 (237-DSC-0325), Samuel Humphreys to John Rodgers, 3 October 1828. Hereinafter cited as Ives Collection, with relevant document references of the museum number and (photo number). This collection contains hundreds of John Lenthall's letters, documents and other personal papers and is a priceless resource for researchers of Lenthall's life. Other sources that state Lenthall served his apprenticeship at Philadelphia are *NCAB,* 26:387-88; Hornsby MS, 2-4; and *DAB,* 11:173.

[20] *NCAB,* 26:387-88; *DAB,* 11:173; Chapelle, *American Sailing Navy,* 353-54; Hornsby MS Docs, transcribed letter, Annette Ives to Miss Morris, 21 September 1926; *ANJ,* "Recent Deaths," 19 (1882): 834.

[21] Edwin L. Dunbaugh and William duBarry Thomas, *William H. Webb, Shipbuilder* (Glen Cove, NY: Webb Institute of Naval Architecture, 1989), 7. Hereinafter cited as Dunbaugh and Thomas, *Webb.*

[22] Genealogy Trails, Washington, D.C., "District of Columbia, Apprenticeship Indentures and Related Documents," http://www.genealogytrails.com/washdc/apprenticedocuments/apprenticeintro.html, accessed October 2019. Hereinafter cited as Apprentice Documents.

[23] Dorothy S. Provine, *District of Columbia Indentures of Apprenticeship, 1801-1893* (Willow Bend Books, 1998).

[24] Historical Manuscripts, Navy Department Library, George W. Much Collection, "Agreement to Apprentice G. W. Much to John Lenthall, Naval Constructor, Philada. May 20, 1839." Hereinafter cited as Much Collection.

[25] Chapelle, *American Sailing Navy,* 277-78, 284, 303, 338-39; Canney, *Sailing Warships,* 52, 87-88.

[26] Chapelle, *American Sailing Navy,* 354.

[27] Hampton L. Carson, "Samuel Humphreys, Chief Constructor of the United States," *The Pennsylvania Magazine of History and Biography,* 8 No. 2 (1884): 216-222. Hereinafter cited as Carson, "Humphreys Constructor."

[28] Geni, "Samuel Humphreys, naval architect," https://www.geni.com/people/samuel-humphreys-naval-architect, accessed September 2019.

[29] Judah Delano, *Washington Directory* (Washington: William Duncan, 1832), 49, 52, 74.

[30] Find A Grave, "William Wade," https://findagrave.com/memorial/33355568/william-wade, accessed November 2021.

CHAPTER 5 *The Philadelphia Navy Yard*

[1] Jeffery M. Dorwart with Jean K. Wolf, *The Philadelphia Navy Yard* (Philadelphia: University of Pennsylvania Press, 2001), 46-47. Hereinafter cited as Dorwart, *PNY.*

[2] Ibid., 55-57.

[3] Henry M. Vallette, "History and Reminiscences of the Philadelphia Navy Yard," *Potter's American Monthly, an Illustrated Magazine of History, Literature, Science and Art,* 6/7 (1876): fourth paper, 256. Hereinafter cited as Vallette, "Reminiscences."

[4] Dorwart, *PNY,* 62-64.

[5] *ANJ,* "Recent Deaths," 19 (1882): 834.

[6] Dorwart, *PNY,* 62. See the detailed inset of the plan of the navy yard's layout.

[7] Gail E. Farr and Brett F. Bostwick, *John Lenthall Naval Architect, A Guide to Plans and Drawings of American Naval and Merchant Vessels 1790-1874* (Philadelphia Maritime Museum, 1991), Brig, FI L90.43.59. Hereinafter cited as Farr and Bostwick, *Guide.*

[8] Canney, *Sailing Navy,* 200.

[9] Russel F. Weigley, Ed., *Philadelphia, A 300-Year History* (New York and London: W. W. Norton & Company, 1982), 3-154. Hereinafter cited as Weighley, *Philadelphia.* Also see J. Thomas Scharf and Thompson Westcott, *History of Philadelphia, 1609-1884* (Philadelphia: L. H. Everts & Co., 1884), 3:2337. Hereinafter cited as Scharf, *History.* Also see Canney, *Sailing Navy,* 17.

[10] Weigley, *Philadelphia,* 205, 214-15, 237; Scharf, *History,* 3:2338.

[11] Weigley, *Philadelphia,* 238-40; Scharf, *History,* 3:2337; Canney, *Sailing Navy,* 108-09.

[12] Weigley, *Philadelphia,* 208-257.

[13] Ives Collection, FICm.002.0001 (242-DSC-1568), American Philosophical Society 100th anniversary circular, 31 March 1843, with an invitation to John Lenthall to present an "Account of the Launch of the Pennsylvania."

[14] Franklin Institute, Faculty Correspondence and Reports 1826 folder, Address of the Committee of Instruction, High School Department.

[15] *ANJ,* "Recent Deaths," 19 (1882): 834.

[16] Bruce Sinclair, *Philadelphia's Philosopher Mechanics, A History of the Franklin Institute, 1824-1865* (Baltimore and London: The Johns Hopkins University Press, 1974), 31-33, 39, 120-29. Hereinafter cited as Sinclair, *Phil Mech.* William H. Wahl, *The Franklin Institute ..., A Sketch of its Organization and History* (Philadelphia: Franklin Institute, 1895), 25-26. Hereinafter cited as Wahl, *Franklin Institute.* Also see Hornsby MS, 3. Hornsby suggests Lenthall attended the high school's full-time courses. The author's search of the Franklin Institute's archives, 14 May 2019, found no documentation of course enrollments but rich anecdotal accounts of its classes.

[17] Carson, "Humphreys Constructor," 216-222.

[18] Vallette, "Reminiscences," fifth paper, 329-30.

[19] Chapelle, *American Sailing Navy,* 353.

[20] *A General Register of the Navy and Marine Corps of the United States.* U.S. government publication, 1827. Hereinafter cited as *Navy Register,* year of issue.

[21] John Lenthall Collection Books.

[22] Ehrenberg, "Mapping," 313.

[23] Ives Collection. FICm.008.0209 (241-DSC-1404), John Rodgers to all whom it may concern, 20 April 1830.

[24] Ibid., FICm.008.0370 (237-DSC-0325), Samuel Humphreys to Commodore John Rodgers, 3 October 1828.

[25] Chapelle, *American Sailing Navy,* 354.

CHAPTER 6 *The Science of Naval Architecture*

[1] Hornsby MS, 4; Chapelle, *American Sailing Navy,* 359; Canney, *Sailing Warships,* 136-37.

[2] Peck, *Round-Shot,* 92.

[3] Genealogy Trails, Washington, D.C., "Washington Navy Yard Employees in April 1829," http://www.genealogytrails.com/washdc/WNY/wny1829aprlemployees.html, accessed October 2019. A listing of the Washington Navy Yard's April 1829 employees.

[4] Ives Collection, FIC.2018.015 (245-DSC-2828), John Murray to John Lenthall, 12 January 1830.

[5] Hornsby MS, 4. Hornsby says that in this period, Lenthall designed the 55 ft long shallop *Stafford* for Denny Vermilion for use on the Potomac and Chesapeake Bay.

[6] Chapelle, *American Sailing Navy,* 360-61; Canney, *Sailing Warships,* 81-82.

[7] Independence Seaport Museum, John Lenthall Collection, John Lenthall Personal Papers Collection, Macedonian (USS) Razee 1851-53. Hereinafter cited as Lenthall Personal Papers, subject.

[8] Jorge Juan y Santacilia, *Examen Maritimo ...* , 2 Vols. (Madrid: Manuel de Mena, 1771). Hereinafter cited as Santacilia, *Examen.* Also see Ferreiro, *Ships and Science,* 256.

[9] Pierre Bouguer, *Traité du Navire, de sa Construction, et de ses Mouvemens* (Paris: Charles-Antoine Jombert, 1746). Hereinafter cited as Bouguer, *Traité*. Fredrik Henrik af Chapman, *Tractat om Skepps-byggeriet* ... (Stockholm: Johan Pfeffer, 1775). Hereinafter cited as Chapman, *Tractat*.

[10] Chapelle, *American Sailing Navy*, 417, 436.

[11] George S. Atwood and M. Vail de Clairbois, "A Disquisition on the Stability of Ships," *Philosophical Transactions of the Royal Society of London*, 88 (1798): 201-310. Hereinafter cited as Atwood, "Disquisition."

[12] Bouguer, *Traité*; Chapman, *Tractat*; Santacilia, *Examen*; Ferreiro, *Ships and Science*, 262-66, 272-78.

[13] Ferreiro, *Ships and Science*, ix, 25-29, 46-58, 217-219. Ferreiro's book admirably documents the lives and work of the early pioneers of naval architecture.

[14] Ibid., 26; Robert Gardiner, Ed., *The Line of Battle, The Sailing Warship 1650-1840* (London: Conway Maritime Press Ltd, 1992), 17-18.

[15] *JFI*, "List of Books Added to the Library during April, May and June, 1883," 116 No. 1 (July 1883): 74-80. An English translation of Chapman's treatise is listed on p. 75 but today is not among Lenthall's books. Larrie Ferreiro provided insight into how rare Bouguer's book was.

[16] Hornsby MS Docs, transcribed letter, Annette Ives to Miss Morris, 21 Sept 1926; Morris, "Owners," 25.

[17] *ANJ*, "Recent Deaths," 19 (1882): 834.

[18] Ives Collection, FICm.007.0131 (240-DSC-1294), John Lenthall to POTUS, 20 April 1830.

[19] Hornsby MS, 5. Hornsby suggests that Humphreys had made such a visit early in his career, but at the time of writing, this has not been independently corroborated.

[20] Ferreiro, *Ships and Science*, 238. An overview of Duhamel du Monceau's book is provided. Also see Farr and Bostwick, *Guide*, 46, for a sampling of Romme's book.

[21] Ives Collection, FICm.007.0005 (240-DSC-1285), John Gardiner to Dr. John Walker, 18 April 1830. Original letter.

[22] Ibid., FICm.001.0038 (240-DSC-1287), John Anderson to Hon William P. Preble, 19 April 1830. Original letter.

[23] Ibid., FICm.007.0131 (240-DSC-1294), John Lenthall to POTUS, 20 April 1830. Copy of letter.

[24] Ibid., FICm.018.0209 (241-DSC-1404), John Rodgers to all whom it may concern, 20 April 1830. Original letter.

[25] Ibid., FICm.022.0010 A (241-DSC-1405), J. J. D'Lagnel to Alf d'Lagnel and M. Van Buren to Louis McLane, 21 April 1830. Copy of letters.

[26] Ibid., FICm.022.0010 B (241-DSC-1406), M. Van Buren to W. C. Rives, Louis Goldsborough to Isaac Cox Barnett, 21 April 1830. Copy of letters.

[27] Ibid., FICm.008.0007 (240-DSC-1288), John H. Hall to Hon. Wm. Pitt Preble. Lenthall's King cousin, Susan, was married to Major Wade. Copy of letter.

[28] Ibid., FICm.022.0010 C (241-DSC-1407), Brig. Gen. Bernard to Col. Laire, Brig. Gen. Bernard to Col. Bagére, 29 April 1830. Copy of letters.

[29] Ibid., FICm.022.0010 D (241-DSC-1408), Poussin to M. Debrotournie, Maj. William Tell Poussin to M. Guerard, 1 May 1830. Copy of letters.

[30] Ibid., FICm.002.0460 (240-DSC-1289), G. Bomford to Hyde de Neuville, 15 July 1830. May be a copy of letter.

[31] Ibid., FICm.004.0280 (240-DSC-1291), Chas Varthaus to Franz Diederich, 23 July 1830. Original letter.

[32] Ibid., FICm.007.0130 (240-DSC-1292), C. Gratiot to Adm. Jurien, 1 August 1830. May be a copy of letter.

[33] John V. Quarstein and Dennis Mroczkowski, *Fortress Monroe, The Key to the South* (Charleston, etc.: Arcadia Publishing, 2000), 13.

[34] *Appleton's,* Poussin.

[35] The author's thanks to Larrie Ferreiro for clarifying the roles of the D'Lagnel brothers and other French players.

[36] Morris, "Owners," 23.

[37] Ives Collection, FICm.005.0050 (241-DSC-1402), H. Eckford to John Lenthall, 10 March 1831.

CHAPTER 7 *European Dockyard Tour*

[1] Ives Collection, FICm.008.0040 (240-DSC-1281), Robert Hunter to W. C. Rives, 11 July 1832; Hornsby MS, 6.

[2] Howard I. Chapelle, *The Search for Speed Under Sail, 1700-1855* (New York: W. W. Norton & Company, Inc., 1967), 258-260. Hereinafter cited as Chapelle, *Search for Speed.*

[3] Ibid.

[4] Ives Collection, FICm.013.0098 (239-DSC-1163), Thos. D. Watter to John Lenthall, 6 September 1831.

[5] Hornsby MS., 7, n. 29.

[6] Ives Collection, FICm.012.0264 (241-DSC-1376), John Lenthall to the Board of Naval Commissioners, 25 March 1835.

[7] Ibid., FICm.012.0318 (240-DSC-1295), Pass ticket issued to John Lenthall for departure from Russia, 10 October 1831.

[8] Ives Collection, FICm.008.0040 (240-DSC-1281), Robert Hunter to W. C. Rives, 11 July 1832. Hunter introduces Lenthall, in mid-1832, as having already visited dockyards in Russia, Denmark and England, and now desiring to do the same in France.

[9] Ives Collection, FICm.001.008 (236-DSC-0147), M. King to John Lenthall, 31 December 1831 through 8 January 1832. Lenthall descendants refer to "the step-mother Mrs. Margaret King" in connection with Scarborough, adding some confusion as to the identity of Aunt Margaret King.

[10] Ibid., FICm.019.0181 (241-DSC-1410), Leon Simpson to John Lenthall, 2 February 1832. This letter, mentioning Lenthall's recent stay, was addressed to him in Chesterfield.

[11] Hornsby MS Docs, transcribed letter, Annette Ives to Miss Morris, 14 November 1926. The Lenthall relatives' letters in the Ives Collection confirm the descendants' claim.

[12] Ives Collection, FICm.023.0354 (240-DSC-1301), Mr. Wood to John Lenthall, 25 May 1832.

[13] Lieutenant Thomas Gedney served on the Coast Survey. In 1835 he discovered Gedney Channel, leading into New York's harbor. Four years later, while in command of the brig *Washington,* he intercepted the Spanish schooner *Amistad* off Long Island, provoking the celebrated trial which led to the liberation of her former slaves.

[14] Ives Collection, FICm.012.0211 (240-DSC-1305-06), Libby Stone to John Lenthall, 11 January 1831 [actually 1832].

[15] Ibid., FICm.012.0519 (239-DSC-1167), Mary Lenthall to John Lenthall, 2 September 1831.

[16] Philip MacDougall, *Royal Dockyards* (Newton, London, North Pomfret, VT: David & Charles (Publishers) Limited, 1982), 124-55. Hereinafter cited as MacDougall, *Dockyards.*

[17] Farr and Bostwick, *Guide,* 20, FI L90.43.72-75.

[18] David Lyon and Rif Winfield, *The Sail & Steam Navy List, All the Ships of the Royal Navy 1815-1889* (London: Chatham Publishing, 2004), 158. Hereinafter cited as Lyon and Winfield, *Navy List.*

[19] Ives Collection, FICm.008.0040 (240-DSC-1281), Robert Hunter to W. C. Rives, 11 July 1832.

[20] Ibid., FICm.013.0098 (239-DSC-1163), Thos. D. Watter to John Lenthall, 6 September 1831.

[21] Ibid., FICm.008.0399 (239-DSC-1159), Robert Hunter to John Lenthall., 3 October 1832. This letter, first sent to the U.S. consul in Paris, was forwarded to Lenthall at Rue de Fosse M. Le Prince, chez Mme. Potel.

[22] *Life of Henry Wadsworth Longfellow,* Samuel Longfellow, Ed. (Boston and New York: Houghton, Mifflin and Company, The Riverside Press, Cambridge, 1891), 1:79-80.

[23] Ives Collection, FICm.019.0305 (239-DSC-1153), Chas. Stewart to John Lenthall, 8 March 1833; Ibid., FICm.012.0731 (239-DSC-1155), Thos. M. Logan to John Lenthall, 30 May 1833.

[24] *ANJ,* "Recent Deaths," 19 (1882): 834.

[25] Etienne Taillemite, "Les archives et le archivists de la Marine des origins à 1870," *Bibliothèque de l'école des chartes,* 127, 1 (1969): 27-89.

[26] Farr and Bostwick, *Guide.*

[27] Patrick Berry, *The Dockyards, Shipyards, and Marine of France* (London: Sampson Low, Son and Marsden, 1864), 37-55, 69-87, 143-162.

[28] Dominique Brisou, *Accueil, introduction et développement de l'énergie vapeur dans la Marine militaire française au XIXe siècle* (Vincennes: Service Historique de la Marine, 2001), 2:423; Rif Winfield and Stephen S. Roberts, *French Warships in the Age of Sail 1786-1861* (Barnsley: Seaforth Publishing, 2015), 318-19. Hereinafter cited as Winfield and Roberts, *French Warships.*

29 Lenthall Personal Papers, Naval Ship Design & Specifications, Letter from John Lenthall to Commodore Morris, 16 July 1835. Written two months after he was hired by the Navy as a master builder, Lenthall's self-promoting three-page letter presented details of *Crocodile*'s trials that could have only been known to an eye-witness.

30 Ives Collection, FICm.012.0468 (240-DSC-1309), Invitation for 4th of July gathering, 22 June 1833.

31 Ibid., FICm.004.0146 (241-DSC-1440), De La Morinièrè to M. Alexandre, 12 July 1833.

32 Ibid., FICm.012.0467 (240-DSC-1311), Marine Royale Lorient, 22 July 1833.

33 Ibid., FICm.022.0001 (240-DSC-1282), A. Vail to John Lenthall, 2 January 1834.

34 McDougall, *Dockyards*, 132-34.

35 Ives Collection, FICm.019.0306 (241-DSC-1369-70), C. Stewart to John Lenthall, 28 March 1834. This is the same Charles Stewart that tagged Lenthall an "artiste mechanique."

BOOK TWO *Constructor*

CHAPTER 8 *Board of Navy Commissioners*

1 Ives Collection, FICm.023.0004 (239-DSC-1157), Susan K. Wade to John Lenthall, 8 November 1832. Cousin Susan reacted to an enclosed photo of Lenthall, "So you flourish a huge pair of whiskers!"

2 Paullin, *History*, 168-173.

3 NARA, RG 45, Entry 310, Chauncey to Lenthall, 14 October 1834.

4 Ibid., Entry 317, Humphreys to Rodgers, 4 October 1834.

5 Ibid., Entry 310, Rodgers to Lenthall, 6 October 1834.

6 Ibid., Entry 312, from John Lenthall, 10 October 1834.

7 Ibid., Entry 310, Chauncey to Lenthall, 14 October 1834.

8 Ives Collection, FICm.030.0127 (240-DSC-1284), Chauncey to Humphreys, 16 October 1834.

9 Ibid., FICm.008.0371 (240-DSC-1312), Humphreys to Lenthall, 17 October 1834.

10 Hornsby MS, 10.

11 Ibid.; NARA, RG 45, E 312, from John Lenthall, 21 October 1834.

12 Historical Manuscripts, Navy Department Library, Work Records of the 1830's of the Moulding Loft at the Washington Navy Yard under Commandant Daniel T. Patterson. Hereinafter cited as WNY Mould Loft Logs.

13 Canney, *Sailing Warships*, 200-203.

14 Theodore D. Wilson, *An Outline of Ship Building, Theoretical and Practical* (New York: John Wiley & Son, 1873), 146. Hereinafter cited as Wilson, *Ship Building*.

15 Basil Greenhill and Sam Manning, *The Evolution of the Wooden Ship* (New York: Facts on File, Inc., 1988), 122-25. This book is told from the English shipbuilding perspective, but gives excellent illustrations of the use of moulds and bevelling boards.

16 Wilson, *Ship Building*, 149.

[17] WNY Mould Loft Logs, 12 November 1834.

[18] Chapelle, *American Sailing Navy*, 352-53.

[19] WNY Mould Loft Logs, 22 and 31 October 1834.

[20] NARA, RG 45, E 317, Humphreys to Rodgers, 19 November 1834.

[21] Ives Collection, FICm.008.0358 (241-DSC-1373), Hull to Lenthall, 9 December 1834.

[22] WNY Mould Loft Logs, 17 November 1834, 25 December 1834, 9 February 1835.

[23] NARA, RG 45, E 317, Lenthall to Humphreys, 19 February 1835; Ibid, Humphreys to Rodgers, 23 February 1835.

[24] WNY Mould Loft Logs, 24 February 1835; NARA, RG 45, E 317, Lenthall to Humphreys, 26 February 1835; Ibid., Humphreys to Rodgers, 26 February 1835.

[25] Ives Collection, FICm.013.0500 (241-DSC-1374), John Murray to John Lenthall, 20 January 1835.

[26] *Navy Register*, 1827-1835; Chapelle, *American Sailing Navy*, 353-55.

[27] See Appendix 12, entries for Samuel Humphreys, Francis Grice and Samuel Hartt.

[28] NARA, RG 45, E 312, from Samuel Humphreys, 10 March 1835; Hornsby MS, 11.

[29] Ives Collection, FICm.012.0264 (241-DSC-1376), John Lenthall to Commo. Rodgers, 25 March 1835; NARA, RG 45, E 312, from John Lenthall, 25 March 1835.

[30] Chapelle, *American Sailing Navy*, 385.

[31] Ives Collection, FICm.018.0194 (241-DSC-1401), Commo. Rodgers to Samuel Humphreys, 28 April 1835; NARA, RG 45, E 317, Humphreys to Rodgers, 28 April 1835.

[32] Ives Collection., FICm.018.0193 (240-DSC-1283), Commo. Rodgers to John Lenthall, 28 April 1835; NARA, RG 45, E 312, from John Lenthall, 28 April 1835; Hornsby MS, 12.

[33] Ives Collection., FICm.018.0192 (241-DSC-1377), Commo. Rodgers to John Lenthall, 1 May 1835; NARA, RG 45, E 310, Rodgers to Lenthall, 1 May 1835.

CHAPTER 9 *Master Builder*

[1] Vallette, "Reminiscences," fifth paper, 332; Scharf, *History*, 3:2340; Dorwart, *PNY*, 69.

[2] ZB Folder, letter by Captain D. W. Knox to Thomas Hornsby, 6 March 1940.

[3] *Navy Register*, 1835, 1836, 1841.

[4] Paul H. Silverstone, *The Sailing Navy, 1775-1854* (Annapolis: Naval Institute Press, 2001), 62-63. Hereinafter cited as Silverstone, *Sailing Navy*.

[5] Chapelle, *American Sailing Navy*, 385-89. *Relief*'s dimensions are from Lenthall's work cited in Appendix 2 and differ from Chapelle's, especially for depth of hold.

[6] NARA, RG 45, E 312, from Samuel Humphreys, 12, 19, 21 and 22 May 1835.

[7] Lenthall Personal Papers, Relief (USS) Store Ship 1835, "Directions for building Store Ship."

[8] Ibid., Macedonian (USS) Razee 1851-53, "General Instructions for Building Frigates of the ~~First~~ 2nd Class." Lenthall signed his copy, marking on it "as built in 1831."

[9] Farr and Bostwick, *Guide*, 21.

[10] Lenthall Personal Papers, Relief (USS) Store Ship 1835, "Calculations of Store Ship 'Relief' built at Phila 1836," "Calculation of Metacenter."

[11] Ives Collection, FICm.012.0218 (244-DSC-2636), Wm. Easby to John Lenthall, 7 June 1835.

[12] Frank M. Bennett, *The Steam Navy of the United States* (Pittsburg: Warren & Co., Publishers, 1896), 16. Hereinafter cited as Bennett, *Steam Navy.* Also see Canney, *OSN1*, 7.

[13] Paolo E. Coletta, Ed., *American Secretaries of the Navy, 1775-1913* (Annapolis: Naval Institute Press, 1980), 1:155-63. Hereinafter cited as Coletta, *Secretaries.*

[14] Canney, *OSN1*, 4; Bennett, *Steam Navy*, 17.

[15] Winfield and Roberts, *French Warships*, 315-18.

[16] Lyon and Winfield, *Navy List*, 148-49, 158.

[17] NARA, RG 45, E 310, Morris and Chauncey to Humphreys and Lenthall, 9 July 1835.

[18] Chapelle, *American Sailing Navy*, 457.

[19] Canney, *OSN1*, 7.

[20] Lenthall Personal Papers, Fulton (USS) Seagoing Steamer 1837, 1850-57. "Called for by Commissioners July 9th 1835."

[21] Ibid., "Probable Cost of Hull July/35."

[22] NARA, RG 45, E 310, Morris and Chauncey to Lenthall, 13 July 1835.

[23] Ibid., E 312, Steamer report from Samuel Humphreys, 14 July 1835.

[24] Canney, *OSN1*, 7-11; Bennett, *Steam Navy*, 7-28. Canney provides a good account of the interactions between the board and the committee as well as a summary of the committee's recommendations.

[25] Lenthall Personal Papers, Naval Ship Design & Specifications, Letter by John Lenthall to Commodore Morris, 16 July 1835.

[26] Ives Collection, FICm.012.0736 (241-DSC-1384), Octavius Longworth to John Lenthall, 9 December 1835.

[27] Franklin Institute, Minutes of Board of Directors, June 9, 1831 to January 18, 1848, 148, 151.

[28] NARA, RG 45, E 310, Rodgers to Lenthall, 15 January 1836.

[29] Ives Collection, FICm.022.0245 (244-DSC-2614), Samuel Barton to John Lenthall, 25 March 1836.

[30] NARA, RG 45, E 312, from John Lenthall, 6 April 1836; Ives Collection, FICm.004.0095 (239-DSC-1151), John Davis to John Lenthall, 19 April 1836.

[31] NARA, RG 45, E 312, from Samuel Humphreys, 21 May 1836.

[32] Vallette, "Reminiscences," eighth paper, 108.

[33] Dorwart, *PNY*, 69.

[34] Naval History and Heritage Command, "Dictionary of American Naval Fighting Ships (DANFS), "Relief I (Store Ship)," https://www.history.navy.mil/research/histories/ship-histories/danfs/r/relief-i.html, accessed September 2019.

CHAPTER 10 *Life in Philadelphia*

[1] Chapelle, *American Sailing Navy,* 354-55.

[2] Hornsby MS Docs, typewritten untitled list of ships designed by or associated with John Lenthall. Hornsby's work reflects much meticulous examination of official records.

[3] Carl C. Cutler, *Queens of the Western Oceans* (Annapolis: United States Naval Institute, 1961), 397, 469. Hereinafter cited as Cutler, *Queens.*

[4] Farr and Bostwick, *Guide,* 21. One drawing of *Georgiana* is listed, a sheer and half breadth plan.

[5] Scharf, *History,* 3:2253, 2255-56.

[6] Augustus C. Buell, *The Memoirs of Charles H. Cramp* (Philadelphia and London: Lippincott Company, 1906), 44. Hereinafter cited as Buell, *Cramp.*

[7] David Budlong Tyler, *The American Clyde* (The University of Delaware Press, 1958), 4, 5.

[8] City of Philadelphia, "Trustees of Ice Boats," https://www.phila.gov/phils/docs/inventor/graphics/archser/S153.htm, accessed November 2021.

[9] Weighley, *Philadelphia,* 270.

[10] Farr and Bostwick, *Guide,* 22; Lenthall Personal Papers, City of Philadelphia Ice Boat 1837. The three drawings are a sheer and half breadth plan, fore and aft body plans and a scale of tonnage.

[11] Lenthall Personal Papers, City of Philadelphia Ice Boat 1837, letter by Lewis Paleski to John Lenthall, 14 May 1837. On a single sheet of folio foolscap, Paleski provided directions for building, specifying the size and material for the ice boat's principal scantling and planking.

[12] Ives Collection, FICm.001.0022 (241-DSC-1380), Wm. Alexander to John Lenthall, 16 December 1836. Alexander's letter is addressed to Lenthall at 318 So. Front St. Also see Hornsby MS, 12, who credits Lenthall's address to an unspecified 1840 city directory.

[13] Hornby MS, 16; Ives Collection, FICm.005.0044 (241-DSC-1390), Joseph Eck to John Lenthall, 14 August 1838. Hornsby says 1835, Eck's letter confirms 1838.

[14] Mary D. Lenthall née Eck died in 1872 and was buried in Washington's Mount Olivet Cemetery. Her headstone gives her age at death as sixty, which yields the birth year of 1812. However, Ancestry suggests that Mary Dugan Eck was born in 1809.

[15] Morris, "Owners," 26.

[16] Ives Collection, FICm.003.0081 (243-DSC-2517-18), Mary A. Cavenaugh to Mary King Lenthall, 16 November 1874. This letter from an old Philadelphia friend of the Eck family gives a good thumbnail sketch of the family's early history.

[17] See the Find A Grave website entries listed in the bibliography for John Peter Eck, Catherine Eck and John Joseph Eck.

[18] Ives Collection. Dozens of letters from Lenthall, his wife and their in-laws are devoid of any mention of their religious differences.

[19] Hornsby MS Docs, transcribed letter, Annette Ives to Miss Morris, 14 November 1926; Morris, "Owners," 26.

[20] Ives Collection, FICm.005.0048 (234-DSC-9472), Indenture, Elenor Daly to Mary D. Eck, 24 February 1837.

[21] Clues offering a glimpse into the discrepancy of Mary Eck's place of residence lie in a number of letters in the Ives Collection to her, her mother and John Lenthall during this same period, the late 1830s. All four are addressed to 318 So. Front Street, which suggests the possibility that Lenthall may have been a boarder in the Eck's now largely empty home. This would also explain how they met and later came to marry.

[22] United States Department of State, Office of the Historian, "Daniel Carroll Brent (1770-1841)," https://history.state.gov/departmenthistory/people/brent-daniel-carroll, accessed July 2020.

[23] Ives Collection, FICm.002.0572 (237-DSC-0324), Daniel Brent to John Lenthall, 22 November 1836.

[24] Ibid., FICm.002.0571 (241-DSC-1375), Daniel Brent to John Lenthall, 21 March 1835.

CHAPTER 11 *Launch of Pennsylvania*

[1] ARSN, 1836, 441.

[2] ZB Folder, letter by Captain D. W. Knox to Thomas Hornsby, 6 March 1940.

[3] Lyon and Winfield, *Navy List*, 88-89; Canney, *Sailing Warships*, 109.

[4] Chapelle, *American Sailing Navy*, 374.

[5] Elijah Baker III, *Introduction to Steel Shipbuilding* (New York, etc.: McGraw-Hill Book Company, Inc., 1953), 225-38. Hereinafter cited as Baker, *Introduction.* Although the book's title implies steel ships, Baker's discussion of the factors affecting a ship's launch are equally applicable to wooden vessels.

[6] ZB Folder, John Rodgers to James Barron, 10 February 1837.

[7] Canney, *Sailing Warshps*, 110.

[8] Lenthall Personal Papers, Pennsylvania (USS) Ship of the Line 1838, "Orders to be Observed," 7 June 1837 and "In Describing the Launch," undated.

[9] Ibid. This account together with those that follow in this chapter were extracted from Lenthall's "In Describing the Launch."

[10] Lenthall Personal Papers, Pennsylvania (USS) Ship of the Line 1838, "Notes on Tide in Delaware at Phila ...," undated.

[11] *Principles of Naval Architecture*, John P. Comstock, Ed. (New York: The Society of Naval Architects and Marine Engineers, 1967), 762. Hereinafter cited as *PNA.*

[12] Baker, *Introduction*, 225-34; *PNA*, 752-64.

[13] Vallette, "Reminiscences," eighth paper, 109.

[14] Canney, *Sailing Navy*, 29.

[15] Baker, *Introduction*, 230-31.

[16] Dorwart, *PNY*, 39.

[17] Ives Collection, FICm.002.0001 (242-DSC-1568), American Philosophical Society 100th anniversary circular, 31 March 1843, with an invitation to John Lenthall to present an "Account of the Launch of the Pennsylvania."

[18] Peter J. Guthorn, *United States Coastal Charts, 1783-1861* (Exton, PA: Schiffer Publishing Limited, 1984), 18-19; Sinclair, *Phil Mech*, 149-52.

[19] John Lenthall, "On the Launching of the Three-deck Ship, the Pennsylvania in 1837," *Proceedings of the American Philosophical Society*, 3 No. 27 (1843): 103-4.

[20] ZB Folder, Isaac Chauncey to John Lenthall, 24 July 1837.

[21] NARA, RG 45, E 312, from John Lenthall, 25 September 1837.

[22] Lenthall Personal Papers, Fulton (USS) Seagoing Steamer 1837, 1850-57, Letter by Isaac Chauncey to Samuel Humphreys, 30 August 1837.

[23] Hornsby MS, 17.

CHAPTER 12 *Naval Constructor*

[1] Chapelle, *American Sailing Navy*, 353.

[2] *DAB*, 11:173.

[3] ZB Folder, Isaac Chauncey to Charles Stewart, 17 January 1838.

[4] Ibid., Isaac Chauncey to John Lenthall, 2 February 1838.

[5] Ibid., Isaac Chauncey to Samuel Humphreys, 2 February 1838.

[6] *Navy Register*, 1844, 1848; ZB Folder, letter by Captain. D. W. Knox to Thomas Hornsby, 6 March 1940.

[7] Ives Collection, FICm.003.0133 (241-DSC-1388), Isaac Chauncey to John Lenthall, 6 March 1838.

[8] Chapelle, *American Sailing Navy*, 418-19.

[9] Ibid., 400-02, 421; Canney, *Sailing Warships*, 142; Silverstone, *Sailing Navy*, 42.

[10] Chapelle, *American Sailing Navy*, 400-02.

[11] Ibid., 403, *Figure 113. Building draught for the 16-gun ship sloops, 1838.*

[12] Canney, *Sailing Warships*, 201; Silverstone, *Sailing Navy*, 42.

[13] Howard I. Chapelle, *The History of American Sailing Ships* (New York: W.W. Norton & Company, Inc., 1935), 118.

[14] Canney, *Sailing Warships*, 142-146; Chapelle, *American Sailing Navy*, 402; Silverstone, *Sailing Navy*, 42-43.

[15] Hornsby MS, 20; Hornsby MS Docs, extensive notes on "Merchant vessels designed by John Lenthall." Independent confirmation that Lenthall designed *Clarion* has not been found.

[16] Lenthall Personal Papers, Clarion, Barque 1841, two pages documenting the results of *Clarion*'s steam trials dated 8 June 1841.

[17] Cedric Ridgely-Nevitt, *American Steamships on the Atlantic* (Newark: The University of Delaware Press, 1981), 83-86. Hereinafter cited as Ridgely-Nevitt, *Steamships*.

[18] Ibid.

[19] Charles Oscar Paullin, *Commodore John Rodgers* (Annapolis: United States Naval Institute, 1967), 396-97.

[20] Ancestry, "Jane Lenthall," https://www.ancestry.com/genealogy/records/jane-lenthall_30285466, accessed November 2017. See Age 58—Return Home.

[21] Ives Collection, FICm.012.0369 (240-DSC-1233), Margaret King to Mary Lenthall, 7 April 1853.

[22] Ibid., FICm.012.0370 (240-DSC-1221), Margaret King to Mary K. Lenthall, 7 March 1859.

CHAPTER 13 *The Sea Steamers*

[1] *United States Statutes at Large*, 25th Cong., 3rd Sess., 1839, Ch. 95, 364; Chapelle, *American Sailing Navy*, 413; Canney, *OSN1*, 11.

[2] Canney, *OSN1*, 11.

[3] "Washington, 15 April," *Richmond Enquirer*, 26 April 1837, as reported from the *National Intelligencer*.

[4] Lenthall Personal Papers, Fulton (USS) Seagoing Steamer 1837, 1850-57, letter by Isaac Chauncey to Samuel Humphreys, Samuel Hartt and John Lenthall, 11 April 1839.

[5] ZB Folder, Isaac Chauncey to John Lenthall, 16 May 1839.

[6] Much Collection, "Agreement to Apprentice G. W. Much to John Lenthall, Naval Constructor, Philada. May 20, 1839." Also see Appendix 12, George Much.

[7] "Board of Engineers and Naval Constructors," *Richmond Enquirer*, 7 June 1839, as reported from the *Army & Navy Chronicle*.

[8] Canney, *OSN1*, 11.

[9] Compiled from various sources, Chapelle, *American Sailing Navy*; Canney, *Sailing Warships*; Canney, *OSN1*; and Silverstone, *Sailing Navy*.

[10] Canney, *OSN1*, 12.

[11] Ibid.; Ridgely-Nevitt, *Steamships*, 105-106.

[12] Canney, *OSN1*, 12, 15; Winfield and Roberts, *French Warships*, 318, General Arrangement of *Sphinx*. With the notable exception of her violin-shaped hull, the similarities between this ship and *Mississippi* are too numerous to be a coincidence. Lenthall likely brought copies of her drawings back to America.

[13] Silverstone, *Sailing Navy*, 73.

[14] Vallette, "Reminiscences," eighth paper, 110; Canney, *Sailing Warships*, 201.

[15] Bennett, *Steam Navy*, 36.

[16] Dorwart, *PNY*, 70-73.

[17] Canney, *OSN1*, 11-12.

[18] Farr and Bostwick, *Guide*, 8; Ives Collection, FIC.2018.012 (245-DSC-2824), John Lenthall to Mary Eck, 29 February 1840. Lenthall's letter was written from Norfolk.

[19] Ives Collection, FICm.001.0083 (242-DSC-1582), Various builders to John Lenthall, 12 October 1842.

[20] Coletta, *Secretaries*, 1:174.

[21] Canney, *OSN1*, 168; Silverstone, *Sailing Navy*, 73; Vallette, "Reminiscences," eighth paper, 110.

[22] Lenthall Personal Papers, Clarion, Barque 1841, two pages documenting the results of *Clarion*'s steam trials dated 8 June 1841.

[23] Ridgely-Nevitt, *Steamships*, 83; Canney, *OSN1*, 22.

[24] William Conant Church, *The Life of John Ericsson* (New York: Charles Scribner's Sons, 1906), 1:92-94. Hereinafter cited as Church, *Ericsson*.

[25] William Avery Baker and Tre Tryckare, *The Engine Powered Vessel* (New York: Grosset & Dunlap, 1965), 42, 49.

[26] Church, *Ericsson*, 1:118-20.

[27] Coletta, *Secretaries*, 1:175-78.

[28] Church, *Ericsson*, 1:119, 121.

[29] Bennett, *Steam Navy*, 62; Coletta, *Secretaries*, 1:184; Farr and Bostwick, *Guide*, 27; Hornsby MS, 22.

[30] Church, *Ericsson*, 1:121-22.

[31] Ibid., 122.

[32] Bennett, *Steam Navy*, 71.

[33] Hornsby MS, 22- 23.

[34] Farr and Bostwick, *Guide*, 27, FI L90.43.191-206; Canney, *OSN1*, 23; Hornsby MS, 23, n. 64, which lists three plans held by NARA.

[35] The Royal Navy's *Rattler* has an equally valid claim to this credit. However, American sources suggest she was designed as a paddle sloop but converted while building to a screw steamer, unlike *Princeton* which was conceived from the start as a screw propelled warship.

[36] Chapelle, *American Sailing Navy*, 476-77.

[37] Canney, *Sailing Warships*, 70; Hornsby MS, 21.

[38] Ives Collection, FICm.019.0331 (242-DSC-1580), R. F. Stockton to John Lenthall, 12 March 1842.

[39] Naval History and Heritage Command, "Dictionary of American Naval Fighting Ships (DANFS), Princeton I (Screw Steamer)," https://www.history.navy.mil/research/histories/ship-histories/danfs/p/princeton-i.html, accessed November 2017. Hereinafter cited as *DANFS*, Princeton I (Screw Steamer).

[40] ARSN, 1841, 374.

[41] Paullin, *History*, 208-13; NARA descriptions for RG 19 and 45. Note that the Bureau of Construction, Equipment and Repairs is in many places, for example in the *Navy Register*, commonly called the Bureau of Construction, Equipment and Repair without the final "s."

[42] Coletta, *Secretaries*, 1:180-183.

[43] Ibid.; Paullin, *History*, 211.

[44] Paullin, *History*, 197; Bennett, *Steam Navy*, 75.

[45] Ives Collection, FICm.021.0018 (242-DSC-1574), A. Upshur to John Lenthall, 6 February 1843.

[46] Hornsby MS, 23; Ives Collection, FICm.018.0034 (242-DSC-1573), George Read to John Lenthall, 13 February 1843.

[47] Dorwart, *PNY*, 74.

[48] Farr and Bostwick, *Guide*, 7. The press reports came from the *United States Gazette*, 14 June 1843.

[49] Dorwart, *PNY*, 74; Vallette, "Reminiscences," eighth paper, 111; Scharf, *History*, 3:2430. All say *Princeton* was launched on 7 September 1843, but *DANFS* says the 5th and Canney, *OSN1*, 22 says the 9th.

[50] *DANFS*, Princeton I (Screw Steamer).

[51] Church, *Ericsson*, 1:140-41; Canney, *OSN1*, 25.

[52] Church, *Ericsson*, 1:139.

CHAPTER 14 *Family and Marriage*

[1] Ives Collection, FIC.2018.012 (245-DSC-2824), John Lenthall to Mary Eck, 29 February 1840.

[2] Ibid., FICm.012.0529 (242-DSC-1583), Mary Eck to Mrs. Ann M. Eck, 12 June 1840.

[3] Hornsby MS Docs, transcribed letter, Annette Ives to Miss Morris, 11 October 1926.

[4] Hornsby MS, 20. We are indebted to Thomas Hornsby for making the connections between Lenthall and private builders but it is regretted that he left little documentation of his local sources. One of them apparently was Philadelphia's custom house records.

[5] Ibid., especially footnotes 53 and 54. Also see Farr and Bostwick, *Guide*, 23, 29; Cutler, *Queens*, 403.

[6] Farr and Bostwick, *Guide*, 23, *Shenandoah*, two plans, FI L90.43.117-118 and 29, *Tuscarora*, one plan, FI L90.43.227.

[7] Chapelle, *American Sailing Navy*, 416-17.

[8] Independence Seaport Museum, "John Lenthall Collection," https://www.phillyseaport.org under Discover/J. Welles Henderson Research Center/Online Catalog/keyword: John Lenthall Collection, accessed October 2017.

[9] *Appleton's*, Poussin.

[10] Ives Collection, FICm.016.0688 (242-DSC-1575-76), Guillaume Tell Poussin to John Lenthall, 6 February 1843.

[11] Ibid., FICm.016.0687 (242-DSC-1572), Guillaume Tell Poussin to John Lenthall, 7 March 1843.

[12] Morris, "Owners," 25, 29.

[13] Ibid., 29-31.

[14] Ives Collection, FICm.012.0535 (241-DSC-1473), M. D. Lenthall to Ann M. Eck, 9 March 1844. The letter is addressed c/o Messrs. Clark & Eck, St. Louis, Mo.

[15] Ibid., FICm.012.620 (242-DSC-1567), M. K. Lenthall to Mary Eck, June 1843.

[16] Ancestry, "John Lenthall," https://www.ancestry.com/family-tree/person/tree/3472171/person/24101637558/facts, accessed on August 2020. Also see Morris, "Owners," 26.

[17] Hornsby MS Docs, transcribed letter, Annette Ives to Miss Morris, 14 November 1926.

[18] *McElroy's Philadelphia Directory for 1845* (Philadelphia: Edward C. & John Biddle, 1845), 205, "Lenthall John, naval constructor, 27 Christian." Also see Ives Collection, FICm.004.0354 (233-DSC-9311-12), C.C. Dunne to Mrs. John Lenthall, 15 April 1845. This letter is one of two in the collection addressed to Christian Street.

[19] Ives Collection, FIC.2018.011 (245-DSC-2822), M. King to John Lenthall, May 1844.

[20] Ancestry, "John Lenthall," https://www.ancestry.com/family-tree/person/tree/3472171/person/24101637558/facts, accessed on August 2020. Also see Morris, "Owners," 26.

[21] Ives Collection, FICm.012.0535 (241-DSC-1473), M. D. Lenthall to Ann M. Eck, 9 March 1844.

[22] Hornsby MS Docs, transcribed letter, Annette Ives to Miss Morris, 21 September 1926.

CHAPTER 15 *Sloop of War Germantown*

[1] Coletta, *Secretaries*, 1:186-87; Chapelle, *American Sailing Navy*, 420-28.

[2] Canney, *Sailing Warships*, 147-49.

[3] Chapelle, *American Sailing Navy*, 541.

[4] Ibid., 444; Canney, *Sailing Warships*, 154.

[5] Farr and Bostwick, *Guide*, 26, FI L90.43.153-190.

[6] *Navy Register*, 1873, 9. Two years after Lenthall's departure, Richard Powell was still the bureau's only draftsman, his original appointment dated 1 November 1849.

[7] Dorwart, *PNY*, 74; Canney, *Sailing Warships*, 202; Silverstone, *Sailing Navy*, 44.

[8] Dorwart, *PNY*, 74-75.

[9] Ives Collection, FICm.019.0332 (241-DSC-1470), R. F. Stockton to John Lenthall, 10 March 1845.

[10] Ibid., FICm.005.0064 (241-DSC-1467), J. D. Elliott to John Lenthall, 25 April 1845.

[11] Lenthall Personal Papers, Macedonian (USS) Razee 1851-53, letter by Silas Stringham to Samuel Humphreys, Samuel Hartt, John Lenthall, Foster Rhodes and Chas. Copeland, 15 August 1845.

[12] Ibid., letter copy by S. Humphreys, S. Hartt, J. Lenthall and F. Rhodes to Silas Stringham, 19 August 1845.

[13] Ancestry, "Jane Lenthall," https://www.ancestry.com/genealogy/records/jane-lenthall_30285466, accessed November 2017; Find A Grave, "Jane *Lenthall* Waggaman," https://www.findagrave.com/memorial/157046156/jane-waggaman, accessed February 2018.

[14] Hornsby MS Docs, transcribed letter, Annette Ives to Miss Morris, 14 November 1926. Also see Morris, "Owners," 26.

[15] Ives Collection, FICm.005.0033 (242-DSC-1610), Joseph Eck to John Lenthall, 12 February 1846.

[16] K. Jack Bauer, *The Mexican War, 1846-1848* (Lincoln and London: University of Nebraska Press, 1974), 66-70. Hereinafter cited as Bauer, *Mexican War*.

[17] Ives Collection, FICm.019.0310 (241-DSC-1457), Commo Chas. Stewart to John Lenthall, 21 May 1846.

[18] Ibid., FICm.012.0205 (242-DSC-1465), Charles Morris to John Lenthall, 24 July 1846.

[19] Chapelle, *American Sailing Navy*, 463; "The Late Samuel Humphreys, Naval Constructor," Philadelphia *Inquirer and National Gazette*, 26 August 1846, a clipping from Lenthall Personal Papers, Naval Personages—Testimonials & Obituaries 1840-70.

[20] "Chief Naval Constructor," *Alexandria Gazette*, 9 September 1846.

[21] *Navy Register*, 1848.

[22] Hornsby MS, 26; Donald L. Canney, *U.S. Coast Guard and Revenue Cutters, 1790-1935* (Annapolis: Naval Institute Press, 1995), 17-18; Canney, *Sailing Warships*, 187.

[23] Bauer, *Mexican War*, 235.

[24] Lenthall Personal Papers, Surf Boats for Mexican War 1846, cover sheet notes /s/ JL.

[25] Bauer, *Mexican War*, 236. Recall earlier discussions about the meaning of 'designer'. The lieutenant is not the same Col. George Totten who was the Panama Railroad's chief engineer.

[26] Lenthall Personal Papers, Surf Boats for Mexican War 1846, untitled sheet with surf boat specifications and a table of dimensions.

[27] Ibid., with weight and oar data from separate sheets.

[28] Bauer, *Mexican War*, 242; Canney, *Sailing Navy*, 154; Vallette, "Reminiscences," ninth paper, 173.

[29] Ives Collection, FICm.007.0018 (241-DSC-1463), Chas. Gauntt to John Lenthall, 30 January 1847; Ibid., FICm.007.0019 (242-DSC-1615), Chas. Gauntt to John Lenthall, 2 March 1847.

[30] 33rd Cong., 1st Sess., House Executive Doc 65, hereinafter cited as H. Doc. 65; Canney, *OSN1*, 31-32.

[31] Ibid.; Chapelle, *American Sailing Navy*, 472.

[32] H. Doc. 65, 114.

[33] Canney, *OSN1*, 32, 173.

[34] Silverstone, *Sailing Navy*, 74.

[35] ZB Folder, Capt. D. W. Knox to Thomas Hornsby, 5 May 1942.

[36] Ives Collection, FICm.019.0205 (242-DSC-1579), Jos. Smith to John Lenthall, 14 July 1847.

[37] Ibid., FICm.012.0250 (235-DSC-0075), Mary K. Lenthall to Mary D. Lenthall, 24 July 1847; Morris, "Owners," 30.

[38] Ives Collection., FICm.012.0478 (235-DSC-0077-78), Mary K. Lenthall to Mary D. Lenthall, 24 November 1847; Ibid., FICm.005.0027 (240-DSC-1250), Ellen M. Eck to Mary K. Lenthall, 28 November 1847.

[39] Ibid., FICm.012.0482 (240-DSC-1256-57), Mary K. Lenthall to Mary D. Lenthall, 20 March 1848.

[40] Ibid., FICm.005.0031 (242-DSC-1599), Ellen Eck to Mary D. Lenthall, 22 March 1849.

[41] *Biography of the Class of 1838, of the College of New Jersey at Princeton, N.J.*, prepared by William Edward Schenck, D.D. (Philadelphia: Jas. B. Rodgers Printing Co., 1889), 26-29.

[42] Brown, *History*, 39.

CHAPTER 16 *Chief Constructor*

[1] *Navy Register*, 1850; Farr and Bostwick, *Guide*, 7.

[2] Ives Collection, FIC.2018.008 (245-DSC-2820), John Lenthall to Mary D. Lenthall, 2 September 1849; Ibid., FICm.005.0039 (234-DSC-9479), Joseph Eck to Mary Lenthall, 23 September 1849.

[3] Chapelle, *American Sailing Navy*, 463.

[4] Ives Collection, FICm.012.0247 (235-DSC-0042), John Lenthall to Mary D. Lenthall, 15 April 1847.

[5] *Navy Register*, 1850.

[6] Ives Collection, numerous letters addressed to John and Mary Lenthall circa 1850-52; Seventh Census of the United States (1850), Washington, D.C.

[7] Canney, *OSN1*, 168; Silverstone, *Sailing Navy*, 74.

[8] Ives Collection, FICm.019.0199 (245-DSC-2802), John Sloat to John Lenthall, 3 February 1850.

[9] Canney, *OSN1*, 168; Dorwart, *PNY*, 76-77. Two other sources, Silverstone, *Sailing Navy*, 23, and Vallette, "Reminiscences," ninth paper, 173, give *Susquehanna*'s launch date as 5 April.

[10] Bennett, *Steam Navy*, 54; Canney, *OSN1*, 27-29.

[11] Bennett, *Steam Navy*, 54-55.

[12] Ives Collection, FICm.007.0017 (241-DSC-1461), Chas. Gauntt to John Lenthall, 5 September 1845. This letter told Lenthall to be ready to inspect and report on the steam tug *Water Witch*.

[13] Bennett, *Steam Navy*, 51-52; Canney, *OSN1*, 27.

[14] James Phinney Baxter III, *The Introduction of the Ironclad Warship* (Annapolis: Naval Institute Press, 2001), 226. This book is a facsimile reissue of the original 1933 edition with a new introduction by Donald Canney. Hereinafter cited as Baxter, *Ironclad Warship*.

[15] William M. Fowler, *Steam Titans* (New York, London, etc.: Bloomsbury USA, 2017), 144-46. Hereinafter cited as Fowler, *Steam Titans*.

[16] *United States Statutes at Large*, Volume 9 (1847), 187-88.

[17] 31st Cong., 1st Sess., Senate Report No. 202, p. 80, Extract from report of Commodore M. C. Perry to the Navy Department, 30 January 1849. Hereinafter cited as Senate Report 202.

[18] Charles B. Stuart, *The Naval and Mail Steamers of the United States* (New York: Charles B. Norton, 1853), 118. Hereinafter cited as Stuart, *Naval and Mail Steamers*.

[19] Lenthall Personal Papers, Mail Steamers 1848-57, John Lenthall to Commodore Perry, 5 April 1850.

[20] Ridgely-Nevitt, *Steamships*, 150, 357.

[21] Lenthall Personal Papers, Mail Steamers 1848-57, John Lenthall to Charles Skinner, 18 March 1852.

[22] Senate Report 202, 76, opening statement of the report.

[23] Fowler, *Steam Titans*, 161.

[24] Senate Report 202, 115, statement by John Lenthall to Secretary Preston, 28 August 1850.

[25] Lenthall Personal Papers, John Lenthall Correspondence regarding Propellers 1851-57, extracts by Lenthall from Mr. Grice's letter to the secretary of the navy, 21 January 1851.

[26] Ibid., letter by John Lenthall "not sent" to the Bureau chief, 6 February 1851; Ibid., letter by John Lenthall to Commo. Stewart, 24 September 1851; Canney, *Sailing Navy*, 71.

[27] Lenthall Personal Papers, John Lenthall Correspondence regarding Propellers 1851-57, letter by John Lenthall to the chief of the BCER, 6 February 1851.

[28] Ibid., endorsement by John Lenthall "on the letter from Mr. Grice of March 28 and sent to Sec. of Navy."

[29] Hornsby MS, 40, n. 74, text of the article dated 3 June 1851 from an "unidentified Philadelphia paper" titled "Important and Valuable Application of a Propeller" is reproduced.

[30] Lenthall Personal Papers, John Lenthall Correspondence regarding Propellers 1851-57, Letter by John Lenthall to Commo. Stewart, 24 September 1851.

[31] Canney, *Sailing Warships*, 71.

[32] Ives Collection, FICm.005.0014 (234-DSC-9462-62), A. M. Eck to Mary D. Lenthall, 14 October 1851.

[33] Ibid., FICm.012.0517 (244-DSC-2657), Mary D. Lenthall to A. M. Eck, 19 December 1851.

[34] Seventh Census of the United States (1850), Washington, D.C.

[35] Morris, "Owners," 23. The conveyed deed was recorded in the District of Columbia on 12 March 1852.

[36] The Church of the Epiphany, "Home-EpiphanyDC," http://epiphanydc.org, accessed October 2019.

[37] Find A Grave, "Ann Maria Eck," https://www.findagrave.com/memorial/157044770/ann-maria-eck, accessed February 2018.

[38] National Register of Historic Places Inventory, Rock Creek Cemetery, under John Lenthall, hereinafter cited as NRHP Rock Creek Cemetery. Also see Find A Grave, "Jane *King* Lenthall," https://www.findagrave.com/memorial/41347682/jane-lenthall, accessed February 2018.

[39] Bennett, *Steam Navy*, 52.

[40] Canney, *OSN1*, 41-42.

[41] Chapelle, *American Sailing Navy*, 466-67; Canney, *Sailing Warships*, 160-64.

BOOK THREE *Bureau Chief*

CHAPTER 17 *Promotion to Bureau Chief*

[1] John H. Schroeder, *Shaping a Maritime Empire* (Westport CT and London: Greenwood Press, 1985), 117-18. Hereinafter cited as Schroeder, *Maritime Empire.*

[2] *Navy Register,* 1853.

[3] Schroeder, *Maritime Empire,* 121; Coletta, *Secretaries,* 1:vii.

[4] Coletta, *Secretaries,* 1:279-300.

[5] Paullin, *History,* 174, 214.

[6] *Navy Register,* 1853.

[7] Office of the United States Trade Representative, "History of the Winder Building," https://ustr.gov/archive/Who_We_Are/History_of_the_Winder_Building,_Home_to_USTR%27s_Washington_DC_Headquarters.html, accessed October 2019.

[8] Alfred Hunter, *The Washington and Georgetown Directory* (Washington: Kirkwood & McGill, 1853), 38, 61.

[9] Paullin, *History,* 212.

[10] Ives Collection, FICm.015.0144 (244-DSC-2646), Wm. Knowles to John Lenthall, 18 May 1853.

[11] Chapelle, *American Sailing Navy,* 457, 472.

[12] Paullin, *History,* 213.

[13] Bennett, *Steam Navy,* 141.

[14] NARA, RG 19, Entry 49, Morris, Smith, Hartt, Lenthall and Copeland to J. C. Dobbin, 31 August 1853.

[15] Canney, *Sailing Warships,* 200; Canney, *OSN1,* 174. Dimensions are rounded to the nearest foot.

[16] Ives Collection, FICm.004.0021 (244-DSC-2649), John Dahlgren to John Lenthall, 19 July 1853.

[17] Ibid., FICm.008.0337 (244-DSC-2647), W. L. Hudson to John Lenthall, 7 October 1853.

[18] Bennett, *Steam Navy,* 56; Kurt Hackemer, *The U.S. Navy and the Origins of the Military-Industrial Complex, 1847-1883* (Annapolis: Naval Institute Press, 2002), 18. Hereinafter cited as Hackemer, *Origins.*

[19] Hackemer, *Origins,* 21-22.

[20] NARA, RG 45, M518, Roll 11, Samuel Hartt to Secretary Dobbin, 17 November 1853.

[21] *Navy Register,* 1854; ZB Folder, letter by Captain D. W. Knox to Thomas Hornsby, 6 March 1940; Paullin, *History,* 210.

[22] Donald L. Canney, *Lincoln's Navy, The Ships, Men and Organization, 1861-65* (Annapolis: Naval Institute Press, 1998), 22. Hereinafter cited as Canney, *Lincoln's Navy.* Also see Paullin, *History,* 211; Hornsby MS, 35-56.

[23] *Navy Register,* 1854.

[24] NARA, RG 45, M518, Roll 25, John Lenthall to Secretary Robeson, 2 February 1870. Note that Lenthall's account designated the clerks by their name and grades, not by numbers.

[25] ARSN, 1853, 16.

[26] Ibid.

[27] *Congressional Globe*, 33rd Cong., 1st Sess., 69, 179, 455, 465, 466, 489 and 490.

[28] Henry Lorenzo Janes, "The Black Warrior Affair," *The American Historical Review*, 12 No. 2 (Jan. 1907): 280-98. *Black Warrior* was seized on 28 February 1854.

[29] NARA, RG 45, M518, Roll 12, John Lenthall to Secretary Dobbin, 6 March 1854.

CHAPTER 18 *The Steam Frigates*

[1] *United States Statutes at Large*, Volume 10, 273.

[2] Canney, *OSN1*, 45; Chapelle, *American Sailing Navy*, 469

[3] Hackemer, *Origins*, 28.

[4] Farr and Bostwick, *Guide*, 20, Frigate, FI L90.63-64. These two body plans, drawn to an enlarged scale and annotated by Lenthall, show just how he was able to use all the precut live oak frames to build the steam frigates.

[5] Canney, *OSN1*, 45.

[6] Lyon and Winfield, *Navy List*, 182-98; Andrew Lambert, *Battleships in Transition, The Creation of the Steam Battlefleet, 1815-1860* (London: Conway Maritime Press, Ltd., 1984), 34-35.

[7] Ives Collection, FICm.999.0126 (239-DSC-1116-7), Donald McKay to John Lenthall, 12 June 1865. McKay wrote Lenthall that Watts "remembered you well when in England on your persevering tour through foreign Dockyards."

[8] Winfield and Roberts, *French Warships*, 66, 67, 115.

[9] NARA, RG 45, M518, Roll 11, John Lenthall to Secretary Dobbin, 14 December 1853; Canney, *OSN1*, 46.

[10] Canney, *OSN1*, 46, 59, 174; Lyon and Winfield, *Navy List*, 185, 199-200; Winfield and Roberts, *French Warships*, 67, 68, 115.

[11] NARA, RG 45, M480, Roll 2, Secretary Dobbin to John Lenthall, 10 June 1854.

[12] That Lenthall was considered by the U.S. Navy as the designer of the lead ship of the class, *Merrimack*, is documented by the inscription on the Navy's official half model of this ship now displayed at the Portsmouth Naval Shipyard Museum, which reads "U.S.S. Merrimac by John Lenthall 1855."

[13] Canney, *OSN1*, 46. 47, 52, 173-74; Bennett, *Steam Navy*, 141-45, 151.

[14] Benjamin F. Isherwood, *Experimental Researches in Steam Engineering* (Philadelphia: William Hamilton, Hall of the Franklin Institute, 1863), 160. Hereinafter cited as Isherwood, *Experimental Researches*.

[15] Easby Biography; Easby-Smith, "Recollections." Also see Appendix 12.

[16] Ancestry, "Joseph Eck," https://www.ancestry.com/family-tree/person/tree/3472171/person/24101253172/facts, accessed February 2020. Joseph Eck died on 31 August 1854; Ives Collection, FICm.007.0096 (243-DSC-2495), D. Gooch to John Lenthall, 24 September 1854.

[17] NARA, RG 45, M480, Roll 2, Secretary Dobbin to John Lenthall et al., 6 September 1854.

[18] For information on the steam frigates' machinery, see Isherwood, *Experimental Researches*; Bennett, *Steam Navy*; Hackemer, *Origins*; and Canney, *OSN1*.

[19] United States Lighthouse Society, "The Development of the American Lightship," https://uslhs.org/development-american-lightship-james-delgado, accessed June 2019.

[20] NARA, RG 45, M480, Reel 2, Charles Welsh to John Lenthall, 13 September 1854.

[21] Ibid., M518, Reel 13, John Lenthall to Secretary Dobbin, 25 August 1855.

[22] Lenthall Personal Papers, Lightships 1854-55, Mould loft dimensions, Costs of light ships, Carpenters days work for lightships.

[23] Ibid., Nantucket Shoals Lightship 1855-56, Cost of Building the U.S. Light Vessel "Nantucket Shoals".

[24] Stephen Chapin Kinnaman, *Merrimack, The Biography of a Steam Frigate* (Wilmington and Malaga: Vernon Press, 2019), 29-37.

[25] Ives Collection, FIC.2018.119 (247-DSC-3104), Daniel Martin to John Lenthall, 25 February 1856. Martin's speeds are in knots and fathoms, a fathom being ⅛ of a knot. Excerpts of Martin's note were published in *The New York Times* on 27 March 1856.

[26] Ibid.; FIC.2018.079 (246-DSC-2989), S. V. Pendergrast to John Lenthall, 29 February 1856.

[27] NARA, RG 24, Deck Log of the U.S.S. *Merrimack*, 26 February 1856. The fifteen knots entry was recorded at 3 p.m. during an unusual "long" hour.

[28] NARA, RG 45, M125, Captain Pendergrast to Secretary Dobbin, 3 March 1856.

[29] Ives Collection, FICm.016.0718 (244-DSC-2609), Captain Pendergrast to John Lenthall, 3 March 1856.

[30] Ibid., FICm.007.0207 (244-DSC-2595), Captain Gregory to John Lenthall, 3 March 1856.

[31] "The New Frigate Merrimac," *The Scientific American*, 11 No. 28 (1856): 222.

[32] Larrie D. Ferreiro, "A Biographical Sketch of John Willis Griffiths from Primary and Secondary Sources," *Nautical Research Journal*, 52 No. 4 (2007): 221-228.

[33] "Trial Trip of the U.S. Steam Frigate Merrimack," *JFI*, 61 No. 4 (1856): 274-278.

[34] Oliver W. Griffiths, Ed., "Screw Steamers of the Navy," *U.S. Nautical Magazine and Naval Journal*, 4 (1857): 65-66. Note that Griffiths' article was written the year following *Merrimack*'s steam trials, after portions of her deck log had been published.

[35] NARA, RG 45, M125, Roll 355, Captain Pendergrast to Secretary Dobbin, 4 March 1856.

[36] Bennett, *Steam Navy*, 148-151.

[37] Greville Bathe, *Ship of Destiny* (St. Augustine, FL: Allen, Lane and Scott), 1951.

CHAPTER 19 *The Steam Sloops*

[1] NARA, RG 45, M518, Roll 13, John Lenthall to Secretary Dobbin, 18 March 1856.

[2] Hackemer, *Origins*, 44-48.

[3] Ibid., 48.

[4] Canney, *OSN1*, 61.

[5] NARA, RG 45, M518, Roll 14, John Lenthall to Secretary Dobbin, 5 February 1857.

[6] Canney, *OSN1*, 61; Bennett, *Steam Navy*, 154; Hackemer, *Origins*, 49.

[7] Coletta, *Secretaries*, 1:296-97.

[8] Ibid., 316.

[9] NARA, RG 45, M518, Roll 14, John Lenthall to Secretary Toucey, 15 June 1857.

[10] Ibid., the preceding letter was numbered 121, this one was numbered 122.

[11] Canney, *Sailing Warships*, 73.

[12] NARA, RG 45, M518, Roll 14, John Lenthall to Secretary Toucey, 18 August 1857.

[13] Hackemer, *Origins*, 49-51.

[14] Bennett, *Steam Navy*, 154.

[15] Hackemer, *Origins*, 55.

[16] Canney, *OSN1*, 61; Hackemer, *Origins*, 50.

[17] Canney, *OSN1*, 61, 63, 174.

[18] Hornsby MS, 43; Canney, *OSN1*, 67; Paul H. Silverstone, *Warships of the Civil War Navies* (Annapolis: Naval Institute Press, 1989), 37. Hereinafter cited as Silverstone, *Civil War Navies.*

[19] Canney, *OSN1*, 67, 70.

[20] ARSN, 1857, 28-32.

[21] Hornsby MS, 39-42.

[22] NARA, RG 45, M518, Roll 14, John Lenthall to Secretary Toucey, 23 April 1858.

[23] *United States Statutes at Large*, 35th Cong., 1st Sess., Chapter 153, 1858, 319, Sect 6.

[24] Canney, *OSN1*, 71-72.

[25] Ibid., 71-84, 174; Bennett, *Steam Navy*, 166-170.

[26] Canney, *OSN1*, 84-87; Bennett, *Steam Navy*, 173.

[27] Canney, *OSN1*, 87-89.

[28] Silverstone, *Civil War Navies*, 24, 38-41.

[29] Canney, *Lincoln's Navy*, 60. Credit goes to Donald Canney for his focus on how the steam sloops of 1858 carried their main battery on their centerlines and why it was so revolutionary.

[30] Spencer Tucker, *Arming the Fleet, U.S. Navy Ordnance in the Muzzle-Loading Era* (Annapolis: Naval Institute Press, 1989), 170-216, 232. Hereinafter cited as Tucker, *Arming the Fleet.*

[31] Canney, *OSN1*, 70-71.

[32] *United States Statutes at Large*, 35th Cong., 1st Sess., Chapter 153, 1858, 319, Sect. 5.

CHAPTER 20 *Gloire and Warrior*

[1] Eighth Census of the United States (1860), Washington, D.C. Appearing two dwellings below the entry for John Lenthall, wife Mary, daughter Jenny and their two servants is the 'family' of Mary K Lenthall and Ann Carson.

[2] "Academy of Visitation," Washington *Evening Star,* 5 July 1860. One of its articles listed Jane Lenthall as a graduating senior queen; on the date the article was written, 4 July, she had just turned sixteen. The academy is now known as the Georgetown Visitation Preparatory School.

[3] The Church of the Epiphany, "Mary King Lenthall," http://epiphanydc.org/2017/03/may-3-mary-king-lenthall-1892/, accessed March 2019.

[4] Ives Collection, FICm.005.0030 (234-DSC-9488-89), Ellen M. Eck to Mary D. Lenthall, 22 July 1858.

[5] Robert Gardiner, Ed., *Steam, Steel & Shellfire, The Steam Warship 1815-1905* (London: Conway Maritime Press Ltd., 1992), 52. Hereinafter cited as Gardiner, *Steam, Steel & Shellfire.* Also see Baxter, *Ironclad Warship,* 69-70.

[6] Baxter, *Ironclad Warship,* 72.

[7] Ibid., 74-90.

[8] Donald L. Canney, *The Old Steam Navy, Volume Two, The Ironclads, 1842-1885* (Annapolis: Naval Institute Press, 1993), 3-6. Hereinafter cited as Canney, *OSN2.*

[9] Baxter, *Ironclad Warship,* 97.

[10] Ibid., 99, 113-14.

[11] Monograph titled *Gloire, Frégate de 900 Chevaux (1859)* (Paris: Association Les Amis des Musées de la Marine, 1968); Baxter, *Ironclad Warship,* 99, 110.

[12] Ives Collection, FICm.012.0313 (235-DSC-0049-52) and FICm.012.0315 (235-DSC-0053-54), six pages of *Gloire* vessel data.

[13] Baxter, *Ironclad Warship,* 110.

[14] Ibid., 116-118; Oscar Parkes, *British Battleships* (London: Seeley Service & Co. Limited, 1973), 11-15. Hereinafter cited as Parkes, *British Battleships.*

[15] Baxter, *Ironclad Warship,* 116-123.

[16] Andrew Lambert, *Warrior, The World's First Ironclad Then and Now* (Annapolis: Naval Institute Press, 1987), 18-23. Hereinafter cited as Lambert, *Warrior.*

[17] Gardiner, *Steam, Steel & Shellfire,* 55.

[18] Lambert, *Warrior,* 18-21; Baxter, *Ironclad Warship,* 130.

[19] Lambert, *Warrior,* 22.

[20] Parkes, *British Battleships,* 19.

[21] Lambert, *Warrior,* 25-26.

[22] Ives Collection, FICm.012.0334 (237-DSC-0334-37), Form No. 211, H.M.S. *Warrior.*

[23] Royal Museums Greenwich, "Objects," (Series of Form No. 211) https://collections.rmg.co.uk/archive/objects/522429.html, accessed August 2020.

[24] Ives Collection, FICm.999.0126 (239-DSC-1116-17), Donald McKay to John Lenthall, 12 June 1865.

[25] *Conway's All the World's Fighting Ships, 1860-1905,* Robert Gardiner, Ed. (New York: Mayflower Books, Inc., 1979), 286. Hereinafter cited as *Conway's Fighting Ships.*

[26] Ives Collection, FICm.020.0146 (238-DSC-0686), Secretary Toucey to John Lenthall, 23 July 1860.

[27] Lambert, *Warrior,* 23.

[28] Gardiner, *Steam, Steel & Shellfire,* 53.

[29] NARA, RG 45, M518, Roll 15, John Lenthall to Secretary Toucey, 8 January 1859.

[30] Ibid.

CHAPTER 21 *War of the Rebellion*

[1] Ives Collection, FICm.004.0310 (238-DSC-0671), Captain Thomas Dornin to John Lenthall, 4 September 1860.

[2] Ibid., FICm.008.0059 (238-DSC-0673-74), William Hanscom to John Lenthall, 12 September 1860.

[3] "Naval," Richmond *Daily Dispatch,* 15 September 1860.

[4] ARSN, 1860, 20; Canney, *OSN1,* 43.

[5] David M. Potter, *The Impending Crisis, 1848-1861* (New York: Harper & Row, Publishers, 1976), 405-447.

[6] Ibid., 486-496.

[7] Ives Collection, FICm.004.0187 (238-DSC-0667-68,) B. F. Delano to John Lenthall, 1 January 1861.

[8] Ibid., FICm.009.0015 (238-DSC-0661-62), B. F. Isherwood to John Lenthall, 19 January 1861.

[9] *Congressional Globe,* 36th Cong., 2nd Sess., 463.

[10] NARA, RG 45, M518, Roll 16, John Lenthall to Secretary Toucey, 1 February 1861.

[11] Bennett, *Steam Navy,* Appendix B. Bennett's appendix supplies the contract cost of a vessel, which covered its hull and machinery, but not its guns, armor, furniture or equipment. Lenthall's estimate for an iron-cased *Iroquois* included all of these costs.

[12] Hagley Museum and Library, Samuel Francis Du Pont Papers, Winterthur Manuscripts, Group 9, Item No. W9-10643, letter by John Lenthall to Samuel Francis Du Pont, 3 February 1861. Hereinafter cited as Du Pont Papers. For context, see *Samuel Francis Du Pont, A Selection of his Civil War Letters,* John D. Hayes, Ed. (Ithaca: Cornell University Press, 1969), 1:30-31. Hereinafter cited as Du Pont, *Civil War Letters.*

[13] Du Pont, *Civil War Letters,* 1:31, n. 7.

[14] *Congressional Globe,* 36th Cong., 2nd Sess., 1039, 1083.

[15] NARA, RG 45, M480, Roll 2, Secretary Welles to John Lenthall, 27 May 1861.

[16] Canney, *OSN1,* 95.

[17] Coletta, *Secretaries,* 1:316.

[18] Ibid., 321; Paullin, *History,* 249, both give the date of Welles' appointment as 5 March 1861. *Navy Register,* 1861, notes the date of 7 March.

[19] Ives Collection, FICm.004.0361 (238-DSC-0657-58), Samuel Francis Du Pont to John Lenthall, 8 March 1861.

[20] Paullin, *History*, 250-52; Coletta, *Secretaries*, 1:321-323.

[21] Baxter, *Ironclad Warship*, 239-40.

[22] NARA, RG 45, M480, Roll 2, Secretary Welles to John Lenthall, 11 April 1861.

[23] Ives Collection, FICm.008.0057 (238-DSC-0696), Isaiah Hanscom to John Lenthall, 11 April 1861.

[24] *Civil War Naval Chronology, 1861-1865* (Washington: Naval History Division, Navy Department, 1971), I-7.

[25] Ephraim Douglass Adams, *Great Britain and the American Civil War* (New York: Russell & Russell, 1924), 93-95. Britain's Proclamation of Neutrality was issued on 13 May 1861, granting the Confederacy *de facto* recognition. France followed Britain's lead on 10 June.

[26] Coletta, *Secretaries*, 1:326-27; Paullin, *History*, 274.

[27] John V. Quarstein, *The CSS Virginia, Sink Before Surrender* (Charleston: The History Press, 2012), 36, 446. Hereinafter cited as Quarstein, *CSS Virginia*.

[28] Ibid., 36-42.

[29] Eighth Census of the United States (1860), Washington, D.C. McCauley, his wife Lelia and four children are listed five dwellings from Lenthall and his family in Washington's 1st Ward as of 11 July 1860.

[30] Paullin, *History*, 261-262.

[31] Ibid., 262; Baxter, *Ironclad Warship*, 241.

[32] Coletta, *Secretaries*, 1:327-28; Ari Hoogenboom, *Gustavus Vasa Fox of the Union Navy, A Biography* (Baltimore: The Johns Hopkins Press, 2008), 72-74. Hereinafter cited as Hoogenboom, *Fox*.

[33] Paullin, *History*, 210.

[34] Admiral David D. Porter, *Naval History of the Civil War* (New York: The Sherman Publishing Company, 1886), 360. Hereinafter cited as Porter, *Naval History*.

[35] *Navy Register*, 1861.

[36] Baxter, *Ironclad Warship*, 242.

CHAPTER 22 *The Ninety-Day Gunboats*

[1] Canney, *OSN1*, 91, 94; K. Jack Bauer and Stephen S. Roberts, *Register of Ships in the U.S. Navy, 1775-1990* (New York, etc.: Greenwood Press, 1991), 72. Hereinafter cited as Bauer and Roberts, *Register*.

[2] Alexander Laing, *American Ships* (New York: American Heritage Press, 1971), 319-320. Hereinafter cited as Laing, *American Ships*.

[3] Edward William Sloan, III, *Benjamin Franklin Isherwood, Naval Engineer* (Annapolis: United States Naval Institute, 1965), 30-31. Hereinafter cited as Sloan, *Isherwood*.

[4] "Proposals for Steam Engines," Washington *National Republican*, 29 May 1861. The notice, under John Lenthall, Chief of the Bureau, was dated 22 May 1861, and referenced the availability to bidders of a cross-section of the vessel.

[5] Silverstone, *Civil War Navies*, 49-54; Canney, *OSN1*, 174-75.

[6] Canney, *OSN1*, 91; Bennett, *Steam Navy*, 221.

[7] *Preliminary Inventory of the Records of the Bureau of Ships (Record Group 19)* (Washington: The National Archives and Records Service, 1961), 225-26, Records of the General Superintendent of Ironclads. Hereinafter cited as *Inventory of RG 19.*

[8] NARA, RG 45, M480, Roll 2, Secretary Welles to John Lenthall, 6 May 1861.

[9] Canney, *OSN1*, 94-97, 175.

[10] NARA, RG 45, M480, Roll 2, Secretary Welles to John Lenthall, 27 May 1861.

[11] Ibid., Secretary Welles to John Lenthall, 3 June 1861.

[12] Bauer and Roberts, *Register*, 64, 66-67.

[13] NARA, RG 45, M480, Roll 2, Secretary Welles to John Lenthall, 30 May 1861.

[14] Hoogenboom, *Fox*, 75.

[15] NARA, RG 45, M480, Roll 2, Secretary Welles to John Lenthall, 1 June May 1861.

[16] *ORA*, III, 2, 814-15.

[17] Canney, *OSN2*, 47-48.

[18] Ives Collection, FICm.004.0370 (238-DSC-0652-54), S. F. Du Pont to John Lenthall, 28 May 1861.

[19] Ibid., FICm.003.0222 (233-DSC-9281), Chas. Copeland to John Lenthall, 3 June 1861.

[20] Ibid., FICm.005.0001 (239-DSC-1148), Mrs. J. W. Easby to John Lenthall, 14 June 1861; Ibid., FICm.005.0002 (238-DSC-0631), Mrs. J. W. Easby to John Lenthall, 25 June 1861.

[21] Hoogenboom, *Fox*, 91. Fox's biographer suggests they were "old colleagues."

[22] *Confidential Correspondence of Gustavus Vasa Fox, Assistant Secretary of the Navy, 1861-1865,* Robert Means Thompson and Richard Wainwright, Eds. (New York: The Naval Historical Society, 1919), 2:73-79. Letter by D. D. Porter to G. V. Fox, 5 July 1861. Spellings and grammar have been corrected. Hereinafter cited as *Fox Correspondence.*

[23] Biographical Directory of the United States Congress, "Mallory, Stephen Russell (1813-1873)," https://bioguideretro.congress.gov/Home/MemberDetails?memIndex=M000084, accessed June 2020.

[24] Porter, *Naval History*, 258, 260.

[25] Ibid., 259.

[26] *Captains of the Old Steam Navy, Makers of the American Naval Tradition, 1840-1880,* James C. Bradford, Ed. (Annapolis: Naval Institute Press, 1986), 243. Hereinafter cited as Bradford, *Captains.* The biographer of Porter's section was Tamara Moser Melia.

[27] NARA, RG 45, M518, Roll 16, John Lenthall to Secretary Welles, 15 July 1861. The bottoms of the first two pages were clipped so it is possible several contracts were missed.

[28] Bauer and Roberts, *Register*, 78-80.

[29] Canney, *OSN1*, 109-113.

[30] NARA, RG 45, M518, Roll 16, John Lenthall to Secretary Welles, 27 August 1861.

[31] Canney, *OSN1*, 97.

[32] Bauer and Roberts, *Register*, 67-68.

[33] NARA, RG 45, M518, Roll 16, John Lenthall to Secretary Welles, 27 July 1861.

[34] Laing, *American Ships*, 325-28.

[35] Ives Collection, FICm.004.0371 (239-DSC-1142-44), S. F. Du Pont to John Lenthall, 24 November 1861; Hornsby MS, 48-49.

CHAPTER 23 *The Ironclad Board*

[1] Baxter, *Ironclad Warship*, 229-30, 245-46.

[2] ARSN, 1861, 22.

[3] 37th Cong., 1st Sess., Senate Executive Document No. 1, 96.

[4] Sloan, *Isherwood*, 50.

[5] Baxter, *Ironclad Warship*, 247-48.

[6] *Report of the Secretary of the Navy in Relation to Armored Vessels* (Washington: Government Printing Office, 1864), 2.

[7] NARA, RG 45, M518, Roll 18, Jos. Smith, H. Paulding and C. H. Davis to Secretary Welles, 16 September 1861.

[8] Rebecca Paulding Meade, *Life of Hiram Paulding, Rear-Admiral, U.S.N* (New York: The Baker & Taylor Company, 1910), 237.

[9] Gideon Welles, *Diary of Gideon Welles, Secretary of the Navy Under Lincoln and Johnson,* with introduction by John T. Morse, Jr., 3 Vols. (Boston and New York: Houghton Mifflin Company, 1911), 1:401. Hereinafter cited as Welles, *Diary.* Also see Hoogenboom, *Fox*, 214; Baxter, *Ironclad Warship*, 275.

[10] Howard J. Fuller, *Clad in Iron, The American Civil War and the Challenge of British Naval Power* (Annapolis: Naval Institute Press, 2008), 57. Hereinafter cited as Fuller, *Clad in Iron.*

[11] Canney, *OSN2*, 21.

[12] William H. Roberts, *USS New Ironsides in the Civil War* (Annapolis: Naval Institute Press, 1999), 16-17. Hereinafter cited as Roberts, *New Ironsides.*

[13] Baxter, *Ironclad Warship*, 264.

[14] NARA, RG 45, M518, Roll 16, Joseph Smith to Secretary Welles, 5 October 1861.

[15] Baxter, *Ironclad Warship,* 264, especially n. 1. Italic emphasis retained from original text. Also see Fuller, *Clad in Iron*, 303 n. 12. Fuller identifies Lenthall as the naval architect who reviewed Ericsson's calculations.

[16] Porter, *Civil War History*, 358, 361.

[17] 38th Cong., 2nd Sess., Senate Report No. 142, Report of the Joint Committee on the Conduct of the War, Light-Draught Monitors, 83. Hereinafter cited as Senate Report No. 142.

[18] Fuller, *Clad in Iron*, 60.

[19] Ibid., 61; Baxter, *Ironclad Warship*, 264 and footnote 1.

[20] Church, *Ericsson,* 1:265-66. Ericsson's biographer says that "the anxious Commodore" estimated *Monitor's* displacement at 1,300 tons but when launched and in fighting trim, she displaced 1,000 tons (the official figure is 987 tons). However, if the reduced armor thickness (172 tons) and outfitting never placed on board (70 tons) are deducted, this leaves a difference of only 58 tons, which could well have come from mill tolerances, design changes, etc.

[21] Fuller, *Clad in Iron,* 61 and n. 18.

[22] Baxter, *Ironclad Warship,* 274.

[23] For the Navy Department ironclad's building instructions and armor specifications, see NARA RG 19, Flat Dash File 142-10-14, the latter of which is also reproduced in Baxter, *Ironclad Warship,* Appendix F; for the steam machinery specifications and drawings, see the New-York Historical Society, Gustavus Vasa Fox Collection, Box 19, Folder 11, "Specifications and Plans: U.S. Iron-plated steam batteries" and Box OS2, Folder 7, "General Plans for U.S. Iron-Plated Steam Batteries," ID Nos. 98041d to 98046d. Hereinafter collectively cited as "Navy Department ironclad specifications and plans."

[24] Captain Louis M. Goldsborough, flag officer of the North Atlantic Blockading Squadron based at Hampton Roads.

[25] Du Pont Papers, Item No. W9-11502, Letter by John Lenthall to Samuel Francis Du Pont, 18 November 1861. For context, see Du Pont, *Civil War Letters,* 1:262.

[26] ARSN, 1861, 22.

[27] *Congressional Globe,* 37th Cong., 2nd Sess., 123, 147-48, 153.

[28] Baxter, *Ironclad Warship,* 281-82.

[29] Du Pont Papers, Item No. W9-11844, Letter by John Lenthall to Samuel Francis Du Pont, 5 January 1862. For context, see Du Pont, *Civil War Letters,* 1:319.

[30] Baxter, *Ironclad Warship,* 278 and Appendix G.

[31] *Congressional Globe,* 37th Cong., 2nd Sess., 696-97.

[32] Baxter, *Ironclad Warship,* 281.

CHAPTER 24 *Monitor Fever*

[1] Fuller, *Clad in Iron,* 88.

[2] Anna Gibson Holloway and Jonathan White, *"Our Little Monitor" The Greatest Invention of the Civil War* (Kent, OH: The Kent State University Press, 2018), 85.

[3] Fuller, *Clad in Iron,* 97.

[4] "Forewarned but not Forearmed," *Burlington Free Press,* 14 March 1862. The article was a reprint from the *Boston Traveller.*

[5] NARA, RG 45, M518, Roll 17, John Lenthall to Secretary Welles, 13 March 1862.

[6] Ibid., John Lenthall, Benjamin Isherwood, Edward Hartt and Daniel Martin to Secretary Welles, 13 May 1862. The quote refers to the "Navy Department ironclad specifications and plans."

[7] Hoogenboom, *Fox,* 118.

[8] Fuller, *Clad in Iron,* 94.

[9] Ibid., 94-9; Hoogenboom, *Fox*, 118-19.

[10] NARA, RG 45, M518, Roll 17, John Lenthall and Benjamin Isherwood to Secretary Welles, 17 March 1862.

[11] Sir Thomas Brassey, *The British Navy: Its Strength, Resources and Administration* (London: Longman, Green, and Co., 1883), 3:3. Hereinafter cited as Brassey, *The British Navy.*

[12] Hoogenboom, *Fox*, 119-20.

[13] Church, *Ericsson*, 2:4.

[14] NARA, RG 45, M518, Roll 17, John Lenthall and Benjamin Isherwood to Secretary Welles, 19 March 1862.

[15] Another reason has been suggested for her selection. "*Roanoke* was never satisfactory, the after part having been broken when launched." See *Conway's Fighting Ships*, p. 120.

[16] Bauer and Roberts, *Register*, 40; Canney, *OSN2*, 59-62.

[17] *Confidential Fox Correspondence*, 2:87, D. D. Porter to G. V. Fox, 11 March 1862.

[18] Du Pont, *Civil War Letters*, 1:383.

[19] Ibid., 417.

[20] *Confidential Fox Correspondence*, 1:114, G.V. Fox to S.F. Du Pont, 3 April 1862.

[21] Bennett, *Steam Navy*, 339-40.

[22] Ibid.; Canney, *OSN2*, 89.

[23] Canney, *OSN2*, 75-93, 119-124.

[24] Ibid., 126-29.

[25] Sloan, *Isherwood*, 65.

[26] Ibid., 55.

[27] Church, *Ericsson*, 2:4.

[28] Paullin, *History*, 257.

[29] Hoogenboom, *Fox*, 120.

[30] Canney, *Lincoln's Navy*, 29; Sloan, *Isherwood*, 66-67; Baxter, *Ironclad Warships*, 263-64.

CHAPTER 25 *Naval Expansion*

[1] *ORN*, I, 12, 813-14.

[2] NARA, RG 45, M480, Roll 2, Secretary Welles to Joseph Smith, John Lenthall, Benjamin Isherwood and Edward Hartt, 26 March 1862. Engineer Daniel Martin was subsequently appointed to the board.

[3] *ORN*, I, 12, 814.

[4] NARA, RG 45, M518, Roll 17, John Lenthall, Benjamin Isherwood, Edward Hartt and Daniel Martin to Secretary Welles, 13 May 1862.

[5] NARA, RG 45, M518, Roll 17, Joseph Smith to Secretary Welles, 10 May 1862.

[6] Bauer and Roberts, *Register*, 42.

[7] Canney, *OSN2*, 62-64.

[8] Ibid.; E. M. Eller and Richard H. Webber, *Monitors of the U.S. Navy 1861-1937* (Washington, D.C.: Naval History Division, Navy Department, 1969), 18-19. Hereinafter cited as Eller, *Monitors.*

[9] Dunbaugh and Thomas, *Webb,* 222; Canney, *OSN2,* 64.

[10] Bauer and Roberts, *Register,* 40-44. Displacements were *Dunderberg* 7,060 tons, the four *Monadnocks* 13,391 tons, the ten *Passaics* 18,750 tons and *Dictator* and *Puritan* 9,350 tons.

[11] Welles, *Diary,* 2:340.

[12] Stephen Chapin Kinnaman, *Captain Bulloch, The Life of James Dunwoody Bulloch, Naval Agent of the Confederacy* (Indianapolis: Dog Ear Publishing, 2013), 289, 302-303.

[13] Canney, *OSN2,* 126-28; Welles, *Diary,* 2:341.

[14] Dunbaugh and Thomas, *Webb,* 92, 222. A Dunderberg scholarship is currently being offered at Webb Institute of Naval Architecture.

[15] Silverstone, *Civil War Navies,* 17.

[16] Canney, *OSN2,* 64.

[17] Ibid., 85.

[18] Ibid., 64-66; Eller, *Monitors,* 19-20.

[19] Senate Report No. 142, 45, 86. This report reviews the failures of the "Light-Draught Monitors." Donald McKay and Assistant Secretary Fox thought highly of the *Monadnocks.*

[20] Porter, *Civil War History,* 361.

[21] Canney, *OSN2,* 66-67, 70; Eller, *Monitors,* 19.

[22] Paullin, *History,* 259-60.

[23] *United States Statutes at Large,* 37th Cong., 2nd Sess., 5 July 1862, Ch. 134, 510-12.

[24] Paullin, *History,* 300-301.

[25] The transfer of responsibility didn't occur until three months later. See NARA, RG 45, M480, Roll 2, Secretary Welles to John Lenthall, 4 October 1862.

[26] Sloan, *Isherwood,* 44.

[27] Hornsby MS, 50. Griffiths' alleged plot involved Army General Herman Haupt and Stuart Gwynn, the inventor of "Union Armor," with the goal of provoking a Senate investigation that would expose Lenthall's shortcomings.

[28] "Confirmations," Washington *National Republican,* 19 July 1862.

[29] NARA, RG 45, M480, Roll 2, Secretary Welles to John Lenthall, 25 July 1862; Ibid., M518, Roll 17, John Lenthall to Secretary Welles, 25 July 1862.

[30] Du Pont, *Civil War Letters,* 2:299-300. Du Pont's letter was dated 4 December 1862. Grimes was the same Senator who initiated the request for the Navy to evaluate an "iron-cased" *Iroquois.*

[31] Sloan, *Isherwood,* 46-47.

[32] The Navy Department's general order was issued on 13 March 1863. For background, see Uniform-Reference.Net, "U.S. Army and Navy Officer Ranks during the Civil War," https://www.uniform-reference.net/ranks/usn/usn_rel_ranks.html, accessed December 2020.

[33] "The Navy Department Has Issued the Following General Order," *New York Times*, 19 April 1863.

[34] *ORN* I, 13, 224-25.

[35] Richard E. Winslow, *"A Race of Shipbuilders," The Hanscoms of Eliot, Maine* (Portsmouth: Portsmouth Marine Society, 2013), 77. Hereinafter cited as Winslow, *The Hanscoms.*

[36] Canney, *OSN1*, 103-108.

[37] Silverstone, *Civil War Navies*, 63-67.

CHAPTER 26 *The Light-Draft Monitors*

[1] Church, *Ericsson*, 2:21.

[2] Senate Report No. 142, 68. Ericsson's testimony.

[3] Canney, *OSN2*, 84-88; Silverstone, *Civil War Navies*, 8.

[4] NARA, RG 45, M480, Roll 2, Secretary Welles to John Lenthall, 8 September 1862.

[5] Canney, *Lincoln's Navy*, 25-26.

[6] Senate Report No. 142, 68-69. Ericsson's testimony.

[7] Ibid., 4. Fox's letter to the committee.

[8] Buell, *Cramp*, 80, 87.

[9] William H. Roberts, "'A Small Margin to Go to Sea With': Alban Stimers and the Union Navy's Light-Draft Monitors, Part I," *Warship International*, 58 No. 3 (September 2021): 228. Roberts casts doubt on Smith's role in encouraging the water tank addition and suggests Stimers had already adopted the plan.

[10] Senate Report No. 142, 69-70. Ericsson's testimony.

[11] Canney, *OSN2*, 120.

[12] Senate Report No. 142, 86-88, 105-107, 116-120. Lenthall and Isherwood's testimony.

[13] Ibid., I-II. Chairman Wade's opening statement.

[14] Church, *Ericsson*, 2:24.

[15] Sloan, *Isherwood*, 69.

[16] Church, *Ericsson*, 2:24-25.

[17] Hackemer, *Origins*, 114.

[18] Senate Report No. 142, 82. Fox's testimony.

[19] Welles, *Diary*, 2:241-42.

[20] Senate Report No. 142, II. Chairman Wade's opening statement.

[21] NARA, RG 45, M518, Roll 19, C. H. Davis, John Lenthall and Benjamin Isherwood to Secretary Welles, 23 July 1863; Canney, *OSN2*, 129.

[22] ARSN, 1863, xvi.

[23] NARA, RG 45, M518, Roll 20, John Lenthall to Secretary Welles, 7 April 1864.

[24] Welles, *Diary*, 2:341.

[25] *Congressional Globe*, 38th Cong., 2nd Sess., 17 February 1865, 866-67.

[26] ARSN, 1863, xii, xvi-xvii.

[27] NARA, RG 45, M480, Roll 2, Secretary Welles to John Lenthall, 5 November 1863.

[28] ARSN, 1875, 303.

[29] Bauer and Roberts, *Register*, 69; Canney, *OSN1*, 127-29.

[30] Bauer and Roberts, *Register*, 59; Canney, *OSN1*, 129-32.

[31] Bauer and Roberts, *Register*, 57-59; Canney, *OSN1*, 133-44; Silverstone, *Civil War Navies*, 32-35; Bennett, *Steam Navy*, Appendix B.

[32] ARSN, 1864, 1001. A letter by John Lenthall to Secretary Welles dated 17 October 1864 is reproduced inside the secretary's message.

[33] Senate Report No. 142, 86-87. Lenthall's testimony.

[34] NARA, RG 19, Entry 64, Admiral Gregory to John Lenthall, 17 July 1863. Letter transmitting bi-weekly report and reporting on ships moved due to New York City riots.

[35] Ibid., Admiral Gregory to John Lenthall, 14 August 1863.

[36] NARA, RG 45, M518, Roll 19, John Lenthall to Secretary Welles, 7 October 1863.

[37] Ibid., M480, Roll 2, Secretary Welles to John Lenthall, 8 October 1863.

[38] NARA., RG 19, Entry 64, Stimers to Lenthall, 27 October 1863. This specification was the 92-page "monitor prayer book" described in Nathanial McKay's Congressional testimony. Ibid., Stimers to Gregory, 29 October 1863.

[39] NARA., RG 45, M480, Roll 2, Secretary Welles to John Lenthall, 14 November 1863.

[40] Ibid., M518, Roll 20, John Lenthall to Secretary Welles, 19 January 1864.

[41] NARA., RG 19, Entry 64, Gregory to Lenthall, 12 May 1864.

[42] Lenthall's "height of vessel in side" of 7'-2"—the molded depth at side—yields a freeboard of 14" on a 6'-0" draft vessel. This appears to be less than the commonly cited dimensions of 15" freeboard and a 6'-5" draft would indicate, perhaps due to differing reference datums.

[43] Senate Report No. 142, 78. Welles' letter to the committee, 15 January 1865. His data implying *Chimo* floated 12 inches too deep seems optimistic but supports Lenthall's conclusions. If anything, she was deeper, a finding reinforced by the remedy adopted: to raise the monitors' decks by 22 inches, which after increasing their draft by 6 inches, yielded an additional 16 inches of freeboard. See 98, Stimers' testimony.

[44] Ibid., 96, 108-109. Stimers' and Lenthall's testimony.

[45] Ibid., 15-16, 31. Adams' and N. McKay's testimony.

[46] Ibid., 96, 108-109. Stimers' and Lenthall's testimony.

[47] Ibid., 94, 103-104. Stimers' testimony.

[48] Ibid., 74. Gregory's testimony.

[49] Welles, *Diary*, 2:108, 350-351.

[50] Senate Report No. 142, 108.

[51] Ibid., 95-96, 108. Stimers' and Lenthall's testimony.

[52] Hoogenboom, *Fox*, 192.

[53] Senate Report No. 142, II, 90. Chairman Wade's opening statement and Lenthall's testimony; Bauer and Roberts, *Register*, 44-45.

[54] Senate Report No. 142, I-IV. Chairman Wade's opening statement.

[55] Sloan, *Isherwood*, 77. Sloan's account of the whole light-draft monitor affair is excellent.

CHAPTER 27 *A Time for Economy*

[1] Ives Collection, FICm.012.0170 (239-DSC-1129), S. P. Lee to John Lenthall, 6 March 1864.

[2] Hoogenboom, *Fox*, 37-46.

[3] NARA, RG 45, M518, Roll 20, John Lenthall to Secretary Welles, 21 June 1864.

[4] Hornsby MS, 51; NARA, RG 45, M518, Roll 20, John Lenthall to Secretary Welles, 9 March 1864.

[5] NARA, RG 45, M518, Roll 20, unaddressed memo by John Lenthall, 10 May 1864.

[6] Ives Collection, FICm.006.0082 (239-DSC-1125-26), A. B. Farwell to John Lenthall, 4 October 1864.

[7] Welles, *Diary*, 1:74.

[8] NARA, RG 45, M518, Roll 21, C. H. Davis and John Lenthall to Secretary Welles, 20 October 1864.

[9] Ibid., John Lenthall to Secretary Welles, 6 December 1864. Welles' instructions are cited in Lenthall's reply.

[10] Ibid.

[11] Silverstone, *Civil War Navies*, 8.

[12] Canney, *OSN2*, 90-91.

[13] William Wirt Henry and Ainsworth R. Spofford, *Eminent and Representative Men of Virginia and the District of Columbia of the Nineteenth Century* (Madison, WI.: Brant & Fuller, 1893), 294-305. Hereafter cited as Henry and Spofford, *Eminent Men.* NRHP Rock Creek Cemetery, under William J. Stone; Morris, "Owners," 30; Burnside, *Sketch*, 18-20.

[14] Eyewitness, American Originals from the National Archives, "Robert Stone King—Assassination of President Abraham Lincoln, 1865," https://www.archives.gov/exhibits/eyewitness/html.php?section=13, accessed November 2018.

[15] Canney, *Lincoln's Navy*, 24.

[16] Ford's Theatre, "The Man Behind the Lincoln Funeral: George R. Harrington," https://www.fords.org/blog/post/the-man-behind-the-lincoln-funeral-george-r-harrington/, accessed November 2018.

[17] Ives Collection, FICm.006.0092 (239-DSC-1118), Assistant Treasury Secretary to Wm. Faxon, 19 April 1865.

[18] Paullin, *History*, 312.

[19] NARA, RG 45, M480, Roll 2, Secretary Welles to John Lenthall, 4 May 1865.

[20] Ibid., M518, Roll 21, Welles to "Sir," 29 June 1865. This unaddressed instruction signed by Welles must have been inserted as a copy in the bureau chiefs' letters.

[21] Ives Collection, FICm.999.0126 (239-DSC-1116-17), Donald McKay to John Lenthall, 12 June 1865.

[22] No record of a British warship matching McKay's description can be found in the Lenthall Collection's drawings or the Ives Collection's documents. McKay may have been referring to plans for one of the big *Mersey* class 40-gun screw frigates attributed to Watts. See Lyon and Winfield, *Navy List*, 203.

[23] "Ironclad Vessels, A Letter from Donald McKay," *New York Times*, 23 March 1862, from the *Boston Daily Advertiser.* McKay's letter was dated from London on 24 January 1862.

[24] Bauer and Roberts, *Register*, 45, 82; Senate Report No. 142, 41.

[25] It has been suggested that the Nova Scotia-born former British subject Donald McKay had a much closer connection to the Royal Navy than indicated by his public letters, and that he supplied drawings of the U.S. Navy's latest warships to the Duke of Somerset, the First Lord of the Admiralty. See Amanda Foreman, *A World on Fire* (New York: Random House, 2010), 740 n.

[26] Kevin J. Weddle, *Lincoln's Tragic Admiral, The Life of Samuel Francis Du Pont* (Charlottesville and London: University of Virginia Press, 2005), 168-69, 204, 211-15. Hereinafter cited as Weddle, *Du Pont.*

[27] "General News," *New-York Daily Tribune*, 7 August 1865; Ives Collection, FICm.016.0641 (239-DSC-1110), Adm. Porter to John Lenthall, 5 August 1865; Weddle, *Du Pont*, 145, 211-12.

[28] Ives Collection, FICm.023.0130 (239-DSC-1109), Secretary Welles to John Lenthall, 15 August 1865,

[29] Paullin, *History*, 312-14.

[30] NARA, RG 45, M518, Roll 22, John Lenthall to Secretary Welles, 23 August 1865; Ibid., John Lenthall to Acting Secretary Fox, 5 September 1865.

[31] Ives Collection, FICm.012.0195 (243-DSC-2478), Jenny Lenthall to her mother, 7 September 1865.

[32] NARA, RG 45, M518, Roll 22, John Lenthall to Secretary Welles, 4 October 1865.

[33] Canney, *Sailing Warships*, 136-38, 199, 201.

CHAPTER 28 *Postwar Years*

[1] Paullin, *History*, 309; Hoogenboom, *Fox*, 284-85.

[2] Paullin, *History*, 309-10.

[3] Silverstone, *Civil War Navies*, 66, 69-70.

[4] *History of the Construction Corps of the United States Navy* (Washington: United States Navy Department, Bureau of Construction and Repair, 1937), 1. Hereinafter cited as *Construction Corps.*

[5] NARA, RG 24, M330, Roll 11. Lenthall's entry is styled: 1380 John Lenthall Aug 18/66 Commissioned (13).

[6] Ibid., RG 45, M518, Roll 23, John Lenthall to Secretary Welles, 6 August 1866. On 18 August, Welles sent Lenthall another commission, this one as a naval constructor.

[7] Ives Collection, FICm.006.0081 (239-DSC-1099), A.B. Farwell to John Lenthall, 13 August 1866.

[8] Bradford, *Captains*, pp. 237-38.

[9] Ives Collection, FICm.016.0640 (238-DSC-0614), David D. Porter to John Lenthall, 16 December 1866.

[10] NARA, RG 45, M518, Roll 23, John Lenthall to Secretary Welles, 7 March 1867.

[11] Canney, *OSN1*, 63-65.

[12] Ibid., 63.

[13] Thomas Gilmer, *Modern Ship Design* (Annapolis: Naval Institute Press, 1975), 244.

[14] Hornsby MS, 56. It was said that together with B.F. Delano, Lenthall visited the Boston Navy Yard during this period.

[15] Ives Collection, FICm.023.0132 (239-DSC-1095), Secretary Welles to John Lenthall, 26 April 1867.

[16] Sloan, *Isherwood*, 165. The quoted phrases are from letters of Isherwood to Fox.

[17] Winslow, *The Hanscoms*, 144.

[18] Ives Collection, FICm.006.0077 (239-DSC-1085), A.B. Farwell to John Lenthall, 7 May 1867.

[19] Ibid., FICm.012.0198 (235-DSC-0017), /s/ RKS (Robert King Stone), 28 April 1867; Ibid., FICm.012.0198 (235-DSC-0013-14), /s/ RKS (Robert King Stone), 1 May 1867.

[20] Richard Henry Dana, *To Cuba and Back: A Vacation Voyage* (Boston: Ticknor and Fields, 1859).

[21] "Marine News, Port of Charleston, Arrived Yesterday," Passengers per Steamship *Champion* from New York, *Charleston Daily News*, 22 May 1867; Ives Collection, FICm.001.0053 (239-DSC-1094), J.F. Armstrong to John Lenthall, 23 May 1867. "Delano said you had returned from Havana and would be in Charleston on the 21st."

[22] Canney, *Lincoln's Navy*, 50.

[23] Ives Collection, FICm.023.0290 (239-DSC-1071), T.D. Wilson to John Lenthall, 3 May 1867. The steamer *Estrella* was later substituted for *Yucca*, as originally proposed by Wilson.

[24] "Obituary Record, Theodore D. Wilson," *New York Times*, 30 June 1896.

[25] Wilson, *Ship Building*.

[26] Ives Collection, FICm.012.0194 (243-DSC-2465), Jenny Lenthall to Aunt Mary, 11 June 1867.

[27] Sloan, *Isherwood*, 166. Cape May would later prove a favorite Lenthall summer vacation destination, as documented in Chapter 30.

[28] Paullin, *History*, 318.

[29] NARA, RG 45, M480, Roll 3, Secretary Welles to John Lenthall, 12 December 1867.

[30] Canney, *OSN1*, 125-26.

[31] NARA, RG 45, M518, Roll 24, John Lenthall to Secretary Welles, 17 January 1868.

[32] Bennett, *Steam Navy*, 627.

33 NARA, RG 45, M518, Roll 24, John Lenthall to Secretary Welles, 2 and 13 April 1868; Bennett, *Steam Navy*, Appendix B.

34 NARA, RG 45, M518, Roll 24, John Lenthall to Secretary Welles, 28 February 1868.

35 Ives Collection, FIC.2018.021 (245-DSC-2837), /s/ RKS (Robert King Stone); Ibid., FICm.012.0198 (235-DSC-0013-21), /s/ R. K. Stone. Several of these prescriptions were written on preprinted forms, one for "Dr. Stone, corner of Fourteenth and F Streets," and another headed "Kidwell & Sons, Pharmacists, Penn. Ave. near cor. 14th Street."

36 Ibid., FICm.023.0131 (239-DSC-1062), G. Welles to John Lenthall, 16 June 1868.

37 *Conway's Fighting Ships*, 380-81.

38 Coletta, *Secretaries*, 1:356-57.

39 Ibid., pp. 363-65; Sloan, *Isherwood*, 230-31.

40 Paullin, *History*, 360; also see Uniform-Reference.Net, "U.S. Army and Navy Officer Ranks during the Civil War," https://www.uniform-reference.net/ranks/usn/usn_rel_ranks.html, accessed December 2020.

41 Coletta, *Secretaries*, 1:365.

42 Bennett, *Steam Navy*, 636-43.

43 Ives Collection, FICm.012.0208 (243-DSC-2482), Daughter Jenny to Father, 22 Aug 1863 [off by 10 years?]; Ibid., FICm.023.0015 (243-DSC-2444), Jenny to Aunt Mary, 22 Aug 1873.

44 For example, see under Smithsonian National Portrait Gallery. *Catalogue of a Collection of Oriental Art Objects belonging to Thomas E. Waggaman of Washington, D.C.*, Ed. by H. Shugio (1896).

45 Ancestry, "Jane Lenthall," https://www.ancestry.com/genealogy/records/jane-lenthall_30285466, accessed November 2017; Morris, "Owners," 26.

46 Paullin, *History*, 322-24; Coletta, *Secretaries*, 1:369.

47 NARA, RG 45, M480, Roll 3, D. D. Porter for Secretary of the Navy to John Lenthall, 19 July 1869.

48 Ibid., RG 24, M330, "Sept 28/69 Placed on the Retired List from the 16th Sept 1869" with a calculation nearby to confirm he was 62; ZB Folder, letter by Captain D. W. Knox to Thomas Hornsby, 6 March 1940.

CHAPTER 29 *Moved Aside*

1 Ives Collection, FICm.012.0262 (238-DSC-0700), John Lenthall to Rear Admiral Gordon, 4 October 1869.

2 Ibid., FICm.004.0190 (233-DSC-9280), D. D. Porter for Secretary of the Navy to John Lenthall, 6 October 1869.

3 Ibid., FICm.006.0079 (238-DSC-0683), A. B. Farwell to John Lenthall, 30 September 1869.

4 John Lenthall Personal Papers, Naval Personages—Testimonials & Obituaries 1840-70.

[5] Ives Collection, FICm.023.0129 (238-DSC-0687-90), Gideon Welles to John Lenthall, 8 November 1869. About half of Welles' eight page letter has been edited out. What remains is a sarcastic commentary on how his former department was now being managed.

[6] Ibid., FICm.018.0154 (238-DSC-0685), Secretary Robeson to John Lenthall. Robeson rather than Porter was now signing orders to the bureau chiefs.

[7] NARA, RG 45, M518, Roll 25, John Lenthall to Secretary Robeson, 8 December 1869. A central paragraph of Lenthall's letter appears in the introduction to Appendix 12.

[8] "Visit of Government Officials to Monarch," *New-York Daily Tribune*, 26 February 1870.

[9] Parkes, *British Battleships*, 130-36. *Captain*, the brain child of the inventor of the Coles type turret, capsized during a tremendous gale off Cape Finisterre seven months later with a loss of 472 officers and men. Her capsizing was caused by her low freeboard which was in turn exacerbated by excess lightship weight. *Monarch*'s turrets were carried a deck higher and so avoided *Captain*'s poor range of stability, an inherent problem of any low freeboard vessel.

[10] *Conway's Fighting Ships*, 121.

[11] Parkes, *British Battleships*, 130; Bennett, *Steam Navy*, Appendix B.

[12] NARA, RG 45, M518, Roll 25, Bureau chiefs to members of Congress, 28 February 1870.

[13] Paullin, *History*, 359.

[14] *United States Statutes at Large*, 41st Cong., 3rd Sess., 1871, Ch. 117, 537.

[15] Winslow, *The Hanscoms*, 131.

[16] See Appendix 12 for details of the Hanscoms' service as naval constructors.

[17] Ives Collection, FICm.006.0129 (241-DSC-1450), G. V. Fox to John Lenthall, 1 March 1870.

[18] Coletta, *Secretaries*, 1:369.

[19] According to the U.S. Naval Academy Museum's senior curator, Tracie Logan, the Ives Collection of John Lenthall's personal papers was donated by Mrs. Eugene Semmes Ives in 1951, in care of her grandson, LCDR Eugene I. Malone.

[20] Ninth Census of the United States (1870), Washington, D.C.

[21] John Lenthall reported $12,000 of real estate owned and $25,000 of personal estate owned; Sister Mary King Lenthall reported $8,000 of real estate and $10,000 of personal estate.

[22] *Navy Register*, 1870.

[23] Ives Collection, FICm.016.0629 (241-DSC-1445), D. D. Porter to John Lenthall, 16 November 1870.

[24] Silverstone, *Civil War Navies*, 119-20.

[25] NARA, RG 45, M518, Roll 25, John Lenthall to Secretary Robeson, 22 November 1870.

[26] Silverstone, *Civil War Navies*, 38.

[27] "The Robeson Investigation," *Wheeling Intelligencer*, 29 March 1872. Lenthall gave testimony about what Charles Dana of the *Sun* called the "Secor steal."

[28] NARA, RG 45, M480, Roll 3, Secretary Robeson to John Lenthall, 19 January 1871.

[29] *Navy Register*, 1873.

[30] NARA, RG 24, M330, a penciled-in note against John Lenthall records "relieved as Chief of Bureau 28 Jany '71," with a formal entry "Jany 29/'71 General Inspector of Ships." Isaiah Hanscom's record formally shows "Jany 28/'71 Commissioned as Chief Bureau of Construction."

[31] Hornsby MS Docs, transcribed letter, Annette Ives to Miss Morris, 21 September 1926.

[32] *Congressional Globe*, 41st Cong., 3rd Sess., 1118-24; Winslow, *The Hanscoms*, 134; NARA, RG 24, M330, William Hanscom's record formally shows "April 17/'71 Reinstated."

[33] "Robeson's Mighty Frauds," New York *Sun*, 8 March 1872.

BOOK FOUR *Inspector*

CHAPTER 30 *Cape May*

[1] Ives Collection, FICm.012.0161, 238-DSC-0612, Secretary Robeson to John Lenthall, 18 April 1871.

[2] *Congressional Globe*, 41st Cong., 3rd Sess., 1122-23; "Robeson's Mighty Frauds," New York *Sun*, 8 March 1872.

[3] "Condition of Steamer Tennessee," Philadelphia *Daily Evening Telegraph*, 3 May 1871.

[4] "Naval Academy Visiting Board," Philadelphia *Daily Evening Telegraph*, 3 May 1871.

[5] Ancestry, "Jane Lenthall," https://www.ancestry.com/genealogy/records/jane-lenthall_30285466, accessed November 2017; Morris, "Owners," 26.

[6] Find A Grave, Mary D. Lenthall," https://www.findagrave.com/memorial/1570 45765/mary-d-lenthall, accessed February 2018; Ancestry, "Mary Dugan Eck," https://www.ancestry.com/search/?name=mary+dugan_eck, accessed February 2018.

[7] Ibid.

[8] Ives Collection, FICm.016.0558 (243-DSC-2457), David Porter to John Lenthall, 10 February 1872.

[9] "Robeson's Mighty Frauds," New York *Sun*, 8 March 1872.

[10] "The Robeson Investigation," *Wheeling Intelligencer*, 29 March 1872.

[11] Ives Collection, numerous letters dated from 1873 through 1880.

[12] Emil R. Salvini, *The Summer City by the Sea: Cape May, New Jersey—An Illustrated History* (Brunswick, NJ: Rutgers University Press, 1998), 7-29. Hereinafter cited as Salvini, *Cape May.*

[13] Ives Collection, FICm.012.0193 (243-DSC-2442), John Lenthall to D. Sister (Mary), 30 June 1874.

[14] Ibid., FICm.012.0537 (235-DSC-0108-9), Mary K. Lenthall to John Lenthall, 16 April 1880. Reference was made to matting Sister Libby found for her Cape May dining room.

[15] Ibid., FICm.001.0036 (241-DSC-1442), D. Ammen to John Lenthall, 30 June 1873.

[16] Ibid., FICm.023.0015 (243-DSC-2448), Jenny Waggaman to Aunt Mary, 22 August 1873.

[17] Ibid., FICm.023.0013 (243-DSC-2446), Jenny Waggaman to Aunt Mary, 26 August 1873.

[18] Ibid., FICm.008.0198 (234-DSC-9523), Joseph Henry to John Lenthall, 13 May 1874.

[19] Wahl, *Franklin Institute*, 25-26.

[20] Farr and Bostwick, *Guide;* also see Independence Seaport Museum, "John Lenthall Collection," https://www.phillyseaport.org under Discover/J. Welles Henderson Research Center/Online Catalog/keyword: John Lenthall Collection, accessed October 2017.

[21] Hornsby MS, between 71 and 72. The copy of Lenthall's letter is in Hornsby's handwriting.

[22] Ives Collection, FICm.012.0193 (243-DSC-2442-43), John Lenthall to Sister Mary, 30 June 1874.

[23] Ibid., FICm.012.0221 (242-DSC-1655), John Lenthall to Sister (Mary), 11 July 1874.

[24] Ibid., FICm.012.0624 (237-DSC-0267), Sister Libby to Sister (Mary), 12 July 1874.

[25] Ibid., FICm.012.0022 (242-DSC-1649), Sister Libby to Sister (Mary), 14 July 1874.

[26] Ibid., FICm.012.0223 (242-DS-1651), John Lenthall to Sister (Mary), 23 July 1874.

[27] Ibid., FICm.012.0224 (243-DSC-2519), John Lenthall to Sister (Mary), 27 July 1874.

[28] Ibid., FICm.012.0226 (242-DSC-1657), John Lenthall to Sister (Mary), 29 July 1874.

[29] Ibid., FICm.012.0193.1 (243-DSC-2441), Jenny Waggaman to Aunt Mary, undated but written shortly before her death. A P.S. at the bottom, probably in Mary K. Lenthall's hand, notes that Jenny died at 1 a.m. on 30 July; Ibid., FIC.2018.019 (245-DSC-2832), John Lenthall to Sister (Mary), dated Monday, likely 27 July 1874, with a note at the bottom, probably in Mary K. Lenthall's hand, giving the time of Jenny's death as 3 a.m. and that she "reached home Friday at 6 a.m." The date of death marked on Jane Lenthall Waggaman's headstone is 29 July 1874.

[30] Ives Collection, FICm.012.0592 (236-DSC-0229-30), Mary Lenthall to Sister (Libby), 3 August 1874.

[31] The church was almost certainly the Saint Stephen Martyr Catholic Church on Pennsylvania Avenue.

[32] Ives Collection, FICm.012.0592 (236-DSC-0229-30), Mary Lenthall to Sister (Libby), 3 August 1874.

[33] Ibid., FICm.012.0546 (243-DSC-2439), Mary Lenthall to Sister (Libby), 5 August 1874.

[34] Ancestry "John Lenthall," https://www.ancestry.com/family-tree/person/tree/3472171/person/24101637558/facts, accessed on August 2020. A copy of Lenthall's will was posted on the website.

[35] Paullin, *History,* 332-334.

[36] *Navy Register,* 1873.

CHAPTER 31 *Monitor Rebuilds*

[1] ARSN, 1876, 4-5.

[2] Paullin, *History*, 341.

[3] Bennett, *Steam Navy*, 544-46.

[4] Paullin, *History*, 341.

[5] Canney, *OSN2*, 131.

[6] Coletta, *Secretaries*, 1:372-73.

[7] "The Spanish Ironclad 'Arapiles' in the Brooklyn Navy-Yard," *Harper's Weekly*, 13 December 1873. *Arapiles* is shown in a graving dock undergoing hull repairs following a grounding.

[8] Donald Macintyre and Basil W. Bathe, *Man-of-War, A History of the Combat Vessel* (New York: Castle Books, 1974), 113.

[9] ARSN, 1878, 26.

[10] 43rd Cong., 2nd Sess., House of Representatives Executive Document 1, Part 3, Report of the Secretary of the Navy ... 1 December 1874, 23.

[11] Canney, *OSN2*, 133.

[12] Ibid.

[13] Bennett, *Steam Navy*, 629, Appendix B.

[14] Paullin, *History*, 346-50.

[15] ARSN, 1876, 4-5.

[16] Paullin, *History*, 350-51; Canney, *OSN2*, 135.

[17] Dorwart, *PNY*, 95-98.

[18] ARSN, 1877, 6.

[19] Ives Collection, FICm.016.0691 (241-DSC-1432), W.J. Powell to John Lenthall, 18 May 1877.

[20] Ibid., A 012.0459 (247-DSC-3107), unidentified newspaper clipping titled "Four Millions. The Most Expensive War Vessel in the World."

[21] Ibid., FIC.2018.098 (247-DSC-3068-69), "Copy, From the Special Report by the Board of Naval Constructors on the Hull of the U.S. Monitor Puritan, made 21 August 1877."

[22] Ibid., FICm.023.0252 (241-DSC-1415), /s/ W.C. Whitthorne, 13 May 1878.

[23] Ibid., FICm.020.0077 (241-DSC-1428), Secretary Thompson to John Lenthall, 24 May 1878.

[24] Ibid., FICm.020.0078 (241-DSC-1414), Secretary Thompson to John Lenthall, 28 May 1878.

[25] Leonard Alexander Swann, Jr., *John Roach, Maritime Entrepreneur* (Annapolis: United States Naval Institute, 1985), 147. Hereinafter cited as Swann, *Roach*.

[26] Ives Collection, A 2018.110 (247-DSC-3091), Memo on new monitors, p. 6; Ibid., A 2018.111 (247-DSC-3092), Memo on new monitors, 7; Ibid., A 2018.112 (247-DSC-3093), Memo on new monitors, 8. These three pages are undated but in Lenthall's hand and clearly relate to a review of *Puritan*, a vessel which the previously mentioned boards found much overweight. They may have been drafts for a report he submitted to the House on 4 June 1878.

[27] Ibid., FICm.009.0016 (241-DSC-1418), B. F. Isherwood to John Lenthall, 16 August 1878. Isherwood's comments about Reed appeared at the beginning of his letter, but they have been placed at the end of the quoted lines in the interest of subject flow.

[28] Ibid., FICm.020.0075 (238-DSC-0630), Secretary Thompson to John Lenthall, 3 February 1879.

[29] "Robeson's Peculations," *St. Paul Globe*, 10 February 1879.

[30] Ives Collection, FICm.020.0079 (238-DSC-0623), Secretary Thompson to John Lenthall, 6 April 1880.

[31] "Naval Boards to Inspect Ironclads," Washington *Evening Star*, 9 April 1880; Canney, *OSN2*, 135.

[32] Ives Collection, FIC.2018.072 (246-DSC-2980), B.F. Isherwood to John Lenthall, 14 April 1880.

[33] Hornsby MS, pp. 62-68. The source for Lenthall's report is unclear; Hornsby notes it to be "Lenthall mss." The report may have come from the Ives Collection but the original documents can no longer be found.

[34] Parkes, *British Battleships*, 175-86, 293-95.

[35] Canney, *OSN2*, 135.

[36] Ives Collection, FICm.023.0253 (240-DSC-1273), Congressman Whitthorne to John Lenthall, 2 June 1880; Ibid., FIC.2018.034 (245-DSC-2868), Congressman Whitthorne to John Lenthall, June 1880.

[37] Ibid., FICm.012.0385 (240-DSC-1262), John Lenthall to Congressman Whitthorne, 17 June 1880.

[38] Ibid., FICm.012.0073 (240-DSC-1271), E. J. Auverien [spelling?] of San Francisco to W. C. Whitthorne, 20 July 1880.

[39] Canney, *OSN2*, 139.

[40] ARSN, 1881, 17-18.

CHAPTER 32 *Twilight*

[1] Burnside, *Sketch*, 18-19.

[2] The Church of the Epiphany, "Elizabeth Jane Lenthall Stone," http://epiphanydc.org/2017/07/31/august-3-elizabeth-jane-lenthall-stone-1892/, accessed February 2019.

[3] Ives Collection, FIC.2018.115 (247-DSC-3098), Annie Hunter to John Lenthall, 16 May 1876. Lenthall paid $50 of Susie's travel expenses to Philadelphia.

[4] Ibid., FICm.012.0583 (243-DSC-2505), Mary K. Lenthall to John Lenthall, 29 May 1876.

[5] "Funeral of Admiral Smith," Washington *National Republican*, 20 January 1877.

[6] Ives Collection, FICm.011.0048 (236-DSC-0150), Samuel Archbold to John Lenthall, 21 June 1877.

[7] Ibid., FICp.601.0299 (241-DSC-1424), Edward Hartt to John Lenthall, 29 June 1877.

[8] Sloan, *Isherwood*, 236-37.

[9] Ives Collection, FICm.006.0130 (241-DSC-1426), G. V. Fox to John Lenthall, 23 June 1877.

[10] Ibid., FICm.012.0546 (236-DSC-0168), Mary K. Lenthall to John Lenthall, 16 October 1877.

[11] Richard S. West, Jr., *Gideon Welles, Lincoln's Navy Department* (Indianapolis and New York: The Bobbs-Merrill Company, 1943), 339-40.

[12] Ives Collection, FICm.012.0541 (236-DSC-0170), Mary K. Lenthall to Annie, 28 March 1879; Ibid., FICm.012.0545 (236-DSC-0162), Mary K. Lenthall to John Lenthall, 7 April 1879.

[13] Ibid., FICm.013.0478 (241-DSC-1446), Geo. W. Much to John Lenthall, 5 June 1879.

[14] Ibid., FICm.023.0273 (237-DSC-0305), Mary K. Lenthall to John Lenthall, 23 June 1879.

[15] Tenth Census of the United States (1880), Washington, D.C.

[16] Ives Collection, FICm.006.0131 (240-DSC-1260), G. V. Fox to John Lenthall, 16 August 1880.

[17] Ibid., FICm.012.0561 (236-DSC-0134), Mary K. Lenthall to John Lenthall, 9 September 1880.

[18] Find A Grave, "Helen *Waldo* Burnside," https://www.findagrave,com/memorial/41347667/helen-burnside, accessed November 2021.

[19] "Building Up the Navy," Washington *Evening Star*, 2 July 1881.

[20] Coletta, *Secretaries*, 1:391-92.

[21] Ibid., 399; Paullin, *History*, 387-90.

[22] Coletta, *Secretaries*, 1:392; Sloan, *Isherwood*, 238-39.

[23] Paullin, *History*, 389.

[24] Baxter, *Ironclad Warship*, 275.

[25] Paullin, *History*, 391-393.

[26] *Inventory of RG 19*, 4.

[27] Swann, *Roach*, 164.

[28] Ives Collection, FICm.023.0288 (239-DSC-1076), T. D. Wilson to John Lenthall, 4 July 1869.

[29] "Sudden Deaths, John Lenthall," Washington *Evening Critic*, 11 April 1882.

[30] Ibid.

[31] "Sudden Death of Mr. John Lenthall," Washington *Evening Star*, 11 April 1882.

[32] E-mail from Tripp Jones, Church of the Epiphany Archivist, to the author, 9 November 2019.

[33] ZB Folder, Memo dated 23 May 1923.

[34] Find A Grave, "John Lenthall," https://www.findagrave.com/memorial/142599741/john-lenthall, accessed February 2020.

[35] *ANJ*, "Recent Deaths," 19 (1882): 834.

[36] Ancestry, "John Lenthall," https://www.ancestry.com/family-tree/person/tree/3472171/person/24101637558/facts, accessed on August 2020.

[37] Burnside, *Sketch*, 22-23.

[38] Find A Grave, "Anna Maria 'Annie' *Waggaman* Ives," https://www.findagrave.com/memorial/5401730/anna-maria-ives, accessed February 2018.
All later formal mentions of Anny give her first name as Anna in contrast to those of Lenthall's era which use Ann.

[39] "Mrs. Cora Semmes Ives Dead," *Washington Post*, 28 January 1916.

[40] Find A Grave, "John Lenthall," https://www.findagrave.com/memorial/142599741/john-lenthall, accessed February 2020.

[41] Find A Grave, "Elizabeth Jane *Lenthall* Stone," https://www.findagrave.com/memorial/41347661/elizabeth-jane-stone, accessed February 2018.

[42] Arizona Historical Society, Eugene Semmes Ives Collection.

[43] Morris, "*Owners*."

[44] Hornsby MS Docs, Letter by Cora Ives to Thomas Hornsby, 26 May 1949.

[45] Ibid., Letter by Cora Ives to Thomas Hornsby, 20 October 1950.

[46] E-mail by Tracie Logan, Senior Curator, U.S. Naval Academy Museum, to the author, 26 April 2018.

APPENDIX 1 *Directions for Building a Store Ship*

[1] Lenthall Personal Papers, Relief (U.S.S.) Store Ship 1835, "Directions for building Store Ship."

APPENDIX 2 *Relief Calculations, Summary and Metacenter*

[1] Lenthall Personal Papers, Relief (U.S.S.) Store Ship 1835, calculation sheets.

[2] Ibid., scan 0025b.

[3] Ibid., scan 0008c.

[4] Atwood, "Disquisition," 269.

[5] Chapman, *Tractat*, 20.

[6] Lenthall Personal Papers, Relief (U.S.S.) Store Ship 1835, calculation sheets, scan 0026a.

APPENDIX 3 *Orders for the Launch of the U.S. Ship Pennsylvania*

[1] Lenthall Personal Papers, Pennsylvania (U.S.S.) Ship of the Line, "Orders to be Observed" and "In Describing the Launch."

[2] John Lenthall, "On the Launching of the Three-deck Ship, the Pennsylvania in 1837," *Proceedings of the American Philosophical Society*, 3 No. 27 (1843): 103-104.

[3] *PNA*, 755.

[4] Lenthall Personal Papers, Pennsylvania (U.S.S.) Ship of the Line, scan 0011b with labels added by R. Thorp.

APPENDIX 4 *Suitability of Mail Steamers as Ships of War*

[1] Lenthall Personal Papers, Mail Steamers 1848-57, John Lenthall to Bureau Chief Captain Charles Skinner, 18 March 1852.

[2] NARA, RG 45, M518, Roll 12, John Lenthall to Secretary Dobbin, 6 March 1854.

APPENDIX 5 *Young, Smart, Spirit of the Age Fellows*

[1] Du Pont Papers, Item No. W9-10643, Letter by John Lenthall to Captain Samuel Francis Du Pont, 3 Feb 1861; for context see Du Pont, *Civil War Letters*, 1:30-31.

[2] NARA, RG 45, M 518, Letter by John Lenthall to Secretary Toucey, dated 1 February 1861.

APPENDIX 6 *The Design and Construction of Naval Vessels of War*

[1] NARA, RG 45, M518, Roll 17, John Lenthall and Benjamin Isherwood to Secretary Welles, 17 March 1862.

[2] Brassey, *The British Navy*, 3:3.

[3] Sloan, *Isherwood*, 52-54. The reader is recommended to Sloan's evaluation of this same letter.

APPENDIX 7 *Evolution of the Double Turreted Ironclad*

[1] *Congressional Globe*, 36th Cong., 2nd Sess., 19 January 1861, 463.

[2] Hoogenboom, *Fox*, 165.

[3] Canney, *Lincoln's Navy*, 60.

[4] NARA, M518, Roll 16, John Lenthall to Secretary Toucey, 1 Feb 1861; Du Pont Papers, letter by John Lenthall to Samuel Francis Du Pont, 3 Feb 1861.

[5] Baxter, *Ironclad Warship*, App. E; Canney, *OSN2*, 57-58; NARA, RG19, Flat Dash File 142-10-14.

[6] NARA, M518, Roll 17, John Lenthall et al. to Secretary Welles, 13 May 1862.

[7] Canney, *OSN2*, 62.

APPENDIX 8 *Ironclad Steamers for Harbor and Coast Defense*

[1] NARA, RG 45, M518, Roll 17, John Lenthall, Benjamin Isherwood, Edward Hartt and Daniel Martin to Secretary Welles, 13 May 1862.

[2] Ibid., Joseph Smith to Secretary Welles, 10 May 1862.

APPENDIX 9 *The Light-Draught Monitors*

[1] Lenthall Personal Papers, Detailed Specifications of Light Draft Monitors 1863, newspaper clipping from the *Boston Daily Advertiser*, dated 4 March 1865.

[2] Senate Report No. 142, 118-20.

APPENDIX 10 *Lenthall's Book and Pamphlet Collection*

[1] Farr and Bostwick, *Guide*, 37-46.

[2] Wahl, *Franklin Institute*, 25-26.

[3] "List of Books Added to the Library during April, May and June, 1883," *JFI*, 116 No. 1 (July 1883): 74-80.

APPENDIX 11 *Ships Constructed, Designed and Specified by John Lenthall*

[1] Chapelle, *American Sailing Navy* and *Search for Speed*; Canney, *OSN1*, *OSN2* and *Sailing Warships*; Silverstone, *Sailing Navy* and *Civil War Navies*; Bennett, *Steam Navy*; Bauer and Roberts, *Register*; Cutler, *Queens*.

[2] ZB Folder, Capt. D.W. Knox to Thomas Hornsby, 5 May 1942.

[3] Ibid.

APPENDIX 12 *Naval Constructors Active During Lenthall's Career*

[1] *Navy Register*, 1825-1882; NARA, RG 24, M330, Roll 11, Abstracts of Service Records of Naval Officers; Lewis R. Hamersly, *The Records of Living Officers of the U.S. Navy and Marine Corps* (Philadelphia: J. B. Lippincott & Co., 1870); Ibid., (New York: L. R. Hamersly & Co., 1898); and sources as listed in Appendix 11.

[2] NARA, RG 45, M518, Roll 25, John Lenthall to Secretary Robeson, 6 December 1869.

* * *

GLOSSARY

Baseline. A longitudinal datum from which vertical heights are measured, BL. On a wooden vessel it is at the upper edge of the keel's rabbet, and on an iron vessel it is at the top edge of plate adjacent to the keel.

Bilge, Bilges. The curved section of a vessel's hull marking the transition from its bottom to its sides.

Breadth. Width of vessel, B; either to the outside of its frame (molded) or to the outside of its planking or plating (extreme).

Center of buoyancy. The centroid of the immersed volume of a vessel's hull, as measured longitudinally (LCB) or vertically (VCB).*

Center of floatation. The centroid of the area of a vessel's waterplane, measured longitudinally (LCF).*

* The transverse component of these centers is usually not considered because of the symmetry of a vessel's hull.

Center of gravity. The centroid of all a vessel's weights, as measured longitudinally (LCG), transversely (TCG) or vertically (VCG).

Coefficients of form. Calculated geometric fractions which yield numeric measures of a hull's shape, most commonly block (C_B), waterplane (C_{WP}) and midship (C_M) coefficients.

Deadrise. The rise or upward angle of the bottom of a vessel's hull, outward from the keel.

Depth (of hold). The height inside a hull, from the top of the keel to the underside of the main deck.

Displacement. The volume of water occupied by a vessel's hull when freely floating, expressed either as volume of displacement (V) in cubic feet or weight of displacement (Δ) in tons.

Double banked. Vessel with two complete gun decks, as applied to a large frigate.

Draft. Depth of water in which a vessel freely floats; more precisely defined as either a vessel's extreme or keel draft, or molded draft to baseline.

Floating line. See load line.

Frames. Transversely arranged bends of timber or iron; the ribs that form the skeleton of a vessel's hull.

Freeboard. For a hull freely floating, the distance from the water's surface to the top of the first open deck or down flooding point.

Frigate. A large, three-masted square-rigged man-of-war with one covered gun deck and mounting from twenty-eight up to fifty large guns; Nelson's "eyes of the fleet."

Hog, hogging. The condition of a ship's hull when strained so that its ends are deformed downward, typically when only its midship section is supported on a wave crest.

Hydrostatic data. Geometric and physical properties of a vessel's hull, usually arranged in tables according to draft, including volumes, displacements, centers of buoyancy and floatation, metacentric heights and other hull data.

Keel. The central, lowermost longitudinal structural member of a vessel; the ship's spine.

Length. Longitudinal distance between a vessel's extremities, L; more precisely defined as length overall (LOA) or length between its fore and aft perpendiculars (LBP).

Lines plan. A drawing documenting a vessel's geometry using three mutually orthogonal views showing its profile (sheer plan), plan view (half-breadth plan) and hull sections (body plan).

Load line. The deepest draft for which the vessel is normally designed to operate.

Longitudinal. Length-wise axis of a vessel.

Metacenter. Height of intersection of the vertical projection of the center of buoyancy with the vessel's centerline, M. In the transverse axis (BM_T), it is a measure of stability; in the longitudinal axis (BM_L), a measure of resistance to pitching.

Midship. Longitudinal center of vessel, usually the geometric mid-point between a vessel's perpendiculars but in sailing vessel hulls, often the widest point of the hull or its 'dead flat'.

Monitor. A low freeboard, light draft coastal warship mounting heavy guns in a turret; originally modeled after John Ericsson's U.S.S. *Monitor.*

Molded (moulded) dimensions. Dimensions taken to the outside of a hull's frame and not including the thickness of its planking, plating, or the volume of its appendages (rudder, keel, etc.), typically shown on a lines plan and replicated on moulds produced in the mould loft.

Offsets. Table of dimensions, usually taken transversely at a given section and elevation, documenting the shape of a hull.

Ordinates. The vertical coordinate or Y function of an X-Y geometric equation.

Perpendiculars. Datums perpendicular to the baseline, the forward perpendicular (FP) defined by the intersection of the load line (or the gun deck) and fore side of the stem rabbet, the aft perpendicular (AP) defined by the intersection of the load line and aft side of the stern post.

Rabbet (of keel, etc.). The groove let into the side of the keel which accepts the first adjacent (garboard) strake of planking.

Razee. A large vessel whose upper deck has been cut down to reduce her height and rating, typically a ship of the line razeed to a frigate or a frigate razeed to a corvette.

Sheer. The upper line of vessel's hull that defines its longitudinal profile.

Ship of the line, Liner. A large, three-masted square-rigged man-of-war with two or three covered gun decks and mounting from seventy-four up to 120 large guns; intended to fight in a fleet's line of battle.

Sloop of war, Sloop. A smaller, square-rigged man-of-war with one (usually) open gun deck and mounting from fourteen up to twenty-four guns; economical compliments to frigates.

Station. A number or lettered longitudinal position on a vessel's hull, often referred to as a frame station, used to define a hull's shape at the named station.

Tonnage. Admeasurement according to the Builder's Old Measurement formula which yielded a legal or customs definition of the capacity of a vessel. Not to be confused with tons displacement which is an accurate calculation of a vessel's weight.

Transverse. Athwartship or cross-wise axis of vessel.

Trim. Difference between forward and after drafts. A vessel trimmed by the head has a deeper forward draft than after draft.

Tumblehome. Inward taper of a vessel's sides above the load line.

Ways. The inclined structures which support a vessel's hull during its launch. Launching or ground ways are lengths of flat planks resting on prepared ground; bilge ways, shaped to fit the hull, sit on the greased launching ways and carry the vessel into the water.

BIBLIOGRAPHY

Government Documents and Publications

Library of Congress:

- Thomas Jefferson papers, Series 3, District of Columbia Miscellany, 1790-1808.

National Archives and Records Administration (NARA), Washington, D.C.:

- *Preliminary Inventory of the Records of the Bureau of Ships (Record Group 19).* Washington: The National Archives and Records Service, 1961.
- Record Group 19, Records of the Bureau of Ships, General Records of the Office of the Chief of the Bureau, Letters Sent to the Secretary of the Navy, 1850-1867, Entry 49.
- Record Group 19, Records of the Bureau of Ships, General Records of the Office of the Chief of the Bureau, Letters Sent to Officers, 1862-1862, Entry 52.
- Record Group 19, Records of the Bureau of Ships, General Records of the Office of the Chief of the Bureau, Letters Sent to the Commandant of the Philadelphia Navy Yard, 1858-1875, Entry 54.
- Record Group 19, Records of the Bureau of Ships, General Records of the Office of the Chief of the Bureau, Letters Received from Superintendents Outside of Navy Yards, 1862-1867, Entry 64.
- Record Group 19, Ship Design and Construction Drawings [Dash Plans].
- Record Group 24, Records of the Bureau of Naval Personnel, Abstracts of Service Records of Naval Officers, 1789-1893, M330.
- Record Group 24, Records of the Bureau of Naval Personnel, Deck Logs, U.S.S. *Merrimack*, 1856-1860.
- Record Group 45, Naval Records Collection of the Office of Naval Records and Library, Records of the Board of Navy Commissioners 1794-1843, Miscellaneous Letters Sent, 1815-1842, Entry 310.
- Record Group 45, Naval Records Collection of the Office of Naval Records and Library, Records of the Board of Navy

Commissioners 1794-1843, Register of Letters Received, 1820-1837, Entry 312.

- Record Group 45, Naval Records Collection of the Office of Naval Records and Library, Records of the Board of Navy Commissioners 1794-1843, Letters Received from Constructors, 1815-1842, Entry 317.
- Record Group 45, Naval Records Collection of the Office of Naval Records and Library, Letters Received by the Secretary of the Navy from Captains, 1805-1861, M125.
- Record Group 45, Naval Records Collection of the Office of Naval Records and Library, Records of the Office of the Secretary of the Navy, Letters Sent by the Secretary of the Navy to Chiefs of Navy Bureaus, 1842-1886, M480.
- Record Group 45, Naval Records Collection of the Office of Naval Records and Library, Records of the Office of the Secretary of the Navy, Letters Received by the Secretary from Chiefs of Navy Bureaus, 1842-1885, M518.
- Record Group 181, Records of Naval Districts and Shore Establishments, Entry 70, Philadelphia Navy Yard.

U. S. Department of the Interior:

- National Register of Historic Places Inventory—Nomination Form, National Park Service, Rock Creek Church Yard and Cemetery.

U. S. Department of the Navy:

- *Civil War Naval Chronology, 1861-1865.* Washington: Naval History Division, Navy Department, 1971.
- *Dictionary of American Naval Fighting Ships* (*DANFS*). Washington, D.C.: Office of the Chief of Naval Operations, Naval History Division, 1969.
- Eller, E. M. and Richard H. Webber, *Monitors of the U.S. Navy 1861-1937.* Washington, D.C.: Naval History Division, Navy Department, 1969.
- Historical Manuscripts, Navy Department Library, Naval History and Heritage Command, Washington, D.C.:

  John Lenthall, ZB folder.

  George Much Collection.

  Work Records of the 1830's of the Moulding Loft at the Washington Navy Yard under Commandant Daniel T. Patterson.

  John Lenthall manuscript collection of data on vessels from the Revolutionary through the Civil War era in the Franklin Institute Library, Philadelphia, PA (microfilm).
- *History of the Construction Corps of the United States Navy.* Washington, D.C.: United States Navy Department, Bureau of Construction and Repair, 1937.

- *Official Records of the Union and Confederate Navies in the War of the Rebellion,* 30 volumes and index. Washington, D.C.: U.S. Government Printing Office, 1894-1927.
- *Register of Commissioned and Warrant Officers of the Navy of the United States, including Officers of the Marine Corps, and Others,* various years.
- *Report of the Secretary of the Navy in Relation to Armored Vessels.* Washington: Government Printing Office, 1864.

U. S. Department of War:

- *The War of the Rebellion: A Compilation of Official Records of the Union and Confederate Armies,* 70 volumes and index. Washington, D.C.: U.S. Government Printing Office, 1880-1901.

U. S. House of Representatives:

- 33rd Cong., 1st Sess., House Executive Document 65.
- 43rd Cong., 2nd Sess., House Executive Document 1.
- 46th Cong., 2nd Sess., House Executive Document 82.

U. S. Senate:

- 31st Cong., 1st Sess., Senate Report No. 202.
- 37th Cong., 1st Sess., Senate Executive Document No. 1.
- 37th Cong., 2nd Sess., Senate Report No. 37.
- 38th Cong., 2nd Sess., Senate Report No. 142.

United States Serial Set

United States Statutes at Large

Published Memoirs and Papers

Ammen, Daniel, *The Old Navy and the New.* Philadelphia: J. B. Lippencott Company, 1891.

Buell, Augustus C., *The Memoirs of Charles H. Cramp.* Philadelphia and London: Lippincott Company, 1906.

Confidential Correspondence of Gustavus Vasa Fox, Assistant Secretary of the Navy, 1861-1865, Robert Means Thompson and Richard Wainwright, Eds. New York: The Naval Historical Society, 1919.

Life of Henry Wadsworth Longfellow, Samuel Longfellow, Ed. Boston and New York: Houghton, Mifflin and Company, The Riverside Press, Cambridge, 1891.

Samuel Francis Du Pont, A Selection from his Civil War Letters, John D. Hayes, Ed. Ithaca: Cornell University Press, 1969.

Welles, Gideon, *Diary of Gideon Welles, Secretary of the Navy under Lincoln and Johnson,* with introduction by John T. Morse, Jr., 3 Vols. Boston and New York: Houghton, Mifflin Company, 1911.

Unpublished Papers Collections

Arizona Historical Society, Library and Archive, Tucson, AZ:

- MS 1381, Eugene Semmes Ives Collection.

California State Library, Sacramento, CA:

- California History Section, Papers regarding Nicholas King, Surveyor of the City of Washington.

Hagley Museum and Library, Wilmington, DE:

- Samuel Francis Du Pont Papers, Winterthur Manuscripts.

Independence Seaport Museum, Philadelphia, PA:

- John Lenthall Collection:

  John Lenthall Ship Plans, loan courtesy of the Franklin Institute.

  John Lenthall Specification Books.

  John Lenthall Personal Papers Collection.

  John Lenthall Library of Books.

  Thomas Hornsby Collection, Biography of John Lenthall, 1958.

  Thomas Hornsby Collection, Manuscript Documents.

Franklin Institute, Philadelphia, PA:

- Faculty Correspondence and Reports 1826 folder.
- Minutes of Board of Directors, June 9, 1831 to January 18, 1848.

U.S. Naval Academy Museum, Annapolis, MD:

- Ives Collection.

Biographical Dictionaries and Encyclopedias

Appleton's Cyclopedia of American Biography. New York: D. Appleton & Company, 1887-1889.

Dictionary of American Biography. New York: Charles Scribner's Sons, 1934.

Dictionary of National Biography. London: Smith, Elder and Co., 1897.

Oxford Dictionary of National Biography. Oxford University Press, 2004, 2005. Also the online edition, 2008.

The National Cyclopedia of American Biography. New York: James T. White & Company, 1937.

Contemporary Newspapers and Serials

Alexandria Gazette

Boston Daily Advertiser

Boston Daily Evening Transcript

Boston Traveller

Burlington Free Press

Charleston Daily News

Congressional Globe

Daily Dispatch (Richmond)

Daily Evening Telegraph (Philadelphia)

Evening Critic (Washington)

Evening Star (Washington)

Harper's Weekly

Inquirer and National Gazette (Philadelphia)

Journal of the Franklin Institute

National Republican (Washington)

Nautical Gazette

New-York Daily Tribune

New York Times

Potter's American Monthly, an Illustrated Magazine of History, Literature, Science and Art

Putnam's Monthly Magazine of American Literature, Science and Art

Richmond Enquirer

St. Paul Globe

Scientific American

Sun (New York)

United States Army and Navy Journal and Gazette

U.S. Nautical Magazine and Naval Journal

Washington Post

Wheeling Intelligencer

Supporting Sources, Books

Adams, Ephraim Douglass., *Great Britain and the American Civil War*, 2 Vols. New York: Russell & Russell, 1925.

Baker, Elijah III, *Introduction to Steel Shipbuilding*. New York, etc.: McGraw-Hill Book Company, Inc., 1953.

Baker, William Avery and Tre Tryckare, *The Engine Powered Vessel*. New York: Grosset & Dunlap, 1965.

Bathe, Greville, *Ship of Destiny*. St. Augustine, FL: Allen, Lane and Scott, 1951.

Battles and Leaders of the Civil War, Robert Underwood Johnson and Clarence Clough Buel, Eds. New York: Century, Co., 1887.

Baudez, Basile, Élisabeth Maisonnier and Emmanuel Pénicaut, *Les hotels de la Guerre et des Affairs étrangères à Versailles*. Paris: Éditions Nicolas Chaudun, 2010.

Bauer, K. Jack, *The Mexican War, 1846-1848.* Lincoln and London: University of Nebraska Press, 1974.

Baxter, James Finney III, *The Introduction of the Ironclad Warship.* Annapolis: Naval Institute Press, 2001.

Bennett, Frank M., *The Steam Navy of the United States.* Pittsburgh, PA: Warren & Co., Publishers, 1896.

Berry, Patrick, *The Dockyards, Shipyards, and Marine of France.* London: Sampson Low, Son, and Marsden, 1864.

Biography of the Class of 1838, of the College of New Jersey at Princeton, N.J., prepared by William Edward Schenck, D.D. Philadelphia: Jas. B. Rodgers Printing Co., 1889.

Bouguer, Pierre, *Traité du Navire, de sa Construction, et de ses Mouvemens.* Paris: Charles-Antoine Jombert, 1746.

Brassey, Sir Thomas, *The British Navy: Its Strength, Resources, and Administration.* London: Longman, Green, and Co., 1883.

Brisou, Dominique, *Accueil, introduction et développement de l'énergie vapeur dans la Marine militaire française au XIXe siècle.* Vincennes: Service Historique de la Marine, 2001.

Brown, David K., *Before the Ironclad, Warship Design and Development, 1815-1860.* Annapolis: Naval Institute Press, 2015.

Brown, Glenn, *History of the United States Capitol.* Washington: Government Printing Office, 1900.

Bryan, Wilhelmus Bogart, *A History of the National Capital,* 2 Vols. New York: The Macmillan Company, 1914.

Burnside, Helen Waldo, *Mrs. Elizabeth J. Stone, Sketch.* Washington, D.C.: Gibson Bros., Printers and Bookbinders, 1893.

Canney, Donald L., *The Old Steam Navy, Volume One, Frigates, Sloops and Gunboats, 1815-1885.* Annapolis: Naval Institute Press, 1990.

—, *The Old Steam Navy, Volume Two, The Ironclads, 1842-1885.* Annapolis: Naval Institute Press, 1993.

—, *U.S. Coast Guard and Revenue Cutters, 1790-1935.* Annapolis: Naval Institute Press, 1995.

—, *Lincoln's Navy, The Ships, Men and Organization, 1861-1865.* Annapolis: Naval Institute Press, 1998.

—, *Sailing Warships of the U.S. Navy.* Annapolis: Naval Institute Press, 2001.

Captains of the Old Steam Navy, Makers of the American Naval Tradition, 1840-1880, James C. Bradford, Ed. Annapolis: Naval Institute Press, 1986.

Catalogue of a Collection of Oriental Art Objects belonging to Thomas E. Waggaman of Washington, D.C., Ed. by H. Shugio. Smithsonian National Portrait Gallery,1896.

Chapelle, Howard I., *The History of American Sailing Ships.* New York: W.W. Norton & Company, Inc., 1935.

—, *The History of the American Sailing Navy.* New York: W.W. Norton & Company, Inc., 1949.

—, *The Search for Speed Under Sail, 1700-1855.* New York: W.W. Norton & Company, Inc., 1967.

Chapman, Fredrik Henrik af, *Tractat om Skepps-byggeriet ....* Stockholm: Johan Pfeffer, 1775.

Church, William Conant, *The Life of John Ericsson,* 2 Vols. New York: Charles Scribner's Sons, 1906.

Coletta, Paolo E., Ed., *American Secretaries of the Navy,* 1775-1972, 2 Vols. Annapolis: Naval Institute Press, 1980.

Conway's All the World's Fighting Ships, 1860-1905, Robert Gardiner, Ed. New York: Mayflower Books Inc., 1979.

Cutler, Carl C., *Queens of the Western Oceans.* Annapolis: United States Naval Institute, 1961.

Dana, Richard Henry, *To Cuba and Back: A Vacation Voyage.* Boston: Ticknor and Fields, 1859.

Delano, Judah, *Washington Directory.* Washington: William Duncan, 1822.

Dorwart, Jeffery M. with Jean K. Wolf, *The Philadelphia Navy Yard.* Philadelphia: University of Pennsylvania Press, 2001.

Du Bois dont on fait les vaisseaux ... 1650-1850, Service historique de la Marine, Chateau de Vincennes, 1997.

Dunbaugh, Edwin L. and William duBarry Thomas, *William H. Webb, Shipbuilder.* Glen Cove, NY: Webb Institute of Naval Architecture, 1989.

Farr, Gail E. and Brett F. Bostwick, *John Lenthall Naval Architect, A Guide to Plans and Drawings of American Naval and Merchant Vessels, 1790-1874.* Philadelphia Maritime Museum, 1991.

Ferreiro, Larrie D., *Ships and Science, the Birth of Naval Architecture and the Scientific Revolution, 1600-1800.* Cambridge and London: The MIT Press, 2007.

—, *Bridging the Seas, The Rise of Naval Architecture in the Industrial Age, 1800-2000.* Cambridge, London: The MIT Press, 2020.

Foreman, Amanda, *A World on Fire.* New York: Random House, 2010.

Fowler, William M., *Steam Titans.* New York, London, etc.: Bloomsbury USA, 2017.

Fuller, Howard J., *Clad in Iron, The American Civil War and the Challenge of British Naval Power.* Annapolis: Naval Institute Press, 2008.

Gardiner, Robert, *The Heavy Frigate, Eighteen-Pounder Frigates: 1778-1800.* London: Conway Maritime Press, 1994.

Gardiner, Robert, Ed., *Steam, Steel and Shellfire, The Steam Warship, 1815-1905.* London: Conway Maritime Press, 1992.

—, *The Line of Battle, The Sailing Warship 1650-1840.* London: Conway Maritime Press Ltd, 1992.

—, *The Naval War of 1812.* Annapolis: Naval Institute Press, 1998.

Gilmer, Thomas, *Modern Ship Design.* Annapolis: Naval Institute Press, 1975.

Gloire, Frégate de 900 Chevaux (1859). Paris: Association Les Amis des Musées de la Marine, 1968.

Green, Constance McLaughlin, *Washington Village and Capital, 1800-1878.* Princeton: Princeton University Press, 1962.

Greenhill, Basil and Sam Manning, *The Evolution of the Wooden Ship.* New York: Facts on File, Inc., 1988.

Guthorn, Peter J., *United States Coastal Charts, 1783-1861.* Exton, PA: Schiffer Publishing Limited, 1984.

Hackemer, Kurt, *The U.S. Navy and the Origins of the Military-Industrial Complex, 1847-1883.* Annapolis: Naval Institute Press, 2001.

Hamersly, Lewis Randolph, *The Records of Living Officers of the U.S. Navy and Marine Corps.* Philadelphia: J. B. Lippincott & Co. 1870.

—, *The Records of Living Officers of the U.S. Navy and Marine Corps.* New York: L. R. Hamersly & Co., 1898.

Hamlin, Talbot, *Benjamin Henry Latrobe.* New York: Oxford University Press, 1955.

Harris, Daniel G., *F. H. Chapman, The First Naval Architect and his Work.* Annapolis: Naval Institute Press, 1989.

Henry, William Wirt and Ainsworth R. Spofford, *Eminent and Representative Men of Virginia and the District of Columbia of the Nineteenth Century.* Madison, WI: Brant & Fuller, 1893.

Hickey, Donald R., *The War of 1812.* Urbana and Chicago: University of Illinois Press, 1989.

Holloway, Anna Gibson and Jonathan White, *"Our Little Monitor" The Greatest Invention of the Civil War.* Kent, OH: The Kent State University Press, 2018.

Hunter, Alfred, *The Washington and Georgetown Directory.* Washington: Kirkwood & McGill, 1853.

Isherwood, Benjamin F., *Experimental Researches in Steam Engineering.* Philadelphia: William Hamilton, Hall of the Franklin Institute, 1863.

Jenkins, Mark Collins and David A. Taylor, *The War of 1812 and the Rise of the U.S. Navy.* Washington, D.C.: National Geographic, 2012.

Kemp, Peter, Ed., *The Oxford Companion to Ships & The Sea.* Oxford University Press, 1979.

Kinnaman, Stephen Chapin, *Captain Bulloch, The Life of James Dunwoody Bulloch, Naval Agent of the Confederacy.* Indianapolis, IN: Dog Ear Publishing, 2013.

—, *Merrimack, The Biography of a Steam Frigate.* Wilmington and Malaga: Vernon Press, 2019.

Laing, Alexander, *American Ships.* New York: American Heritage Press, 1971.

Lambert, Andrew, *Battleships in Transition: The Creation of the Steam Battlefleet, 1815-1860.* London: Conway Maritime Press, Ltd., 1985.

—, *Warrior, The World's First Ironclad Then and Now.* Annapolis: Naval Institute Press, 1987.

—, *The Challenge, Britain Against America in the Naval War of 1812.* London: Faber and Faber Limited, 2012.

Lyon, David and Rif Winfield, *The Sail and Steam Navy List, All the Ships of the Royal Navy, 1815-1889.* London: Chatham Publishing, 2004.

MacDougall, Philip, *Royal Dockyards.* Newton Abbot, London, North Pomfret VT: David & Charles (Publishers) Limited, 1982.

Macintyre, Donald and Basil W. Bathe, *Man-of-War, A History of the Combat Vessel.* New York: Castle Books, 1974.

Mahan, Alfred Thayer, *The Influence of Sea Power upon History, 1660-1783.* Boston: Little, Brown and Co., 1890.

Marine Engineering, Herbert L. Seward, Ed. New York: The Society of Naval Architects and Marine Engineers, 1968.

Marolda, Edward J., *The Washington Navy Yard, An Illustrated History.* Washington: The Naval Historical Center, 1999.

McElroy's Philadelphia Directory for 1845. Philadelphia: Edward C. & John Biddle, 1845.

Meade, Rebecca Paulding, *Life of Hiram Paulding, Rear-Admiral, U.S.N.* New York: The Baker & Taylor Company, 1910.

Parkes, Oscar, *British Battleships.* London: Seeley Service & Co. Limited, 1973.

Paullin, Charles Oscar, *Commodore John Rodgers.* Annapolis: United States Naval Institute, 1967.

—, *Paullin's History of Naval Administration 1775-1911.* Annapolis: U.S. Naval Institute, 1968.

Peck, Taylor, *Round-Shots to Rockets, The History of the Washington Navy Yard and the United States Naval Gun Factory.* Annapolis: United States Naval Institute, 1949.

Pitch, Anthony S., *The Burning of Washington, The British Invasion of 1814.* Annapolis: Naval Institute Press, 1998.

Porter, Admiral David D., *Naval History of the Civil War.* New York: The Sherman Publishing Company, 1886.

Potter, David M., *The Impending Crisis, 1848-1861.* New York: Harper & Row, Publishers, Inc., 1976.

Powell, William and Edward Shippen, Eds., *Officers of the Army and Navy (regular) who served in the Civil War.* Philadelphia: L. R. Hamersly, 1892.

Principles of Naval Architecture, John P. Comstock, Ed. New York: The Society of Naval Architects and Marine Engineers, 1967.

Provine, Dorothy S., *District of Columbia Indentures of Apprenticeship, 1801-1893.* Willow Bend Books, 1998.

Quarstein, John V., *The CSS Virginia, Sink Before Surrender.* Charleston and London: The History Press, 2012.

Quarstein, John V. and Dennis Mroczkowski, *Fortress Monroe, The Key to the South.* Charleston, etc.: Arcadia Publishing, 2000.

Ridgely-Nevitt, Cedric, *American Steamships on the Atlantic.* Newark: University of Delaware Press, 1981.

Roberts, William H., *USS New Ironsides in the Civil War.* Annapolis: Naval Institute Press, 1999.

—, *Civil War Ironclads, The U.S. Navy and Industrial Mobilization.* Baltimore: The Johns Hopkins Press, 2002.

Salvini, Emil R., *The Summer City by the Sea: Cape May, New Jersey—An Illustrated History.* New Brunswick, NJ: Rutgers University Press, 1998.

Santacilia, Jorge Juan y, *Examen Maritimo ...* , 2 Vols. Madrid: Manuel de Mena, 1771.

Scharf, J. Thomas, *History of the Confederate States Navy, from its Organization to the Surrender of its Last Vessel.* New York: Rogers & Sherwood, 1887.

Scharf, J. Thomas and Thompson Westcott, *History of Philadelphia, 1609-1884.* Philadelphia: L. H. Everts & Co., 1884.

Schroeder, John H., *Shaping a Maritime Empire, The Commercial and Diplomatic Role of the American Navy, 1829-1861.* Westport, CT and London: Greenwood Press, 1985.

Silverstone, Paul H., *Warships of the Civil War Navies.* Annapolis: Naval Institute Press, 1989.

—, *The Sailing Navy, 1775-1854.* Annapolis: Naval Institute Press, 2001.

Sinclair, Bruce, *Philadelphia's Philosopher Mechanics, A History of the Franklin Institute, 1824-1865.* Baltimore and London: The Johns Hopkins University Press, 1974.

Sloan, Edward William, III, *Benjamin Franklin Isherwood, Naval Engineer.* Annapolis: United States Naval Institute, 1965.

Stuart, Charles B., *The Naval and Mail Steamers of the United States.* New York: Charles B. Norton, 1853.

Swann, Leonard Alexander, Jr., *John Roach, Maritime Entrepreneur.* Annapolis: United States Naval Institute, 1985.

Tucker, Spencer, *Arming the Fleet, U.S. Navy Ordnance in the Muzzle-Loading Era.* Annapolis: Naval Institute Press, 1989.

Tucker, Spencer and Frank T. Reuter, *Injured Honor, The Chesapeake-Leopard Affair, 22 June 1807.* Annapolis: Naval Institute Press, 1996.

Tyler, David Budlong, *The American Clyde.* The University of Delaware Press, 1958.

Wahl, William H., *The Franklin Institute ... , a Sketch of its Organization and History.* Philadelphia: Franklin Institute, 1895.

Walker, Fred M., *Ships & Shipbuilders, Pioneers of Design and Construction.* Barnsley: Seaforth Publishing, 2010.

Weddle, Kevin J., *Lincoln's Tragic Admiral, The Life of Samuel Francis Du Pont.* Charlottesville and London: University of Virginia Press, 2005.

Weigley, Russell F., Ed. *Philadelphia, A 300-Year History.* New York and London: W. W. Norton & Company, 1982.

West, Richard S., Jr., *Gideon Welles, Lincoln's Navy Department.* Indianapolis and New York: The Bobbs-Merrill Company, 1943.

Wilson, Theodore D., *An Outline of Ship Building, Theoretical and Practical.* New York: John Wiley & Son, 1873.

Winfield, Rif and Stephen S. Roberts, *French Warships in the Age of Sail 1786-1861.* Barnsley: Seaforth Publishing, 2015.

Winslow, Richard E., *"A Race of Shipbuilders" The Hanscoms of Eliot, Maine.* Portsmouth: Portsmouth Marine Society, 2013.

Supporting Sources, Articles

Atwood, George S. and M. Vail de Clairbois, "A Disquisition on the Stability of Ships," *Philosophical Transactions of the Royal Society of London,* Vol. 88 (1798): 201-310.

Carson, Hampton L., "Samuel Humphreys, Chief Constructor of the United States," *The Pennsylvania Magazine of History and Biography,* Vol. 8, No. 2 (June 1884): 216-222.

—, "The Humphreys Family," *Publications of the Genealogical Society of Pennsylvania,* Vol. 8, No. 2 (1922): 121-138.

Carter, Edward C. II, "Benjamin Henry Latrobe and the Growth and Development of Washington, 1798-1818," *Records of the Columbia Historical Society, Washington, D.C.,* Vol. 71/72 (1971/1972): 128-149.

Easby-Smith, Wilhelmina M., "Personal Recollections of Early Washington with a Sketch of the Life of Captain William Easby," *The Association of the Oldest Inhabitants of the District of Columbia* (1913): 10-28.

Ehrenberg, Ralph E., "Mapping the Nation's Capital, The Surveyor's Office, 1791-1818," *The Quarterly Journal of the Library of Congress,* Vol. 36, No. 3 (Summer 1979): 279-319.

Ferreiro, Larrie D., "The Naval Constructors of France, Great Britain and the United States," *Naval Engineers Journal* (September 1998): 99-132.

—, "A Biographical Sketch of John Willis Griffiths from Primary and Secondary Sources," *Nautical Research Journal,* Vol. 52, No. 4 (Winter 2007): 221-228.

Griffiths, Oliver W., Ed., "Screw Steamers of the Navy," *U. S. Nautical Magazine and Naval Journal,* Vol. VI (April—September 1857): 59-66.

Hansen, Stephen A., "The Lenthall Houses: A Moving Tale of Historic Preservation," *TheInTowner* (9 November 2012).

Janes, Henry Lorenzo, "The Black Warrior Affair," *The American Historical Review*, Vol. 12, No. 2 (Jan. 1907): 280-98.

Lenthall, John, "On the Launching of the Three-deck Ship, the Pennsylvania in 1837," *Proceedings of the American Philosophical Society*, Vol. III, No. 27 (May 25-30, 1843): 103-4.

"List of Books Added to the Library during April, May and June, 1883," *Journal of the Franklin Institute*, Vol. 116, Issue 1 (July 1883): 74-80.

Morris, Maud Burr, "The Lenthall Houses and Their Owners," *Records of the Columbia Historical Society, Washington, D.C.*, Vol. 31/32 (1930): 1-35.

"New American Steamships of War," *Journal of the Franklin Institute*, Vol. 31 (February 1857): 125-32.

"Recent Deaths," *The United States Army and Navy Journal and Gazette ...*, Vol. 19 (15 April 1882): 834.

Roberts, William H., "'A Small Margin to Go to Sea With': Alban Stimers and the Union Navy's Light-Draft Monitors, Part I," *Warship International*, Vol. 58, No. 3 (September 2021): 223-247.

Taillemite, Etienne, "Les archives et les archivists de la Marine des origins à 1870," *Bibliothèque de l'école des chartes*, tome 127, livraison 1 (1969): 27-89.

"The New Frigate Merrimac," *The Scientific American*, Vol. XI, No. 28 (22 March 1856): 222.

"Trial Trip of the United States Steam Frigate Merrimack," *Journal of the Franklin Institute*, Vol. 61, Issue 4 (April 1856): 274-78.

Vallette, Henry M., "History and Reminiscences of the Philadelphia Navy Yard," *Potter's American Monthly, an Illustrated Magazine of History, Literature, Science and Art*, Vols. VI and VII (1876).

Museums, Libraries, Etc.

Fondren Library, Rice University, Houston, Texas

Hampton Roads Naval Museum, Norfolk, Virginia

Independence Seaport Museum, Philadelphia, Pennsylvania

Mariners' Museum, Newport News, Virginia

National Maritime Museum, Greenwich, United Kingdom

National Museum of the Royal Navy, Portsmouth, United Kingdom

National Museum of the United States Navy, Washington, D.C.

New-York Historical Society, New York, New York

Portsmouth Naval Shipyard Museum, Portsmouth, Virginia

Science Museum, London, United Kingdom

Smithsonian Institution, National Museum of American History, Washington, D.C.

U. S. Naval Academy Museum, Annapolis, Maryland

Websites

Ancestry:

"Joseph Eck," https://www.ancestry.com/family-tree/person/tree/3472171/person/24101253172/facts, accessed February 2020.

"Mary Dugan Eck," https://www.ancestry.com/search/?name=mary+dugan_eck, accessed February 2018.

"Nicholas King," https://www.ancestry.com/family-tree/person/tree/84101958/person/100189780502/facts, accessed March 2020.

"Robert King Sr.," https://www.ancestry.com/family-tree/person/tree/84101958/person/100169920188/facts, accessed March 2020.

"Jane King," https://www.ancestry.com/family-tree/person/tree/25725267/person/272136990093/facts, accessed March 2020.

"Jane Lenthall," https://www.ancestry.com/genealogy/records/jane-lenthall_30285466, accessed November 2017.

"John Lenthall," https://www.ancestry.com/family-tree/person/tree/3472171/person/24101637558/facts, accessed on August 2020.

Biographical Directory of the United States Congress, "Mallory, Stephen Russell (1813-1873)," https://bioguideretro.congress.gov/Home/MemberDetails?memIndex=M000084, accessed June 2020.

City of Philadelphia, "Trustees of Ice Boats," https://www.phila.gov/phils/docs/inventor/graphics/archser/S153.htm, accessed November 2021.

Eyewitness, American Originals from the National Archives, "Robert Stone King—Assassination of President Abraham Lincoln, 1865," https://www.archives.gov/exhibits/eyewitness/html.php?section=13, accessed November 2018.

Find A Grave:

"Helen *Waldo* Burnside," https://www.findagrave,com/memorial/41347667/helen-burnside, accessed November 2021.

"Ann Maria Eck," https://www.findagrave.com/memorial/157044770/ann-maria-eck, accessed February 2018.

"Catherine Eck," https://www.findagrave.com/memorial/183365639/catherine-eck, accessed February 2018.

"Ellen Eck," https://www.findagrave.com/memorial/157043961/ellen-eck, accessed February 2018.

"John Joseph Eck," https://www.findagrave.com/memorial/115672431/john-joseph-eck, accessed February 2020.

"John Peter Eck," https://www.findagrave.com/memorial/115672301/john-peter-eck, accessed November 2021.

"Anna Maria 'Annie' *Waggaman* Ives," https://www.findagrave.com/memorial/5401730/anna-maria-ives, accessed February 2018.

"Nicholas King," https://www.findagrave.com/memorial/19608130/nicholas-king, accessed March 2020.

"Jane *King* Lenthall," https://www.findagrave.com/memorial/41347682/jane-lenthall, accessed February 2018.

"John Lenthall," https://www.findagrave.com/memorial/142599741/john-lenthall, accessed February 2020.

"Mary D. Lenthall," https://www.findagrave.com/memorial/157045765/mary-d-lenthall, accessed February 2018.

"Elizabeth Jane *Lenthall* Stone," https://www.findagrave.com/memorial/41347661/elizabeth-jane-stone, accessed February 2018.

"William Wade," https://www.findagrave.com/memorial/33355568/william-wade, accessed November 2021.

"Jane *Lenthall* Waggaman," https://www.findagrave.com/memorial/157046156/jane-waggaman, accessed February 2018.

"Thomas Ennals Waggaman," https://www.findagrave.com/memorial/6130951/thomas-ennals-waggaman, accessed February 2018.

Ford's Theatre, "The Man Behind the Lincoln Funeral: George R. Harrington," https://www.fords.org/blog/post/the-man-behind-the-lincoln-funeral-george-r-harrington/, accessed November 2018.

Genealogy Trails, Washington, D.C.:

"Captain William Easby, 1791-1854," http://www.genealogytrails.com/washdc/biographies/bio5.html, accessed October 2019.

"District of Columbia, Apprenticeship Indentures and Related Documents," http://www.genealogytrails.com/washdc/apprenticedocuments/apprenticeintro.html, accessed October 2019.

"Washington Navy Yard Employees in April 1829," http://www.genealogytrails.com/washdc/WNY/wny1829aprlemployees.html, accessed October 2019.

Geni, "Samuel Humphreys, naval architect," https://www.geni.com/people/samuel-humphreys-naval-architect, accessed September 2019.

Independence Seaport Museum, "John Lenthall Collection," https://www.phillyseaport.org under Discover/J. Welles Henderson Research Center/Online Catalog/keyword: John Lenthall Collection, accessed October 2017.

Naval History and Heritage Command,

"A Brief History of Civilian Personnel in the U.S. Navy Department," http://www.history.navy.mil/library/special/civilian_personnel.htm, accessed May 2020.

"Annual Reports of the Secretary of the Navy (ARSN)," https://www.history.navy.mil/content/history/nhhc/research/library/online-reading-room/title-list-alphabetically/a/secnav-reports.html, accessed 2017-2021.

"Dictionary of American Naval Fighting Ships (DANFS)," https://www.history.navy.mil/research/histories/ship-histories/danfs.html, accessed 2017-2021.

"Officers - Continental & US Navy/Marine Corps 1775-1900," https://www.history.navy.mil/research/library/online-reading-room/title-list-alphabetically/o/officers-continental-usnavy-mc-1775-1900.html, accessed 2017-2021.

Office of the United States Trade Representative, "History of the Winder Building," https://ustr.gov/archive/Who_We_Are/History_of_the_Winder_Building,_Home_to_USTR%27s_Washington_DC_Headquarters.html, accessed October 2019.

Royal Museums Greenwich, "Objects," (Series of Form No. 211) https://collections.rmg.co.uk/archive/objects/522429.html, accessed August 2020.

The Church of the Epiphany:

"Home-EpiphanyDC," http://epiphanydc.org, accessed October 2019.

"John Lenthall," http://epiphanydc.org/2017/04/10/april-11-john-lenthall-1882/, accessed February 2019.

"Mary King Lenthall," http://epiphanydc.org/2017/03/may-3-mary-king-lenthall-1892/, accessed March 2019.

"Elizabeth Jane Lenthall Stone," http://epiphanydc.org/2017/07/31/august-3-elizabeth-jane-lenthall-stone-1892/, accessed February 2019.

Uniform-Reference.Net, "U.S. Army and Navy Officer Ranks during the Civil War," https://www.uniform-reference.net/ranks/usn/usn_rel_ranks.html, accessed December 2020.

United States Department of State, Office of the Historian, "Daniel Carroll Brent (1770-1841)," https://history.state.gov/departmenthistory/people/brent-daniel-carroll, accessed July 2020.

United States Lighthouse Society, "The Development of the American Lightship," https://uslhs.org/development-american-lightship-james-delgado, accessed June 2019.

Virginia Places, "Before the Pentagon, Where Were the Military Headquarters," http://www.virginiaplaces.org/military/beforethepentagon.html, accessed February 2019.

* * *

INDEX

NOTE: Officers' ranks or diplomatic assignments described herein are those held during the period of this book's narrative and may not fully reflect that officer's ultimate rank or that diplomat's subsequent service. Naval constructors are U.S. Navy unless otherwise noted.

A

B

C

D

E

F

G

H

I

J

K

L

M

N

O

P

Q

R

S

T

U

V

W

Y

CPSIA information can be obtained
at www.ICGtesting.com
Printed in the USA
BVHW012358090422
633858BV00007B/61/J